T0155657

Lecture Notes in Computer Science

Lecture Notes in Artificial Intelligence   14274

Founding Editor

Jörg Siekmann

Series Editors

Randy Goebel, *University of Alberta, Edmonton, Canada*
Wolfgang Wahlster, *DFKI, Berlin, Germany*
Zhi-Hua Zhou, *Nanjing University, Nanjing, China*

The series Lecture Notes in Artificial Intelligence (LNAI) was established in 1988 as a topical subseries of LNCS devoted to artificial intelligence.

The series publishes state-of-the-art research results at a high level. As with the LNCS mother series, the mission of the series is to serve the international R & D community by providing an invaluable service, mainly focused on the publication of conference and workshop proceedings and postproceedings.

Huayong Yang · Honghai Liu · Jun Zou ·
Zhouping Yin · Lianqing Liu · Geng Yang ·
Xiaoping Ouyang · Zhiyong Wang
Editors

Intelligent Robotics and Applications

16th International Conference, ICIRA 2023
Hangzhou, China, July 5–7, 2023
Proceedings, Part VIII

Springer

Editors
Huayong Yang
Zhejiang University
Hangzhou, China

Jun Zou 🆔
Zhejiang University
Hangzhou, China

Lianqing Liu 🆔
Shenyang Institute of Automation
Shenyang, Liaoning, China

Xiaoping Ouyang 🆔
Zhejiang University
Hangzhou, China

Honghai Liu 🆔
Harbin Institute of Technology
Shenzhen, China

Zhouping Yin
Huazhong University of Science
and Technology
Wuhan, China

Geng Yang 🆔
Zhejiang University
Hangzhou, China

Zhiyong Wang
Harbin Institute of Technology
Shenzhen, China

ISSN 0302-9743   ISSN 1611-3349 (electronic)
Lecture Notes in Artificial Intelligence
ISBN 978-981-99-6500-7   ISBN 978-981-99-6501-4 (eBook)
https://doi.org/10.1007/978-981-99-6501-4

LNCS Sublibrary: SL7 – Artificial Intelligence

© The Editor(s) (if applicable) and The Author(s), under exclusive license
to Springer Nature Singapore Pte Ltd. 2023

This work is subject to copyright. All rights are reserved by the Publisher, whether the whole or part of the material is concerned, specifically the rights of translation, reprinting, reuse of illustrations, recitation, broadcasting, reproduction on microfilms or in any other physical way, and transmission or information storage and retrieval, electronic adaptation, computer software, or by similar or dissimilar methodology now known or hereafter developed.
The use of general descriptive names, registered names, trademarks, service marks, etc. in this publication does not imply, even in the absence of a specific statement, that such names are exempt from the relevant protective laws and regulations and therefore free for general use.
The publisher, the authors, and the editors are safe to assume that the advice and information in this book are believed to be true and accurate at the date of publication. Neither the publisher nor the authors or the editors give a warranty, expressed or implied, with respect to the material contained herein or for any errors or omissions that may have been made. The publisher remains neutral with regard to jurisdictional claims in published maps and institutional affiliations.

This Springer imprint is published by the registered company Springer Nature Singapore Pte Ltd.
The registered company address is: 152 Beach Road, #21-01/04 Gateway East, Singapore 189721, Singapore

Paper in this product is recyclable.

Preface

With the theme "Smart Robotics for Sustainable Society", the 16th International Conference on Intelligent Robotics and Applications (ICIRA 2023) was held in Hangzhou, China, July 5–7, 2023, and designed to encourage advancement in the field of robotics, automation, mechatronics, and applications. It aimed to promote top-level research and globalize quality research in general, making discussions and presentations more internationally competitive and focusing on the latest outstanding achievements, future trends, and demands.

ICIRA 2023 was organized and hosted by Zhejiang University, co-hosted by Harbin Institute of Technology, Huazhong University of Science and Technology, Chinese Academy of Sciences, and Shanghai Jiao Tong University, co-organized by State Key Laboratory of Fluid Power and Mechatronic Systems, State Key Laboratory of Robotics and System, State Key Laboratory of Digital Manufacturing Equipment and Technology, State Key Laboratory of Mechanical System and Vibration, State Key Laboratory of Robotics, and School of Mechanical Engineering of Zhejiang University. Also, ICIRA 2023 was technically co-sponsored by Springer. On this occasion, ICIRA 2023 was a successful event after the COVID-19 pandemic. It attracted more than 630 submissions, and the Program Committee undertook a rigorous review process for selecting the most deserving research for publication. The Advisory Committee gave advice for the conference program. Also, they help to organize special sections for ICIRA 2023. Finally, a total of 431 papers were selected for publication in 9 volumes of Springer's Lecture Note in Artificial Intelligence. For the review process, single-blind peer review was used. Each review took around 2–3 weeks, and each submission received at least 2 reviews and 1 meta-review.

In ICIRA 2023, 12 distinguished plenary speakers delivered their outstanding research works in various fields of robotics. Participants gave a total of 214 oral presentations and 197 poster presentations, enjoying this excellent opportunity to share their latest research findings. Here, we would like to express our sincere appreciation to all the authors, participants, and distinguished plenary and keynote speakers. Special thanks are also extended to all members of the Organizing Committee, all reviewers for peer-review, all staffs of the conference affairs group, and all volunteers for their diligent work.

July 2023

Huayong Yang\
Honghai Liu\
Jun Zou\
Zhouping Yin\
Lianqing Liu\
Geng Yang\
Xiaoping Ouyang\
Zhiyong Wang

Organization

Conference Chair

Huayong Yang   Zhejiang University, China

Honorary Chairs

Youlun Xiong   Huazhong University of Science and Technology, China

Han Ding   Huazhong University of Science and Technology, China

General Chairs

Honghai Liu   Harbin Institute of Technology, China

Jun Zou   Zhejiang University, China

Zhouping Yin   Huazhong University of Science and Technology, China

Lianqing Liu   Chinese Academy of Sciences, China

Program Chairs

Geng Yang   Zhejiang University, China

Li Jiang   Harbin Institute of Technology, China

Guoying Gu   Shanghai Jiao Tong University, China

Xinyu Wu   Chinese Academy of Sciences, China

Award Committee Chair

Yong Lei   Zhejiang University, China

Publication Chairs

Xiaoping Ouyang	Zhejiang University, China
Zhiyong Wang	Harbin Institute of Technology, China

Regional Chairs

Zhiyong Chen	University of Newcastle, Australia
Naoyuki Kubota	Tokyo Metropolitan University, Japan
Zhaojie Ju	University of Portsmouth, UK
Eric Perreault	Northeastern University, USA
Peter Xu	University of Auckland, New Zealand
Simon Yang	University of Guelph, Canada
Houxiang Zhang	Norwegian University of Science and Technology, Norway
Duanling Li	Beijing University of Posts and Telecommunications, China

Advisory Committee

Jorge Angeles	McGill University, Canada
Tamio Arai	University of Tokyo, Japan
Hegao Cai	Harbin Institute of Technology, China
Tianyou Chai	Northeastern University, China
Jiansheng Dai	King's College London, UK
Zongquan Deng	Harbin Institute of Technology, China
Han Ding	Huazhong University of Science and Technology, China
Xilun Ding	Beihang University, China
Baoyan Duan	Xidian University, China
Xisheng Feng	Shenyang Institute of Automation, Chinese Academy of Sciences, China
Toshio Fukuda	Nagoya University, Japan
Jianda Han	Nankai University, China
Qiang Huang	Beijing Institute of Technology, China
Oussama Khatib	Stanford University, USA
Yinan Lai	National Natural Science Foundation of China, China
Jangmyung Lee	Pusan National University, Korea
Zhongqin Lin	Shanghai Jiao Tong University, China

Hong Liu	Harbin Institute of Technology, China
Honghai Liu	University of Portsmouth, UK
Shugen Ma	Ritsumeikan University, Japan
Daokui Qu	Siasun Robot and Automation Co., Ltd., China
Min Tan	Institute of Automation, Chinese Academy of Sciences, China
Kevin Warwick	Coventry University, UK
Guobiao Wang	National Natural Science Foundation of China, China
Tianmiao Wang	Beihang University, China
Tianran Wang	Shenyang Institute of Automation, Chinese Academy of Sciences, China
Yuechao Wang	Shenyang Institute of Automation, Chinese Academy of Sciences, China
Bogdan M. Wilamowski	Auburn University, USA
Ming Xie	Nanyang Technological University, Singapore
Yangsheng Xu	Chinese University of Hong Kong, China
Huayong Yang	Zhejiang University, China
Jie Zhao	Harbin Institute of Technology, China
Nanning Zheng	Xi'an Jiaotong University, China
Xiangyang Zhu	Shanghai Jiao Tong University, China

Contents – Part VIII

Intelligent Inspection Robotics

Robotics in Sustainable Manufacturing for Carbon Neutrality

**Innovative Design and Performance Evaluation of Robot
Mechanisms - II**

Physical and Neurological Human-Robot Interaction

Scene-Level Surface Normal Estimation from Encoded Polarization Representation

Yifei Zhang$^{(\boxtimes)}$, Minxiang Ye, Senwei Xiang, and Anhuan Xie

Research Center for Intelligent Robot, Zhejiang Lab, Hangzhou 311121, China
`yifeiz@zhejianglab.com`

Abstract. Scene-level surface normal estimation is crucial for robot perception and navigation. However, it is challenging to obtain the geometric information of the scene from a single view. Different from previous object-level Shape from Polarization (SfP) methods, we focus on potential scene-level indoor and outdoor environments for robot navigation. In this work, we introduce a novel learning-based SfP method that allows efficient polarization information encoding for accurate prediction of surface normals. The proposed encoding method adopts the feature representation of HSV-like data format, and integrates Pauli-inspired four feature channels. In order to evaluate the effectiveness of the proposed method, we conduct extensive experiments on the SPW dataset. The experimental results and comparative analysis show that our model outperforms all baselines by a large margin in terms of angular error and accuracy, and exhibits promising generalization ability in outdoor scenes. Furthermore, the encoded polarization representation has the potential to be used in various polarization vision tasks.

Keywords: Surface Normals · Polarization Image · Scene Understanding · Robot Vision

1 Introduction

Accurate environmental perception is crucial for various robots to achieve intelligent behavior. To name a few, mobile robots perceive outdoor or indoor environment information for path planning and obstacle avoidance, so as to ensure safe navigation. Intelligent systems with robotic arm are able to perform fine manipulations based on visual perception, such as grasping objects. Therefore, research on scene perception for robots is valuable and necessary. To tackle the challenge, we study scene-level surface normal estimation task in this work, which can provide accurate geometric information of scenes for semantic understanding [1], decision-making and subsequent control.

Current research on surface normals mainly focuses on object-level prediction. A major reason is that the scene-level groundtruth of surface normals is

© The Author(s), under exclusive license to Springer Nature Singapore Pte Ltd. 2023
H. Yang et al. (Eds.): ICIRA 2023, LNAI 14274, pp. 3–14, 2023.
https://doi.org/10.1007/978-981-99-6501-4_1

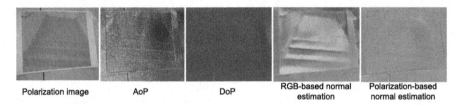

| Polarization image | AoP | DoP | RGB-based normal estimation | Polarization-based normal estimation |

Fig. 1. An image example from SPW dataset [4] showing the importance of polarization. Note that the staircase in the illustration is a printed photo. The RGB-based method [28] is difficult to accurately identify in this case, while the correct prediction based on the polarization image comes from our method.

relatively difficult to obtain. Some works use sensors such as photometric stereo camera [2] and lidar to collect geometric information of scenes. However, normal estimation algorithms trained on such data may perform poor generalization [4] in different scenarios due to the limited sensor working range. In this work, we explore the estimation of surface normals from a single polarization image as input. The advantage of polarization images is that it allows the acquisition of changes in the state of light, thus describing both the diffuse and specular parts of the scene [3]. Therefore, it contains not only light intensity information but also rich prior physical information. Especially for smooth and reflective surfaces, polarization images are more conducive to visual perception than traditional RGB images. Figure 1 gives an example to illustrate the importance of polarization information.

The phenomenon of polarization is ubiquitous in nature and is less affected by scene changes. Therefore, polarization images have significant potential for estimation and reconstruction of scene geometric information. Several methods [4,5] attempt to extract polarization image information in a data-driven manner. To some extent, these learning-based methods perform better than physics-based ones. However, how to encode polarization information more efficiently remains an open problem.

In summary, the contribution of our work is threefold. First, we propose a novel method for encoding polarization images. The proposed encoding adopts feature representation in HSV-like (Hue, Saturation, Value) format and integrates complementary four feature channels, which are Pauli-inspired mix on intensity images at four polarization directions. Then, targeting complex scenes in robotic navigation, we apply the encoded polarization representation to the task of scene-level surface normal estimation. Finally, quantitative evaluation and qualitative analysis demonstrate the effectiveness of the proposed method, which also generalizes well to outdoor scenes.

2 Related Work

Shape from Polarization. The task of reconstructing the 3D shape of an object using polarization cues is referred to as Shape from Polarization (SfP) [6], including surface normal and depth estimation. Since the polarization phenomenon of light acting on the surface of an object can be described by the Fresnel equation, early SfP algorithms utilize the physics-based approach to estimate the surface normals, such as [8,11]. However, these methods all have the problem of π-ambiguity. To tackle this problem, researchers propose to use the coarse depth map [9], two-view stereo [10], multi-view stereo [11], specific illumination conditions [12], etc. Learning-based methods effectively avoid π-ambiguity problem. For example, [13] build a real-world object-level dataset for normal estimation and the proposed network significantly outperforms physics-based methods. Other typical work can be found in [14].

Normal Estimation from a Single RGB Image. A large number of algorithms for surface normal estimation based on RGB images have been developed in recent years. RGB images contain rich color and texture information of the scene. The related works, such as [15,16], train an elaborated neural network on large-scale datasets. However, these methods are prone to performance degradation due to the lack of physical information of the scene. To solve this problem, some works attempt to involve supplementary cues, such as depth [17], planes and edges [18], semantics [19], etc. These methods are usually more complex and increase the application cost.

Polarization Representation. Among data-driven approaches, several works have attempted to improve prediction accuracy by encoding polarization images. To name a few, [14] takes as input AoP, DoP and I_{un} computed from raw polarization image. Considering the ambiguity in the azimuth angle α and uncertainty in the zenith angle θ, DeepSfP [13] calculates possible solutions under the assumption of orthographic projection $n = ([sin\theta cos\alpha \ sin\theta sin\alpha \ cos\theta])^\top$. In recent work, [4] encodes the raw AoP representation by $\phi_e = (cos2\phi \ sin2\phi)$. In other polarization vision tasks, [20,21] also attempt different encoding methods such as HSV and HSL, and made a detailed comparison.

3   Polarization Formalism

The polarization of light is ubiquitous in nature. Polarization information can be obtained by rotating a polarizer in front of the camera or by a sensor exploiting the division of focal plane (DoFP). Polarimetry has unique and valuable properties due to its ability to describe both the diffuse and specular of a scene, especially reflective surfaces. Based on these advantages, polarization imaging has great potential to be applied to various computer vision tasks, such as scene understanding and 3D reconstruction.

Assuming that using a DoFP sensor, we can simultaneously obtain the intensity of light under four polarizer angles ($0°$, $45°$, $90°$, $135°$), denoted as I_0, I_{45}, I_{90}, I_{135}. Light determined by scattering or reflection is generally unpolarized or partially linearly polarized and can be described by the linear Stokes vector, $S = [S_0 \ S_1 \ S_2]^\top$. S_0 represents the total light intensity, S_1 represents the superiority of parallel polarized portion against the perpendicular polarized portion, and S_2 stands for the superiority of $45°$ polarized portion against $135°$ polarized portion. They can be derived by [3, 22]:

$$S = \begin{bmatrix} S_0 \\ S_1 \\ S_2 \end{bmatrix} = \begin{bmatrix} I_0 + I_{90} \\ I_0 - I_{90} \\ I_{45} - I_{135} \end{bmatrix}. \tag{1}$$

Depending on the Stokes parameters in Eq. 1, we can determine the Angle of Polarization (AoP) and the Degree of Polarization (DoP) as:

$$AoP = \frac{1}{2}atan2(S_2, S_1), \tag{2}$$

$$DoP = \frac{\sqrt{S_1^2 + S_2^2}}{S_0}. \tag{3}$$

The AoP means the orientation of the polarized light with regards to the incident plan, while the DoP indicates the quantity of polarized light in a wave. In this work, AoP and DoP are referred as ϕ and ρ, and their value ranges are $[-\frac{\pi}{2}, \frac{\pi}{2}]$ and $[0, 1]$.

4   The Proposed Method

Polarization sensors are able to capture physical prior information in complex scenes. Our goal is to obtain more accurate surface normal predictions by efficiently encoding polarization image information. This work employs a learning-based approach to extract features from encoded polarization representation. In the following, we describe the proposed encoding method and the overall network architecture in detail.

4.1   Polarization Representation Encoding

Compared with traditional three-channel color images, polarization images contain valuable physical prior information of the scene. Especially in recent years, the rapid development of data-driven methods has enabled the efficient extraction of image features. Therefore, this work aims to efficiently encode polarization representation to make full use of the image information. Overall, the proposed polarization representation consists of two parts: three-channel feature map in HSV-like (Hue, Saturation, Value) format and complementary four feature channels with a mix of the intensity at different polarization angle.

In previous work [20], it is possible to encode polarization features in the form of HSV. The HSV color space is developed from the RGB color space, which clearly separate color components from intensity. For polarization images, standard HSV encoding usually correspond Hue, Saturation, and Value to angle of polarization ϕ, degree of polarization ρ, and intensity of polarization S_0, respectively. We adopt the HSV encoding and map the radian of ϕ to [0,1]. Besides, we employ the unpolarized intensity of light $I_{un} = \frac{1}{2}S_0$ in Value channel, which is also normalized to [0,1]. Based on Eqs. 2, 3, the relationship of these parameters can be verified as follows [6]:

$$I_\theta = I_{un}(1 + \rho\cos(2\phi - 2\theta)), \tag{4}$$

where I_θ indicates the intensity image from the polarizer oriented at θ.

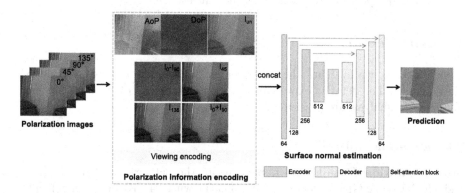

Fig. 2. Overview of network architecture. The polarization images consist of four intensity images captured at $0°$, $45°$, $90°$, $135°$ polarization angle. The encoded polarization representation contains the angle of polarization (AoP), degree of polarization (DoP), unpolarized image (I_{un}), and complementary four feature channels. An encoder-decoder network with self-attention block is used for surface normal prediction.

Furthermore, the mix on the intensities are less considered in existing work of polarization encoding. In the processing of Synthetic Aperture Radar (SAR) data, Pauli decomposition is often applied to polarimetric SAR images [20,23]. Using this data format, images can be encoded as $(I_{HH}, I_{HV}, I_{VH}, I_{VV})$, in which H and V denote the orientations of the received and the transmitted light wave, respectively. The original Pauli decomposition usually adopts $I_{HH} - I_{VV}$, I_{HV} and $I_{HH} + I_{VV}$ as the RGB configuration. Inspired by Pauli decomposition and Eq. 1, we employ a mix on the intensities as follow:

$$(I_0 - I_{90}, I_{45}, I_0 + I_{90}, I_{135}). \tag{5}$$

In this way we correspond the light intensity to the horizontal and the vertical filters. Note that all channels are normalized between 0 and 1. Finally, we concatenate all encoded polarization feature channels for further feature extraction. An illustration of the proposed polarization representation can be found in Fig. 2.

4.2 Overall Network

As shown in Fig. 2, we tackle the surface normal estimation task with a learning-based method. This work adopts a similar network architecture in [4], which consists of an encoder, a decoder and an elaborated self-attention block. The self-attention block contains multi-head self-attention [24] and a series of convolutional layers for global context cues extraction. Furthermore, the network model receives the encoded polarization representation as the main input. Considering non-orthogonal projections in scene-level surface normal estimation, we keep the 3-channel view encoding [4] as part of the input, thus avoiding the negative impact of viewing direction. We also conduct an ablation study on view encoding, and report the relevant experimental results in Sect. 5.3.

5   Experiments

In this section, we evaluate the effectiveness of the proposed method on the SPW dataset. The detailed experimental setup and a series of experiments with comparative analysis are presented.

5.1   Experimental Setup

Implementation Details. We implement all the networks with PyTorch on a single NVIDIA GPU (GeForce RTX 3090Ti with 24 GB of memory). The network models are trained for 1000 epochs with a batch size of 8 and optimized by the Adam optimizer [25] with an initial learning rate 10^{-4}. A cosine decay scheduler is used to automatically adjust the learning rate. We also employ a cosine similarity loss [13] for training. Our model takes as input 512×512 resolution images and outputs surface normals of the same size.

Dataset. We conduct various evaluation experiments on the SPW (Shape from Polarization in the Wild) dataset [4]. It consists of 522 sets of images from 110 different scenes, which is the first scene-level real-world dataset for polarization-based surface normal estimation. Different from object-level DeepSfP dataset [13] and synthetic scene-level Kondo dataset [14], SPW is closer to the real environment for robot navigation and perception. For a fair comparison, we use the same train/test splits as previous work, i.e. 403 and 119 images for training and evaluation, respectively.

Evaluation Metrics. In this work, we employ six common evaluation metrics [16] for surface normal estimation, including Mean, Median, RMSE, $11.25°$, $22.55°$, and $30.05°$. The first three represent the Mean absolute of the angle error, Median of absolute error, and Root mean square error respectively, thus the lower the better. While the last three indicate the percentage of pixels with angular error below a specific threshold, in which the higher the better.

5.2   Comparisons to Baselines

We compare the proposed method with six baselines, including three physics-based SfP methods and three learning-based SfP methods. The experimental results for these baselines are mainly re-implemented and reported in [4]. It is

Table 1. Quantitative evaluation for various baselines on the SPW dataset. Mean, Median and RMSE represent the Mean absolute of the angle error, Median of absolute error, and Root mean square error respectively. 11.25°, 22.55°, and 30.05° indicate the percentage of pixels with angular error below a specific threshold.

Method	Angular Error↓			Accuracy↑		
	Mean	Median	RMSE	11.25°	22.55°	30.05°
Physics-based methods						
Miyazaki [7]	55.34	55.19	60.35	2.6	10.4	18.8
Mahmoud [26]	52.14	51.93	56.97	2.7	11.6	21.0
Smith [27]	50.42	47.17	55.53	11.0	24.7	33.2
Learning-based methods						
DeepSfP [13]	28.43	24.90	33.17	18.8	48.3	62.3
Kondo [14]	28.59	25.41	33.54	17.5	47.1	62.6
sfp-wild [4]	17.86	14.20	22.72	44.6	76.3	85.2
Ours	**16.39**	**12.72**	**21.30**	**49.5**	**79.5**	**87.6**

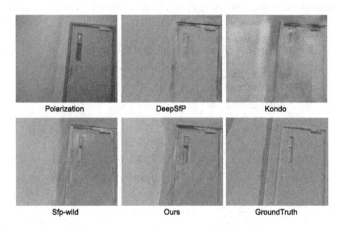

Fig. 3. An example showing the performance of each method on the SPW dataset.

worth noting that most of the previous SfP methods focus on object-level geometric reconstruction. Sfp-wild is the only scene-level surface normal estimation method that is driven by real-world polarization data.

Table 1 presents the quantitative results of all the methods on the SPW dataset. Obviously, our method outperforms all baselines by a large margin in terms of the angular error and accuracy. Compared with the second place, our model reduces the mean angular error by 1.47 and improves the accuracy by 4.9 at the 11.25° threshold. To be more intuitive, we provide an example showing the performance of each baseline for surface normal prediction in Fig. 3.

5.3   Comparisons of Different Polarization Representation

To further evaluate the effectiveness of the proposed polarization encoding method, we conduct experiments on the SPW dataset with different polarization input. Table 2 provides the quantitative results in terms of angular error. In general, methods that take polarization information as input perform better than methods that do not. And taking the raw polarization information directly as input cannot make full use of the prior physical information in the scene. Compared with the other three polarization inputs (mentioned in Sect. 2), our model with the proposed polarization representation achieves the best performance.

Furthermore, we compare the prediction accuracy of the proposed method and sfp-wild with/without viewing encoding. As shown in Fig. 4, our model still outperforms without viewing encoding. It is worth noting that our method performs better when the angle threshold is smaller, namely, it has more advantages at edges and details. For clarity, we provide two examples in Fig. 5 to show the prediction comparison of details.

Table 2. Quantitative evaluation for different polarization representation on the SPW dataset.

Input	Channel	Angular Error↓		
		Mean	Median	RMSE
w/o polarization	3	27.52	-	-
Raw polarization	4	21.77	-	-
P from [14]	3	18.26	-	-
P from [13]	3	18.05	-	-
P from [4]	4	17.86	14.20	22.72
Ours	7	**16.39**	**12.72**	**21.30**

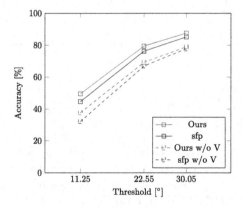

Fig. 4. Comparison between our method and sfp-wild with/without viewing encoding.

5.4   Qualitative Analysis on Outdoor Scenes

Mobile robots not only work in indoor environments, but also navigate between indoors and outdoors. Therefore, we provide some experimental results on outdoor scenes to demonstrate the generalization of our model. In general, surface normal estimation from a single RGB image has poor generalization ability to scenes due to different scene views and texture variations. As shown in Fig. 6, We can find that although the training data comes from indoor scenes, our model still performs well in outdoor scenes. It can be seen that our method has great potential for environmental perception and navigation of robots due to the ability to take advantage of prior physical information.

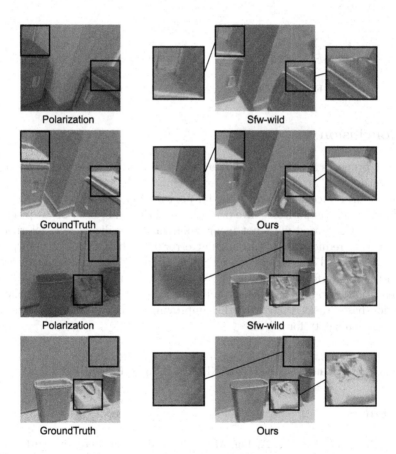

Fig. 5. Two examples showing the prediction details of the proposed method.

Input

Output

Fig. 6. Qualitative results on outdoor scenes.

6   Conclusion

This work proposes an effective polarization-based method for scene-level surface normal estimation. In order to fully extract and utilize the polarization information, we introduce a novel encoding for polarization representation. Extensive experiments and comparisons have demonstrated the superiority of the proposed method: (a) Compared with not using polarization, utilizing our polarization representation reduces the mean angular error 11°; (b) Our method surpasses other physics-based and learning-based SfP methods by a large margin, achieving state-of-the-art performance on the SPW dataset. In addition, our polarization representation encoding has the great potential to be used in various polarization vision-based tasks, thereby further improving the environmental perception and navigation safety for robots.

Acknowledgments. This work is supported by the Key Research Project and Youth Foundation of Zhejiang Lab (No. G2021NB0AL03, No. K2023NB0AA05).

References

1. Fan, R., Wang, H., Cai, P., Liu, M.: SNE-RoadSeg: incorporating surface normal information into semantic segmentation for accurate freespace detection. In: Vedaldi, A., Bischof, H., Brox, T., Frahm, J.-M. (eds.) ECCV 2020. LNCS, vol. 12375, pp. 340–356. Springer, Cham (2020). https://doi.org/10.1007/978-3-030-58577-8_21
2. Chen, G., Han, K., Shi, B., Matsushita, Y., Wong, K.-Y.K.: Deep photometric stereo for non-lambertian surfaces. IEEE Trans. Pattern Anal. Mach. Intell. **44**(1), 129–142 (2020)

3. Wolff, L.B., Andreou, A.G.: Polarization camera sensors. Image Vis. Comput. **13**(6), 497–510 (1995)
4. Lei, C., Qi, C., Xie, J., Fan, N., Koltun, V., Chen, Q.: Shape from polarization for complex scenes in the wild. In: Proceedings of the IEEE/CVF Conference on Computer Vision and Pattern Recognition (CVPR), pp. 12632–12641 (2022)
5. Gao, D., et al.: Polarimetric pose prediction. In: Avidan, S., Brostow, G., Cissé, M., Farinella, G.M., Hassner, T. (eds.) ECCV 2022. LNCS, vol. 13669, pp. 735–752. Springer, Cham (2022). https://doi.org/10.1007/978-3-031-20077-9_43
6. Collett, E.: Field guide to polarization. SPIE, Bellingham (2005)
7. Miyazaki, D., Tan, R.T., Hara, K., Ikeuchi, K.: Polarization-based inverse rendering from a single view. In: ICCV (2003)
8. Rahmann, S., Canterakis, N.: Reconstruction of specular surfaces using polarization imaging. In: CVPR (2001)
9. Kadambi, A., Taamazyan, V., Shi, B., Raskar, R.: Polarized 3D: high-quality depth sensing with polarization cues. In: ICCV (2015)
10. Fukao, Y., Kawahara, R., Nobuhara, S., Nishino, K.: Polarimetric normal stereo. In: CVPR (2021)
11. Miyazaki, D., Shigetomi, T., Baba, M., Furukawa, R., Hiura, S., Asada, N.: Surface normal estimation of black specular objects from multiview polarization images. Opt. Eng. **56**(4), 041303 (2016)
12. Deschaintre, V., Lin, Y., Ghosh, A.: Deep polarization imaging for 3D shape and SVBRDF acquisition. In: CVPR (2021)
13. Ba, Y., et al.: Deep shape from polarization. In: Vedaldi, A., Bischof, H., Brox, T., Frahm, J.-M. (eds.) ECCV 2020. LNCS, vol. 12369, pp. 554–571. Springer, Cham (2020). https://doi.org/10.1007/978-3-030-58586-0_33
14. Kondo, Y., Ono, T., Sun, L., Hirasawa, Y., Murayama, J.: Accurate polarimetric BRDF for real polarization scene rendering. In: Vedaldi, A., Bischof, H., Brox, T., Frahm, J.-M. (eds.) ECCV 2020. LNCS, vol. 12364, pp. 220–236. Springer, Cham (2020). https://doi.org/10.1007/978-3-030-58529-7_14
15. Li, B., Shen, C., Dai, Y., Van Den Hengel, A., He, M.: Depth and surface normal estimation from monocular images using regression on deep features and hierarchical CRFs. In: CVPR (2015)
16. Wang, X., Fouhey, D.F., Gupta, A.: Designing deep networks for surface normal estimation. In: CVPR (2015)
17. Qi, X., Liu, Z., Liao, R., Torr, P.H., Urtasun, R., Jia, J.: Geonet++: iterative geometric neural network with edge-aware refinement for joint depth and surface normal estimation. IEEE Trans. Pattern Anal. Mach. Intell. **44**(2), 969–984 (2020)
18. Huang, J., Zhou, Y., Funkhouser, T., Guibas, L.J.: Framenet: learning local canonical frames of 3D surfaces from a single RGB image. In: ICCV (2019)
19. Zhang, Z., Cui, Z., Xu, C., Yan, Y., Sebe, N., Yang, J.: Pattern-affinitive propagation across depth, surface normal and semantic segmentation. In: CVPR (2019)
20. Blin, R., Ainouz, S., Canu, S., Meriaudeau, F.: A new multimodal RGB and polarimetric image dataset for road scenes analysis. In: Proceedings of the IEEE/CVF Conference on Computer Vision and Pattern Recognition Workshops, pp. 216–217 (2020)
21. Blanchon, M., et al.: Polarimetric image augmentation. In: Proceedings of the 2020 25th International Conference on Pattern Recognition (ICPR), Milan, Italy, 10–15 January 2021, p. 9 (2021)
22. Li, L., Li, Z., Li, K., Blarel, L., Wendisch, M.: A method to calculate stokes parameters and angle of polarization of skylight from polarized CIMEL sun/sky radiometers. J. Quant. Spectrosc. Radiat. Transfer **149**, 334–346 (2014)

23. Shimoni, M., Borghys, D., Heremans, R., Perneel, C., Acheroy, M.: Fusion of polsar and polinsar data for land cover classification. Int. J. Appl. Earth Obs. Geoinf. **11**(3), 169–180 (2009)
24. Vaswani, A., et al.: Attention is all you need. In: NeurIPS (2017)
25. Kingma, D.P., Ba, J.: Adam: a method for stochastic optimization. In: ICLR (2015)
26. Mahmoud, A.H., El-Melegy, M.T., Farag, A.A.: Direct method for shape recovery from polarization and shading. In: ICIP (2012)
27. Smith, W.A.P., Ramamoorthi, R., Tozza, S.: Height-from-polarisation with unknown lighting or albedo. IEEE Trans. Pattern Anal. Mach. Intell. **41**(12), 2875–2888 (2019)
28. Do, T., Vuong, K., Roumeliotis, S.I., Park, H.S.: Surface normal estimation of tilted images via spatial rectifier. In: Vedaldi, A., Bischof, H., Brox, T., Frahm, J.M. (eds.) ECCV 2020. LNCS, vol. 12349, pp. 265–280. Springer, Cham (2020). https://doi.org/10.1007/978-3-030-58548-8_16

Configuration Synthesis of 4 DOF Knee Rehabilitation Parallel Mechanism Based on Multiset Theory

Zhongxin Zhang[1,2,3], Bin Yu[1,2,3], Jinbao Wang[1,2,3], Jingke Song[1,2,3], and Jun Wei[1,2,3(✉)]

[1] School of Mechanical Engineering, Hebei University of Technology, Tianjin 300401, China
jun.wei@hebut.edu.cn
[2] Intelligent Rehabilitation Device and Detection Technology Engineering Research Center of the Ministry of Education, Tianjin 300130, China
[3] Key Laboratory of Robot Perception and Human–Machine Fusion, Hebei Province, Tianjin 300130, China

Abstract. The occurrence of diseases and accidental damage cause many people to have knee motion dysfunction, the synthesis design of the knee joint rehabilitation mechanism is of great significance. This paper proposes a new 4 DOF (degree-of-freedom) motion equivalent model of knee joint, and the limb synthesis and configuration synthesis of 4 DOF parallel rehabilitation mechanism of knee joint are carried out. Firstly, according to the physiological characteristics of the knee joint and the three non-negligible motion characteristics of the knee joint, a 4 DOF motion equivalent model of the knee joint that is more in line with the knee joint motion is obtained, and the motion screw system and constraint screw system of this model are obtained, Configuration synthesis conditions are proposed. Second, the type of limb constraint is obtained according to the configuration synthesis conditions, and the limb synthesis is carried out by using screw correlation and reciprocity. Finally, the constraint types of the moving platform are classified by using the constraint screw multiple set theory, and the configuration synthesis of each type is carried out, a large number of knee joint 4 DOF parallel rehabilitation mechanisms that meet the requirements are obtained.

Keywords: Knee rehabilitation · Screw theory · Constraint screw multiset · Configuration synthesis

1 Introduction

The occurrence of population aging, various diseases and accidental damage cause many people to have knee motion dysfunction, it is an important problem to be solved urgently in today 's society to restore their athletic ability and freedom, the comprehensive design of the knee joint rehabilitation mechanism is of great significance. It is common to fit knee joint motion with planar four-bar mechanism [1–3], Some researchers have also proposed a five-bar mechanism [4] and Gear-five bar mechanism [5] for knee rehabilitation mechanism. In addition, Lee K M [6], Wang D [7] proposed the cam mechanism for knee rehabilitation.

© The Author(s), under exclusive license to Springer Nature Singapore Pte Ltd. 2023
H. Yang et al. (Eds.): ICIRA 2023, LNAI 14274, pp. 15–24, 2023.
https://doi.org/10.1007/978-981-99-6501-4_2

Configuration synthesis is to find all the mechanisms that meet the requirements. Researchers have proposed a variety of configuration synthesis methods, including Lie group synthesis, displacement set synthesis, constraint screw multiple set theory, geometric algebra synthesis, screw synthesis and Grassmann Line Geometry synthesis. Wei et al. [8] used Lie groups to synthesize a large number of mechanisms that can switch between plane motion and spherical motion. Li and Hervé [9] proposed the type synthesis of 3-DOF RPR equivalent parallel mechanisms based on the Lie group algebraic properties of rigid body displacement sets. Song, Han and Wang [10] proposed geometric algebraic method to study the synthesis of parallel mechanisms. Jun Wei et al. [11] synthesized Equivalent UU Parallel Mechanisms with Two Virtual Center-of-Motion based on Grassmann Line Geometry. Based on the displacement subgroup theory, Li Qinchuan et al. [12] synthesized a series of parallel mechanisms with equivalent SP virtual limbs. Because of its good kinematic performance and kinematic characteristics, it is applied to minimally invasive surgical robots. Xie Fugui et al. [13] proposed a configuration synthesis method based on Grassmann line geometry and Atlas method, and used this method to synthesize a series of 1T2R parallel mechanisms [14]. Then, under the guidance of the improved method of Grassmann line geometry and Atlas method, a parallel robot TH-HR4 was proposed [15].

The configuration synthesis design of knee rehabilitation mechanism is of great significance. However, the existing rehabilitation mechanism fails to consider the movement of the knee joint outside the sagittal plane, resulting in poor patient comfort and inability to adapt to different individuals. Researchers have synthesized a large number of mechanisms that meet the requirements by using various configuration synthesis methods. Based on the full analysis of the physiological structure and motion characteristics of the knee joint, this paper will obtain a more realistic knee joint motion equivalent model, and synthesize the configuration of the knee joint rehabilitation mechanism.

The paper is arranged in the following structure. Section 2 analyzes the physiological structure and motion characteristics of the knee joint, and obtains the 4 DOF motion equivalent model of the knee joint. Limb is synthesized based on correlation and reciprocity of screws in Sect. 3. Section 4 applies the screw multiset theory to synthesize the configuration, and Sect. 5 is the conclusion.

2   4 DOF Knee Joint Motion Equivalent Model

The knee joint is the most complex joint in the human body. It is mainly composed of the lower end of the femur, the upper end of the tibia and the patella. It also includes ligaments and muscles attached to the bone joint cavity, as shown in Fig. 1(a). The lower end of the femur can be approximately regarded as two arcs, and the upper end of the tibia is approximately flat.

The main movement of the knee joint is the flexion and extension movement in the sagittal plane, it means that the knee joint rehabilitation mechanism should have a large rotation angle, but it cannot be simply regarded as the fixed axis revolute of the revolute joint. The knee joint has three motion characteristics that cannot be ignored. First, as shown in Fig. 2, the relative motion between the femur and the tibia is a combined motion of rolling and sliding [16], secondly, the rotation axis in the sagittal plane of the human knee joint is not fixed, and it changes with the rotational angle of the knee joint. This requires that the knee rehabilitation mechanism must have two DOF in the same plane to adapt to the variable axis motion of the knee joint [17–19]. Third, the knee joint also has a spiral homing mechanism [20]. During the bending and straightening process, the calf has an outward rotation of about 10° relative to the thigh, which requires the rehabilitation mechanism to increase a revolute DOF to adapt to this feature of the calf. Therefore, the knee rehabilitation mechanism should have 4 DOF, including two revolute DOF and two mobile DOF. The motion equivalent model is shown in Fig. 1(b). According to the knee joint motion equivalent model, the rehabilitation mechanism is designed, which can accurately fit the complex motion of the knee joint and can also solve different problems of knee joint trajectory of different individuals.

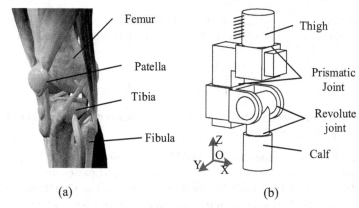

Fig. 1. (a) Physiological structure of knee joint (b) Knee joint motion equivalent model

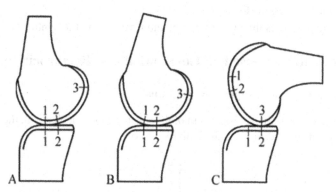

Fig. 2. The combination of rolling and sliding in knee flexion and extension movement [16]

According to the equivalent model of knee joint motion, the motion screw system of knee joint rehabilitation mechanism. $\mathbb{S}$ indicates the constraint screw system of the knee joint rehabilitation mechanism:

$$\mathbb{S} = \ominus \begin{cases} S_1 = (0\ 0\ 0;\ 1\ 0\ 0) \\ S_2 = (0\ 0\ 0;\ 0\ 0\ 1) \\ S_3 = (0\ 1\ 0;\ 0\ 0\ 0) \\ S_4 = (0\ 0\ 1;\ 0\ 0\ 0) \end{cases} \tag{1}$$

The reciprocal product of constraint screw and motion screw is zero:

$$\mathbb{S} \circ S^r = 0 \tag{2}$$

The constraint screw system of knee rehabilitation mechanism is obtained. $\mathbb{S}^r$ indicates the constraint screw system of the knee joint rehabilitation mechanism:

$$\mathbb{S}^r = \begin{cases} S_1^r = (0\ 1\ 0;\ 0\ 0\ 0) \\ S_2^r = (0\ 0\ 0\ 1\ 0\ 0) \end{cases} \tag{3}$$

The configuration synthesis conditions can be known from the motion model of knee rehabilitation mechanism:

(1) The knee rehabilitation mechanism should be 2R2T 4 DOF, that is, it has a constraint force and a constraint moment; the constraint force axis passes through the VCM (Virtual Center-of-Motion) and the direction does not change with the motion of the moving platform. The direction of the constraint moment changes with the rotation of the moving platform;
(2) There is a VCM to ensure that the motion center of the mechanism coincides with the motion center of the knee joint;
(3) This article only uses the prismatic joint and revolute joint to synthesis.

3 Limbs Synthesis Based on Correlation and Reciprocity of Screws

3.1 Classification and Composition of Limbs

According to the constraint screw system of the rehabilitation mechanism, the constraint screw systems of the four limbs can be divided into:

$$\mathbb{S}^r = \begin{cases} \varnothing \\ (S_1^r) \\ (S_2^r) \\ (S_1^r;\ S_2^r) \end{cases} \tag{4}$$

From the 4 DOF motion model of the knee joint, the motion screw system and the constraint screw system of the knee joint rehabilitation mechanism, the four limbs motion and constraint characteristics are as follows:

(1) Limbs I: Six DOF limbs, does not provide constraints;
(2) Limbs II: A five DOF limbs composed of five linearly independent motion screws, provide a constraint force and a VCM, the direction of the constraint force does not change due to the rotation of the moving platform and passes through the VCM;
(3) Limbs III: A five DOF limb composed of five linearly independent motion screws, provide a constraint moment, the direction of the constraint moment changes with the rotation of the moving platform;
(4) Limbs IV: A 4 DOF limb composed of four linearly independent motion screws, provide a constraint force, a VCM and a constraint moment, the direction of the constraint force does not change due to the rotation of the moving platform and passes through the VCM, the direction of the constraint moment changes with the rotation of the moving platform;

3.2 Correlation and Reciprocity of Screws Based Limbs Synthesis

According to Table 1, there are at most three linearly independent coplanar screws of the same pitch, at most three linear independences for concurrent screws of the same pitch, at most three linear independences for parallel screws of the same pitch, and at most two linearly independent screws of the same pitch with coplanar concurrent or coplanar parallel. Therefore, when the limbs are synthesized, there are at most three coplanar, concurrent or parallel screws with the same pitch, and there are at most two coplanar concurrent or coplanar parallel screws with the same pitch. Therefore, $[RRR]_{\parallel}$, $[RR]_{\parallel}$, $[RRR]_{\wedge}$, $[RR]_{\wedge}$ is linearly independent.

Table 1. Correlation with the same pitch screw

Number of screws	Geometric conditions of screw linear correlation
Two	The axis is collinear
Three	The axis is coplanar concurrent or coplanar parallel
Four	The axis concurrent or parallel or coplanar
Five	The axis is contained in a line congruence composed of two linear linear complex
Six	The axis is in a linear linear complex

The reciprocal product of two screws equal to zero is called the reciprocal screw. Two zero-pitch screws are reciprocal when they intersect or parallel, zero-pitch screw and infinite-pitch screw are reciprocal when vertical, two infinite-pitch screws are reciprocal under any conditions.

The limb I is an unconstrained limb, and the UPS limb with better performance is selected in this paper. According to the different types of kinematic joints, limb II can be divided into three types: RRRRR, RRRRP, and RRRPP. Limb III can be divided into four types: RRRRR, RRRRP, RRRPP and RRPPP, limb IV can be divided into three types: RRRR, RRRP and RRPP. Based on the correlation of the screws with the same

Table 2. Limb synthesis results of 4 DOF knee rehabilitation parallel mechanism

Category of limbs	Kinematic screws composition	Constraint limb meeting the constraint requirements
I	UPS	UPS
II	RRRRR	$[RRR]_\parallel[RR]_\wedge$ $[RR]_\parallel[RRR]_\wedge$
	RRRRP	$[RP]_\perp[RRR]_\wedge$ $[PR]_\perp[RRR]_\wedge$ $[[RR]_\parallel P]_\perp[RR]_\wedge$ $[P[RR]_\parallel]_\perp[RR]_\wedge$
	RRRPP	$PP[RRR]_\wedge$
III	RRRRR	$[RRR]_\parallel[RR]_\parallel$ $[RR]_\parallel[RRR]_\parallel$
	RRRRP	$[RRRP]_\parallel R$ $[RRPR]_\parallel R$ $[RPRR]_\parallel R$ $[PRRR]_\parallel R$ $R[RRRP]_\parallel$ $R[RRPR]_\parallel$ $R[RPRR]_\parallel$ $R[PRRR]_\parallel$ $P[RR]_\parallel[RR]_\parallel$ $[RR]_\parallel P[RR]_\parallel$ $[RR]_\parallel[RR]_\parallel P$
	RRRPP	$P\left[RR^\parallel\right]_\wedge R^\parallel P$ $\left[RR^\parallel\right]_\wedge R^\parallel PP$ $PP\left[RR^\parallel\right]_\wedge R^\parallel$ $PR^\parallel\left[R^\parallel R\right]_\wedge P$ $R^\parallel\left[R^\parallel R\right]_\wedge PP$ $PPR^\parallel\left[R^\parallel R\right]_\wedge$
	RRPPP	$RR[PPP]_\perp$ $R[PPP]_\perp R$ $[PPP]_\perp RR$
IV	RRRR	$\left[RRR^\wedge\right]_\parallel R^\wedge$
	RRRP	$\left[PR^\parallel\right]_\perp\left[R^\parallel R\right]_\wedge$
	RRPP	$PP[RR]_\wedge$

pitch to ensure the linear independence between the kinematic joints. According to the geometric relationship between the two screws reciprocity, the limb is guaranteed to meet the constraint requirements. There are 7 kinds of limb II, 21 kinds of limb III and 3 kinds of limb IV that meet the requirements. The results of limb synthesis are shown in Table 2. [ ]$_\wedge$ indicates that the axis of the kinematic joints in [] are intersect, [ ]$_\perp$ indicates that the axis of the kinematic joints in [] are perpendicular, [ ]$_\parallel$ indicates that the axis of the kinematic joints in [] are parallel, $R^\parallel R^\parallel$ indicates that the axis of the kinematic joints are parallel.

4   Constraint Screw Multiset Based Configuration Synthesis

Parallel mechanism can be divided into the exactly constrained parallel mechanism and the redundant constrained parallel mechanism according to the constraint type. The constraint screw of moving platform is expressed by multiset theory, which corresponds to the constraint screw basic set and the constraint screw multiset respectively [21]. The parallel mechanism needed to be synthesized in this paper needs at least one constraint force and one constraint moment, and is limited to four limbs, then there are at most four always coincident constraint forces and four constraint moments with the same direction. Therefore, the constraint conditions of the moving platform of the parallel mechanism needed to be synthesized in this paper are expressed as one constraint screw basic set and fifteen types by constraint screw multiset theory. The constraint screw basic set screw can be expressed as $\{S_1^r,\ S_2^r\}$ and the constraint screw multiset is shown in Eq. (5), $\langle S^r \rangle$ indicates the constraint screw multiset of the limbs to the moving platform.

$$
\langle \mathbb{S}^r \rangle =
\begin{cases}
\langle S_1^r,\ S_1^r,\ S_2^r \rangle \\
\langle S_1^r,\ S_2^r,\ S_2^r \rangle \\
\langle S_1^r,\ S_1^r,\ S_2^r,\ S_2^r \rangle \\
\langle S_1^r,\ S_1^r,\ S_1^r,\ S_2^r \rangle \\
\langle S_1^r,\ S_2^r,\ S_2^r,\ S_2^r \rangle \\
\langle S_1^r,\ S_1^r,\ S_1^r,\ S_2^r,\ S_2^r \rangle \\
\langle S_1^r,\ S_1^r,\ S_2^r,\ S_2^r,\ S_2^r \rangle \\
\langle S_1^r,\ S_1^r,\ S_1^r,\ S_1^r,\ S_2^r \rangle \\
\langle S_1^r,\ S_2^r,\ S_2^r,\ S_2^r,\ S_2^r \rangle \\
\langle S_1^r,\ S_1^r,\ S_1^r,\ S_1^r,\ S_2^r,\ S_2^r \rangle \\
\langle S_1^r,\ S_1^r,\ S_2^r,\ S_2^r,\ S_2^r,\ S_2^r \rangle \\
\langle S_1^r,\ S_1^r,\ S_1^r,\ S_2^r,\ S_2^r,\ S_2^r \rangle \\
\langle S_1^r,\ S_1^r,\ S_1^r,\ S_1^r,\ S_2^r,\ S_2^r,\ S_2^r \rangle \\
\langle S_1^r,\ S_1^r,\ S_1^r,\ S_2^r,\ S_2^r,\ S_2^r,\ S_2^r \rangle \\
\langle S_1^r,\ S_1^r,\ S_1^r,\ S_1^r,\ S_2^r,\ S_2^r,\ S_2^r,\ S_2^r \rangle
\end{cases}
\tag{5}
$$

The parallel mechanism is obtained by selecting and combining the limbs according to 16 constraints. For the redundant constraint parallel mechanism, the constraint forces provided by different limbs are judged according to the geometric relationship one by one to determine whether the constraint forces provided by different limbs are always coincident, and whether the constraint forces provided by different limbs are always in the same direction, so as to determine whether the mechanism is full cycle. The arrangement and combination of a full-cycle mechanisms is arranged to obtain all mechanisms under the redundant constraints, and then all the 4 DOF knee joint parallel rehabilitation mechanisms that meet the requirements are obtained. In this way, a large number of mechanisms can be synthesized, two of which are shown in Fig. 3.

The mechanism diagram of the $[RR]_{\parallel}[RRR]_{\wedge}\&[RRR]_{\parallel}[RR]_{\parallel}\&$ 2-UPS parallel mechanism is shown in Fig. 4. $A_1, B_1, C_1, D_1, E_1, A_2, B_2, C_2, D_2$ and E_2 represent the feature points of the revolute joint respectively, and refer to the revolute joint with them. A_3 and A_4 are the center of the S joint respectively, and refer to the S joint with them. E_3 and E_4 are the intersection points of the two axes of the U joint respectively, and refer to the U joint with them. The revolute joint A_1, B_1, C_2, D_2 and E_2 is always parallel, and the revolute joint C_1, D_1 and E_1 axis intersects at point O. The coordinate system O-XYZ is established with O as the coordinate origin, where the X axis coincides with the revolute joint C_1, the Z axis is perpendicular to the fixed platform, and the Y axis is determined by the right-handed criterion. Do the vertical line of the revolute joint A_1, the vertical line passes through O and intersects the revolute joint A_1 at point F. Do

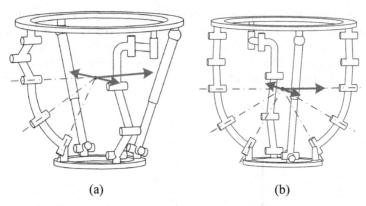

(a)   (b)

Fig. 3. (a) $[RR]_\parallel [RRR]_\wedge \& [RRR]_\parallel [RR]_\parallel \&$ 2-UPS mechanism (b) 2- $[RR]_\parallel [RRR]_\wedge$
$\& [RRR]_\parallel [RR]_\parallel \&$ UPS mechanism.

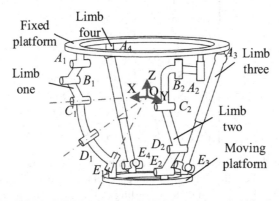

Fig. 4. $[RR]_\parallel [RRR]_\wedge \& [RRR]_\parallel [RR]_\parallel \&$ 2-UPS knee joint rehabilitation mechanism

the vertical line of the revolute joint B_1, the vertical line passes through O and intersects the revolute joint B_1 at point G. Then the motion screw system in the branch-global coordinate system is:

$$\mathbb{S} = \begin{cases} S_{11} = (r_{A_1F}; r_{OF} \times r_{A_1F}) \\ S_{12} = (r_{B_1G}; r_{OB_1} \times r_{B_1G}) \\ S_{13} = (r_{OC_1}; \mathbf{0}) \\ S_{14} = (r_{OD_1}; \mathbf{0}) \\ S_{15} = (r_{OE_1}; \mathbf{0}) \end{cases} \quad (6)$$

Do the vertical line of the revolute joint A_2, the vertical line passes through O and intersects the revolute joint A_2 at point H. Do the vertical line of the revolute joint B_2, the vertical line passes through O and intersects the revolute joint B_2 at point K. Do the vertical line of the revolute joint C_2, the vertical line passes through O and intersects the revolute joint C_2 at point M. Do the vertical line of the revolute joint D_2, the vertical line passes through O and intersects the revolute joint D_2 at point N. Do the vertical line of the revolute joint E_2, the vertical line passes through O and intersects the revolute joint E_2 at point P. Then the motion screw system in the branch-global coordinate system is:

$$\mathbb{S} = \ominus \begin{cases} S_{21} = (r_{A_2H} \quad ; r_{OH} \times r_{A_2H}) \\ S_{22} = (r_{B_2K} \quad ; r_{OB_2} \times r_{B_2K}) \\ S_{23} = \quad (r_{C_2M} ; r_{OC_2} \times r_{C_2M}) \\ S_{24} = \quad (r_{D_2N} ; r_{OD_2} \times r_{D_2N}) \\ S_{25} = \quad (r_{E_2P} \quad ; r_{OE_2} \times r_{E_2P}) \end{cases} \tag{7}$$

Then the constraint screw system in the global coordinate system of the knee joint rehabilitation mechanism is:

$$\mathbb{S}^r = \begin{cases} S_1^r = (r_{OX} ; 0) \\ S_2^r = (0; r_{OY}) \end{cases} \tag{8}$$

Therefore, the mechanism has a constraint force and a constraint moment. The constraint force parallel to the X-axis, the movement of the moving platform along the X-axis is limited, and the constraint force intersects the three rotation axes to form a VCM, The constraint moment parallel to the Y-axis at the initial position, and the direction of the constraint moment changes with the motion of the moving platform, limits a revolute DOF of the moving platform, Therefore, this mechanism has 4 DOF of 2R2T, which meets the requirements of knee joint rehabilitation and proves the correctness of configuration synthesis.

5 Conclusion

In this paper, a 4 DOF motion model of the knee joint was obtained on the basis of fully analyzing the unique physiological structure of the knee joint and its three motion characteristics that cannot be ignored. According to the knee joint motion model, the motion screw system and constraint screw system of the knee joint 4 DOF rehabilitation mechanism were obtained, and the synthesis condition of the mechanism configuration was obtained. By used screw correlation and reciprocity, there were 7 kinds of limb II, 21 kinds of limb III and 3 kinds of limb IV that meet the requirements. The constraint condition of the moving platform of the parallel rehabilitation mechanism was classified by the constraint screw multiset, and 16 kinds of constraint screw multiset types were obtained. Finally, a large number of 4 DOF knee rehabilitation parallel mechanisms were obtained.

Acknowledgment. This research work was supported by the Natural Science Foundation of Hebei Grant Numbers E2022202130.

References

1. Hyun, D.J.: Biomechanical design of an agile, electricity-powered lower-limb exoskeleton for weight-bearing assistance. Robot. Auton. Syst. **95**, 181–195 (2017)
2. Hamon, A., Aoustin, Y., Caro, S.: Two walking gaits for a planar bipedal robot equipped with a four-bar mechanism for the knee joint. Multibody Sys.Dyn. **31**(3), 283–307 (2014)
3. Aoustin, Y.: Human like trajectory generation for a biped robot with a four-bar linkage for the knees. Robot. Auton. Syst. **61**(12), 1717–1725 (2013)
4. Buśkiewicz, J.: Use of shape invariants in optimal synthesis of geared five-bar linkage. Mechanism and Machine Theory **45**(2), 273–290 (2010)
5. Sun, Y.: Design and evaluation of a pros-thetic knee joint using the geared five-bar mechanism. IEEE Trans. Neural Sys. Rehabilit. Eng. **23**(6), 1031–1038 (2015)
6. Lee, K.M.: Kinematic and dynamic analysis of an anatom-ically based knee joint. J. Biomech. **43**(7), 1231–1236 (2010)
7. Wang, D.: Adaptive knee joint exoskeleton based on biological geometries. IEEE/ASME Trans. Mechatron. **19**(4), 1268–1278 (2014)
8. Wei, J.: Reconfiguration-aimed and manifold-operation based type synthesis of metamorphic parallel mechanisms with motion between 1R2T and 2R1T. Mech. Mach. Theory **139**, 66–80 (2019)
9. Li, Q.: Type synthesis of 3-DOF RPR-equivalent parallel mechanisms. IEEE Trans. Rob. **30**(6), 1333–1343 (2014)
10. Song, Y.: Type synthesis of 1T2R and 2R1T parallel mechanisms employing conformal geometric algebra. Mech. Mach. Theory **121**, 475–486 (2018)
11. Jun, W.: Grassmann line geometry based configuration synthesis of equivalent Uu parallel mechanisms with two virtual center-of-motion. Mechan. Machi. Theo. **181**, 105208 (2023)
12. Li, Q.: Type synthesis of a special family of remote center-of-motion parallel manipulators with fixed linear actuators for minimally invasive surgery. J. Mech. Robot. **9**(3), 031012 (2017)
13. Xie, F.: Type synthesis of 4-DOF parallel kinematic mechanisms based on Grassmann line geometry and atlas method. Chinese J. Mechan. Eng. **26**(6), 1073–1081 (2013)
14. Chong, Z.: Design of the parallel mechanism for a hybrid mobile robot in wind turbine blades polishing. Robo. Comp.-Integ. Manuf. **61**, 101857 (2020)
15. Meng, Q.: Design and development of a Schönflies-motion parallel robot with articulated platforms and closed-loop passive limbs. Robo. Comp.-Integr. Manuf. **77**, 102352 (2022)
16. Masouros, S.: (i) Biomechanics of the knee joint. Orthopaedics and Trauma **24**(2), 84–91 (2010)
17. Varela, M.J.: A kinematic characterization of human walking by using CaTraSys. Mechan. Machi. Theo. **86**, 125–139 (2015)
18. Patel, V.V.H.K.: A three-dimensional MRI analysis of knee kinematics. J. Orthopa. Res. **22**(2), 283–292 (2004)
19. Komistek, R.D., Dennis, D.A., Mahfouz, M.: In vivo fluoroscopic analysis of the normal human knee. Clini. Orthopae. Rela. Res. **410**(410), 69–81 (2003)
20. Yao, Y.: Review of research on knee-postoperative rehabilitation training robot. J. Mecha. Eng. **57**(05), 1–18 (2021)
21. Dai, J.S.: Geometrical foundations and screw algebra for mechanisms and robotics. Higher Education Press, Beijing, China (2014)

Design and Analysis of Four-Finger Three-Joint Underactuated Hand Rehabilitation Mechanism

Shuaibang Wang, Mingjie Dong, Ran Jiao, Shuwen Sun$^{(\boxtimes)}$, and Jianfeng Li

Beijing Key Laboratory of Advanced Manufacturing Technology, Faculty of Materials and Manufacturing, Beijing University of Technology, Beijing 100124, China
sshwen@bjut.edu.cn

Abstract. To solve the rehabilitation problem of hand dysfunction caused by stroke and other accidental injuries, an underactuated four-finger three-joint hand rehabilitation mechanism with good physical human-robot interaction performance was designed. The configuration design and operation principle of the mechanism were introduced at first. At the same time, the statics analysis and kinematics simulation of the mechanism were carried out. Finally, the prototype was developed to complete the performance test and operation reliability experiment. The robot innovatively designs a power transmission system using only connecting rod mechanism. Compared with the traditional gear drive or hybrid drive ones, it has a simple structure and can realize synchronous movement of three joints driven by a motor. The experimental results of the prototype show that the mechanism can meet the needs of human finger rehabilitation and effectively improve the physical human-robot interaction performance.

Keywords: Hand rehabilitation training · underactuated mechanism · physical human-robot interaction · design and analysis

1 Introduction

Stroke is a common cerebrovascular disease that poses a great threat to people's life and health, and most patients show symptoms of hemiplegia [1]. Among them, lack of hand function will seriously affect people's daily life and thus reduce their quality of life [2]. However, patients with impaired hand function have a small probability of recovery. At present, in addition to drug therapy, patients with impaired hand function mainly rely on repetitive rehabilitation for symptom relief [3]. Compared with artificial rehabilitation training by medical practitioners, robotic rehabilitation training has more advantages because it can provide more complex multi-joint movements [4].

Hand rehabilitation robot can be divided into active rehabilitation and passive rehabilitation ones, during which, the active rehabilitation robot is designed to stimulate patients to carry out autonomous exercise by setting specific scenes, while passive rehabilitation robot is designed to drive patients to carry out passive rehabilitation training [5]. Among them, active rehabilitation systems include the game rehabilitation system based on ADLs [6], the wearable grip force sensor integrated with the Music Glove

© The Author(s), under exclusive license to Springer Nature Singapore Pte Ltd. 2023
H. Yang et al. (Eds.): ICIRA 2023, LNAI 14274, pp. 25–37, 2023.
https://doi.org/10.1007/978-981-99-6501-4_3

game [7], and the music ultrasonic therapy [8], etc. For passive rehabilitation robots, there are flexible ones and rigid ones, among which, flexible hand rehabilitation robots include sensory gloves [9], rehabilitation robot gloves with brain-computer interface [10], wearable one-sided remote control robot [11], and Carolina Soft robot based on textiles [12], robot orthotic gloves [13], etc., while rigid ones include 3DP-MFHD multifunctional hand device [14], hand rehabilitation exoskeleton [15], force feedback hand rehabilitation trainer [16], wearable hand rehabilitation robot [17], and ANA RobHand system [18], etc. From the current research-es on hand rehabilitation robots, we can see that current hand rehabilitation robots generally have shortcomings such as low motion accuracy, less freedom and lack of sensing ability [19]. It can be found that rigid rehabilitation robots generally have large volume, heavy weight and complex control system, while flexible robots generally have some defects such as poor accuracy, inaccurate angle control, and unable to achieve force feedback and interaction due to their fewer degrees of freedom (DOFs).

In this paper, we designed a four-finger three joint underactuated hand rehabilitation robot to solve problems existing in current researches and improve physical human-robot interaction.

2   Mechanism Design of Underactuated Rehabilitation Robot

The human hand has a complex structure, among which the index finger, middle finger, ring finger and little finger have the same structure. Therefore, in the design of hand rehabilitation robot, the four fingers have similar mechanism. The hand re-habilitation robot designed in this paper only involves the rehabilitation of the four fingers. Therefore, the following analysis on the structure and movement characteristics of the fingers focuses on the four fingers, and the index finger is taken as an example here.

2.1   Kinematic Model of Hand Index Finger

The index finger has three joints with four DOFs, the distal knuckle joint (DIP), the proximal knuckle joint (PIP), and the metacarpophalangeal joint (MCP), as in Fig. 1. The DIP and PIP can only achieve flexion and extension of the index finger, while the MCP can not only achieve flexion and extension, but also achieve a small range of abductive and adductive movements of the index finger.

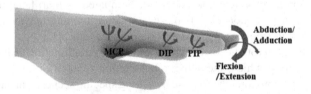

Fig. 1. Schematic diagram of finger joint.

2.2 Configuration Design of Coupling Mechanism of Hand Rehabilitation Robot

The designed robot has four fingers for the rehabilitation of the index, middle, ring and little fingers, respectively. Each robot finger has three DOFs and can perform flexion and extension training of four fingers simultaneously. Due to the small range of abduction and adduction movements, the training is of little significance, and the rehabilitation training of abduction and adduction will greatly increase the complexity of the robot. Therefore, this paper mainly focuses on the rehabilitation training of flexion and extension of four fingers. According to the structural similarity of the four fingers, the mechanism adopts the same design to reduce its overall complexity. The following uses one of the fingers for structural analysis, statics and kinematics analysis.

Each finger of the robot is powered by a linear motor, so the robot uses a total of four power sources to provide torque for 12 rotating pairs. The power output end of the linear motor is fixed to proximal phalanx, which directly provides rotating power to it. At the same time, the power is transmitted through the connecting rod mechanism along the direction of the proximal phalanx – middle phalanx – distal phalanx. The structure diagram of the underactuated mechanism is shown in Fig. 2, from which, F1, F2 and F3 represent proximal phalanx, middle phalanx and distal phalanx, respectively; L1, L2, L3, L4 represent the force transfer linkage at each finger phalanxes; S1 and S2 represent the sub-center points of rotation of the slider on the proximal and middle phalanx, respectively; and O1 and O2 are both bases; A1 and A2 are the center of rotation of middle phalanx and the center of rotation of distal phalanx. F is the driving force of linear motor.

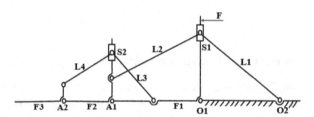

Fig. 2. Schematic diagram of underactuated linkage mechanism.

When it works, the linear motor directly exerts the driving force on proximal phalanx F1 to make F1 rotate counterclockwise around the frame O1. Since one end of the connecting rod L1 is fixed in the frame, it will pull the slider S1 down in the direction of F1, thus driving one end of the connecting rod L2 to move synchronously. Due to the fixed length of L2, a force along the middle phalanx F2 direction will be generated at the other end of connecting rod L2, thus generating a rotating torque to make middle phalanx rotate at the PIP joint, so as to realize the coupling drive of proximal phalanx and middle phalanx. Similarly, when middle phalanx F2 rotates around the PIP joint A1, the power can be transmitted to distal phalanx F3 through the connecting rod, so that F3 rotates around the DIP joint. In conclusion, the mechanism can realize the function of using one power source to carry out the coupling motion of three knuckles.

For the underactuated mechanism, there are 9 components and 13 low pairs. Therefore, the total DOF of one underactuated linkage mechanism is 1 according to (1).

$$F = n - 2P_l - P_h \tag{1}$$

As shown in Fig. 3, thumb rehabilitation requires more freedom of design, which will greatly increase the complexity of the robot. To balance single-finger rehabilitation performance and multi-finger compatibility, this robot is designed with four fingers. The above underactuated mechanism is respectively applied to the index finger, middle finger, ring finger and little finger, and the coupled motion of each finger is powered by one linear motor. At the same time, the robot palm is used as the base to connect the four fingers of the robot and the linear motor.

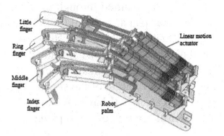

Fig. 3. Robot 3D model.

2.3   Design of Human-Robot Connection Mechanism

In the design of hand rehabilitation robot, the problem of human-robot compatibility has to be discussed, that is, the finger joints of the robot will be misaligned with the finger joints of the human during rehabilitation, which may cause the secondary injury to the fingers. To solve this problem, we designed a separate human-robot connection mechanism, which can act as an intermediary, connecting the robot and the human hand, so as to realize the isolation of their relation. The human-robot connection mechanism can provide three passive sliding pairs, which are located at proximal phalanx, middle phalanx and distal phalanx of the robot. Two passive prismatic pairs are located at middle phalanx and distal phalanx of the robot, respectively, as shown in Fig. 4, in which, the yellow mechanism is the coupling transmission mechanism, and the red is the human-robot connection mechanism. The human-robot connection mechanism has three passive prismatic pairs, so the robot can adapt to different sizes of hands in a certain range, thus improving the applicability of the hand rehabilitation robot.

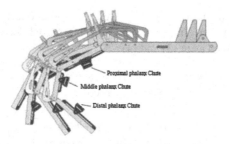

Fig. 4. Human-robot connection mechanism.

3 Analysis and Simulation

3.1 Statics Analysis

In the process of statics analysis, the dead weight of the bar and the friction force between the components are ignored to simplify the calculation process. The parameters used in the following analysis and their meanings are shown in Table 1.

Table 1. Each parameter and its meaning

Parameter	Parameter meaning
F_0	Driving force of linear motor
F_1	Contact force on middle phalanx when grasping objects (N)
F_2	Contact force on distal phalanx when grasping objects (N)
P_1	Position coordinates of middle phalanx contact point
P_2	Position coordinates of distal phalanx contact point
θ_1	Angle between palm bottom plate and proximal phalanx chute (rad)
θ_2	Angle between Proximal phalanx bottom plate and middle phalanx chute (rad)
θ_3	Angle between middle phalanx bottom plate and vertical bar of distal phalanx (rad)
h_1	The distance between F_1 contact point and proximal phalanx (mm)
h_2	The distance between F_2 contact point and middle phalanx (mm)
x_1	Height of slide block in proximal phalanx chute (mm)
x_2	Height of slide block in middle phalanx chute (mm)
Δl	Length of linear motor expansion (mm)

According to the principle of virtual work, the (2) can be obtained:

$$\begin{bmatrix} F_1 & F_2 \end{bmatrix} \begin{bmatrix} \delta P_1 \\ \delta P_2 \end{bmatrix} = F_0 \Delta l \tag{2}$$

The left side of (2) is the sum of the virtual work of the contact force on the far finger and middle finger, and the right side is the virtual work done by the driving force.

For the virtual displacement of the contact force, according to its horizontal and vertical coordinates in the plane cartesian coordinate system, partial derivatives of P_1, P_2 and θ_1, θ_2, and θ_3 are obtained as in (3) and (4).

$$\delta P_1 = \begin{bmatrix} -l_3 \sin \theta_1 & -h_1 \sin \theta_2 \\ l_3 \cos \theta_1 & h_1 \cos \theta_2 \end{bmatrix} \begin{bmatrix} \delta \theta_1 \\ \delta \theta_2 \end{bmatrix} \tag{3}$$

$$\delta P_2 = \begin{bmatrix} -l_3 \sin \theta_1 & -l_6 \sin \theta_2 & -h_2 \sin \theta_3 \\ l_3 \cos \theta_1 & l_6 \cos \theta_2 & h_2 \cos \theta_3 \end{bmatrix} \begin{bmatrix} \delta \theta_1 \\ \delta \theta_2 \\ \delta \theta_3 \end{bmatrix} \tag{4}$$

Through (3) and (4), the relation between the derivative of the position of the contact force and the angle of each knuckle can be established:

$$\begin{bmatrix} \delta P_1 \\ \delta P_2 \end{bmatrix} = \begin{bmatrix} -l_3 \sin \theta_1 & -h_1 \sin \theta_2 & 0 \\ l_3 \cos \theta_1 & h_1 \cos \theta_2 & 0 \\ -l_3 \sin \theta_1 & -l_6 \sin \theta_2 & -h_2 \sin \theta_3 \\ l_3 \cos \theta_1 & l_6 \cos \theta_2 & h_2 \cos \theta_3 \end{bmatrix} \begin{bmatrix} \delta \theta_1 \\ \delta \theta_2 \\ \delta \theta_3 \end{bmatrix} \tag{5}$$

The coefficient matrix in (5) is named J_1, and the formula of relation between $\delta \theta_1$ and Angle derivative is given:

$$\begin{bmatrix} \delta \theta_1 \\ \delta \theta_2 \\ \delta \theta_3 \end{bmatrix} = J_2[\delta \theta_1] \tag{6}$$

In (6), J_2 is a 3×1 matrix. In addition, the functional relation between θ_1 and linear motor elongation Δl is:

$$[\delta \Delta l] = J_3[\delta \theta_1] \tag{7}$$

In (7), J_3 is a 1×1 matrix. The relationship between the driving force of linear motor and the two contact forces can be obtained by connecting (2) and (7).

$$\begin{bmatrix} F_{1x} \\ F_{1y} \\ F_{2x} \\ F_{2y} \end{bmatrix} = [F_0]J_3(J_1J_2)^{-1} \tag{8}$$

In (8), the left side is a matrix with 4×1, which are the components of contact force F_1 and contact force F_2 in the x and y directions in the coordinate system.

The matrix J_2 is used to describe the relation between $\delta \theta_1$, $\delta \theta_2$ and $\delta \theta_3$. So, it is necessary to discuss the relation between θ_1 and θ_2, θ_1 and θ_3. The relationship between these angles can be found in statics models through geometric constraints.

For θ_1 and θ_2, the relation between the length of rod x_1 and the angle of θ_1 can be obtained by using the triangle $x_1 l_1 l_2$ in the statics model, as in (9).

$$x_1 = \frac{2 \cos \theta_1 l_1 \pm \sqrt{(2 \cos \theta_1 l_1)^2 - 4(l_1^2 - l_2^2)}}{2} \tag{9}$$

Since the rod length x_1 is greater than 0, the subtraction of molecules in (9) is discarded. In order to facilitate expression and calculation, quadrilateral $x_1 l_3 l_4 l_5$ is constructed. Add auxiliary lines for the quadrilateral $x_1 l_3 l_4 l_5$ to facilitate subsequent calculations, as shown in Fig. 5.

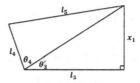

Fig. 5. The diagram of Auxiliary line

In this quadrangle, the trigonometric functions of θ_3' and θ_4 are obtained first, then the final relation between θ_2 and θ_1 is obtained, as in the followings.

$$\cos \theta_3' = \frac{l_3}{\sqrt{x_1^2 + l_3^2}} \tag{10}$$

$$\sin \theta_3' = \frac{x_1}{\sqrt{x_1^2 + l_3^2}} \tag{11}$$

$$\cos \theta_4 = \frac{l_4^2 + x_1^2 + l_3^2 - l_5^2}{2 l_4 \sqrt{x_1^2 + l_3^2}} \tag{12}$$

$$\sin \theta_4 = \sqrt{1 - (\cos \theta_4)^2} \tag{13}$$

$$\cos \theta_2 = \cos \theta_3' \cos \theta_4 - \sin \theta_3' \sin \theta_4 \tag{14}$$

The above (10) to (13) are trigonometric functions of θ_3' and θ_4. By combining the above four equations, (14) can be obtained. The relation between θ_2 and θ_1 can be obtained by linking (9). The relation between $\delta\theta_2$ and $\delta\theta_1$ can be obtained by calculating partial derivatives of θ_2 and θ_1 respectively in (14).

The relation between θ_3 and θ_2 can be obtained by the same method because of the similarity of the structure before and after the mechanical finger. Meanwhile, the geometric relation of the quadrangle $x_2 l_6 l_7 l_8$ is given, as shown in Fig. 6.

The trigonometric functions of θ_5 and θ_6 can be obtained through the geometric constraints. The expression of θ_3 obtained as the followings.

$$\cos \theta_3 = \cos \theta_5 \cos \theta_6 - \sin \theta_5 \sin \theta_6 \tag{15}$$

Similarly, in the above equations, the trigonometric functions of θ_5 and θ_6 can be expressed by θ_2. The relationship between θ_3 and θ_2 can be deduced by connecting with (15). The relation between $\delta\theta_3$ and $\delta\theta_2$ can be obtained by calculating partial derivatives of θ_3 and θ_2 respectively in (15). The relation between $\delta\theta_3$ and $\delta\theta_1$ can be obtained by the relation between $\delta\theta_2$ and $\delta\theta_1$ obtained above.

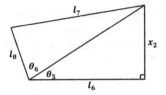

Fig. 6. The diagram of geometric.

Let's say A and B be matrices with 1×1, respectively, and list the following equations.

$$[\delta\theta_2] = A[\delta\theta_1] \tag{16}$$

$$[\delta\theta_3] = B[\delta\theta_1] \tag{17}$$

Thus, the expression of J_2 matrix can be obtained as in (18).

$$J_2 = \begin{bmatrix} 1 \\ A \\ B \end{bmatrix} \tag{18}$$

The relationship between $\delta\Delta l$ and $\delta\theta_1$ is derived by using the geometric relation of the hand part in the statics model, and the matrix J_3 is obtained. Here, we extract a quadrilateral $\Delta l l_{12} l_{13} l_{14}$ from the statics model and add an auxiliary line, as in Fig. 7.

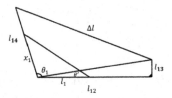

Fig. 7. The diagram of Auxiliary line.

In Fig. 7, angle θ' is a part of angle θ_1. The trigonometric function expression of θ' can be expressed by the length of the sides of the quadrilateral as follows.

$$\cos\theta' = \frac{l_{12}}{\sqrt{l_{12}^2 + l_{13}^2}} \tag{19}$$

$$\sin\theta' = \frac{l_{13}}{\sqrt{l_{12}^2 + l_{13}^2}} \tag{20}$$

The denominator in (19) and (20) is the diagonal length of $\Delta l l_{12} l_{13} l_{14}$.

The relationship between the length of linear motor Δl and angle θ_1 can be obtained by cosine theorem and difference angle formula, as in (21).

$$\Delta l^2 = l_{14}^2 + l_{12}^2 + l_{13}^2 - 2l_{14}\sqrt{l_{12}^2 + l_{13}^2}(\cos\theta'\cos\theta_1 + \sin\theta'\sin\theta_1) \tag{21}$$

In (21), l_{12}, l_{13} and l_{14} are known quantities, and the trigonometric function of angle θ' can be replaced by the expression expressed by the known quantities. Therefore, this formula can be used to describe the relationship between linear motor length Δl and Angle θ_1. The relation between $\delta\Delta l$ and $\delta\theta_1$ can be obtained by calculating partial derivatives of Δl and θ_1 respectively in (21). The expression of matrix J_3 can be obtained by coupling (7).

3.2   Statics Simulation

According to (12) in the above statics analysis results, the final equation of the contact force matrix can be obtained by combining the matrix J_1, J_2 and J_3. Through MATLAB simulation, the three-dimensional function diagram between the contact force F_1, the angle θ_2 and θ_3 of middle phalanx, and the position h_1 and h_2 of the contact force can be obtained. The specific image is shown in Fig. 8.

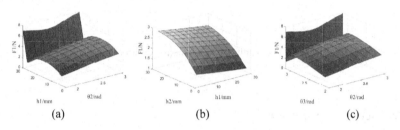

(a)   (b)   (c)

Fig. 8. The results of MATLAB analysis

It can be seen from Fig. 8(a) that with the increase of the contact point h_1, the contact force F_1 firstly increases and then decreases, reaching the lowest point at 27mm Proximal phalanx and then rising rapidly. However, the contact force F_1 is less affected by the change of angle θ_2, and generally shows a gentle upward trend. It can be seen from Fig. 8(b) that the contact force F_1 increases with the increase of h_2. As can be seen from Fig. 8(c), F_1 first increase and then decrease with increasing θ_3, and rise abruptly when approaching the boundary.

3.3   Kinematic Simulation

As shown in Fig. 3, the three-dimensional model of the robot, all parts are connected by rotating pairs, and middle phalanx and distal phalanx are coupled with proximal phalanx through connecting rod mechanism. In this section, kinematics simulation analysis will be conducted on the coupling motion of metacarpophalangeal joint MCP, proximal joint PIP and distal joint DIP, so as to explore the relationship between PIP and DIP and the movement of MCP joint.

ADAMS software was used for this simulation. The angular velocity of 10°/s was applied to the MCP joint, and the simulation time was 6.3s. Therefore, the MCP Angle change curve is a straight line with a amplitude of 63°. Figure 9(a), Fig. 9(b), and Fig. 9(c) represent the angular changes of MCP, PIP and DIP, respectively. Their horizontal axis represents the simulation time of the robot, and the vertical axis represents the rotation Angle of the corresponding joint. According to Fig. 9, the motion Angle amplitudes of PIP joint and DIP joint are 90° and 72° respectively, and the motion Angle curve is smooth and approximately linear, so it can meet the needs of human finger rehabilitation training.

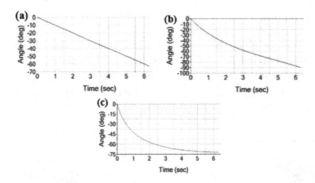

Fig. 9. The results of joint kinematics simulation

4   Prototype Production

4.1   The Construction of Experimental Platform

To reduce the complexity of the robot's overall system, the four power sources of the robot used the linear drive electric cylinders of INSPIRE-ROBOTS company. The model of electric cylinders is LAF30-024D (INSPIRE-ROBOTS, China).

The motor is driven by the USB to LVTTL3.3V debugging board. It is equipped with USB interface, which can be connected to the upper computer to realize the serial communication between the upper computer and the linear motor. The debugging board has six PWM (Pulse Width Modulation) output interfaces and can control six linear motors at the same time. The data monitoring software uses the linear motor debugging software of INSPIRE-ROBOTS company to monitor and analyze the data. The interface of the software is shown in Fig. 10.

4.2   Physical Experiment

By using three passive prismatic pairs to connect with the human hand, the robot has strong wearing adaptability, which can be used for different sizes of human hands within a certain range. Two fitness experiments with larger male hand and smaller male hand were conducted, smaller male hand, as shown in Fig. 11(a) and Fig. 11(b), respectively.

We carried out four finger independent rehabilitation experiment and four finger simultaneous rehabilitation experiment respectively. Figure 12(a)-(d) show the independent rehabilitation of the index finger, middle finger, ring finger and little finger,

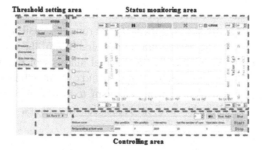

Fig. 10. The developed human-robot interface

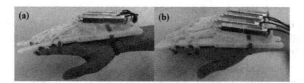

Fig. 11. Wearing diagram

respectively. Figure 12(e) shows the four-finger simultaneous rehabilitation experiment. At the same time, we made the experimenters relax their hands and enabled them to grab daily objects by wearing the hand rehabilitation robot, so as to verify the force transfer performance of the rehabilitation robot, as shown in Fig. 12(f).

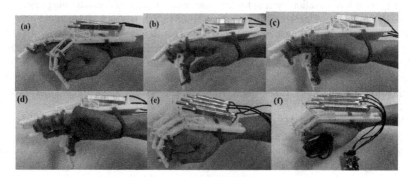

Fig. 12. Robot rehabilitation experiment

5   First Section

In this paper, a hand rehabilitation robot is proposed to improve the human-robot physical interaction performance. The reasonable structure makes the robot realize the coupling movement of three finger phalanxes through a relatively simple mechanical structure. The human-robot connection mechanism adds three passive prismatic pairs and two passive rotating pairs to the robot, which solves the human-robot compatibility. The statics analysis and kinematic simulation verify the running feasibility of the robot, and the real experiment verifies the performance and reliability of the robot.

In the future, we will complete the mechanical analysis of the human-robot connection mechanism, calibrate the mechanism [20] and optimize the structural design. In addition, we will add some sensors to the mechanism, to further improve its human-robot interaction performance on the basis of our researches in sensors.

References

1. Dong, M., Zhou, Y., Li, J., et al.: State of the art in parallel ankle rehabilitation robot: a systematic review. J. NeuroEng. Rehabil. **18**(52) (2021)
2. Li, C., et al.: Quantitative assessment of hand motor function for post-stroke rehabilitation based on HAGCN and multimodality fusion. IEEE Trans. Neural Syst. Rehabil. Eng. **30**, 2032–2041 (2022)
3. Li, J., Fan, W., Dong, M., et al.: Implementation of passive compliance training on a parallel ankle rehabilitation robot to enhance safety. Indus. Robot Int. J. Robo. Res. Appl. **47**(5), 747–755 (2020)
4. Vermillion, B.C., Dromerick, A.W., Lee, S.W.: Toward restoration of normal mechanics of functional hand tasks post-stroke: subject-specific approach to reinforce impaired muscle function. IEEE Trans. Neural Syst. Rehabil. Eng. **27**(8), 1606–1616 (2019). Aug.
5. Sarac, M., Solazzi, M., Frisoli, A.: Design requirements of generic hand exoskeletons and survey of hand exoskeletons for rehabilitation, assistive, or haptic use. IEEE Trans. Haptics **12**(4), 400–413 (2019). Oct.
6. Song, X., Van De Ven, S.S., Liu, L., Wouda, F.J., Wang, H., Shull, P.B.: Activities of daily living-based rehabilitation system for arm and hand motor function retraining after stroke. IEEE Trans. Neural Syst. Rehabil. Eng. **30**, 621–631 (2022)
7. Sanders, Q., Chan, V., Augsburger, R., Cramer, S.C., Reinkensmeyer, D.J., Do, A.H.: Feasibility of wearable sensing for in-home finger rehabilitation early after stroke. IEEE Trans. Neural Syst. Rehabil. Eng. **28**(6), 1363–1372 (2020). Jun.
8. Colombo, R., et al.: The SonicHand protocol for rehabilitation of hand motor function: a validation and feasibility study. IEEE Trans. Neural Syst. Rehabil. Eng. **27**(4), 664–672 (2019). Apr.
9. Chen, X., et al.: A wearable hand rehabilitation system with soft gloves. IEEE Trans. Ind. Inform. **17**(2), 943–952 (2021). Feb.
10. Guo, N., et al.: SSVEP-based brain computer interface controlled soft robotic glove for post-stroke hand function rehabilitation. IEEE Trans. Neural Syst. Rehabil. Eng. **30**, 1737–1744 (2022)
11. Kim, D.H., Lee, Y., Park, H.-S.: Cooperative hand therapy via a soft, wearable, and unilateral telerobotic system. IEEE Trans. Biomed. Eng. **70**(1), 366–377 (2023). Jan.
12. Correia, C., et al.: Improving grasp function after spinal cord injury with a soft robotic glove. IEEE Trans. Neural Syst. Rehabil. Eng. **28**(6), 1407–1415 (2020). Jun.
13. Yurkewich, A., Hebert, D., Wang, R.H., Mihailidis, A.: Hand Extension Robot Orthosis (HERO) glove: development and testing with stroke survivors with severe hand impairment. IEEE Trans. Neural Syst. Rehabil. Eng. **27**(5), 916–926 (2019). May
14. Chen, Z.-H., Yang, Y.-L., Lin, K.-W., Sun, P.-C., Chen, C.-S.: Functional assessment of 3D-printed multifunction assistive hand device for chronic stroke patients. IEEE Trans. Neural Syst. Rehabil. Eng. **30**, 1261–1266 (2022)

15. Wang, D., Meng, Q., Meng, Q., Li, X., Yu, H.: Design and development of a portable exoskeleton for hand rehabilitation. IEEE Trans. Neural Syst. Rehabil. Eng. **26**(12), 2376–2386 (2018). Dec.
16. Yang, L., Zhang, F., Zhu, J., Fu, Y.: A portable device for hand rehabilitation with force cognition: design, interaction, and experiment. IEEE Trans. Cogn. Dev. Syst. **14**(2), 599–607 (2022). Jun.
17. Cheng, L., Chen, M., Li, Z.: Design and control of a wearable hand rehabilitation robot. IEEE Access **6**, 74039–74050 (2018)
18. Cisnal, A., Perez-Turiel, J., Fraile, J.-C., Sierra, D., De La Fuente, E.: RobHand: a hand exoskeleton with real-time EMG-driven embedded control. quantifying hand gesture recognition delays for bilateral rehabilitation. IEEE Access **9**, 137809–137823 (2021)
19. Li, J., Kong, Y., Dong, M., et al.: Development of a linear-parallel and self-adaptive underactuated hand compensated for the four-link and sliding base mechanism. Robotica **40**(6), 2047–2064 (2022)
20. Dong, M., Kong, Y., Li, J., et al.: Kinematic calibration of a parallel 2-UPS/RRR ankle rehabilitation robot. Journal of Healthcare Engineering, Article ID 3053629 (2020)
21. Dong, M., Fang, B., Li, J., et al.: Wearable sensing devices for upper limbs: a systematic review. Proc. Inst. Mech. Eng. Part H-J. Eng. Med. **235**(1), 117–130 (2021)
22. Dong, M., Yao, G., Li, J., et al.: Calibration of low cost IMU's inertial sensors for improved attitude estimation. J. Intell. Robot. Syst. **100**, 1015–1029 (2020)

Human-Computer Interactive Digital-Twin System Driven by Magnetic-Inertia Fusion Data

Minghao Zhou, Ruikang Ge, Xiaotong Cai, and Huimin Shen[✉]

School of Mechanical Engineering, University of Shanghai for Science and Technology,
Shanghai 200093, China
hmshen@usst.edu.cn

Abstract. As the basic interface for human-computer interaction, human hand allows us to operate digital devices in a natural and intuitive way. With the advent of touch screens, gestures and other forms of gesture recognition technology, the role of the hand in human-computer interaction has become even more important. From mobile devices to game consoles, virtual reality systems to industrial systems, it enables us to quickly manipulate objects and perform complex tasks that are difficult to achieve with traditional input devices. In this paper, we develop a digital twin system based on magnetic inertial data driven data glove, and build a personalized 3D virtual hand model in Solidworks. Import Simulink through the United Robotics Description Format (URDF) plug-in. Then Simscpae Multibody is used to drive the virtual hand model in real time. The simulation results show that the virtual finger model obtained by the inverse solution of magnetic positioning can follow the human hand to complete the corresponding action under the interface of Simulink, and the real-time performance is good.

Keywords: Data gloves · Magneto-inertial sensing unit · Solidworks · Simulink · Digital Twin · URDF

1 Background

Human-computer interaction (HCI) [1] refers to the study of human-computer interaction with the purpose of designing, implementing, and evaluating computer systems that are easy to use, efficient, and enjoyable. With the increase of human dependence on technology, it has become an important branch of computer science, psychology, engineering, design and other related disciplines. Compared with the early command line interface and text input, modern human-computer interaction systems have achieved great improvements: graphical user interface (GUI), touch screen, speech recognition, virtual reality and other interaction methods, so that users can interact with computer systems in a more natural, convenient, flexible way. Meanwhile, human-computer interaction also covers user experience design [2], artificial intelligence, machine learning [3] and other fields, so as to improve the computer system's understanding of user requirements and the quality of interactive experience [4].

© The Author(s), under exclusive license to Springer Nature Singapore Pte Ltd. 2023
H. Yang et al. (Eds.): ICIRA 2023, LNAI 14274, pp. 38–46, 2023.
https://doi.org/10.1007/978-981-99-6501-4_4

Research at the intersection of physics and neuroscience plays an increasingly important role in HCI. Physicists and neuroscientists have provided many valuable insights into human-computer interaction by studying the interaction between biological and physical principles. In physics [5], we study phenomena such as object motion, force and energy conversion, which are central to human-computer interaction. For example, physicists can study how to design the right gamepads, buttons, touch screens, and other controllers for more natural and efficient human-computer interaction. In neuroscience [6], we study the mechanisms of how the brain processes information and controls the actions of the body. This helps us understand the nature of human perception, attention, learning, thinking and action. This knowledge can be translated into better methods and tools for designing, developing, and evaluating human-computer interaction systems.

A data glove is a smart glove that can capture and record human hand movements and finger positions. It can interact with a computer or other device, enabling users to control interfaces and applications through gestures. The design and development of data gloves have received a lot of attention due to their physical and neuroscientific properties. As an interface between the physical and nervous systems, data gloves have the following advantages:

Biological signal acquisition ability [7]: Data gloves can collect and record biological signals of human hands, such as muscle activity and electrical signals. The collection of these signals can provide information to help designers better understand the user's gesture and interaction needs, making the design more accurate and user-friendly.

High accuracy [8]: Data gloves can provide more accurate hand and finger position, recognize close to real natural gestures, and accurately reproduce these natural gestures. This kind of high precision simulation will further promote the development of virtual reality and augmented reality technology.

Natural perception [9]: Hand control using data gloves has a more natural perception and response, and does not require learning new control languages or techniques. This kind of natural perception makes the user smoother to use in human-computer interaction.

Real-time feedback [10]: Data glove can provide real-time feedback to track, record and feedback various gestures of users in real time. This real-time feedback allows users to get immediate feedback, better adjust gestures and improve interaction efficiency.

In this paper, the simulation platform system is built to verify the practical feasibility of the glove driven by magnetic inertial sensing data as the interface between the physical system and the nervous system.

2 Information-Driven Digital-Twin System for Human-Computer Interaction

As an important natural medium for human interaction with the external environment, hand has a high degree of flexibility and can realize complex hand movements. Therefore, efficient and accurate recognition of hand posture is of great significance for hand human-machine environment interaction. This paper verifies the feasibility of hand as an interface between human and environment through real-time acquisition and processing of hand motion data through experimental equipment.

2.1 Data Processing Terminal

The overall structure of human-computer interaction simulation system based on data glove is shown in Fig. 1. The control of data glove on virtual hand is realized in Simulink. The basic function of Simscape Multibody[11] plug-in in Simulink is to simulate the motion of mechanical parts. Relying on Simulink, the data in J-Link can be transmitted in real time, and the data of each joint Angle we need can be read and then sent to the rotating joint of each virtual hand to realize the control of virtual finger movement.

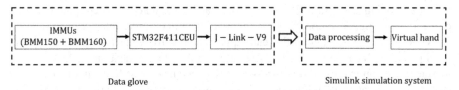

Fig. 1. System overall structure diagram.

In order to better and faster read the inverse data, J-Link is selected as the data transfer station, Simulink can directly read the data, which makes us in the real-time simulation of the extension greatly reduced. Keil was used to write and process the F411 microcontroller, and the obtained data was packaged and sent to the transfer station in a matrix way for the convenience of subsequent operations. Hal library was used for data upload programming.

2.2 Virtual Hand 3D Model

Simscape Multibody's built-in modeling capability is poor and does not work well with the component finger and joint model, but its solid module can import the model from outside. It is inefficient to import not only each knuckle, but also to set the rotating joint between the knuckles. And easy to cause problems after import. Therefore, this simulation adopts the plug-in United Robotics Description Format (URDF) [12] to import the model. This plug-in is a unified description format for robots, and relevant parameters can be designed in advance after the modeling is completed. The length of each knuckle obtained according to the inverse magnetic positioning model is modeled with Solidworks. Because the knuckle length has the greatest influence on the movement of the hand, the thickness of the finger is not considered. During the exercise of the hand, the valgus/introversion Angle of the fingertip depends on the valgus/introversion Angle of the root joint of the finger. Therefore, in order to reduce simulation interference, we use a rotating pair for the interphalangeal connection except the root of the finger, while the root joint is closed with a ball axis. Three-dimensional modeling was conducted according to the above conditions, and the hand assembly drawing was shown in Fig. 2.

After the 3D model is established, we need to pre-process the model in Solidworks, so that after exporting the URDF file, Simulink can read the 3D virtual hand model smoothly as we expected. For the preprocessing of the model, the axis of rotation with pitch Angle formed by the rotation motion of all finger joints around the axis should be defined first.

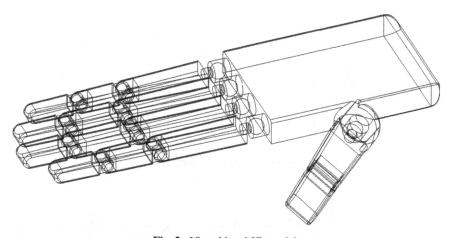

Fig. 2. Virtual hand 3D model.

In the assembly drawing, the coaxial axis connected with the hole axis between each knuckle should be taken as the axis of rotation. Secondly, the Cartesian coordinate system should be established with the center point of each joint as the coordinate origin. The other joints except the root joint are connected by the rotation pair in Simscape Multibody. The definition of the rotation pair by this plug-in is rotation around the Z-axis. In order to realize the simulation of finger movement without the phenomenon of mold penetration, nine Cartesian coordinate systems were established. For the movement of the root joint of five fingers, the yaw Angle has little influence on the direct movement of fingers, so the influence of this Angle is ignored, and the root joint movement only receives the influence of two angles, namely the pitch Angle and the Angle of convergence/valgus, that is, the rotational freedom in two directions. For the accuracy of real-time simulation, In Simscape Multibody, a double universal hinge is selected as the connection element between finger root and palm. The two axes of rotation defined by the double universal hinge element system are X and Y axes. Therefore, the motion directions of hand pitch and valgus/introversion are defined as X and Y axes when the coordinate system is established. Therefore, five Cartesian coordinate systems at the joint of finger root are established. Taking the middle finger as an example, the pretreatment of coordinate axes and rotation axes is shown in Fig. 3.

After the axis of rotation and coordinate system of each finger joint are determined, the URDF plug-in is used in Solidworks to define each joint of the pretreated finger model as joint, and define the global fixed coordinate system, so as to carry out relative motion in the follow-up real-time simulation. Finally, the URDF file is exported to prepare for the follow-up simulation. When Simscape Multibody plug-in is used to read the URDF model file, in order to generate the model more easily and quickly, the code is input in MATLAB, and the simulation hand model can be directly generated in Simscape Multibody as shown in Fig. 4.

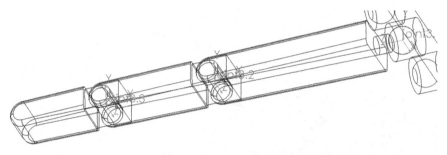

Fig. 3. Finger joint definition preconditioning.

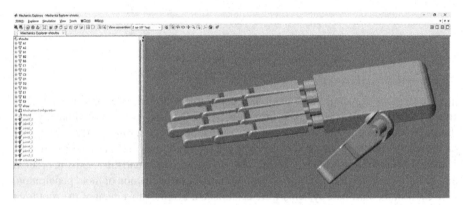

Fig. 4. Simscape Multibody hand simulation.

2.3 Virtual Hand Simulation Network

The subsequent processing of the imported model was carried out in Simulink. In order to realize real-time dynamic simulation, the Motion data supply mode in the rotating pair and double universal hinge was set to be provided externally, and then each joint directly read the matrix data uploaded in J-Link-v9 to drive the motion. However, it is necessary to process the data when reading the data. The data provided by the data glove is the input signal, while the driving data required by the virtual hand movement is the physical signal. Therefore, in data reading, Simulink-PS Converter should be used to realize the transformation from the input signal to the physical signal [13]. In addition, in order to avoid errors in the signal converter solver, we will set up the automatic second-order filtering of the input signal, using the default filtering time constant of 0.001s. The above analysis of this step of data processing is completed in this paper. Taking the knuckle of the middle finger root as an example, the simulation network in Simscape Multibody is shown in Fig. 5. C1 is the model of knuckle, and the left end is double universal hinge, one end is connected to the palm and the other is connected to the knuckle. Run the program to observe the simulation results.

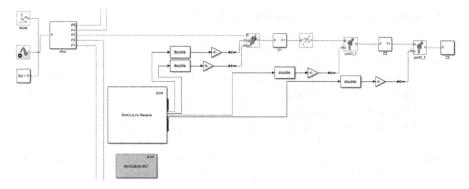

Fig. 5. Simscape Multibody Hand simulation network diagram.

3 Magnetic-Inertia Fusion Hand Motion Data Acquisition

The working principle of data glove is based on full attitude information inversion of smart finger unit based on magnetic and inertial sensing fusion [14], which will not be elaborated here. The overall hardware components of the data glove twin system include 3 magnetic-inertial sensor units, 12 inertial sensor units, a STM32F411 single chip microcomputer and a J-Link-V9 module. The physical picture of the overall device is shown in Fig. 6 (J-Link module is not included in the figure). In order to more accurately measure the bending Angle of the knuckle, the biological model of human finger knuckle is adopted. Each sensing unit is placed in the distribution as shown in the figure below, in order to measure the more accurate attitude of each joint. Sensors placed at each knuckle output acceleration and angular velocity information as well as spatial euler angles. Then the data fusion algorithm [15] based on gradient descent algorithm can obtain the pitch Angle and the Angle of convergence/outswing of each joint.

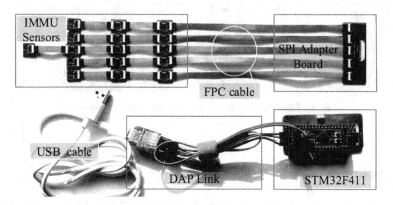

Fig. 6. Data glove physical picture.

4 System Effectiveness Simulation Verification

Figure 7 shows the real picture of the data glove. The end of the glove is connected to J-Link-v9, and then J-Link-v9 is connected to the computer through the data cable, so as to realize real-time data transmission of the data glove and continuous data reading by the virtual hand in Simscape Multibody. The operator wears data gloves and makes specific gestures. The control effect of human hand movements on virtual hand movements is shown in Fig. 8. It can be seen that when the human hand makes a specific gesture, the data glove will map the measured data into the virtual model after processing, and the virtual manipulator will also make corresponding actions. In the actual system verification, because the MCU timing interrupt program is set for 0.1s to upload a data to J-Link-v9, in addition to Simulink data reading and Simulink-ps Converter filter there is a time difference, so there is a delay in the actual simulation system.

Fig. 7. Data glove wearing physical picture.

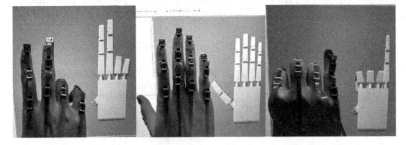

Fig. 8. Data gloves correspond to virtual hand movements.

5 Conclusion

In this paper, based on the magnetic-inertial measurement unit (IMU), a data glove is designed to be used as the interface of human-computer interaction. The finger model is built in Solidworks through the inverse knuckle-length of the finger, and the system is imported by URDF plug-in and built in Simulink for experiments. The experimental results show that the virtual hand model simulation system based on Simscape Multibody can simulate the movement of human hand more realistically, and the system has low delay and good real-time performance. It can provide a platform for human-computer interaction, and make the connection between human and machine more flexible and closer. Through the simulation experiment, we can experience the advantages of data glove in human-computer interaction:

More natural and intuitive interaction: Through data gloves, users can directly control the computer system by using their hand movements and posture. This interaction is closer to human's daily action habits, so as to be more natural and intuitive.

Improve interaction accuracy and response speed: The data glove can record and feedback hand movements and posture in real time through the sensor. This interactive mode can capture the user's movements more accurately and achieve very fast response speed.

Increase user immersion and engagement: Data gloves increase user immersion and engagement by allowing users to become more deeply involved in the interaction process. For example, the use of data gloves in virtual reality systems allows users to control virtual objects through hand movement and posture, thus enhancing the immersion and realism of virtual reality.

As a physical and nervous system interface, data gloves offer new possibilities and improved directions for human-computer interaction with advantages such as biological signal acquisition capability, high accuracy, natural perception and real-time feedback.

Acknowledgement. This work is supported by National Natural Science Foundation of China (No. 52175055).

References

1. Mohammed, Y.B., Karagozlu, D.: A review of human-computer interaction design approaches towards information systems development. BRAIN-Broad Res. Artif. Intell. Neurosci. **12**(1), 229–250 (2021)
2. Vera Anaya, D.F., Yuce, M.R.: A hands-free human-computer-interface platform for paralyzed patients using a TENG-based eyelash motion sensor. In: 2020 42nd Annual International Conference of the IEEE Engineering in Medicine & Biology Society (EMBC), pp. 4567–4570. Montreal, QC, Canada (2020)
3. Cai, J., Cai, J.: Human-computer interaction-based robotic design and development and control system testing —Prototyping and implementation testing study of a robotic hand. In: 2022 IEEE Asia-Pacific Conference on Image Processing, Electronics and Computers *(IPEC)*, pp. 471–475. Dalian, China (2022)
4. Liu, X.: Earth Environ. Sci. **252**, 042090 (2019)
5. Królak, A., Strumiłło, P.: Eye-blink detection system for human–computer interaction. Univ. Access Inf. Soc. **11**, 409–419 (2012)
6. Hao, Z., et al.: Biofabrication of a Low Modulus Bioelectroprobe for Neurons to Grow Into. Materials (2012)
7. Jiang, S., Kang, P., Song, X., Lo, B.P.L., Shull, P.B.: Emerging wearable interfaces and algorithms for hand gesture recognition. In: IEEE Reviews in Biomedical Engineering, vol. 15, pp. 85–102 (2022)

8. Pan, M., Tang, Y., Li, H.: State-of-the-art in data gloves: a review of hardware, algorithms, and applications. In: IEEE Transactions on Instrumentation and Measurement, vol. 72, pp. 1–15 (2023). Art no. 4002515

9. Almeida, L., et al.: Towards natural interaction in immersive reality with a cyber-glove. In: 2019 IEEE International Conference on Systems, Man and Cybernetics (SMC), pp. 2653–2658. Bari, Italy (2019)

10. Chou, W., Wang, T., Hu, L.: Design of data glove and arm type haptic interface. In: 11th Symposium on Haptic Interfaces for Virtual Environment and Teleoperator Systems, 2003. HAPTICS 2003. Proceedings, pp. 422–427. Los Angeles, CA, USA (2003)

11. Michał, S., Leszek, B., Jarosław, P., Wojciech, K.: Modeling and simulation of movement of dispersed group of mobile robots using Simscape multibody software. In: AIP Conference Proceedings (2019)

12. Jiang, Y., Peng, P., Wang, L., Wang, J., Liu, Y., Wu, J.: Modeling and Simulation of Unmanned Driving System for Load Haul Dump Vehicles in Underground Mines. Sustainability (2022)

13. Kaur, G., Kumar, S.: Comparison: Matrix Converter, Cycloconverter, and DC Link Converter. In: Singh, S., Wen, F., Jain, M. (eds.) Advances in Energy and Power Systems. Lecture Notes in Electrical Engineering, vol. 508. Springer, Singapore (2018)

14. Shen, H., Ge, R., Gu, X., Cai, X., Gan, Y., Yang, G.: Method of dexterous finger unit full-pose modeling based on magnetic-inertial sensor fusion. Jixie Gongcheng Xuebao **58**(18), 133–140 (2022)

15. Zhu, X., Tian, W., Li, G., Yu, J.: Research on localization vehicle based on multiple sensors fusion system. In: 2017 International Conference on Computer Network, Electronic and Automation (ICCNEA), pp. 491–494. Xi'an, China (2017)

Motion Planning for Pelvis-Assisted Walking Training Robot

Qianpeng Wang[1,2], Jia Wang[1,2], Jinxing Qiu[1,2], Mo Yang[1,2], and Tao Qin[1,2(✉)]

[1] Xiangyang Key Laboratory of Rehabilitation Medicine and Rehabilitation Engineering Technology, Xiangyang 441053, Hubei, China
heu_qt@163.com
[2] School of Mechanical Engineering, Hubei University of Arts and Science, Xiangyang 441053, Hubei, China

Abstract. A pelvic-assisted walking training robot is proposed for individuals with walking difficulties, such as hemiplegic patients and the elderly. Firstly, an innovative overall structure of the pelvic-assisted walking training robot with a symmetric layout is designed based on the requirements of rehabilitation robotics and clinical rehabilitation training. Secondly, according to the analysis of human gait, the gait cycle is divided into Initial Step, Continuous Cycle Step and Terminal Step, and the motion planning of these three parts is carried out reasonably. Finally, a semi-physical simulation analysis is conducted to validate the influence of different gait cycle durations on the swing of the lower limb assistive linkages, ensuring the fulfillment of walking rehabilitation training requirements.

Keywords: Walking training robot · Pelvic-assisted · Motion planning

1 Introduction

Stroke, also known as cerebrovascular accident (CVA), is a common condition characterized by the interruption of blood supply to the brain due to ruptured or blocked blood vessels. Stroke leads to oxygen deprivation and death of brain cells, resulting in various neurological and functional impairments. Motor dysfunction, such as abnormal muscle tone, weakness, or hemiparesis, often occurs in stroke patients [1]. Walking rehabilitation training plays a critical role in restoring the neuromuscular memory, improving balance, and enhancing coordination [2]. However, traditional walking rehabilitation training heavily relies on manual guidance and support from rehabilitation physicians or devices, which poses limitations and challenges. Firstly, the limited time and resources of rehabilitation physicians hinder the provision of long-duration, continuous, and accurate training for each patient. Secondly, traditional rehabilitation devices often lack intelligent and personalized features, making it difficult to adjust training plans according to individual needs and progress [3]. Additionally, manual guidance and support methods may vary subjectively, leading to inconsistencies and impacting the stability and comparability of rehabilitation outcomes.

© The Author(s), under exclusive license to Springer Nature Singapore Pte Ltd. 2023
H. Yang et al. (Eds.): ICIRA 2023, LNAI 14274, pp. 47–57, 2023.
https://doi.org/10.1007/978-981-99-6501-4_5

To overcome these limitations, walking training robots have been introduced as novel rehabilitation assistance tools. These robots can provide prolonged, continuous, precise, and fatigue-free treatment to patients based on predefined programs and parameters [4]. Additionally, robots equipped with sensing devices can monitor patients' training status and progress in real-time, record relevant data, and provide objective and independent indicators for rehabilitation treatment, supporting the development of personalized rehabilitation plans.

Among the existing walking training robots, exoskeleton-based and treadmill-based robots have been the main research directions [5, 6]. Exoskeleton-based robots facilitate walking training by tracking the leg movements of patients using mechanical legs, such as Lokomat by Hocoma (Switzerland) [7] and BLEEX designed by the University of California [8]. Treadmill-based robots simulate human walking and stair climbing processes using multiple motors, such as GaitMaster developed by Tsukuba University (Japan) [9] and G-EO-system by MediCal Park (Germany) [10]. Although these robots have made significant progress in meeting the rehabilitation needs of the elderly and hemiparetic patients, their applications in community and home environments are limited due to design, cost, and clinical requirements. Moreover, they often overlook the importance of pelvic-assisted lower limb coordination during human walking training, which may lead to pathological gait patterns. This aspect is particularly crucial in the walking rehabilitation of stroke patients because pelvic stability and coordination are vital for restoring normal gait patterns.

Therefore, this paper presents a unilateral single-drive dual-output pelvic-assisted walking training robot for rehabilitation training of stroke hemiparetic patients. The robot, driven by a single motor, controls pelvic motion and assists knee flexion during walking to meet the requirements of walking rehabilitation training. Through innovative mechanisms based on the coordination between pelvic and lower limb movements during human walking, the robot aims to provide rehabilitation training that closely mimics natural gait patterns.

2 Gait Analysis

As shown in Fig. 1, When humans walk, the stationary upright posture of both feet is the starting point of the entire movement. One leg on the side of the body swings forward, entering the single-support phase until the heel touches the ground. This marks the beginning of the alternating movement of the legs, forming a complete walking process. The entire process consists of three steps: the stance phase, the swing phase, and the stance phase.

The stance phase refers to the process where one foot is on the ground while the other foot begins to swing forward. This phase has a relatively short duration. Next is the swing phase, which involves the continuous alternating movement of both feet in a cyclic walking motion until the legs return to an upright position. Lastly, there is the stance phase, where one foot remains on the ground while the other foot is off the ground.

Each gait cycle consists of two phases: the stance phase and the swing phase. The stance phase represents the period when the foot is in contact with and bearing weight on the ground. It accounts for 60% of the entire gait cycle. In the stance phase, the

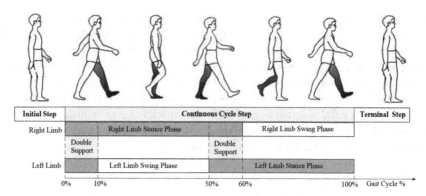

Fig. 1. A complete process of human walking on level ground

ball, sole, and heel of the foot respectively make contact with the ground, supporting the body weight while maintaining spring-like elasticity. At the same time, the body propels forward. The swing phase, which accounts for 40% of the gait cycle, represents the period when the foot is off the ground and swinging forward. In this phase, the knee bends forward, and the lower leg and foot swing back and forth, propelling the body forward.

Pelvic coordination refers to the coordinated movement of various parts of the pelvis in different motion modes to ensure smooth and effective movement. Pelvic stability refers to the ability of the structure and muscle strength of the pelvic region to resist external forces and maintain normal posture. By targeting rehabilitation training to the pelvic region, pelvic coordination and stability can be improved and restored, thereby improving overall function and movement efficiency. Movement pattern training is an effective method, and training for specific movement patterns can promote the coordination of the pelvic region. For example, gait training by simulating gait movements or functional training by simulating specific movements (such as squats, turns, etc.) can enhance synergistic movement in the pelvic area. This training method helps improve the function of the pelvic area and enhances the efficiency of overall body movement.

The pelvis connects the trunk and lower limbs and plays a key role in supporting and balancing the body. In the double support phase, when one foot hits the ground, the pelvis is tilted slightly to bear the weight of the body and ensure stability. At the same time, the other foot begins to swing forward and the pelvis needs to be fine-tuned to maintain balance. In the swing phase, the legs circulate and alternate, and the movement of the pelvis pushes the body forward. The pelvis rotates and tilts slightly, so that the legs can swing freely and promote the body to move forward. The analysis of normal gait rules is helpful to analyze how to use the pelvis to assist walking training and motion planning.

3 Pelvis-Assisted Walking Training Robot

Through the analysis of the gait cycle and the existing research status, a pelvic-assisted walking training robot, as shown in Fig. 2, was designed and researched by members of our laboratory, and the feasibility and rationality has been proved [11]. It consists of four main components: the auxiliary support unit, pelvic-assisted walking unit, self-tightening seat backrest, and medical treadmill. The auxiliary support unit consists of a fixed frame and a height-adjustable device, allowing the robot to better accommodate the patient's body characteristics and improve comfort. The pelvic-assisted walking unit includes the pelvic motion mechanism and lower limb assistive mechanism, aiming to assist the patient's pelvic motion and enhance the training effect. The self-tightening seat backrest adopts a parallelogram linkage mechanism with clamping pads at both ends to automatically secure the patient's pelvic position. This design ensures the patient's stability and comfort, enhancing the safety of the robot.

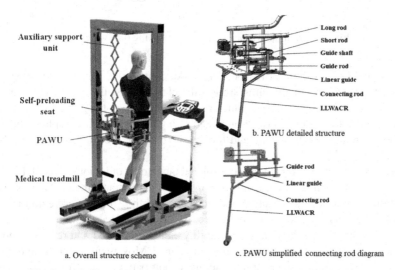

Fig. 2. Overall structure scheme of pelvis-assisted walking training robot

The motion of the pelvis along the sagittal axis and vertical axis is consistent with the law of sine and cosine motion, and the projection on the sagittal plane is approximately elliptical, pelvis-assisted walking training robots can refer to the structural design of elliptical machines. The detailed structure of the pelvic assisted walking unit is shown in Fig. 2, which is composed of long rod, drive shaft, short rod, guide shaft, guide rod, linear guide, connecting rod and lower limb walking assist connecting rod (LLWACR).

The main function of the LLWACR is that when there is leg lifting action in the rehabilitation training process of the patient, the LLWACR will exert an appropriate force on the patient's thigh to help the patient better complete the stepping movement and walk. This can make full use of the coordination and linkage between the joints of normal human walking, and ensure that the structure and driving form of the designed pelvis-assisted walking training robot are more consistent with the movement law of human walking, so as to improve the rehabilitation effect of walking training for patients.

4 Motion Planning

The walking motion planning of the pelvis-assisted walking training robot is a set of time-based motion trajectories determined by combining human movement patterns and robot motion principles. The purpose of walking planning is to ensure balance of the patient's limbs in contact with the robot during normal human movement, while also ensuring the stability and continuity of the robotic mechanism during assisted rehabilitation training, without generating sudden or abnormal situations that could harm the patient. Based on the time-dependent correlation of the robot-assisted continuous walking training, this study investigates the influence of walking cycle duration on the effectiveness of assistance.

4.1 Motion Planning of Continuous Cycle Step

During normal human walking, there is typically a distinct acceleration and deceleration phase between the stance and swing phases. To ensure that the pelvis-assisted walking training robot does not exhibit abrupt changes during these phase transitions and considering the movement pattern of the human pelvic center of mass in the sagittal plane, a cosine function can be employed to simulate the rotational speed profile of the driving shaft during the cyclic gait phase. Therefore, the rotational speed profile of the driving shaft of the right-side pelvic motion mechanism can be planned as follows:

$$\omega_{R1} = \begin{cases} \frac{1}{T}\left[A\cos\left(\frac{2\pi t}{\lambda T}\right) - \omega_0 - A\right], 0 \le t \le \lambda T \\ \frac{1}{T}\left[B\cos\left(\frac{2\pi t}{(1-\lambda)T} + M\right) - \omega_0 - B\right], \lambda T \le t \le T \end{cases} \tag{1}$$

In this equation, T represents the walking cycle, λ represents the proportion of the swing phase within one walking cycle, and it satisfies $0 < \lambda < 1$. A and B are constants, while ω_0 represents the initial value of the rotational speed of the driving shaft in the pelvic motion mechanism. When $t = \lambda T$, the duration of the stance and swing phases within a single gait cycle, ω_{R1}, should be equal. Additionally, according to the normal human walking pattern, it is recognized that the bilateral lower limbs exhibit coordinated motion with a 50% time interval between them within a walking cycle.

Therefore, we have the following equation:

$$\frac{1}{T}\left[A\cos\left(\frac{2\pi t}{\lambda T}\right) - \omega_0 - A\right]\Bigg|_{t=\lambda T} = \frac{1}{T}\left[B\cos\left(\frac{2\pi t}{(1-\lambda)T} + M\right) - \omega_0 - B\right]\Bigg|_{t=\lambda T} \tag{2}$$

$$\omega_{L1} = \begin{cases} \frac{1}{T}\left[B\cos\left(\frac{2\pi t}{(1-\lambda)T} + \frac{2-4\lambda}{1-\lambda}\pi\right) - \omega_0 - B\right], 0 \le t \le \lambda T \\ \frac{1}{T}\left[A\cos\left(\frac{2\pi t}{\lambda T}\right) - \omega_0 - A\right], \lambda T \le t \le T \end{cases} \tag{3}$$

$$\begin{cases} \int_0^T \omega_{R1}dt = 4\pi \\ \int_0^T \omega_{L1}dt = 4\pi \end{cases} \tag{4}$$

The unique structure of the pelvis-assisted walking training robot utilizes an indirect gear mechanism with a gear ratio of 2. Let $\lambda = 0.5$ be the variable representing this ratio, while $T = 10$s can also be taken into account. Based on this, the planned walking motion curve of the drive shafts of the bilateral pelvic motion mechanism during the cyclic step phase can be described as follows:

$$\omega_{R1} = \begin{cases} 13.94395\cos\left(\frac{2\pi t}{5}\right) - 25.94395, 0 \le t \le 5 \\ -39.83185\cos\left(\frac{2\pi t}{5}\right) - 51.83185, 5 \le t \le 10 \end{cases} \tag{5}$$

$$\omega_{L1} = \begin{cases} -39.83185\cos\left(\frac{2\pi(t+5)}{5}\right) - 58.803825, 0 \le t \le 5 \\ 13.94395\cos\left(\frac{2\pi(t-5)}{5}\right) - 32.915925, 5 \le t \le 10 \end{cases} \tag{6}$$

4.2 Motion Planning of Initial and Terminal Step

The initial and terminal step phases mark the beginning and end of the walking cycle, and they have shorter durations compared to the cyclic step phase. In order to fully consider the characteristics of the initial and terminal step phases and ensure smooth transitions between them and the cyclic step phase, a cubic spline curve can be employed to plan the walking motion in these two phases. Therefore, the planned drive shaft speed of the pelvis motion mechanism during the initial and terminal step phases can be described as follows:

$$\begin{cases} \omega_{R1-1} = a_1 t^3 + a_2 t^2 + a_3 t + a_4, 0 \le t \le T_0 \\ \omega_{R1-2} = b_1 t^3 + b_2 t^2 + b_3 t + b_4, 0 \le t \le T_1 \end{cases} \tag{7}$$

To ensure the formation of a complete walking motion cycle and smooth transitions between the initial step phase, cyclic step phase, and terminal step phase, it is required that the drive shaft speed of the pelvis motion mechanism during the initial and terminal step phases also satisfies the following conditions:

$$\begin{cases} \omega_{R1-1}|_{t=0} = 0 \\ \omega_{R1-1}|_{t=T_0} = \omega_{R1}|_{t=0} \\ \omega'_{R1-1}|_{t=T_0} = 0 \\ \int_0^{T_0} \omega_{R1-1}dt = \Delta\theta_{R1-1} \end{cases} \quad \begin{cases} \omega_{R1-2}|_{t=0} = \omega_{R1}|_{t=nT} \\ \omega_{R1-2}|_{t=T_1} = 0 \\ \omega'_{R1-2}|_{t=0} = 0 \\ \int_0^{T_1} \omega_{R1-2}dt = \Delta\theta_{R1-2} \end{cases} \tag{8}$$

where:

θ_{R1-T0} represents the starting position of the cyclic step phase, θ_{R1-10} represents the initial position of the initial step phase, $\Delta\theta_{R1-1} = \theta_{R1-T0} - \theta_{R1-10}$. Z represents the ending position of the cyclic step phase, and C represents the initial position of the terminal step phase, $\Delta\theta_{R1-2} = \theta_{R1-10} - \theta_{R1-Te}$.

In the equation, by selecting the initial phase duration T_0 and termination phase duration T_1, the corresponding drive shaft speeds ω_{R1-1} and ω_{R1-2} can be determined. Similarly, the drive shaft speeds ω_{L1-1} and ω_{L1-2} of the left pelvic motion mechanism during the initial and termination phases can be obtained. Summarizing the planned drive shaft speed patterns of the pelvic motion mechanism during the initial phase, cyclic phase, and termination phase, a complete model of the walking motion cycle can be integrated as follows:

$$\begin{cases} \omega_{RT} = \begin{cases} \omega_{R1-1}, 0 \le t \le T_0 \\ \omega_{R1}, 0 \le t \le T \\ \omega_{R1-2}, 0 \le t \le T_1 \end{cases} \\ \omega_{LT} = \begin{cases} \omega_{L1-1}, 0 \le t \le T_0 \\ \omega_{L1}, 0 \le t \le T \\ \omega_{L1-2}, 0 \le t \le T_1 \end{cases} \end{cases} \quad (9)$$

Based on the previous analysis, it can be determined that there is a certain correlation between the initial phase and termination phase on the right side, as well as the intermediate cyclic phase. Assuming the gait cycle time is $T = 10s$, the following derivation can be obtained:

$$\begin{cases} \omega_{R1-1} = -9.777778t^3 + 60.0t^2 - 96.0t, 0 \le t \le 3 \\ \omega_{R1-2} = 1.036t^3 - 1.774667t^2 - 12, 0 \le t \le 3 \end{cases} \quad (10)$$

Similarly, the motion planning curves for the initial phase and termination phase on the left side can be calculated as follows with respect to $T = 10s$:

$$\begin{cases} \omega_{L1-1} = -1.786081t^3 + 12.82449t^2 - 28.72272t, 0 \le t \le 3 \\ \omega_{L1-2} = 11.3623t^3 - 31.9789t^2 - 18.971975, 0 \le t \le 3 \end{cases} \quad (11)$$

4.3 Simulation Analysis

Based on the previous analysis, a Simscape model of the pelvis-assisted walking training robot can be constructed using MATLAB, as shown in Fig. 3, to conduct a semi-physical simulation analysis and verify the influence of different gait cycle durations on the swing motion of the lower limb assistive links.

In Sect. 4.2 of this paper, certain parameters, including $\lambda = 0.5$ and $T = 10s$, were defined. Within the gait cycle, the motion planning equations for the unilateral and bilateral pelvis motion mechanisms can be expressed as Eqs. (5) and (6). Similarly, the planning equations for the pelvis motion mechanisms in the initial and termination phases are equally important and can be represented by Eqs. (10) and (11). For ease of analysis, two gait cycle lengths were selected, and the velocity curves of the left and right pelvis motion mechanisms obtained from MATLAB simulations are shown in Fig. 4. From the graph, it can be observed that the planned curves are smooth without significant discontinuities, ensuring the smooth motion of the lower limb assistive links. According to the planned velocity patterns, the corresponding angular changes of the lower limb assistive links during the rotation of the bilateral pelvis motion mechanisms are depicted in Fig. 5. During the stance phase, the bilateral lower limb assistive links remain stationary, and they start to move with the driving axes only when entering the swing phase. The graph illustrates continuous and uninterrupted angular profiles of the lower limb assistive links, and the motion patterns of the bilateral lower limb assistive links are consistent with the planned assistive gait sequence. Furthermore, in Fig. 6,

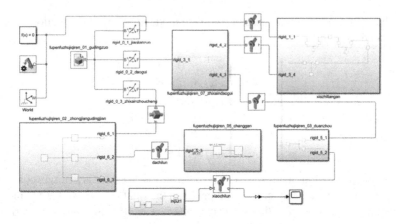

Fig. 3. Simscape model of pelvic assisted walking training robot

which shows the variation of angular velocities of the bilateral lower limb assistive links, the left and right lower limb assistive links maintain an interval of 50% of the gait cycle, aligning with the analysis in Sect. 4.2.

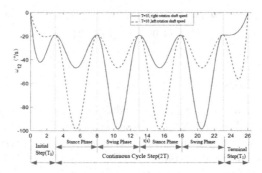

Fig. 4. Planned left and right crank speed curves when $T_0 = 3s$, $T = 10s$, $T_1 = 3s$

In actual walking training, there are significant differences in walking speeds among different patients. Therefore, this study investigated the influence of different gait cycle durations (T) on the lower limb assistive mechanism, as shown in Fig. 7, where the planned curves of the left and right pelvis driving axes are presented for various T values. It can be observed that when the gait cycle duration T is larger, the rate of change in the driving axes' rotational speed is lower, resulting in a decrease in the patient's walking speed. Figure 8 illustrates the pattern of angular changes in the lower limb assistive links, where the range of achievable angular motion for the lower limb assistive links is fixed, and different gait cycle durations T only affect the rate of rotation of the lower limb assistive links. Figure 9 represents the pattern of angular velocity changes in the lower limb assistive links, indicating the mutual relationship between the angular velocity of the lower limb assistive links and the driving axes during the swing phase. Therefore, through simulation analysis and by adjusting the gait cycle duration T, it is

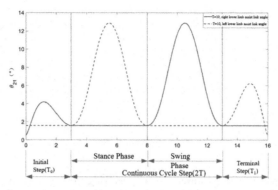

Fig. 5. The rotation angle curves of lower extremity link when $T_0 = 3s$, $T = 10s$, $T_1 = 3s$

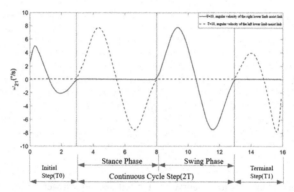

Fig. 6. The angular velocity curves of lower extremity link when $T_0 = 3s$, $T = 10s$, $T_1 = 3s$

possible to enhance or decrease the assistance provided by the assistive mechanism, thereby adjusting the walking speed of the patients.

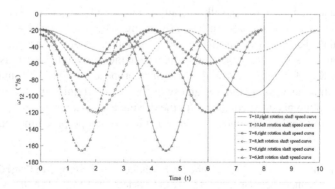

Fig. 7. The planned rotation angle curves of the left and right rotating shafts at different synchronous periods T

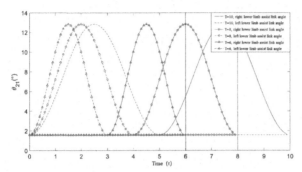

Fig. 8. The planned left and right lower extremity walking aid link rotation curves at different walking cycles T

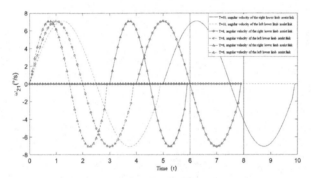

Fig. 9. The planned angular velocity curves of the left and right lower limb walking assistance links at different walking cycles T

5 Conclusion

This study analyzed the assisted walking training process of the pelvis-assisted walking training robot. Based on the normal human walking patterns, the process was divided into the initial phase, gait cycle phase, and termination phase. To accommodate the rehabilitation training needs of different patients and the structural characteristics of the pelvis-assisted walking training robot, researchers proposed a motion planning method using the continuous walking training and swing assistance training modes of the robot, and determined the planning equations for the driving axis rotational speed. The results of the simulation analysis demonstrate the feasibility of the proposed motion planning method.

Acknowledgments. This work was supported by Scientific Research Project of Education Department of Hubei Province under Grant No. D20222603, Science and Technology Innovation Team of Hubei University of Arts and Science under Grant 2022pytd01, Graduate Innovation Project of Hubei University of Arts and Science under Grant YCX202305.

References

1. Lou, Y.T., Yang, J.J., Ma, Y.F., et al.: Effects of different acupuncture methods combined with routine rehabilitation on gait of stroke patients. World Journal of Clinical Cases **8**(24), 14 (2020)
2. Jiang, G.: Early rehabilitation nursing for stroke patients with hemiplegia in neurology department. J. Clini. Nurs. Res. **5**(6), 5 (2021)
3. Tao, R., Ocampo, R., Fong, J., et al.: Modeling and emulating a physiotherapist's role in robot-assisted rehabilitation. Adv. Intell. Sys. **2**(7), 1900181 (2020)
4. Zou, Y.P., Zhang, A.D., Zhang, Q., et al.: Design and experimental research of 3-RRS parallel ankle rehabilitation robot. Micromachines **13**, 950 (2022)
5. Shi, D., Zhang, W., Zhang, W., et al.: A review on lower limb rehabilitation exoskeleton robots. Chinese J. Mecha. Eng. **32**(1), 1–11 (2019)
6. Lu, J., Guo, S., Zhou, M.: Weight loss system of lower limb rehabilitation robot based on force/position control. Metrology & Measurement Technique (2019)
7. Cherni, Y., Hajizadeh, M., Maso, F.D., et al.: Effects of body weight support and guidance force settings on muscle synergy during Lokomat walking. European J. Appl. Physiol. 1–14 (2021)
8. Zoss, A.B., Kazerooni, H., Chu, A.: Hybrid control of the berkeley lower extremity exoskeleton (BLEEX). IEEE/ASME Trans. Mechatron. **11**(2), 128–138 (2006)
9. Tanaka, N., Saitou, H., Takao, T., et al.: Effects of gait rehabilitation with a footpad-type locomotion interface in patients with chronic post-stroke hemiparesis: a pilot study. Clin. Rehabil. **26**(8), 686 (2012)
10. Andrenelli, E., Capecci, M., Biagio, L.D., et al.: Improving gait function and sensorimotor brain plasticity through robotic gait training with G-EO system in Parkinson's disease. Ann. Phys. Rehabil. Med. **61**, e79–e80 (2018)
11. Ma, Y.M., Xia, M., Qin, T., et al.: Design and motion planning of a pelvic-assisted walking training robot. In: Proceedings of 15th International Conference of Intelligent Robotics and Applications, ICIRA2022, pp. 694–704. Harbin, China (August 1–3, 2022)

Advanced Motion Control Technologies for Mobile Robots

Research on Motion Control of Underwater Robot Based on Improved Active Disturbance Rejection Control

Zhijie Hua[1], Haobin Ruan[1], Dawei Tu[1(✉)], Xu Zhang[1,2], and Kaiwei Zhang[1]

[1] School of Mechatronic Engineering and Automation, Shanghai University, Shanghai, China
tdw@shu.edu.cn
[2] Wuxi Research Institute, Huazhong University of Science and Technology, Jiangsu, China

Abstract. The underwater robot based on visual guidance is disturbed by ocean currents, wind waves and other disturbances in the process of moving to the target position, which makes its motion nonlinear and uncertain. In this paper, an active disturbance rejection controller (ADRC) based on nonlinear function was proposed, which utilize the engineering practice concept of "large error, small gain" and "small error, large gain", to improve the motion control of visual-guided underwater robot. Firstly, the control model of the underwater robot is established. Next, an extended state observer based on the nfal function is designed and its convergence is verified by Lyapunov stability theory. Finally, the anti-disturbance comparison experiment of the proposed ADRC was carried out on the simulation platform, and the controller was applied to the specific practice. The experimental results show that the controller can eliminate the influence of external factors faster and has better anti-interference ability.

Keywords: Underwater robot · Active disturbance rejection controller · nonlinear function · anti-interference · Lyapunov

1 Introduction

Visual-guided underwater robots have a facilitating role in the exploration and exploitation of marine resources. These robots collect underwater images through their onboard cameras, identify and locate underwater targets in the images, and then guide themselves to approach the targets, adjust their posture, and perform underwater tasks. However, underwater robots are subject not only to hydrodynamic resistance during their motion towards targets but also to disturbances caused by dark currents, wind and waves, and ocean currents, making stable control difficult [1]. Developing a control system with good dynamic and stability performance is crucial for underwater robots. Currently, there are several methods for motion control of underwater robots, such as PID control [2], adaptive control [3], sliding mode variable structure control [4], fuzzy logic control [5], and neural network control [6]. Among them, PID control is widely used in underwater robot control due to its simple structure and superior control performance.

© The Author(s), under exclusive license to Springer Nature Singapore Pte Ltd. 2023
H. Yang et al. (Eds.): ICIRA 2023, LNAI 14274, pp. 61–73, 2023.
https://doi.org/10.1007/978-981-99-6501-4_6

However, the limitations of PID controllers are gradually becoming evident, such as poor environmental adaptability and low accuracy. To address this limitation, Professor Han Jingqing first proposed the Active Disturbance Rejection Control (ADRC) [7]. ADRC integrates modern control theory with the PID controller, treating the disturbances and wave errors in each control loop as the total disturbance of the system.

Traditional ADRCs employ the fal function as the nonlinear control function of the Extended State Observer (ESO). Although increasing the error feedback gain coefficient of the function can enhance the convergence and observation efficiency, the amplification of system noise due to high error feedback gain coefficients can also adversely affect the normal control of underwater robots [8]. Many studies [9–13] have been conducted on underwater robot control based on advanced ADRC. Yuxuan Shen et al. [9] proposed a new tracking differentiator of the ADRC, which can provide better noise attenuation performance and avoid the chattering phenomenon. Yan Z et al. [10] proposed a novel ADRC based on support vector regression(SVR), which uses SVR algorithm to adjust the coefficients of the nonlinear state error feedback part in ADRC to deal with nonlinear variations at different operating points. Tao Chen et al. [11] used the recurrent networks model (RNM) to optimize the parameters of ADRC, which can realize real-time optimizing to reject the disturbances much better. The majority of the work discussed above focuses on improving the motion control of underwater robots using traditional ADRC techniques, without delving into the internal workings of the ESO's nonlinear control function.

In this paper, an active disturbance rejection controller based on nfal function was proposed to improve the motion control of Visual-guided underwater robot. Using the heading control of an underwater robot as an example. Firstly, the heading control model of the underwater robot is established. Next, an extended state observer based on the nfal function is designed and its convergence is verified. Finally, the anti-interference performance of the controller is experimentally verified.

2 Heading Control Model of Underwater Robot

Maintaining a stable heading is a prerequisite for underwater robots to accurately complete underwater operations. When yaw occurs, the underwater robot needs to adjust its course by turning the bow to ensure that the movement is on the established route. The horizontal motion of the underwater robot mainly refers to the surge, sway and yaw motion on the XnY plane. The motion is related to the parameters u、$\dot{u}$、v、$\dot{v}$、r and $\dot{r}$. Ignoring other motion states, the meaning of each parameter is shown in Table 1. Suppose that $w = \dot{w} = p = \dot{p} = q = \dot{q} = 0$, and stipulates:

(1) The center of gravity position $P(x_g, y_g, z_g)$ of the underwater robot coincides with the center of buoyancy position $P(x_p, y_p, z_p)$, and both are located at the origin of the coordinates, that is,

$$\begin{cases} x_g = x_p = 0 \\ y_g = y_p = 0 \\ z_g = z_p = 0 \end{cases} \tag{1}$$

Table 1. Parameter definition

Degree of freedom	Motion	Linear velocity and angular velocity	Linear acceleration and angular acceleration	Position and Attitude
1	surge	u	$\dot{u}$	x
2	sway	v	$\dot{v}$	y
3	heave	w	$\dot{w}$	z
4	roll	p	$\dot{p}$	ϕ
5	pitch	q	$\dot{q}$	θ
6	yaw	r	$\dot{r}$	ψ

(2) The connection between the center of gravity and the center of buoyancy is located in the vertical position. At this time, the roll angle ϕ and the pitch angle θ of the robot are 0, that is,

$$\phi = \theta = 0 \tag{2}$$

Under the condition of meeting the above requirements, the motion equation of the underwater robot on the horizontal plane can be obtained as follows:

$$\left(n_{s1}^2 K_{P\prime} + n_{s2}^2 K_P + n_{s3}^2 K_{P\prime} + n_{s4}^2 K_P\right)\rho D^2 \sin\phi l_1 + N_r r + N_{r|r|} r|r| - \lambda_{6,6}\dot{r} = I_z\dot{r} \tag{3}$$

where, the thrust coefficient is K_P when the propeller rotates forward, and $K_{P\prime}$ when the propeller rotates backward. P is the driving force output when the propeller rotates forward, $P\prime$ is the driving force output when the propeller rotates backward, D is the diameter of the propeller, ρ is the density of the water, n_{st} is the rotation speed of the propeller, N_r and $N_{r|r|}$ are viscous hydrodynamic parameters, I_z is the rotational inertia around the Z axis, and $\lambda_{6,6}$ is the hydrodynamic coefficient of yaw inertia.

To simplify the motion equation, the smaller viscous hydrodynamic parameter $N_{r|r|}$ is ignored, and the real-time output speeds of the four thrusters are assumed to be the same. Combined with the kinematics model of underwater robot:

$$\dot{\psi} = \left(\frac{\sin\phi}{\cos\theta}\right)q + \left(\frac{\cos\phi}{\cos\theta}\right)r \tag{4}$$

The state-space equation of heading control can be derived as:

$$\begin{bmatrix} \dot{\psi} \\ \ddot{\psi} \end{bmatrix} = \begin{bmatrix} 0 & 1 \\ 0 & \frac{N_r}{\lambda_{6,6}+I_z} \end{bmatrix} \begin{bmatrix} \psi \\ \dot{\psi} \end{bmatrix} + \begin{bmatrix} 0 \\ \frac{2(K_P+K_P')\rho D^2 l_1 \sin\varphi}{\lambda_{6,6}+I_z} \end{bmatrix} n_{st}^2 \tag{5}$$

$$y = \begin{bmatrix} 1 & 0 \end{bmatrix} \begin{bmatrix} \psi \\ \dot{\psi} \end{bmatrix} \tag{6}$$

3   Method

3.1   The Principle of Active Disturbance Rejection Control

Active Disturbance Rejection Control (ADRC) is composed of Tracking Differentiator (TD), Extended State Observer (ESO) and Nonlinear State Feedback Law (NLSEF). The second-order heading control model with single input and single output is:

$$\begin{cases} \dot{\psi}_1(t) = \psi_2(t) \\ \dot{\psi}_2(t) = f(\psi_1(t), \psi_2(t), t, d(t)) + bn_{st}(t) \\ y(t) = \psi_1(t) \end{cases} \tag{7}$$

where, $\psi_1(t)$, $\psi_2(t)$ represent the state variables of each order of the system, $y(t)$ represents the output of the system, $n_{st}(t)$ represents the input of the system, $f(\psi_1(t), \psi_2(t), t, d(t))$ represents the total disturbance of the controlled system, which includes internal disturbance and external nonlinear disturbance $d(t)$, b represents the control gain.

The architecture of the ADRC is depicted in Fig. 1. Initially, the controller leverages a tracking differentiator to extract the differential signal of the heading input. Subsequently, an extended state observer is employed to monitor the output and disturbance of the heading control model. Ultimately, the NLSEF module accomplishes the heading control of the underwater robot. The three modules are independent of each other and are designed accordingly.

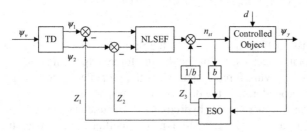

Fig. 1. The architecture of the ADRC

(1) **Tracking Differentiator**

The TD module, which synchronously produces the differential signal and tracks the input signal in a rapid manner, is an appropriate choice for the transitional stage. The transitional process can be mathematically expressed as:

$$\begin{cases} \psi_1(t+h) = \psi_1(t) + h\psi_2(t) \\ \psi_2(t+h) = \psi_2(t) + hfhan(\psi_2(t) - \psi_v(t), \psi_2(t), r, h_0) \end{cases} \tag{8}$$

where, ψ_i denotes the tracked heading angle of the underwater robot, r represents the speed coefficient, and h signifies the sampling step size, which correlates with the tracking velocity. Meanwhile, h_0 indicates the filtering coefficient of the controller, which is contingent upon the filtering capacity of the TD module. The central component is the optimal velocity control function, denoted as *fhan*(∗):

$$
fhan(*) =
\begin{cases}
a_0 = \sqrt{d^2 + 8r|h|} \\
a = \begin{cases} \psi_2 + \frac{(a_0 - d)}{2} sign(y), |y| > d_0 \\ \psi_2 + \frac{y}{h_0}, |y| \le d_0 \end{cases} \\
d = rh_0 \\
d_0 = h_0 d \\
y = \psi_1 + h\psi_2 \\
fhan = -\begin{cases} rsign(a), |a| > d \\ r\frac{a}{d}, |a| \le d \end{cases}
\end{cases}
\tag{9}
$$

(2) Extended State Observer

The extended state observer employs the input signal $n_{st}(t)$ and the output signal $\psi_y(t)$ of the heading control model of the underwater robot to observe the various-order state variables of the controlled system. Specifically, for the second-order heading control system of the underwater robot, the corresponding extended state observer is established as follows:

$$
\begin{cases}
e = z_1 - \psi_y \\
\dot{z}_1 = z_2 - \beta_1 e \\
\dot{z}_2 = z_3 - \beta_2 fal(e, \alpha_1, \delta) + bn_{st} \\
\dot{z}_3 = -\beta_3 fal(e, \alpha_2, \delta)
\end{cases}
\tag{10}
$$

where, z_1 denotes the tracking signal of the output value $\psi_y(t)$, whereas z_2 and z_3 represent differential signals of different orders. The gain coefficients of the control system are represented by $\beta_1, \cdots, \beta_3$. The fal function is a nonlinear power function that effectively mitigates high-frequency vibrations during the heading control process of underwater robot. The function is mathematically expressed as:

$$
fal(e, \alpha, \delta) =
\begin{cases}
\frac{e}{\delta^{\alpha-1}}, |e| \le \delta \\
|e|^{\alpha} sign(e), |e| > \delta
\end{cases}
\tag{11}
$$

where, e represents the system bias, δ represents the width of the interval within the linear range, α represents the exponent, and its value range is [0, 1]. The fal function has different derivative values when the independent variable takes values inside or outside the interval $[-\delta, \delta]$.

(3) Nonlinear State Feedback Law

In the control of the heading direction of an underwater robot, the output signal of the tracking differentiator ψ_1 is taken as the desired signal, while $\psi_2 \sim \psi_n$ are its differential signals. $z_1 \sim z_2$ are the state variables of the control system, and the difference between these two sets of variables is the system state error value ε_i:

$$
\varepsilon_i = \psi_i - z_i (i = 1, \cdots, n)
\tag{13}
$$

The system state error obtained in the above formula is nonlinearly combined:

$$
n_{st}(t) = \sum_{i=1}^{n} \mu_i fal(\varepsilon_i, r_i, \delta)(i = 1, \cdots, n)
\tag{14}
$$

where, μ_i, r_i, δ are the adjustable parameters of the controller, and the nonlinear control of the heading of the underwater robot is completed by reasonable parameter adjustment.

3.2 Extended State Observer Based on Nfal Function and its Convergence Verification

The extended state observer serves as the core module of the self-disturbance rejection controller, enabling real-time estimation of feedback and disturbance signals in underwater robotic systems. The continuity and smoothness of the nonlinear function in the ESO are directly related to its observational performance, which in turn impacts the overall controller's performance. The selection criteria for the nonlinear function in the ESO are specified as follows [14]:

(1) The function curve is required to be symmetric about the origin, exhibiting continuity and differentiability at all points.
(2) The function must possess a parsimonious set of tuning parameters, allowing for adjustment in accordance with the "large error, small gain; small error, large gain" control strategy.
(3) The function curve must demonstrate exceptional continuity, smoothness, and convergence properties.

The conventional extended state observer leverages the fal function as the nonlinear control function. The fal function adheres to criterion (1), exhibiting a symmetrical curve about the origin, as well as continuity and differentiability throughout its domain. However, the function requires an excessive number of tuning coefficients, leading to a cumbersome adjustment process during practical engineering applications. Additionally, the fal function is prone to chattering near the origin, rendering it unsuitable to meet the continuity and smoothness prerequisites of criterion (3) with respect to the function curve. Accordingly, a novel ESO based on the nfal nonlinear function was devised to enhance the tracking performance and disturbance rejection capability of the controller. The mathematical expression for the nfal function is presented below:

$$
nfal(x, \sigma, \mu) = \begin{cases} \mu \dfrac{e^{xe^{-\frac{x^2}{2\sigma^2}}} - 1}{e^{xe^{-\frac{x^2}{2\sigma^2}}} + 1}, & |x| \le 1 \\[4mm] \mu \dfrac{e^{sign(x)e^{-\frac{1}{2\sigma^2}}} - 1}{e^{sign(x)e^{-\frac{1}{2\sigma^2}}} + 1}, & |x| > 1 \end{cases}
\tag{15}
$$

where, x represents the system error, σ and μ are the adjustable parameters of nfal function, which are greater than 0. The nfal function is a composite function, where the exponential function of e is infinitely differentiable, and its curve is symmetric about the origin, conforming to the criterion (1). The nfal function contains two parameters that need to be tuned, which are related to the amplitude and frequency of the state observer. By tuning the parameters according to the adjustment rule, it conforms to the criterion (2).

The application of the nfal nonlinear function to the ESO yields an improved state observer model, which is presented in Eq. (16):

$$\begin{cases} e_1 = z_1 - y \\ \dot{z}_1 = z_2 - \beta_1 e_1 \\ \dot{z}_2 = z_3 - \beta_2 nfal(e_1, \sigma_1, \mu_1) + bu \\ \dot{z}_3 = -\beta_3 nfal(e_1, \sigma_2, \mu_2) \end{cases} \tag{16}$$

To ensure that the modified extended state observer can be applied in the ADRC, stability verification of the observer is required. Firstly, it is necessary to recalculate the system's error equation, which is shown in Eq. (17):

$$\dot{e} = -A(e)e \tag{17}$$

The expression of $A(e)$ is:

$$A(e) = \begin{bmatrix} \beta_1 & -1 & 0 \\ \beta_2 \frac{nfal(e_1,\sigma_1,\mu_1)}{e_1} & 0 & 1 \\ \beta_3 \frac{nfal(e_1,\sigma_2,\mu_2)}{e_1} & 0 & 0 \end{bmatrix} \tag{18}$$

Lemma 1 [15], If there exists a matrix D:

$$D = \begin{bmatrix} d_{11} & d_{12} & d_{13} \\ -d_{12} & d_{22} & d_{23} \\ -d_{13} & -d_{23} & d_{33} \end{bmatrix} \tag{19}$$

The diagonal elements of D are positive and the matrix $DA(e)$ is positive definite and symmetric, then the trivial solution (17) of the equation is asymptotically stable in the sense of Lyapunov. Therefore, it is necessary to construct a matrix D that satisfies the given conditions. Computing the matrix $DA(e)$ yields:

$$DA(e) = \begin{bmatrix} D_{11} & -d_{11} & -d_{12} \\ D_{21} & d_{12} & -d_{22} \\ D_{31} & d_{31} & d_{23} \end{bmatrix} \tag{20}$$

The expressions for D_{11}, D_{21}, and D_{31} are given by:

$$\begin{cases} D_{11} = d_{11}\beta_1 + d_{12}\beta_2 F_1 + d_{13}\beta_3 F_2 \\ D_{21} = -d_{12}\beta_1 + d_{22}\beta_2 F_1 + d_{23}\beta_3 F_2 \\ D_{31} = -d_{13}\beta_1 - d_{23}\beta_2 F_1 + d_{33}\beta_3 F_2 \\ F_1 = \frac{nfal(e_1,\sigma_1,\mu_1)}{e_1} \\ F_2 = \frac{nfal(e_1,\sigma_2,\mu_2)}{e_1} \end{cases} \tag{21}$$

The expressions for F_1 and F_2 in the equation denote the slope of the line connecting the origin to an arbitrary point on the function curve. Therefore, F_1 and F_2 are bounded and have finite value ranges, with $0 < F_1 < \mu$ and $0 < F_2 < \mu$. To ensure that $DA(e)$

is positive definite and symmetric, with equal diagonal elements and all three leading principal minors positive, the following equivalent conditions can be derived:

$$d_{22} = -d_{13} \tag{22}$$

$$D_{31} = -d_{12} \tag{23}$$

$$D_{21} = -d_{11} \tag{24}$$

$$D_{11} > 0 \tag{25}$$

$$\begin{vmatrix} D_{11} & -d_{11} \\ -d_{11} & d_{12} \end{vmatrix} > 0 \tag{26}$$

$$\begin{vmatrix} D_{11} & -d_{11} & d_{12} \\ -d_{11} & d_{12} & d_{22} \\ -d_{12} & -d_{22} & d_{23} \end{vmatrix} > 0 \tag{27}$$

By setting $d_{11} = 1$, and $d_{22} = d_{33} = \varepsilon$, where ε is a positive number approaching zero. Combining Eqs. (20) and (22), we obtain:

$$d_{13} = -\varepsilon \tag{28}$$

By combining the definition of D_{31} in Eq. (20) with the condition specified in Eq. (23), we can conclude that:

$$d_{12} = -\varepsilon\beta_1 + d_{23}\beta_2 F_1 - \varepsilon\beta_3 F_2 \tag{29}$$

By utilizing the definition of D_{21} presented in Eq. (20) and Eq. (29), in conjunction with the condition stated in (24), it can be inferred that:

$$d_{23} = \frac{1 + \varepsilon\beta_1^2 + \varepsilon\beta_2 F_1 + \varepsilon\beta_1\beta_3 F_2}{\beta_1\beta_2 F_1 - \beta_3 F_2} \tag{30}$$

Combining Eqs. (28) to (30) with the definition in Eq. (20), Eq. (25) is equivalent to:

$$D_{11} = \beta_1 - \varepsilon\beta_1\beta_2 F_1 + \frac{1 + \varepsilon\beta_1^2 + \varepsilon\beta_2 F_1 + \varepsilon\beta_1\beta_3 F_2}{\beta_1\beta_2 F_1 - \beta_3 F_2}\beta_2^2 F_1^2 - \varepsilon\beta_2\beta_3 F_1 F_2 - \varepsilon\beta_3 F_2 > 0 \tag{31}$$

Furthermore, as F_1 and F_2 are bounded and ε tends towards zero infinitely, the Eq. (31) can be simplified to:

$$D_{11} \approx \beta_1 + \frac{\beta_2^2 F_1^2}{\beta_1\beta_2 F_1 - \beta_3 F_2} > 0 \tag{32}$$

The necessary and sufficient condition for Eq. (32) to hold is:

$$\beta_1\beta_2 F_1 - \beta_3 F_2 > 0 \tag{33}$$

or

$$\begin{cases} \beta_1\beta_2 F_1 - \beta_3 F_2 < 0 \\ \beta_1(\beta_1\beta_2 F_1 - \beta_3 F_2) + \beta_2^2 F_1^2 < 0 \end{cases} \tag{34}$$

The following will discuss the conditions under which Eqs. (33) and (34) hold, respectively:

As ε approaches zero infinitely, it follows from Eqs. (29) and (30) that:

$$d_{23} \approx \frac{1}{\beta_1\beta_2 F_1 - \beta_3 F_2} > 0 \tag{35}$$

$$d_{12} \approx d_{23}\beta_2 F_1 > 0 \tag{36}$$

If condition (34) holds, then $d_{23} < 0$ and $d_{12} < 0$. This contradicts the property of a symmetric positive definite matrix, so condition (34) is excluded.

Assuming that condition (33) holds, it is consistent with the property that the diagonal elements of a symmetric positive definite matrix are greater than 0, as expressed in Eqs. (35) and (36). To determine if condition (33) can further ensure the validity of conditions (26) and (27), we substitute Eqs. (29) to (31) into condition (26) and set $d_{11} = 1$. This yields:

$$\begin{aligned} D_{11}d_{12} - 1 &= \frac{\beta_1^2\beta_2^2 F_1^2 - \beta_1\beta_2\beta_3 F_1 F_2 + \beta_2^3 F_1^3}{(\beta_1\beta_2 F_1 - \beta_3 F_2)^2} - 1 \\ &= \frac{(\beta_1\beta_2 F_1 - \beta_3 F_2)^2 + (\beta_1\beta_2 F_1 - \beta_3 F_2)(\beta_3 F_2) + \beta_2^3 F_1^3}{(\beta_1\beta_2 F_1 - \beta_3 F_2)^2} - 1 > 0 \end{aligned} \tag{37}$$

From Eq. (37), it follows that condition (33) is sufficient to ensure the validity of condition (26).

Expanding the determinant of condition (27), we obtain:

$$D_{11}(d_{12}d_{23} - d_{22}^2) - 2d_{11}d_{12}d_{22} - d_{12}^3 - d_{11}^2 d_{23} > 0 \tag{38}$$

Substituting $d_{11} = 1$, $d_{22} = d_{33} = \varepsilon(\varepsilon \to 0^+)$ into Eq. (38), we obtain:

$$D_{11}d_{12}d_{23} - d_{12}^3 - d_{23} > 0 \tag{39}$$

Substituting Eqs. (32), (35), and (36) into the left-hand side of Eq. (39), and simplifying, yields:

$$\begin{aligned} D_{11}d_{12}d_{23} - d_{12}^3 - d_{23} &= \frac{(\beta_1\beta_2 F_1 - \beta_3 F_2)(\beta_1\beta_2 F_1) + (\beta_1\beta_2 F_1 - \beta_3 F_2)^2}{(\beta_1\beta_2 F_1 - \beta_3 F_2)^3} \\ &= \frac{\beta_3 F_2}{(\beta_1\beta_2 F_1 - \beta_3 F_2)^2} > 0 \end{aligned} \tag{40}$$

Therefore, condition (33) can make inequality (27) hold.

In conclusion, when condition (33) holds, a matrix D that satisfies the requirements of Lemma 1 can be found, such that the matrix $DA(e)$ is symmetric positive definite. Then, it can be obtained that the trivial solution of system (17) is Lyapunov asymptotically stable.

4   Experiment

4.1   The Simulation Experiment of Underwater Robot Motion Control

To authenticate the efficacy of the ADRC based on the nfal function for regulating the heading control of an underwater robot, simulations were conducted in the Matlab R2018b/Simulink environment. The simulations were compared to PID controllers and traditional ADRC under the same conditions.

Figure 2 illustrates the schematic diagram of the heading control simulation. By utilizing the PID Tuner plugin embedded in Matlab, the parameters of the PID controller for the heading control simulation were configured to $K_P = 405.5, K_I = 253, K_D = 95$. The ADRC based on fal function and the ADRC based on the nfal function underwent parameter tuning within the control simulation, with a simulation time step of 0.01 s.

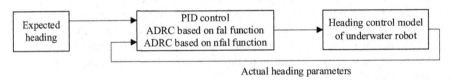

Actual heading parameters

Fig. 2. The schematic diagram of the heading control simulation

To compare the control performance of different controllers without interference, the heading change is added to the heading motion control simulation of the underwater robot at the beginning of 1s. The tracking response of the three controllers to the heading is shown in Fig. 3(a).

From the simulation curve of pursuit in Fig. 3(a), it can be seen that the ADRC based on nfal function has obvious advantages over PID controller and ADRC based on fal function in terms of transient characteristics control. The specific transient characteristics of the underwater robot when the heading is 60° is shown in Table 2.

Table 2. The transient characteristics table at 60° heading

Transient Characteristics	PID controller	The ADRC based on fal function	The ADRC based on nfal function
Rise time t_r/s	0.155	0.129	0.189
Peak value y_m/m	72.126	65.323	64.568
Peak time t_m/s	0.240	0.352	0.321
Settling time t_s/s	2.112	2.325	2.095
Overshoot $\sigma/\%$	18.60	12.30	10.05

The transient characteristics table for the prescribed heading of 60°shows that the ADRC based on nfal function has the shortest settling time and the smallest overshoot, with a reduction of 18.3% compared to the ADRC based on fal function. In motion control simulations of the underwater robot under undisturbed conditions, it exhibits the best tracking performance for the heading.

To assess the resilience of the ADRC based on nfal function, a bounded white noise signal is employed to replicate the effects of water flow during underwater operations. The response profiles of diverse controllers subjected to interference were exhibited in Fig. 3(b).

Figure 3(b) indicates that, under the influence of bounded white noise, the PID controller attains steady-state with a heading difference between the peak and valley, denoted by y_Δ of 20.5°. In contrast, the ADRC based on fal function yields a difference of 9.8°, whereas the ADRC based on nfal function manifests a significantly reduced difference of 7.6°. Thus, in the presence of white noise interference, the ADRC based on nfal function evinces an impressive capacity to swiftly counteract the external hydrodynamic factors, while concurrently preserving its ability to maintain the reference path's stability, thereby exemplifying an exceptional anti-interference prowess.

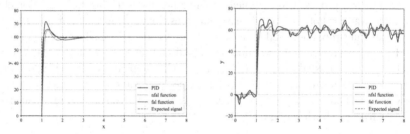

Fig. 3. (a) The response curve of heading motion control. (b) Response curve of heading motion control under noise interference

4.2 Autonomous Target Tracking Experiment of Underwater Robot

Figure 4(a) illustrates the experimental environment for autonomous target tracking by underwater robot. The Aohai Marine Autonomous Submersible Vehicle model, BlueROV2 Standard, was selected as the underwater robot for the experiment. As for the visual component, a proprietary underwater stereo camera was implemented to furnish the system with two-dimensional and three-dimensional information of underwater targets.

The underwater robot obtains the three-dimensional coordinates of the target in the underwater robot motion coordinate system by image coordinates and the depth information. Then, the yaw motion of the underwater robot is controlled to ensure that the underwater robot moves steadily to the same depth as the starfish. The starfish movement trajectory is shown in Fig. 4(b), with the initial position of the starfish at position 1. When the underwater robot tracks to a steady state, it moves the starfish to position 2. Afterwards, the underwater robot's motion and the starfish's movement alternate, and the starfish ends up at position 4.

72   Z. Hua et al.

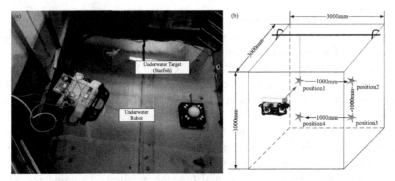

Fig. 4. (a) Autonomous target tracking experimental environment for underwater robot (b) Starfish motion diagram

By leveraging the electronic compass feedback on the mounted underwater robot, and utilizing the Matlab R2018b toolbox, the heading curve of the underwater robot during the target tracking process was obtained. Figure 5 illustrates the heading variation chart of the underwater robot. At 25s, the sea star transitioned from position 1 to position 2, the underwater robot adjusted its heading from 30° to 70° based on visual cues. At 125s, the sea star moved from position 3 to position 4, and the heading control signal was subsequently adjusted from 70° to 27°. The red line depicts the actual heading value feedback from the electronic compass. When the heading control command changes, the underwater robot can rapidly achieve steady-state with an overshoot of less than 10%, thereby realizing stable heading control.

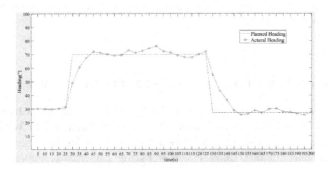

Fig. 5. Heading change diagram of underwater robot

5   Conclusion

This paper details the design of a controller for underwater robot, utilizing the engineering practice concept of "large error, small gain" and "small error, large gain." To enhance the extended state observer in the ADRC, a novel nonlinear function was proposed. Simulation experiments were conducted to compare the control performance and anti-interference ability of various controllers. Results demonstrate that the ADRC based on the nfal function outperforms both the PID controller and the traditional ADRC in terms of error tracking and control effectiveness under external noise interference. This provides a viable control scheme for the motion control system of vision-guided underwater robot.

Acknowledgements. This research was supported by the National Natural Science Foundation of China (Nos. 62176149, 61673252, and 51975344).

References

1. Lapierre, L.: Robust diving control of an AUV. Ocean Eng. **36**(1), 92–104 (2009)
2. Gonzalez-Vazquez, S., Moreno-Valenzuela, J.: A new nonlinear PI/PID controller for quadrotor posture regulation. Electronics, Robotics and Automotive Mechanics Conf. Morelos: IEEE, 642–647 (2010)
3. Divine, M., Ahmed, C., et al.: Adaptive depth and pitch control of an underwater vehicle with real-time experiments. Ocean Engineering (2015)
4. Zheng, E.H., Xiong, J.J., Luo, J.L.: Second order sliding mode control for a quadrotor UAV. Isa Transactions **53**(4), 1350–1356 (2014)
5. Chen, Y., Zhang, R., Zhao, X., et al.: Adaptive fuzzy inverse trajectory tracking control of underactuated underwater vehicle with uncertainties. Ocean Engineering **121**(JUL.15), 123–133 (2016)
6. Wang, Y., Zhang, M., Wilson, P.A., et al.: Adaptive neural network-based backstepping fault tolerant control for underwater vehicles with thruster fault. Ocean Engineering **110**(DEC.1PT.A), 15–24 (2015)
7. Han, J.Q.: Active disturbance rejection controller and its application. Control and Decision **13**(1), 19–23 (1998)
8. Orozco-Soto, S.M., Ibarra-Zannatha, J.M., Malo-Tamayo, A.J., et al.: Active disturbance rejection control for UAV hover using ROS. In: 2018 XX Congreso Mexicano de Robótica (COMRob), pp. 1–5. IEEE (2018)
9. Shen, Y., Shao, K., Ren, W., et al.: Diving control of autonomous underwater vehicle based on improved active disturbance rejection control approach. Neurocomputing **173**(JAN.15PT.3), 1377–1385 (2016)
10. Yan, Z., Liu, Y., Zhou, J., et al.: Path following control of an AUV under the current using the SVR-ADRC. J. Appl. Math. (2014-3-13), 1–12 (2014)
11. Chen, T., Gao, H., Xu, D., et al.: Trajectory-keeping control of AUV based on RNM-ADRC method under current disturbances for terrain survey mission. Lecture Notes in Computer Science (2017)
12. Zca, B., Bq, A., Ms, A., et al.: Q-Learning-based parameters adaptive algorithm for active disturbance rejection control and its application to ship course control. Neurocomputing **408**, 51–63 (2020)
13. Li, H., He, B., Yin, Q., et al.: Fuzzy Optimized MFAC Based on ADRC in AUV Heading Control. Electronics **8**(6), 608(2019)
14. Xiong, S., Wang, W., Liu, X., et al.: A novel extended state observer. ISA Trans. **58**, 309–317 (2015)
15. Lozgachev, G.I.: On a method of construction of Lyapunov functions. Autom. Remote. Control. **10**(10), 101–111 (1998)

Autonomous Navigation of Tracked Robot in Uneven Terrains

Gang He[1], Juntian Shi[1], Chao Liu[1], Weichao Guo[2], and Xinjun Sheng[1,2(✉)]

[1] State Key Laboratory of Mechanical System and Vibration, School of Mechanical Engineering, Shanghai Jiao Tong University, Shanghai 200240, China
xjsheng@sjtu.edu.cn
[2] Meta Robotics Institute, Shanghai Jiao Tong University, Shanghai 200240, China

Abstract. Since microdosing of chemical, biological, radiological, and nuclear (CBRN) contaminants is enough to cause great damage to humans, operating robots are widely used to handle CBRN-related tasks. However, how to improve the automation capabilities of these robots in uneven environments, such as autonomous navigation, is still a huge challenge. Current navigation methods usually set the scene as flat pavement, without considering the situation that the land slope exceeds a certain threshold. In order to explore ways of autonomous navigation in uneven environments, a 3D path planning and navigation method for the tracked robot is proposed in this paper, respecting applicable traversability constraints in uneven terrains. Firstly, a 3D graph-based map is built according to the occupancy map of the uneven environment. A set of spatial points, ensuring collision-avoidance of the robot, is randomly sampled in free space, and a vertex map is generated based on these vertices for robot traversing. Then, regarding the robot's climbing and obstacle crossing ability as constraints, a path planning algorithm is used to search for the best path based on the Dijkstra algorithm. Finally, a fusion SLAM method based on LiDAR, IMU and RGB-D camera is used to achieve real-time localization, and the pure pursuit algorithm is used for navigation. The simulation results show that the proposed method can provide a safe and effective 3D path for the tracked robot and enable the robot's autonomous navigation in uneven environments.

Keywords: Path planning · Navigation · Uneven terrains

1 Introduction

The environment with contamination of CBRN agents is known as a CBRN threat. These hazardous substances may be released during system failure or natural disasters and cause great harm to surroundings. With the development of robotics technology, robots with various functions have been put into the CBRN environment to carry out target searching or sampling, and these works have achieved remarkable results [1]. However, most robots still rely on human operation in practice, which poses potential hazards during the robot operation.

© The Author(s), under exclusive license to Springer Nature Singapore Pte Ltd. 2023
H. Yang et al. (Eds.): ICIRA 2023, LNAI 14274, pp. 74–84, 2023.
https://doi.org/10.1007/978-981-99-6501-4_7

Since the environment is unfamiliar to the operator, the operator's experience may be ineffective. High attention demands or repetitive tasks can lead to operator's fatigue and cause failures. Meanwhile, when the sensor is degraded (such as that the camera fails due to darkness), operational errors may occur due to the operator's inability to obtain environmental information in time. How to reduce requirements of the operator's skill and improve the automation capabilities of robots, including environment-detecting, path planning and navigation, has been widely concerned by researchers [2].

Autonomous navigation is an important part of robotic automation, connecting the progress from departure to operating in the target area. Autonomous navigation methods with a high applicability can effectively reduce the technical requirements of operators. At present, most robots are still limited to flat terrain [3]. But when facing slopes or stairs, they eventually have to rely on manual operation due to planning failures. Therefore, in order to improve the safety and stability of robot's navigation, it is necessary to develop 3D path planning and navigation methods suitable for uneven terrains.

Some robots, with a certain degree of path planning and autonomous navigation capabilities, have been applied to CBRN-related works. Guzman et al. [4] developed a CBRN robot called "RESCUER" for intervention, sampling, and situation awareness. It is able to build 2D maps and enable autonomous navigation. However, when dealing with slopes and stairs, human operation is still required. Liu et al. [5] used a robot equipped with a LIDAR and a nuclear-radiation-detection sensor, applying the Cartographer to 2D mapping and autonomous navigation in unknown environments, and verified the method in simulation and real world. Huang et al. [6] proposed an autonomous navigation method for nuclear emergency robots. They achieved real-time autonomous navigation by building a 2.5D multi-layer costmap including costmaps of terrain slope and nuclear radiation quantity, and then using A* algorithm for global path planning. Lazna et al. [7] proposed an autonomous robotic system for radiation detection. It contains functions like radiometric mapping, and explore areas of interest. They proposed a path planning and navigation method to realize the robot's exploration of areas of interest. Jonasson et al. [8] applied LIDAR-Vision fusion-based measurement and navigation solutions to the robot to map inside the Joint European Torus. Some researchers have tried to optimize path planning algorithms, such as A* algorithm [9] and RRT* algorithm [10], to improve navigation efficiency in CBRN environments. But most of these robots and autonomous navigation methods are still limited to flat terrain and are not suitable for uneven terrains.

Other researchers have focused on solving the problem of autonomous navigation in uneven terrains. Wang et al. [11] obtained a 2D traversable map based on 3D Octomap projection for the uneven and unstructured indoor environment, which calculated the slope of occupancy voxels, and then verified their navigation algorithm through simulation and real-world experiments in the indoor uneven environment. Kulkarni et al. [12] used a legged robot and an aerial robot for collaborative mapping and used the Dijkstra algorithm for path planning and navigation on the established 3D path map. Atas et al. [13] evaluated the sampling-based path planner in the Open Motion Planning Library (OMPL) to validate and compare robotic path planning in a 3D environment. It turns out that sampling-based methods tend to cause large computations and poor real-time performance. Neubert et al. [14] used a sampling-based method to assist in the robot's camera-based navigation in a given 3D map and complete the verification in the corridor dataset. Ratnayake et al. [15] proposed an exploration and navigation system based on Octomap, which can identify unexplored areas and complete autonomous navigation and exploration by robots. Maier et al. [16] proposed a 3D environment robot localization and path planning method based on a depth camera, and completed the verification on humanoid robots. Some researchers have also used machine-learning-related algorithms to achieve autonomous navigation [17–19], but these methods are not applicable because of the difficulty in obtaining the data set of CBRN environment.

Hence, to explore the problem of robot autonomous navigation in 3D uneven environment, a 3D path planning and navigation method for tracked robots is proposed herein. The method takes the robot's traversal capabilities as constraints, and realizes the path planning in the 3D uneven environment, which ensures high versatility. Then, based on a real-time localization method and pure pursuit algorithm, the autonomous navigation is realized. Simulation shows that uneven terrain and even slopes with large slopes can be planned and crossed by robots, which further verifies the effectiveness of the proposed method.

The paper is organized as followed: In Sect. 2, a graph-based map is generated, based on the occupancy map. It consists of traversable vertices and edges. In Sect. 3, the path planning algorithm incorporates the robot's terrain traversal capability into the planning in the form of edge weights, and then generates a global path suitable for the robot's traversal. In Sect. 4, a real-time localization method based on LIDAR and IMU is used to offer the robot's position in complex and uneven environments. In Sect. 5, a simulation study is conducted and verifies the technical feasibility of the method.

2   3D Graph-Based Map

Consistent and accurate maps are an important foundation for autonomous systems. For 3D environments, pre-establishing graphs consisting of vertices and edges can effectively improve the efficiency of robots in path planning and navigation. In this work, a graph-based map for robot path planning is built, based on the occupancy map. As for an occupancy map, let the occupied voxel be $V_{occupied}$, the free voxel be V_{free}, and the unknown voxel be $V_{unknown}$. First, a series of spatial points (s_i) are sampled, which are distributed in the robot's adjacent space, as shown in Fig. 1(a). However, there are some constraints in selecting these points, and those that do not meet these constraints will be considered invalid samples. Constraints are listed as: 1. For tracked robots, the height above the ground exceeds the set threshold; 2. Due to the geometric size of the robot itself, it is too close to the obstacle or wall; 3. On the path connected to the initial vertex (v_i), it will collide with the obstacle.

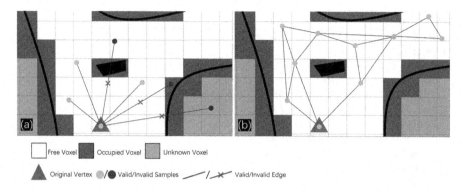

Fig. 1. The Graph-based map: (a) Samples in the robot's adjacent space; (b) Graph with valid vertices and edges.

$$samples\{s_0, s_1, \cdots, s_n\} = \begin{cases} invalid\,samples, & s_i\,not\,meets\,constraints \\ valid\,samples, & others. \end{cases} \quad (1)$$

$$\mathbb{G} = \{v_0, v_1, \cdots, v_n\},\,with\,valid\,edges. \quad (2)$$

After removing the invalid samples, the remaining samples are regarded as path vertices and connected with edges. Based on this sampling and graph building process, a Graph-based map $\mathbb{G}$ is also created, as shown in Fig. 1(b), which contains the path points and paths that the robot can pass through.

3 Path Planning and Autonomous Navigation of Tracked Robot

The weights of the valid edges in $\mathbb{G}$ are adjusted according to the maximum climbing angle of the robot. The Dijkstra algorithm is then used for global path planning, and the pure pursuit algorithm is used for autonomous navigation, based on a LIDAR-Inertial fusion SLAM method to achieving real-time localization.

3.1 Path Planning of Tracked Robot

In the 3D path planning process, the robot's ability to cross obstacles and climb hills must be taken into account. When the robot encounters a slope or obstacle, it must judge whether its traversal capability can make it cross the corresponding terrain. Otherwise, the path should be considered impassable. For each edge in $\mathbb{G}$, its slope can be thought of as the angle of inclination as the robot travels along it. Therefore, by adding the edge's slope as an impact factor to the calculation of the weight, the global path that can avoid large slopes can be effectively planned. More importantly, when the slope of the edge exceeds the robot's maximum climbing angle, its weight is set to a very large value, thus avoiding the edge in planning.

Algorithm 1. ObtainGlobalPath

Input: $\mathbb{G}$, $MaximunClimbingAngle$
Output: GP
    for all $v_i \in \mathbb{G}$ **do**
        for all $v_j nexttov_i$ **do**
            if $SLOPE(v_i, v_j) \leq MaximunClimblingAngle$ **then**
                $weight(v_i, v_j) = LENGTH(v_i, v_j) + SLOPE(v_i, v_j)$
            else
                $weight(v_i, v_j) = MaxValue$
            end if
        end for
    end for
    $GP \leftarrow GetDijkstraPath(\mathbb{G})$
    return GP

Then, on $\mathbb{G}$ improved by the robot's traversal capabilities, Dijkstra algorithm is used for obtaining global path ($GP = \{v'_0, v'_1, \cdots, v'_k\}, v'_j \in \mathbb{G}$), as shown in Algorithm 1.

3.2   Autonomous Navigation of Tracked Robot

The 2D localization method such as AMCL would fail in 3D environment, because the terrain is not flat. Therefore, in this work, a real-time localization method based on tightly-coupled LIDAR-Inertial odometry [20] is used to complete robot positioning in uneven terrains. A 3D LIDAR and an IMU are employed by the algorithm. Its framework is shown in Fig. 2. Let $\hat{\omega}_t$ and $\hat{a}_t$ be angular velocity and acceleration at time t. Respectively, they are affected by a slowly varying bias b_t and noise n_t.

$$\hat{\omega}_t = \omega_t + b_t^\omega + n_t^\omega \tag{3}$$

$$\hat{a}_t = R_t(a_t - g) + b_t^a + n_t^a \tag{4}$$

R_t is the rotation matrix from the coordinate of world to the robot's coordinate. Based on above formulas, the estimation of the robot's pose over time can be obtained through the IMU.

$$v_{t+\Delta t} = v_t + g\Delta t + R_t(\hat{a}_t - b_t^a - n_t^a)\Delta t \tag{5}$$

$$P_{t+\Delta t} = P_t + v_t\Delta t + \frac{1}{2}g\Delta t^2 + \frac{1}{2}R_t(\hat{a}_t - b_t^a - n_t^a)\Delta t^2 \tag{6}$$

$$R_{t+\Delta t} = R_t exp((\hat{\omega}_t - b_t^\omega - n_t^\omega)\Delta t) \tag{7}$$

Based on the pose estimation provided by the IMU, relatively accurate results can be obtained quickly in LIDAR odometry pointcloud-matching algorithm.

However, due to the very high echo rate of 3D LIDAR, if the pointcloud is directly used for the subsequent matching algorithm, it will lead to low computational efficiency and not meet the real-time requirements. So, the received LIDAR information needs to be processed.

First, feature extractions are performed on LIDAR frames. By calculating roughness of points over a local region [21], edge and plane features are extracted, which effectively reduces the number of points to be matched. Let c be the average roughness of the point p_i and S be the set of neighboring points p_j. The larger the value of c, the more likely it is that p_i is an edge point; The closer the value of c to 0, the more likely it is that p_i is a plane point.

$$c = \frac{1}{|S| \|p_i\|} \sum_{j \in S, j \neq i} \|p_i - p_j\| \tag{8}$$

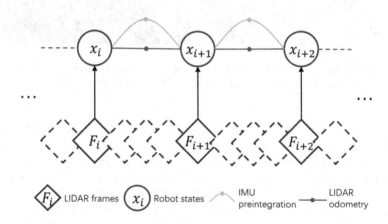

Fig. 2. The framework of the localization method

Further, every certain number of LIDAR frames are discarded, and the remaining two frames are selected as LIDAR key frames for estimation. This can effectively reduce the amount of computing in the system and improve the real-time performance of the localization algorithm. Base on the real-time localization, the Pure Pursuit algorithm is then used for autonomous navigation, which can control the robot's motion based on fewer parameters and can be simply and directly arranged on the robot.

4   Experiments and Results

To verify the proposed 3D path planning and navigation method, a simulation study is conducted in an environment with uneven terrain built in Gazebo. The composition of the tracked robot and its key capability parameters are confirmed. It shows that the path planning and navigation method can realize the functions of graph-based map establishment, 3D path planning and autonomous navigation in a 3D uneven environment.

4.1   Simulation Environment and 3D Robot Model

In this work, a narrow corridor (length: 40 m, width: 5 m) is built, with uneven terrain, a higher step, and scattered obstacles, as shown in Fig. 3(a). In this simulation environment, the robot needs to cross from the starting area to the area in red as the target for sampling or searching tasks. The occupancy map of the simulation environment is shown in Fig. 3(b), and its resolution is set to 0.15 m for increasing speed and maintaining accuracy.

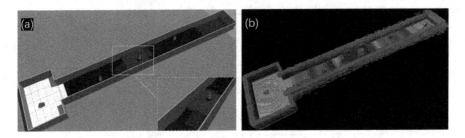

Fig. 3. (a) Simulation Environment (a corridor with uneven terrains in black and a higher step in blue and green); (b) Occupancy Map (Color figure online)

Due to robot capabilities and protection costs, the construction of the robot is subject to certain constraints, such as the robot's ability to cross obstacles, and the redundancy of sensors. In order to meet most needs of special scenarios, the principle for the robot construction is to have higher traversal capacity and fewer sensors. A 3D model of the CBRN robot is shown in Fig. 4. A tracked chassis serves as a mobile platform to provide more robust handling and better obstacle crossing capabilities. To reduce protection costs, only a 3D LIDAR, an IMU, and an RGB-D camera are used for situation awareness and autonomous navigation. Table 1 provides the key capability indicators of the robot, which are used as important constraints in subsequent path planning and navigation.

4.2   Graph-Based Map and Path Planning

On the occupancy map, a graphed-based map for robot path planning and navigation is obtained, as shown in Fig. 5(a). Due to the narrow corridor, the established vertices are more concentrated, and are distributed around the obstacle above the step, indicating that the robot can pass from both sides. In the uphill and downhill positions of the step, vertices and edges are tucked in on the slope, indicating that the robot can only pass through the step through the uphill/downhill.

Table 1. The key capability indicators of the robot

Capability Indicator	Maximum obstacle crossing	Maximum leap	Maximum climbing angle	Speed
-	120 mm	250 mm	≥30°	0–5 km/h

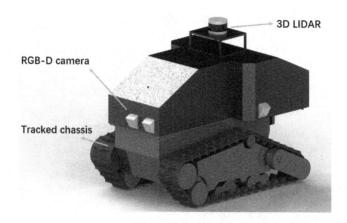

Fig. 4. 3D model of the tracked robot

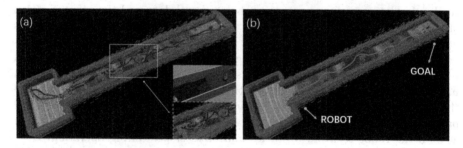

Fig. 5. (a) Graph-based map: vertices are represented by gray spheres and edges are represented by orange lines; (b) The global path is represented by a pink line. (Color figure online)

The global path from the starting point to the target area is generated, as shown in Fig. 5(b), and the average planning time is about 2.31 s. In order to verify the speed of the path planning algorithm, different lengths of crossing distance are applied to the planning algorithm, and according to Algorithm 1 and experimental results, it is shown that the algorithm has a time complexity $O(n^2)$. Since the longer the distance, the more vertices participate in the planning progress, which means that the amount of computation increases at the same time. Therefore, path planning over a long distance can lead to an unacceptable planning time or even failures (Fig. 6).

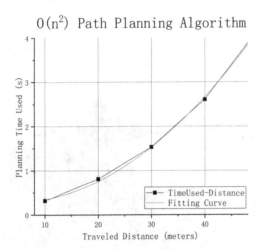

Fig. 6. The time used in planning varies by the traveled distance.

4.3 Autonomous Navigation

In the simulation environment, the robot sensors' data and the robot position obtained by the localization algorithm are used as input to realize autonomous navigation.

In order to reach the designated target area, the robot must pass through an uneven narrow corridor, and the entire simulation movement process is shown in Fig. 7, showing the robot's movement, the information of maps and sensors, and the global path (shown in a pink line in Fig. 7). It can be seen that the global path obtained based on Graph-based map and the path planning algorithm enables the robot to avoid obstacles and cross slopes during operation. Even under the limits of maximum speed (1.5 m/s, 2 rad/s), the robot can smoothly cross a distance of more than 40 m to reach the target area, which lasts about 108 s.

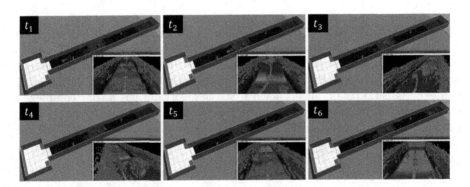

Fig. 7. The simulation of the CBRN robot: avoid obstacles at t_1, t_3, t_5; climb up/down the step at t_2, t_4; arrive at target area at t_6.

5   Conclusions

In this work, a 3D path planning and navigation method for the tracked robot is proposed, respecting applicable traversability constraints in uneven terrains, and accomplish the path planning and navigation. Firstly, a graph-based map is built, which serves as a graph that contains a set of vertices for robot traversing. Then, a path planning method, considering the robot's climbing and obstacle crossing ability as constraints, is proposed, in which the Dijkstra algorithm is used. Finally, a fusion SLAM method is used to achieve real-time localization, and the pure pursuit algorithm is used for navigation. The simulation results show that the proposed method is technically feasible and can enable the robot's autonomous navigation in uneven environments.

The result shows that the path planning method has a time complexity $O(n^2)$ and the cases in real world will be more complex, which means the importance of simplifying algorithms and real-time performance. The autonomous exploration and target sampling are challenging problem, which will be also considered in future research.

Acknowledgement. This work is jointly supported by National Natural Science Foundation of China (U1813224).

References

1. Tsitsimpelis, I., Taylor, C.J., Lennox, B., Joyce, M.J.: A review of ground-based robotic systems for the characterization of nuclear environments. Prog. Nucl. Energy **111**(3), 109–124 (2019)
2. Chang, F., et al.: Research status and key technologies analysis of operating robots for nuclear environment. Opto Electron. Eng. **47**(10), 200338 (2020)
3. Yang, L., Qi, J., Song, D., Xiao, J., Han, J., Xia, Y.: Survey of robot 3D path planning algorithms. J. Control Sci. Eng. **2016**, 1–22 (2016)
4. Guzman, R., Navarro, R., Ferre, J., Moreno, M.: Rescuer: development of a modular chemical, biological, radiological, and nuclear robot for intervention, sampling, and situation awareness. J. Field Robot. **33**(7), 931–945 (2016)
5. Liu, X., Cheng, L., Yang, Y., Yan, G., Xu, X., Zhang, Z.: An alpha/beta radiation mapping method using simultaneous localization and mapping for nuclear power plants. Machines **10**(9), 800 (2022)
6. Huang, Y., Shi, X., Zhou, Y., Xiong, Z.: Autonomous navigation of mobile robot in radiation environment with uneven terrain. Int. J. Intell. Robot. Appl. (2022)
7. Lazna, T., Fisera, O., Kares, J., Zalud, L.: Localization of ionizing radiation sources via an autonomous robotic system. Radiat. Prot. Dosimetry. **186**(2–3), 249–256 (2019)
8. Jonasson, E.T., et al.: Reconstructing JET using LIDAR-vision fusion. Fusion Eng. Des. **146**, 110952 (2019)
9. Chen, C., Cai, J., Wang, Z., Chen, F., Yi, W.: An improved A* algorithm for searching the minimum dose path in nuclear facilities. Prog. Nucl. Energy **126**, 103394 (2020)

10. Chao, N., Liu, Y.-K., Xia, H., Ayodeji, A., Bai, L.: Grid-based RRT* for minimum dose walking path-planning in complex radioactive environments. Ann. Nucl. Energy **115**, 73–82 (2018)
11. Wang, C., et al.: Autonomous mobile robot navigation in uneven and unstructured indoor environments. In: 2017 IEEE/RSJ International Conference on Intelligent Robots and Systems (IROS), pp. 109–116 (2017)
12. Kulkarni, M., et al.: Autonomous teamed exploration of subterranean environments using legged and aerial robots. In: 2022 International Conference on Robotics and Automation (ICRA), pp. 3306–3313 (2022)
13. Atas, F., Grimstad, L., Cielniak, G.: Evaluation of Sampling-Based Optimizing Planners for Outdoor Robot Navigation. arXiv preprint arXiv:2103.13666 (2021)
14. Neubert, P., Schubert, S., Protzel, P.: Sampling-based methods for visual navigation in 3D maps by synthesizing depth images. In: 2017 IEEE/RSJ International Conference on Intelligent Robots and Systems (IROS), pp. 2492–2498 (2017)
15. Ratnayake, K., Sooriyaarachchi, S., Gamage, C.: OENS: an octomap based exploration and navigation system. In: 2021 5th International Conference on Robotics and Automation Sciences (ICRAS), pp. 230–234 (2021)
16. Maier, D., Hornung, A., Bennewitz, M.: Real-time navigation in 3D environments based on depth camera data. In: 2012 12th IEEE-RAS International Conference on Humanoid Robots (Humanoids 2012), pp. 692–697 (2012)
17. Tsiakas, K., Kostavelis, I., Gasteratos, A., Tzovaras, D.: Autonomous vehicle navigation in semi-structured environments based on sparse waypoints and LiDAR road-tracking. In: 2021 IEEE/RSJ International Conference on Intelligent Robots and Systems (IROS), pp. 1244–1250 (2021)
18. Pfeiffer, M., Schaeuble, M., Nieto, J., Siegwart, R., Cadena, C.: From perception to decision: a data-driven approach to end-to-end motion planning for autonomous ground robots. In: 2017 IEEE International Conference on Robotics and Automation (ICRA), pp. 1527–1533 (2017)
19. Weerakoon, K., Sathyamoorthy, A.J., Patel, U., Manocha, D.: TERP: reliable planning in uneven outdoor environments using deep reinforcement learning. In: 2022 International Conference on Robotics and Automation (ICRA), pp. 9447–9453 (2022)
20. Shan, T., Englot, B., Meyers, D., Wang, W., Ratti, C., Rus, D.: LIO-SAM: tightly-coupled lidar inertial odometry via smoothing and mapping. In: 2020 IEEE/RSJ International Conference on Intelligent Robots and Systems (IROS), pp. 5135–5142 (2020)
21. Zhang, J., Singh, S.: Low-drift and real-time lidar odometry and mapping. Auton. Robot. **41**(2), 401–416 (2017)

DR-Informed-RRT* Algorithm: Efficient Path Planning for Quadruped Robots in Complex Environments

Haoyu Jiang[1], Qiao Zhou[1], Yulong Zhang[1], Xungao Zhong[1,3(✉)], and Xunyu Zhong[2(✉)]

[1] School of Electrical Engineering and Automation, Xiamen University of Technology, Xiamen 361024, China
zhongxungao@163.com
[2] School of Aerospace Engineering, Xiamen University, Xiamen 361005, China
zhongxunyu@xmu.edu.cn
[3] Xiamen Key Laboratory of Frontier Electric Power Equipment and Intelligent Control, Xiamen 361024, China

Abstract. Quadruped robotics system possesses superior trafficability. However, path planning for these robots in complex environments continues to present challenges. We propose a DR-Informed-RRT* (Dual-attached and reconstructed informed-RRT*) algorithm to address issues such as poor search optimality, low sampling efficiency, and excessive planning time. The path planning process is divided into two parts: initial path generation and path optimization. In the initial path generation phase, a dual sampling point approach with multiple sampling probabilities is employed to sample random points, reducing the number of futile node expansions and providing directionality to the growth of the random tree, thereby improving the algorithm's efficiency. Furthermore, the reconstruction of parent nodes and the elimination of redundant nodes are incorporated in the path optimization phase, introducing different types of parent nodes to optimize the path and reducing redundancy in the planned path. Our algorithm showed promising performance in simulations and successfully validated its feasibility on a quadruped robot.

Keywords: Quadruped robot navigation · Path planning · Informed-RRT* · Path optimization

1 Introduction

With the continuous advancement of robotics technology, various types of robot platforms are now frequently appearing in areas such as terrain exploration, disaster response, and healthcare services. Quadruped robots, with their superior terrain adaptability and enhanced maneuverability, are attracting increasing attention. The goal of global path planning for quadruped robots is to quickly and efficiently find the shortest path based on a known priori environmental map. However, current navigation algorithms for

© The Author(s), under exclusive license to Springer Nature Singapore Pte Ltd. 2023
H. Yang et al. (Eds.): ICIRA 2023, LNAI 14274, pp. 85–95, 2023.
https://doi.org/10.1007/978-981-99-6501-4_8

quadruped robots still face challenges such as high path planning costs and long navigation times. Common path planning algorithms can be categorized as search-based (Dijkstra [1], A* [2]) and bio-inspired (genetic algorithm [3], ant colony algorithm [4]). However, traditional path planning algorithms are unable to adapt to the complex and dynamic environments encountered today, and their planning efficiency is low.

In recent years, sampling-based algorithms have proven to be an effective approach for addressing path planning in high-dimensional environments for mobile robots. The Rapidly-Exploring Random Tree (RRT) algorithm proposed by LaValle in 1998 [5] is known for its fast planning speed and strong adaptability to dynamic environments. However, it suffers from high search randomness and a tendency to get trapped in local minima. In 2011, Karaman et al. introduced the RRT* algorithm [6], which combines completeness and asymptotic optimality but exhibits low search efficiency in large-scale scenarios. In 2013, LaValle proposed the Bi-RRT algorithm [7], which improves search speed by simultaneously generating RRT trees from the start and goal points. Building upon this, the RRT-connect algorithm [8] was introduced, incorporating a directional expansion strategy. However, the lack of an optimization process in RRT-connect leads to excessive redundant sampling and long planning times. The methods mentioned above involve random searches across the entire environment map and may not effectively reduce planning time. In 2014, Gammell et al. proposed the Informed-RRT* algorithm [9]. This method restricts the search space to an ellipsoidal subset after obtaining an initial path, iteratively refining it to obtain an optimal planning solution. It shares the completeness and optimality characteristics of RRT* while demonstrating superior path planning capability. Ryu et al. introduced an improved version of Informed RRT* [10] by skeletonizing the search space into a grid graph. This approach enables fast acquisition of initial solutions and significantly improves algorithm convergence rate. To address the low efficiency in generating paths of Informed RRT* in mobile robot navigation, Dai et al. proposed an optimization using a greedy algorithm and potential parent node reconstruction [11] in 2022. Mashayekhi et al. presented an improved Informed RRT* path planning algorithm based on node optimization [12]. By introducing an adaptive t-distribution function to alter the distribution probability of random points in different environments, the algorithm's efficiency is enhanced. These advancements aim to enhance the performance and efficiency of Informed RRT* algorithm, providing more effective and optimized solutions for mobile robot path planning.

Drawing on existing research findings, we propose a DR-Informed-RRT* algorithm to address the limitations of traditional algorithms in complex environments. The proposed algorithm divides the entire path planning process into two stages. In each planning stage, a strategy employing dual-sample points and multiple sampling probabilities is utilized during the sampling process. This strategy effectively balances the randomness of sampling with the directional guidance towards the goal. In the initial search path determination stage, a bidirectional search strategy is introduced, where two trees are generated separately from the start and goal positions, significantly accelerating the path search process. Furthermore, in the path optimization stage, a multi-level parent node reselection strategy is designed. Cost functions are assigned to these potential optimal parent nodes to minimize unnecessary collision detections, thereby reducing the optimization time.

2 Design of the Algorithm

2.1 Problem Description

First, let's concretize the concepts involved in the path planning process for quadruped robots and provide their respective definitions. Assuming $S \in R^n$ represents the global environmental space, S_{obs} denotes the space occupied by obstacles after inflation in the environmental space, S_{free} represents the space available for the free movement of the robot, where the robot can reach any two-dimensional spatial position without any restrictions, $x_{start} \in S_{free}$ denotes the initial position for path planning, while $x_{goal} \in D_{free}$ represents the destination position for path planning, $\sigma : (0, n) \in D$ represent a collision-free path in the environmental space, connecting points x_{start} and x_{goal} using n intermediate waypoints, and $p(x)$ denote the cost function that evaluates the cost of a path. The optimal path is achieved when $p(x)$ is minimized, and it can be represented as Eq. (1).

$$\sigma = \arg\{p(\sigma)|\sigma(0) = x_{start}, \sigma(n) = x_{goal}, \forall d \in [0, n], \sigma(d) \in S_{free}\} \qquad (1)$$

The algorithm generates a random tree denoted as $T = (V, E)$, where $V \in S_{free}$ represents all the nodes in the tree, and $E \in S_{free}$ represents all the branches in the tree.

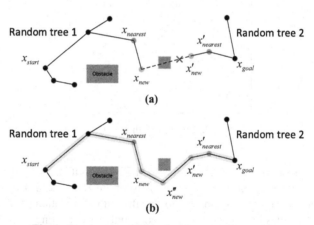

Fig. 1. Random tree bidirectional connection process

2.2 Informed-RRT* Algorithm Improvement Strategy

Dual Attachment. During the search process, two random search trees are created from the start and goal positions, respectively. The newly added sample point, denoted as x_{new}, expands the first random tree, while the new node x'_{new} in the second random tree is expanded in the direction of the line connecting nodes x_{new} and $x'_{nearest}$. In each iteration, both random trees are expanded, and attempts are made to connect the two trees. In Fig. 1(a), the connection process between x_{new} and x'_{new} is obstructed by an obstacle, resulting in a failed connection. In the next iteration of random tree expansion, the priority of expanding the two trees is swapped or generate another sample point, and the process is repeated. Once the two trees are successfully connected, a feasible path from the start to the goal position is obtained, as shown in Fig. 1(b).

Multiple Sampling Probability. During the path planning process, it is important to set different sampling probabilities for points in different regions of the map. Therefore, we define three regions with four different sampling probabilities: (1) In the region with a radius of r_{center} centered at the midpoint of the line connecting the start and goal points, the sampling probability is set as P_a. (2) Around the goal point, a region with a radius of r_{center} is defined, and the sampling probability is set as P_b. The sampling probability near the goal position P_{goal} is slightly higher than P_b to allow the random tree to approach the goal point more quickly. (3) For other regions in the environment map, a sampling probability of P_c is set for random sampling. The sum of the sampling probabilities in the three regions is $P_a + P_b + P_c = 1$. Combining the multi-sampling probabilities with the dual attachment algorithm can effectively expedite the initial path-solving processs (Fig. 2).

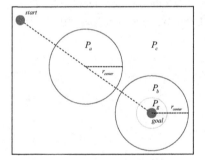

Fig. 2. Probability distribution

Parent Node Reconstruction. The Informed RRT* algorithm uses a fixed depth for selecting ancestor nodes and rewire strategies to optimize the path. However, using a fixed depth for ancestor nodes can lead to insufficient optimization of the path. When there are few obstacles in the environment space, only reconnecting the new node with the first-level parent nodes reduces the utilization of nodes. On the other hand, when there are many obstacles in the environment, expanding the search range for parent nodes results in significant computational time spent on collision detection. To address these issues, we propose a multi-level parent node reconnection strategy and assigns a cost function to these parent nodes. The potential optimal parent nodes with lower cost values will be excluded from the collision detection phase, eliminating some potential optimal parent nodes that do not contribute to improving the path while improving the efficiency of path optimization. The process of the multi-level parent node reconnection strategy is as follows:

Modify the Parent Node Selection Range. After adding the new node x_{new} to the random tree, we need to find all nodes that are within a distance of r_{near} from x_{new} and collect them in the set U_1. Then, we iterate through the nodes x_{near} to find their first-level ancestor nodes and record these parent nodes in the set U_2. The set U_3 only contains the starting position x_{start}. Next, we create the set U_{all}, which includes all the nodes from U_1, U_2, and U_3. We remove any duplicate nodes in U_{all} and keep only one instance of each node.

Calculate the Parent Node Generation Value. We evaluate the nodes in the set U_{all} using a cost function $P(x)$. If the cost value of a node is less than the threshold value ζ_t, these nodes will be excluded from the path optimization phase. Additionally, we create the set U_{useful} to keep track of the nodes with cost values greater than the threshold ζ_t. Typically, these removed nodes are very close to the new node and do not have a significant impact on path optimization. The specific expression for the cost function is given by Eq. (2).

$$P(x) = |1 - \frac{1}{e^{\tan[\frac{d}{\gamma} \cdot (\frac{\pi}{2} - |\varepsilon|)]}}|$$ (2)

The expression with the given parameters for the cost function $P(x)$ is as follows: $d = \|x_{new} - x\|_2$, γ is the adjustment parameter based on the r-disc RGG model [13], $\eta \geq 1$ is the adjustment variable, and ε is a small constant.

Path Optimization. After selecting the potential optimal parent node set in the previous two steps, we proceed to the path optimization phase by reselecting the parent nodes. As shown in Fig. 3, The original path is ABCD with a cost of 12. Point D is the newly added node x_{new} in the random tree and needs to be optimized. According to the mentioned parent node optimization strategy, referring to Fig. 3(b), we can see that all the parent nodes of point D are in the set $U_{all} = \{U_1 = \{C, F, I, J\}, U_2 = \{B, E, H, K\}, U_3 = \{A\}\}$. Assuming that after calculating the node cost function px, point F is found to be below the threshold ζ_t. Therefore, point F is removed, and the set U_{all} is updated to obtain the set $U_{useful} = \{U_1 = \{E, J, K\}, U_2 = \{B, F, I, D\}, U_3 = \{A\}\}$, which consists of potential optimal parent nodes for point K. Then, collision detection is performed on the nodes in the set U_{useful}. As shown in Fig. 3(b), paths BD, AD, and KD collide with obstacles. Hence, nodes A, B, and K are removed from the path, as shown in Fig. 4(c). Subsequently, the cost of connecting each node in U_{useful} with point K is calculated, and finally, the new path AGHK with the minimum path cost is obtained. The path cost is 11, which represents the optimal path between the current nodes, as depicted in Fig. 3(d).

3 Results and Analysis

In this section, we will evaluate the effectiveness of this algorithm from two perspectives: simulation experiment and quadruped robot platform. The hardware and software configurations used in the experiment are shown in Table 1.

3.1 Simulation

To validate the effectiveness of the DR-Informed-RRT* algorithm in improving path planning efficiency, we conducted comparative experiments on various simulated maps.

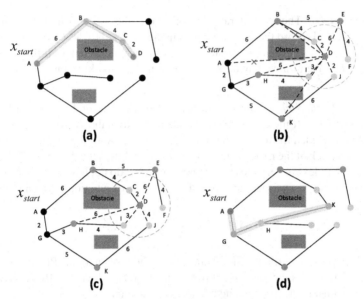

Fig. 3. Process of reselecting the parent node

Table 1. Hardware and software configuration

Category	Type
CPU	11th Gen Intel Core"m i7-11800H @230GHz
Memory	16GB
Software version	PyCharm Community Edition 2023.1.2
2D LiDAR	PRLIDAR M2M1

The performance of the DR-Informed-RRT* algorithm was compared with that of the Informed-RRT* algorithm and the RRT-Connect algorithm.

In the experiments, the quadruped robot was treated as a point mass, neglecting its motion characteristics but considering its geometric dimensions. This was done to prevent collisions between the robot's limbs and obstacles in real-world navigation scenarios. To make the simulation experiments more relevant, the obstacle regions in the simulated maps were inflated by a certain proportion of the reduced body width of the real quadruped robot. Two types of maps, including simple maps and maze maps, were used in the simulation experiments. Different numbers of algorithm iterations were set according to the complexity of each map. The environmental parameters, as well as the parameters for the start and goal positions in the path planning, are summarized in Table 2.

Initial Path Search Experiment. The global path planning consists of two stages: initial path search and path optimization. When the number of algorithm iterations is fixed,

Table 2. Environment parameters and path planning parameters

Scene	Start	Goal	Number of iterations	Number of obstacles
Simple map	(5,2)	(48,30)	2000	9
Maze map	(50,700)	(800,25)	3000	23

reducing the number of iterations in the initial path search allows for more iterations in the path optimization stage. Therefore, it is important to validate the effectiveness of the improved initial path search method proposed by the DR-Informed-RRT* algorithm through simulation experiments. The initial path search algorithm was tested on a simple map with dimensions of 50 × 35 units (meters). Figure 4. Illustrates the path search results of the three algorithms in the simple map. The obstacles are represented by gray squares, the blue square in the lower-left corner of the map represents the start position, the green square in the upper-right corner represents the goal position, and the optimal paths generated by the three algorithms are depicted by red lines.

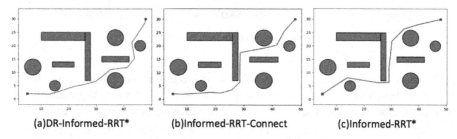

(a)DR-Informed-RRT*   (b)Informed-RRT-Connect   (c)Informed-RRT*

Fig. 4. Simple map path search results

According to the experiment, each algorithm (Informed-RRT*, RRT-Connect, and DR-Informed-RRT*) was iterated 2000 times. The simulation experiments were conducted 50 times, and the time and iteration count were recorded for each experiment. The results are shown in Fig. 5. From the table, it can be observed that the DR-Informed-RRT* algorithm, which incorporates the bidirectional sampling and multi-sampling probability strategy, has a better average search time compared to the other two algorithms.

Global Path Planning Experiment. The global path planning experiment was conducted in a maze map. As shown in Fig. 6, the experimental results of the three algorithms in this map were presented. In order to validate the effectiveness of the algorithms, obstacles were placed at the start and end points of the complex map to block the robot's path, and dense and numerous obstacles of different shapes were distributed throughout the map.

Since the global path planning experiment aims to obtain the optimal path within a fixed number of iterations, the evaluation metrics are focused on the length of the planned path and the time taken for path planning. Each algorithm was run 50 times in the complex map, and the results of time and length for each path planning were statistically analyzed, as shown in Fig. 7 and Fig. 8.

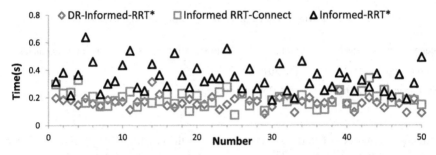

Fig. 5. Initial path search time of three algorithms

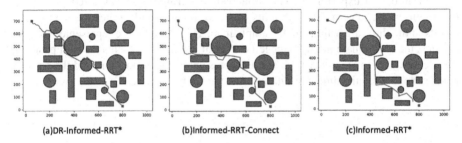

(a)DR-Informed-RRT*   (b)Informed-RRT-Connect   (c)Informed-RRT*

Fig. 6. Maze map path search results

From the Fig. 7 and Fig. 8, we can observe that our proposed DR-Informed-RRT* algorithm, benefiting from the adoption of multi-sample probability and bidirectional sampling methods, significantly reduces the average planning time compared to the other two algorithms. Due to the improved parent node selection strategy, the algorithm is able to eliminate redundant nodes and shorten the length of the planned path. The simulation results demonstrate that the DR-Informed-RRT* algorithm outperforms the other two algorithms and is better suited for four-legged robot path planning tasks.

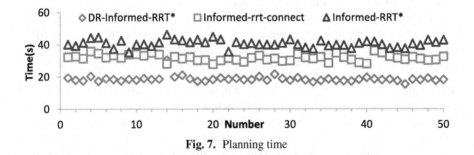

Fig. 7. Planning time

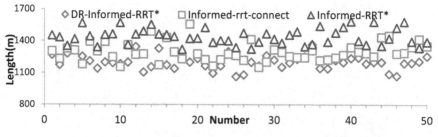

Fig. 8. Planning distance

3.2 Quadruped Robot Experiment

In the quadruped experiment, a comparative study was conducted between the DR-Informed-RRT* algorithm and Informed-RRT* in a laboratory setting. The robot used in the experiment has a width of approximately 0.35 m and a length of approximately 0.64 m. The maximum running speed of the robot was set to 0.3 m/s, while the minimum running speed was set to 0.1 m/s. The experimental environment covered an area of 162.8 m^2, with the obstacles occupying approximately 84.48 m^2, resulting in an occupancy ratio of approximately 48.10%. The prior map of the environment was constructed using Gmapping [14] in the ROS platform. Quadruped robot platform and the experimental environment are depicted in Fig. 9.

Fig. 9. Quadruped robot platform and experimental environment

Figure 10 presents the optimal paths generated by the two algorithms for the quadruped robot in three different start and goal configurations. The blue lines represent the paths generated by the algorithms, while the red lines indicate the current position of the robot during its movement. Finally, Table 3 presents the time taken and the distance covered by the four-legged robot. From Table 3, it can be observed that the DR-Informed-RRT* algorithm consistently generates the shortest paths in different environments. Compared to Informed-RRT*, the improved algorithm achieved a 16.16% and 21.03% improvement in actual runtime and motion distance, respectively. Therefore, it can be concluded that our proposed path planning algorithm is capable of generating optimal paths for quadruped robots.

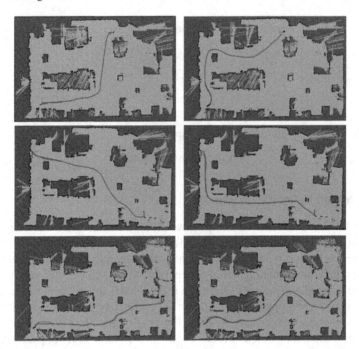

Fig. 10. The running track. DR-Informed-RRT* on the left and Informed-RRT* on the right

Table 3. The distance and time of actual movement of the quadruped robot

Number	Algorithm	Running Time (s)	Movement distance (m)
1	DR-Informed-RRT*	84.17	13.25
	Informed-RRT*	101.26	16.88
2	DR-Informed-RRT*	101.59	15.86
	Informed-RRT*	120.74	19.75
3	DR-Informed-RRT*	96.27	14.56
	Informed-RRT*	114.22	18.64

4 Conclusion

In this work, we propose a DR-Informed-RRT* path planning algorithm suitable for quadruped robots. Compared to traditional sampling-based algorithms, our algorithm improves the efficiency of path planning by incorporating bidirectional search strategy, multi-sampling probability, and parent node reconstruction. Experimental results demonstrate that the algorithm is capable of generating effective initial paths within the shortest time frame, exhibiting remarkable performance in reducing both the overall path planning time and path length. By deploying our algorithm on a quadruped robot, we achieve a notable improvement of 16.16% in planning time and 21.03% in distance compared to the informed-RRT* method, showcasing the algorithm's exceptional performance and effectiveness.

Acknowledgments. This work was supported in part by the National Natural Science Foundation of China under Grant (NO. 61703356), in part by the Natural Science Foundation of Fujian Province under Grant (NO. 2022J011256), in part by the Innovation Foundation of Xiamen under Grant (NO. 3502Z20206071).

References

1. Ye, Y., Wei, F., Cai, X.: Research on fast Dijkstra's algorithm based on parallel computing. Comput. Eng. Appl. **56**(6), 58–65 (2020)
2. Hong, Z., Sun, P., Tong, X.: Improved A-star algorithm for long-distance off-road path planning using terrain data map. ISPRS Int. J. Geo Inform. **10**(11), 785 (2021)
3. Rahmaniar, W., Rakhmania, A.E.: Mobile robot path planning in a trajectory with multiple obstacles using genetic algorithms. J. Robot. Control **3**(1), 1–7 (2022)
4. Dorigo, M.: The Any System Optimization by a colony of cooperating agents. IEEE Trans. System, Man Cybernet. Part B **26**(1), 1–13 (1996)
5. LaValle, S.M., Kuffner, J.J., Jr.: Randomized kinodynamic planning. Int. J. Robot. Res. **20**(5), 378–400 (2001)
6. Karaman, S., Frazzoli, E.: Sampling-based algorithms for optimal motion planning. Int. J. Robot. Res. **30**(7), 846–894 (2011)
7. Karaman, S., Walter, M.R., Perez, A., Frazzoli, E., Teller, S.: Anytime motion planning using the RRT. In: 2011 IEEE International Conference on Robotics and Automation, Shanghai (ICRA), China, pp. 1478–1483 (2011)
8. Chen, J., Zhao, Y., Xu, X.: Improved RRT-connect based path planning algorithm for mobile robots. IEEE ACCESS. **9**, 145988–145999 (2021)
9. Gammell, J.D., Srinivasa, S.S., Barfoot, T.D.: Informed RRT: optimal sampling-based path planning focused via direct sampling of an admissible ellipsoidal heuristic. In 2014 IEEE/RSJ International Conference on Intelligent Robots and Systems (IROS), Chicago, Illinois, USA, pp. 2997–3004 (2014)
10. Ryu, H., Park, Y.: Improved informed RRT* using gridmap skeletonization for mobile robot path planning. Int. J. Precis. Eng. Manuf. **20**, 2033–2039 (2019)
11. Dai, J., Li, Z., Li, Y., Zhao, J.: Robot path planning based on improved informed-RRT* algorithm. J. Henan Univ. Technol. (Nat. Sci. Edn.) (1), 1–11 (2021)
12. Mashayekhi, R., Idris, M.Y.I., Anisi, M.H., Ahmedy, I., Ali, I.: Informed RRT*-connect: an asymptotically optimal single-query path planning method. IEEE Access **8**, 19842–19852 (2020)
13. Gammell, J.D., Srinivasa, S.S., Barfoot, T.D.: Batch Informed Trees (BIT): sampling-based optimal planning via the heuristically guided search of implicit random geometric graphs, pp. 3067–3074. In: 2015 IEEE International Conference on Robotics and Automation (ICRA), Seattle, Washington, USA (2015)
14. Tian, C., Liu, H., Liu, Z., Li, H., Wang, Y.: Research on multi-sensor fusion SLAM algorithm based on improved gmapping. IEEE Access **11**, 13690–13703 (2023)

Game-Theoretic Motion Planning for Multiple Vehicles at Unsignalized Intersection

Youjie Guo$^{(\boxtimes)}$ and Xiaoqiang Ren

Shanghai University, Shanghai 200444, China
{lakiguo,xqren}@shu.edu.cn

Abstract. The paper addresses the challenges posed by unsignalized intersections, particularly in situations involving multiple autonomous vehicles. Specifically, it focuses on motion planning for multi-vehicle scenarios at such intersections. To this end, we formulate the problem as a M-player general-sum dynamic game with a finite horizon. Given the criticality of efficiency and safety, we adopt a maximum-over-time cost structure and approximate the original game to a linear-quadratic game in the reach-avoid setting, enabling the use of dynamic programming. Game theory allows for a shared information view and consideration of all vehicles' states. However, traditional methods are not suitable for large numbers of vehicles that meet at intersections. Therefore, we propose a matching policy that decomposes the game into two-player sub-games, allowing for scalability and efficient computation. By conducting simulation verification on our algorithm, we demonstrate its effectiveness in motion planning for multiple autonomous vehicles. Overall, the proposed approach provides a promising solution for motion planning at unsignalized intersections with multiple autonomous vehicles. Our method is released on https://github.com/lakiGuo/Reach-Avoid-Games.

Keywords: Motion planning · Unsignalized intersection · Game theory · Matching policy

1 Introduction

One of the most complicated urban scenarios for autonomous driving involve unsignalized intersections, where vehicles interact with other traffic participants without the guidance of traffic lights [17]. At an intersection, autonomous vehicles make consecutive maneuvers to reach their target lanes while avoiding collisions. For reason of safety and efficiency, motion planning is an important task for autonomous multi-vehicles.

With the development of cooperative vehicle-infrastructure systems and communication technology, we can consider applying a game theory framework to address vehicle interaction issues. Game theory provides an analytical framework for tackling the interactions among decision-makers. Differential games cover

© The Author(s), under exclusive license to Springer Nature Singapore Pte Ltd. 2023
H. Yang et al. (Eds.): ICIRA 2023, LNAI 14274, pp. 96–107, 2023.
https://doi.org/10.1007/978-981-99-6501-4_9

a wide range of applications [9,12,15], and they originated with Isaacs, who focused on zero-sum games and proposed Hamilton-Jacobi-Isaacs partial differential equations for deriving Nash feedback strategies [13]. Finding an appropriate strategy for one player in relation to the decisions of other players is equivalent to finding an equilibrium. For non-cooperative games with players making decisions simultaneously, Nash equilibrium is a typical solution. Nash equilibrium can be interpreted as a situation that no player can increase the reward or decrease the cost by unilaterally altering its strategy within strategy sets. However, compared with zero-sum games, the interests of players in general-sum cases are not diametrically opposed, and Nash equilibrium may not be unique for general-sum games with different payoff structures.

While solving partial differential equations is a classical method for finding the equilibrium, most of these equations cannot be solved analytically [3]. Thus, linear quadratic (LQ) differential games [4,6–8] are chosen due to practical considerations, as LQ games allow for efficient closed-form solutions [2]. When encountering with nonlinear dynamics and non-quadratic costs, Fridovich-Keil *et al.* [10] propose an iterative algorithm that is based on the iterative linear-quadratic regulator (ILQR) [5]. Fridovich and Tomlin [11] finds the limitation of a LQ game with time-additive objective and proposes a reach-avoid game with maximum-over-time objective which maintains LQ structure.

Our research is primarily focused on reach-avoid games based on the work of Fridovich-Keil *et al.* [11] due to the concise and effective modeling. We approach the motion planning problem of multiple vehicles at intersections by formulating it as a finite horizon game with maximum-over-time costs as the objective. Since the conventional method cannot be applied to scenarios where a large number of vehicles converge at intersections as in Fig. 4(a), we present a matching policy that decomposes the game into two-player sub-games or one-player optimal control problems. The decomposition process involves a maximum bipartite matching problem (8), which we solve using the Hungarian algorithm. Our main contribution is the inclusion of the matching policy in the game formulation, which allows for an extension of the original algorithm to handle more than three players in practical applications.

2   Problem Formulation

Due to the interaction of vehicle trajectories, motion planning at an unsignalized intersection can be considered as a M-player finite horizon general-sum differential game characterized by nonlinear system dynamics

$$\dot{\mathbf{x}} = \mathbf{f}(\mathbf{x}, \mathbf{u}^{1:M}, t), \ t \in [0, T], \tag{1}$$

where $\mathbf{x} \in \mathbb{R}^n$ is the state of the system, and $\mathbf{u}^i \in \mathbb{R}^{m^i}, i \in \mathcal{I}$ is the control input of player i, and $\mathbf{u}^{1:M} = (\mathbf{u}^1, \mathbf{u}^2, \dots, \mathbf{u}^M)$, and $\mathbf{f} \in \mathbb{C}^1$ is a vector function. Each player has a cost functional $J^i : \mathcal{X} \times U^1 \times \dots \times U^M \to \mathbb{R}$. Figure 1 illustrates the specific scenario. If there is only one player, the dynamic game formulation

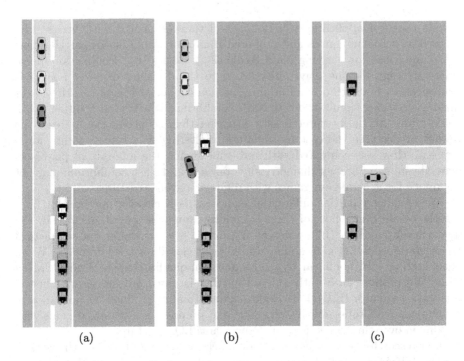

Fig. 1. Model of a T-shaped unsignalized intersection with matching areas. The matching areas are highlighted in color. (a) Cars in the green area turn left, while those in the red area go straight. (b) A sub-game with two players is solved by matching the white and red cars, and the resulting trajectory is feasible. (c) Another sub-game is played between the pink and blue cars. For the purple car, the game formulation degenerates into an optimal control problem. (Color figure online)

reduces to an optimal control problem. To solve the game problem, we have established two types of game objective functions. One type is time-additive cost structure (2), and another one is maximum-over-time cost structure (4). There are mature solving methods for the first type of objective formulation while the assurance of safety requires many constraints. Then, maxmium-over-time structure is considered which makes a concise formulation [11].

2.1 Time-Additive Cost Structure

Cost function J^i is usually designed as an integral of running costs c^i since the structure is easily amenable to both locally optimal and globally optimal control methods [11]:

$$J^i = \int_0^T c^i(\mathbf{x}(t), \mathbf{u}^{1:M}(t), t), \quad \mathbf{x}(t_0) = \mathbf{x}_0, \ \forall i \in \mathcal{I}. \tag{2}$$

2.2 Maximum-Over-Time Cost Structure

Time-additive cost structure is not applicable to collision-avoidance scenarios due to introducing extra constraints which complicates the solution approaches [11]. Hence, maximum-over-time cost structure is introduced. Expression of extreme-over-time sets the problem as a reach-void formulation which is concerned with entering the target sets and avoiding the failure sets. Here, a target set is denoted by $\mathcal{T} \subset \mathcal{X}$ and a failure set is denoted by $\mathcal{F} \subset \mathcal{X}$. $\mathcal{X}$ denotes set of states. For practical application, two Lipschitz continuous functions, $\ell, g : \mathcal{X} \to \mathbb{R}$ are used [1], as follows:

$$
\begin{aligned}
\ell\left(\mathbf{x}(t)\right) \leq 0 &\iff \mathbf{x}(t) \in \mathcal{T}, \\
g\left(\mathbf{x}(t)\right) > 0 &\iff \mathbf{x}(t) \in \mathcal{F}.
\end{aligned}
\tag{3}
$$

At unsignalized intersections, autonomous vehicles are expected to remain in their designated lanes, maintaining a safe distance from the boundaries of the roadway, in order to reach their intended destination, as illustrated in Fig. 2. Then, maximum-over-time structure of the game can be designed as follows:

$$
J_s^i = \max_{t \in \{s, T\}} \left(\ell^i\left(\mathbf{x}(t)\right), \max_{\tau \in \{s, t\}} g^i\left(\mathbf{x}(\tau)\right) \right), \ \forall i \in \mathcal{I},
\tag{4}
$$

where $s \in [0, T]$. If $\ell^i(x(t)) > 0$, it means that vehicle i has not yet reached its goal, while $g^i(x(\tau)) > 0$ indicates that the states of vehicle i have entered the failure set. The extreme structure allows for consideration of the worst-case scenario. Therefore, the ideal condition is when $\ell^i(x(t)) \leq 0$ and $g^i(x(\tau)) \leq 0$. To achieve this, a control strategy is needed to minimize the objective with a maximum-over-time structure.

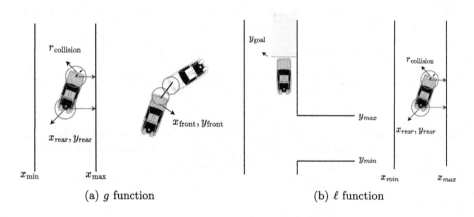

(a) g function   (b) ℓ function

Fig. 2. The selection of the margin function.

2.3   Time Consistency

Time consistency is a key property of an optimal control strategy, which ensures its optimality for sub-problems that arise at intermediate times during its execution, regardless of any sub-optimal actions taken earlier. In this work, we use the extension of time consistency [1] instead of the traditional definitions used in dynamic game literature [2].

Definition 1. Solution of the general-sum differential game: $\gamma^i \in \Gamma$, $\forall i \in \mathcal{I}$ *indicates an admissible strategy which inherently is a mapping:* $\mathcal{X} \to \mathcal{U}$, *and* $\gamma = (\gamma^1, \ldots, \gamma^M)$ *is a strategy tuple.* $\mathcal{U}$ *denotes the set of admissible control inputs, which is the Cartesian product* $\{U^1 \times \ldots \times U^M\}$ *of M sets* $U^1, \ldots, U^M$.

Definition 2. Strong time consistency [1]: *An optimal strategy* $\gamma^* \in \Gamma$ *is said to be strongly time-consistent if it remains optimal for the truncated reach-avoid problem when restricted to begin at an intermediate time s from an arbitrary state denoted by* $\tilde{\mathbf{x}}$. *Specifically, if we apply any other feasible strategy γ defined at subsequent times $t \in [s, T]$, the following inequality holds:*

$$J_s\left(\mathbf{x}_{s,\tilde{x}}^{\gamma^*}\right) \leq J_s\left(\mathbf{x}_{s,\tilde{x}}^{\gamma}\right), \ \forall s \in [0, T], \ \forall \tilde{\mathbf{x}} \in \mathcal{X}_s. \tag{5}$$

J_s is the objective of the truncated reach-avoid problem after applying γ^* on the set $\{0, 1, \ldots, s-1\}$ in the discrete case.

In other words, regardless of the feasible strategy β applied in the time interval $[0, s-1]$, γ^* can always find the optimal state that minimizes J_s.

2.4   Local Nash Equilibrium

Definition 3. Local Nash equilibrium: *A strategy tuple γ^* which is a solution to the game is local Nash equilibrium, then the following inequality must hold for each* $\gamma^i \in \tilde{\Gamma}^i$:

$$\exists \tilde{\Gamma}^i \subset \Gamma^i : \gamma^{i*} \in \tilde{\Gamma}^i \wedge$$
$$J_0^i\left(\mathbf{x}_{\mathbf{x}_0}^{\gamma^*}\right) \leq J_0^i\left(\mathbf{x}_{\mathbf{x}_0}^{\left(\gamma^{-i*}, \gamma^i\right)}\right), \ \forall \gamma^i \in \tilde{\Gamma}^i, \ \forall \mathbf{x}_0 \in \mathcal{X}_0. \tag{6}$$

Time consistency is a complementary to the Nash equilibrium. For a solution to be time-consistent, the players should have no rational reason to deviate from the adopted policy at any future stage of the game.

2.5   Problem of Interest

Our goal is to identify the local Nash equilibrium for the reach-avoid game. In other words, our goal is to develop a method for finding a time-consistent strategy that satisfies the following optimization problem, using the objective function and dynamics definition mentioned earlier:

$$
\begin{aligned}
\underset{\mathbf{x},\mathbf{u}}{\text{minimize}}\quad & J_s \\
\text{s.t.}\quad & u_t \in \mathcal{U}_t,\ \mathcal{U}_t \subset \mathcal{U},\ \forall t \in \{0,1,\ldots,T\}, \\
& x_t \in \mathcal{X}_t,\ \mathcal{X}_t \subset \mathcal{X},\ \forall t \in \{0,1,\ldots,T\}, \\
& \delta x_t = \mathbf{f}_t\left(x_t, u_t\right),\ \forall t \in \{0,1,\ldots,T-1\}, \\
& \mathbf{x}_0 \in \mathcal{X}_0,\ \text{(initial state is given)},
\end{aligned}
\tag{7}
$$

where, $\mathbf{x}_t$ denotes $x(t)$, and $\mathbf{u}_t$ denotes $u(t)$. The objective function J_s is formulated to take the maximum value over time (4). We assume that we are operating in a vehicle-to-infrastructure communication context, with the assistance of an edge cloud to facilitate communication between vehicles.

Algorithm 1. ILQ with matching policy

Input: $\mathbf{x}_0, \mathrm{T}, \left(\ell_t^i(\cdot), g_t^i(\cdot)\right)_{i=1}^N$

1: $\mathcal{I}_1, \mathcal{I}_2, \mathrm{CostMatrix} \leftarrow \text{generateBipartiteGraph}(\mathbf{x}_0)$;

2: cargroups $\leftarrow \text{HungarianAlgorithm}(\mathcal{I}_1, \mathcal{I}_2, \mathrm{CostMatrix})$

3: Initialize: $\gamma^i \leftarrow \left(\mathbf{u}^i, P^i, \alpha^i\right)$

4: **for** (j,k) in cargroups **do**

5:     **while** not converged **do**

6:         $\mathbf{x} \leftarrow \text{RolloutTrajectory}\left(\mathbf{x}_0^j, \mathbf{x}_0^k, \mathbf{u}^j, \mathbf{u}^k\right)$;

7:         $\left(\tilde{P}^i, \tilde{\alpha}^i\right)_{i \in \{j,k\}} \leftarrow \mathbf{ReachAvoidLQSolve}\left(\mathbf{x}, \mathbf{u}^j, \mathbf{u}^k)\right)$; [1]

8:         $(\gamma^i)_{i \in \{j,k\}} \leftarrow \text{ILQStrategyUpdate}\left(\mathbf{x}_0^j, \mathbf{x}_0^k, \left(\mathbf{u}^i, \tilde{P}^i, \tilde{\alpha}^i\right)_{i \in \{j,k\}}\right)$;

9:     $\gamma \leftarrow \text{append}(\gamma^i)$

Return: converged strategies γ

---

3 Technical Approach

Our approach to solving problem (7) involves using the locally strongly time-consistent algorithm [1], and augmenting it with a matching policy, which is our original contribution as in Algorithm 1. Our approach consists of three key steps. First, we propose a matching policy that breaks down a game with M players into sub-games consisting of either two players or one player, which increases the efficiency of solving the original game. Secondly, we outline three key steps for the efficient method for solving a classical game with the objective defined in (2) and establish a link with the maximum-over-time structure of the problem. Finally, we apply a locally strongly time-consistent algorithm specifically tailored to reach-avoid problems. This algorithm compensates for the deficiencies of the approach described above, and satisfies local consistency requirements, making it particularly well-suited for real-world applications. To apply the method, we discretize the model using fourth-order Runge-Kutta integration.

3.1 Matching Mechanism

As mentioned in Sect. 1, a system with large scale of dimensions is hard to solve. To solve the dynamic game problem efficiently, we can decompose the whole games into many sub-games. We divide the vehicles into two parts, represented as a bipartite graph in Fig. 3. Here, we use a matrix to represent the result of matching and formulate the matching problem in optimization form:

$$\underset{P}{\text{minimize}} \quad \sum_{i=1}^{m} \sum_{j=1}^{n} (PC)_{ij}$$
$$\text{subject to} \quad \sum_{j=1}^{n} P_{ij} \leq 1 \qquad\qquad (8)$$
$$P_{ij} \in \{0, 1\}$$

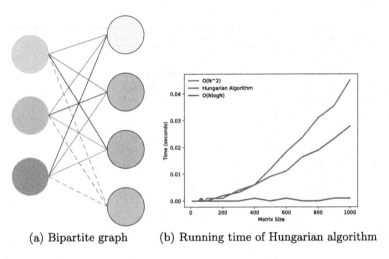

(a) Bipartite graph   (b) Running time of Hungarian algorithm

Fig. 3. (a) The cars at T-shaped intersections are divided into two groups. Each car is abstracted as a node. The red line means that the result of our matching policy. (b) If the matrix dimension is less than 200×200, a quick matching result can be achieved. (Color figure online)

Here, $|\mathcal{I}_1| = m$, $|\mathcal{I}_2| = n$ and $P \in \mathbb{R}^{m \times n}$ denotes the matching matrix, while $C \in \mathbb{R}^{m \times n}$ denotes the cost matrix. The cost matrix is designed based on two main factors: vehicle velocity and position. When matching vehicles, priority is given to those with similar speeds and minimized differences in distances from the center of the road. The design of the matching cost is as follows:

$$C_{ij} = a|2y_{\text{center}} - y^j - y^i| + b|v^i - v^j|, \ i \in \mathcal{I}_1, \ j \in \mathcal{I}_2,$$

where a and b is the manually set parameters.y^i and y^j represent the vertical position of the vehicles. y_{center} is calculated by $(y_{\text{min}} + y_{\text{max}})/2$. To find the minimum total cost, we can apply the Hungarian algorithm [16].

3.2   Iterative LQ Game Regulator

Since the dynamics (1) of the game are possibly nonlinear, we can compute a linear system by assumption that function $\mathbf{f}$ is continuously twice differentiable. First, we start with an operating state $\hat{\mathbf{x}}$ and an initial control strategies $\hat{\gamma}$. Then, we can get variations $\delta\mathbf{x}(t) = \mathbf{x}(t) - \hat{\mathbf{x}}(t)$ and $\delta u(t) = u(t) - \hat{u}(t)$ in which $\hat{u} = \hat{\gamma}(\mathbf{x}_0)$. At last, we can get an approximation as follows:

$$\dot{\delta\mathbf{x}}(t) \approx A(t)\delta\mathbf{x}(t) + \sum_{i\in\mathcal{I}} B^i(t)\delta u^i(t), \tag{9}$$

where $A(t)$ is the Jacobian matrix $D_{\hat{\mathbf{x}}}\mathbf{f}\left(\hat{\mathbf{x}}, \hat{u}_{1:M}, t\right)$ and $B^i(t)$ is likewise $D_{\hat{u}^i}\mathbf{f}\left(\cdot\right)$. Similarly to procedure of getting dynamics linearization, we can obtain a quadratic cost from the running costs (2):

$$c^i\left(t,\ x(t), u^{1:M}(t)\right) \approx$$
$$c^i\left(t, \hat{\mathbf{x}}(t), \hat{u}^{1:M}(t)\right) + \frac{1}{2}\delta\mathbf{x}(t)^T\left(Q^i(t)\delta\mathbf{x}(t) + 2q^i(t)\right) +$$
$$\frac{1}{2}\sum_{j\in[M]}\delta u^j(t)^T\left(R^{ij}(t)\delta u^j(t) + 2r^{ij}(t)\right), \tag{10}$$

where vector $q^i(t)$ is Jacobian matrix $D_{\hat{\mathbf{x}}}c^i$, $r^{ij}(t)$ is likewise $D_{\hat{u}^j}c^i$, and $Q^i(t)$ and $R^{ij}(t)$ are Hessian matrices $D^2_{\hat{\mathbf{x}}\hat{\mathbf{x}}}c^i$ and $D^2_{\hat{u}^j\hat{u}^j}c^i$, respectively. Since we have already formulated LQ game, we can derive the procedure to find an optimal strategy as follows [10]:

$$\tilde{\gamma}^i_k(t, \mathbf{x}(t)) = \hat{u}^i(t) - P^i_k(t)\delta\mathbf{x}(t) - \alpha^i_k(t), \tag{11}$$

where k denotes the k-th iteration, $P^k_i(t) \in \mathbb{R}^{m_i\times n}$ denotes gains and $\alpha^k_i(t) \in \mathbb{R}^{m^i}$ denotes affine terms. $P^k_i(t)$ and $\alpha^k_i(t)$ represent the solutions obtained from the traditional game. In order to adapt the method to the reach-avoid setting described in Eq. (7), we can transform the maximum-over-time cost structure into the running-cost form as shown in Eq. (10). Subsequently, we identify the critical time, denoted as τ, at which the objective function J_s in Eq. (4) achieves its maximum value. During each iteration, we set Q^i and q^i to zero for the remaining time steps. The approach, referred to as the pinch-point method, is characterized as time-inconsistent according to Anthony et al. [1]. More specifically, if the target is a set with boundary such as a circle region and there is a sufficiently long horizon T, we may find that an agent which has passed the target set at the time τ, $0 < \tau \le T$ can reduce the cost J_τ by turning back into target set again due to only recording the maximum value. That is, J_τ is not minimized by the pinch-point method. To address the time inconsistency flaw of the pinch-point method, we introduced the time-consistent reach-avoid LQ solver. The details of the solver can be found in [1].

4   Simulations

We compares the time-consistent algorithm that uses a matching policy to one that does not use a matching policy in software simulation. We use vehicle dynamics in [14], as followings:

$$\dot{x}^i = v\cos(\theta^i)$$
$$\dot{y}^i = v\sin(\theta^i)$$
$$\dot{\theta}^i = \frac{v}{L}\tan(\phi^i)$$
$$\dot{v}^i = a,$$

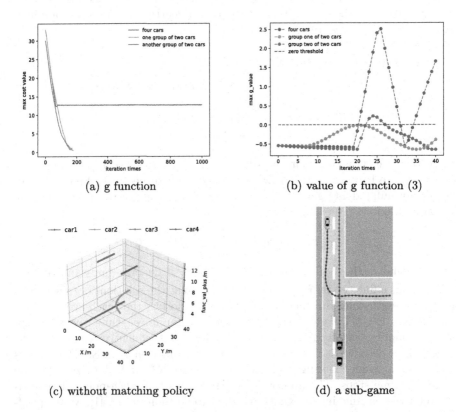

(a) g function   (b) value of g function (3)

(c) without matching policy   (d) a sub-game

Fig. 4. (a) While the time-consistent algorithm without a matching policy does converge (as shown by the blue line), its cost value does not reach zero. In contrast, the time-consistent algorithm that incorporates a matching policy can converge much faster to a point close to zero (as shown by the orange and green lines). (b) The value of g being above zero indicates that the vehicle has reached the failure set. Comparing the g function demonstrates the effectiveness of the matching policy. (c) The cost value of four cars at last iteration is high. (d) The planned trajectory of two cars presents the solution of the sub-game. (Color figure online)

where $i \in \mathcal{I}$, x^i and y^i are the position of the car i, θ^i is the heading angle, v^i is speed, ϕ^i is the steering angle, L^i is the distance between the front and rear axles of car i, and a^i is the acceleration. All the experiments are conducted on a laptop with an Intel i7-8750H CPU (2.2 GHz).

4.1   The Selection of Margin Function

The $g(\mathbf{x}_t)$ depends on the road rules and collision penalty as in Fig. 2(a). The $\ell(\mathbf{x}_t)$ depends on the goal and the road rules as in Fig. 2(b).

$$g_1 = y_{\text{rear}} - y_{\text{max}} + r_{\text{collision}} > 0$$
$$g_2 = y_{\text{front}} - y_{\text{max}} + r_{\text{collision}} > 0$$
$$g_3 = 2r_{\text{collision}} - (x_1 - x_2)^2 - (y_1 - y_2)^2 > 0$$
$$g = \max(g_1, g_2, g_3)$$
$$\ell_1 = y_{\text{goal}} - y_{\text{rear}} < 0$$
$$\ell_2 = y_{\text{max}} - y_{\text{rear}} - r_{\text{collision}} < 0$$
$$l = \max(\ell_1, \ell_2)$$

4.2   Computational Complexity

To apply the classical ILQ game [10], it is assumed that the state dimension n is greater than the control dimension m_i for each player $i \in \mathcal{I}$, and that the solution requires N_{iter} iterations. This approach involves linearizing the system dynamics and converting the costs into a quadratic form, which entails a computational complexity of $\mathcal{O}(n^2)$ and $\mathcal{O}(Mn^2)$ at each time step, respectively. Furthermore, solving the coupled Riccati equations of the classical LQ game at each time step has a complexity of $\mathcal{O}(Mn^3)$. Therefore, the total time complexity of the solution is $\mathcal{O}(N_{iter}Mn^3)$.

4.3   The Efficiency of Matching Policy

Not utilizing the matching policy could result in a substantial increase in computing time and hinder the generation of feasible trajectories. This is evident in the blue line of Fig. 4(a), which represents the maximum cost incurred by the four players in each iteration. The high cost implies that the car has failed to reach its intended destination even after 1000 steps. Furthermore, the trajectories may not be able to avoid the failure set, as shown in Fig. 4(b).

As in Fig. 1, we set the matching area which is colored red or green due to the consideration of velocity matching of two cars. If the velocities of two cars in the matching area differ significantly, such as one being at 0 m/s and the other at 7 m/s, it becomes impossible to find feasible trajectories for both cars, as demonstrated in the Table 1. Therefore, we incorporate the velocity difference into the matching algorithm. When the velocity difference is too large, we shift from solving a game-theoretic problem to a sequential optimal control problem for individual vehicles. The result is shown in the last two rows of the table.

Table 1. Comparison of the time-consistent algorithm that uses a matching policy to one that does not use a matching policy

M-player	iterations	time (seconds)	average time (each iteration)	feasible
4	1000	13463	13.46	no
2	177	198	1.12	yes
2	157	276	1.76	yes
2	1000	13153	13.15	no
1	22	7.56	0.34	yes
1	81	70.2	0.87	yes

5   Conclusion

This paper presents a novel approach to address the challenges posed by unsignalized intersections involving multiple autonomous vehicles. By formulating the problem as a M-player general-sum dynamic game, the proposed approach allows for a shared information view and consideration of all vehicles' states. The adoption of a maximum-over-time cost structure and approximation of the original game to a linear-quadratic game in the reach-avoid setting enables the use of dynamic programming, which enhances both efficiency and safety. Additionally, the proposed matching policy decomposes the game into two-player sub-games, ensuring scalability and efficient computation. In future, we will explore more methods such as reinforcement learning to accelerate computing optimal trajectory.

Acknowledgements. The work was supported in part by the National Natural Science Foundation of China under Grant 62273223, and the Project of Science and Technology Commission of Shanghai Municipality under Grant 22JC1401401.

References

1. Anthony, D.R., Nguyen, D.P., Fridovich-Keil, D., Fisac, J.F.: Back to the future: efficient, time-consistent solutions in reach-avoid games. In: 2022 International Conference on Robotics and Automation (ICRA), pp. 6830–6836. IEEE (2022)
2. Başar, T., Olsder, G.J.: Dynamic noncooperative game theory. SIAM (1998)
3. Bellman, R.: Dynamic programming. Science **153**(3731), 34–37 (1966)
4. Bressan, A., Nguyen, K.T.: Stability of feedback solutions for infinite horizon non-cooperative differential games. Dyn. Games Appl. **8**, 42–78 (2018)
5. Chen, J., Zhan, W., Tomizuka, M.: Constrained iterative LQR for on-road autonomous driving motion planning. In: 2017 IEEE 20th International Conference on Intelligent Transportation Systems (ITSC), pp. 1–7. IEEE (2017)
6. Engwerda, J.: Feedback nash equilibria in the scalar infinite horizon LQ-game. Automatica **36**(1), 135–139 (2000)
7. Engwerda, J.: LQ Dynamic Optimization and Differential Games. Wiley, Hoboken (2005)

8. Engwerda, J.: Linear quadratic differential games: an overview. In: Advances in Dynamic Games and Their Applications: Analytical and Numerical Developments, pp. 1–34 (2009)

9. Foley, M., Schmitendorf, W.: A class of differential games with two pursuers versus one evader. IEEE Trans. Autom. Control **19**(3), 239–243 (1974)

10. Fridovich-Keil, D., Ratner, E., Peters, L., Dragan, A.D., Tomlin, C.J.: Efficient iterative linear-quadratic approximations for nonlinear multi-player general-sum differential games. In: 2020 IEEE International Conference on Robotics and Automation (ICRA), pp. 1475–1481. IEEE (2020)

11. Fridovich-Keil, D., Tomlin, C.J.: Approximate solutions to a class of reachability games. In: 2021 IEEE International Conference on Robotics and Automation (ICRA), pp. 12610–12617. IEEE (2021)

12. Garcia, E., Casbeer, D.W., Pachter, M.: Design and analysis of state-feedback optimal strategies for the differential game of active defense. IEEE Trans. Autom. Control **64**(2), 553–568 (2018)

13. Isaacs, R.: Differential games: a mathematical theory with applications to warfare and pursuit, control and optimization. Courier Corporation (1999)

14. Kong, J., Pfeiffer, M., Schildbach, G., Borrelli, F.: Kinematic and dynamic vehicle models for autonomous driving control design. In: 2015 IEEE Intelligent Vehicles Symposium (IV), pp. 1094–1099. IEEE (2015)

15. Lin, W.: Differential games for multi-agent systems under distributed information (2013)

16. Mills-Tettey, G.A., Stentz, A., Dias, M.B.: The dynamic Hungarian algorithm for the assignment problem with changing costs. Robotics Institute, Pittsburgh, PA, Technical report, CMU-RI-TR-07-27 (2007)

17. Tian, R., Li, N., Kolmanovsky, I., Yildiz, Y., Girard, A.R.: Game-theoretic modeling of traffic in unsignalized intersection network for autonomous vehicle control verification and validation. IEEE Trans. Intell. Transp. Syst. **23**(3), 2211–2226 (2022). https://doi.org/10.1109/TITS.2020.3035363

To Improve the Energy Efficiency: Modeling and Control for Quadrotor with Tiltable Wing

Fulin Song[1], Zhan Li[1,2(✉)], Hai Li[1], Yuan Li[1], Quman Xu[1], and Bingkai Xiu[1]

[1] The Research Institute of Intelligent Control and Systems,
Harbin Institute of Technology, Harbin, China
`zhanli@hit.edu.cn`
[2] Department of Mathematics and Theories, Peng Cheng Laboratory,
No. 2, Xingke 1st Street, Nanshan, Shenzhen, China

Abstract. In this article, a new configuration of vertical take-off and landing (VTOL) UAV is proposed aiming at improving the energy utilize efficiency. In this configuration, a tiltable wing is installed at the center of the H-configuration quadrotor, and the orientation of the wing surface and the attitude of the quadrotor body are adjusted according to the orientation and magnitude of the target velocity. A state feedback + model feedforward flight controller capable of controlling the quadrotor with tiltable wing (QTW) throughout the entire flight envelope is proposed, without the need to switch between several mode. The performance of the proposed configuration and controller is demonstrated through a set of numerical simulations on the model of the QTW.

Keywords: VTOL UAV · quadrotor with tiltable wing · energy efficiency · model feedforward

1 Introduction

With the rapid development of the UAV logistics industry, the problem of the short battery endurance of the quadrotor has attracted more and more attention [2,11]. In order to increase the endurance time of vertical take-off and landing (VTOL) UAV, various new configurations of aerial vehicle have been proposed to reduce the energy consumption, including fixed wing hybrid quadrotor, monoplane wing tail-sitter, biplane-quadrotor, tilt-rotor aircraft, etc.

The most classic VTOL UAV is the fixed wing hybrid quadrotor. It is a hard combination of quadrotor and fixed wing [9]. When taking off and landing, the quadrotor mode is used. When steady-level forward flight, the four rotors stop, and the thrust is provided by the fixed wing motor. In [12], a minimum power control allocation for the fixed wing hybrid quadrotor is proposed to reduce

This work was supported by the National Natural Science Foundation of China (Grant No. 62273122).

© The Author(s), under exclusive license to Springer Nature Singapore Pte Ltd. 2023
H. Yang et al. (Eds.): ICIRA 2023, LNAI 14274, pp. 108–119, 2023.
https://doi.org/10.1007/978-981-99-6501-4_10

the energy consumption. However, the fixed wing hybrid quadrotor always has a propulsion system that is not used during flight, which increases the dead weight of the aircraft.

The monoplane wing tail-sitter does not have two sets of propulsion systems like fixed wing hybrid quadrotor, which reduces dead weight [1]. It achieves hovering and forward flying through two motors and two rudder surfaces [13]. However, during the VTOL and hovering phases, the vertical wing surface is easily disturbed by various external gusts [17]. Therefor, many anti-disturbance algorithms have been proposed to solve the problem that the monoplane wing tail-sitter is easily disturbed by wind, such as [15]. However, at low speeds, the torque generated by the rudder surface is very limited, so the disturbance can easily saturate the actuator.

The biplane-quadrotor no longer relies on the rudder surface to generate torques, but generate torques by rotors just like the quadrotor [5]. Backstepping control, integral terminal sliding mode control, and hybrid control is used on the biplane-quadrotor in [6] respectively to compare the performance of different controllers. The biplane-quadrotor realizes the switching between vertical and horizontal flight by rotating the body, and the intermediate transition process is controlled by position open loop [16]. This will lead to uncontrollable position during the transition mode, reducing the tracking accuracy. Moreover, the two wings will increase the moment of inertia of the fuselage, reduce the lift of each wing, increase the drag, and reduce the energy utilization efficiency [10].

The tilt-rotor aircraft realizes the vertical and horizontal conversion of the propulsion system by tilting the rotors [4]. This configuration can ensure both the disturbance resistance during hovering and the aerodynamic efficiency during horizontal flight [8]. In [3], a tilt-rotor aircraft controller that can smoothly and seamlessly transition from hovering to horizontal flight is proposed. This configuration can reduce energy consumption while maintaining tracking accuracy. However, the wing of tilt-rotor aircraft is kept in a fixed attitude. It will bring additional air resistance during vertical take-off, and it will form a serious ground effect under the wing when landing, resulting in drift when the aircraft approaches the ground.

Inspired by the above VTOL UAV, a new vehicle configuration called quadrotor with tiltable wing (QTW) is proposed aiming at reducing the energy consumption of the quadrotor aerial vehicle. Install freely tiltable wing surface on the middle of the quadrotor, and change the orientation of the wing surface according to the target speed direction, so as to increase lift and reduce energy consumption. The control of the four rotors adopts a method of state feedback + model feedforward, which ensures that the system has no steady-state error. There are two main innovation of this work:

1. A new aerial vehicle configuration named QTW is proposed, which supports VTOL, hovering and has high energy utilization efficiency.
2. A flight controller that is able to control the QTW throughout its whole flight envelope is proposed, without the need to switch between several flight controllers.

2   System Description

In this section, the configuration and the coordinate of the QTW are presented and the mathematical model of the QTW is established. As shown in Fig. 1, the center of the H-configuration quadrotor is equipped with a free-tilting wing surface that can rotate along the y_b axis 360°. The angle between the wing surface and the body surface $x_b O_b y_b$ can be controlled by the steering gear. The control strategy for the quadrotor part in QTW is the same as that for a conventional quadrotor, where pitch causes forward or backward translation, roll causes left or right translation, and yaw affects the heading direction of the vehicle. Figure 1 also shows the coordinate system of the QTW. $O_g x_g y_g z_g$ is the ground coordinate frame, whose x_g, y_g, z_g coordinate axes point to the north (N), east (E), and down (D). $O_b x_b y_b z_b$ is the body coordinate frame, whose x_b, y_b, z_b coordinate axes fix on the head (H), right (R), and bottom (B) of the body. $O_b x_a y_a z_a$ is the airflow coordinate frame, the x_a axis coincides with the airspeed direction, the z_a axis is in the body symmetry plane, perpendicular to the x_a axis, and pointing to the bottom of the body. The y_a axis is determined using the right-hand rule. $O_b x_w y_w z_w$ is the wing coordinate frame, the y_w axis coincides with y_b axis, the z_w axis is perpendicular to the wing surface pointing to the bottom of the body. The x_w axis is determined using the right-hand rule.

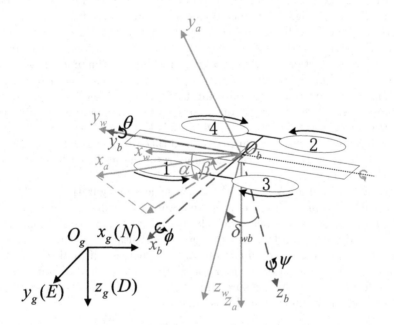

Fig. 1. The coordinate system of the QTW.

The forces acting on the QTW include gravity, aerodynamics force (lift, sideforce and drag), and propulsion, which can be resolved along the QTW body axis. the dynamic of the QTW can be formulated as:

$$\begin{bmatrix} \ddot{x}_g \\ \ddot{y}_g \\ \ddot{z}_g \end{bmatrix} = \begin{bmatrix} 0 \\ 0 \\ mg \end{bmatrix} + R_{bg}^T \left(\begin{bmatrix} 0 \\ 0 \\ -T \end{bmatrix} + R_{wb}^T R_{aw}^T \begin{bmatrix} -D \\ Y \\ -L \end{bmatrix} \right) \tag{1}$$

where $[x_g, y_g, z_g]^T$ is the position of the center of mass of the QTW, R_{bg} is the rotation matrix from the ground frame to the body frame, R_{wb} is the rotation matrix from the body frame to the wing frame, R_{aw} is the rotation matrix from wing frame to the airflow frame, m is the mass of the QTW, g is the standard acceleration of gravity, T is the resultant thrust acting on the QTW, $[L, D, Y]$ are the aerodynamic forces, representing lift, drag and side-force respectively. R_{bg} is as follows:

$$R_{bg} = R_x(\phi) R_y(\theta) R_z(\psi) \tag{2}$$

where

$$R_x(\phi) = \begin{bmatrix} 1 & 0 & 0 \\ 0 & \cos\phi & \sin\phi \\ 0 & -\cos\phi & \cos\phi \end{bmatrix} \tag{3}$$

$$R_y(\theta) = \begin{bmatrix} \cos\theta & 0 & -\sin\theta \\ 0 & 1 & 0 \\ \sin\theta & 0 & \cos\theta \end{bmatrix} \tag{4}$$

$$R_z(\psi) = \begin{bmatrix} \cos\psi & \sin\psi & 0 \\ -\sin\psi & \cos\psi & 0 \\ 0 & 0 & 1 \end{bmatrix} \tag{5}$$

where ϕ, θ, ψ are the Euler angles of the QTW body. R_{wb} is as follows:

$$R_{wb} = \begin{bmatrix} \cos\delta_{wb} & 0 & -\sin\delta_{wb} \\ 0 & 1 & 0 \\ \sin\delta_{wb} & 0 & \cos\delta_{wb} \end{bmatrix} \tag{6}$$

where δ_{wb} is the rotation angle from the body frame to the wing frame. R_{aw} is as follows:

$$R_{aw} = \begin{bmatrix} \sin\alpha\cos\beta & -\sin\alpha\sin\beta & \cos\alpha \\ \sin\beta & \cos\beta & 0 \\ -\cos\alpha\cos\beta & \cos\alpha\sin\beta & \sin\alpha \end{bmatrix} \tag{7}$$

where α is the angle of the attack, β is the sideslip angle.

The aerodynamic force $[L, D, Y]$ is as follows:

$$L = \frac{1}{2}C_L \rho V_a^2 S \tag{8}$$

$$D = \frac{1}{2}C_D \rho V_a^2 S \tag{9}$$

$$Y = \frac{1}{2}C_Y \rho V_a^2 S \tag{10}$$

where ρ is the atmospheric air density, $V_a = \sqrt{v_x^2 + v_y^2 + v_z^2}$ is the airspeed, S is the wing reference area, C_L, C_D, C_Y are the dimensionless aerodynamic coefficients. According to [14], they can be calculated by:

$$C_L = C_{L_\alpha}(\alpha) + \frac{c}{2V_a} C_{L_q} q \tag{11}$$

$$C_D = C_{D_\alpha}(\alpha) + \frac{c}{2V_a} C_{D_q} q \tag{12}$$

$$C_Y = C_{Y_\beta}\beta + \frac{b}{2V_a}\left(C_{Y_p} p + C_{Y_r} r\right) \tag{13}$$

where C_{L_α} and C_{D_α} are functions of angle of attack α, $C_{L_q}, C_{D_q}, C_{Y_\beta}, C_{Y_p}$ and C_{Y_r} are all constants which are related to the airfoil, b is the wing span, c is the wing mean geometric chord, p, q, r are the angular velocities of the wing coordinate frame.

The task of the control method can be described as follows: By designing reasonable $\phi_d, \theta_d, \psi_d, \delta_{wb}$ and T, let the current position $[x_g, y_g, z_g]^T$ of the QTW track the reference position $[x_{gd}, y_{gd}, z_{gd}]^T$, while ensure the reduction of energy consumption.

3   Control Method

In this work, a state-feedback controllers with model feedforward for reducing the energy consumption of the QTW is developed. Initially, error variables are defined as:

$$e_{x_g} \triangleq x_{gd} - x_g, \quad e_{y_g} \triangleq y_{gd} - y_g, \quad e_{z_g} \triangleq z_{gd} - z_g \tag{14}$$

$$e_{vx} \triangleq v_{xd} - \dot{x}_g, \quad e_{vy} \triangleq v_{yd} - \dot{y}_g, \quad e_{vz} \triangleq v_{zd} - \dot{z}_g \tag{15}$$

where the intermediate variables $v_{xd} = k_{p1} e_{x_g} + \dot{x}_{gd}, v_{yd} = k_{p2} e_{y_g} + \dot{y}_{gd}, v_{zd} = k_{p3} e_{z_g} + \dot{z}_{gd}$ are properly defined through parameters k_{p1}, k_{p2}, k_{p3}.

Determine the orientation of the wing coordinate system according to the target velocity vector, so the pitch angle of the wing frame θ_{wd} can be designed as follows:

$$\theta_{wd} = \arctan\left(\frac{-v_{zd}}{v_{xd}\cos\psi + v_{yd}\sin\psi}\right) + \alpha_d \tag{16}$$

where α_d is the target attack angle, which set as a reasonable constant value according to the function C_{L_α} in this paper. According to the relationship between the body coordinate frame and the wing coordinate frame, δ_{wb} can be calculated as

$$\delta_{wb} = \theta_{wd} - \theta \tag{17}$$

Let the target force in ground frame as intermediate control variables, they can be designed as:

$$F_{xg} = m(k_{v1} e_{vx} + \ddot{x}_{gd}) \tag{18}$$

$$F_{yg} = m(k_{v2} e_{vy} + \ddot{y}_{gd}) \tag{19}$$

$$F_{zg} = m(k_{v3} e_{vz} - g + \ddot{z}_{gd}) \tag{20}$$

Considering that the aerodynamic force and the speed of the QTW have the same differential order, and the speed of the vehicle will not change suddenly when the rotor propulsion changes, so the aerodynamic force can be considered as a constant when calculating the target rotor thrust.

According to (1), the target force of the QTW is as follows:

$$\begin{bmatrix} F_x \\ F_y \\ F_z \end{bmatrix} = R_z(\psi) \begin{bmatrix} F_{xg} \\ F_{yg} \\ F_{zg} \end{bmatrix} - R_y(\theta)^T R_x(\phi)^T R_{wb}^T R_{aw}^T \begin{bmatrix} -D \\ Y \\ -L \end{bmatrix} \tag{21}$$

Let the four rotors turn to the direction of the target force, the target tilt angle of the QTW body can be calculated as follows:

$$\theta_d = -\text{atan2}(F_x, -F_z) \tag{22}$$

$$\phi_d = \text{atan2}(F_y, -F_z) \tag{23}$$

the target torsion angle of the QTW body is as follows:

$$\psi_d = \text{atan2}(v_{yd}, v_{xd}) \tag{24}$$

where the expression of atan2 is as follows:

$$\text{atan2}(y, x) = \begin{cases} \arctan\left(\frac{y}{x}\right) & x > 0 \\ \arctan\left(\frac{y}{x}\right) + \pi & y \geq 0, x < 0 \\ \arctan\left(\frac{y}{x}\right) - \pi & y < 0, x < 0 \\ \frac{\pi}{2} & y > 0, x = 0 \\ -\frac{\pi}{2} & y < 0, x = 0 \\ 0 & y = 0, x = 0 \end{cases} \tag{25}$$

Finally, we project the target force vector onto the actual body frame z_b axis in order to compute the target thrust for the QTW:

$$T = \frac{-F_z}{\cos\theta \cos\phi} \tag{26}$$

4   Simulation Result

In order to verify the tracking performance and energy-saving advantages of the new aerial vehicle configuration, we let the QTW and a quadrotor of the same quality track the same spiral trajectory, and finally compare the tracking accuracy and energy consumption of the two. The expression for the trajectory is:

$$\begin{cases} x_{gd} = R\cos(\omega t) \\ y_{gd} = R\sin(\omega t) \\ z_{gd} = -2\omega t - h \end{cases} \tag{27}$$

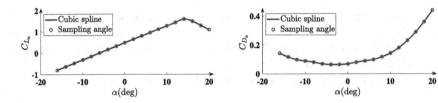

Fig. 2. The function curves of C_{L_α} and C_{D_α} with respect to α.

Table 1. The parameters of the QTW and the environment

Parameters	Values	Unit	Parameters	Values	Unit
m	1.2	kg	b	0.700	m
S	0.082	m^2	c	0.117	m
ρ	1.225	kg/m^3	g	9.81	m/s^2

Table 2. The dimensionless aerodynamic coefficients of the QTW

Parameters	Values	Parameters	Values	Parameters	Values
C_{L_q}	0.0516	C_{Y_p}	−0.0401	C_{Y_r}	−0.2349
C_{D_q}	0	C_{Y_β}	−0.3438		

Table 3. The controller parameters of the QTW and quadrotor

Parameter	Value	Parameter	Value	Parameter	Value
k_{p1}	1.4	k_{p2}	1.4	k_{p3}	1.4
k_{v1}	2	k_{v2}	2	k_{v3}	2

where $\omega = 0.2$, $R = 50$, $h = 100$. The inertia parameters of the QTW and environment parameters are shown in Table 1. The dimensionless aerodynamic coefficients of the QTW measured by Xflr5 [7] are shown in Table 2, where C_{L_α} and C_{D_α} as functions of α are plotted in Fig. 2. The controller parameters of the QTW and quadrotor are given in Table 3. The target attack angle $\alpha_d = 10$deg. The simulations run on a personal computer host (Intel(R) Core(TM) i7-8700K at 3.7 GHz CPU) with Windows 10 operating system. The simulations are configured to use the fourth-order Runge-Kutta method with a step size of 0.001s.

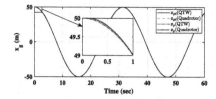

Fig. 3. Responses of position x_g of the QTW and quadrotor.

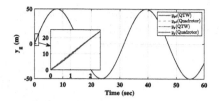

Fig. 4. Responses of position y_g of the QTW and quadrotor.

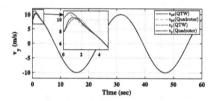

Fig. 5. Responses of position z_g of the QTW and quadrotor.

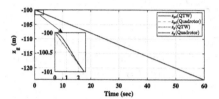

Fig. 6. Responses of velocity v_x of the QTW and quadrotor.

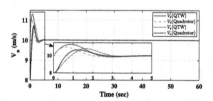

Fig. 7. Responses of velocity v_y of the QTW and quadrotor.

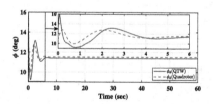

Fig. 8. Responses of velocity v_z of the QTW and quadrotor.

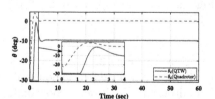

Fig. 9. The airspeed V_a of the QTW and quadrotor.

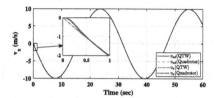

Fig. 10. The target roll angle ϕ_d of the QTW and quadrotor.

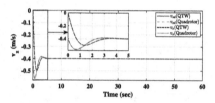

Fig. 11. The target pitch angle θ_d of the QTW and quadrotor.

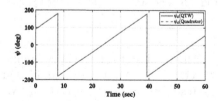

Fig. 12. The target yaw angle ψ_d of the QTW and quadrotor.

Mean, Maximum and Root Mean Square Error (RMSE) of the tracking process are used to indicate the tracking accuracy. They are obtained by

$$\text{Mean} = \frac{1}{n}\sum_{i=1}^{n}\|\boldsymbol{p}_i - \boldsymbol{r}_d\|$$

$$\text{Maximum} = \max_{i=1,2,\ldots,n}\|\boldsymbol{p}_i - \boldsymbol{r}_d\| \qquad (28)$$

$$\text{RMSE} = \sqrt{\frac{1}{n}\sum_{i=1}^{n}(\|\boldsymbol{p}_i - \boldsymbol{r}_d\|)^2}$$

where $\boldsymbol{p}_i$ is the actual position of the QTW, $\boldsymbol{r}_d$ is the reference position.

In order to compare the energy utilization efficiency of the QTW and quadrotor, the following expression is used to calculate energy consumption:

$$E_C = \int_{t_0}^{t_f} T(t)V_a(t)dt \qquad (29)$$

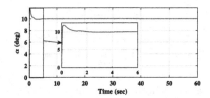

Fig. 13. The target thrust T of the QTW and quadrotor.

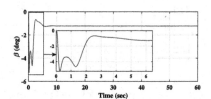

Fig. 14. The target δ_{wb} of the QTW.

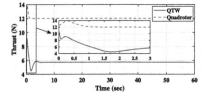

Fig. 15. The attack angle α of the QTW.

Fig. 16. The sideslip angle β of the QTW.

The results of the tracking simulation are shown in Figs. 3, 4, 5, 6, 7, 8, 9, 10, 11, 12, 13, 14, 15, 16 and 17 and Table 4. Figure 3, 4 and 5 demonstrate the responses of position of the QTW and quadrotor in the ground coordinate frame. Figure 6, 7, 8 and 9 demonstrate the responses of velocity of the QTW and quadrotor in the ground coordinate frame. Figure 10, 11 and 12 show the evolutions of attitude of the QTW and quadrotor, respectively. Figure 13 shows

Table 4. Tracking error of the QTW and Quadrotor

	Mean	Maximum	RMSE
QTW	0.0359	0.9291	0.1274
Quadrotor	0.0248	0.6973	0.0855

the evolution of thrust of the QTW and quadrotor. Figure 14 shows the evolution
of δ_{wb} of the QTW. Figure 15 and 16 demonstrate the aerodynamic angles of the
QTW. Figure 17 demonstrate the trajectory of the QTW and quadrotor. From
Fig. 17 and the data in Table 4, one can get that the tracking errors of the QTW
and quadrotor are not much different. Substituting the data in Fig. 9 and Fig. 13
into (29), yields that:

$$E_{C_{QTW}} = 3438.6\text{J}, \quad E_{C_{QR}} = 7222.8\text{J} \tag{30}$$

where $E_{C_{QTW}}$ is the energy consumption of the QTW, $E_{C_{QR}}$ is the energy consumption of the quadrotor. It can be seen that the energy consumption of the
QTW is much smaller than that of quadrotor. This shows that the new configuration of the aerial vehicle we proposed can effectively save energy and increase
endurance flight time.

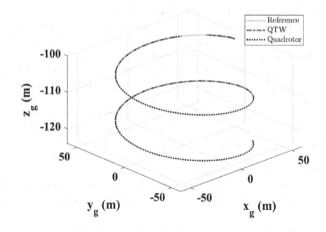

Fig. 17. The tracking trajectory of the QTW and quadrotor.

5 Conclusion

In this paper, a novel configuration of the aerial vehicle named QTW is presented aiming at reducing the energy consumption by adding tiltable wing on
the quadrotor. The QTW can use the airflow flowing over the wing to generate

lift to reduce the magnitude of the target thrust. We have modeled the translational dynamics and designed a state feedback + model feedforward controller for the proposed QTW vehicle. A set of simulation result has shown the efficiency of the new configuration and the controller. From the simulation results, it can be seen that the QTW consumes less than half of the energy of a quadrotor of the same quality when the position tracking performance is similar.

References

1. Argyle, M.E., Beard, R.W., Morris, S.: The vertical bat tail-sitter: dynamic model and control architecture. In: 2013 American Control Conference, pp. 806–811. IEEE (2013)
2. Bauersfeld, L., Scaramuzza, D.: Range, endurance, and optimal speed estimates for multicopters. IEEE Robot. Autom. Lett. **7**(2), 2953–2960 (2022)
3. Bauersfeld, L., Spannagl, L., Ducard, G.J.J., Onder, C.H.: MPC flight control for a tilt-rotor VTOL aircraft. IEEE Trans. Aerosp. Electron. Syst. **57**(4), 2395–2409 (2021). https://doi.org/10.1109/TAES.2021.3061819
4. Chen, Z., Jia, H.: Design of flight control system for a novel tilt-rotor UAV. Complexity **2020**, 1–14 (2020)
5. Dalwadi, N., Deb, D., Ozana, S.: Dual observer based adaptive controller for hybrid drones. Drones **7**(1) (2023). https://doi.org/10.3390/drones7010048
6. Dalwadi, N., Deb, D., Rath, J.J.: Biplane trajectory tracking using hybrid controller based on backstepping and integral terminal sliding mode control. Drones **6**(3) (2022). https://doi.org/10.3390/drones6030058
7. Drela, M.: XFOIL: an analysis and design system for low reynolds number airfoils. In: Mueller, T.J. (ed.) Low Reynolds Number Aerodynamics, pp. 1–12. Springer, Cham (1989). https://doi.org/10.1007/978-3-642-84010-4_1
8. Flores, G.R., Escareño, J., Lozano, R., Salazar, S.: Quad-tilting rotor convertible MAV: modeling and real-time hover flight control. J. Intell. Robot. Syst. **65**(1–4), 457–471 (2012)
9. kalpa Gunarathna, J., Munasinghe, R.: Development of a quad-rotor fixed-wing hybrid unmanned aerial vehicle. In: 2018 Moratuwa Engineering Research Conference (MERCon), pp. 72–77. IEEE (2018)
10. Jones, R., Cleaver, D., Gursul, I.: Aerodynamics of biplane and tandem wings at low reynolds numbers. Exp. Fluids **56**, 1–25 (2015)
11. Liu, B., Li, J., Yang, Y., Zhou, Z.: Controller design for quad-rotor UAV based on variable aggregation model predictive control. Flight Control Detect. **4**(3), 1–7 (2021)
12. Pfeifle, O., Fichter, W.: Minimum power control allocation for incremental control of over-actuated transition aircraft. J. Guid. Control. Dyn. **46**(2), 286–300 (2023)
13. Smeur, E.J., Bronz, M., de Croon, G.C.: Incremental control and guidance of hybrid aircraft applied to a tailsitter unmanned air vehicle. J. Guid. Control. Dyn. **43**(2), 274–287 (2020)
14. Stevens, B.L., Lewis, F.L., Johnson, E.N.: Aircraft Control and Simulation: Dynamics, Controls Design, and Autonomous Systems. Wiley, Hoboken (2015)
15. Sun, J., Li, B., Wen, C.Y., Chen, C.K.: Model-aided wind estimation method for a tail-sitter aircraft. IEEE Trans. Aerosp. Electron. Syst. **56**(2), 1262–1278 (2020). https://doi.org/10.1109/TAES.2019.2929379

16. Swarnkar, S., Parwana, H., Kothari, M., Abhishek, A.: Biplane-quadrotor tail-sitter UAV: flight dynamics and control. J. Guid. Control. Dyn. **41**(5), 1049–1067 (2018)
17. Xi, L., Zhu, Q., Zhang, D.: Sliding mode control design based on fuzzy reaching law for yaw angle of a tail-sitter UAV. In: 2016 22nd International Conference on Automation and Computing (ICAC), pp. 238–243 (2016). https://doi.org/10. 1109/IConAC.2016.7604925

Balance Control for Inverted Pendulum System via SGCMG

Bowen Tang, Xinrong Yan, and Ming Chu$^{(\boxtimes)}$

School of Modern Post (School of Automation), Beijing University of Posts and
Telecommunications, Beijing 100876, China
chuming_bupt@bupt.edu.cn

Abstract. It is crucial to study the self-balance problem of an inverted pendulum
with non-holonomic constraints. For the balance control of inverted pendulum
systems, there are now issues with insufficient robustness, a short control range,
and a complex controller design. The fuzzy PD control method is a new control approach that is proposed in this paper. Firstly, with a single gimbal control
moment gyro (SGCMG), a dynamic model of the inverted pendulum is established
and a dynamic analysis is carried out. Secondly, certain important parameters are
specified, including PID control parameters and fuzzy domain, and variables like
SGCMG pitch rate and inverted pendulum rolling angle are defined. Thirdly,
some important variables are configured, like the fuzzy domain and PID control parameters. Finally, using the Matlab-Adams co-simulation, the effects of
this technique on the stability of the inverted pendulum is confirmed. The simulation results ultimately demonstrate the effectiveness and viability of the suggested fuzzy PD control method, which can effectively increase the stability of
the inverted pendulum.

Keywords: SGCMG · Inverted pendulum · PID control · Fuzzy control · Fuzzy
PD control

1 Introduction

The inverted pendulum is an underactuated, non holonomic constraint system, and
second-order dynamic coupling constraints are placed on its lateral tilt angle. The academic community has acknowledged the difficulty of achieving nonlinear management
of the equilibrium of the entire system without using the inverted pendulum or other
mechanical auxiliary structures [1–3].

A crucial control moment output method is the single gimbal control moment gyroscope (SGCMG) [4]. It is frequently employed in aircraft control, satellite attitude control, and other fields due to its high control precision and stability [5]. Relevant studies
on bicycles and inverted pendulum systems were undertaken in 2014 by Harun Yetkin
et al. from Ohio State University [6]. They proved that control moment gyroscopes may
be utilized to stabilize inverted pendulum systems and have good robustness by creating
dynamic equations and designing controllers.

© The Author(s), under exclusive license to Springer Nature Singapore Pte Ltd. 2023
H. Yang et al. (Eds.): ICIRA 2023, LNAI 14274, pp. 120–129, 2023.
https://doi.org/10.1007/978-981-99-6501-4_11

In 2012, Dr. Pom Yuan Lam of the National University of Singapore created a self-balancing bicycle that is comparable to a real-world model of an inverted pendulum system. By comparing the effects of PID and PD controllers on system stability, Dr. Pom Yuan Lam showed how effective PID control is at controlling the inverted pendulum system [7]. Later, for the control effects of the inverted pendulum, people started looking into different control approaches, like fuzzy control. To achieve full automatic control, Saeed, Hashemnia, and others make choices based on fuzzy rules. The reaction tracking of the control system is subpar, and the output of a simple fuzzy controller exhibits severe phase lag [8].

It is shown that the inverted pendulum system with the SGCMG stabilizer may be controlled in a variety of methods, the two most common being PID control and fuzzy control. But PID control is improper for nonlinear systems since it has a broad range of ideal parameters that depend on the situation. Phase delays and lengthy adjustment times are issues with fuzzy control. The inverted pendulum system cannot be controlled effectively or reliably using any of these two control techniques.

The fuzzy PD control method that is proposed in this article combines the benefits of fuzzy and PID control. Fuzzy PD control is more accurate and resilient than classical PID control, especially for nonlinear, time-varying, and multivariable complex systems [9]. Using fuzzy PD control in inverted pendulum systems can increase steady-state control precision and lower steady-state errors as compared to fuzzy control.

2 Dynamic Analysis for Inverted Pendulum with SGCMG

By regulating the gyroscopic moment produced during precession, the balancing problem of an inverted pendulum system based on the SGCMG precession effect is studied in this research. In relation to a gyroscope, an object that is spinning will remain spinning in its original orientation. The spin axis takes on the shape of a cone when exposed to an external torque. Gyroscopic precession is the name given to this occurrence. In the gyro frame of reference, the combined torque of the control torque and the Coriolis torque produced by precession is zero (Fig. 1).

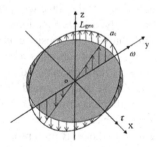

Fig. 1. Distribution of Gyroscopic Rotor Gees Acceleration.

Symbol definitions are provided below:

Lgyro: The constant angular momentum (spin vector) of the gyro.

ω: The precession angular velocity vector of the gyro.

ac: The Coriolis acceleration at each mass element.

τ: The sum of external moments.

Euler's dynamical equations may be used to determine the effects of control torque on a single-frame gyro. The motion of a rigid body is described by Euler's dynamical equations, which also show how angular acceleration and torque relate to one another.

The following equation can be expressed using Euler's dynamics equation under the assumption that the gyro is a rigid body with no additional external forces or disturbances, such as air resistance or friction:

$$\frac{dL}{dt} = \tau$$

This indicates that the control torque supplied to the gyro equals the rate of change of the angular momentum of the gyro over time. Assuming that the gyroscope's axis rotates at an angle of "ω" with respect to a specific axis, the formula for angular momentum's rate of change is:

$$\frac{dL}{dt} = \omega \times Lgyro$$

The cross-product operation is indicated by "$\times$" The subsequent equation can be created by equating these two equations equally:

$$\omega \times Lgyro = \tau$$

The rotor of the gyroscope also applies an equal and opposite reaction torque to the surrounding environment in accordance with the action and reaction principle. This reactive torque is often referred to as the gyroscopic torque.

$$M gyro = -\omega \times Lgyro$$

Similarly, the dynamic equation of the inverted pendulum system, including SGCMG, can be determined Euler's dynamical equations.

To avoid ambiguity, the coordinate system's positive direction is defined as follows: the positive direction of the X-axis is the outward direction of the vertical paper surface; the positive direction of the Y-axis is the right direction of the parallel paper surface; and the positive direction of the Z-axis is the upward direction of the parallel paper surface. All angles are measured with the coordinate axis as the beginning position and the positive direction being counterclockwise.

More variables that will be used in the derivation procedure are defined below.

I: The entire system's moment of inertia around the rotational joint (aka. X-axis).

θ: The roll angle of the entire system.

m: The entire system's mass.

l: The distance from the center of mass of the system to the axis of rotation.

g: The acceleration of gravity.

M': Moments other than gravitational moments, such as disturbance moments.

The experiment's inverted pendulum has just one degree of freedom for rotation about the X-axis. Rewrite the angular momentum rate of change along the X-axis:

$$\frac{dL}{dt} = \omega \times Lgyro + I\dddot{\theta}$$

Replace the external torque "τ" with:

$$\tau = mglsin\theta + M'$$

According to the Euler's dynamical equations:

$$\omega \times Lgyro + I\ddot{\theta} = mglsin\theta + M'$$

The dynamic equation of the inverted pendulum system is obtained by simplifying the above equation:

$$I\ddot{\theta} = -\omega \times Lgyro + mglsin\theta + M'$$

The inverted pendulum system's dynamic behavior is described by the equation above. This dynamic equation can be used in practical applications to construct controllers that will control the inverted pendulum.

3 PID Control

Proportional, integration, and differentiation control are collectively referred to as PID (proportional-integral-derivative) control. Due to its strong robust performance and convenient tweaking techniques, this algorithm is a key application technology in the field of autonomous control theory.

The upright control of the inverted pendulum requires high speed when a single gimbal control moment gyroscope stabilizer is used to control it. There is no need for an integral coefficient in this situation because of the huge proportional coefficient and the system's low static error. The integral coefficient is therefore 0.

In the Adams dynamic simulation software, create a model of an inverted pendulum system. A SGCMG, a gyroscope support, and an inverted pendulum platform make up the entire apparatus. The gyroscope rotor is connected to the rotating shaft through bearings, and the same applies to the SGCMG and the gyroscope support. Other items are fixedly connected to one another. The inverted pendulum system has a symmetrical construction and a homogenous overall mass distribution. Finally, the precession angle of SGCMG is used as the input interface of the system. The inclination angle relative to the plane of reference and angular velocity of the inverted pendulum are used as the output interface of the system to create a co-simulation between Matlab and Adams (Fig. 2).

With a force of 5N in the horizontal direction to the left, a disturbance is established in Adams' upright inverted pendulum system at a time of 0.1 s. To stabilize the system, the ultimate control effect should reduce overshoot, and reduce initial disturbances to

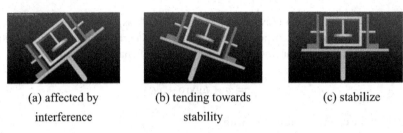

(a) affected by   (b) tending towards   (c) stabilize

interference   stability

Fig. 2. Model of an inverted pendulum system equipped with SGCMG (a) affected by interference. (b) tending towards stability (c) stabilize

enhance robustness. The proportional coefficient was found to be 80 and the differential coefficient to be 10, following experimental testing. At this point, the overshoot had greatly decreased, and the oscillation amplitude after interference was roughly 40% of that without control, which was the desired outcome. As demonstrated in the accompanying graphic, simulation results demonstrate how the PID controller affects the balancing of the inverted pendulum system.

The PID controller can speed up the system's return to equilibrium effectively in the presence of disturbances. But the PID controller is not applicable for inverted pendulum systems due to the nonlinear nature of the system.

4   Fuzzy Control

The inverted pendulum is a well-known control problem with nonlinear and unstable properties. Fuzzy control can handle complex and nonlinear systems and has good robustness and adaptability by fuzzifying input and output, designing fuzzy inference rules, and de-fuzzification.

The three core stages of fuzzy control design are fuzzification, fuzzy inference, and de-fuzzification. The input variables for the fuzzification stage are the inverted pendulum inclination angle in relation to the reference plane and the angular velocity, while the output variable is the pitch angular velocity of the SGCMG. The input values are converted to corresponding fuzzy sets using membership functions, and the membership degrees of each fuzzy set are calculated.

The domain of the inverted pendulum inclination angle E is set to [−1.05, 1.05] rad, and the domain of the inverted pendulum oscillation speed EC is chosen to be [−2.618, 2.618] rad/s since the goal of this experiment is to study the control effect of the big angle inclination of the inverted pendulum. The fuzzy language is chosen as {NB, NM, NS, ZO, PS, PM, PB}, and the output domain is set as [−50, 50].

Fuzzy rules describe the fuzzy relationship between input and output. By calculating the membership degree of a fuzzy set and the condition part of fuzzy rules, the activation degree or weight of each rule can be obtained (Fig. 3).

The process then moves on to the de-fuzzification stage, where the centroid approach is employed in this experiment to translate the fuzzy output into true output values. Figure 4 displays the fuzzy controller's final control surface.

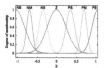 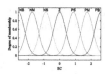 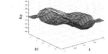

Fig. 3. Membership functions for tilt angle and angular velocity

Fig. 4. Fuzzy rule surface for proportional coefficient

Fig. 5. Tilt change curve after employing fuzzy control

The inverted pendulum's tilt angle changes with and without fuzzy control can be compared by importing the fuzzy file into the MATLAB workspace and simulating it (as shown in Fig. 5).

Fuzzy sets and fuzzy logic are two effective control methods that can be used to solve control issues in complex, nonlinear, and fuzzy systems. It is a versatile and reliable tool that works well for solving control issues in a variety of fields. The fuzzy control design approach can produce suitable and stable control strategies by constructing appropriate fuzzy rules and membership functions.

5   Fuzzy PD Control

The traditional PID controller has the benefits of being straightforward and widely applicable but it might struggle to handle nonlinear, complicated systems. Nonlinear and fuzzy issues can be resolved using traditional PID control by introducing the concepts and methodologies of fuzzy control. Fuzzy control has considerable robustness and can manage fuzzy and unpredictable input-output correlations. Fuzzy logic and traditional PID control can be used to improve control performance and system durability while overcoming the constraints of the latter in nonlinear systems.

5.1   Determination of Input and Output Parameters

The inclination angle "θ" and angular velocity "$\dot{\theta}$" of the inverted pendulum system with respect to the reference plane are selected as inputs, and the two parameters that call for on-line adjustment for the fuzzy PD controller are selected as outputs based on the requirements of the information gathering and the actual needs. As a result, the inputs chosen are the inverted pendulum system angular velocity EC and the tilt angle deviation E. Proportional coefficient and differential coefficient are the outputs.

5.2   Determination of Fuzzy Domain

According to the actual situation and requirements, the range of the inverted pendulum tilt angle is selected as [−1.77 1.77] rad, and the output domain is {−6, −4, −2, 0, 2, 4, 6}. The range of the inverted pendulum angular velocity is selected as [−2.6 2.6] rad/s, and the output domain is {−6, −4, −2, 0, 2, 4, 6}. Referring to the parameters of the PID controller and its corresponding actual operation, the value range of proportional coefficient is set to [–155 155], and the output domain is {0, 1, 2, 3, 4, 5, 6}. The value range of differential coefficient is selected as [–8 8], and the output domain is {0, 1, 2, 3, 4, 5, 6}.

5.3 Fuzzy Segmentation

The fundamental domain is subdivided into seven fuzzy sets: PB (positive big), PM (positive medium), PS (positive small), ZE (zero), NS (negative small), NM (negative medium), and NB (negative big).

There are many different membership functions in fuzzy control, but the Gaussian function is most frequently used because it has the benefit of fitting the normal distribution. The expression used by this system, which chooses the Gaussian function to calculate membership degree.

$$\mu(x) = e^{-\left(\frac{x-a}{b}\right)^2}$$

The membership functions of the input and output variables can be changed by utilizing the membership function editor. Figure 6 displays the membership functions for the input variables tilt angle and angular velocity. Figure 7 displays the membership functions for the output variables proportional coefficient and differential coefficient.

 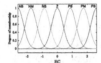 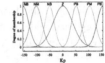

Fig. 6. Membership functions for tilt angle and angular velocity

Fig. 7. Membership functions for proportional coefficient and differential coefficient

5.4 Determining Control Rules

The following five control rules can be distilled based on the properties of the inverted pendulum system as well as the actual application effects and system response.

1. A bigger proportional coefficient should be employed when the inverted pendulum system's tilt angle is large in order to swiftly rectify the inverted pendulum posture. Currently, a smaller differential coefficient should be utilized if angular velocity results in a balance trend, whereas a bigger differential coefficient should be employed if an imbalance trend of greater magnitude develops.
2. The inverted pendulum system must have strong static performance and reduce control overshoot when the tilt angle is minimal. Use a smaller proportional coefficient instead. At this point, a smaller differential coefficient value is required if angular velocity is small. A higher differential coefficient value is required if angular velocity is significant.

Table 1. Fuzzy rule table for proportional coefficient

E \ EC	NB	NM	NS	ZO	PS	PM	PB
NB	PB	PM	ZO	NS	NB	NS	ZO
NM	PB	PM	NS	NM	NB	ZO	PS
NS	PM	PS	NM	NB	NB	ZO	PS
ZO	PM	PS	NM	NB	NM	PS	PM
PS	PS	ZO	NB	NB	NM	PS	PM
PM	PS	ZO	NB	NM	NS	PM	PB
PB	ZO	NS	NB	NS	ZO	PM	PB

Table 2. Fuzzy rule table for differential coefficient

E \ EC	NB	NM	NS	ZO	PS	PM	PB
NB	PB	NM	NM	NS	NM	NS	NB
NM	PM	NM	NM	NM	NS	ZO	NM
NS	PS	NM	NM	NB	ZO	PS	NS
ZO	ZO	NB	NB	NB	NB	NB	ZO
PS	NS	PS	ZO	NB	NM	NM	PS
PM	NM	ZO	NS	NM	NM	NM	PM
PB	NB	NS	NM	NS	NM	NM	PB

3. It is important to ensure response time and limit excessive overshoot when the tilt angle and angular velocity are both of medium magnitude. It is best to utilize a moderate proportional coefficient and a modest or lesser differential coefficient.
4. If tilt angle and angular velocity have the opposite signs, the inverted pendulum system tends to accept a lower proportional coefficient as it approaches equilibrium.
5. If the indications of the tilt angle and angular velocity are the same, the inverted pendulum system must act fast to restore the posture as it moves out of balance and will often require a greater proportional coefficient (Table 1 and Table 2).

5.5 Fuzzy Inference and Defuzzification

Fuzzy instructions are created from the aforementioned rules and submitted to the fuzzy controller. As shown in Fig. 8, the output surface viewer enables users to recognize the connections between the proportional coefficient, differential coefficient, and input variables as a result of fuzzy inference.

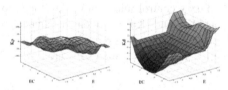

Fig. 8. Fuzzy rule surface for proportional coefficient and differential coefficient.

The forward route of the system should also include the setup fuzzy controller and the PD controller after being imported into Simulink. In Fig. 9, the inverted pendulum's tilt angle variation curves are depicted (Fig. 10).

It can be concluded from comparing the inverted pendulum inclination angle change process under three different control methods that fuzzy PD control can effectively suppress disturbances compared to fuzzy control, stabilizing the angle at 1.57 radians with a steady-state error of essentially 0, while fuzzy control ultimately has a steady-state error of 0.01 to 0.02 radians. The experimental results mentioned above show that fuzzy PD control surpasses basic fuzzy controllers and conventional PID controllers in terms of robustness, accuracy of steady-state control.

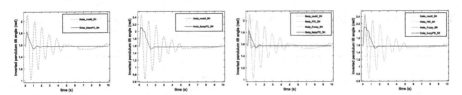

Fig. 9. Tilt change curve after adding Fuzzy PD control.

Fig. 10. Comparing the control effects.

6 Conclusion

Based on the aforementioned information, it can be inferred that fuzzy PD control offers higher robustness and steady-state control accuracy when compared to PID control and fuzzy control. Furthermore, the parameters of fuzzy PD control may automatically change with the structural and characteristic changes of the system by defining simple fuzzy domains and fuzzy rules according to the actual situation, considerably decreasing the difficulty of controller design. Fuzzy PD control has been proven to be highly feasible and successful in resolving the balancing issue of the inverted pendulum system based on SGCMG through simulation.

The Fuzzy PD controller's design is very important in this essay. The inclination angle "θ" and angular velocity "$\dot{\theta}$" of the inverted pendulum with regard to the reference plane are the variables to be regulated in fuzzy PD control, according to relevant materials combined with the actual scenario. Additionally, the Fuzzy PD controller needs to dynamically modify two parameters, "Kp" and "Kd". The design of the fuzzy domain is also significant since it influences whether certain parameter adjustments are near to ideal in some situation. The appropriate domains for the parameters in the Fuzzy PD controller can be discovered using the experience of altering parameters in the previously employed PID controller.Fuzzy control rules can be developed to identify the method for dynamically modifying "Kp" and "Kd" based on the balance process and adjustment requirements of the inverted pendulum system after disturbance. The controller and associated circuits are built using the simulation software Fuzzy Toolbox and Simulink in Matlab.

Acknowledgments. This research is supported by Research Innovation Fund for Collage Students of Beijing University of Posts and Telecommunications (Project No. 202212048).

References

1. Abut, T.: Real-time control and application with self-tuning PID-type fuzzy adaptive controller of an inverted pendulum. Ind. Robot. **46**(1), 159–170 (2019)
2. Trentin, J.F.S.: Variable speed control moment gyroscope in an inverted pendulum. J. Dyn. Syst. Measur. Control, Transactions of the ASME **141**(11) (2019)
3. Messikh, L.: Stabilization of the cart-inverted-pendulum system using state-feedback pole-independent mpc controllers. Sensors **22**(1), (2022)
4. Huang, Z.L.: Analysis of output characteristics of single frame control moment gyroscope. J. Mech. **53** 2), 511–523+I0004 (2021)

5. Salleh, M.B., Suhadis, N.M.: Three-axis attitude control performance of a small satellite using control moment gyroscope. In: 56th AEROTECH Conference 2014, pp. 286–290. Trans Tech Publications Ltd, Malaysia (2016)

6. Yetkin, H., Kalouche, S.: Gyroscopic stabilization of an unmanned bicycle. In: American Control conference, ACC 2014, pp. 4549–4554. Institute of Electrical and Electronics Engineers Inc., United States (2014)

7. Lam, P.Y.: Gyroscopic stabilization of a self-balancing robot bicycle. Int. J. Autom. Technol. 5(6), 916–923 (2011)

8. Hashemnia, S.: Unmanned bicycle balancing via Lyapunov rule-based fuzzy control. Multibody Sys. Dyn. 31(2), 147–168 (2014)

9. Wang, L.X., Wang, Y.J.: Tutorial on Fuzzy Systems and Fuzzy Control. Tsinghua University Press, Beijing (2017)

Robot Human-Lateral-Following Method with Adaptive Linear Quadratic Regulator

Chaoqun Wang, Wenfeng Li$^{(\boxtimes)}$, Jinglong Zhou, and Anning Yang

School of Transportation and Logistics Engineering, Wuhan University of Technology,
Wuhan 430063, China
liwf@whut.edu.cn

Abstract. For following robots in a human-machine cooperative context, a lateral following method based on Adaptive Linear Quadratic Regulator (ALQR) control method is proposed in this paper. Compared to conventional following techniques, this method is more adaptable and may be used in a variety of contexts. First, Non-Uniform Rational B-Splines (NURBS) curves are employed to enhance the lateral following theoretical trajectory of the robot. Further, fuzzy control is used to optimize the traditional LQR controller. Finally, experiments are carried out to verify the reliability of the ALQR algorithm. The experimental results show that the lateral following method proposed in this paper is improved compared with other algorithms. The real-time performance of forward error and lateral error is improved by 43.9% and 62.1% respectively. In terms of stability, it increased by 55.2% and 71.8% respectively.

Keywords: Mobile Robot · Adaptive Linear Quadratic Regulator · Lateral Following · Soft Following

1 Introduction

In recent years, robot technology has advanced in the direction of high intelligence, and human-machine integration will be a key component of the next generation of industrial robots. The field of lateral following robot is a significant subset of the following robot, which is widely employed in industrial applications [2]. The lateral following robot can assist humans in moving products rapidly and safely on the production line and in storage facilities. Robots with lateral following capabilities can follow inspectors to verify equipment in huge factories and warehouses. Additionally, lateral following robots can assist humans in the sector of customized production by completing intricate tasks and increasing productivity. The lateral following robot exhibits excellent potential and application value when looking at the industrial landscape [3]. Consequently, the advancement of robot lateral following technology can result in more effective, reliable, and intelligent warehousing and logistics solutions for industry.

Currently, the robot follows the target primarily in front and back follow modes, and research into the best way to manage this behavior is ongoing. In terms of following stability, Yan et al. [4] proposed a crutch robot system, which can assist users to walk

© The Author(s), under exclusive license to Springer Nature Singapore Pte Ltd. 2023
H. Yang et al. (Eds.): ICIRA 2023, LNAI 14274, pp. 130–141, 2023.
https://doi.org/10.1007/978-981-99-6501-4_12

by estimating human intention. Gong et al. [5] proposed an algorithm based on point cloud, which enables robots to follow human beings in complex environments. Chen et al. [6] used laser radar point clouds to distinguish human legs, and then used PID algorithm to make crutch robots follow human movements. Aguirre et al. [7] proposed a method of leg detection and classification through machine learning, which improves the accuracy of detection and tracking. In terms of following comfort, Julio et al. [8] designed a new type of following controller, which introduces the user space state and speed state to improve the following comfort. Feng et al. [9] proposed a target following method based on virtual spring model, which improves the robustness of following in complex environments. Nguyen et al. [10] proposed a stable following mothod based on fuzzy control, which combines obstacle information to control the output of the robot.

The performance of the following robot and the algorithm have both been enhanced by the aforementioned research. The actual use of the following technology is still constrained by issues including poor tracking accuracy, high cost, high computing effort, and following lag. In order to solve these problems, a lateral following method of robot based on ALQR is proposed in this paper. Based on the real-time speed of the robot, the LQR controller is adjusted by fuzzy control. Realize the adaptive adjustment of weight matrix. And combined with the NURBS curve to optimize the tracking trajectory to achieve stable and compliant lateral tracking of the robot. The robustness and real-time performance of the robot's lateral following are confirmed through simulation trials, both for regular and erratic user movements.

The main contributions of this paper are summarized as follows.

(1) A robot lateral following system based on user's state is suggested to test the viability of the lateral following method, taking into account the need for robot following in environments including human-machine interaction.
(2) A robot soft following method is proposed. It can optimize the lateral following trajectory via the NURBS curve, which significantly minimizes the lateral following's range of fluctuation when the user's state is considered.
(3) Considering the influence of robot speed on lateral following control, the ALQR controller is proposed. The Q and R weight matrix is continuously optimized using the fuzzy control theory, which enhances the motion's stability and responsiveness in real time.

2 Robotic Motion Planning for the Lateral Following

2.1 Robotic Model for Lateral Following

The robot must imitate the situation of human contact and move forward side by side in the lateral following mode, which is different from the conventional navigator-following mode. To create a safe and stable lateral following mode, the forward following error is minimized under the assumption that the safe distance is maintained. Figure 1 depicts the robot's lateral following.

The orange portion of Fig. 1 represents the human, and the blue portion represents the two-wheel differential robot. The monocular camera carried by the robot can be used to determine the positions $(x_{p(t)}, y_{p(t)})$ and $(x_{r(t)}, y_{r(t)})$ of the human and robot at the

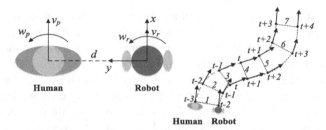

Fig. 1. Robot lateral following schematic diagram (Color figure online)

time t. Combining the human position $(x_{p(t-1)}, y_{p(t-1)})$ at time $t-1$ yields the robot's location $(x_{r(t+1)}, y_{r(t+1)})$ at time $t+1$.

The human position vector $\boldsymbol{P}_{(t)}\boldsymbol{R}_{(t-1)}$ can be expressed in the following formula:

$$
\boldsymbol{P}_{(t)}\boldsymbol{R}_{(t-1)} = \begin{bmatrix} \cos\frac{\pi}{2} & -\sin\frac{\pi}{2} \\ \sin\frac{\pi}{2} & \cos\frac{\pi}{2} \end{bmatrix} \begin{bmatrix} x_{p(t)} - x_{p(t-1)} \\ y_{p(t)} - y_{p(t-1)} \end{bmatrix} \tag{1}
$$

with the help of the trajectory vector, determine the robot's position $t+1$ at the moment $(x_{r(t+1)}, y_{r(t+1)})$:

$$
x_{r(t+1)} = x_{p(t)} + \frac{d(y_{p(t-1)} - y_{p(t)})}{\sqrt{(y_{p(t-1)} - y_{(t)})^2 + (x_{p(t)} - x_{p(t-1)})^2}} \tag{2}
$$

$$
y_{r(t+1)} = y_{p(t)} + \frac{d(x_{p(t)} - x_{p(t-1)})}{\sqrt{(y_{p(t-1)} - y_{(t)})^2 + (x_{p(t)} - x_{p(t-1)})^2}} \tag{3}
$$

where d is the desired lateral separation between the robot and the human.

2.2 Robot Motion Planning for the Soft Following

Due to the randomness of human motion, the trajectory to be followed by the robot calculated by the traditional geometric method fluctuates violently, and the robot fails to follow when the human turns suddenly. Therefore, it is necessary to consider the human real-time trajectory state and optimize the trajectory to be followed by the robot.

To follow the robot's trajectory, it is therefore required to soften it in accordance with the human real-time trajectory, changing the theoretical trajectory point that will be followed by the robot's trajectory point to the optimal intended trajectory point. In this paper, we introduce NURBS curves, a representation based on B-Spline curves, for robots following trajectory optimization. NURBS curve has superior accuracy and efficiency when dealing with human random trajectories than curves like the Bezier curve and B-Spline.

The following equation describes the B-Spline curve:

$$
C(u) = \sum_{i=0}^{n} N_{i,p}(u)\boldsymbol{P}_i \tag{4}
$$

$$N_{i,p}(u) = \frac{u - u_i}{u_{i+p} - u_i} N_{i,p-1}(u) + \frac{u_{i+p+1} - u}{u_{i+p+1} - u_{i+1}} N_{i+1,p-1}(u) \tag{5}$$

where P_i stands for the control point of the B-Spline, $N_{i,p}$ for the basis function, p for the order of the basis function, which represents the number of curves. Select the track point of n history to be followed and record it as:

$$P_i = \begin{bmatrix} X_{r(t)} \ X_{r(t+1)} \cdots X_{r(t+n)} \\ Y_{r(t)} \ Y_{r(t+1)} \cdots Y_{r(t+n)} \end{bmatrix}^T \tag{6}$$

to get the coordinate point P_i^w in the flush coordinate state, set the weight vector of the NURBS curve to $w = [w_0, w_1, w_2 \cdots w_n]^T$ and multiply the coordinates of P_i by the weight w_i:

$$P_i^w = \begin{bmatrix} w_i x_i \ w_i y_i \ w_i z_i \ w_i \end{bmatrix}^T \tag{7}$$

since in the chi-square coordinates, P_i and P_i^w represent the same position. As a result of substituting this new chi-squared form into the equation $C(u)$, and convert the chi-squared coordinate form back to Cartesian coordinates:

$$C(u) = \frac{\sum_{i=0}^{n} N_{i,p}(u)w_i P_i}{\sum_{i=0}^{n} N_{i,p}(u)w_i} \tag{8}$$

because of the nature of the NURBS curve, we use the weighted average method to find the corresponding point of each original trajectory point on the NURBS curve. Specifically, for the original trajectory point P_i of i. We can find the corresponding parameter value u_i' on the NURBS curve by solving the following optimization problem:

$$u_i' = \underset{u_i}{argmin} \left\| \frac{C(u_i) - P_i}{w_i} \right\|^2 \tag{9}$$

the formula $\|\cdot\|$ means the L_2 parametrization of the vector.

Then by substituting u_i' into the expression for the NURBS curve, the actual tracking point after optimization is obtained as follows:

$$P_i' = C(u_i') \tag{10}$$

the above methods can optimize the trajectory points to be tracked by the robot. On the premise of ensuring the timeliness of following, the trajectory of the robot is more flexible. Through this method, the security and stability of human-computer interaction are improved.

2.3 Robot Lateral Following with LQR

Following the foregoing description of the lateral following, the analysis of robot lateral following using kinematic modeling is now completed. Taking a robot with two-wheel differential motion as an example, a lateral following kinematic model is constructed as shown in Fig. 2.

As shown in Fig. 2, building a two-wheel differential robot positive kinematic model using the left and right driving wheels' speeds.

$$\begin{bmatrix} v \\ w \end{bmatrix} = \begin{bmatrix} \frac{v_r+v_l}{2} \\ \frac{v_r-v_l}{d_{wb}} \end{bmatrix} = \begin{bmatrix} \frac{1}{2} & \frac{1}{2} \\ \frac{1}{d_{wb}} & -\frac{1}{d_{wb}} \end{bmatrix} \begin{bmatrix} v_r \\ v_l \end{bmatrix} \tag{11}$$

in the robot's continuous time domain, the state space model is thus stated as:

$$\begin{cases} \dot{x} = v\cos(\theta) \\ \dot{y} = v\sin(\theta) \\ \dot{\theta} = w \end{cases} \tag{12}$$

for a system with A degree of freedom subject to B constraints, its dynamic equation can be expressed as follows:

$$M(q)\ddot{q} + C_m(q, \dot{q})\dot{q} + G(q) + F(\dot{q}) + \tau_d = B(q)\tau - J^T(q)\lambda \tag{13}$$

in the formula, $M(q)$ is a positive definite symmetric symmetric inertial matrix. $C_m(q, \dot{q})$ is the centrifugal force and Coriolis force matrix of the robot. $G(q)$ is the gravity matrix. $F(\dot{q})$ is the friction matrix of the robot. τ_d is an uncertain external disturbance and τ is a torque control input. $B(q)$ is the input transformation matrix. $J(q)$ is a nonholonomic constraint matrix. λ is the binding matrix.

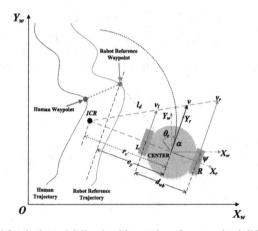

Fig. 2. Model for the lateral following kinematics of a two-wheel differential robot

Combined with the kinematic model, it can be deduced that:

$$\overline{M}\dot{u} + \overline{C}u + S^T(F(\dot{q}) + \tau_d) = \overline{B}\tau \tag{14}$$

in the formula, $\overline{M} = \begin{bmatrix} m_r & 0 \\ 0 & I_r \end{bmatrix}, \overline{C} = \begin{bmatrix} 0 & 0 \\ 0 & 0 \end{bmatrix}, \overline{B} = \frac{1}{r}\begin{bmatrix} 1 & 1 \\ -b & b \end{bmatrix}$. m_r is the total mass of the mobile robot. I_r is its total moment of inertia. r is the radius of the driving wheel. b is half the distance between the two driving wheels.

Because of the uncertainty of external friction, friction $F(\dot{q})$ is regarded as a kind of external interference in this paper. The unknown external disturbance τ_d is called external disturbance, and $d = -S^T(F(\dot{q}) + \tau_d)$ is defined. The equation of state of the available dynamic model is as follows:

$$\dot{u} = \overline{M}^{-1}\left[\overline{B}\tau + d\right] \tag{15}$$

a discrete-time system can be represented as follows:

$$X_{(k+1)} = AX_{(k)} + Bu_{(k)} \tag{16}$$

in this scenario, X represents the state vector, u represents the control vector, A represents the state recurrence matrix, and B represents the control coefficient matrix. The reference points $X = [x, y, \theta]^T$, $u = [v, w]^T$ in the robot's kinematic model $X_r = [x_r, y_r, \theta_r]^T$, $u_r = [v_r, w_r]^T$ are used. This leads to the following expression for the robot motion model.

$$X_{e(k+1)} = \begin{bmatrix} 1 & 0 & -Tv_r \sin\theta_r \\ 0 & 1 & Tv_r \cos\theta_r \\ 0 & 0 & 1 \end{bmatrix} X_{e(k)} + \begin{bmatrix} T\cos\theta_r & 0 \\ T\sin\theta_r & 0 \\ 0 & T \end{bmatrix} u(k) \tag{17}$$

the discrete system's state equation allows us to derive the objective function of the LQR as follows:

$$J = \sum_{k1}^{N}(X^TQX + u^TRu) \tag{18}$$

the two matrices, Q and R, which are typically considered diagonal arrays, represent a semi-positive definite state loss function matrix and a positive definite control loss function matrix, respectively.

In the optimization function in lateral following, the first term represents the cumulative magnitude of the deviation, and the second term represents the loss of control energy. In this way, the trajectory tracking control problem is transformed into an optimal control problem. The optimal control law u is a linear function concerning the state variable X for the optimal solution of the aforementioned objective function.

$$u = [-(R + B^TPB)^{-1}B^TPA]X = KX \tag{19}$$

where P is the solution of the Riccati equation:

$$P = A^TPA - A^TPB(R + B^TPB)^{-1}B^TPA + Q \tag{20}$$

the goal of robot lateral following human can be achieved by using the above equation to compute the target trajectory point to be tracked by the trajectory vector, and then following the target trajectory point by solving for the optimal control quantity u.

3 ALQR Controller

The LQR controller's fundamental components are the weighting matrices $\mathbf{Q}$ and $\mathbf{R}$. The majority of recent studies have concentrated on manipulating the robot's mobility state using a fixed weight matrix. The lateral following system is more complicated and significantly different from ideal settings in the real world. In particular, the rapid variations in human speed have a significant impact on the robot's speed variation and the lateral following control effect. The LQR controller with fixed weights is unable to more effectively adjust to changes in robot speed. The LQR controller weight settings are adaptively adjusted in this paper's solution to this issue, ensuring the performance of lateral tracking at various speeds.

3.1 Variable Design

Two weight matrices, $\mathbf{Q}$ and $\mathbf{R}$, which stand in for the state and control quantities, respectively, are present in the LQR controller:

$$\begin{cases} \mathbf{Q} = \text{diag}[q_1, q_2, q_3] \\ \quad \mathbf{R} = \text{diag}[r_1, r_2] \end{cases} \tag{21}$$

in the formula q_1, q_2 and q_3 are the weight parameters of the lateral error, forward error and heading error of the robot, respectively. r_1 and r_2 are the weight coefficients of the speed and angle of the robot, respectively.

The controller primarily accounts for three factors including robot lateral error, robot forward error, and robot turning angle when the robot follows the human laterally. The relative size of the weight coefficient determines the level of control the controller has over each variable, and the larger the weight coefficient, the stronger its restricting influence is on the associated variables. The larger the weight coefficient of the error, the higher the tracking accuracy. The larger the weight coefficient of the corner is, the smaller the change of the angle is, and the better the stability and security of tracking is.

The robot moves smoothly in settings similar to low-speed human motion, so the error weight should be adjusted primarily to ensure tracking accuracy. Under the condition of human high-speed movement, the position of the robot changes greatly in a short time, so the corner weight should be increased to prevent swinging left and right due to overshoot.

The adaptive controller for the change in vehicle speed is achieved in this paper by setting q_3 and r_1 to fixed values. And modifying q_1, q_2, and r_2 to vary the relative magnitudes of the weights. The input variable of fuzzy adjustment is set to robot speed v_x. The output variable is the control coefficient q_1, q_2, and r_2, and the adjustment is expressed as Δq_1, Δq_2, and Δr_2.

3.2 Fuzzy Processing and Defuzzification

The set of fuzzy linguistic variables in this paper is divided into seven fuzzy subsets in accordance with fuzzy theory. Negative Big (NB), Negative Medium (NM), Negative Small (NS), Zero (O), Positive Small (PS), Positive Medium (PM), and Positive Big

(PB). High tracking precision and stability are necessary given the complexity of the surrounding environment. Therefore, the membership function is selected as a Gaussian function, as follows:

$$g(x, \sigma, c) = e^{-\frac{(x-c)^2}{2\sigma^2}} \tag{22}$$

where x is the variable, σ denotes the standard deviation, and c is the centre position of the Gaussian function.

Figure 3 displays the results of the independent fuzzing of the input and output variables.

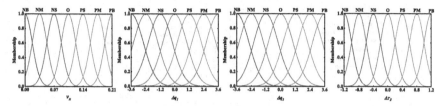

Fig. 3. Membership function of v_x, q_1, q_2 and r_2

The degree of lateral error and forward error restriction should be reduced as robot speed increases while turning angle restriction should be increased. As a result, overshooting oscillation is avoided and lateral following stability is preserved.

The output values after fuzzy inference may be fuzzy according to the generated fuzzy rules, so the weighted average method of defuzzification is used to get the precise output quantities Δq_1, Δq_2, and Δr_2. The following is the defuzzification formula:

$$\overline{A} = \frac{\sum_{i=1}^{n} w_i A_i}{\sum_{i=1}^{n} w_i} \tag{23}$$

where $A_1, A_2, \ldots, A_n$ is the final fuzzy evaluation value achieved by weighted average, $w_1, w_2, \ldots, w_n$ is the equivalent weight. And $\overline{A}$ is the fuzzy evaluation value gained by fuzzy evaluation of n indications.

The optimal control weight coefficients q_1^*, q_2^*, and r_2^* can be calculated as follows for lateral error, lateral error, and turning angle for various robot speeds:

$$\begin{cases} q_1^* = q_{10} + \Delta q_1 \\ q_2^* = q_{20} + \Delta q_2 \\ r_2^* = r_{20} + \Delta r_2 \end{cases} \tag{24}$$

where q_{30} and r_{10} are the optimal weight coefficients of heading error and speed error at the reference vehicle speed, respectively.

4   Lateral Following Experimental Results and Analysis

The ALQR control algorithm was built in python to test the viability of the lateral following method proposed in this paper. The "8" and random trajectories were employed in the experiment. The maximum following speed was 0.22 m/s, the maximum deflection angular speed was 2.84 rad/s, and the safe lateral distance between human and robot was 0.5 m.

4.1 Optimization of the Lateral Following Trajectory

In order to simulate the effect of real human random trajectories under NURBS curve optimization, this paper adopted a sliding window approach to optimize the nearest 20 trajectory points. The comparison between before and after optimization in a window at a certain moment is shown in Fig. 4.

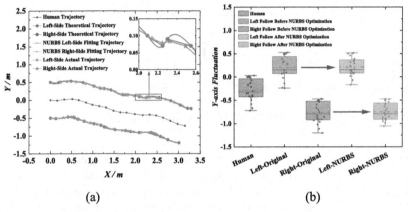

Fig. 4. Lateral following trajectory optimization. (a) Schematic diagram of trajectory point optimization. (b) Comparison diagram of fluctuation before and after optimization

As shown in Fig. 4(a), the human random trajectory and the left following method are used as examples. The black dotted line is the human trajectory. The red dotted line and the yellow pentagram are the robot following trajectory before and after optimization, respectively. It is obvious that the following trajectory is smoother after the NURBS curve optimization in this paper. Figure 4(b) depicts the fluctuations of the trajectory before and after optimization more significantly. The following fluctuations before optimization are shown in yellow and blue box plots, and the following fluctuations after optimization are shown in green and purple box plots. Both in terms of mean value and distribution density, better results are achieved after optimization. Specifically, the left following and right following improve 21% and 17%, respectively, compared to the softness before optimization.

4.2 Experiment of Lateral Following

In this paper, we focused on the development of the robot's lateral following function. Under the "8" type and random trajectory, the following trajectory was optimized by NURBS curve. Then the following effects of PurePersuit, PID, LQR and ALQR were compared. The feasibility of ALQR control algorithm in lateral tracking of robot was verified.

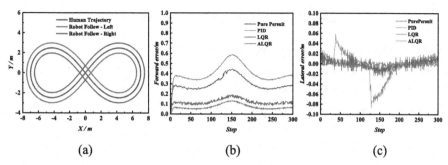

Fig. 5. Comparison of "8" type trajectory following results. (a) Lateral following result. (b) Forward error. (c) Lateral error.

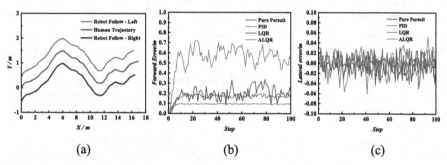

Fig. 6. Comparison of random trajectory following results. (a) Lateral following result. (b) Forward error. (c) Lateral error.

Figure 5 depicts the robot's subsequent impact on the "8" trajectory. Figure 5 (a) shows the effect of lateral following in ALQR, and the robot follows humans well on the left and right sides. PurePersuit, PID, LQR, and ALQR are contrasted in Fig. 5(b) and Fig. 5 (c), respectively, in terms of forward error and lateral error. Similar to Fig. 5, Fig. 6 depicts the robot's reaction to a human random course. The lateral following results, forward error comparison, and lateral error comparison under the random trajectory are shown in Fig. 6 (a), Fig. 6 (b), and Fig. 6 (c), respectively.

The "8" type and the random trajectory are given a weight of 40% and 60% respectively according to experience, and the mean squared error is weighted to indicate the fluctuation degree. This is done because the control difficulty under the random trajectory is greater than that under the regular trajectory. The specifics are displayed in Table 1.

The algorithm in this paper performs better than the first three algorithms in terms of timeliness and stability of lateral following, as shown in Table 1.

In comparison to the LQR algorithm, there has been an improvement in timeliness of 43.9% and 62.1%, respectively. In terms of stability, the variance of forward error and lateral error can be kept at 3.74E-04m and 2.31E-05m, respectively. These values are better than the LQR algorithm in each case by 55.2% and 71.8%. As a result, the ALQR algorithm suggested in this paper is superior and can satisfactorily serve the needs of the robot that is lateral following a human.

Table 1. Experimental results and comparison

Type	Error (m)	PurePersuit	PID	LQR	ALQR
Average	Forward error	0.236	0.495	0.150	0.0841
	Lateral error	-3.14E-03	-2.06E-03	9.06E-04	-3.44E-04
Variance	Forward error	4.50E-03	1.07E-02	8.34E-04	3.74E-04
	Lateral error	2.20E-04	6.16E-04	2.34E-04	2.31E-05

5 Conclusion

In this paper, an ALQR robot lateral following method is presented, which uses NURBS curves to optimize the trajectory points to be tracked and soften the following trajectory. The weight matrix of LQR is optimized based on robot speed, and the lateral following of robot in multi-state is realized. The experimental findings demonstrate the stability and real-time performance of the lateral following approach proposed in this paper, which can maintain a safe distance from the user. In order to better solve the problem of large forward error, the follow-up work is prepared to consider the historical walking trajectory of the target, combined with walking habits to predict the trajectory.

Acknowledgements. This work was supported by the National Natural Science Foundation of China (No.62173263) and Hainan Provincial Natural Science Foundation of China (No.621CXTD1013).

References

1. Song, P., Yu, Y.Q., Zhang, X.P.: A tutorial survey and comparison of impedance control on robotic manipulation. Robotica 37(5), 801–836 (2019)
2. Zaman, U.K.U., Aqeel, A.B., Naveed, K., et al.: Development of automated guided vehicle for warehouse automation of a textile factory. In: 2021 International Conference on Robotics and Automation in Industry (ICRAI), pp. 1–6. IEEE (2021)
3. Zhang, H., Ge, Y.H., Li, W.F.: Human following of mobile robot with a low-cost laser scanner. In: 2019 International Conference on Systems, Man and Cybernetics (SMC), pp. 3987–3992. IEEE (2019)
4. Yan, Q.Y., Huang, J., Yang, Z.H., et al.: Human-following control of cane-type walking-aid robot within fixed relative posture. IEEE/ASME Trans. Mechatron. 27(1), 537–548 (2021)
5. Gong, L.X., Cai, Y.F.: Human following for outdoor mobile robots based on point-cloud's appearance model. Chin. J. Electron. 30(6), 1087–1095 (2021)
6. Chen, N., Chen, X.X., Chen, C., et al.: Research on the human-following method, fall gesture recognition, and protection method for the walking-aid cane robot. In: 2022 IEEE International Conference on Cyborg and Bionic Systems (CBS), pp. 286–291. IEEE (2023)
7. Aguirre, E., García-Silvente, M.: Detecting and tracking using 2D laser range finders and deep learning. Neural Comput. Appl. 35(1), 415–428 (2023)
8. Montesdeoca, J., Toibero, J.M., Jordan, J., et al.: Person-following controller with socially acceptable robot motion. Robot. Auton. Syst. 153, 104075 (2022)

9. Feng, T., Yu, Y., Wu, L., et al.: A human-tracking robot using ultra wideband technology. IEEE Access **6**, 42541–42550 (2018)
10. Nguyen, T.V., Do, M.H., Jo, J.: Robust-adaptive-behavior strategy for human-following robots in unknown environments based on fuzzy inference mechanism. Industr. Robot: Int. J. Robot. Res. Appl. **49**(6), 1089–1100 (2022)

Research on Outdoor AGV Localization Method Based on Adaptive Square Root Cubature Kalman Filter

Feng Gao[1,2], Kaiguo Yan[1,2], Jihao Duan[1,2], Tingguang Chen[1,2], and Yan Li[1,2(✉)]

[1] School of Mechanical and Precision Instrument Engineering, Xi'an University of Technology, Xi'an 710048, China
54280239@qq.com
[2] Key Lab of Manufacturing Equipment of Shaanxi Province, Xi'an, China

Abstract. Accurate and reliable positioning is crucial for the safe operation of AGVs in complex and dynamic outdoor environments. An adaptive square root Cubature Kalman strong tracking filtering algorithm based on multi-sensor data fusion is proposed to address the positioning challenges faced by AGVs. The algorithm utilizes the AGV's motion model as the state equation and incorporates GPS and IMU data as the observation equation, whose object is to handle issues such as inconsistent sampling frequencies among sensors and the influence of initial parameters. Simulation results demonstrate that the positioning accuracy real-time performance are improved, making the proposed algorithm suitable for outdoor AGV navigation.

Keywords: Outdoor AGVs · Square root Cubature Kalman Filter · Strong tracking algorithm · multiple fading factors

1 Introduction

Outdoor AGVs(Automatic Guided Vehicle) are widely used for logistics handling in factories or terminals. Accurate positioning information is an important guarantee for routine work. Outdoor AGVs usually rely on GPS sensors to obtain positioning information which is incoherent and not accurate enough [1]. Therefore, IMU(Inertial Measurement Unit) sensors are extensively applied in aircrafts track reckoning, which has characteristics of low latency and high accuracy in short-distance calculation. But there is a cumulative error that increases along with the time [2].

Single-source sensor cannot meet the demand on low latency, high accuracy and high robustness of positioning system of outdoor AGVs [3]. Presently, the widely used multi-sensor data fusion has more advantages in navigation and positioning [4]. The main multi-sensor data fusion methods include gradient descent [5, 6], complementary filter [7, 8] and Kalman filter [9], etc., in which Kalman filter has the advantages of optimal unbiased estimation and minimum variance under Gaussian noise [10, 11].

© The Author(s), under exclusive license to Springer Nature Singapore Pte Ltd. 2023
H. Yang et al. (Eds.): ICIRA 2023, LNAI 14274, pp. 142–152, 2023.
https://doi.org/10.1007/978-981-99-6501-4_13

As the Kalman filter state equation, the AGV kinematic model has strong non-linear characteristics. Truong-Ngoc Tan used EKF (Extended Kalman Filter) to approximate the non-linear system, and the established model was only applicable to for the case of weak nonlinearity [12]. Cheng et al. used UKF (Unscented Kalman Filter) to improve the accuracy by approximating probability distribution. Using the unscenter transform, the UKF could achieve third-order approximation accuracy [13].

Li proposed a SRCKF(square root Cubature Kalman filter) to approximate the mean and covariance of non-linear system with Gaussian noise based on multi-dimensional integrals criterion, which had better filtering accuracy and filtering stability [14]. All of the above methods are discussed based on accurate system model and measurement model. The system noise is usually assumed to be known in filtering algorithms. However, the system parameters are generally unknown in actual system. The AGV positioning accuracy is reduced due to the large errors of parameters. Therefore, Zhu proposed an adaptive Sage-Husa based Kalman filter method to real-time estimate system noise and measurement noise, which could reduce the impact of model errors and obtain better filtering results without too much prior knowledge of system motion and sensor error model [15–17].

To solve the problem of sudden changes of AGV position and orientation angle caused by slippery road surface, Xu proposed a strong tracking filtering algorithm to real-time adjust the covariance matrix gain by adding a fading factor to the calculation of predicted covariance matrix. Thereby, the system had strong robustness and tracking capability for sudden state changes [18, 19]. But the different states of the system were affected differently by system uncertainty, so that single fading factor cannot guarantee a high tracking ability for each variate [20].

Accordingly, in order to meet the needs of low latency, high accuracy and high robustness of outdoor AGVs positioning, this study adopts sequential filtering to autonomously select different error matrix transfer states and update the error covariance matrix based on CKF(Cubature Kalman Filter). And an improved Sage-Husa adaptive algorithm is proposed to reduce the sensitivity of the positioning accuracy to the initial system values. The adaptive adjustment method of system initial parameters is obtained at the expense of lower accuracy using biased estimation. In the event of sudden changes of AGV position due to skidding or other external forces during driving, the orthogonality of residuals is used to determine whether the system is in a stable state. And multiple fading factors are introduced to adjust the Kalman gain matrix so as to ensure strong tracking performance when the AGV state changes suddenly.

2   ASRCKF Algorithm Based on Multiple Fading Factors

2.1   Kinematic Model

Information such as velocity, acceleration and angular rate is used to calculate the pose of the AGVs. Describing the pose of the AGVs moving in the plane requires x, y and θ coordinates, but x, y and θ alone cannot accurately calculate the state values at each moment, so the state space need to be extended. The equation is expressed as follows:

$$\begin{cases} x_k = x_{k-1} + \left(\Delta t \cdot v_{k-1} + \frac{1}{2} \Delta t^2 a_v \right) \cdot \cos \theta_{k-1} \\ y_k = y_{k-1} + \left(\Delta t \cdot v_{k-1} + \frac{1}{2} \Delta t^2 a_v \right) \cdot \sin \theta_{k-1} \\ \theta_k = \theta_{k-1} + \Delta t \cdot w_{k-1} + \frac{1}{2} \Delta t^2 a_w \\ v_k = v_{k-1} + \Delta t \cdot a_v \\ w_k = w_{k-1} + \Delta t \cdot a_w \end{cases} \quad (1)$$

where x_k, y_k are the position coordinates of AGV, θ_k is the orientation angle, v_k, w_k are the linear velocity and angular velocity at moment k respectively; Δt is the filter period, a_v is the linear acceleration, a_w is the angular acceleration.

2.2 SRCKF Based on QR Decomposition

The system state equations are a non-linear system of equations, and the CKF is used as the basic filtering. The process of updating the error covariance matrix by the SRCKF involves matrix opening, and this paper uses the QR decomposition method to update the error covariance, which solves the problem that the filtering accuracy decreases due to the failure of the decomposition when the error covariance matrix is a semi-positive definite matrix.

QR decomposition process: $(Q,R) = Tria(A)$, where A is the matrix to be decomposed in the Cubature Kalman filter, Q is the orthodox matrix, R is the upper triangle matrix. $S = R^T$. Assuming that $S_{Q,k}$ and $S_{R,k}$ are the square root of the system noise and the measurement noise, there is $Q_k = S_{Q,k} S_{Q,k}{}^T$, $R_k = S_{R,k} S_{R,k}{}^T$.

2.3 Sequential Filtering Based Data Fusion of Different Frequency Sensors

During the actual process, the frequency of the sensor is different, and the system receives different numbers of information at different times.

When only IMU data exists, T_j contains θ, v, w, when GPS data exists, T_j contains x and y, when IMU and GPS data exist at the same time, T_j contains x, y, θ, v and w. The sensor information obtained at different times is used to calculates the T_j according to the measuring data of different lengths. And distributes different measurement noise matrix R_j and different observation equation $h(\cdot)$ based on T_j.

2.4 Strong Tracking Algorithm Based on Multiple Fading Factors

In the complex outdoor environment, due to the external forces or other interference the AGV in the process of operation creates sudden changes in position, speed or direction, if the Kalman gain coefficient is near to stable, the system slowly responds to sudden changes in state, resulting in a large positioning error within a certain time, therefore the AGV needs to have a strong tracking capability for positioning information against sudden changes.

The strong tracking filter should satisfy the requirements on a robust system model despite parameter mismatch. The strong tracking filter for a non-linear system is expressed as follows:

$$\hat{x}_{k+1|k+1} = \hat{x}_{k+1|k} + K_k \cdot \gamma_k \quad (2)$$

where $\hat{x}_{k+1|k}$ is the state estimation value of $k + 1$ moment at k moment; K_k is the gain coefficient at the time of k; γ_k is the residual at the time of k.

Based on the strong tracking characteristics of Eq. 2 and the real-time orthogonal of the optimal estimated time residual sequence, determine the time-varying gain matrix K.

$$E\left[\varepsilon_{k+j}\varepsilon_k^T\right] = 0 \quad k = 1, 2, \cdots ; j = 1, 2, \cdots \tag{3}$$

For sudden changes in the state of the system due to road and other external forces while the AGV is in motion, the orthogonal property of the residual sequence determines whether the state of the AGV changes abruptly.

When the residual series lose orthogonality and are in a non-stationary state, the fading memory filtering is introduced, and multiple fading factors are used to independently estimate and correct for different states.

A one-step approximation algorithm of the sub-optimal fading factor is expressed as follows:

$$\zeta_k = \text{diag}\left[\zeta_k^1, \zeta_k^2, \cdots, \zeta_k^n\right] \tag{4}$$

where ζ_k is the n-dimension fading factor matrix.

The system model should meet the following conditions:

(1) Q_k is a semi-positive definite symmetric matrix. R_k and P_k are positive definite symmetric matrices;
(2) $H(x)$ is a non-singular matrix.

The sub-optimal fading factor is expressed as follows:

$$\begin{cases} \zeta_k^i = \max(1, \alpha_i c_k) \\ c_k = tr N_k / \sum_{i=1}^{n} \alpha_i M_k^{ii} \\ V_k = \begin{cases} e_1 e_1^T, k = 1 \\ \dfrac{\rho V_{k-1} + e_k e_k^T}{1 - \rho}, k > 1 \end{cases} \\ N_k = V_k - \left[P_{x,k|k-1}^{(l)}\right]^T \left[P_{k|k-1}^{(l)}\right]^{-1} Q_{k-1} \left[P_{k|k-1}^{(l)}\right]^{-1} P_{xz|k-1}^{(l)} - R_k \\ M_k = \left(P_{k|k-1}^{(l)} - Q_{k-1}\right) \left[P_{k|k-1}^{(l)}\right]^{-1} P_{xx,k|k-1}^{(l)} \left[P_{xz,k|k-1}^{(l)}\right] \left[P_{k|k-1}^{(l)}\right]^{-1} \end{cases} \tag{5}$$

where $\zeta_k^i \geq 1$, the fading factor for each state; α_i is the scale factor. Which can be obtained from prior knowledge and chosen to be larger if the state function of state variable x_i fluctuates sharper or if x_i is unstable, it can be chosen to be 1 if no prior knowledge is available. $0 < \rho < 1$, the smaller ρ is, the stronger the adaptability of the measurement noise change, and the more drastic the change of the estimated result. In order to prevent the noise estimation result from jumping sharply, it is often taken between 0.9 and 1, we taking as 0.95. V_k is a variance matrix estimated by a time series. $M_k - N_k - V_k$ is the theoretical value of the variance matrix. Here, the two variance matrices are shifted to facilitate the calculation of the fading factor matrix.

2.5 Sage-Husa Based Adaptive Filtering Algorithm

AGVs operate in an outdoor unstructured environment where system noise varies over time. The adaptive algorithm with improved Sage-Husa is used to dynamically estimate the system and sensor noise characteristics by using real-time measurement data to correct the sensor noise measurement parameters [21].

The conventional Sage-Husa adaptive algorithm is an equal-weighted recursive estimation method, as shown in Eq. 6, when k approaches infinity, the adaptive ability is weakened until the adaptive ability is almost lost.

$$
\begin{cases}
\widehat{Q}_k = \left(1 - \dfrac{1}{k}\right)\widehat{Q}_{k-1} + \dfrac{1}{k}\left(K_k e_k e_k^{\mathrm{T}} K_k^{\mathrm{T}} + P_k - \Phi_{k,k-1} P_{k-1} \Phi_{k,k-1}^{\mathrm{T}}\right) \\
\widehat{R}_k = \left(1 - \dfrac{1}{k}\right)\widehat{R}_{k-1} + \dfrac{1}{k}\left(e_k e_k^{\mathrm{T}} - H_k P_{k/k-1} H_k^{\mathrm{T}}\right)
\end{cases}
\tag{6}
$$

Change the equal-weighted recursive estimation method to the exponential-weighted recursive estimation method, as shown in Eq. 7, when k is sufficiently large, $d_k \approx 1 - b$, and the adaptive ability of appropriate size can be maintained as filtering progresses [22].

$$
\begin{cases}
\widehat{Q}_k = (1 - d_k)\widehat{Q}_{k-1} + d_k\left(K_k e_k e_k^{\mathrm{T}} K_k^{\mathrm{T}} + P_k - \Phi_{k,k-1} P_{k-1} \Phi_{k,k-1}^{\mathrm{T}}\right) \\
\widehat{R}_k = (1 - d_k)\widehat{R}_{k-1} + d_k\left(e_k e_k^{\mathrm{T}} - H_k P_{k/k-1} H_k^{\mathrm{T}}\right) \\
d_k = (1 - b)/(1 - b^{k+1}), 0 < b < 1
\end{cases}
\tag{7}
$$

In Eq. 7, when the measured noise of the actual system deviates greatly from the theoretical modeling value, it will cause $\widehat{R}_k$ to lose positive certainty, resulting in abnormal filtering, and the biased estimation method of $\widehat{R}_k$ and $\widehat{Q}_k$ is used instead of Eq. 8 to ensure the symmetry and positive determinism of $\widehat{R}_k$ and $\widehat{Q}_k$ in the process of filtering.

$$
\begin{cases}
\widehat{Q}_k = \dfrac{1-d_k}{k-1}[(k-1)\widehat{Q}_{k-1} + K_k e_k e_k^{\mathrm{T}} K_k^{\mathrm{T}} + P_{k/k}] \\
\widehat{R}_k = \dfrac{1 - d_k}{k - 1}[(k - 1)\widehat{R}_{k-1} + e_k e_k^{\mathrm{T}}] \\
d_k = (1 - b)/(1 - b^{k+1}), 0 < b < 1
\end{cases}
\tag{8}
$$

3 Case Sudies

3.1 Comparison Simulation of Different On-board Sensor Filters

Owing to the different frequencies of the sensors, the system obtains three different measurement information at different moments, so according to the three different measurement information, three groups of control experiments are conducted, and the improved algorithm is set as the experimental group comparing to the other three groups for simulation experiments (see Tables 1 and 2).

Figure 1 shows a comparison of the filtering errors for the four sets of experiments, from which we can see:

Table 1. Sampling period

Type	Time/s
System period	0.01
GPS period	0.05
IMU period	0.03

Table 2. Experimental group settings

Group	Measured data
GPS	$(x, y)^{\mathrm{T}}$
IMU	$(\theta, v, w)^{\mathrm{T}}$
L(G + I)	$(x, y, \theta, v, w)^{\mathrm{T}}$
G + I	$(x, y)^{\mathrm{T}} + (\theta, v, w)^{\mathrm{T}} + (x, y, \theta, v, w)^{\mathrm{T}}$

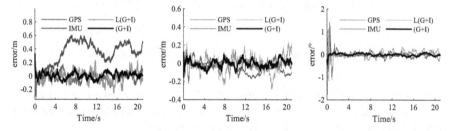

Fig. 1. Filtering error of the pose

(1) The IMU group has a large filtering error in the x and y directions as it relies only on information such as θ, v, w.

(2) The GPS group only receives information on x and y, so there is a large error at the beginning of θ. Although it is converged gradually there is still large fluctuations.

(3) The L(G + I) group only receives two measurement values at the same time for positional positioning, and has the largest filtering period and fluctuations.

Figure 2 shows the quantitative analysis of the positioning error for each group by mathematical statistical principle. The state quantities (x, y, θ, v, w) The error confidence intervals of the experimental group are 92.3%, 97.2%, 96.4%, 99.5% and 99% Respectively. Compared to the IMU group, the confidence levels of x and y are increased by 88.2% and 20.6%, respectively; Compared to the GPS group, the confidence level of θ is enhanced by 31.3%; Compared to the L(G + I) group, the confidence level of x, y and θ are improved by 15.0%, 21.3% and 35.9%, respectively.

From the mean error analysis in Fig. 3, the mean error of the experimental group's state is decreased by 40.8% compared to that of the GPS group, 71.7% to that of the IMU group, and 45.1% to that of the L(G + I) group.

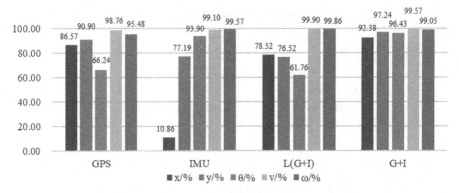

Fig. 2. Confidence interval calculation for pose estimation

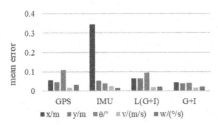

Fig. 3. Mean state error

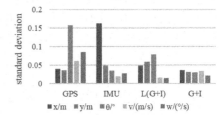

Fig. 4. State standard deviation comparison

Figure 4 shows error standard deviation of each group, The standard deviation of the state values in the experimental group was 58.3%, 60.4% and 47.6% lower than that in the GPS group and the IMU group L(G + I) group, respectively.

3.2 Comparison Simulations

Experimental Setup
Table 3 shows the initial values and the real values for the sensor noise properties. Design experiments to compare ASRCKF(adaptive square root Cubature Kalman filter) and SRCKF for verifying the superiority of the ASRCKF algorithm.

Discussion of Simulation Results
The ASRCKF group with the improved Sage-Husa algorithm can adjust the system parameters according to the sensor measurement data when the initial parameters of the system have large errors, so as to ensure the estimation accuracy of the vehicle posture.

It is not possible to make a quantitative judgement on the improved adaptive algorithm from Fig. 5, for which statistical error data are available, and a comparison of the mean error values in Fig. 6 shows that the experimental group using the adaptive algorithm has 81.6%, 89.3%, 84.3%, 50.0% and 55.2% declined in the mean error values for each state quantity (x, y, θ, v, w).

Table 3. Noise parameter setting

Variance	Real value	Initial value
x/m^2	0.1	11
y/m^2	0.1	13
$\theta/°^2$	0.15	10
$v/(m/s)^2$	0.1	14
$w/(°/s)^2$	0.1	11

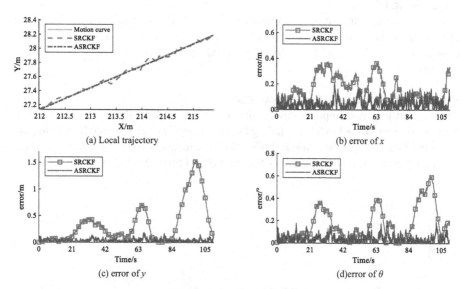

(a) Local trajectory

(b) error of x

(c) error of y

(d) error of θ

Fig. 5. Pose filtering error

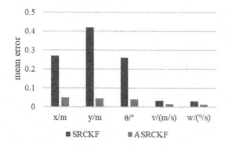

Fig. 6. Mean positioning error

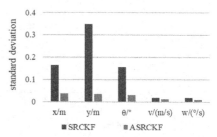

Fig. 7. Standard deviation of positioning error

Comparing the standard deviation of the error in Fig. 7, the error distribution for each state in the experimental group with the Sage-Husa adaptive algorithm decreased by 77.2%, 90.1%, 80.5%, 32.1% and 37.3% compared to the CKF respectively.

The filtering accuracy of the state vector is not guaranteed or even divergent when the AGV drives in a complex outdoor environment, where the system noise and measurement noise change with time and external conditions. The improved Sage-Husa adaptive algorithm is used to dynamically estimate the system and measurement noise characteristics by using real-time measurement data, overcoming the problem of filtering accuracy degradation due to initial model errors or environmental changes.

3.3   Comparative Simulation of Sudden Changes in AGV Position during Driving

Experimental Setup

The experimental simulation condition is that the AGV is in uniformly accelerated curvilinear motion, and at 80s of the AGV's travel time, the AGV encounters a sudden change of state of $y + 5$. Two sets of positional positioning error are observed and analyzed.

Comparative Analysis of Simulation Results

The recovery time is an important indicator of the strong tracking algorithm. The recovery time of the MSTSRCKF(Multiple fading factors Strong Tracking Square Root Cubature Kalman Filter) in the y-direction is 0.67s; while the recovery time of the SRCKF in the y-direction is 10.28 s; so the recovery time is reduced by 93.5% (see Fig. 8).

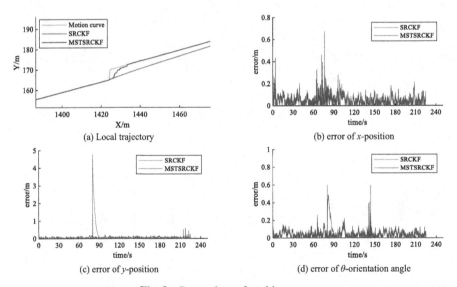

Fig. 8.   Comparison of position errors

The algorithm incorporating strong tracking can effectively reduce the impact of abrupt changes in the face of large uncertainties in the system model, using its orthogonality to residual sequences to provide strong tracking capabilities for abrupt state changes. When the residual sequence loses orthogonality and is in a non-stationary state, the idea of fading memory filtering is introduced, and a multiple fading factor is introduced for state-by-state correction while calculating the state prediction error covariance matrix, thus realizing the adjustment of the filter gain matrix and forcing the filter residual sequence to remain mutually orthogonal in real time, and the strong tracking capability of the filter is greatly improved by using multiple fading factors for independent estimation and adjustment of different states due to the different degrees of influence of the sudden change situation on each quantity of the state.

4 Conclusion

In this study, the adaptive square root volumetric Kalman filtering strong tracking filtering algorithm is investigated for the positioning of AGV in unstructured outdoor complex and variable environments for safe driving. The main conclusions:

(1) For the problem of inconsistent frequency of on-board sensors, by using sequential filtering, the confidence intervals of each state is an average improvement of 35.3% compared to that of the SRCKF, indicating that the positioning algorithm improves the sensor information utilization and greatly enhances localization accuracy.
(2) The proposed method can estimate the correction parameters in real time using the residual. The average positioning error variance of each state quantity is a 52.6% decrease in data error compared to SRCKF localization, indicating stable localization despite large errors in the initial values of the parameters, reflecting the robustness of the algorithm.
(3) MSTSRCKF has a strong sensitivity to the sudden state change situation of AGV caused by the road surface status or external force, whose recovery time is 93.5% less than that of SRCKF algorithm, which improves the real-time tracking of the AGV's position.

Acknowledgements. This study was supported by the Key Research and Development Program of Shaanxi (2021ZDLGY09-01).

References

1. Sirish Kumar, P., Srilatha Indira Dutt, V.B.S., Ganesh Laveti.: A novel kinematic positioning algorithm for GPS applications in urban canyons. In: Materials Today: Proceedings, pp. 33 (2020) (prepublish)
2. Wei, S.W.X.C.: Optimization method for integrated train positioning accuracy based on IMU calibration compensation **02**(42), (2020) 57–64
3. Titterton, D.H., Weston, J.L.: Strapdown inertial navigation technology. Aerosp. Electron. Syst. Mag. IEEE **7**(20), 33–34 (2004)
4. Konstantin, N., Andrey, K., Andrey, M., et al.: Investigation into the nonlinear Kalman filter to correct the INS/GNSS integrated navigation system. GPS Solutions **27**(2) (2023)
5. Madgwick Sebastian, O.H., Harrison Andrew, J.L., Vaidyanathan Andrew.: Estimation of IMU and MARG orientation using a gradient descent algorithm. In: IEEE International Conference on Rehabilitation Robotics: [proceedings] (2011)

6. Shuaihua, Z., Fang, Z., Xia, L., et al.: An attitude algorithm based on variable- step-size momentum gradient descent method. Electron. Opt. Control. **27**(09), 66–70 (2020)

7. Du, C., Pengfei, H., Chao, C., et al.: Rolling angle measurement algorithm based on adaptive complementary filtering. J. Detect. Control **42**(01), 17–20 (2020)

8. Qinyu, N., Song, M., Kejian, C., et al.: Attitude algorithm of optimal complementary filter for omnidirectional AGV. Mech. Sci. Technol. Aerosp. Eng. **40**(05), 794–800 (2021)

9. Tanizaki, H., Mariano, R.S.: Nonlinear filters based on taylor series expansions. Commun. Stat. Theory Methods **25**(6), 1261–1282 (1996)

10. Nada, D., Bousbia-Salah, M., Bettayeb, M.: Multi-sensor data fusion for wheelchair position estimation with unscented Kalman filter. Int. J. Autom. Comput. **15**(02), 207–217 (2018)

11. Kwon, S., Yang, K., Park, S., et al.: A Kalman filter localization method for mobile robots. In: Proceedings of the International Conference of the Society for Control and Robot Systems (2005)

12. Tan, T.-N., Khenchaf, A., Comblet, F., et al.: Robust-extended kalman filter and long short-term memory combination to enhance the quality of single point positioning. Appl. Sci. **10**(12), 4335 (2020)

13. Jianhua, C., Nuo, W., Xiuneng, S.: Research on course angle estimation method of integrated navigation system based on improved UKF. Navig. Positioning Timing **7**(03), 112–119 (2020)

14. Xiaoming, L., Changsheng, Z., Xinglong, T.: Improved integrated navigation and positioning algorithm based on cubature Kalman filter. Sci. Surveying Mapp. **45**(09), 25–30 (2020)

15. Wenchao, Z., Fei, H.: Adaptive Kalman filtering based on variable weight innovation covariance. J. Xihua Univ. (Nat. Sci. Ed.) **38**(04), 83–87 (2019)

16. Yanhui, W., Jing, L., Shenggong, H.: SINS/DVL integrated navigation system based on improved adaptive filtering algorithm. Autom. Instrum. **34**(05), 95–100 (2019)

17. Wang, Z., Liu, Z., Tian, K., et al.: Frequency-scanning interferometry for dynamic measurement using adaptive Sage-Husa Kalman filter. Opt. Lasers Eng. **165**, 107545 (2023)

18. Shusheng, X., Xiaogong, L., Xinfei, L.: Strong tracking adaptive square-root cubature Kalman filter algorithm. Acta Electron. Sin. **42**(12), 2394–2400 (2014)

19. Donghua, Z., Yugeng, X., Zhongjun, Z.: Suboptimal fading extended kalman filtering for nonlinearsystems. Control Decis. **05**, 1–6 (1990)

20. Pan, C., Gao, J., Li, Z., et al.: Multiple fading factors-based strong tracking variational Bayesian adaptive Kalman filter. Measurement **176**, 109139 (2021)

21. Zhao, F., Wu, F.: Adaptive integrated navigation based artificial intelligence. J. Beijing Univ. Posts Telecommun. **45**(2), 1–8 (2022)

22. Xiaoyan, L., Liuqing, Y., Jin, G., et al.: Application of improved sage-husa adaptive filtering algorithm in MEMS AHRS. Navig. Control **18**(02), 105–112 (2019)

Optimization-based Coordinated Motion Planning for Redundant Wheeled Mobile Manipulator

Wenji Jia[1,2], Weili Peng[1,2], Che Hou[1,2], and Wenjie Chen[1,2(✉)]

[1] Blue-Orange Lab, Midea Group, Foshan 528300, China
chenwj42@midea.com
[2] Midea Corporate Research Center, Foshan 528300/, Shanghai 201702, China

Abstract. Due to the combination of mobility and dexterity, the mobile manipulator has great application potential in many fields such as manufacturing, logistics and service. The motion planning for the mobile manipulator becomes more challenging due to the high degree of redundancy. An optimization-based method is proposed to solve the coordinated motion planning problem. The optimization goal is to enhance the manipulability while considering the distinct kinetic characteristics of the manipulator and the mobile platform. Since the manipulator has superior performance in respond speed and accuracy, a motion distribution weighting matrix is employed to increase the motion proportion of the manipulator for a given task. Moreover, the joint range and velocity constraints are formulated in a unified form for calculation efficiency. Simulation and experiment are presented to validate the proposed method. The algorithm can generate feasible trajectories in configuration space without violating the constraints, and the adjustable motion distribution between the manipulator and the mobile platform is achieved. The trajectory tracking accuracy can be improved when the configuration space motion distribution between the manipulator and the mobile platform is regulated appropriately.

Keywords: Mobile Manipulator · Motion Planning · Optimization

1 Introduction

Mobile manipulator (MM) is an integrated system with a manipulator mounted on a mobile platform. The manipulator can perform sophisticated tasks while the mobile platform can dramatically enlarge its workspace. The MM has been employed in various applications, including manufacturing [1], service [2], medical [3, 4], and space [5]. Instead of regarding the manipulator and the mobile platform as two independent sub-systems, coordinated planning and control are performed to the MM in order to fully utilize the combination performance of mobility and dexterity. However, this will bring many new challenges due to two major reasons. The first reason is that the strongly coupled manipulator and the mobile platform have significantly different dynamic characteristics, and the second is that the MM is usually a relatively high redundant system.

© The Author(s), under exclusive license to Springer Nature Singapore Pte Ltd. 2023
H. Yang et al. (Eds.): ICIRA 2023, LNAI 14274, pp. 153–165, 2023.
https://doi.org/10.1007/978-981-99-6501-4_14

This work mainly focuses on the motion planning problem of the MM with high redundancy. The fundamental issue for solving such a problem is how to coordinate the manipulator and the mobile platform, as well as use the redundancy of the system to achieve sub-tasks (the primary task is typically the end-effector trajectory tracking). Many redundancy resolution methods for the traditional redundant manipulator can be extended to the MM, such as the damped least-square inverse Jacobian method [6] and weighted Jacobian method [7]. These methods are based on the pseudo-inverse of the Jacobian matrix which may cause the singularity issue. Sample-based methods are also widely adopted by many researchers for solving the motion planning problem of the MM, such as Rapid-Exploring Radom Trees (RRT) [8, 9], Probabilistic Roadmap (PRM) [10, 11], and Random Profile Approach (RPA) [12]. However, in these methods the sample-based methods focus more on path planning instead of trajectory, and the feasibility of the path is more important than the optimality. The path generated by the sample-based methods may have low smoothness problem and smoothing techniques need to be applied during the process. Optimization-based motion planning methods have been taken much attention from the researchers recently, the target is to search a trajectory that minimizes (or maximizes) a given objective function while satisfying the constraints. The objective function is formulated to enhance the performance of the robot, such as manipulability [13], force exertion capability [14], and stability [15]. Since the manipulator and the mobile platform have significant different kinematic and dynamic characteristics, the coordination between the two sub-systems also needs to be considered for improving the entire performance of the MM.

In this paper, an optimization-based motion planning method for the MM is proposed. The unified kinematic model of the MM which is developed in our laboratory is derived at first. The manipulability and motion distribution between the manipulator and the mobile platform are considered in the objective function. The manipulator is expected to contribute more in the entire motion since it moves faster and more accurate than the mobile platform. For the constraints, the joint range and velocity limits are established in a unified way for computational efficiency. The interior-point optimization method is applied for solving the problem. Finally, simulation and experiment are performed to validate the proposed method.

2 Modelling

In order to establish the optimization scheme, the kinematic analysis for the MM should be fulfilled first. The MM is shown in Fig. 1, it consists of a two-wheel non-holonomic mobile platform and a 7-DOF redundant robot arm, and the total DOF of the system is 9. The kinematic modelling usually contains two phases: the first is the forward kinematics, which calculates the end-effector pose and velocity by giving the joint angles and rates, and the second is the inverse kinematics, which calculates the joint variables by giving the target end-effector pose and velocity. Since there exists non-holonomic constrains in the motion of the mobile platform, it is infeasible to directly derive the kinematic model which maps the wheels' rotational angles to the platform pose, the kinematic analysis for the optimization is mainly concerned in velocity level.

2.1 The Manipulator

The 7-DOF manipulator mounted on the mobile platform is shown in Fig. 1a, and its kinematic model will be formulated in this subsection. Here we denote two reference frames, Σ_e and Σ_b, as the end-effector frame and the arm base frame respectively. The forward kinematics of the manipulator can be derived by the POE (product of exponentials) formula

$$T_m(q_m) = e^{[S_1]q_1} e^{[S_2]q_2} \cdots e^{[S_7]q_7} T_m(0) \tag{1}$$

where $q_m = [q_1, q_2, \cdots q_7]^T$ denotes the joint angles of the manipulator, $T_m(0) \in SE(3)$ is the end-effector frame configuration when the manipulator is in zero position. $S_i (i = 1, 2, \cdots, 7)$ represent the screw axes of each joint, which are determined by the configuration parameters shown in Fig. 1a.

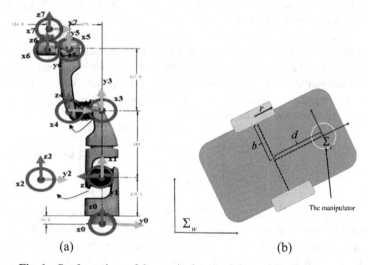

(a)   (b)

Fig. 1. Configurations of the manipulator and the mobile platform.

The spatial twist V_s is given by $[V_s] = \dot{T}T^{-1}$, by calculating $\dot{T}T^{-1}$ we obtain the spatial Jacobian of the manipulator

$$V_s = \begin{bmatrix} J_{S_1} & J_{S_2} & \cdots & J_{S_7} \end{bmatrix} \begin{bmatrix} \dot{q}_1 \\ \dot{q}_2 \\ \vdots \\ \dot{q}_7 \end{bmatrix} \tag{2}$$

$$= J_S \cdot \dot{q}_m$$

where the column component J_{S_i} is calculated by

$$J_{S_i} = Ad_{e^{[S_1]q_1} \cdots e^{[S_{i-1}]q_{i-1}}} (S_i) \tag{3}$$

In order to formulate the whole-body kinematics of the MM, it is convenient to transform the spatial Jacobian to the body Jacobian for which the end-effector velocity is represented in its own frame. This transformation can be achieved by

$$J_b = Ad_{T_{be}^{-1}}(J_S) \tag{4}$$

where $Ad_{T_{be}^{-1}} \in R^{6 \times 6}$ is the adjoint representation of the inverse of the transformation matrix T_{be}.

2.2 The Mobile Platform

The kinematics of the mobile platform shown in Fig. 1b will be discussed in this subsection. Two additional reference frames, Σ_w and Σ_c, are denoted as the fixed world frame and the manipulator installation point of the mobile platform respectively. When the manipulator is mounted on the mobile platform, Σ_c is coincident with Σ_b. The mobile platform is driven by two independent wheels, four passive castor wheels are located at the corners of the rectangular shape chassis to keep stable and balanced. The radius of each driving wheel is denoted by r, $\dot{\varphi}_R$ and $\dot{\varphi}_L$ denote the velocity of the right and left wheels, h denotes the height of the mobile platform. In addition, b and d represent the horizontal distance from the driving wheel and the manipulator base to the center of the mobile platform, respectively. The velocity of the point on the mobile platform where the manipulator installed can be calculated as

$$V_c = J_c \cdot \dot{q}_c = \begin{bmatrix} r/2 & r/2 \\ -(r*d)/2b & (r*d)/2b \\ -r/2b & r/2b \end{bmatrix} \begin{bmatrix} \dot{\varphi}_L \\ \dot{\varphi}_R \end{bmatrix} \tag{5}$$

where $V_c = \begin{bmatrix} \dot{x}_c & \dot{y}_c & \dot{\phi}_c \end{bmatrix}^T$ denotes the planar velocity, including two translational and one rotational velocity components, J_c denotes the body Jacobian of the mobile platform. The kinematics of the mobile platform is formulated under the assumption that no slippery and slide occur to it. And the vertical movement due to the uneven ground is also neglected in this paper.

2.3 System Model

In this subsection the whole-body kinematics of the MM will be presented. The homogeneous transform matrix of the end-effector frame Σ_e with respect to the world frame Σ_w can be described as

$$
\begin{aligned}
T_{mmr} &= T_p \cdot T_{offset} \cdot T_m \\
&= \begin{bmatrix} \cos(\phi_c) & -\sin(\phi_c) & 0 & x_c \\ \sin(\phi_c) & \cos(\phi_c) & 0 & y_c \\ 0 & 0 & 1 & h \\ 0 & 0 & 0 & 1 \end{bmatrix} \begin{bmatrix} & & & d \\ I_{3\times3} & & & 0 \\ & & & 0 \\ 0_{1\times3} & & & 1 \end{bmatrix} \cdot T_m
\end{aligned} \tag{6}
$$

where T_p is the transform matrix of the center of the mobile platform (the middle point between two driving wheels) with respect to the world frame, T_{offset} denotes the fix offset of the manipulator installation point from the center of the mobile platform.

Furthermore, the velocity of the end-effector of the MM can be calculated as

$$V_e = J_{mmr\_b} \cdot \dot{q}_{mmr} = \begin{bmatrix} J_b \ Ad_{T_m^{-1}}(J_c) \end{bmatrix} \begin{bmatrix} \dot{q}_m \\ \dot{q}_c \end{bmatrix} \tag{7}$$

where $Ad_{T_m^{-1}} \in R^{6\times6}$ is the adjoint representation of the transformation matrix T_m^{-1} which translates the mobile platform velocity expressed in its own frame to the velocity expressed in the end-effector frame. $J_{mmr\_b} \in R^{6\times9}$ is the Jacobian matrix of the MM. It should be note that J_{mmr_b} represents the body Jacobian, since the Cartesian space trajectory of the end-effector is often expressed in the global frame, it is intuitive to use the Jacobian which maps the joint velocity to the Cartesian velocity expressed in the global frame. This can be done by

$$J_{mmr} = \begin{bmatrix} R_{mmr} & 0 \\ 0 & R_{mmr} \end{bmatrix} J_{mmr\_b} \tag{8}$$

where $R_{mmr} \in SO(3)$ denotes the 3×3 rotational matrix in T_{mmr}.

3 Methodology

In this section, the coordinated motion planning for the MM will be presented. Based on the unified kinematic model derived before, the method is to generate configuration space trajectory for a given end-effector task. Due to the high redundancy of the MM, some sub-tasks can be executed simultaneously via the null space. The motion planning of the MM will be formulated as a nonlinear optimization problem.

3.1 Optimization Target

To formulate the optimization model there are two main aspects must be considered, one is the objective function formulation, and the other is the constraints determination. A general pseudo-inverse type of a redundant robot system can be written as

$$\dot{q} = J^\dagger \dot{x}_d + \left(I - J^\dagger J \right) \dot{q}_0 \tag{9}$$

where $J^\dagger$ denotes the pseudo-inverse of the Jacobian matrix, $\dot{x}_d$ denotes the desired Cartesian space velocity. $\dot{q}_0$ is an arbitrary vector which is projected into the null space and it is usually determined by the selected optimization criteria.

The manipulability index quantifies the distance between the current configuration and the singular configuration. Moreover, higher manipulability also implies that the robot requires lower joint velocity for a given end-effector twist. It is defined as

$$m(q) = \sqrt{\det\left(JJ^T\right)} \tag{10}$$

The gradient of $m(q)$ is expressed as

$$\nabla m = \left[\frac{\partial m}{\partial q_1}, \cdots, \frac{\partial m}{\partial q_1} \right]^T \tag{11}$$

Then it can be calculated in the analytical way as

$$\frac{\partial m}{\partial q_i} = m(q) tr\left(\left(JJ^T\right)^{-1} J \left(\frac{\partial J}{\partial q_i}\right)^T \right) \tag{12}$$

where $tr(\cdot)$ denotes the trace of the matrix. The manipulability can be maximized by adding the term

$$-\omega \cdot \nabla m \cdot \dot{q} \tag{13}$$

as part of the objective function to be formulated, where ω is a constant nonnegative scalar weight. The negative sign in (13) ensures the manipulability index is maximized.

The mobile platform and the manipulator are strongly coupled resulting complicated kinematic and dynamic behavior. Meanwhile, the two subsystems have significantly different kinetic characteristics. The manipulator has quicker response and higher accuracy while the mobile platform has much wider range of motion but is confined by the nonholonomic constraint. To fully utilize the performance of the MM by considering the respective characteristics of the two sub-systems, the motion distribution between the manipulator and the mobile platform during a task is involved in the planning. In (9), $J^{\dagger}\dot{x}_d$ represents the particular solution of the configuration space velocity and the rest part represents the homogenous solution, which maximizes the manipulability index here. The optimization problem for the configuration space motion is original formulated as

$$\min_{\dot{q}} \dot{q}^T W_q \dot{q} - \omega \cdot \nabla m \cdot \dot{q} \tag{14}$$

subject to

$$J \cdot \dot{q} = \dot{x}_d \tag{15}$$

where $W_q \in R^{9 \times 9}$ is the weighting matrix for joint motion distribution and it is defined as

$$W_q = \begin{bmatrix} (1-\alpha) I_{2 \times 2} & 0_{2 \times 7} \\ 0_{7 \times 2} & \alpha I_{7 \times 7} \end{bmatrix} \tag{16}$$

where $\alpha \in [0, 1]$ is the motion distribution parameter. $\alpha = 1$ means only the manipulator is involved in the minimized objective function and the more joint motion is assigned to the mobile platform. Conversely, $\alpha = 0$ means more joint motion is assigned to the manipulator. Since the manipulator has superior kinetic performance than the mobile platform, it is desirable to distribute more motion to the manipulator in lots of scenarios. The joint velocity constraint is denoted as

$$\dot{q}_{m\ min} \leq \dot{q}_m \leq \dot{q}_{m\ max} \tag{17}$$

where $\dot{q}_{m\ min}$ and $\dot{q}_{m\ max}$ are the lower and upper bounds joint velocities of the manipulator respectively. If the joint velocity of the manipulator approaches the limit, it means the mobile platform should contribute more motion to keep the end-effector follow the desire trajectory. The parameter λ is set to evaluate the joint velocity of the manipulator

$$\lambda = \max\left\{\frac{|\dot{q}_{m,i}|}{|\dot{q}_{m\ max,i}|}, \frac{|\dot{q}_{m,i}|}{|\dot{q}_{m\ min,i}|}\right\} \tag{18}$$

with $i = 1, 2, \ldots, 7$. The parameter α can be adjusted as

$$\alpha = \begin{cases} \lambda & \text{if } \lambda \leq \varepsilon \\ 1 & \text{if } \lambda > \varepsilon \end{cases} \tag{19}$$

where ε is a threshold value used to determine whether the mobile platform needs to be fully engaged into the entire motion. After formulating the objective function, the constraints have to be considered. The detailed description of the constraints will be provided in the next subsection.

3.2 Optimization Scheme

The joint angles of the robot are limited by their mechanical structure and they are usually confined to certain regions. Besides, the joint velocity also has to be limited since excessive velocity may damage the structure. Generally the robot joint range and velocity constraints are expressed as

$$q_{min} \leq q \leq q_{max} \tag{20}$$

$$\dot{q}_{min} \leq \dot{q} \leq \dot{q}_{max} \tag{21}$$

where q_{min} and q_{max} denote the lower and upper bounds of the joint range(two wheel joints of the mobile platform are unlimited), $\dot{q}_{min}$ and $\dot{q}_{max}$ denote the lower and upper bounds of the joint velocity. In order to improve the computational efficiency of the optimization algorithm, here we adopt the method which incorporates the joint range and velocity in a unified form

$$\hat{\dot{q}}_{min} \leq \dot{q} \leq \hat{\dot{q}}_{max} \tag{22}$$

where $\hat{\dot{q}}_{min}$ and $\hat{\dot{q}}_{max}$ are generalized minimal and maximal joint limits respectively. They are defined as

$$\hat{\dot{q}}_{min,i} = \begin{cases} \dot{q}_{min,i}^{\frac{(q_i - q_{min,i}) - \rho_s}{\rho_j - \rho_s}} & \text{if } q_i - q_{min,i} \leq \rho_j \\ \dot{q}_{min,i} & \text{otherwise} \end{cases}$$

$$\hat{\dot{q}}_{max,i} = \begin{cases} \dot{q}_{max,i}^{\frac{(q_{max,i} - q_i) - \rho_s}{\rho_j - \rho_s}} & \text{if } q_{max,i} - q_i \leq \rho_j \\ \dot{q}_{max,i} & \text{otherwise} \end{cases} \tag{23}$$

where the subscript i denotes the ith joint, ρ_j and ρ_s are user-defined constant used to determine the safety margin away from the joint range limits. It can be proven that, with the constraints expressed in (23), the robot joint motion will yield not only the velocity limits but also the safety joint range depend on ρ_s.

$$q_{min,i} + \rho_s \leq q_i \leq q_{max,i} - \rho_s \tag{24}$$

From the above, the optimization scheme can be summarized as

$$
\begin{aligned}
minimize \quad & F(\dot{q}_{mmr}) \\
subject\ to \quad & J_{mmr}\dot{q}_{mmr} = \dot{x}_d \\
& \hat{\dot{q}}_{min} \leq \dot{q}_{mmr} \leq \hat{\dot{q}}_{max}
\end{aligned}
\tag{25}
$$

where $F(\dot{q}_{mmr}) = \dot{q}_{mmr}^T W_q \dot{q}_{mmr} - \omega \cdot \nabla m \cdot \dot{q}_{mmr}$ is the objective function. Equation (25) is a typical nonlinear optimization problem and various methods can solve it, such as recurrent neural networks, sequential quadratic programming method and interior point method. The interior point method achieves optimization by going through the middle of the solid defined by the problem rather than around its surface. It is adopted in a variety of nonlinear optimization problems [16, 17] and has good performance in rate of convergence and completeness. Thus, the interior point method is selected to solve the motion planning problem described in (25) in this paper, and the simulation and experimental results will be presented in the next section.

4   Simulation and Experiment Results

For validating the proposed motion planning optimization algorithm, simulation and experiment are performed. The MM is developed in our laboratory, it is composed of a 7-DOF manipulator and a non-holonomic two-wheel differential drive mobile. The configuration parameters of the manipulator are provided in Fig. 1a, and the parameters of the mobile platform are given as follows $r = 0.125m$, $b = 0.2325m$, $d = 0.316m$, $h = 0.269m$. Moreover, the joint range and velocity limits are given as

$$
\begin{aligned}
q_{min} &= \left[-\inf, -\inf, -130°, -90°, -120°, -120°, -100°, -100°, -160° \right] \\
q_{max} &= \left[+\inf, +\inf, +130°, +90°, +120°, +120°, +100°, +100°, +160° \right] \\
\dot{q}_{min} &= \left[-360°, -360°, -90°, -90°, -80°, -90°, -120°, -120°, -120° \right] \\
\dot{q}_{max} &= \left[+360°, +360°, +90°, +90°, +80°, +90°, +120°, +120°, +120° \right]
\end{aligned}
\tag{26}
$$

4.1   Simulation

The motion planning simulation is implemented by the MATLAB and the robot simulator Coppeliasim. We also integrate the optimization tool CasADi into the MATLAB program. CasADi [18] is a symbolic framework for nonlinear optimization and algorithmic differentiation. The desired trajectory of the end-effector moves along a Rhodonea-curve expressed as

$$\begin{cases} v_x^d = \alpha \dfrac{\pi^2}{T} \sin(\dfrac{\pi t}{T})(2\sin(2\beta)\cos(\beta) + \cos(2\beta)\sin(\beta)) \\ v_y^d = \alpha \dfrac{\pi^2}{T} \sin(\dfrac{\pi t}{T})(2\sin(2\beta)\cos(\beta) - \cos(2\beta)\sin(\beta)) \\ v_z^d = 0 \end{cases} \tag{27}$$

where $\alpha = 0.5$ and $\beta = 2\pi \sin^2(\pi t/(2T))$, the orientation of the end-effector remains constant. The total simulation time is 5 s and the simulation frequency is 100 Hz.

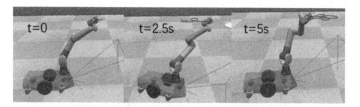

Fig. 2. The simulation process of the MM

Figure 2 shows the trajectory tracking process and the proposed algorithm generates feasible configuration space motion for the MM to accomplish the task. Figure 3a-b illustrates the joint motion of the manipulator during the simulation process, the dashed lines denote the joint limits. It is clear that none of the joints violate the joint constraints, and joint 1, 3, 4, and 6 have approached to their constraint lines but instead of hitting them. The reason for it is that we set the safety margin $\rho_s = 0.05$ in the constraint described in (23). Figure 3c illustrates the wheel joint velocities of the mobile platform, since there is no safety margin in the velocity constraints, the peak velocities of the two driving wheels have reached to their limits and kept on the limits for a short period of time. Figure 4 shows the manipulability measurements of the robot during the trajectory with different values of ω. If ω is too small ($\omega = 50$), the manipulability term in the objective function has little effect in the optimization result. The manipulability maximization becomes more effective when ω is set to a larger value. However, ω should be within an appropriate range (around 15000 on this occasion), since the optimization becomes infeasible when ω is too large.

4.2 Experiment

The proposed optimization algorithm is also verified via experiment. The self-developed MM is shown in Fig. 5 and the end-effector is commanded to follow a cosine curve in space. The trajectory of the task is expressed as

$$\begin{cases} v_x^d = 0.5 * \sin(1.5t) \\ v_y^d = 0 \\ v_z^d = 0.15 * \sin(6t) \end{cases} \tag{28}$$

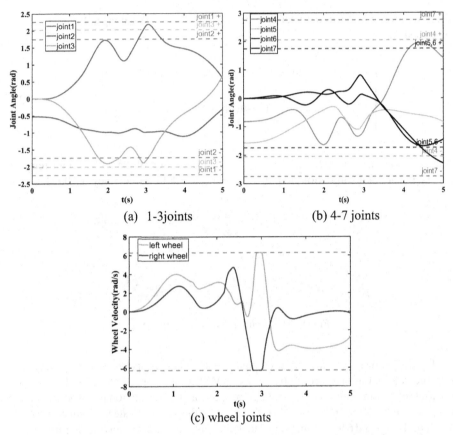

(a) 1-3joints

(b) 4-7 joints

(c) wheel joints

Fig. 3. The configuration space motion of the MM during the simulation

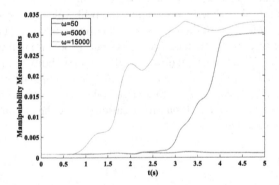

Fig. 4. Manipulability measurements during the simulation

The MM is designed as a fully unified system and the two subsystems share one central controller. It is worth noting that though the appearance of the real MM is different with the model in the simulation, they have exactly the same kinematic configuration parameters. The running time for the given task is 2 s and the control frequency is 1000 Hz in the experiment.

Fig. 5. The experiment process of the MM

In the experiment, the effectiveness of the joint motion distribution matrix is verified. Figure 6 illustrates the joint velocities of the manipulator generated by the algorithm, two conditions that $\varepsilon = 0.15$ and $\varepsilon = 0.85$ are considered. From the results we know that a smaller value of ε is corresponding to more joint motion distribution of the mobile platform. That outcome also means less motion distribution of the wheels. Figure 7 shows the position tracking error of the end-effector in the two situations. The tracking error is calculated by the joint encoder information of the manipulator as well as the mobile platform. Since the manipulator has higher accuracy, the tracking error becomes smaller when the manipulator has more degree of participation in configuration space.

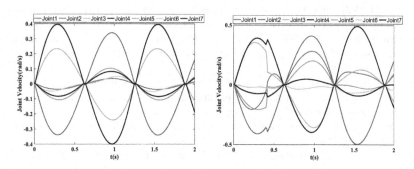

Fig. 6. The joint velocities of the manipulator during the experiment

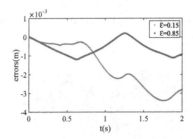

Fig. 7. Tracking errors of the end-effector

5 Conclusion

In this paper, an optimization-based motion planning method for the MM is proposed. The MM is conducted as a unified system in modelling and planning. The optimization goal is to enhance the manipulability while considering the configuration space motion distribution between the manipulator and the mobile platform. In order to accelerate the optimization process, the joint range and velocity constraints are formulated in a unified form. Simulation and experiment are provided to validate the proposed method. The algorithm can generate feasible trajectories in configuration space without violating the constraints, and the adjustable motion distribution between the manipulator and the mobile platform is achieved. For improving the tracking accuracy of the system, more joint motion can be distributed to the manipulator. In the future study, the real-time implementation of the proposed method will be focused.

References

1. Outón, J.L., Villaverde, I., Herrero, H., Esnaola, U., Sierra, B.: Innovative mobile manipulator solution for modern flexible manufacturing processes. Sensors **19**(24), 5414 (2019)
2. Caselli, S., Fantini, E., Monica, F., Occhi, P., Reggiani, M.: Toward a mobile manipulator service robot for human assistance. In: Proceedings of the 1st Robocare Workshop. ISTC-CNR, Roma, Italy, 30 October (2003)
3. Li, Z., Moran, P., Dong, Q., Shaw, R.J., Hauser, K.: Development of a tele-nursing mobile manipulator for remote care-giving in quarantine areas. In: 2017 IEEE International Conference on Robotics and Automation (ICRA) (2017)
4. Seo, K.-H., Lee, J.-J.: The development of two mobile gait rehabilitation systems. IEEE Trans. Neural Syst. Rehabil. Eng. **17**(2), 156–166 (2009)
5. Zereik, E., Sorbara, A., Casalino, G., Didot, F.: Autonomous dual-arm mobile manipulator crew assistant for surface operations: force/vision-guided grasping. In: 2009 4th International Conference on Recent Advances in Space Technologies (2009)
6. Nakamura, Y., Hanafusa, H.: Inverse kinematic solutions with singularity robustness for robot manipulator control. J. Dyn. Syst. Meas. Contr. **108**(3), 163–171 (1986)
7. Chan, T.F., Dubey, R.V.: A weighted least-norm solution based scheme for avoiding joint limits for redundant joint manipulators. IEEE Trans. Robot. Autom. **11**(2), 286–292 (1995)
8. Karaman, S., Frazzoli, E.: Sampling-based algorithms for optimal motion planning. Int. J.Rob.Res. **30**(7), 846–894 (2011)
9. Lavalle, S.M.: Rapidly-exploring random trees: a new tool for path planning (1999)

10. Kavraki, L.E., Svestka, P., Latombe, J.-C., Overmars, M.H.: Probabilistic roadmaps for path planning in high-dimensional configuration spaces. IEEE Trans. Robot. Autom. **12**(4), 566–580 (1996)
11. Mbede, J., Ele, P., Mvehabia, C., Toure, Y., Graefe, V., Ma, S.: Intelligent mobile manipulator navigation using adaptive neuro-fuzzy systems. Inf. Sci. **171**(4), 447–474 (2005)
12. Haddad, M., Chettibi, T., Hanchi, S., Lehtihet, H.E. (n.d.). Optimal motion planner of mobile manipulators in generalized point-to-point task. In: 9th IEEE International Workshop on Advanced Motion Control (2006)
13. Zhang, Y., Yan, X., Chen, D., Guo, D., Li, W.: QP-based refined manipulability-maximizing scheme for coordinated motion planning and control of physically constrained wheeled mobile redundant manipulators. Nonlinear Dyn. **85**(1), 245–261 (2016)
14. Xing, H., Torabi, A., Ding, L., Gao, H., Deng, Z., Tavakoli, M.: Enhancement of force exertion capability of a mobile manipulator by kinematic reconfiguration. IEEE Rob. Autom. Lett. **5**(4), 5842–5849 (2020)
15. Huang, Q., Tanie, K., Sugano, S.: Coordinated motion planning for a mobile manipulator considering stability and manipulation. Int. J. Robot. Res. **19**(8), 732–742 (2000)
16. Liao, J., Huang, F., Chen, Z., Yao, B.: Optimization-based motion planning of mobile manipulator with high degree of kinematic redundancy. Int. J. Int. Rob. Appl. **3**(2), 115–130 (2019)
17. Fan, Q., Gong, Z., Tao, B., Gao, Y., Yin, Z., Ding, H.: Base position optimization of mobile manipulators for machining large complex components. Rob. Comput.-Integr. Manuf. **70**, 102138 (2021)
18. Andersson, J.A.E., Gillis, J., Horn, G., Rawlings, J.B., Diehl, M.: CasADi: a software framework for nonlinear optimization and optimal control. Math. Program. Comput. **11**(1), 1–36 (2018)

Efficient and Hierarchical Quadrotor Planner for Fast Autonomous Flight

Hongyu Nie[1,2,3(✉)], Jiantan Chen[1,2,3], Guangyu Zhang[1,2], Decai Li[1,2], and Yuqing He[1,2]

[1] State Key Laboratory of Robotics, Shenyang Institute of Automation, Chinese Academy of Sciences, 110016 Shenyang, China
{chenjiantan,niehongyu}@sia.cn
[2] Institutes for Robotics and Intelligent Manufacturing, Chinese Academy of Sciences, 110016 Shenyang, China
[3] University of Chinese Academy of Sciences, Beijing 100049, China

Abstract. In this paper, we propose an effective and hierarchical planning framework for quadrotor fast autonomous flight. In the front-end, we propose an efficient guided sampling strategy by topology graph. In the back-end, the traditional trajectory optimization problems are formulated as minimising an objective function such as total energy cost while considering safety and dynamic feasibility constraints. However, the time characteristic is ignored. In this paper, the time optimal trajectory is studied, the time optimal trajectory problem is transformed to a convex optimization problem with a time optimal guidance trajectory based on the Pontryagin's Minimum Principle. The simulation experimental results demonstrate the feasibility and validity of the proposed motion planning method.

Keywords: hierarchical planning · trajectory optimization · time optimal

1 Introduction

Fast autonomous flight, especially quadrotors, has received a large amount of interest in recent years. Thanks to their mobility, agility, and flexibility, quadrotors are able to fly rapidly and safely through complex environments while avoiding any unexpected collisions. The trajectory generation system is consisted of two parts: path searching (frondend) and trajectory optimization (back-end). The framework is shown in Fig. 1. Path searching can be divided into two classical methods: graph searching-based planner and sample-based planner. Graph-based searches, such as Dijkstra's algorithm [4]and A* [6], and sampling-based methods, such as Probabilistic Roadmaps (PRM) [10]and Rapidly Exploring Random Trees (RRT) [8]. The basic idea of a kinodynamic RRT algorithm is to maintain a tree rooted at the initial state and to grow the tree by randomly sampling the state space. RRT method will ideally cover the entire reachable state space if given time is enough. RRT addresses a planning problem by progressively constructing a tree through free space. RRT* [9]enhances this process by incrementally

© The Author(s), under exclusive license to Springer Nature Singapore Pte Ltd. 2023
H. Yang et al. (Eds.): ICIRA 2023, LNAI 14274, pp. 166–175, 2023.
https://doi.org/10.1007/978-981-99-6501-4_15

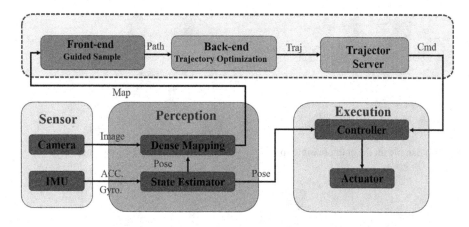

Fig. 1. The framework of motion planning.

rewire the tree during its sample. However, this approach is rather inefficient on large-scale and aggressive environment. In this paper, we adopt a guided sampling strategy base on the topology graph to improve sample efficiency.

In the back-end, the widely used method is that combing the differentially flat property of multi-rotor dynamics or simple point-mass dynamics with time-parameterized high order polynomial in the trajectory optimization [2,5,11,15]. The differential flatness property implies that quadrotor's states and control inputs can be computed by the flat outputs, i.e., position and yaw angle, and their high order derivatives [12]. So, the differential flatness characteristic has significant significance and advantages in trajectory optimization. Traditional trajectory optimization is formulated as minimum an objective function such as total energy cost while considering safety and dynamic feasibility. However, these works, such as gradient-based trajectory optimization [3,5,13,16,19,20] and control-based method [1,7,14], the time characteristics of dynamics are ignored. In our previous work [17,18], the time-optimal control problem is reformulated as an Model Predictive Control problem, but it is not suitable for wild environment with complex obstacles. Algorithms generating a minimum-time trajectory while need to guarantee smoothness, safely and dynamic feasibility at the same time is still a complex and non-convex problem. In this paper, we propose an efficient guided sampling strategy by topology graph, and in the back-end, the time optimal trajectory problem is transformed to a convex optimization problem with a time optimal guidance trajectory.

The main contributions of this article are as follows:

- We introduce a geometrically guided sample method based the topological map. The sample region is focused on the smaller space than the entire feasible space to improve sample efficiency.
- The optimal time is used in trajectory optimization to generate a safe, dynamic feasibility and minimum-time trajectory. The simulation experimental results demonstrate the feasibility and validity of the proposed motion planning method.

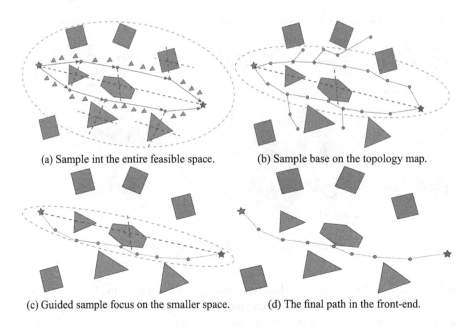

(a) Sample int the entire feasible space.   (b) Sample base on the topology map.

(c) Guided sample focus on the smaller space.   (d) The final path in the front-end.

Fig. 2. The process of geometrically guided sample.

In what follows, we design the hierarchical planning framework works in Sect. 2, include the guided RRT* searching in the front-end and trajectory optimization in the back-end. Experiments and results are given in Sect. 3. Section 4 concludes this article.

2   Motion Planning

2.1   Geometrically Guided Kinodynamic RRT*

In order to improve the sample efficiency, we construct a topological tree of the environment to focus on sample region. Sampling-based motion planners rely on incremental densification to discover progressively shorter paths. The sample space can be densified uniformly to find shorter paths, After computing feasible path between start position x_s and target position x_g, the guided sample prunes the sample space by conservatively eliminating points that cannot yield shorter paths. The geometrically guided sample space is defined as follow:

$$X_{gs} = \{x|x \in X, h(x_s, x) + h(x, x_t) \leq c(\eta)\} \tag{1}$$

where $c(\eta)$ is the cost of the current path, h is the Euclidean heuristic function. The overall sample process is shown in Algorithm 1 (Fig. 2).

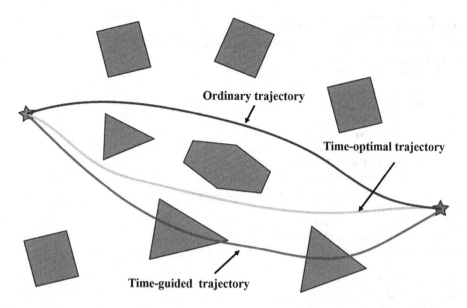

Fig. 3. Three trajectory generate by different methods, red one is the time-guided trajectory base on Pontryagin's Minimum Principle, blue one is the ordinary trajectory, green one is the time-optimal trajectory base our method. (Color figure online)

2.2 Time Optimal Trajectory Generation

The differential flatness of quadrotor systems allows us to represent the trajectory by three independent 1-D time-parameterized polynomial functions.

$$p(t) = \begin{bmatrix} p_x(t) \; p_y(t) \; p_z(t) \end{bmatrix}^T \quad p_u(t) = \sum_{k=0}^{K} a_k t^k \tag{2}$$

In the back-end, a lightweight yet effective trajectory optimization method based on the optimal time and dynamic constrained, which converges quickly to generate a safe, dynamically feasible trajectory. Based on the aforementioned optimization variable indicators, the cost function is designed:

$$f_{total} = \lambda_1 f_s + \lambda_2 f_t \tag{3}$$

where f_s is the smoothness cost of total trajectory, f_t is the time optimal cost of total trajectory, and λ_1 and λ_2 are the weights coefficient, respectively.

Smoothness Cost Function. The cost function is the integral of the square of the kth derivative. In this paper, we minimize the snap along the global trajectory, so k is 4.

$$f_s = \sum_{u \in [x,y,z]} \int_0^T \left(\frac{d^k f_u(t)}{dt^k} \right) dt, \tag{4}$$

Algorithm 1. Geometrically guided sample

Input: sample space ξ, tree τ, start position x_{start}, target position x_{goal}
Output: path : $P = p_0, p_1, p_2 \cdots, p_n$
  1: **function** GUIDE_SAMPLE($\xi, \tau, x_{start}, x_{goal}$)
  2:      **initalize:** $\tau \leftarrow [x_{start}]^T$
  3:      **for** $i \in [0, 1, \cdots, n]$ **do**
  4:         $x_{new} \leftarrow$ **Sample**(ξ)
  5:         $x_{near} \leftarrow$ **Near**(x_{new}, τ).
  6:         $x_{min} \leftarrow$ **ChooseParent**(x_{new}, x_{near}).
  7:         $\tau \leftarrow \tau \cup$ **ChooseParent**(x_{new}, x_{near}).
  8:         **if TryConnectGoal**(x_{new}, x_{near}) **then**
  9:            $c_i(\eta) \leftarrow$ **ComputeCostFunc**(x_{start}, x_i, x_{goal})
10:         **end if**
11:         **if** $c_{min} < c_i(\eta)$ **then**
12:            Update sample space using ($c_i(\eta)$)
13:            **return** P
14:            break
15:         **end if**
16:      **end for**
17: **end function**

Time Optimal Cost Function. Fast flight from a start position to a target position in the minimum time with dynamic and acceleration constraints can be formulated as following optimal problem:

$$\min_{a(t)} \int_{t_0}^{t_f} dt = \min_{a(t)} \left(t_f - t_0\right) \tag{5}$$

where, t_0 is the start time, t_f is the final time. In order to covert the non-convex time optimal 5 into a convex optimal problem on the trajectory optimization, the guided time optimal objective function is defined based the closed-form guided trajectory.

$$f_t = \int_0^T \left(\rho_0 \|p(t) - p^*(t)\|^2 + \rho_1 \|\dot{p}(t) - \dot{p}^*(t)\|^2\right) dt \tag{6}$$

where, ρ_0 and ρ_1 are the weight of zero-order and first-order proximity respectively. We call it as guidance time optimal cost function. If the optimal problem (5) replaces the time objective function $\int_{t_0}^{t_f} dt$ by f, then it will be converted into a convex optimal problem on the trajectory optimization. The time guided trajectory is shown in Fig. 3.

Continuity Constraints. The position(p), velocity(v) and acceleration(a) must be continuous at all the connecting point between two piecewise trajectory. The continuity constraints are enforced by setting hard constraints between two piecewise trajectory j^{th} and $(j+1)^{th}$ pieces curves, the continuity constraints is defined as:

$$\begin{cases} p_{u,j}^n = e_{u,j}^{0,n}, & p_{u,j}^n = p_{u,j+1}^0, \\ v_{u,j}^n = e_{u,j}^{1,n}, & v_{u,j}^n = v_{u,j+1}^0, \\ a_{u,j}^n = e_{u,j}^{2,n}, & a_{u,j}^n = a_{u,j+1}^0, \end{cases} \tag{7}$$

Dynamic Feasibility Constraints. We penalize velocity or acceleration along the trajectory exceeding maximum allowable value v_{max} and a_{max} with a dynamic feasibility constraints:

$$f_v(v) = \begin{cases} \left(v_u^2 - v_{max}^2\right), & v_u^2 > v_{max}^2 \\ 0, & v_u^2 < v_{max}^2 \end{cases} \tag{8}$$

$$f_a(a) = \begin{cases} \left(a_u^2 - a_{max}^2\right), & a_u^2 > a_{max}^2 \\ 0, & a_u^2 < a_{max}^2 \end{cases} \tag{9}$$

The continuity constraints and high order dynamical constrains are reformulated as linear equality constraints ($A_{eq}c = b_{eq}$) and linear inequality constraints ($A_{ie}c \leq b_{ie}$), here $\left[c_j^0, c_j^1, \cdots, c_j^n\right]$. The total cost function is reformulated as Q_0. Then the trajectory generation problem is reformulated as:

$$\begin{aligned} \min \quad & c^T Q_0 c, \\ s.t. \quad & A_{eq}c = b_{eq}, \\ & A_{ieq}c \leq b_{ie}, \end{aligned} \tag{10}$$

Table 1. Params of Simulation Experiment

Symbol	Description	Value
m	take-off weight	2.1 kg
ρ_0	The resolution of grid map	0.1
d_{max}	tha maximum sensing range	5 m
v_{max}	Maximum velocity	$5\,\mathrm{m/s}^2$
a_{max}	Maximum acceleration	$4\,\mathrm{m/s}^3$

which is a convex quadratic program (QP), and can be solved by OSQP (Fig. 4).

Table 2. Performance Comparison of the Trajectory

Method	Total Time	Traj Length	Average v	Average a
Proposed	23.96 s	2.47 m	2.12 m/s	$2.73\,\mathrm{m/s}^2$
Zhou	27.309 s	2.31 m	1.99 m/s	$2.56\,\mathrm{m/s}^2$
Chen	30.15 s	2.39 m	1.69 m/s	$2.36\,\mathrm{m/s}^2$
Ye	34.6 s	2.39 m	2.03 m/s	$2.49\,\mathrm{m/s}^2$

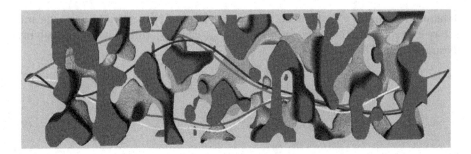

Fig. 4. Trajectory generation by different methods. The red trajectory is generated by our method, the green trajectory is generated by Zhou's method, the blue trajectory is generated by Ye's method, the yellow trajectory is generated by Chen's method. (Color figure online)

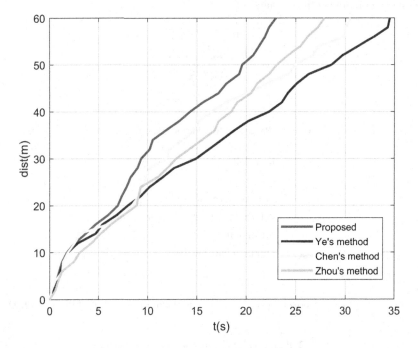

Fig. 5. Four trajectory generate by different methods, Track the different trajectory by the same SE(3) controller, the flight time comparison show our method has the minimum-time performance.

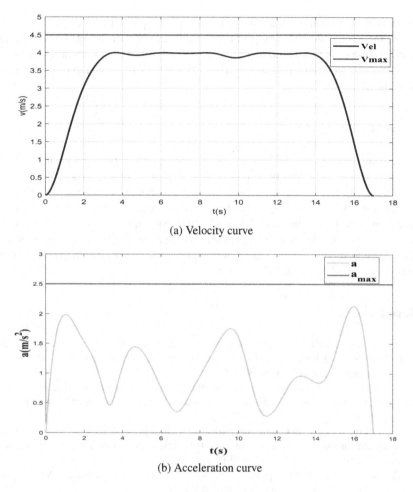

(a) Velocity curve

(b) Acceleration curve

Fig. 6. The simulation experiment results.

3 Experiment

3.1 Experiments Setting

We conduct a ROS simulation in a $80 \times 40 \times 3$ m environment with 50 randomly deployed obstacles and starting and goal positions. The start and final goal position are: $p_0 = [0, -30, 2]$, $v_0 = [0, 0, 0]^T$ $p_f = [0, 30, 2]^T$, $v_f = [0, 0, 0]^T$, respectively. The main parameters of simulation experiment are list in Table 1.

3.2 Simulation Experiments

We design a flight task to validate the proposed method can fast autonomous flight in the clutter 3-D environment with time-optimal policies. The start-to-goal Euclidean

Distance is $E_{dist} = 60$ m, we track the different online replanning trajectory by the same params SE(3) controller. The experimental results are shown in Fig. 5 and Fig. 6, the total flight time of the proposed method is 23.96 s, the zhou's, Chen's and ye's method are 27.309 s, 30.15 s and 34.6 s, respectively. The results of simulation experiment are list in Table 2.

4   Conclusion

In this paper, we propose an effective guided sample in the front-end to improve sample efficiency in the smaller optimal space than the entire feasible space. We propose a optimal time trajectory method for the trajectory generation in the back-end. The time-optimal trajectory is used in trajectory optimization to generate a safe, dynamic feasibility and minimum-time trajectory. The simulation experimental results and benchmark shows our method has the best flight performance on time. The feasibility and efficiency of the proposed method are validated in numerical simulations. In the future, we will validate the method on the real experiment.

References

1. Arrizabalaga, J., Ryll, M.: Towards time-optimal tunnel-following for quadrotors. In: 2022 International Conference on Robotics and Automation (ICRA), pp. 4044–4050 (2022). https://doi.org/10.1109/ICRA46639.2022.9811764
2. Beul, M., Behnke, S.: Analytical time-optimal trajectory generation and control for multirotors. In: 2016 International Conference on Unmanned Aircraft Systems (ICUAS), pp. 87–96. IEEE (2016)
3. Chen, J., Liu, T., Shen, S.: Online generation of collision-free trajectories for quadrotor flight in unknown cluttered environments. In: 2016 IEEE International Conference on Robotics and Automation (ICRA), pp. 1476–1483. IEEE (2016)
4. Dijkstra, E.W.: A note on two problems in connexion with graphs. In: Edsger Wybe Dijkstra: His Life, Work, and Legacy, pp. 287–290 (2022)
5. Gao, F., Wang, L., Zhou, B., Zhou, X., Pan, J., Shen, S.: Teach-repeat-replan: a complete and robust system for aggressive flight in complex environments. IEEE Trans. Rob. **36**(5), 1526–1545 (2020)
6. Hart, P.E., Nilsson, N.J., Raphael, B.: A formal basis for the heuristic determination of minimum cost paths. IEEE Trans. Syst. Sci. Cybern. **4**(2), 100–107 (1968)
7. Hehn, M., Ritz, R., D'Andrea, R.: Performance benchmarking of quadrotor systems using time-optimal control. Auton. Robot. **33**, 69–88 (2012)
8. Hsu, D., Kindel, R., Latombe, J.C., Rock, S.: Randomized kinodynamic motion planning with moving obstacles. Int. J. Robot. Res. **21**(3), 233–255 (2002)
9. Karaman, S., Frazzoli, E.: Sampling-based algorithms for optimal motion planning. Int. J. Robot. Res. **30**(7), 846–894 (2011)
10. Kavraki, L.E., Svestka, P., Latombe, J.C., Overmars, M.H.: Probabilistic roadmaps for path planning in high-dimensional configuration spaces. IEEE Trans. Robot. Autom. **12**(4), 566–580 (1996)
11. Liu, S., Atanasov, N., Mohta, K., Kumar, V.: Search-based motion planning for quadrotors using linear quadratic minimum time control. In: 2017 IEEE/RSJ International Conference on Intelligent Robots and Systems (IROS), pp. 2872–2879. IEEE (2017)

12. Mellinger, D., Kumar, V.: Minimum snap trajectory generation and control for quadrotors. In: 2011 IEEE International Conference on Robotics and Automation, pp. 2520–2525. IEEE (2011)
13. Romero, A., Penicka, R., Scaramuzza, D.: Time-optimal online replanning for agile quadrotor flight. IEEE Robot. Autom. Lett. **7**(3), 7730–7737 (2022)
14. Romero, A., Sun, S., Foehn, P., Scaramuzza, D.: Model predictive contouring control for time-optimal quadrotor flight. IEEE Trans. Rob. **38**(6), 3340–3356 (2022)
15. Van Loock, W., Pipeleers, G., Swevers, J.: Time-optimal quadrotor flight. In: 2013 European Control Conference (ECC), pp. 1788–1792. IEEE (2013)
16. Ye, H., Zhou, X., Wang, Z., Xu, C., Chu, J., Gao, F.: TGK-planner: an efficient topology guided kinodynamic planner for autonomous quadrotors. IEEE Robot. Autom. Lett. **6**(2), 494–501 (2020)
17. Zhang, G., He, Y., Dai, B., Gu, F., Yang, L., Han, J., et al.: Optimal trajectory planning of a quadrotor toward free flying target catching. Inf. Control **48**, 469–476 (2019)
18. Zhang, G., et al.: Guided time-optimal model predictive control of a multi-rotor. IEEE Control Syst. Lett. **7**, 1658–1663 (2023). https://doi.org/10.1109/LCSYS.2023.3277319
19. Zhou, B., Gao, F., Wang, L., Liu, C., Shen, S.: Robust and efficient quadrotor trajectory generation for fast autonomous flight. IEEE Robot. Autom. Lett. **4**(4), 3529–3536 (2019)
20. Zucker, M., et al.: Chomp: covariant hamiltonian optimization for motion planning. Int. J. Robot. Res. **32**(9–10), 1164–1193 (2013)

Formation Control of Unmanned Ground Vehicles Based on Broad Learning

Zhanwei Yang[1], Hui Xu[1(✉)], Feng Pan[2], and Yintao Wang[1]

[1] School of Marine Science and Technology,
Northwestern Polytechnical University, Xi'an 710072, China
xuhui@nwpu.edu.cn
[2] The 716th Research Institute of China Shipbuilding Industry Corporation,
Lianyungang 222061, China

Abstract. This paper studies the distributed formation control of Multiple unmanned ground vehicle systems with input saturation. Based on the bionic coupling mechanism, a multi-agent model is established; The bionic coupling mechanism can determine the interaction weight according to the distance between agents. The closer the distance is, the greater the weight is, which can reduce the impact of external interference on communication. A distributed active controller is designed based on dynamic surface control, eliminating differential explosion in backstepping control. Due to the nonlinear dynamics of the system model caused by the mismatch between the assumed conditions and the actual environment, broad learning is used to estimate and compensate it. In order to solve the problem of input saturation caused by limited input in actual system, an input saturation auxiliary system is introduced to eliminate its adverse effects. The stability of the formation control scheme is proved by using the Lyapunov method. Simulation results verify the effectiveness of the controller.

Keywords: Multiple Unmanned Ground Vehicle Systems · Bionic Coupling Mechanism · Formation Control · Broad Learning

1 Introduction

Multi-agent has many advantages over a single agent in practical applications, such as high efficiency and low cost [1], so more and more research has been done on multi-agent in recent years. At the same time, multi-agent systems (MASs) are complex and require high reliability and stability when they cooperate to complete tasks. Currently, MASs have some problems, such as communication coupling, nonlinear dynamics and input saturation [2]. The solution to these problems is necessary to improve the stability and reliability of MASs. Therefore,

This work was supported by the National Natural Science Foundation of China under Grant U2141238.

© The Author(s), under exclusive license to Springer Nature Singapore Pte Ltd. 2023
H. Yang et al. (Eds.): ICIRA 2023, LNAI 14274, pp. 176–187, 2023.
https://doi.org/10.1007/978-981-99-6501-4_16

the formation control of the multiple unmanned ground vehicle system with input saturation is studied in this paper.

Nonlinear MASs are one of the current research hotspots. Adaptive formation control was studied in many aspects [3]. In the actual control process, there are usually nonlinear dynamics. Many scholars have used neural networks, fuzzy logic and other algorithms to solve such problems. For example, for the formation tracking control of nonlinear MASs, a fuzzy logic system is used to approach the mismatched nonlinear dynamics [4]. For distributed formation control problem, the neural network is used to fit the unknown nonlinear dynamics [5,6]. Based on the Lyapunov sliding mode theory and the online learning of broad learning (BL) for system uncertainty, an adaptive distributed formation control method is proposed to realize asymptotic formation control in the presence of uncertainty [7].

At present, some achievements have been made in the research of multiple unmanned ground vehicles(UGVs), but most of them are aimed at the input saturation and nonlinear dynamics of multiple unmanned ground vehicles [8,9]. There are few studies on real-time changing the coupling strength of unmanned workshops, and each has its shortcomings. An event-triggered control protocol is proposed that uses a nonlinear function with passive features for the couple, thus extending existing control methods and allowing greater flexibility [10]. Time-varying formation control method is constructed by using the adaptive output feedback method for fixed and switched communication topologies and coupling weight based on an adaptive algorithm is introduced to achieve formation control relying on local information [11]. The traditional communication topology switching process is processed by using the smooth step function to avoid communication discontinuity of MASs in switching communication topologies [12,13]. The above studies mainly focus on the topology switching problem of MASs under directed or undirected graphs and do not study the coupling problem existing in the topology in depth [14,15].

Based on the above contents, this paper has the following advantages: 1)The bionic coupling mechanism can determine the interaction weight between UGVs according to the distance between UGVs in real-time. The closer the distance is, the greater the interaction weight is, thus avoiding the impact of poor communication quality caused by long-distance communication on UGVs. 2)Based on dynamic surface control and BL, an adaptive formation controller is designed, which can solve the input saturation and nonlinear dynamic problems in the multi-unmanned ground vehicle system simultaneously, providing a theoretical basis for the formation control algorithm to be applied to the actual system.

The other parts of the paper are as follows: Part 2 describes the preliminary knowledge of graph theory and BL. In the third part, the design of the adaptive controller and the proof of its stability are mainly introduced. In the fourth part, the simulation parameters and result analysis are given. The fifth part summarizes the research contents.

2 Preliminaries and Problem Formulation

2.1 Graph Theory

The communication topology can be represented as a directed graph $G = \{V, E, A\}$, where $V = \{v_1, v_2, \ldots, v_N\}$ denotes the set of nodes, $E = \{(v_i, v_j) | v_i, v_j \in V\} \subseteq V \times V$ stands for the line between points, $A = [a_{ij}] \in R^{N \times N}$ is the weighted adjacency matrix, where a_{ij} is the weight between two points (v_i, v_j). If the directed edge $(v_i, v_j) \in G$, $a_{ij} > 0$, otherwise $a_{ij} = 0$. If v_j is a neighbor of v_i and $(v_i, v_j) \in E$, $N_i = \{v_j | v_j \in V, (v_i, v_j) \in E\}$ represents all the neighbors of v_i. $D = diag\{d_1, d_2, \ldots, d_N\}$ is the degree matrix, and $d_i = \sum_{j \in N_i} a_{ij}$. Laplacian matrix L is obtained by the degree matrix from subtracting the weighted adjacency matrix. The exchange matrix is $B = diag\{b_1, b_2, \ldots, b_N\}$. $b_i = 1$ when the follower can establish a direct relationship with the leader, otherwise $b_i = 0$.

Lemma 1: There is a continuous bounded function $Z(t) \geq 0, \forall t \geq 0$. If

$$\dot{Z}(t) \leq -\kappa_1 Z(t) + \kappa_2, \tag{1}$$

then the following formula is valid

$$Z(t) \leq Z(0)e^{-\kappa_1 t} + \frac{\kappa_2}{\kappa_1}(1 - e^{-\kappa_1 t}) \tag{2}$$

where κ_1 and κ_2 are positive constants.

Lemma 2: There have two arbitrary vectors $x \in R^n$ and $y \in R^n$. If $r > 0$ and $q > 0$ meet $(r-1)(q-1) = 1$, the following formula is valid

$$x^T y \leq \frac{a^r}{r}\|x\|^r + \frac{1}{qa^q}\|y\|^q \tag{3}$$

The equal sign establishes when $x=y$.

2.2 Broad Learning

BL can be used to approach a continuous nonlinear function $\Gamma(x) : R^p \to R^q$. If BL has enough mapped and augmented nodes, then there exist three bounded and optimally weighted matrices Φ_e^*, Φ_f^* and Φ^* such that

$$\Gamma(z) = \Phi^{*T} S(z) + \delta \tag{4}$$

where $z = [z_1, z_2, \ldots, z_p]^T \in R^p$ denotes the input vector, $\Gamma(z) = [\Gamma_1, \Gamma_2, \ldots, \Gamma_q]^T \in R^q$ represents output vector, $S(z) = [s_1(z), s_2(z), \ldots, s_\ell(z)]^T \in R^\ell$ stands for output vector, $\delta \in R^q$ is bounded approximation error and meets $\|\delta\| \leq \delta^*$ and δ^* is the maximum value. The output of BL is $\hat{\Gamma}(x) = \hat{\Phi}^T S(x)$. The network structure of BL can be found in reference [7]. The mapping layer weights, enhancement layer weights and output layer weights are $\tilde{\Phi}_f = \Phi_f^* - \hat{\Phi}_f$, $\tilde{\Phi}_e = \Phi_e^* - \hat{\Phi}_e$ and $\tilde{\Phi} = \Phi^* - \hat{\Phi}$, then

$$\Gamma(z) = \hat{\Gamma}(z) + \tilde{\Gamma}(z) \tag{5}$$

Define the approximate error as

$$\tilde{\Gamma}(z) = \tilde{\Phi}^T \frac{\partial \tilde{\Gamma}}{\partial \Phi} + \frac{\partial \tilde{\Gamma}}{\partial \Phi_f} \tilde{\Phi}_f + \frac{\partial \tilde{\Gamma}}{\partial \Phi_e} \tilde{\Phi}_e + h_t = \tilde{\Phi}^T S + \hat{\Phi}^T \frac{\partial S}{\partial \Phi_f} \tilde{\Phi}_f + \hat{\Phi}^T \frac{\partial S}{\partial \Phi_e} \tilde{\Phi}_e + h_t \quad (6)$$

where $h_t = \tilde{\Phi}^T \tilde{S} + \delta$ and $\|h_t\| < h_m$

2.3 Bionic Coupling Mechanism

In nature, birds will change their formation during migration, and each bird will change according to the change of its neighbors. The closer the two birds are, the greater their influence on each other. This relationship is the same in MASs, so the bionic coupling mechanism is designed as

$$c_{ij} = \begin{cases} 1, & if\,|N_i| = 1 \\ \dfrac{-d_{ij} + \sum\limits_{j \in N_i} d_{ij}}{(|N_i| - 1) \sum\limits_{j \in N_i} d_{ij}}, & if\,|N_i| \geq 2 \end{cases} \quad (7)$$

where d_{ij} represents the distance between two agents, $\sum_{j \in N_i} d_{ij}$ denotes the sum of the distances between the agent and its neighbors, and $|N_i|$ is the number of neighbors.

2.4 Problem Formulation

This subsection builds a multiple UGVs system model based on the UGV dynamics model and then designs the formation tracking state error to prepare for the later controller design. The system model of multiple UGVs is established as follows

$$\begin{cases} \dot{x}_i = v_i + f_{i,1}(x_i, v_i) \\ \dot{v}_i = T(\varphi_i) J^+ M^{-1} sat(\tau_i) + f_{i,2}(x_i, v_i) - T(\varphi_i) J^+ M^{-1} F_f\left(\dot{\theta}_i\right) R \\ \quad - \left[D_\theta R^2 T(\varphi_i) J^+ M^{-1} J T^{-1}(\varphi_i) + T(\varphi_i) T^{-1}(\dot{\varphi}_i) \right] v_i \end{cases} \quad (8)$$

where x_i and v_i denote the position and speed state of UGV respectively, $f_{i,1}(x_i, v_i)$ and $f_{i,2}(x_i, v_i)$ are the nonlinear dynamics caused by the condition mismatch and abbreviated as $f_{i,1}$, $f_{i,2}$ in the following text; R is the radius of the wheel; φ_i is the included angle between the body coordinate system and the world coordinate system; $\dot{\theta}$ is the wheel angular speed; $F_f\left(\dot{\theta}\right) = \vartheta mg \cdot sign\left(\dot{\theta}\right) \big/ 4$ represents the vehicle wheel friction. ϑ and D_θ are respectively static and viscous friction coefficient. g is the acceleration of gravity; $T(\varphi_i)$ denotes the conversion matrix from the body coordinate system to the world coordinate system, J^+ and J denote Jacobian matrix of forward and inverse kinematics model respectively; To facilitate theoretical derivation later, η_i and μ_i are respectively designed as

$$\begin{cases} \eta_i = - T(\varphi_i) J^+ M^{-1} F_f\left(\dot{\theta}_i\right) R \\ \quad - \left[D_\theta R^2 T(\varphi_i) J^+ M^{-1} J T^{-1}(\varphi_i) + T(\varphi_i) T^{-1}(\dot{\varphi}_i) \right] v_i \\ \mu_i = T(\varphi_i) J^+ M^{-1} \end{cases} \quad (9)$$

The actual drive torque of UGV is $sat\left(\tau_i\right)$, τ_i denotes the drive torque calculated by control algorithm.

$$sat\left(\tau_i\right) = \begin{cases} \tau_i & if \ |\tau_i| \leq \tau_m \\ \text{sgn}\left(\tau_i\right)\tau_m & if \ |\tau_i| > \tau_m \end{cases} \tag{10}$$

where τ_m represents the maximum boundary value.

3   Main Results

This section plans to design the formation controller according to the formation tracking state error and proves the system's stability. Firstly, The state error vectors between followers and leader are

$$\begin{cases} e_{i,1} = \displaystyle\sum_{j \in N_i} \bar{a}_{ij}\left(t\right)\left[\left(x_i - y_i\right) - \left(x_j - y_j\right)\right] + b_i\left[\left(x_i - y_i\right) - r\left(t\right)\right], \\ e_{i,2} = v_i - \bar{\beta}_i - \lambda_i. \end{cases} \tag{11}$$

where y_i stands for the state deviation vector and has the first derivative. $\bar{a}_{ij}\left(t\right) = a_{ij} \cdot c_{ij}$. λ_i represents the compensation for input saturation. β_i is a virtual controller designed by backstepping control. To avoid differential explosion in backstepping control, an instruction filter is used to filter β_i. $\bar{\beta}_i$ is the filtered output of β_i. The form of instruction filter is

$$\varpi_i \dot{\bar{\beta}}_i + \bar{\beta}_i = \beta_i, \bar{\beta}_i\left(0\right) = \beta_i\left(0\right) \tag{12}$$

where ϖ_i denotes the bandwidth of the filter and meets the requirements of $\varpi_i > 0$.

The derivative of $e_{i,1}$ is as follows

$$\begin{aligned} \dot{e}_{i,1} = &\sum_{j \in N_i} \dot{\bar{a}}_{ij}\left(t\right)\left[\left(x_i - y_i\right) - \left(x_j - y_j\right)\right] + \left(\sum_{j \in N_i} \bar{a}_{ij}\left(t\right) + b_i\right)\left[\left(\bar{\beta}_i + e_{i,2} + \lambda_i\right) - \dot{y}_i\right] \\ &- \sum_{j \in N_i} \bar{a}_{ij}\left(t\right)\left(v_j - \dot{y}_j\right) - b_i\left(t\right)\dot{r}\left(t\right) + \varGamma_{i,1}\left(Z_{i,1}\right) \end{aligned} \tag{13}$$

where $Z_{i,1} = \left[x_i^T \ v_i^T \ x_j^T \ v_j^T\right]^T$ $\left(j \in N_i\right)$, and $\varGamma_{i,1}(Z_{i,1}) = \sum_{j \in N_i} \bar{a}_{ij}(f_{i,1} - f_{j,1}) + b_i f_{i,1}$ is the unknown nonlinear function, which can be approximated by BL. Due to limited space, the detailed design process is not given here, and the specific process can be referred to reference [7]. In the following, according to the Lyapunov function, we design the BL learning weight update rate for estimating nonlinear functions, and make it satisfy the Lyapunov stability theorem.

Because filtering β_i will produce filtering error $\tilde{\beta}_i = \bar{\beta}_i - \beta_i$, in order to reduce its impact on tracking error, the compensation for filtered error is designed

$$\dot{\rho}_{i,1} = -k_{i,1}\rho_{i,1} + \left(\sum_{j \in N_i} \bar{a}_{ij}\left(t\right) + b_i\right)\left(\bar{\beta}_{i,1} - \beta_{i,1} + \rho_{i,2}\right), \rho_{i,1}\left(0\right) = 0 \tag{14}$$

where $k_{i,1}$ denotes the design parameters related to filter compensation and meets $k_{i,1} > 0$. After filtering compensation, the tracking error can be obtained as follows

$$\bar{e}_{i,1} = e_{i,1} - \rho_{i,1}, \bar{e}_{i,2} = e_{i,2} - \rho_{i,2} \tag{15}$$

The derivative of $\bar{e}_{i,1}$ is

$$\dot{\bar{e}}_{i,1} = \sum_{j \in N_i} \dot{\bar{a}}_{ij}(t) \left[(x_i - y_i) - (x_j - y_j) \right] + \left(\sum_{j \in N_i} \bar{a}_{ij}(t) + b_i \right) \left[(\beta_i + \bar{e}_{i,2} + \lambda_i) - \dot{y}_i \right]$$
$$- \sum_{j \in N_i} \bar{a}_{ij}(t) (v_j - \dot{y}_j) - b_i(t) \dot{r}(t) + \Gamma_{i,1} + k_{i,1}\rho_{i,1} \tag{16}$$

According to (16) and Lyapunov's stability theorem, the virtual controller $\beta_{i,1}$ is defined as follows

$$\beta_{i,1} = -\lambda_i + \dot{y}_i + \frac{1}{\sum_{j \in N_i} \bar{a}_{ij}(t) + b_i} \left(\begin{array}{c} -k_{i,1}e_{i,1} - \sum_{j \in N_i} \dot{\bar{a}}_{ij}(t) \left[(x_i - y_i) - (x_j - y_j) \right] \\ + \sum_{j \in N_i} \bar{a}_{ij}(t)(v_j - \dot{y}_j) + b_i \dot{r}(t) - \hat{\Gamma}_{i,1} - \frac{1}{2}\bar{e}_{i,1} \end{array} \right) \tag{17}$$

where $\hat{\Gamma}_{i,1}$ is the estimate obtained by BL fitting the unknown nonlinear function $\Gamma_{i,1}$.

Bringing (17) into (16) yields

$$\dot{\bar{e}}_{i,1} = -k_{i,1}\bar{e}_{i,1} + \tilde{\Gamma}_{i,1} + \left(\sum_{j \in N_i} \bar{a}_{ij}(t) + b_i \right)\bar{e}_{i,2} - \frac{1}{2}\bar{e}_{i,1} \tag{18}$$

The Lyapunov function candidate is designed as

$$V_1 = \sum_{i=1}^{N} \left(\begin{array}{c} \frac{1}{2}\bar{e}_{i,1}^T \bar{e}_{i,1} + \frac{1}{2\gamma_{i,1}} Tr\left(\tilde{\Phi}_{i,1}^T \tilde{\Phi}_{i,1} \right) + \frac{1}{2\gamma_{ei,1}} Tr\left(\tilde{\Phi}_{ei,1}^T \tilde{\Phi}_{ei,1} \right) \\ + \frac{1}{2\gamma_{fi,1}} Tr\left(\tilde{\Phi}_{fi,1}^T \tilde{\Phi}_{fi,1} \right) \end{array} \right) \tag{19}$$

where $\gamma_{i,1}$, $\gamma_{ei,1}$ and $\gamma_{fi,1}$ are the design parameters and positive constants. Taking the derivative of V_1 and combing (18), we can obtain

$$\dot{V}_1 = \sum_{i=1}^{N} \left(\begin{array}{c} \bar{e}_{i,1}^T (-k_{i,1}\bar{e}_{i,1} + \tilde{\Gamma}_{i,1} - \frac{1}{2}\bar{e}_{i,1} + (\sum_{j \in N_i} \bar{a}_{ij}(t) + b_i)\bar{e}_{i,2}) \\ -\frac{1}{\gamma_{i,1}} Tr\left(\tilde{\Phi}_{i,1}^T \dot{\hat{\Phi}}_{i,1} \right) - \frac{1}{\gamma_{ei,1}} Tr\left(\tilde{\Phi}_{ei,1}^T \dot{\hat{\Phi}}_{ei,1} \right) - \frac{1}{\gamma_{fi,1}} Tr\left(\tilde{\Phi}_{fi,1}^T \dot{\hat{\Phi}}_{fi,1} \right) \end{array} \right) \tag{20}$$

Based on Lemma 2 and (6), the following inequality can be obtained

$$\bar{e}_{i,1}^T \tilde{\Gamma}_{i,1} \leq \frac{1}{2}\bar{e}_{i,1}^T \bar{e}_{i,1} + \frac{1}{2}\tilde{\Gamma}_{i,1}^T \tilde{\Gamma}_{i,1}$$
$$\leq \frac{1}{2}\bar{e}_{i,1}^T \bar{e}_{i,1} + \frac{1}{2}\tilde{\Gamma}_{i,1}^T (h_{ti,1} + \hat{\Phi}_{i,1}^T \frac{\partial S_{i,1}}{\partial \Phi_{fi,1}} \tilde{\Phi}_{fi,1} + \tilde{\Phi}_{i,1}^T S_{i,1} + \hat{\Phi}_{i,1}^T \frac{\partial S_{i,1}}{\partial \Phi_{ei,1}} \tilde{\Phi}_{ei,1}) \tag{21}$$
$$\tilde{\Gamma}_{i,1}^T h_{ti,1} \leq \delta_{i,1}^* h_{mi,1} \tag{22}$$

Taking (21) (22) into (20) yields

$$
\dot{V}_1 \leq \sum_{i=1}^{N}
\begin{pmatrix}
-k_{i,1}\bar{e}_{i,1}^T\bar{e}_{i,1} + \frac{1}{2}\delta_{i,1}^* h_{mi,1} + Tr(\tilde{\Phi}_{i,1}^T(-\frac{\dot{\hat{\Phi}}_{i,1}}{\gamma_{i,1}} + \frac{1}{2}\tilde{\Gamma}_{i,1}S_{i,1}^T)^T) \\
+(\sum_{j\in N_i}\bar{a}_{ij}(t) + b_i)\bar{e}_{i,1}^T\bar{e}_{i,2} + Tr(\tilde{\Phi}_{ei,1}^T(\frac{1}{2}\tilde{\Gamma}_{i,1}\frac{\partial S_{i,1}}{\partial \Phi_{ei,1}}^T\hat{\Phi}_{i,1} - \frac{\dot{\hat{\Phi}}_{ei,1}}{\gamma_{ei,1}})^T) \\
+Tr(\tilde{\Phi}_{fi,1}^T(\frac{1}{2}\tilde{\Gamma}_{i,1}\frac{\partial S_{i,1}}{\partial \Phi_{fi,1}}^T\hat{\Phi}_{i,1} - \frac{\dot{\hat{\Phi}}_{fi,1}}{\gamma_{fi,1}})^T)
\end{pmatrix}
\tag{23}
$$

According to (23), the adaptive learning laws of BL are designed as

$$
\dot{\hat{\Phi}}_{i,1} = \gamma_{i,1}\bar{e}_{i,1}S_{i,1}^T, \dot{\hat{\Phi}}_{ei,1} = \gamma_{ei,1}\bar{e}_{i,1}\frac{\partial \hat{\Gamma}_{i,1}}{\partial \Phi_{ei,1}}^T, \dot{\hat{\Phi}}_{fi,1} = \gamma_{fi,1}\bar{e}_{i,1}\frac{\partial \hat{\Gamma}_{i,1}}{\partial \Phi_{fi,1}}^T \tag{24}
$$

Substituting (24) into (23) yields

$$
\dot{V}_1 \leq \sum_{i=1}^{N}((\sum_{j\in N_i}\bar{a}_{ij}(t) + b_i(t))\bar{e}_{i,1}^T\bar{e}_{i,2} - k_{i,1}\bar{e}_{i,1}^T\bar{e}_{i,1} + \delta_{i,1}^* h_{mi,1}) \tag{25}
$$

The derivative of $e_{i,2}$ yields

$$
\dot{e}_{i,2} = \dot{v}_i - \dot{\beta}_i - \dot{\lambda}_i = \mu_i sat(\tau_i) + \eta_i + \Gamma_{i,2} - \dot{\beta}_i - \dot{\lambda}_i \tag{26}
$$

In the theoretical control algorithm, sometimes the control input given will exceed the boundary of the actual control input, which leads to the instability of the system control. In order to facilitate the application of the control algorithm in practice, the effect of input saturation needs to be eliminated, so the assist system is designed

$$
\dot{\lambda}_i = -k_{i,2}\lambda_i + \mu_i(sat(\tau_i) - \tau_i), \lambda_i(0) = 0 \tag{27}
$$

The auxiliary system can reduce the number of input saturation occurrences and make the system run more stable. When the system appears input saturation, the auxiliary system will act and pull the control input back within the input boundary. When there is no input saturation in the system, the auxiliary system will rapidly converge to zero, which has no impact on the control.

The compensation for the filtered error is defined as

$$
\dot{\rho}_{i,2} = -k_{i,2}\rho_{i,2} \tag{28}
$$

where $k_{i,2} > 0$ and $\rho_{i,2}(0) = 0$.

Based on (27) and (28), the derivative of $\bar{e}_{i,2}$ is as follows

$$
\dot{\bar{e}}_{i,2} = \dot{e}_{i,2} - \dot{\rho}_{i,2} = \mu_i\tau_i + \eta_i + \Gamma_{i,2} - \dot{\beta}_i + k_{i,2}\lambda_i + k_{i,2}\rho_{i,2} \tag{29}
$$

where $Z_{i,2} = \begin{bmatrix} x_i^T & v_i^T \end{bmatrix}^T$. $\Gamma_{i,2}(Z_{i,2}) = f_{i,2}$ is the unknown nonlinear function, which can be fitted by BL.

According to (29) and Lyapunov's stability theorem, the formation controller τ_i is designed as follows

$$\tau_i = \mu_i^- \left(-(\sum_{j \in N_i} \bar{a}_{ij}(t) + b_i)\bar{e}_{i,1} + \dot{\hat{\beta}}_{i,1} - \eta_i - k_{i,2}\lambda_i - k_{i,2}e_{i,2} - \hat{\Gamma}_{i,2} - \tfrac{1}{2}\bar{e}_{i,2} \right)$$

$$(30)$$

Bringing (30) into (29) gives

$$\dot{\bar{e}}_{i,2} = -(\sum_{j \in N_i} \bar{a}_{ij}(t) + b_i)\bar{e}_{i,1} + \tilde{\Gamma}_{i,2} - k_{i,2}\bar{e}_{i,2} - \frac{1}{2}\bar{e}_{i,2} \qquad (31)$$

The Lyapunov function candidate is defined as

$$V_2 = V_1 + \sum_{i=1}^{N} \left(\begin{array}{c} \frac{1}{2}\bar{e}_{i,2}^T\bar{e}_{i,2} + \frac{1}{2\gamma_{i,2}}Tr\left(\tilde{\Phi}_{i,2}^T\tilde{\Phi}_{i,2}\right) + \frac{1}{2\gamma_{ei,2}}Tr\left(\tilde{\Phi}_{ei,2}^T\tilde{\Phi}_{ei,2}\right) \\ + \frac{1}{2\gamma_{fi,2}}Tr\left(\tilde{\Phi}_{fi,2}^T\tilde{\Phi}_{fi,2}\right) \end{array} \right) \qquad (32)$$

where $\gamma_{i,2} > 0$, $\gamma_{ei,2} > 0$ and $\gamma_{fi,2} > 0$ are the design parameters.

Take the derivative of V_2 to get

$$\dot{V}_2 = \dot{V}_1 + \sum_{i=1}^{N} \left(\begin{array}{c} \bar{e}_{i,2}^T(-(\sum_{j \in N_i} \bar{a}_{ij}(t) + b_i)\bar{e}_{i,1} + \tilde{\Gamma}_{i,2} - k_{i,2}\bar{e}_{i,2} - \tfrac{1}{2}\bar{e}_{i,2}) \\ -\frac{1}{\gamma_{i,2}}Tr\left(\tilde{\Phi}_{i,2}^T\dot{\hat{\Phi}}_{i,2}\right) - \frac{1}{\gamma_{ei,2}}Tr\left(\tilde{\Phi}_{ei,2}^T\dot{\hat{\Phi}}_{ei,2}\right) \\ -\frac{1}{\gamma_{fi,2}}Tr\left(\tilde{\Phi}_{fi,2}^T\dot{\hat{\Phi}}_{fi,2}\right) \end{array} \right) \qquad (33)$$

According to (33), the adaptive learning laws of BL are designed as

$$\dot{\hat{\Phi}}_{i,2} = \gamma_{i,2}\bar{e}_{i,2}S_{i,2}^T, \dot{\hat{\Phi}}_{ei,2} = \gamma_{ei,2}\bar{e}_{i,2}\frac{\partial\hat{\Gamma}_{i,2}}{\partial\Phi_{ei,2}}^T, \dot{\hat{\Phi}}_{fi,2} = \gamma_{fi,2}\bar{e}_{i,2}\frac{\partial\hat{\Gamma}_{i,2}}{\partial\Phi_{fi,2}}^T. \qquad (34)$$

Here the inequality conversion is the same as (21) and (22). Substituting (25) (34) into (33) gives get

$$\dot{V}_2 \leq \sum_{i=1}^{N}(-\sum_{\iota=1}^{2} k_{i,\iota}\bar{e}_{i,\iota}^T\bar{e}_{i,\iota} + \frac{1}{2}\sum_{\iota=1}^{2}\delta_{i,\iota}^*h_{mi,\iota}) \leq -\alpha_1 V_n + \alpha_2 \qquad (35)$$

where $\alpha_1 = \min\{2k_{i,1}, 2k_{i,2},\} > 0$, $\alpha_2 = \frac{1}{2}\sum_{i=1}^{N}\sum_{\iota=1}^{n}\delta_{i,\iota}^*h_{mi,\iota} > 0$.

Based on (32) and (35), we can get $\dot{V}_2 \leq 0$ when $\alpha_1 \gg \alpha_2$. From Lyapunov's second theorem, we know the system will achieve asymptotic stability. Through (32) and lemma 1, the inequality can be obtained as follows

$$\bar{E}_1^T\bar{E}_1 \leq 2V_2(t) \leq 2V_2(0)e^{-\alpha_1 t} + 2\frac{\alpha_2}{\alpha_1}\left(1 - e^{-\alpha_1 t}\right) \qquad (36)$$

where $\bar{E}_1 = \left[\bar{e}_{1,1}^T, \cdots, \bar{e}_{N,1}^T\right]^T$. It means $\|\bar{E}_1\| \leq \sqrt{2V_2(0)e^{-\alpha_1 t} + 2\frac{\alpha_2}{\alpha_1}\left(1 - e^{-\alpha_1 t}\right)}$
When $\lim_{t \to \infty} e^{-\alpha_1 t} = 0$, $\lim_{t \to \infty} \|\bar{E}_1\| \leq \sqrt{2\frac{\alpha_2}{\alpha_1}}$.

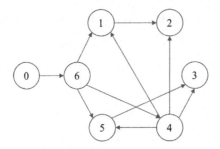

Fig. 1. Communication topology between UGVs.

From (15), to prove that $e_{i,1}$ is bounded, we need to continue to prove that $\rho_{i,1}$ is bounded. The Lyapunov function candidate can be defined as

$$\bar{V} = \sum_{i=1}^{N} \sum_{\tau=1}^{2} \frac{1}{2} \rho_{i,\tau}^{T} \rho_{i,\tau} \tag{37}$$

Taking the derivative of $\bar{V}$ and combing (14) and (28), we can get

$$\dot{\bar{V}} = \sum_{i=1}^{N} \left(-k_{i,1} \rho_{i,1}^{T} \rho_{i,1} - k_{i,2} \rho_{i,2}^{T} \rho_{i,2} + \left(\sum_{j \in N_i} \bar{a}_{ij} + b_i \right) \rho_{i,1}^{T} \left(\bar{\beta}_i - \beta_i + \rho_{i,2} \right) \right) \tag{38}$$

According to Lemma 2, the inequality can be obtained as follows

$$\rho_{i,1}^{T} \left(\bar{\beta}_i - \beta_i + \rho_{i,2} \right) \leq \rho_{i,1}^{T} \rho_{i,1} + \frac{1}{2} \rho_{i,2}^{T} \rho_{i,2} + \frac{1}{2} \left\| \bar{\beta}_{i,1} - \beta_{i,1} \right\|^2 \tag{39}$$

where $\left\| \bar{\beta}_i - \beta_i \right\| \leq \sigma$, σ is a minimal positive number. Bringing (27) into (26) gives

$$\dot{\bar{V}} \leq \sum_{i=1}^{N} \left(- \sum_{\tau=1}^{2} \bar{k}_{i,\tau} \rho_{i,\tau}^{T} \rho_{i,\tau} + \left(\frac{1}{2} \left(\sum_{j \in N_i} \bar{a}_{ij} + b_i \right) v^2 \right) \right) \leq -\bar{\alpha}_1 \bar{V} + \bar{\alpha}_2 \tag{40}$$

where $\bar{k}_{i,1} = k_{i,1} - \left(\sum_{j \in N_i} \bar{a}_{ij} + b_i \right)$, $\bar{k}_{i,2} = k_{i,2} - \frac{1}{2} \left(\sum_{j \in N_i} \bar{a}_{ij} + b_i \right)$, $\bar{\alpha}_1 = \min\{\bar{k}_{i,1}, \bar{k}_{i,2}\}$, $\bar{\alpha}_2 = \sum_{i=1}^{N} \frac{1}{2} \left(\sum_{j \in N_i} \bar{a}_{ij} + b_i \right) \sigma^2 > 0$.
Similar to the analysis of (35) and (36), we can get

$$\lim_{t \to \infty} \|\rho_1\| \leq \sqrt{2 \frac{\bar{\alpha}_2}{\bar{\alpha}_1}} \tag{41}$$

Then the inequality can be deduced as follows

$$\lim_{t \to \infty} \|E_1\| \leq \lim_{t \to \infty} \|\bar{E}_1\| + \lim_{t \to \infty} \|\rho_1\| \leq \sqrt{2 \frac{\alpha_2}{\alpha_1}} + \sqrt{2 \frac{\bar{\alpha}_2}{\bar{\alpha}_1}} \tag{42}$$

Therefore, the above analysis can prove that the system is asymptotically stable and the tracking error is bounded.

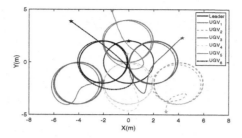

Fig. 2. Formation trajectories of UGVs.

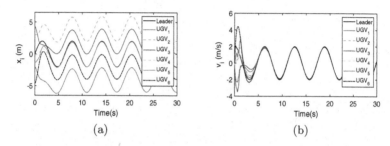

Fig. 3. (a) X-direction positions of UGVs(m). (b) X-direction velocities of UGVs (m/s).

4 Simulation Example

In order to prove the feasibility of the controller designed in the third part, we are going to select six UGVs for simulation. The specific characteristic parameters of UGV are in [16]. The communication relationship between UGVs is shown in Fig. 1. The initial value of UGV is $x_1 = [2.0332 \ -1.8122 \ 0]^T, x_2 = [3.0101 \ -4.7078 \ 0]^T, x_3 = [4.2885 \ 2.3033 \ 0]^T, x_4 = [-0.1139 \ 0.7853 \ 0]^T, x_5 = [-1.3256 \ 4.8798 \ 0]^T, x_6 = [-4.6226 \ 3.8717 \ 0]^T$. The global reference signal is $r(t) = [2\sin(t) \ 2\cos(t) \ 0]^T$, the bandwidth and compensation design parameters of the filter are respectively $\varpi_i = 0.01$, $k_{i,1} = 2$ and $k_{i,2} = 1.5$. The position deviation vector between six UGVs and the leader is $y_1 = [-4 \ -2 \ 0]^T, y_2 = [4 \ -2 \ 0]^T, y_3 = [2 \ 0 \ 0]^T, y_4 = [0 \ -2 \ 0]^T, y_5 = [0 \ 2 \ 0]^T, y_6 = [-2 \ 0 \ 0]^T$. The nonlinear dynamics are $f_{i,1} = 0.01 * sin(x_i)$ and $f_{i,2} = 0.01 * cos(x_i + v_i)$. Figure 2 shows the movement track of six UGVs and one leader. From it, we can see that from the starting position, UGVs have completed the task of formation and maintenance through their learning.   Figure 3 shows the positions and speeds of UGVs in the X direction. At the fifth second, the speed tends to be consistent, and the position keeps a fixed interval, indicating that the formation of UGV has formed at this time. The six UGVs generally maintain stable movement in a fixed formation. Figure 4a shows the driving torques of the first wheels of the six UGVs. In the beginning, the driving torque is enormous. Because the input saturation auxiliary system is introduced, the torque will not exceed the maximum

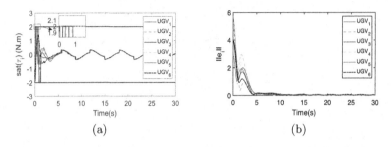

Fig. 4. (a) Torques of the first wheel (N·m), (b) Tracking errors of UGVs.

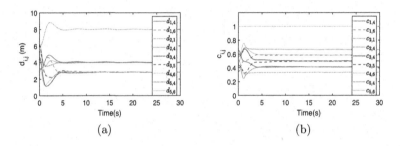

Fig. 5. (a) The distance between UGVs (m), (b) Coupling degrees between UGVs.

boundary, which means that the auxiliary system plays a role. In Fig. 4b, the norm of the position error vector is given, which approaches 0 at the fifth second, indicating that the controller has a good control effect. Figure 5 shows the coupling degree and distance between UGVs. It can be seen that when the coupling degree of UGVs is related to the distance between UGVs, the coupling degree also tends to be stable when the distance is constant. Therefore, the nonlinear coupling mechanism based on distance is effective.

5 Conclusion

In this paper, a UGV formation control model has been established which has unknown nonlinear dynamics and input saturation. A bionic coupling mechanism based on relative distance is proposed to optimize the communication coupling problem. BL is used to approximate the unknown nonlinear dynamics, and an auxiliary system is introduced to eliminate the input saturation problem. Then The dynamic surface controller is designed, the state tracking error is bounded, and the stability of the system is proved. Finally, a system composed of six UGVs is simulated, and the results show the availability of the controller.

References

1. Yu, D., Xu, H., Chen, C.L.P., Bai, W., Wang, Z.: Dynamic coverage control based on k-means. IEEE Trans. Ind. Electron. **69**(5), 5333–5341 (2021)

2. Yu, D., Chen, C.L.P.: Automatic leader-follower persistent formation generation with minimum agent-movement in various switching topologies. IEEE Trans. Cybern. **50**(4), 1569–1581 (2020)

3. Zhou, Q., Shi, P., Tian, Y., Wang, M.: Approximation-based adaptive tracking control for MIMO nonlinear systems with input saturation. IEEE Trans. Cybern. **45**(10), 2119–2128 (2015)

4. Chen, Z., Li, Z., Chen, C.L.P.: Disturbance observer-based fuzzy control of uncertain MIMO mechanical systems with input nonlinearities and its application to robotic exoskeleton. IEEE Trans. Cybern. **47**(4), 984–994 (2017)

5. He, W., Chen, G., Han, Q.-L., Qian, F.: Network-based leader-following consensus of nonlinear multi-agent systems via distributed impulsive control. Inf. Sci. **380**, 145–158 (2017)

6. Ma, J., Ge, S.S., Zheng, Z., Hu, D.: Adaptive NN control of a class of nonlinear systems with asymmetric saturation actuators. IEEE Trans. Neural Netw. Learn. Syst. **26**(7), 1532–1538 (2015)

7. Tsai, C.-C., Yu, C.-C., Wu, C.-W.: Adaptive distributed BLS-FONTSM formation control for uncertain networking heterogeneous omnidirectional mobile multi-robots. J. Chin. Inst. Eng. **43**(2), 171–185 (2019)

8. Wen, C., Zhou, J., Liu, Z., Su, H.: Robust adaptive control of uncertain nonlinear systems in the presence of input saturation and external disturbance. IEEE Trans. Autom. Control **56**(7), 1672–1678 (2011)

9. Field, J.R., Salman, M.U.: Multi-agent approach to analyzing kinetics of a multi-actuated OmniDirectional mobile robot for control system development. In: 2018 9th IEEE Annual Ubiquitous Computing, Electronics & Mobile Communication Conference (UEMCON). IEEE (2018)

10. Jia, Q., Tang, W.K.S.: Event-triggered protocol for the consensus of multi-agent systems with state-dependent nonlinear coupling. IEEE Trans. Circuits Syst. I: Regul. Pap. **65**(2), 723–732 (2018)

11. Dong, X., Li, Y., Lu, C., Hu, G., Li, Q., Ren, Z.: Time-varying formation tracking for UAV swarm systems with switching directed topologies. IEEE Trans. Neural Netw. Learn. Syst. **30**(12), 3674–3685 (2019)

12. Yu, D., Chen, C.L.P., Ren, C.-E., Sui, S.: Swarm control for self-organized system with fixed and switching topology. IEEE Trans. Cybern. **50**(10), 4481–4494 (2020)

13. Yu, D., Chen, C.L.P.: Smooth transition in communication for swarm control with formation change. IEEE Trans. Ind. Inform. **16**(11), 6962–6971 (2020)

14. Dong, X., Xi, J., Lu, G., Zhong, Y.: Formation control for high-order linear time-invariant multiagent systems with time delays. IEEE Trans. Control Netw. Syst. **1**(3), 232–240 (2014)

15. Dong, X., Yu, B., Shi, Z., Zhong, Y.: Time-varying formation control for unmanned aerial vehicles: theories and applications. IEEE Trans. Control Syst. Technol. **23**(1), 340–348 (2015)

16. Yu, D., Chen, C.L.P., Xu, H.: Fuzzy swarm control based on sliding-mode strategy with self-organized omnidirectional mobile robots system. IEEE Trans. Syst. Man Cybern. Syst. **52**, 1–13 (2021)

Equilibrium-Compensation-Based Sliding Mode Control for Accurate Steering Tracking of a Single-Track Two-Wheeled Robot

Boyi Wang⬤, Yang Deng⬤, Feilong Jing⬤, Yu Tian⬤, Zhang Chen$^{(\boxtimes)}$⬤, and Bin Liang⬤

Department of Automation, Tsinghua University, Beijing, China
{by-wang19,jfl21,yu-tian18}@mails.tsinghua.edu.cn,
dengyang@mail.tsinghua.edu.cn, {cz_da,bliang}@tsinghua.edu.cn

Abstract. This paper presents an equilibrium-compensation-based sliding mode control scheme for achieving accurate steering angle tracking in a single-track two-wheeled robot subject to mismatched disturbances. To mitigate the impact of these disturbances, we propose a novel module called the equilibrium compensator. Additionally, to deal with the non-minimum phase characteristic of the system, the output redefinition method is employed to transform the system into a minimum phase system. A nominal sliding mode controller is then designed for the external subsystem, and an extended state observer is utilized to estimate the system state and disturbance. Altogether, accurate steering tracking is achieved by applying the nominal sliding mode controller to the compensated state. The effectiveness of the proposed control scheme is validated through experiments conducted on a robot prototype.

Keywords: Sliding mode control · Mismatched disturbance · Equilibrium compensation · Single-track two-wheeled robot

1 Introduction

The dynamics of single-track two-wheeled (STTW) robots, such as unmanned motorcycles and bicycles, exhibit several interesting properties, including under-actuated characteristic [8], non-minimum phase behavior [4], nonholonomic kinematic constraints [5], low-speed instability [17], and coupling between kinematics and dynamics [10], which have attracted considerable attentions of researchers.

In recent decades, many researchers have been devoted to the development of prototypes of STTW robots. Yu et al. [17] had studied the effect of the trail length of bicycles and developed an autonomous bicycle with a negative trail that

This work was supported in part by National Natural Science Foundation of China under Grant 62073183 and 62203252.

© The Author(s), under exclusive license to Springer Nature Singapore Pte Ltd. 2023
H. Yang et al. (Eds.): ICIRA 2023, LNAI 14274, pp. 188–201, 2023.
https://doi.org/10.1007/978-981-99-6501-4_17

can keep balance at speeds as low as 0.58 m/s. Wang et al. [11] achieved simultaneous trajectory tracking and balance control with prototype demonstration using a controller based on the external/internal convertible (EIC) structure. He et al. [8] developed a learning-based control framework for a bicycle robot with a pendulum balancer, which attained trajectory tracking and balance control.

However, these researches have primarily concentrated on balancing control and trajectory tracking control, paying little attention to steering angle tracking control. This gap can be attributed to two main factors. Firstly, the handlebar serves the dual purpose of maintaining balance and steering the direction, resulting in a significant coupling between these two tasks. As a result, it is challenging to achieve accurate steering angle tracking control. Secondly, there has been a lack of emphasis on the application of steering angle tracking. By decoupling the balancing and trajectory tracking tasks, accurate steering angle tracking capability can enable an STTW vehicle to exhibit behavior similar to a four-wheeled robot.

In practical steering angle tracking tasks, the presence of mismatched disturbances introduces a steady-state error in the controlled output. While sliding mode control (SMC) techniques have been developed for systems with such disturbances [6,12,13], they are limited to systems formulated as chains of integrators and cannot be applied to non-minimum phase systems. Various approaches, such as output redefinition, have been devised to handle non-minimum phase systems, but they typically employ basic techniques like integral control to address the disturbances [14]. Consequently, there is a lack of general methods to effectively tackle mismatched disturbances in non-minimum phase system.

To address this challenge, this paper proposes a novel control scheme that combines sliding mode control, output redefinition and equilibrium compensation (EC). First, the original system is transformed into a minimum phase system using output redefinition technique. Then a nominal sliding mode controller is designed for the external dynamic system. Subsequently, an extended state observer (ESO) [3,7] is employed to estimate the state and disturbance, which are used to calculate the equilibrium that ensures zero steady-state error in the output. Finally, the proposed equilibrium compensation technique is utilized to apply the nominal controller on the compensated state, achieving zero steady-state error while preserving nominal performance.

The main contributions of this paper are threefold: (1) extending the sliding mode controller to non-minimum phase systems like STTW robots based on output redefinition; (2) proposing an accurate steering angle tracking algorithm based on equilibrium point compensation for STTW robots; (3) validating the proposed algorithm on a physical robot prototype. To the best of our knowledge, there have been no reported demonstrations of accurate steering tracking on physical STTW robots without assisted balancers.

The remainder of this paper is organized as follows: Sect. 2 presents the dynamic modeling of an STTW robot based on the Newton-Euler method. Section 3 provides a detailed description of the proposed equilibrium-compensation-based sliding mode controller (EC-SMC), analyzes the stability of the controller, and proves that the controller ensures zero steady-state error in the controlled output. In Sect. 4, we introduce the STTW robot prototype and experimental setup, and analyzes the experimental results, thereby demonstrating the effectiveness of the proposed method. The final chapter summarizes the whole work.

2 System Model

The dynamics of the STTW robot had been extensively studied in the past century [2,15–18], most of which are derived using Lagrange method, losing the physical interpretation of the terms in the equations of motion. In this paper, we adopt the Newton-Euler method to derive the dynamics of the STTW robot, aiming to retain the physical significance of the equation terms.

The schematic of the STTW robot is depicted in Fig. 1. To establish a simplified model, we make the following assumptions: (i) Both the front and rear suspension are locked; (ii) There is no lateral slippage between the wheels and the ground; (iii) The wheels possess negligible thickness. The world coordinate system is denoted as $O - XYZ$. The coordinate system undergoing translation and rotation about the Z axis relative to the world frame is denoted as $o - xyz$, with x axis attached to the robot body. Then the robot rotates a roll angle φ about the x axis of frame $o - xyz$.

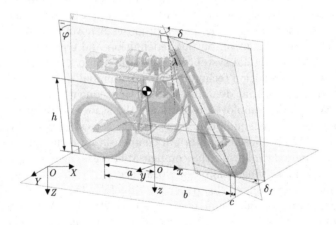

Fig. 1. Schematic of the STTW robot.

From the top view of the robot, as depicted in Fig. 2, in the case of zero steering angle, P_1, P_2 represent the rear and front wheel-ground contact points, respectively. P_3 denotes the intersection point of the steering axis with the ground plane, while P_4 represents the projection point of center of mass onto the wheelbase line. When the handlebar is turned at an angle δ, we assume there is no movement of P_1 and P_2, and the corresponding moved points P_3 and P_4

are denoted as P_3' and P_4', respectively. The projection of steering angle δ on the ground is denoted as δ_p, which satisfies

$$\tan \delta_p \cos \varphi = \tan \delta \cos \lambda. \tag{1}$$

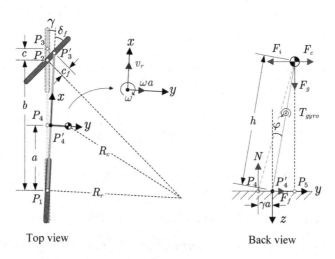

Top view   Back view

Fig. 2. Top view and Back view of the STTW robot.

According to [2], the relationship between the trail length c_f and the steering angle δ can be expressed as

$$c_f = r_f \tan \lambda \cos \delta - \frac{\sqrt{1 - (\sin \delta \sin \lambda)^2}}{\cos \lambda} d \approx c + r_f \tan \lambda (\cos \delta - 1), \tag{2}$$

where c denotes the trail length corresponding to zero steering angle and r_f denotes the front wheel radius. The small angle γ resulting from the steering rotation satisfies

$$\gamma \approx \sin \gamma = \frac{c_f}{b} \sin \delta_f. \tag{3}$$

The turning radius of the rear wheel, denoted as R_r, can be determined by

$$R_r = \frac{b + c - c_f / \cos \delta_f}{\tan \delta_f} \approx \frac{b}{\tan \delta_f}. \tag{4}$$

To obtain the equation of roll motion, we analyse the forces acting on the robot. As illustrated in the back view of the robot in Fig. 2, observing along x axis from the moving frame $o - xyz$, the robot is subject to the gravity F_g, the fictitious inertial force F_i caused by the translational acceleration of frame $o - xyz$, the centrifugal force F_c generated by the rotation of frame $o - xyz$, the normal force N and frictional force F_f between the ground and the wheels. These forces are governed by

$$F_g = mg, \quad F_i = ma_{o,y}, \quad F_c = m\omega^2 h \sin \varphi, \quad N = mg - mh\ddot{\varphi} \sin \varphi, \tag{5}$$

where m is the total mass of the robot, $a_{o,y}$ is translational acceleration of frame $o - xyz$ along the y axis, and ω is the yaw angular velocity of the robot. The translational velocity of P_4 expressed in the $o - xyz$ frame can be described by $\boldsymbol{v}_o = [v_r, \omega a, 0]^T$, where v_r is the forward velocity of the rear wheel, satisfying $v_r = \omega R_r$. Given that frame $o - xyz$ is rotating with an angular velocity $\boldsymbol{\omega} = [0, 0, \omega]^T$, the acceleration of $o - xyz$ relative to the world frame satisfies

$$\boldsymbol{a}_o = \dot{\boldsymbol{v}}_o + \boldsymbol{\omega} \times \boldsymbol{v}_o. \tag{6}$$

Only the component $a_{o,y}$ has an effect on the roll motion. It can be derived as

$$
\begin{aligned}
a_{o,y} &= \omega v_{o,x} + \dot{v}_{c,y} = \omega v_r + \dot{\omega} a \\
&= \frac{v_r^2 \tan \delta \cos \lambda}{b \cos \varphi} + \frac{a \cos \lambda}{b \cos \varphi} \left(\dot{v}_r \tan \delta + \frac{v_r \dot{\delta}}{\cos^2 \delta} \right) + \frac{a v_r \tan \delta \cos \lambda \tan \varphi}{b \cos \varphi} \dot{\varphi}.
\end{aligned}
\tag{7}
$$

By selecting $o - x$ as the axis of rotation and applying Euler's rotation equation, the following equation is obtained:

$$(I_t + mh^2)\ddot{\varphi} = F_g h \sin \varphi + F_c h \cos \varphi + N\gamma a - F_i h \cos \varphi, \tag{8}$$

where I_t is the total moment of inertia about the roll axis through the COM. Collecting Eqs. (1)–(8), the equation of roll motion can be derived as

$$
\begin{aligned}
\left(I_t + mh^2 + mha\gamma s_\varphi \right) \ddot{\varphi} &= -\frac{mhc_\lambda \tan \delta v_r^2}{b} \left(1 - \frac{hc_\lambda \tan \delta \tan \varphi}{b} \right) \\
&- \frac{mahc_\lambda}{b} \left(\left(\tan \delta \dot{v}_r + \frac{\dot{v}_r}{c_\delta^2} \right) + v_r \tan \delta \tan \varphi \dot{\varphi} \right) + mghs_\varphi + \frac{mgac_f s_{\delta_f}}{b},
\end{aligned}
\tag{9}
$$

where the abbreviations s_x and c_x represent $\sin x$ and $\cos x$, respectively.

3   Controller Design

In this paper, small angle approximations and other unmodeled dynamics are treated as a lumped disturbance. We choose $\boldsymbol{x} = [\delta \quad \varphi \quad \dot{\varphi}]^T$ as the state and $u = \dot{\delta}$ as the input. Assuming the robot moves at a constant velocity, after linearizing around the origin, the following linear system is obtained:

$$
\begin{aligned}
\dot{\boldsymbol{x}} &= \boldsymbol{A}\boldsymbol{x} + \boldsymbol{b}_u u + \boldsymbol{b}_d d \\
\boldsymbol{y}_m &= \boldsymbol{C}_m \boldsymbol{x} + \boldsymbol{e}_m g \\
y_o &= \boldsymbol{c}_o \boldsymbol{x},
\end{aligned}
\tag{10}
$$

where

$$
\boldsymbol{A} = \begin{bmatrix} 0 & 0 & 0 \\ 0 & 0 & 1 \\ a_1 & a_2 & 0 \end{bmatrix}, \boldsymbol{b}_u = \begin{bmatrix} 1 \\ 0 \\ b_1 \end{bmatrix}, \boldsymbol{b}_d = \begin{bmatrix} 0 \\ 0 \\ 1 \end{bmatrix}, \boldsymbol{C}_m = \begin{bmatrix} 1 & 0 & 0 \\ 0 & 1 & 0 \end{bmatrix}, \boldsymbol{e}_m = \begin{bmatrix} 0 \\ 1 \end{bmatrix}, \boldsymbol{c}_o = \begin{bmatrix} 1 & 0 & 0 \end{bmatrix},
$$

$\boldsymbol{y}_m, \boldsymbol{y}_o, d$ and g represent the measurable output vector, the controlled output, the lumped disturbance and the constant sensor error in the measurement of roll angle, respectively. a_1, a_2 and b_1 are nonzero coefficients. It should be noted that the error g cannot be calibrated in advance due to the movement of the COM caused by the variation of the payload. Additionally, d satisfies the following assumption.

Assumption 1. *The disturbance d is differentiable and bounded, and converges to a steady value as t increases, i.e. $\lim_{t \to \infty} d = d^*$. Its derivative $h = \dot{d}$ is bounded and converges to zero, i.e. $\lim_{t \to \infty} h = 0$.*

This system exhibits the following distinguishing characteristics compared to the systems studied in SMC, which are often formulated as chains of integrators: (i) This system incorporates the presence of sensor errors in the measurable output, which has received limited consideration in previous studies. (ii) The STTW robot is a non-minimum phase system, which cannot be transformed into the typical form of chain of integrators. (iii) The disturbance d encountered in this system is identified as a mismatched disturbance since $\boldsymbol{b}_u$ and $\boldsymbol{b}_d$ are linearly independent. As a result, direct compensation of the disturbance using the control input is not feasible (see [1]). To tackle these challenging issues, the EC-SMC scheme is proposed, as illustrated in Fig. 3. The design procedure of the controller can be summarized in three steps.

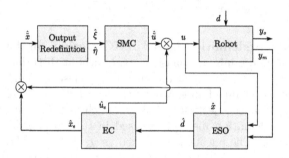

Fig. 3. Block diagram of EC-SMC.

Step 1: State Transformation and ESO Design. To simultaneously handle the disturbance and sensor error, the following new state $\boldsymbol{x}'$ is introduced:

$$\boldsymbol{x}' = \boldsymbol{x} + \boldsymbol{x}_g, \boldsymbol{x}_g = \begin{bmatrix} 0 & g & 0 \end{bmatrix}^T. \tag{11}$$

Then system (10) can be transformed into

$$\begin{aligned} \dot{\boldsymbol{x}}' &= \boldsymbol{A}\boldsymbol{x}' + \boldsymbol{b}_u u + \boldsymbol{b}_d d' \\ \boldsymbol{y}_m &= \boldsymbol{C}_m \boldsymbol{x}' \\ \boldsymbol{y}_o &= \boldsymbol{c}_o \boldsymbol{x}', \end{aligned} \tag{12}$$

where $d' = d + a_2 g$ represents the equivalent disturbance. This transformation implies that the sensor error can be treated as an additive disturbance in the roll channel.

By defining the extended state as $\bar{x} = [x'^T, d'^T]^T$, the extended system is written as

$$\dot{\bar{x}} = \bar{A}\bar{x} + \bar{b}_u u + \bar{b}_d h$$
$$y_m = \bar{C}_m \bar{x}, \tag{13}$$

where $h = \dot{d}'$ and

$$\bar{A} = \begin{bmatrix} A & b_d \\ 0 & 0 \end{bmatrix}, \bar{b}_u = \begin{bmatrix} b_u \\ 0 \end{bmatrix}, \bar{b}_d = \begin{bmatrix} 0 \\ 1 \end{bmatrix}, \bar{C}_m = [C_m \ 0].$$

The ESO is designed as

$$\dot{\hat{\bar{x}}} = \bar{A}\hat{\bar{x}} + \bar{b}_u u + L(y_m - \hat{y}_m)$$
$$\hat{y}_m = \bar{C}_m \hat{\bar{x}}, \tag{14}$$

where $\hat{\bar{x}} = [\hat{x}', \hat{d}']$ is the estimation of the extended state $\bar{x}$ and the matrix L is the observer gain, which is appropriately designed to ensure that the matrix $\bar{A}_c = \bar{A} - L\bar{C}_m$ is Hurwtiz. Subtracting (14) from (13) results in

$$\dot{\bar{e}} = \bar{A}_c \bar{e} + \bar{b}_d h, \tag{15}$$

$$\bar{e} = \bar{x} - \hat{\bar{x}}, e_x = x' - \hat{x}', e_d = d' - \hat{d}'. \tag{16}$$

Step 2: Output-Redefinition-Based SMC Design. In this step, a nominal SMC for the non-minimum phase system without disturbance is designed. Given that the STTW robot is a non-minimum phase system that cannot be transformed into a chain of integrators, the conventional SMC method with mismatched disturbance rejection techniques, such as [13], cannot be applied.

The output redefinition method, as used in [14], is applied to the STTW robot in this paper. The output is redefined as $y'_o = [0 \ -a_2/a_1 \ 0]x$ satisfying $\lim_{t\to\infty} y'_o = \lim_{t\to\infty} y_o$. Then the system can be transformed into its *normal form* represented by

$$\dot{\xi} = \begin{bmatrix} 0 & 1 \\ a_2 & \dfrac{a_1}{b_1} \end{bmatrix} \xi + \begin{bmatrix} 0 \\ -a_2 \end{bmatrix} \eta + \begin{bmatrix} 0 \\ -\dfrac{a_2 b_1}{a_1} \end{bmatrix} u$$

$$\dot{\eta} = -\frac{a_1}{b_1}\eta + \begin{bmatrix} \dfrac{a_1}{b_1} & \dfrac{a_1^2}{b_1^2 a_2} \end{bmatrix} \xi, \tag{17}$$

where $\xi = [y'^T_o, \dot{y}'^T_o]^T$ and $\eta = x'_1 - b_1^{-1} x'_3$ are the external state and the internal state, respectively. Since $a_1/b_1 > 0$ is determined by the physical model, the zero dynamics is asymptotically stable. Therefore, our primary objective becomes stabilizing the external dynamics. To achieve this, the sliding surface is defined as

$$s = \xi_2 + \alpha\xi_1 = 0, \tag{18}$$

and the nominal control law is designed as

$$u_n(\boldsymbol{\xi}, \eta) = \frac{a_1}{b_1 a_2} \left(a_2 \xi_1 + \left(\frac{a_1}{b_1} + \alpha \right) \xi_2 - a_2 \eta + \beta \text{sign}(s) \right), \tag{19}$$

with $\alpha > 0$, $\beta > 0$ being the tuning parameters.

Step 3: Equilibrium-Compensation-Based Control. In order to achieve accurate tracking control, it is necessary to drive the system towards the equilibrium $(\boldsymbol{x}'_e, u_e)$, satisfying

$$\begin{bmatrix} \boldsymbol{A} & \boldsymbol{b}_u \\ \boldsymbol{c}_o & 0 \end{bmatrix} \begin{bmatrix} \boldsymbol{x}'_e \\ u_e \end{bmatrix} + \begin{bmatrix} \boldsymbol{b}_d \\ 0 \end{bmatrix} d' = 0. \tag{20}$$

In practical applications, the actual disturbance d' is not available. Thus we are restricted to achieving the estimated equilibrium as

$$\begin{bmatrix} \hat{\boldsymbol{x}}'_e \\ \hat{u}_e \end{bmatrix} = - \begin{bmatrix} \boldsymbol{A} & \boldsymbol{b}_u \\ \boldsymbol{c}_o & 0 \end{bmatrix}^{-1} \begin{bmatrix} \boldsymbol{b}_d \\ 0 \end{bmatrix} \hat{d}'. \tag{21}$$

Subsequently, the compensated state is constructed as

$$\hat{\tilde{\boldsymbol{x}}}' = \hat{\boldsymbol{x}}' - \hat{\boldsymbol{x}}'_e, \hat{\tilde{u}} = u - \hat{u}_e. \tag{22}$$

As depicted in Fig. 3, we apply the nominal controller based on the compensated state and control. Thus, the control input applied to the robot is formulated as

$$u = \hat{\tilde{u}} + \hat{u}_e = u_n(\tilde{\boldsymbol{\xi}}, \hat{\eta}) + \hat{u}_e, \tag{23}$$

where

$$\tilde{\boldsymbol{\xi}} = -\frac{a_2}{a_1} \begin{bmatrix} \hat{\tilde{x}}'_2 \\ \hat{\tilde{x}}'_3 \end{bmatrix}, \tilde{\eta} = \hat{\tilde{x}}'_1 - b_1^{-1} \hat{\tilde{x}}'_3. \tag{24}$$

Substituting (16) into (22) yields

$$\hat{\tilde{\boldsymbol{x}}}' = \boldsymbol{x}' - \boldsymbol{e}_x - \hat{\boldsymbol{x}}'_e, \tag{25}$$

Through the combination of (12), (15), (21) and (23), the derivative of $\hat{\tilde{\boldsymbol{x}}}'$ can be derived as

$$\begin{aligned} \dot{\hat{\tilde{\boldsymbol{x}}}}' &= \left(\boldsymbol{A}\boldsymbol{x}' + \boldsymbol{b}_u u + \boldsymbol{b}_d d' \right) - \left(\boldsymbol{A}\boldsymbol{e}_x + \boldsymbol{b}_d e_d - \boldsymbol{L}_x \boldsymbol{C}_m \bar{\boldsymbol{e}} \right) - \dot{\hat{\boldsymbol{x}}}'_e - \left(\boldsymbol{A}\hat{\boldsymbol{x}}'_e + \boldsymbol{b}_u \hat{u}_e + \boldsymbol{b}_d \hat{d}' \right) \\ &= \boldsymbol{A}(\boldsymbol{x}' - \boldsymbol{e}_x - \hat{\boldsymbol{x}}'_e) + \boldsymbol{b}_u (u - \hat{u}_e) + \boldsymbol{b}_d (d' - e_d - \hat{d}') + \boldsymbol{L}_x \boldsymbol{C}_m \bar{\boldsymbol{e}} - \dot{\hat{\boldsymbol{x}}}_e \\ &= \boldsymbol{A}\hat{\tilde{\boldsymbol{x}}}' + \boldsymbol{b}_u u_n(\tilde{\boldsymbol{\xi}}, \tilde{\eta}) + \boldsymbol{L}_x \boldsymbol{C}_m \bar{\boldsymbol{e}} - \dot{\hat{\boldsymbol{x}}}_e. \end{aligned} \tag{26}$$

For the sake of simplicity, (26) can be concisely expressed as

$$\dot{\hat{\tilde{\boldsymbol{x}}}}' = \boldsymbol{A}\hat{\tilde{\boldsymbol{x}}}' + \boldsymbol{b}_u u_n(\tilde{\boldsymbol{\xi}}, \tilde{\eta}) + \varepsilon \tag{27}$$

$$\varepsilon = \boldsymbol{L}_x \boldsymbol{C}_m \bar{\boldsymbol{e}} - \dot{\hat{\boldsymbol{x}}}_e. \tag{28}$$

The disturbance ε satisfies the following lemma:

Lemma 1. *Assume that Assumption 1 is satisfied. Consider system* (10) *under the ESO* (14), *the disturbance ε in the error system* (27) *is bounded and satisfies* $\lim_{t \to \infty} \varepsilon = 0$.

Proof. Since the observation error system (15) has a globally exponentially stable equilibrium point at the origin and the function $\sigma(e, h) = \bar{A}_c \bar{e} + \bar{b}_d h$ is globally Lipschitz, it can be deduced from [9, Lemma 4.5] that system (15) is input-to-state stable (ISS). Therefore, under the assumption that h remains bounded and $\lim_{t \to \infty} h = 0$, it follows that $\bar{e}$ is also bounded and $\lim_{t \to \infty} \bar{e} = 0$, implying $\hat{d}'$ is bounded and $\lim_{t \to \infty} \hat{d}' = d'$. Furthermore, by utilizing (21), we can conclude that $\dot{\hat{x}}_e$ is bounded and $\lim_{t \to \infty} \dot{\hat{x}}_e = 0$. Therefore, $\varepsilon = L_x C_m \bar{e} - \dot{\hat{x}}_e$ is bounded, and $\lim_{t \to \infty} \varepsilon = 0$.

By denoting the upper bound of ε as $|\varepsilon| \le U_\varepsilon$, we can establish the following theorem:

Theorem 1. *Assume that Assumption 1 holds. Consider system* (10) *under the ESO* (14), *if the parameters of the controller* (23) *satisfy $\alpha > 0$ and $\beta > \alpha U_{\varepsilon,1} + U_{\varepsilon,2}$, then system* (26) *is asymptotically stable and the controlled output of system* (10) *has no steady error, i.e.* $\lim_{t \to \infty} y_o = 0$.

Proof. Substituting the control law (19) into system (27) yields

$$\dot{\tilde{\xi}} = f_\xi(\tilde{\xi}) + \varepsilon_\xi, \tag{29}$$

$$\dot{\tilde{\eta}} = f_\eta(\tilde{\eta}, \xi) + \varepsilon_\eta. \tag{30}$$

where

$$\tilde{s} = \tilde{\xi}_2 + \alpha \tilde{\xi}_1, \quad f(\tilde{\xi}) = \begin{bmatrix} \tilde{\xi}_2 \\ -\beta \mathrm{sign}(\tilde{s}) - \alpha \tilde{\xi}_2 \end{bmatrix}, \quad f(\tilde{\eta}, \tilde{\xi}) = -\frac{a_1}{b_1} \tilde{\eta} + \begin{bmatrix} \frac{a_1}{b_1} & \frac{a_1^2}{b_1^2 a_2} \end{bmatrix} \tilde{\xi}. \tag{31}$$

Consider a Lyapunov candidate function $V(\tilde{s}) = 1/2 \tilde{s}^2$ of the external subsystem (29). Taking the derivative of $V(\tilde{s})$ along the trajectories of (29)–(31) yields

$$
\begin{aligned}
\dot{V} &= \tilde{s}(-\beta \mathrm{sign}(\tilde{s}) + (\alpha \varepsilon_1 + \varepsilon_2)) \\
&\le -(\beta - \alpha U_{\varepsilon,1} - U_{\varepsilon,2})|\tilde{s}| \le -\sqrt{2}(\beta - \alpha U_{\varepsilon,1} - U_{\varepsilon,2})\sqrt{V}.
\end{aligned}
\tag{32}
$$

Since $\beta > \alpha U_{\varepsilon,1} + U_{\varepsilon,2}$, the state will reach and stay at the sliding surface in finite time. Then the sliding dynamics and the internal dynamics satisfy

$$\dot{\tilde{\xi}}_1 = -\alpha \tilde{\xi}_1$$

$$\dot{\tilde{\eta}} = -\frac{a_1}{b_1} \tilde{\eta} + \begin{bmatrix} \frac{a_1}{b_1} & \frac{a_1^2}{b_1^2 a_2} \end{bmatrix} \tilde{\xi}. \tag{33}$$

Under the condition that $\alpha > 0$ and $a_1/b_1 > 0$, according to [9, Lemma 4.5], system (33) is ISS, resulting in $\lim_{t \to \infty}(\tilde{\hat{x}}') = 0$. Consequently, we obtain $\lim_{t \to \infty}(x') = \lim_{t \to \infty}(\hat{\hat{x}}' + e_x + \hat{x}'_e) = x'_e$. By applying (20), it follows that the controlled output satisfies $\lim_{t \to \infty}(y_o) = 0$, indicating the absence of steady-state error.

4   Experimental Validations

The outdoor experiments are conducted on an autonomous motorcycle prototype depicted in Fig. 4(a), with the robot's parameter values provided in Table 1. The robot is equipped with an IMU, providing a static roll accuracy of 0.2° and a dynamic roll accuracy of 0.6°. The steering joint incorporates a 37:1 reducer and an encoder with a resolution of 19 bits. To validate the effectiveness of the proposed control method, both the EC-SMC and the conventional SMC without EC are implemented on a real-time Linux computer. The controller operates at a frequency of 200 Hz. In order to mitigate the chattering problem associated with SMC, we replace the sign function in (19) with a saturation function defined as $\text{sat}(s) = \text{sign}(s) \cdot \min(|s|/\epsilon, 1), \epsilon > 0$. In the experiments, the controller parameters are chosen as $\alpha = 2.3, \beta = 6, \epsilon = 1$. The experiments are carried out in an outdoor environment as illustrated in Fig. 4(b), characterized by uneven terrain with a slight inclination and occasional potholes. Moreover, the robot is exposed to gusts, which pose a substantial external disturbance.

(a)   (b)

Fig. 4. (a) The STTW robot prototype. (b) Experimental environment.

Table 1. Parameter values of the STTW robot

Parameter	h (m)	a (m)	b (m)	c (m)	λ (°)	r_r (m)	m (kg)	I_t (kg $\cdot$ m^2)
Value	0.743	0.534	1.3	0.08	23	0.319	97	8.44

Figure 5 presents the comparative experimental results of tracking a step signal under the two controllers, conventional SMC and EC-SMC. The reference signal for the steering angle begins at 0° for the first 7 s, then steps up to 10° and remains constant for approximately 20 s. Afterward, it returns to 0° and remains there for about 10 s. Subsequently, it steps down to −10° and maintains that value for about 20 s. Finally, it returns back to 0°. It should be noted that, due to size limitations of the experimental environment, the reference signal is provided via a 2.4 GHz remote controller. As a result, the reference signals for the two experiments cannot be entirely identical.

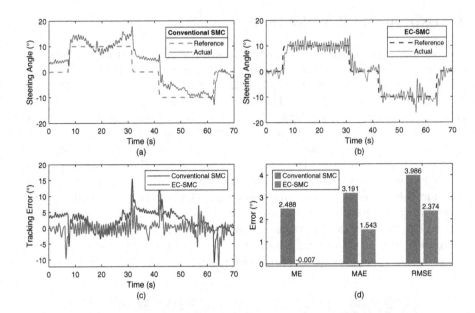

Fig. 5. Comparison of the conventional SMC and the EC-SMC tracking a step reference signal. (a)–(b) Steering angle tracking under conventional SMC and EC-SMC. (c) Steering angle tracking errors under two controllers. (d) ME, MAE and RMSE of tracking errors under two controllers.

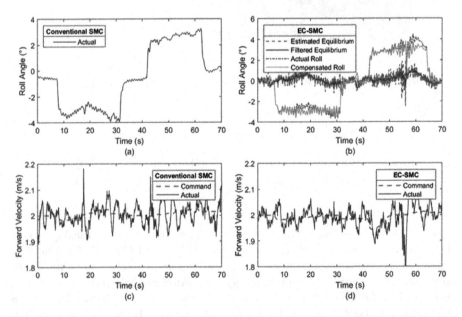

Fig. 6. Key variables during steering tracking. (a) Roll angle under conventional SMC. (b) Roll angle related variables under EC-SMC. (c) and (d) are the rear velocity under conventional SMC and EC-SMC respectively. (Color figure online)

Figures 5(a)–(b) depict the contrasting tracking performance of the conventional SMC and the EC-SMC. The conventional SMC fails to accurately track the reference, whereas the EC-SMC demonstrates accurate tracking capabilities. To further analyze and compare the tracking performance in detail, Fig. 5(c) illustrates the tracking errors and Fig. 5(d) presents several statistics of errors including ME (mean error), MAE (mean absolute error) and RMSE (root mean square error). Notably, the tracking error of the EC-SMC oscillates around zero, with an almost negligible mean error of $-0.007°$, indicating that the EC-SMC achieves zero steady-state error. In contrast, the conventional SMC exhibits a maximum error exceeding $15°$ and a mean error of $2.488°$. Additionally, the EC-SMC demonstrates approximately a 50% reduction in both MAE and RMSE compared to the corresponding metrics of the conventional SMC.

The variations of other key variables during steering angle tracking are plotted in Fig. 6. From Fig. 6(a) and Fig. 5(a), it can be observed that the roll angle and the steering angle exhibit the same trend under the conventional SMC. This observation provides an insight into the underlying cause of the inaccurate tracking performance of conventional SMC. It reveals that the disturbances exert an influence on the roll angle, and subsequently affects the steering angle. Figure 6(b) illustrates the variations of roll angle related variables under the EC-SMC, where the red dashed line represents the roll angle element of the original estimated equilibrium, $\hat{\varphi}_e$, which is significantly affected by high-frequency disturbances, such as the forward velocity variation shown in Fig. 6(d). To mitigate the impact of high frequency noise, a low-pass filter is applied and the filtered signal is represented by the blue solid curve. The magenta dashed line corresponds to the actual roll angle φ, which exhibits a trend similar to the one of the conventional SMC in Fig. 6(a). The green solid line represents the compensated roll angle $\hat{\bar{\varphi}}$ after utilizing equilibrium compensation, showing a consistent trend with the reference signal, which leads to accurate steering tracking.

5   Conclusion

This paper proposes the EC-SMC control scheme for a non-minimum phase STTW robot with mismatched disturbances and sensor errors. This approach not only ensures accurate tracking and disturbance rejection performance of the STTW robot, but also provides a framework for addressing a wide range of systems. By elaborately integrating the EC, output redefinition technique and ESO, the EC-SMC scheme presents a comprehensive solution that expands the applicability of conventional SMC to general non-minimum systems with mismatched disturbances. Experimental results validate the effectiveness of proposed controller, demonstrating its capability of accurate steering tracking. In the future, we will extend the equilibrium compensation method to general controllers and general systems, thereby expanding the applicability of this method.

References

1. Chen, W.H., Yang, J., Guo, L., Li, S.: Disturbance-observer-based control and related methods–an overview. IEEE Trans. Industr. Electron. **63**(2), 1083–1095 (2015)
2. Cossalter, V.: Motorcycle Dynamics. Lulu.com (2006)
3. Gao, Z., et al.: Scaling and bandwidth-parameterization based controller tuning. In: Proceedings of the 2003 American Control Conference, pp. 4989–4996 (2003)
4. Getz, N.: Control of balance for a nonlinear nonholonomic non-minimum phase model of a bicycle. In: Proceedings of 1994 American Control Conference, vol. 1, pp. 148–151. IEEE (1994)
5. Getz, N.H., Marsden, J.E.: Control for an autonomous bicycle. In: Proceedings of 1995 IEEE International Conference on Robotics and Automation, vol. 2, pp. 1397–1402. IEEE (1995)
6. Ginoya, D., Shendge, P., Phadke, S.: Sliding mode control for mismatched uncertain systems using an extended disturbance observer. IEEE Trans. Industr. Electron. **61**(4), 1983–1992 (2013)
7. Han, J.: From PID to active disturbance rejection control. IEEE Trans. Industr. Electron. **56**(3), 900–906 (2009)
8. He, K., Deng, Y., Wang, G., Sun, X., Sun, Y., Chen, Z.: Learning-based trajectory tracking and balance control for bicycle robots with a pendulum: a gaussian process approach. IEEE/ASME Trans. Mechatron. **27**(2), 634–644 (2022)
9. Khalil, H.K.: Nonlinear Control, vol. 406. Pearson, New York (2015)
10. Tian, Y., Chen, Z., Deng, Y., Wang, B., Liang, B.: Steady-state manifold of riderless motorcycles. In: 2022 IEEE/RSJ International Conference on Intelligent Robots and Systems (IROS), pp. 3491–3496. IEEE (2022)
11. Wang, P., Yi, J., Liu, T., Zhang, Y.: Trajectory tracking and balance control of an autonomous bikebot. In: 2017 IEEE International Conference on Robotics and Automation (ICRA), pp. 2414–2419. IEEE (2017)
12. Yang, J., Li, S., Su, J., Yu, X.: Continuous nonsingular terminal sliding mode control for systems with mismatched disturbances. Automatica **49**(7), 2287–2291 (2013)
13. Yang, J., Li, S., Yu, X.: Sliding-mode control for systems with mismatched uncertainties via a disturbance observer. IEEE Trans. Industr. Electron. **60**(1), 160–169 (2012)
14. Ye, L., Zong, Q., Crassidis, J.L., Tian, B.: Output-redefinition-based dynamic inversion control for a nonminimum phase hypersonic vehicle. IEEE Trans. Industr. Electron. **65**(4), 3447–3457 (2017)
15. Yi, J., Song, D., Levandowski, A., Jayasuriya, S.: Trajectory tracking and balance stabilization control of autonomous motorcycles. In: Proceedings of 2006 IEEE International Conference on Robotics and Automation, pp. 2583–2589. IEEE (2006)
16. Yi, J., Zhang, Y., Song, D.: Autonomous motorcycles for agile maneuvers, part I: Dynamic modeling. In: Proceedings of the 48h IEEE Conference on Decision and Control (CDC) held jointly with 2009 28th Chinese Control Conference, pp. 4613–4618. IEEE (2009)
17. Yu, Y., Zhao, M.: Steering control for autonomously balancing bicycle at low speed. In: 2018 IEEE International Conference on Robotics and Biomimetics (ROBIO), pp. 33–38. IEEE (2018)

18. Zheng, X., Zhu, X., Chen, Z., Sun, Y., Liang, B., Wang, T.: Dynamic modeling of an unmanned motorcycle and combined balance control with both steering and double CMGs. Mech. Mach. Theory **169**, 104643 (2022)

Adaptive Attitude Controller for a Six Wheel-Legged Robot Based on Impedance Control

Haotian Zhi[1], Lin Zhang[1], Jihao Liu[1], Jianping Jing[1,2], and Yanzheng Zhao[1,2(✉)]

[1] School of Mechanical Engineering, Shanghai Jiao Tong University, 800 Dongchuan Road, Shanghai, China
yzh-zhao@sjtu.edu.cn

[2] State Key Laboratory of Mechanical System and Vibration, Shanghai Jiao Tong University, 800 Dongchuan Road, Shanghai, China

Abstract. To remain the attitude of the robot during moving, an adaptive controller is proposed for a wheeled-legged robot on an irregular terrain. Our contributions are as follows: we develop a six-wheeled legged robot based on PRR structure and an adaptive attitude controller. The controller is comprised of three modules: which are adaptive impedance controller module, attitude controller module and centroid height controller module. When moving in wheeled mode, attitude adjustment primarily relies on elongation of each leg, it is crucial to avoid any suspended legs. An adaptive impedance control (AIC) is employed to track the leg force, adapt to terrain changes-induced disturbances, and compensate for terrain uncertainty by self-adaptively adjusting target damping. The comparative simulations were conducted to verify the effectiveness and robustness of the proposed adaptive controller in maintaining the robot's attitude stability across various motion modes. AIC could track the desired force within 0.3 s and the force error is less than 20 N. The robotic attitude angles are maintained within a range of $\pm0.5°$ and the centroid height error fluctuates within -2 mm to $+5$ mm.

Keywords: Six wheel-legged robot · Adaptive attitude controller · Adaptive impedance control

1 Introduction

Mobile robots can be categorized into wheeled robots and legged robots based on their locomotion methods. Wheeled robots are suitable for operating on flat terrain, with smooth, efficient and fast characteristics. However, they encounter difficulties in navigating complex terrains. Legged robots' bionic structures provide a high degree of versatility and exhibit significant advantages in locomotion within irregular environments [1]. Nonetheless, legged robots generally have slower movement speeds compared to wheeled robots.

Wheel-legged robots combine the advantages of both types, maintaining high maneuverability on flat surfaces while demonstrating adaptability to complex terrains. Kun,

© The Author(s), under exclusive license to Springer Nature Singapore Pte Ltd. 2023
H. Yang et al. (Eds.): ICIRA 2023, LNAI 14274, pp. 202–213, 2023.
https://doi.org/10.1007/978-981-99-6501-4_18

X. et al. [2, 3] designed a six wheel-legged variable-structure robot called NOROS. It can switch between wheel and leg locomotion modes by changing the leg configuration. Similar robots include PAW [4], ANYmal [5], and Momaro [6], all featuring a combination of wheels and articulated legs, enabling swift switches between legged motion and wheeled motion. Liu D C et al. [7] designed BITNAZA, a robot with strong load capacity, where each leg is a Stewart platform with a wheel attached at the end.

To operate effectively in irregular environments, it is essential to maintain the stability of wheeled-legged robots to avoid issues such as foot suspension, wheel slippage, and tilting. Grand, C. et al. [8] proposed a velocity-based robot attitude control algorithm for their wheel-legged robot named Hylos, to enable walking control on irregular sloped terrains. Cui, L et al. [9] explored adaptive optimal control for wheel-legged robots using reinforcement learning, providing a learning-based solution for adaptive optimal control. The first method does not consider the interaction force between the robot and the environment, and the second method uses reinforcement learning method. Although the final result is good, the control process is complex. The impedance control theory proposed by Hogan et al. [10–12] has been widely applied to robot stability control. Irawan, A. et al. [13] applied impedance control to a hexapod robot, achieving body attitude stability control during walking on uneven terrains. However, uncertain environmental information can result in force tracking errors that affect stability. Jung S. [14] and Duan J. [15] proposed adaptive impedance control with adjustable damping parameter for stable control of the robotic manipulator. However, they neglected the stiffness term in impedance theory, making it unsuitable for controlling wheeled-legged robots that interact with the environment through multiple contact points. Xu, K. et al. [16] applied adaptive impedance control with adjustable stiffness parameters to BITNAZA [7], but theoretically, alterations to the stiffness may impact the robot's compliance. Therefore, in this paper, we propose an adaptive impedance control with adjustable damping parameter while retaining the stiffness term for our six wheel-legged robot. The primary contributions of this paper are summarized as follows:

1. We have developed a new structure of a six-legged wheeled robot.
2. We propose a novel adaptive attitude controller based on adaptive impedance controller module for the stable body control of the six-legged wheeled robot, including attitude controller module and centroid height controller module.
3. Simulation experiments demonstrate that our controller ensures the stability of the robot's body and exhibits fast, stable, and accurate performance.

The rest of the paper is organized as follows: In Sect. 2, a six wheeled-legged robot system is briefly introduced. Section 3 introduces adaptive attitude controller based on adaptive impedance controller module. Section 4 shows the simulation results, to confirm the effectiveness of the proposed controller. Finally, conclusions are made to summarize and discuss in Sect. 5.

2 Six Wheel-Legged Robot System

2.1 Mechanism of Six Wheel-Legged Robot

As shown in Fig. 1, the proposed six wheel-legged robot is designed for operations inside box girder, the control system is equipped with six electric cylinders and eighteen motors. The model of steel box girder is shown in Fig. 2.

Each leg of the robot consists of three-degree-of-freedom PRR linkage mechanism and one active wheel, where P denotes the prismatic joint, R denotes the revolute joint. As shown in Fig. 1 (b), R1 and R2 represent the first and second revolute joint on each leg, respectively. The main properties of the proposed robot are listed in Table 1. Each linkage is driven by one electric cylinder and two motors, respectively.

The robot can stably walk in wheeled mode, when encountering lower obstacles such as rocks and the speed hump. We adjust the linkage to regulate the robot posture, which means we remain the robot attitude by the adaptive leg posture on a rough terrain. When encountering high obstacles such as internal partitions inside the box girder, it can transition into legged mode to overcome them: The front two legs raise prismatic joints (P), R1 rotate the wheel to the forward direction, after stepping over the internal partition, P drops to make the wheel touch the ground. The middle and back legs move in this way in turn.

For the proposed robot, the combination of wheeled mode and legged mode is helpful to realize a flexible movement.

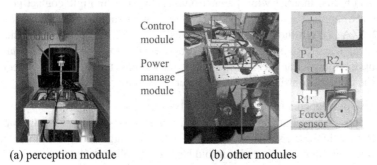

        (a) perception module   (b) other modules

Fig. 1. Six wheel-legged robot.

The robot system consists of the motion module, control module, perception module, and power manage module. The control module is developed based on the Beckhoff platform with TwinCAT 3. Due to the high-level real-time capability offered by the TwinCAT 3 software, we can realize precise motion and posture control with exceptional accuracy.

To maintain balance and stability subject to various terrains, the perception module is developed to include a laser radar, an inertial measuring unit (IMU), feet force sensors, and a depth camera, etc. The robot can perceive its environment to achieve a function of navigation. The IMU is utilized for obtaining attitude angles of the robot. Meanwhile, force sensors are employed to measure the ground reaction forces.

Table 1. Main properties of the proposed robot.

Item	Values	Item	Values
Length (m)	1.52	Motion Mode	2
Width (m)	0.67	Max Velocity (m/s)	2
Height (m)	0.86	Self-weight (kg)	180
Stroke of Electric Cylinder (mm)	900	Load Capacity (kg)	100
Stroke of R1 (°)	−180–180	Stroke of R2 (°)	−180–180

In addition, the communication network includes EtherCAT network and RS485 network. The communication between IMU and CPU relies on RS485 network, other cases rely on EtherCAT network.

2.2 Ground Reaction Model of Wheel-Legs

To model the contact force between the leg and the ground, the leg is regarded as a second-order mass-spring-damper system, while the ground is equivalent to a spring, as shown in Fig. 3. Meanwhile, coordinates systems are defined for the derivation, where the coordinate system {B} represents the robot's body coordinate system, and the coordinate system {W} represents the world coordinate system. The Z axis is defined by the gravid direction. Unless specified otherwise, the parameters in this article are assumed to be defined in the z-direction.

Fig. 2. The wooden model of steel box girder

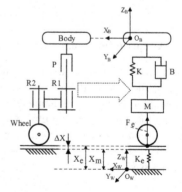

Fig. 3. Ground reaction model

Further, the model can be expressed as follows:

$$F_e = K_e(X_e - X_m) \tag{1}$$

where K_e is the stiffness of the ground, X_m and X_e are the positions of the wheel the environment respectively. F_e is the interaction force obtained by a force sensor.

3   Adaptive controller for various terrains

To realize a stable robot attitude, we develop an adaptive controller including an adaptive impedance controller (AIC) module, an attitude controller module, and a centroid height controller module, as shown in Fig. 4.

The operator gives the desired forces F_d and the desired height Z_C^d, the adaptive impedance controller module combines the contact forces F_e and the positions of wheel X_m, then the controller generates the command position X_c; the attitude controller module generates the position correction amount Δl_i according to the attitude angles *roll* and *pitch*; finally, the centroid height controller module generates the position of each leg P_i by combining the desired height Z_C^d, Δl_i and X_c. The position controller receives the position of each leg P_i and adjusts the linkage to regulate the robot posture.

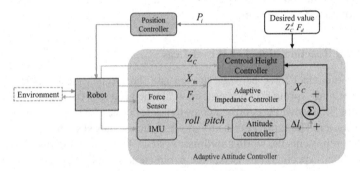

Fig. 4. Overview of the adaptive attitude control system

3.1   Adaptive Impedance Controller Module

During moving, the occurrence of wheel suspension state can introduce some disturbances, such as insufficient driving force and body oscillations. To overcome these problems, it is crucial to adaptively regulate the leg posture. Further, by tracking the contact force of the leg, we utilize the position-based impedance control law to realize the stead contacting state between the wheel and the ground. According to the impedance control theory, the relationship between the contact force F_e and the position error E can be expressed as follows:

$$M\ddot{E}(t) + B\dot{E}(t) + KE(t) = F_e(t) \tag{2}$$

where M, D and K refer to the target mass, damping, stiffness parameters in the z-direction respectively. $E = X_m - X_d$ refers to position disturbance caused by contact forces, X_d refer to desired position. In the position control mode, the command position $X_c = X_m$, thus E can be used to modify X_d to produce $X_c = X_d + E$, which is then tracked by the servo driver system.

To maintain the contact force within a desired range, a desired force F_d is introduced. The force-tracking error is $\Delta F = F_e - F_d$, which is the input of the impedance model.

As a result, the model for impedance control as follows:

$$M\ddot{E}(t) + B\dot{E}(t) + KE(t) = \Delta F(t) \tag{3}$$

The transfer-function $G(s) = 1/(Ms^2 + Bs + K)$, then the force-tracking error is expressed as:

$$\Delta F = F_e - F_d = K_e(X_e - X_c) - F_d = K_e X_e - K_e(X_d + G(s)\Delta F) - F_d \tag{4}$$

Submitting $G(s)$ into Eq. (4), yields:

$$\Delta F(Ms^2 + Bs + K + K_e) = (Ms^2 + Bs + K)[K_e(X_e - X_d) - F_d] \tag{5}$$

The steady-state force tracking error is $\Delta F_{ss} = K[K_e(X_e - X_d) - F_d]/(K + K_e)$, if ΔF_{ss} error is to be zero, it is necessary to satisfy: $X_d = X_e - F_d/K_e$. Therefore, desired position X_d can be designed to achieve F_d only if K_e and X_e are accurately known. However, K_e and X_e are not accurately known, which can lead to force tracking errors.

It is difficult to obtain desired position X_d, because of the unknown environmental information. Therefore, replacing X_d with the initial contact location X_e, the new impedance equation can be written as follows:

$$M\left(\ddot{X}_c - \ddot{X}_e\right) + B\left(\dot{X}_c - \dot{X}_e\right) + K(X_c - X_e) = F_e - F_d \tag{6}$$

Due to the complexity of the virtual ground, X_e is time-varying, $\dot{X}_e \neq 0$ and $\ddot{X}_e \neq 0$, so estimation on the contact location may be not accurate. Therefore, suppose the environment location is $\tilde{X}_e = X_e - \delta X_e$, where $\delta X_e > 0$ to ensure contact between the robot and the environmental surface. The position error can be expressed as $\tilde{E} = E + \delta X_e$, replacing E with $\tilde{E}$ in Eq. (6) yields:

$$\Delta F = F_e - F_d = M\ddot{\tilde{E}} + B\dot{\tilde{E}} + K\tilde{E} = M\ddot{E} + B\dot{E} + KE + \delta\left(M\ddot{X}_e + B\dot{X}_e + KX_e\right) \tag{7}$$

To compensate for the error term in Eq. (7) and ensure system stability [13], AIC is proposed, the damping parameter is adjusted according to the force error in real time:

$$\begin{cases} F_e(t) - F_d(t) = M\ddot{\tilde{E}}(t) + \tilde{B}(t)\dot{\tilde{E}}(t) + K\tilde{E}(t) \\ \tilde{B}(t) = B(t) + \Delta B(t) \\ \Delta B(t) = B \cdot \Phi(t)/\dot{\tilde{E}}(t) \\ \Phi(t) = \Phi(t - \tau) + \alpha[F_d(t - \tau) - F_e(t - \tau)]/B \end{cases} \tag{8}$$

where τ is the sampling period of the controller and α is the update rate.

To facilitate the process of programming control systems, Eq. (8) can be converted to discrete format as:

$$\begin{cases} \ddot{X}_c(t) = \ddot{X}_e(t) + [\Delta F(t) - \tilde{B}(t)\left(\dot{X}_c(t-1) - \dot{X}_e(t)\right) - K(X_c(t-1) - X_e(t))]/M \\ \dot{X}_c(t) = \dot{X}_c(t-1) + \ddot{X}_c(t)T \\ X_c(t) = X_c(t-1) + \dot{X}_c(t)T \end{cases} \tag{9}$$

where T is the system communication period between the controller and the cylinder drivers. Then the adaptive impedance control block diagram is shown in Fig. 5.

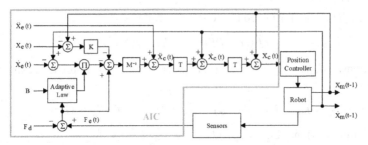

Fig. 5. The adaptive impedance control block diagram

3.2 Attitude Controller Module and h Controller Module

To satisfy the requirement on the stable operation on the mobile platform, it is essential to remain a steady robot attitude of the robot. Thus, we develop an attitude controller for adaptive attitude regulation. As shown in Fig. 6, the origin of the coordinate system O_B is located at the COG (Center Of Geometry) of the six legs, the *roll* angle is around the X-axis, and the *pitch* angle is around the Y-axis.

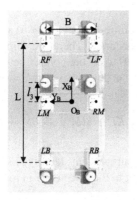

Fig. 6. 3D model diagram of the robot

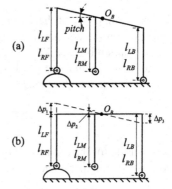

Fig. 7. Illustration of posture adjustment

Figure 7 (a) represents the alteration in body posture when the two front legs *LF* and *RF* of the robot across the obstacle at the same time, when *pitch* < 0. To remain the robot attitude, the lengths of six legs are regulated. As shown in Fig. 7 (b), the front legs *LF* and *RF* are shortened simultaneously by Δp_1, *LM* and *RM* are shortened by Δp_2, *LB* and *RB* are elongated by Δp_3.

It can be considered that each leg is elongated, and the degree of elongation can be written as follows:

$$\begin{cases} \Delta p = (L/2 + l_3) \sin(pitch) \\ \Delta p' = l_3 \sin(pitch) \end{cases} \tag{10}$$

The elongations of the front, middle and back legs are $\Delta p_1 = \Delta p$, $\Delta p_2 = \Delta p'$, $\Delta p_3 = -\Delta p$, respectively.

Similarly, if the left side of the robot's body is higher than the right side, when *roll* > 0, the left legs *LF*, *LM*, *LB* can be shortened and the right leg can be elongated respectively. It can be considered that each leg is elongated, and the elongations of the left and right legs are $\Delta r_1 = -\Delta r$, $\Delta r_2 = \Delta r$, respectively. Δr can be written as follows:

$$\Delta r = B \cdot \sin(roll)/2 \tag{11}$$

Meanwhile, if the AIC module of the six wheel-legged robot is already capable of accurately tracking the desired force, while the body attitude controller maintains attitude of the robot's body, simultaneously shortening and elongating all six legs would still meet the requirements of both controllers. However, the movement joints of the legs maybe exceed their strokes, thereby affecting the normal operation of the impedance controller and attitude controller. So it is crucial for the centroid height controller to continuously regulate the leg lengths to remain the desired height Z_C^d. The input to output of the central controller is shown as follows:

$$P_i = Z_C^d - Z_C + \Delta l_i + X_c \tag{12}$$

Therefore, the specific algorithm is shown in Algorithm 1.

Algorithm 1: attitude control and centroid height controller algorithm

---

1: Acquire attitude angle (*roll, pitch*) and centroid height Z_C ;

2: Send *pitch* to Eq.(10) and *roll* to Eq.(11), send Z_C and Z_C^d to Eq.(12);

3: Obtain Δp , $\Delta p'$, Δr ; ΔZ ;

4: Calculate elongations of each leg:
   $\Delta l_{LF} = -\Delta r + \Delta p$, $\Delta l_{LM} = -\Delta r + \Delta p'$, $\Delta l_{LB} = -\Delta r - \Delta p$,
   $\Delta l_{RF} = \Delta r + \Delta p$, $\Delta l_{RM} = \Delta r + \Delta p'$, $\Delta l_{RB} = \Delta r - \Delta p$;

5: Send Z_C , Z_C^d , Δl_i and X_c to Eq.(12)

6: **return** P_i, $i = LF, LM, LB, RF, RM, RB$.

---

4 Simulation Verification

Simulations were carried out based on the CoSimulation software (MATLAB and CoppeliaSim). In CoppeliaSim, a simulation environment featuring the six wheel-legged robot and the various rough terrains was created, as shown in Fig. 8.

To evaluate the performance of the proposed adaptive controller, simulations were carried out. A comparison between the adaptive impedance control (AIC) and constant parameter impedance control (CIC) is conducted in terms of the force tracking error.

4.1 Simulation Model Construction

In this simulation, the command parameters were as follows:

The forward speed of wheeled movement was 0.1 m/s, the angular speed of rotation was 0.02 rad/s, so the motion trajectory was a circle C of 5 m radius, the turning mode was Ackermann steering, and the R2 joint of each leg turned the wheel by the corresponding angle. The desired forces F_d of *LF, LM, LB, RF, RM, RB* were 86.6N, 92.5 N, 103 N, 87.3 N, 93.0 N, 103.0 N, respectively. They were determined by the weight distributed on the six legs of the robot during flat ground motion in the simulation environment. The desired height $Z_C^d = 948.5$ mm.

The parameters of the environment were as follows:

Both obstacles were $\dot{X}_e \neq 0$ and $\ddot{X}_e \neq 0$, with the length, width and height of 1000 mm × 345 mm × 100 mm, 500 mm × 300 mm × 50 mm, respectively. In addition, they were located at 20, 30° of the motion trajectory, respectively.

The target impedance parameters were selected as $M = 1$, initial $B = 200$, $K = 2500$. For the AIC, the sampling period of the controller $\tau = 5 \times 10^{-3}s$, the update rate $\alpha = 0.1$.

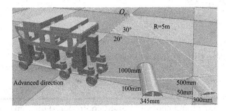

Fig. 8. Simulation environment in CoppeliaSim

4.2 Simulation Results

The process of obstacle traversal during the robot's circular motion by using AIC is shown in Fig. 9. During the motion when encountering obstacles, the wheels were unable to fully adhere to the obstacle surface. Moreover, when encountering longer obstacles, the same leg pair did not cross simultaneously. These scenarios pose significant challenged in terms of controlling the robot to track desired forces and maintain attitude balance.

The simulation results under the control of the adaptive attitude controller are illustrated in Figs. 10–13.

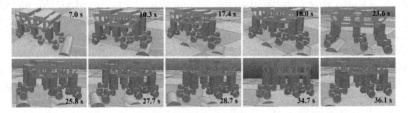

Fig. 9. Simulation scenes of robot motion based on AIC

Figure 10 and 11 depict the forces acting on the LB of the robot during the obstacle traversal process while turning, using CIC and AIC, respectively. The red line represents the desired force, while the blue line represents the contact force.

As shown in Fig. 10, during the traversal of the two obstacles, the contact forces experience significant disturbances. The first disturbance was caused by LF overcome the first obstacle at 7.0 s, the contact force on LB was unable to track the desired force of 103 N and was perturbed for nearly 5 s. Particularly, at 28.7 s, when LB overcame the first obstacle, it resulted in a maximum tracking error of −90 N. It was challenging for CIC to track the desired forces within a short period.

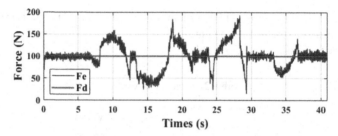

Fig. 10. Force tracking of the left back leg (LB) based on CIC

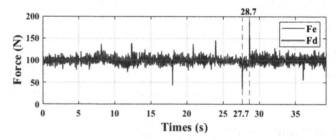

Fig. 11. Force tracking of the left back leg (LB) based on AIC

Compared with CIC, AIC performed very well. The force exerted on LB displays multiple peaks as shown in Fig. 11, corresponding to the moments when wheel overcame the obstacle. The minimum force peak and maximum peak occur at 27.7 s and 28.7 s, corresponding to RB and LB overcame the first obstacle, respectively. Each peak lasted only within 0.3s. During the movement, AIC could track the desired force of 103 N with negligible force errors of less than 20 N during the movement. The result demonstrates a significant improvement compared to CIC. Therefore, the AIC was robust to the various rough terrains.

The variations in centroid height and robotic attitude angle by using adaptive attitude controller based on AIC are illustrated in Fig. 12 and 13, respectively. The robotic attitude angles were maintained within a tolerance of ±0.5° and gradually returned to a horizontal state after being disturbed. The centroid height fluctuates within a narrow range of approximately −2 mm to +5 mm around the desired value. Compared to the

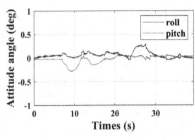

Fig. 12. Robotic attitude angle

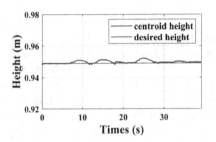

Fig. 13. Centroid height

heights of obstacles (100 mm and 50 mm), the change in centroid height is minimal and gradually adjusted to the desired height.

Simulation results are listed in Table 2.

Table 2. Simulation results.

Item	Values
Max force errors of the CIC (N)	90
Max force errors of the AIC (N)	20
Reaction time of the CIC (s)	5
Reaction time of the AIC (s)	0.3
Range of the centroid height (mm)	−2–5
Range of the attitude angle (°)	±0.5

5   Conclusion and Future Work

This paper introduces a six wheel-legged robot with PRR mechanisms for operating inside the box girder. To maintain robotic attitude and avoid the lack of driving force caused by the suspension state of legs, the adaptive attitude controller based on AIC is proposed. This controller can adjust the length of leg adaptively by force tracking, thus ensuring the solution of the robotic attitude stability on an irregular terrain.

Superior to CIC, the proposed controller performs fast, stable, and accurate. Each leg under the control of AIC can track the desired force within 0.3 s, and the force error fluctuates within 20 N. In addition, with the attitude angles error of less than 0.5° and the centroid height error of less than 5 mm, the adaptive attitude controller ensures the horizontal stability of the robot's body and adaptability to different terrains.

Future research directions involve experimental validation of the proposed control framework for force tracking and attitude control. Additionally, the application of environmental perception information from sensor systems to the adaptive impedance control can be explored to enhance the positioning accuracy of desired positions, enabling six wheel-legged robot to adapt to more complex and unknown terrains.

Acknowledgments. The supports of National Natural Science Foundation of China (No. 52004034) in carrying out this research are gratefully acknowledged.

References

1. Bledt, G., Powell, M.J., Katz, B., Di Carlo, J., Wensing, P.M., Kim, S.: MIT Cheetah 3: design and control of a robust, dynamic quadruped robot. In: 2018 IEEE/RSJ International Conference on Intelligent Robots and Systems (IROS), Madrid, Spain, pp. 2245–2252 (2018)
2. Kun, X., Yi, Z., Xilun, D.: Structure design and motion mode analysis of a six wheel-legged robot. J. Beijing Univ. Aeronaut. Astronaut. **42**(1), 59–71 (2016)
3. Xilun, D., Kejia, L., Kun, X.: Dynamics and wheel's slip ratio of a wheel-legged robot in wheeled motion considering the change of height. Chin. J. Mech. Eng. **25**(5), 1060–1067 (2012)
4. Smith, J.A., Sharf, I., Trentini, M.: PAW: a hybrid wheeled-leg robot. In: Proceedings 2006 IEEE International Conference on Robotics and Automation (ICRA 2006), Orlando, FL, USA, pp. 4043–4048 (2006)
5. Bjelonic, M.: Keep rollin'—whole-body motion control and planning for wheeled quadrupedal robots. IEEE Rob. Autom. Lett. **4**(2), 2116–2123 (2019)
6. Schwarz, M., Rodehutskors, T., Schreiber, M., Behnke, S.: Hybrid driving-stepping locomotion with the wheeled-legged robot Momaro. In: 2016 IEEE International Con-ference on Robotics and Automation (ICRA 2016), Stockholm, Sweden, 2016, pp. 5589–5595 (2016)
7. Liu, D.C., Wang, J.Z., Wang, S.K., Shen, W., Peng, H.: An electric wheel-legged robot based on parallel 6-DOF structure. Chin. J. Rob. **40**, 01–02 (2018)
8. Grand, C., Benamar, F., Plumet, F., Bidaud, P.: Stability and traction optimization of a reconfigurable wheel-legged robot. Int. J. Robot. Res. **23**(10–11), 1041–1058 (2004)
9. Cui, L., Wang, S., Zhang, J., Zhang, D., et al.: Learning-based balance control of wheel-legged robots. IEEE Robot. Automat. Lett. **6**(4), 7667–7674 (2021)
10. Hogan, N.: Impedance control - an approach to manipulation. I - theory. II - implementa-tion. III - applications. J. Dyn. Syst. Measure. Control **107**, 1–24 (1985)
11. Raibert, M., Craig, J.J.: Hybrid position/force control of manipulators. ASME J. Dynamic Syst. Meas. Control **102**, 126–133 (1981)
12. Anderson, R., Spong, M.W.: Hybrid impedance control of robotic manipulators. IEEE J. Robot. Autom., 1073–1080 (1987)
13. Irawan, A., Nonami, K., Ohroku, H., Akutsu, Y., Imamura, S.: Adaptive impedance control with compliant body balance for hydraulically driven hexapod robot. J. Syst. Des. Dyn. **5**(5), 893–908 (2011)
14. Seul Jung, T.C.H., Bonitz, R.G.: Force tracking impedance control of robot manipulators under unknown environment. IEEE Trans Control Syst Technol **12**(3), 474–483 (2004)
15. Duan, J., Gan, Y., Chen, M.: Adaptive variable impedance control for dynamic contact force tracking in uncertain environment. Robot. Auton. Syst. **102**, 54–65 (2018)
16. Xu, K., et al.: Adaptive impedance control with variable target stiffness for wheel-legged robot on complex unknown terrain. Mechatronics **69**(7), 102388 (2020)

Design and Simulation of a Reconfigurable Multimode Mobile Robot with Folding Platform

Wenqian Li and Chunyan Zhang$^{(\boxtimes)}$

Shanghai University of Engineering Since, Shanghai, China
2500164499@qq.com

Abstract. To enable mobile robots to have multiple motion modes during task execution and achieve significant reconstruction, deformation, and folding, a reconfigurable multimodal mobile robot with a folding platform was designed. The adjacency matrix is used to analyze the mode topology of quadrangle rolling, hexagon rolling, quadruped crawling and overall folding of the robot, and calculate the degrees of freedom of each mode. By combining the topology analysis results of each mode with the time-sharing control of the motor, the robot's motion gait is generated. Finally, simulation experiments were conducted on different motion modes of a reconfigurable multimodal mobile robot with a folding platform using ADAMS software, verifying the correctness and feasibility of the robot design.

Keywords: Multimodal mobile robot · Reconfigurable · Folding · Topology analysis

1 Introduction

Mobile robots, as an important branch of the field of robotics, play a significant role in engineering operations, exploration and survey, emergency rescue and disaster relief, medical transportation, and other fields. Traditional robots with a single mode of movement are increasingly unable to meet the conditions for working in special multiple application environments. Designing and researching multimodal mobile robots with multiple working modes is becoming a difficult and hot topic in the field of mobile robots.

Yao Yan'an et al. designed a multi mode two wheel mobile robot with a wheeled platform and a deformable body, which has a certain ability to deform and fold during operation. Shi Zhixin et al. proposed a multimodal mobile robot with multiple combinations for collaborative work in unstructured work environments. Zhang et al. designed a 3-RSR multi-mode mobile parallel robot with rolling mode and self traversal characteristics. Liu Xiangyu et al. designed and proposed a reconfigurable multi-mode walking and rolling mobile robot that integrates walking and rolling capabilities to meet the needs of multiple complex terrain environments. Guo Sheng et al. designed and proposed a new multimodal wheel legged composite robot that can perform multiple tasks in complex environments and switch between wheeled and footed movements. Although these mobile robots increase the diversity of motion modes during the movement process, they

© The Author(s), under exclusive license to Springer Nature Singapore Pte Ltd. 2023
H. Yang et al. (Eds.): ICIRA 2023, LNAI 14274, pp. 214–228, 2023.
https://doi.org/10.1007/978-981-99-6501-4_19

also result in larger overall structural volume, weight, and inability to achieve significant folding deformation.

Therefore, this article integrates platform folding with mobile mechanisms for design. In response to the limitations of the aforementioned multimode mobile robots, platform folding is integrated with the structure of the mobile robot, and a reconfigurable multimode mobile parallel robot with a planar folding platform is designed. The robot integrates modes such as quadrilateral rolling, hexagonal rolling, quadruped crawling, and overall folding, and can switch between different motion modes, greatly enhancing the robot's mobility and folding deformation ability.

2 Institutional Description

A reconfigurable multimode mobile robot with a folding platform is shown in Fig. 1. The robot mechanism is composed of the same upper and lower folding platforms and four equally distributed branch chains connecting the upper and lower platforms. With the upper folding platform $A_1A_2A_3A_4O_1$ meeting the requirements $A_1O_1 = A_2O_1 = A_3O_1 = A_4O_1$ and the lower folding platform $C_1C_2C_3C_4O_2$ being a scalable platform. The four branch chains are symmetrically distributed and have identical structural dimensions. The branch chains $i = 1 \sim 4$ contain $A_iB_iC_i$ and the motion pairs at the points are all rotational pairs, among which $D_1D_2D_3D_4O_2$ are moving pairs.

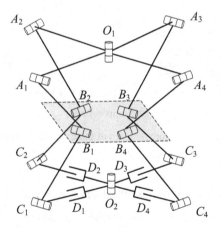

Fig. 1. Schematic diagram of a reconfigurable multimode mobile robot mechanism with a folding platform

2.1 Design of Robot Folding Platform

Design the upper folding platform with a composite hinge at the O_1 rotation joint, which requires the robot folding platform members to be in the same plane. Therefore, the upper platform connecting rod A_1O_1, A_2O_1, A_3O_1, A_4O_1 is designed with a layered hinge relative to the rotation joint O_1. Install the upper platform motor O_1 at the rotation joint of the upper folding platform M_1, M_2 and fix it with a motor bracket. Install the motor A_1O_1, A_2O_1, A_3O_1, A_4O_1 at the end of the platform connecting rod $M_3 \sim M_6$. The structure of the upper folding platform is shown in Fig. 2

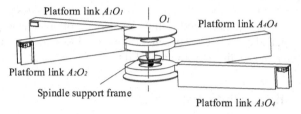

Fig. 2. Structure diagram of the folding platform

Design the down folding platform with a composite hinge at the O_2 rotating pair. Similarly, design the layered hinge of the connecting rod C_1O_2, C_2O_2, C_3O_2, C_4O_2 of the down folding platform relative to the rotating pair O_2, as shown in Fig. 3. Design the $D_1D_2D_3D_4O_2$ moving pair inside the lower folding platform link, fix the motor on the slider of the slider guide rail, and drive the slider to move in a straight line through the gear and rack meshing at the end of the motor output shaft, thus forming the moving pair as shown in Fig. 3.

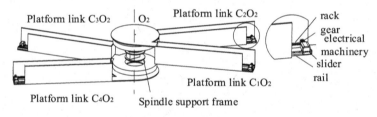

Fig. 3. Structure diagram of the foldable platform

2.2 Overall Design of Robot Folding Platform and Branch Chain

Design the branch chain $A_iB_iC_i$ that connects the upper and lower folding platforms, and arrange the A_i, C_i symmetrically through the rotating pair B_i. The rotating pair A_iO_1 that connects one end of the connecting rod A_iB_i to the upper platform connecting rod is installed with a motor $M_3 \sim M_6$ at A_i, one end of the branch chain connecting rod B_iC_i is connected to the motor $M_9 \sim M_{12}$ installed at B_i point, and the other end is connected to the motor $M_9 \sim M_{12}$ installed at the end of the lower platform connecting rod C_iO_2. The specific connection method is shown in Fig. 4 (a). The rotating pair $A_iB_iC_i$ is parallel to each other, so the designed branch chain can achieve both inward storage as shown in Fig. 4 (b) and outward folding as shown in Fig. 4.

By using a motor $M_3 \sim M_6$, $M_9 \sim M_{16}$ for time-sharing drive, the mechanism can complete different modes of motion.

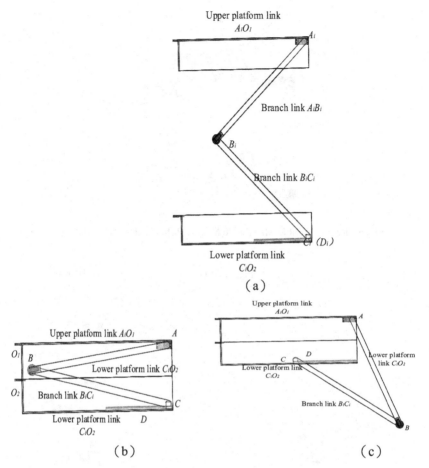

Fig. 4. Schematic diagram of mechanism branch chain design motion

2.3   Multi Mode Mobile Robot

The connecting rods of the robot mechanism are connected by rotating pairs, and each rotating pair is equipped with an electric motor, as shown in Fig. 5. Through time-sharing control of the motor, the folding of the robot platform can be achieved, thereby completing various modes of motion, as shown in Fig. 6.

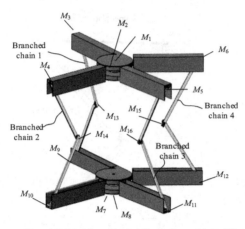

Fig. 5. Reconfigurable Multimode Mobile Robot with Folding Platform

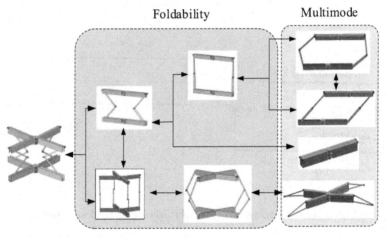

Fig. 6. Schematic diagram of multiple motion modes of mobile robots

3 Various Motion Modes of the Robot

3.1 Quadrilateral Rolling Mode of the Robot

In order to realize the quadrilateral rolling mode of the constructed multi-mode mobile parallel robot, the relative bar of the mechanism is always parallel under this mode, and the angular displacement, angular velocity and angular acceleration of the two links are always equal, which can amplify the displacement.

When the mechanism transitions from a general state to a quadrilateral mode, it is necessary to merge and reconstruct the mechanism members. That is, the upper and lower platforms of the mechanism drive the rotating pair O_1, O_2 through the motor M_1, M_2, M_7, M_8, which converts the mechanism from a three-dimensional mode to a two-dimensional mode. The other rotating pair positions of the mechanism are then driven by the motor to rotate the rotating pair, completing the merger and reconstruction of the mechanism members. The conversion process is shown in Fig. 7.

The robot moves and rolls in the quadrilateral mode, with member A_1O_1, A_3O_1, C_1O_2, C_3O_2 overlapping with member A_2O_1, A_4O_1, C_2O_2, C_4O_2 and the support chain $A_iB_iC_i (i = 1 \sim 4)$ and platform member transforming into the four edges of the quadrilateral, denoted as $A_{1(2)}A_{3(4)}$, $C_{1(2)}C_{3(4)}$, $A_{1(2)}C_{1(2)}$, $A_{3(4)}C_{3(4)}$. During the movement, the four edges come into contact with the ground in order to provide the required support area. In this mode, the main reliance is on the motor $M_3 \sim M_6$, $M_9 \sim M_{12}$ to drive the corresponding rotating pair to rotate, driving the connecting rod to achieve angle changes, and thus completing the robot's movement.

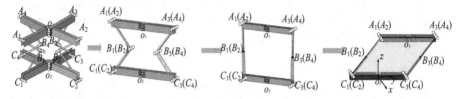

Fig. 7. Transformation process diagram of quadrilateral rolling mode of the robot

3.2 Hexagonal Rolling Mode of the Robot

The hexagonal mode of the robot is a planar hexagonal mechanism, with parallel and equal opposing edges. On the basis of the quadrangular mode of the robot, the motor $M_{13} \sim M_{16}$ can drive the rotating pair B_j to fold outward, achieving the merger of branch chains and completing the conversion of the hexagonal mode of the mechanism. The conversion process is shown in Fig. 8.

The movement mode of the mechanism in the hexagonal mode is also rolling. During the movement process, each edge of the hexagonal contacts the ground in order to provide the required support area. In this mode, the motion is mainly driven by the corresponding rotating pair A_i, B_j, C_k through the motor $M_3 \sim M_6$, $M_9 \sim M_{12}$, $M_{13} \sim M_{16}$, achieving the angle transformation between the connecting rods, and thus achieving the rolling of the robot.

Among them, the six edges in the hexagonal mode are formed by A_1O_1, A_3O_1, C_1O_2, C_3O_2 overlapping with member A_2O_1, A_4O_1, C_2O_2, C_4O_2, and the branch chain $A_iB_iC_i (i = 1 \sim 4)$ is transformed from the platform member. The six edges are the branch chain $A_{1(2)}B_{1(2)}$, $B_{1(2)}C_{1(2)}$, $C_{1(2)}C_{3(4)}$, $C_{3(4)}B_{3(4)}$, $B_{3(4)}A_{3(4)}$.

3.3 The Quadruped Crawling Mode of the Robot

In order to enable spatial multimode mobile mechanisms to achieve quadruped crawling mode, the general state mechanisms were merged and reconstructed to form a quadruped crawling mechanism, as shown in Fig. 9.

In the quadruped crawling mode of the robot, motor $M_3 \sim M_6$, $M_9 \sim M_{12}$, $M_{13} \sim M_{16}$ is in a locked state, mainly relying on motors M_1, M_2 and M_7, M_8 to drive composite

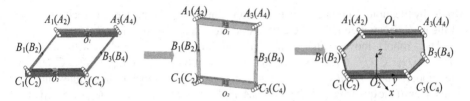

Fig. 8. Transformation process diagram of hexagonal rolling mode

hinges O_1 and O_2, achieving the rotational motion of platform links $O_1A_i (i = 1 \sim 4)$, $O_2C_i (i = 1 \sim 4)$ and H, and thus the robot's gait advances.

Branch chain $A_iB_iC_i (i = 4)$ and platform members are transformed into four robot legs, each with $O_1(O_2)A_i(C_i)B_i$. During the movement, each leg sequentially contacts the ground to provide the required support area.

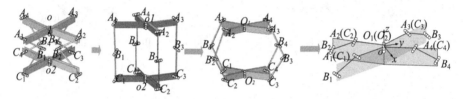

Fig. 9. Transformation process diagram of hexagonal rolling mode

3.4 Single Pole Like Mode of Robots

In order to enable the spatial multimode mobile mechanism to achieve overall folding and storage mode, the mechanism in general state is merged and reconstructed into a similar single bar mechanism. In this mode, the branch chain $A_iB_iC_i (i = 1 \sim 4)$ and the platform member are converted into a single bar A_1A_3. The reconstruction process is shown in Fig. 10.

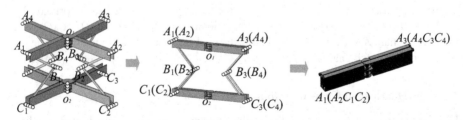

Fig. 10. Process Diagram of Mechanism Single Rod Mode Conversion

4 Topological Analysis of Various Motion Modes of the Robot

Based on the spatial geometric relationships of each motion pair of the above mechanism, the mechanism can achieve multiple different motion modes by transforming joint constraints. Due to the spatial symmetry of the mechanism structure, the implementation of each motion mode of the mechanism relies on the coordinated motion between the upper and lower folding platforms and the support chains. Therefore, in order to facilitate the analysis of the equivalent motion models under different motion modes, each mode of the mechanism uses the adjacency matrix encoded by the motion pair for topological structure analysis.

Analyze and establish the mechanism platform adjacency matrix, branch chain adjacency matrix and overall mechanism adjacency matrix. The overall mechanism adjacency matrix of the mechanism in general position state is:

$$A_{OC} = \begin{bmatrix} O_{2\times2} & N_{2\times2} & N_{2\times2} & N_{2\times2} & N_{2\times2} \\ N_{2\times2} & A_{OL1} & M_{2\times2} & M_{2\times2} & M_{2\times2} \\ N_{2\times2} & M_{2\times2} & A_{OL2} & M_{2\times2} & M_{2\times2} \\ N_{2\times2} & M_{2\times2} & M_{2\times2} & A_{OL3} & M_{2\times2} \\ N_{2\times2} & M_{2\times2} & M_{2\times2} & M_{2\times2} & A_{OL4} \end{bmatrix} \tag{1}$$

where, A_{OL1}, A_{OL2}, A_{OL3}, A_{OL4} is the branch chain matrix of the relationship between the links in branch chain 1, branch chain 2, branch chain 3 and branch chain 4, $O_{2\times2}$ is the platform adjacency matrix of the robot, and C is the auxiliary matrix.

$$O_{2\times2} = \begin{bmatrix} O_1A_1A_2A_3A_4 & 0 \\ 0 & O_2C_1C_2C_3C_4 \end{bmatrix} \tag{2}$$

$$M_{2\times2} = \begin{bmatrix} 1 & 0 \\ 0 & 1 \end{bmatrix} \tag{3}$$

The topology of the mechanism in different modes can be obtained by transformation equation, that is, by using EU elementary matrix. The EU meaning of elementary matrix in mathematics is extended to the relationship between members in the mechanism. According to the $U_{i,j}$ transposition of adjacency matrix left multiplied by elementary matrix $U_{i,j}$ and right multiplied by elementary matrix in mathematics, the definition is to j add row to i row in the matrix i and column to column in the matrix respectively; The diagonal element of the adjacency matrix represents the link, and the non diagonal element represents the j connection between the link i. Therefore, the $U_{i,j}$ role of the elementary matrix is to i combine the first j link and the third link in the mechanism, and give the connection between the first link and other links to the first link. According to the E_j transposition of adjacency matrix left multiplied by elementary matrix E_j and right multiplied by elementary matrix in mathematics, the j row in the matrix is deleted and the j column in the matrix is deleted respectively; Correspondingly, the i first j connecting rod in the mechanism is deleted after merging with the second connecting rod. Therefore, the EU use of elementary matrix means to transfer the link connection relationship for the mechanism. Through EU elementary matrix transformation of the adjacency matrix of the whole mechanism, the equivalent motion models of the mechanism in different motion modes are obtained.

$$
U_{i,j} = \begin{bmatrix} I & 0 & \cdots & 0 & 0 & \cdots & 0 \\ 0 & I & \cdots & 0 & 0 & \cdots & 0 \\ \vdots & \vdots & & \vdots & \vdots & & \vdots \\ 0 & 0 & & I_{i,i} & I_{j,j} & & 0 \\ 0 & 0 & & & I_{j,j} & & 0 \\ \vdots & \vdots & & \vdots & & & \vdots \\ 0 & 0 & \cdots & 0 & 0 & \cdots & I \end{bmatrix} \tag{4}
$$

$$
E_j = \begin{bmatrix} I & 0 & \cdots & 0 & 0 & 0 & \cdots & 0 \\ 0 & I & \cdots & 0 & 0 & 0 & \cdots & 0 \\ \vdots & \vdots & & \vdots & \vdots & \vdots & & \vdots \\ 0 & 0 & \cdots & I_{j-1,j-1} & 0 & 0 & \cdots & 0 \\ 0 & 0 & \cdots & 0 & 0 & I_{j+1,j+1} & \cdots & 0 \\ \vdots & \vdots & & \vdots & \vdots & \vdots & & \vdots \\ 0 & 0 & \cdots & 0 & 0 & 0 & \cdots & I \end{bmatrix} \tag{5}
$$

Among them $I = diag(1, 1, \cdots, 1)$.

Based on the above analysis, the topological analysis of each motion mode of the mechanism is carried out through the topological analysis of the adjacency matrix of the foldable platform.

4.1 Topological Analysis of the Quadrilateral Rolling Mode of the Mechanism

The changes between the bars follow the elementary transformation formula, that is, the equivalent combination of the bars. According to the elementary transformation equation, the adjacency matrix of the mechanism under the quadrilateral rolling mode is as follows:

$$
A_{OC'} = \begin{bmatrix} A_{1(2)}A_{3(4)} & 1 & 0 & 1 \\ 1 & A_{3(4)}C_{3(4)} & 1 & 0 \\ 0 & 1 & C_{3(4)}C_{1(2)} & 1 \\ 1 & 0 & 1 & C_{1(2)}A_{1(2)} \end{bmatrix} \tag{6}
$$

From Formula 6, it can be seen that as shown in Fig. 11, the mechanism can be regarded as an equivalent parallelogram in the quadrilateral rolling mode, with a degree of freedom of 1.

4.2 Topological Analysis of Various Motion Modes of the Mechanism

The changes between the bars of each motion mode of the mechanism follow the elementary transformation formula, that is, the equivalent combination of the bars. According to the elementary transformation equation, the adjacency matrix of each motion mode of the mechanism can be obtained, as shown in Table 1.

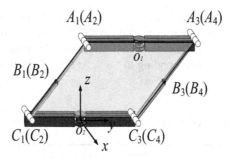

Fig. 11. Schematic diagram of quadrilateral rolling mode

Table 1. Adjacency matrix of mechanism under each motion mode

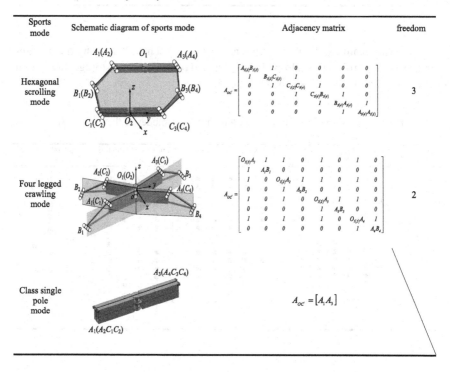

5 Motor Time-Sharing Control and Gait Generation of the Mechanism

The motion control of composite mobile robots often faces problems such as difficulty in coordination and control. The mobile robot adopts segmented control of motors, greatly reducing the control difficulty. Using a "binary like" chart combined with to illustrate the control of mobile robots. As shown in Table 2, the motor marked with a black circle is in an energized driving state, which corresponds to the binary "1" of the corresponding class. At this time, the rod is in an active input state; The motor marked with a white circle is in a self-locking state, corresponding to "0". At this time, there is no movement between the connecting rods of the motor; The motor with a cross mark inside the circle is in a power failure state, corresponding to " ×", At this point, the rod connected to the motor is a passive motion pair.

Table 2 Binary representation method for motor time-sharing control class

Category Serial number	Motor marking symbols	Class binary	Motor status
1	●	1	Power on drive
2	○	0	Self locking state
3	⊗	×	Power failure

The driving status and gait generation process of each motor in the quadrangular rolling, hexagonal rolling, quadruped crawling, and overall folding storage modes of the robot mechanism are shown in Tables 3 and 4.

Table 3 Time sharing control of motors in various modes of the mechanism

Sports mode	Quadrilateral scrolling mode					Hexagonal scrolling mode					Four legged crawling mode					Overall folding mode	
	1	2	3	4	5	1	2	3	4	5	1	2	3	4	5	1	2
M_{16}	○	○	○	○	○	○	○	○	○	○	⊗	○	○	○	○	⊗	○
M_{15}	○	○	○	○	○	●	●	●	●	●	⊗	○	○	○	○	⊗	○
M_{14}	○	○	○	○	○	●	●	●	●	●	⊗	○	○	○	○	⊗	○
M_{13}	○	○	○	○	○	○	○	○	○	○	⊗	○	○	○	○	⊗	○
M_{12}	○	○	○	○	○	⊗	⊗	⊗	⊗	⊗	⊗	○	○	○	●	⊗	○
M_{11}	○	○	○	○	○	⊗	⊗	⊗	⊗	⊗	⊗	○	○	●	○	⊗	○
M_{10}	○	○	○	○	○	●	●	●	●	●	⊗	○	●	○	○	⊗	○
M_9	○	○	○	○	○	●	●	●	●	●	⊗	●	○	○	○	⊗	○
M_8	○	○	○	○	○	○	○	○	○	○	○	○	○	○	●	⊗	●
M_7	○	○	○	○	○	○	○	○	○	○	○	○	○	●	○	⊗	●
M_6	●	●	●	●	●	●	●	●	●	●	●	○	○	○	○	●	○
M_5	●	●	●	●	●	●	●	●	●	●	●	○	○	○	○	●	○
M_4	●	●	●	●	●	⊗	⊗	⊗	⊗	⊗	●	○	○	○	○	●	○
M_3	●	●	●	●	●	⊗	⊗	⊗	⊗	⊗	●	○	○	○	○	●	○
M_2	○	○	○	○	○	○	○	○	○	○	○	○	●	○	○	⊗	●
M_1	○	○	○	○	○	○	○	○	○	○	○	●	○	○	○	⊗	●

Motor drive status — step

Table 4 Motor Time Sharing Control and Gait Analysis for Each Mode of Motion

Gait Generation for Quadrilateral Rolling					
Time sharing drive	Initial state	Step1	Step2	Step3	Step4
Motor status	[001111000000 0000]	[0011110000000000]			
Formed gait					

Gait Generation for Hexagonal Rolling					
Time sharing drive	Initial state	Step1	Step2	Step3	Step4
Motor status	[00××110011× ×0110]	[00××110011××0110]			
Formed gait					

Gait generation in quadruped crawling					
Time sharing drive	Initial state	Step1	Step2	Step3	Step4
Motor status	[00111100 ××××××××]	[101111001 0000000]	[01111100 01000000]	[00111110 00100000]	[00111101 00010000]
Formed gait					

Gait generation for overall folding and storage			
Time sharing drive	Initial state	Step1	Step1
Motor status	[××1111×××××××××]	[××1111×××××××××]	[1100001100000000]
Formed gait			

6 Robot Simulation

This robot integrates multiple motion modes and can switch between multiple modes through time-sharing control between motors. Compared with traditional mobile robots, this robot has the advantages shown in Table 5.

The robot is expected to achieve four motion modes and walk over obstacles on uneven roads, using ADAMS software for motion simulation, as shown in Tables 6, 7, 8, 9.

(1) Quadrilateral scrolling mode
(2) Hexagonal scrolling mode
(3) Four legged crawling mode
(4) Folding storage mode

Table 5 Integration of Various Modes of Reconfigurable Multimode Mobile Parallel Robot with Folding Platform

	Quadrilateral scrolling mode	Hexagonal scrolling mode	Four legged crawling mode	Overall folding storage mode
Sports mode				
Integrated technology	Multi motion mode integration, folding and storage, and motor time-sharing control strategy			
Performance advantages	Fast movement, strong ground adaptability, multiple motion modes, good concealed passability, and convenient storage and transportation			
Terrain suitability	Complex terrain environment with multiple features (such as flat land, sandy land, gravel roads, gullies, etc.)			
Engineering application	Military reconnaissance platform, complex environment survey platform, engineering transportation platform			

Table. 6 Quadrilateral Rolling Simulation Process

time	T=0s	T=2.4s	T=3.2s	T=7.1s	T=9.2s
plane					
space					

Table 7 Hexagonal Rolling Simulation Process

time	T=0s	T=1.5s	T=5.5s	T=11s	T=20s
plane					
space					

Table 8 Simulation process of quadruped crawling

time	T=0s	T=1.2s	T=2.4s	T=4s	T=5.6s
plane					
space					

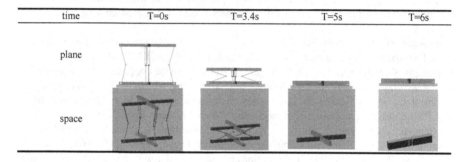

Table 9 Folding Storage Simulation Process

time	T=0s	T=3.4s	T=5s	T=6s
plane				
space				

7 Summary

A new type of reconfigurable multi-mode mobile parallel robot with folding and unfolding platform is designed based on the concept of multi-mode, folding and unfolding, and reconfigurable. The robot integrates multiple motion modes such as quadrilateral rolling, hexagonal rolling, quadruped crawling, folding and storing, and can switch between different modes without the need for reassembly. It can also be transformed into a single rod like shape through folding and storing mode, which has strong concealment and storage portability, It has strong adaptability to ground environment and can achieve small volume folding storage function. Simulation experiments were conducted using ADAMS software, and the simulation results showed that each motion mode was feasible and could switch between different modes.

In summary, exploring and innovating the design concept of a robot structure that can achieve multiple motion modes without the need for reassembly, combined with the design concept of reconfigurable and foldable mechanisms, we have developed and produced a mobile robot that can adapt to different complex working environments and have multiple motion modes, which has certain practical significance.

References

1. History, Z.N.: Current situation, and trends of robot development. J. Harbin Instit. Technol. (06), 4 (1989)
2. Hai, Z., Bing, Y.: The development status and application prospects of robots. Equipment Manuf. Technol. **09**, 47–49 (2017)
3. Wenying, Z.: Current situation and prospects of mobile robot technology. Inf. Recording Mater. **21**(10), 24–25 (2020)
4. Yuanxun, Z., Zedong, H., Han Liangliang, G., Chengpeng, Z.W.: Design and analysis of crawling and rolling characteristics of climbing and rolling robots suitable for extreme terrain on the lunar surface. J. Mech. Eng. **57**(03), 35–48 (2021)
5. Chunyan, Z., An, P.: Design and kinematic characteristics analysis of a multi-mode mobile parallel mechanism with folding and unfolding platform. J. Agric. Mach. **53**(03), 449–458 (2022)
6. Liu, R., Yao, Y.A., Ding, W.: Locomotion optimization and manipulation planning of a tetrahedron-based mobile mechanism with binary control. Chin. J. Mech. Eng. **31**(1), 11–20 (2018)
7. Yanying, H., Li Yezhuo, W., Jianxu, L.X., Yan'an, Y.: Design and motion analysis of multimodal two wheeled mobile robots. J. Mech. Eng. **55**(23), 83–92 (2019)
8. Dongfu, X., Yufeng, L., Zhixin, S., Yande, L.: Research on the cooperative mode of multiple mobile robots and their tipping stability. China Mech. Eng. **31**(20), 2472–2485 (2020)
9. Zhang, C., Wan, Y., Zhang, D., et al.: A new mathematical method to study the singularity of 3-RSR multimode mobile parallel mechanism. Math. Problems Eng. (2019)
10. Xiangyu, L., Chunyan, Z., Mingjuan, X., Cong, N., Maosheng, L., Wan, Y.: A reconfigurable multi mode stepping and rolling mobile robot. Mech. Transm. **43**(06), 158–164 (2019)
11. Chengyu, Z., Sheng, G., Fuqun, Z.: Motion analysis and gait research of a new type of wheel leg composite robot. J. Mech. Eng. **55**(15), 145–153 (2019)

RBSAC: Rolling Balance Controller Based on Soft Actor-Critic Algorithm of the Unicycle Air Robot

Chunzheng Wang, Yunyi Zhang, Chenlong Zhang, Qixiang Zhao, and Wei Wang[✉]

Beihang University, Beijing, China
wangwei701@buaa.edu.cn

Abstract. Due to the complexity of the robot's dynamics model coupled with multiple outputs, most model-based or proportional-integral-derivative type controllers are unable to effectively solve the problem of attitude control of a Unicycle Air Robot (UAR) rolling in ground mode. In this paper, we formulate the attitude control problem in ground mode as a continuous-state, continuous-action Markov decision process with unknown transfer probabilities. Based on deterministic policy gradient theorems and neural network approximations, we propose RBSAC: a model-free rolling balance Reinforcement Learning (RL) controller based on Soft Actor-Critic (SAC) algorithm, which learns the state feedback controller from the attitude sampling of the ground mode. To improve the performance of the algorithm, we further integrate a batch learning method by playing back previously prioritized trajectories. We illustrate through simulations that our model-free approach RBSAC outperforms a feedback-based linear PID controller. After conducting simulation verification, it has been observed that the RBSAC controller enables stable rolling of the UAR on the ground, resulting in a 60% improvement in speed compared to the PID controller. Moreover, the RBSAC controller exhibits enhanced robustness and autonomous response to external disturbances during motion.

Keywords: Unicycle Air Robot · Reinforcement Learning · Attitude Control

1 Introduction

Unicycle Air Robots (UARs) have been widely studied in recent years due to their higher energy efficiency compared to flight modes and higher trafficability in narrow spaces [1–5]. However, in ground mode, these robots' multiple power unit inputs generate control coupling, and their interaction with the ground forces is non-linearly complex, which poses great challenges to the attitude control.

The conventional Proportional-Integral-Derivative (PID) algorithm, renowned for its simplistic architecture, lucid principles, and straightforward implementation, has demonstrated commendable control outcomes when applied to address rudimentary control quandaries characterized by linearity and time-invariant attributes [6]. However, when the controlled system is a complex, non-linear system that is difficult to linearise and

© The Author(s), under exclusive license to Springer Nature Singapore Pte Ltd. 2023
H. Yang et al. (Eds.): ICIRA 2023, LNAI 14274, pp. 229–240, 2023.
https://doi.org/10.1007/978-981-99-6501-4_20

establish an accurate mathematical model, linear PID control is often unable to achieve satisfactory control results. Furthermore, in the case of controlled systems characterized by numerous state variables, a multitude of actuators, and elevated task complexity, exemplified by the UAR system proposed in the seminal work by paper [7], the necessity arises to concurrently regulate multiple channels while considering the existence of inter-channel coupling. This intricate scenario entails the utilization of multiple PID controllers and entails a substantial number of parameters to be calibrated, rendering the task of identifying the optimal parameter combination arduous.

In the past few years, the field of Reinforcement Learning (RL) has witnessed noteworthy accomplishments in various domains, encompassing diverse applications ranging from high-level path planning and navigation [8, 9] to fine-grained attitude control [10–12]. RL emerges as a particularly promising technique for multi-rotor robots, offering valuable insights in mitigating the intricate nonlinear airflow ramifications stemming from rotor blades [13]. Additionally, RL proves advantageous in operating within uncertain environments, characterized by variables like wind patterns and obstacles. Notably, the model-free paradigm within RL holds a distinct edge, enabling agents to interact with intricate environments devoid of explicit dynamics models [14].

Wang. C. etc. [7] use the conventional method for UAR attitude control, which is the conventional proportional-integral link and controller based on model decomposition. The work in this paper is a direct continuation of that paper. We design RBSAC: a model-free rolling balance reinforcement learning controller based on Soft Actor-Critic algorithm [15], for the stable control of the ground mode rolling attitude of the UAR proposed in the literature. And we verify the excellent performance of RBSAC controller in a simulation environment.

After designing the network, we built a simulation environment based on the actual physical model parameters, sampled the UAR attitude, and trained it to avoid the possible hazards of physical UAR experiments and the problem of long and time-consuming data acquisition. To improve data efficiency, we proposed a batch learning scheme by playing back previous experiences [16] (Fig. 1).

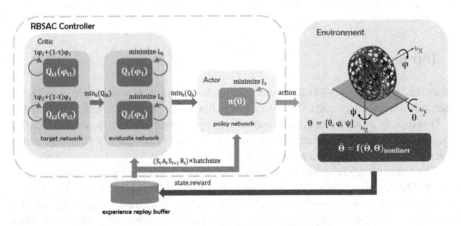

Fig. 1. The altitude control task of UAR used RBSAC controller.

The main contributions of this paper are summarized as follows:

1) Pioneeringly, we formulate the three attitude angle control problems for UAR as a Markov Decision Process (MDP), integrating meticulously crafted state and reward functions.

2) We build a realistic, testable RBSAC controller for a UAR simulation environment that can efficiently acquire observation space, state space, action space, and rewards at update rates of up to 100 Hz.

3) We design an attitude controller of the UAR called RBSAC, which is based on the SAC algorithm that uses a circular experience buffer to store past experiences. The agent uses small batches of randomly sampled experiences from the buffer to update the actor and critic networks.

This paper is organized as follows: First, in Sect. 2, we decompose the defined UAR control problem, introduce a nonlinear dynamics model of the UAR, and transform it into a MDP; in Sect. 3, we propose RBSAC agent that interacts iteratively with the UAR's MDP to optimize the neural network attitude control strategy. Finally, in Sect. 4, we build a UAR simulation environment and evaluate the advantages of the RBSAC controller over conventional PID controllers for the UAR attitude tracking task.

2 Preliminary

2.1 Introduction of UAR

This paper innovatively integrates the multi-rotor structure with the unicycle structure and proposes a new UAR design that has the advantages of both multi-rotors and unicycle structures. The weight of the UAR is about 2.8 kg, the diameter of the wheel is 460 mm and the width is 170 mm.

We design the inner ring of the UAR as the center of gravity eccentric structure, and install the rolling motor between the inner and outer ring, as shown in Fig. 2. The output torque of the rolling motor makes the inner ring rotate at a certain angle and overcome its gravity moment, and the reaction torque of the motor acts on the outer ring to drive it to roll. The inner ring of the system produces a torque that is directly correlated to the rotation angle. As a consequence, the reaction torque exerted on the outer ring is likewise contingent upon the rotation angle of the inner ring. Through the manipulation of the motor to regulate the magnitude of the rotation angle of the inner ring, it becomes possible to achieve control over the rolling speed of the outer ring. The rolling balance motion is schematically shown in Fig. 3.

In particular, the camera can be fixed to the inner ring, and the rotation angle of the inner ring can be kept stable by rolling motors, which means the camera can be kept facing forward to facilitate functional expansion, such as autonomous navigation and target detection, which is a better design than the robot in reference [3].

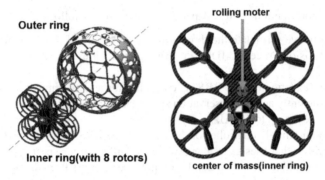

Fig. 2. Structure of the UAR

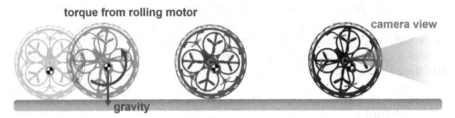

Fig. 3. Process of rolling balance motion

2.2 Task Definition

Since the control method of UAR in flight mode is similar to that of a conventional quadrotor, we will focus on the control in ground mode.

To characterize the ground motion, a coordinate system is established concerning the fixed inner circle. Euler angles are adopted to describe the attitude of the Unified Actuator-Retaining (UAR) system during the ground motion. The design of the rolling controller aims to ensure that the UAR's attitude aligns with the input command, with the expected Euler angles serving as the inputs to the controller.

2.3 Definition of Observation Space

The main onboard measurement elements of the UAR are an accelerometer, gyroscope, magnetometer, and barometer, while an encoder of the rolling motor is set to measure the angle and speed of outer rings for the control of rolling speed. According to the design goals of the controller, the desired Euler angles should also be used as the observation information provided to the agent. The defined observation space is shown in Table 1.

Table 1. Definition of the observation space

Observation space variables	Meaning
$\Theta = \begin{pmatrix} \phi & \theta & \psi \end{pmatrix}^{T}$	3 measured Euler angles for the inner circle coordinate system
$\Theta_d = \begin{pmatrix} \phi_d & \theta_d & \psi_d \end{pmatrix}^{T}$	3 desired Euler angles for the inner circle coordinate system
$\omega = \begin{pmatrix} \omega_x & \omega_y & \omega_z \end{pmatrix}^{T}$	Tri-axial angular velocity of the inner ring
$\dot{\phi}_{\text{Outer}}$	The rotational speed of the outer ring relative to the ground around its central axis
$\mathbf{u}_{t-1}$	The intelligent body output action of the previous step

2.4 Definition of Action Space

The actuators of the UAR are the 8-rotor motors and the rolling motors between the inner and outer rings. Since there is a mapping relationship between the combined force and moment generated by the 8 rotors and the speed of each rotor represented by the power distribution matrix, it is sufficient to define the combined force and moment of the 8 rotors and the moment of the rolling motor in the action space (Table 2).

Table 2. Definition of the action space

Action space variables	Meaning
F	Combined force generated by rotors
τ_x, τ_y, τ_z	Combined torque generated by rotors
T	Rolling motor torque

2.5 Definition of Reward Function

The reward function for the training process is designed according to the design goals of the controller to encourage the deviation of each Euler angle measurement from the desired value to be as small as possible, to penalize too fast rotation or vibration of the inner ring to prevent interference with the measurement elements attached to the inner ring and devices such as the camera and to penalize the agent for using too much control to obtain a reward. The reward function includes both continuous and sparse rewards and includes both reward and penalty terms. The expression of the reward function is shown below:

$$r_1 = -(\varphi - \varphi_d)^2 - (\theta - \theta_d)^2 - (\psi - \psi_d)^2$$
$$r_2 = 0.25 \ (\text{if}|\varphi - \varphi_d| < 0.05)$$
$$r_3 = 0.25 \ (\text{if}|\theta - \theta_d| < 0.05)$$
$$r_4 = 0.25 \ (\text{if}|\varphi - \varphi_d| < 0.05)$$
$$r_5 = 20 \ (\text{if}|\varphi - \varphi_d| < 0.05 \&\& |\theta - \theta_d| < 0.05 \&\& |\varphi - \varphi_d| < 0.05)$$
$$r_6 = -\|\mathbf{u}_{t-1}\|$$
$$r_7 = 250 \frac{T_s}{T_f}$$
$$r_8 = -1000 \cdot \text{isdone}$$
$$R_t = \sum_{i=1}^{8} r_i$$

(1)

The maximum training time of each round is denoted as T_f and the interval of each time step is denoted as T_f. Two parameters are set as follows:

$$T_f = 10\,\text{s}, T_s = 0.01\,\text{s}$$

"Isdone" means that if a control quantity deviates too much, it means that the strategy used in this round is poor and the training round needs to be terminated early. The conditions for triggering isdone are defined as:

1) Any angular deviation greater than 1 rad.
2) Inside circle instantaneous speed greater than 5 rad/s.

3   Design of the Algorithm

3.1   Algorithm Principle

The SAC algorithm is a model-free, online learning, heterogeneous strategy, reinforcement learning algorithm based on an actor-critic structure [17]. The SAC algorithm computes an optimal strategy that maximizes both the long-term desired reward and the policy entropy (policy entropy) [18]. Policy entropy is a measure of the uncertainty of a policy for a given state [19, 20]. The entropy of the policy distribution for a given state s is $\pi(a|s)$, the probability distribution of different actions selected by an intelligence in the action space A, which is defined as:

$$h(\pi(\cdot|s)) = -\int_A \pi(a|s) \ln(\pi(a|s)) da$$

(2)

Obviously, a higher entropy value promotes the agent to try more exploration in the action space. To the single-step reward R_{t+1} calculated from the reward function, add the term determined by the strategy entropy:

$$R_{t+1}^{\text{entropy}} = R_{t+1} + \alpha^{\text{entropy}} h(\pi(\cdot|s_t))$$

(3)

And the state value function with entropy and action value function are derived according to the usual method. The SAC algorithm maintains a total of 5 deep neural networks (Table 3):

In the training, SAC performs the following operations:

Table 3. Meaning of Network Symbols

Network Symbols	Meaning
$\pi(A\|S;\theta)$	The stochastic policy network containing the parameter θ is output as an policy (actor) to output action values in the action space according to a normal distribution
$Q_k(S, A; \varphi_k), k = 1, 2$	Double Q-networks with the same structure containing parameters φ_1, φ_2 respectively, avoiding overestimation of the value function
$Q_{tk}(S, A; \varphi_{tk}), k = 1, 2$	Double target networks Q_{t1} and Q_{t2} corresponding to Q_1 and Q_2 networks, respectively, improving the stability of the parameter updating process

1) Update the actor and critic attributes periodically during the learning process.
2) Estimate the mean and standard deviation of the Gaussian probability distribution of the continuous action space, and then randomly select actions based on this distribution.
3) Update the entropy weight term to balance the expected return.
4) Use a circular experience buffer to store past experiences, while the agent uses a random sampling of experiences from the buffer to update the networks.

Algorithm 1 Soft Actor-Critic Algorithm

Input: θ, φ_k and φ_{tk}

$\varphi_{tk} \leftarrow \varphi_k$, $D \leftarrow \varnothing$

for each iteration **do**

    for each environment step do

        $a_t \sim \pi_\theta(a_t \mid s_t)$

        $s_{t+1} \sim p(s_{t+1} \mid s_t, a_t)$, p is the state transition probability.

        $D \leftarrow D \cup \{(s_t, a_t, r(s_t, a_t), s_{t+1})\}$, D is the experience pool.

    end for

    for each gradient step **do**

        $\varphi_k \leftarrow \varphi_k - \lambda_Q \hat{\nabla}_{\varphi_i} J_Q(\varphi_i)$ for $i \in \{1,2\}$, λ is learning rate, J is loss,

and $\hat{\nabla}$ is gradient.

        $\theta \leftarrow \theta - \lambda_\pi \hat{\nabla}_\theta J_\pi(\varphi)$

        $\alpha \leftarrow \alpha - \lambda \hat{\nabla}_\alpha J(\alpha)$

        $\varphi_{tk} \leftarrow \tau \varphi_k + (1-\tau) \varphi_{tk}$ for $i \in \{1,2\}$, τ is smoothing factor.

    end for

end for

Output: θ, φ_k and φ_{tk}

4 Experiments and Results

4.1 Simulation Environment

In this paper, Matlab Simulink is selected as the simulation environment, and Simscape Multibody is used to build the mechanical structure of the UAR. Based on the physical test data, mathematical modeling is conducted for the input-output relationship of the UAR rotor motor, rolling motor and the aerodynamic characteristics of the propeller, and the physical interaction, sensor signals and control signals are simulated, and finally the 3D visualization simulation of the UAR motion on land and in the air is realized (Fig. 4).

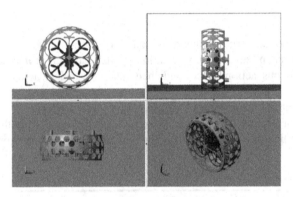

Fig. 4. 3D simulation interface

4.2 PID Controller Design

We partition the pitch and yaw angles into a single channel and assigned the roll angle to another separate channel. To achieve UAR attitude control, we develop two P-PID controllers. The architecture of these controllers is depicted below:

1) The pitch and yaw controller takes input from the measured pitch and yaw angles, as well as their angular velocities, obtained through an Inertial Measurement Unit (IMU). It outputs the desired torque in the two directions, ultimately determining the throttle for the rotor motors.
2) The pitch and yaw controller takes input from the measured pitch and yaw angles, as well as their angular velocities, obtained through an Inertial Measurement Unit (IMU). It outputs the desired torque in the two directions, ultimately determining the throttle for the rotor motors.

4.3 RBSAC Controller Design

The connection relationship between the layers of Critic and Actor networks with the number of nodes and the activation function is set as shown in Fig. 5. Critic networks fit the value of the action and Actor outputs the action according to the current state.

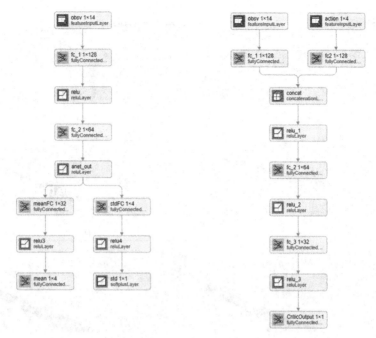

Fig. 5. Networks of RBSAC controller

4.4 Experimental Result

The following actions are designed to test the control effect of the trained reinforcement learning controller:

1) The initial state of the UAR is stationary and upright on the ground.
2) Set the desired rotation angle (i.e., roll angle) of the inner ring to $-30°$, and the outer ring of the UAR starts to roll on the ground under the action of the rolling motor torque.
3) After rolling for some time, the desired pitch angle of the inner ring is set to $30°$, and the UAR is tilted at a certain angle by the aerodynamic force of the rotor and steadily tilted forward to roll.
4) During the tilt forward roll, a raised obstacle appears on the ground, and the UAR rolls over the obstacle while keeping the tilt angle (i.e. pitch angle) constant at $30°$.
5) After the obstacle, the inner ring is set to expect the pitch angle to be $0°$, and the UAR changes to an upright forward roll again.
6) The control force generated by the UAR through the rotor always keeps the yaw angle near $0°$ during the whole motion, i.e., it keeps the forward direction not affected by the pitch angle and obstacles, and the control torque generated by the motor always keeps the inner ring rotation angle near $-30°$.

The 3D visual motion simulation verification of the above motion process is shown in Fig. 6, and the video of the camera fixed on UAR is on the top left.

The variation curve of each attitude angle with time is shown in Fig. 7.

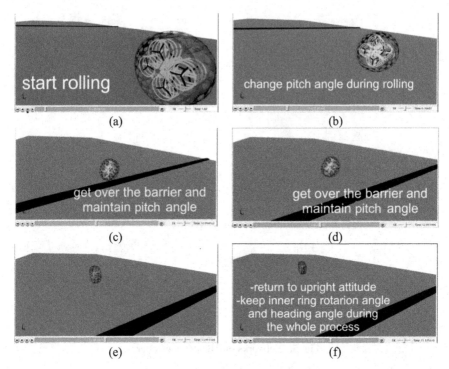

Fig. 6. Simulation of the designed motion

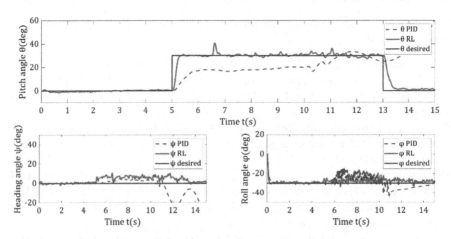

Fig. 7. The desired value and measured value of 3 Euler angles

The experiments demonstrate that the RBSAC controller can acquire an improved control strategy through a sufficient number of training iterations during fully autonomous exploration. Regarding pitch angle control, the RBSAC controller achieves approximately 60% reduction in adjustment time compared to the PID controller, with nearly zero steady-state error, whereas the PID controller exhibits a significant steady-state error of approximately 70%. Concerning the inner ring rotation angle control, when simultaneous control of the pitch angle is required, the PID controller takes considerable oscillation, whereas the RBSAC controller consistently maintains minimal angle changes. Consequently, the designed RBSAC controller offers superior control over stable rolling and flexible attitude changes for UAR on the ground, effectively leveraging the advantages of its single-wheel structure.

In addition, when we train the network, the UAR rolls on flat terrain, but in the testing environment, roadblocks are set on the ground to verify the robustness of the controller. It was observed that at approximately 12 s, the UAR encountered a collision with the roadblock. As a result, the PID controller failed to maintain stability of the flywheel, leading to divergence in all Euler angles. However, it was noted that the RBSAC controller had a minimal impact on the movement of the UAR, thereby indicating the robustness of RBSAC controllers.

After extensive testing in the simulation environment, the trained policy network will be directly deployed on the physical platform in the future.

5   Conclusion

In this paper, we propose a RBSAC controller to keep the balance of UAR while rolling in ground mode. In order to simulate the motion of the UAR more realistically, this paper selects MATLAB/Simulink as the simulation environment, uses Simscape Multibody to build the mechanical structure of the UAR, and simulates physical interaction and sensor signals. The simulation is carried out to realize the 3D visualization simulation of the UAR motion on land and in the air.

This paper uses the Soft Actor-Critic algorithm as the basic principle of the controller and designs the controller for rolling motion according to the specific structure and task characteristics of the UAR, relying on the simulation platform to train the intelligent body a lot so that the agent learns the optimized control algorithm. After simulation verification, the controller designed in this paper can make the UAR roll stably on the ground and change its attitude flexibly, and at the same time, it has certain robustness and can cope with external interference to the motion autonomously, achieving the design goal.

References

1. Kawasaki, K., Zhao, M., Okada, K., Inaba, M.: MUWA: multi-field universal wheel for airland vehicle with quad variable-pitch propellers. In: 2013 IEEE/RSJ International Conference on Intelligent Robots and Systems, pp. 1880–1885. IEEE, Tokyo, Japan (2013)
2. Fan, D.D., Thakker, R., Bartlett, T., et al.: Autonomous hybrid ground/aerial mobility in unknown environments. In: 2019 IEEE/RSJ International Conference on Intelligent Robots and Systems (IROS), pp. 3070–3077. IEEE, Macau, China (2019)
3. Jia, H., et al.: A quadrotor with a passively reconfigurable airframe for hybrid terrestrial locomotion. IEEE/ASME Trans. Mechatron. **27**(6), 4741–4751 (2022)
4. Zhang, R., Wu, Y., Zhang, L., et al.: Autonomous and adaptive navigation for terrestrial-aerial bimodal vehicles. IEEE Rob. Autom. Lett. **7**(2), 3008–3015 (2022)

5. Jia, H., Ding, R., Dong, K., Bai, S., Chirarattananon, P.: Quadrolltor: a reconfigurable quadrotor with controlled rolling and turning. IEEE Rob. Autom. Lett., 1–8 (2023)
6. Borase, R.P., Maghade, D.K., Sondkar, S.Y., et al.: A review of PID control, tuning methods and applications. Int. J. Dynam. Control **9**, 818–827 (2021)
7. Wang, C., Zhang, Y., Li, C., Wang, W., Li, Y.: A rotor flywheel robot: land-air amphibious design and control. In: IEEE/RSJ International Conference on Intelligent Robots and System (2023)
8. Richter, D.J., Calix, R.A.: Using double deep q-learning to learn attitude control of fixed-wing aircraft. In: 2022 16th International Conference on Signal-Image Technology & Internet-Based Systems (SITIS), Dijon, France, pp. 646–651 (2022)
9. Tong, G., Jiang, N., Biyue, L., Xi, Z., Ya, W., Wenbo, D.: UAV navigation in high dynamic environments: a deep reinforcement learning approach. Chin. J. Aeronaut. **34**(2), 479–489 (2021)
10. Hodge, V.J., Hawkins, R., Alexander, R.: Deep reinforcement learning for drone navigation using sensor data. Neural Comput. Appl. **33**(6), 2015–2033 (2021)
11. Jiang, Z., Lynch, A.F.: Quadrotor motion control using deep reinforcement learning. J. Unmanned Veh. Syst. **9**(4), 234–251 (2021)
12. Koch, W., Mancuso, R., West, R., Bestavros, A.: Reinforcement learning for UAV attitude control. ACM Trans. Cyber-Phys. Syst. **3**(2), 1–21 (2019)
13. Waslander, S.L., Hoffmann, G.M., Jang, J.S., Tomlin, C.J.: Multi-agent quadrotor testbed control design: integral sliding mode vs. reinforcement learning. In: 2005 IEEE/RSJ International Conference on Intelligent Robots and Systems, pp. 3712–3717. IEEE (2005)
14. Sun, Z., Wang, Z., Liu, J., Li, M., Chen, F.: Mixline: a hybrid reinforcement learning framework for long-horizon bimanual coffee stirring task. In: Liu, H., et al. (eds.) Intelligent Robotics and Applications. ICIRA 2022. LNCS, vol. 13455. Springer, Cham (2022). https://doi.org/10.1007/978-3-031-13844-7_58
15. Haarnoja, T., Zhou, A., Hartikainen, K., et al.: Soft actor-critic algorithms and applications. arXiv preprint arXiv:1812.05905 (2018)
16. Mysore, S., Mabsout, B., Mancuso, R., Saenko, K.: Regularizing action policies for smooth control with reinforcement learning. In: 2021 IEEE International Conference on Robotics and Automation (ICRA), pp. 1810–1816. IEEE, Xi'an, China (2021)
17. Choi, M., Filter, M., Alcedo, K., Walker, T.T., Rosenbluth, D., Ide, J.S.: Soft actor-critic with inhibitory networks for retraining UAV controllers faster. In: 2022 International Conference on Unmanned Aircraft Systems, Dubrovnik, Croatia, pp. 1561–1570 (2022)
18. He, L., Li, H.: Quadrotor aerobatic maneuver attitude controller based on reinforcement learning. In: 2022 13th Asian Control Conference, Jeju, Korea, pp. 2450–2453 (2022)
19. Brunori, D., Colonnese, S., Cuomo, F., Iocchi, L.: A reinforcement learning environment for multi-service UAV-enabled wireless systems. In: 2021 IEEE International Conference on Pervasive Computing and Communications Workshops and other Affiliated Events (PerCom Workshops), Kassel, Germany, pp. 251–256 (2021)
20. Liaq, M., Byun, Y.T.: Autonomous UAV navigation using reinforcement learning. Int. J. Mach. Learn. Comput. **9**, 756–761 (2019)

Design and Control of a Mobile Cable-Driven Manipulator with Experimental Validation

Ju Lao, Renjie Ju, Yan Gai, and Dong Zhang[✉]

Beijing University of Chemical Technology, Beijing 100029, China
1053073999@qq.com

Abstract. Cable-driven manipulators (CDMs) can move in confined spaces due to their continuous bodies and multiple degrees of freedom (DOFs). However, most CDMs are only used to execute detecting tasks due to their single end effectors. Besides, their workspace are not large enough due to their fixed bases. In order to improve their workspace, flexibility and adaptability, this work designs a novel mobile CDM (MCDM) combined by a CDM and a wheeled platform. In addition, a lightweight cable-driven gripper is designed as an end effector for the novel robot to improve its operational capabilities. To control MCDM accurately, a multi-sensor system is designed and a close-loop control strategy is proposed. For further validation, a simulated and a physical prototypes of MCDM are conducted to execute a grasp task. Results verify the proposed mechanism and close-loop control method.

Keywords: Mobile cable-driven manipulator · multi-sensor · close-loop control

1 Introduction

With the development of manipulators in the past years, they can replace humans to complete some structural tasks [1,2]. Compared to traditional manipulators, hyper-redundant cable-driven manipulator (CDM) has great advantages of slender, flexible, stable, continuous body and strong obstacle avoidance abilities. Due to these features, they are widely used in many fields, such as nuclear [3,4], aerospace exploration [5,6] and medical treatment [7,8].

Motion accuracy is important for manipulators to complete complex tasks. Research of manipulators achieves significant progress in the past decades, but there still remain difficulties in their accurately control due to absence of feedbacks [5]. There are various reasons for causing motion errors in CDM, e.g., deviations between actual sizes and planned sizes of prototypes, differences between desired changes of cable lengths and executed movement, and errors of cable

This work is supported by the National Natural Science Foundation of China (52105005), and the China Postdoctoral Science Foundation (2021M690320), and State Key Laboratory of Robotics and System (SKLRS-2022-KF-15).

ⓒ The Author(s), under exclusive license to Springer Nature Singapore Pte Ltd. 2023
H. Yang et al. (Eds.): ICIRA 2023, LNAI 14274, pp. 241–253, 2023.
https://doi.org/10.1007/978-981-99-6501-4_21

elongation. External force including gravity of links and friction of cables is another important factor that reduces control accuracy. These factors may cause irreversible damages to CDM prototypes. Besides, these errors are difficult to be measured and compensated timely due to the absence of feedbacks.

In order to achieve higher accuracy in motion of manipulators, some work is carried out through close-loop control of manipulators' motion. To achieve precise control, Cui [9] propose a close-loop control system of CDM. Thuruthel work out a algorithm in [10] for close-loop predictive control of a soft robotic manipulator, the algorithm uses a model-based policy. In [11], a close-loop path planning method is designed for multi-DOF snake robots. Power packet dispatching system application of a close-loop manipulator control system is researched in [12]. In [13], a puller-follower controller is proposed, the puller is considered as being primarily responsible for the motion, while the follower prevents its tendon from becoming slack by maintaining its tendon force at some non-zero level. Using joint angle and cable tension sensors, a puller-follower controller is developed in [14] to realize close-loop control of universal joints. A close-loop and compliant controller of the manipulator is designed in [15], and it using a magnetic encoder in the gimbal and a tensile force sensor at the end of the cable. However, the sensors will definitely increase the load weight to reach the maximum capacity limit, there may also be interference between different sensors and encoders, these factors are all challenges that need to be faced by close-loop control of manipulators.

Inspired by above papers, this paper designs a mobile cable-driven manipulator (MCDM) consisted of a 6-DOF CDM, a 3-finger gripper at the end and a wheeled mobile platform at the bottom. To improve its control accuracy, several sensors are integrated on MCDM. Angle sensors are used to measure rotate angles of joints and fingers of gripper. Tension sensors are used to measure cables' tensions. Pressure sensors are installed on the inner side of gripper's fingers to measure contact states between the gripper and targets.

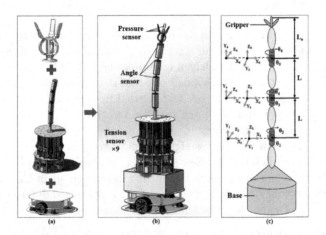

Fig. 1. Design of a MCDM and its D-H coordinate system. (a) Three parts of MCDM. (b) Sensor installation position. (c) D-H coordinate system.

The remainder of this paper is organized as follows. A structure and a kinematic model of MCDM are briefly described in Sect. 2. Section 3 introduces the designed multi-sensor system and feedback control method. Results of experiments are given in Sect. 4. Finally, Sect. 5 concludes this paper.

2 Design and Kinematics Model of MCDM

2.1 Mechanism of MCDM

As shown in Fig. 1, a novel MCDM is designed in this work. The robot consists of a 6-DOF CDM, a 3-finger gripper and a mobile platform. The designed CDM is consisted of 3 joints and 4 rigid links. Each joint can rotate in both pitch and yaw directions by controlling its corresponding 3 cables.

The base of CDM consists of 12 motors distributed in a circular array. Mobile platform can move flexible and fast, and installing CDM on mobile platform can greatly increase the workspace of CDM. The gripper controlled by three cables is installed as an actuator at CDM's end. By combining these parts together, it is possible for MCDM to complete grasping tasks in wider ranges.

2.2 Kinematics of CDM

Kinematics of CDM includes three mappings between cable driven space, joint space and task space. Research on forward kinematics is basis of control of manipulator. In this work, a kinematics model of CDM is derived by using a classical D-H theory. To simplify the model, CDM is hypothesized as a system with 4 links connected by 3 joints as shown in Fig. 1(b). D-H coordinate system is shown in Fig. 1(c). Mathematical symbols and D-H parameters used in this work are listed in Tables 1 and 2, respectively.

To derive a relationship between joint space and task space, a relative position matrix of adjacent discs i and $i-1$ can be computed by using D-H theory:

$$^{i-1}T_i = \begin{bmatrix} C_{\theta_i} & -S_{\theta_i}C_{\gamma_i} & S_{\theta_i}S_{\gamma_i} & a_iC_{\theta_i} \\ S_{\theta_i} & C_{\theta_i}C_{\gamma_i} & -C_{\theta_i}S_{\gamma_i} & a_iS_{\theta_i} \\ 0 & S_{\gamma_i} & C_{\gamma_i} & \kappa_i \\ 0 & 0 & 0 & 1 \end{bmatrix}, \tag{1}$$

where a_i refers to the length of link, γ_i refers to the torsion angle of link, κ_i refers to the joint offset and θ_i is the joint angle.

A transformation relationship between CDM's end coordinate and base coordinate can be obtained by multiplying matrixes sequentially:

$$^0T_n = {}^0T_1 \cdot {}^1T_2 \cdots {}^{n-1}T_n. \tag{2}$$

To derive a relationship between driven space and joint space, kinematics model of a joint is established and analyzed. As shown in Fig. 2, take the first joint as an example, a joint can be simplified as two adjacent discs driven by

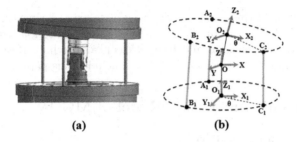

Fig. 2. Kinematics parameters of a joint.

Table 1. Mathematical notations of MCDM.

Symbol	Description
r	Radius of discs
h	Distance of two adjacent parallel discs
α_i	Joint i pitch angle
β_i	Joint i yaw angle
C_α, S_α	$\cos\alpha, \sin\alpha$

Table 2. D-H parameters of CDM.

Link i	$\kappa_i(mm)$	$\theta_i(°)$	$a_i(mm)$	$\gamma_i(°)$
1	0	θ_1	0	−90
2	0	θ_2	L	90
3	0	θ_3	0	−90
4	0	θ_4	L	90
5	0	θ_5	0	−90
6	0	θ_6	L_e	90

three cables. As shown in Fig. 2(b), planes $A_1B_1C_1$ and $A_2B_2C_2$ are adjacent discs, cables A_1A_2, B_1B_2 and C_1C_2 are corresponding cables of the joint. Center of mass (CM) of the joint locates at O.

As shown in Fig. 2(b), plane $A_1B_1C_1$ rotates α around the axis X_1, and then shift $\frac{h}{2}$ upward, and the origin O_1 coincides with point O. Homogeneous change matrix between $A_1B_1C_1$ and O is:

$$^{1}T_0 = Trans(0,0,\frac{h}{2})\, Rot(X,\alpha) = \begin{bmatrix} 1 & 0 & 0 & 0 \\ 0 & 1 & 0 & 0 \\ 0 & 0 & 1 & \frac{h}{2} \\ 0 & 0 & 0 & 1 \end{bmatrix} \begin{bmatrix} 1 & 0 & 0 & 0 \\ 0 & C_\alpha & -S_\alpha & 0 \\ 0 & S_\alpha & C_\alpha & 0 \\ 0 & 0 & 0 & 1 \end{bmatrix} = \begin{bmatrix} 1 & 0 & 0 & 0 \\ 0 & C_\alpha & -S_\alpha & 0 \\ 0 & S_\alpha & C_\alpha & \frac{h}{2} \\ 0 & 0 & 0 & 1 \end{bmatrix}. \quad (3)$$

The point (O) coincides with O_2 after rotating β around its Y axis and translating upward $\frac{h}{2}$. A homogeneous transformation matrix between $A_2B_2C_2$ and

(O) can be obtained:

$$
{}^{0}T_2 = Rot(Y,\beta)\,Trans(0,0,\tfrac{h}{2}) =
\begin{bmatrix} C_\beta & 0 & S_\beta & 0 \\ 0 & 1 & 0 & 0 \\ -S_\beta & 0 & C_\beta & 0 \\ 0 & 0 & 0 & 1 \end{bmatrix}
\begin{bmatrix} 1 & 0 & 0 & 0 \\ 0 & 1 & 0 & 0 \\ 0 & 0 & 1 & \tfrac{h}{2} \\ 0 & 0 & 0 & 1 \end{bmatrix}
=
\begin{bmatrix} C_\beta & 0 & S_\beta & 0 \\ 0 & 1 & 0 & 0 \\ -S_\beta & 0 & C_\beta & \tfrac{h}{2} \\ 0 & 0 & 0 & 1 \end{bmatrix}.
\tag{4}
$$

Therefore, a homogeneous transformation matrix of coordinate system $A_1B_1C_1$ and coordinate system $A_2B_2C_2$ is:

$$
{}^{1}T_2 = {}^{1}T_0\,{}^{0}T_2 =
\begin{bmatrix} C_\beta & 0 & S_\beta & 0 \\ 0 & 1 & 0 & 0 \\ -S_\beta & 0 & C_\beta & \tfrac{h}{2} \\ 0 & 0 & 0 & 1 \end{bmatrix}
\begin{bmatrix} 1 & 0 & 0 & 0 \\ 0 & C_\alpha & -S_\alpha & 0 \\ 0 & S_\alpha & C_\alpha & \tfrac{h}{2} \\ 0 & 0 & 0 & 1 \end{bmatrix}
=
\begin{bmatrix} C_\beta & S_\alpha S_\beta & C_\alpha S_\beta & S_\beta h \\ 0 & C_\alpha & -S_\alpha & 0 \\ -S_\beta & C_\beta S_\alpha & C_\alpha C_\beta & C_\beta h \\ 0 & 0 & 0 & 1 \end{bmatrix}.
\tag{5}
$$

In coordinate system $A_1B_1C_1$, representation of point C_1 is:

$$
{}^{1}C_1 = \begin{bmatrix} rC_\theta & rS_\theta & 0 & 1 \end{bmatrix}^{T}.
\tag{6}
$$

In coordinate system $A_2B_2C_2$, representation of point C_2 is:

$$
{}^{2}C_2 = \begin{bmatrix} rC_\theta & rS_\theta & 0 & 1 \end{bmatrix}^{T},
\tag{7}
$$

where θ represents angle between C_1 and axis X_1, as well as angle between C_2 and axis X_2. In plane $A_2B_2C_2$, ${}^{2}C_2$ can be expressed as:

$$
{}^{1}C_2 = {}^{1}T_2\,{}^{2}C_2 =
\begin{bmatrix} hS_\beta + rC_\beta C_\theta + rS_\alpha S_\beta S_\theta \\ rC_\alpha S_\theta \\ hC_\beta - rC_\theta S_\beta + rC_\beta S_\alpha S_\theta \\ 1 \end{bmatrix}.
\tag{8}
$$

Thus, distance between C_1 and C_2 is:

$$
|C_1C_2| =
\begin{vmatrix} hS_\beta + rC_\beta C_\theta + rS_\alpha S_\beta S_\theta - rS_\theta \\ rC_\alpha S_\beta - rS_\theta \\ hC_\beta - rC_\theta S_\beta + rC_\beta S_\alpha S_\theta \\ 0 \end{vmatrix}.
\tag{9}
$$

Similarly, distance between points A_1 and A_2 and another one between B_1 and B_2 can be computed by:

$$
|A_1A_2| =
\begin{vmatrix} hS_\beta + rC_\beta C_{\theta+2\pi/3} + rS_\alpha S_\beta S_{\theta+2\pi/3} - rC_{\theta+2\pi/3} \\ rC_\alpha S_\beta - rS_{\theta+2\pi/3} \\ hC_\beta - rC_{\theta+2\pi/3}S_\beta + rC_\beta S_\alpha S_{\theta+2\pi/3} \\ 0 \end{vmatrix},
\tag{10}
$$

and

$$
|B_1B_2| =
\begin{vmatrix} hS_\beta + rC_\beta C_{\theta+4\pi/3} + rS_\alpha S_\beta S_{\theta+4\pi/3} - rC_{\theta+4\pi/3} \\ rC_\alpha S_\beta - rS_{\theta+4\pi/3} \\ hC_\beta - rC_{\theta+4\pi/3}S_\beta + rC_\beta S_\alpha S_{\theta+4\pi/3} \\ 0 \end{vmatrix}.
\tag{11}
$$

2.3 Kinematics of Cable-Driven Gripper

The gripper is also controlled by cables. When cables are relaxed, springs push the slicing and locking cable device upwards, and fingers open, causing gripper to be in a released state. When cables are tightened, the locking cable device presses down on the slice, causing springs to tighten and fingers to approach center of palm (CP), placing gripper in a grasping state.

To illustrate the kinematics of the gripper, Fig. 3 shows a single finger of the gripper and its kinematics parameters. As shown in Fig. 3, point A locates at the base remains fixed, $\angle BCD = \angle B'C'D'$. When the gripper is in a released state as shown in Fig. 3(a), relationships are established:

$$\sin \angle DCE = \frac{e}{d}, \tag{12}$$

$$\angle DCE + \angle BCD + \angle ACB = 180°, \tag{13}$$

$$a^2 = b^2 + c^2 - 2bc \cos \angle ACB. \tag{14}$$

By combining (12)–(14), distance from fingertip D to CP can be calculated as:

$$e = d\sin(180° - \angle BCD - acos(\frac{b^2 + c^2 - a^2}{2bc})). \tag{15}$$

As shown in Fig. 3(b), when corresponding cables are stretched tight, the gripper is in a contract status, relationships are established:

$$a'^2 = b'^2 + c'^2 - 2b'c' \cos \angle AC'B', \tag{16}$$

$$b' + s = b, \tag{17}$$

$$\angle CC'D' + \angle B'C'D' + \angle AC'B' = 180°, \tag{18}$$

$$\sin \angle CC'D' = \frac{e'}{d'}. \tag{19}$$

Distance from D' to the gripper's CP is:

$$e' = d'\sin(180° - \angle B'C'D' - acos(\frac{(b - s')^2 + c'^2 - a'^2}{2(b - s')a'})). \tag{20}$$

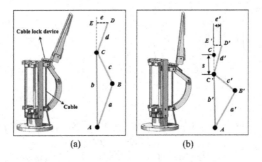

Fig. 3. Single finger of the cable-driven gripper. (a) Release status. (b) Contract status.

Therefore, the distance of D to the gripper's CP can be expressed as:

$$D_x = e - e' = d\sin(180° - \angle BCD - acos(\frac{b^2 + c^2 - a^2}{2bc}))$$
$$- d'\sin(180° - \angle B'C'D' - acos(\frac{(b-s)^2 + c'^2 - a'^2}{2(b-s)c'})) \quad . \tag{21}$$

Using above computation, states of the gripper finger's tip D_x can be derived from a cable change s. Motion of cables can be calculated according to changes of the gripper's tip:

$$s = \frac{-B + \sqrt{B^2 - 4C}}{2}. \tag{22}$$

To simplify computation, A, B and C are abbreviated as:

$$A = 180° - \angle B'C'D' - asin(\frac{d\sin(\pi - \angle BCD - a\cos(\frac{b^2+c^2-a^2}{2bc})) - D_x}{d}),$$
$$\tag{23}$$
$$B = 2c'\cos A - 2b, \tag{24}$$
$$C = b^2 + c'^2 - a'^2 - 2bc'\cos A. \tag{25}$$

2.4 Kinematics of Mobile Platform

In the novel MCDM, a dual-wheel differential driven robot is selected as a mobile platform. The platform has two driving wheels locate in its axis and four passive wheels distributed at four corners. Its kinematics model is shown in Fig. 4. (x, y) is the coordinate of CM of the mobile platform in global coordinate system, θ is the platform's heading angle, the radius of driven wheels is l, and the distance between two driven wheels is d, ω is the turning angular speed of the mobile platform. States of the mobile platform can be expressed as $\boldsymbol{p} = [x, y, \theta]^T$.

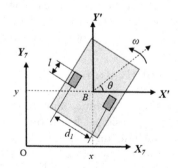

Fig. 4. Kinematics parameters of the mobile platform.

Assuming angular velocities of the left and right driven wheels is ω_l and ω_r, the following relationship holds:

$$x' = \frac{l(\omega_l + \omega_r)C_\theta}{2},$$

$$y' = \frac{l(\omega_l + \omega_r)S_\theta}{2}, \tag{26}$$

$$\theta' = \frac{l(\omega_l + \omega_r)}{2}.$$

Then B is taken as the reference point to obtain the kinematic model of the mobile platform:

$$\begin{bmatrix} x' \\ y' \\ \theta' \end{bmatrix} = \begin{bmatrix} \frac{1}{2}lC_\theta & \frac{1}{2}lC_\theta \\ \frac{1}{2}lS_\theta & \frac{1}{2}lS_\theta \\ -\frac{l}{d_1} & -\frac{l}{d_1} \end{bmatrix} = \begin{bmatrix} \omega_l \\ \omega_r \end{bmatrix}. \tag{27}$$

According to (27), the mobile platform's position can be expressed as:

$$x_{i+1} = x_i + \frac{l}{2}C_{\theta i} \int_{t_i}^{t_{i+1}} (\omega_l(t) + \omega_r(t))dt,$$

$$y_{i+1} = y_i + \frac{l}{2}S_{\theta i} \int_{t_i}^{t_{i+1}} (\omega_l(t) + \omega_r(t))dt, \tag{28}$$

$$\theta_{i+1} = \theta_i + \frac{l}{d_1} \int_{t_i}^{t_{i+1}} (\omega_l(t) + \omega_r(t))dt.$$

States of the mobile platform can be got by discretizing (28):

$$\begin{bmatrix} x(k+1) \\ y(k+1) \\ \theta(k+1) \end{bmatrix} = \begin{bmatrix} x(k) + \frac{l}{2}TC_\theta(\omega_{ri} + \omega_{li}) \\ y(k) + \frac{l}{2}TS_\theta(\omega_{ri} + \omega_{li}) \\ \theta(k) + \frac{l}{d_1}T(\omega_{ri} - \omega_{li}) \end{bmatrix}. \tag{29}$$

From above derivations, it can be got that the control vector of the mobile platform is $[\omega_l, \omega_r]^T$. Therefore, direction of the mobile platform can be controlled by adjusting the speed difference of the two driving wheels.

3   Close-Loop Control System

Close-loop control is necessary for accuracy motion of MCDM. In this work, a close-loop control framework is designed based on a multi-sensor system. The important states of MCDM include angles of CDM's joints, pressures of fingers, position of mobile platform and tensions of cables. To get these information, a multi-sensor system is designed as shown in Fig. 5. Gyroscopes are installed on discs of joints and gripper's fingers to measure their angles. Tension sensors are installed at the connection between driven-cables and guide rails. Pressure sensors are installed on the inner side of the gripper's fingertips, stick sponge tape on it to prevent damage.

3.1 Angle Sensor

To measure angles of joints and gripper's fingers, gyroscopes MPU6050 are used in this work. There are two ways to measure angles by using the sensor. The first one is inverting acceleration to obtain Euler angles. The second one is integrating angular velocities. Each method has merits and shortcomings. Due to the first method cannot measure roll angles, the second method is used to measure angles in this work. An Arduino mega 2560 is used as an acquisition board to transfer signals. The angle subsystem includes 6 sets of data, e.g., pitch and yaw angles of three CDM joints, and angles of three fingers of gripper.

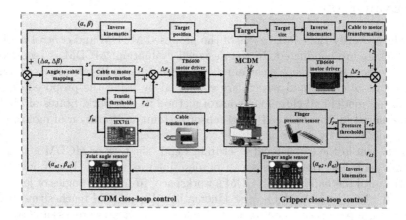

Fig. 5. Close-loop control framework of MCDM.

3.2 Tension Sensor

In the application scenario of CDM, the pulling situation of the cable directly determines the accuracy of joint angle. Accuracy of joints' motion is decided by movements of cables. It is necessary to obtain tensions of cables and judge their degree of tightness. This work will measure the tensions by using ZNLBS-VII S-type tension sensors. Arduino board is selected as their controller unit. The measured signals are converted to digital signals and transmitted to MCU by using a HX711 module. The tension level and motor compensation value are shown in the Table 3.

Table 3. Tension thresholds.

sensor indication	tension level	motor compensation
>80	too tight	<−300
(0, 80]	tight	0
[−80, 0]	loose	0
<−80	too loose	>300

3.3   Pressure Sensor

End effector of MCDM is a 3-finger gripper. Each finger is controlled by a cable. In order to obtain contact degrees between the gripper and target objects, a membrane pressure sensor is installed in the fingertip to measure grasping forces. A RP-L membrane resistive pressure sensor is selected in this work. The resistance value of the sensor decreases as the finger's pressure increases. The pressure contact level and motor compensation value are shown in Table 4. Installation of sensors is shown in Fig. 6.

4   Evaluation

In order to verify the effectiveness of the proposed MCDM and control method, experiments are conducted. In the designed evaluation, MCDM is required to grasp a object which keeps a certain distance from itself. Rotate angles of joints, movements of cables and wheels are computed by using the proposed derived kinematics model and close-loop control method in this work. States of MCDM are measured by the designed multi-sensor system, and position of mobile platform is obtained by an Optitrack 3D capture system.

As shown in the experimental setup in Fig. 7, the task of MCDM is to grasp a tennis ball. The task process can be described as follows. The robot moves forward until the ball is within CDM's workspace. Rotational angles of joints are calculated based on CDM's inverse kinematics. When CDM reaches the desired pose, the gripper grasps the target. Prototype experimental process and sensors' data are shown in Figs. 7 and 8, respectively.

Table 4. Pressure thresholds.

sensor indication	contact level	motor compensation
$(0, 150]$	light touch	500
$(150, 300]$	medium touch	300
$(300, 500]$	big touch	0
>500	big squeeze	< -300

(a)   (b)   (c)

Fig. 6. Sensors installation.

Control compensations are computed by using feedback data. As shown in Fig. 8(a), large errors in the joints' angles are detected at 95 s and 136 s. Consequently, they are compensated until the error reduce to an acceptable range. In Fig. 8(c), it is observed that the pressure between finger 3 and object is too low at 311 s. As a result, compensations are applied to finger 3 based on Table 4. Furthermore, Fig. 8(d) reveals that tensions of the cables of motor 10 and motor 2 are too loose at 244 s. Hence, it is compensated according to Table 3. As far as the current experiments are concerned, no interferences between different sensors are found.

Fig. 7. Prototype experiment.

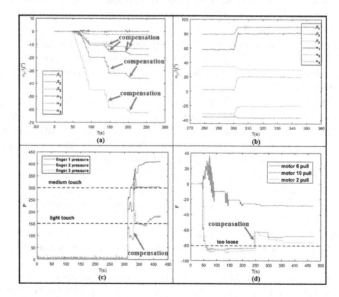

Fig. 8. Sensors data. (a) Joints angles. (b) Gripper fingers angles. (c) Gripper fingers pressure and (d) Cables tension.

5   Conclusion and Future Work

Most CDMs are designed without feedbacks, this lead to imprecise control. Besides, their workspace are limited by fixed bases. In order to improve performances of CDM, this paper proposed a MCDM and a feedback control method based on a multi-sensor system. Firstly, we designed a MCDM and analyzed its kinematics. After that, a close-loop control system of MCDM was then designed. Finally, experiments on MCDM were conducted to verify the effectiveness of the proposed method. The experiments show that MCDM has high accuracy in motion with the close-loop control.

In our future work, we will research control methods for MCDM in more complex environments with multi-obstacle.

References

1. Du, Z., Ouyang, G., Xue, J., Yao, Y.: A review on kinematic, workspace, trajectory planning and path planning of hyper-redundant manipulators. In: IEEE International Conference on Cyber Technology in Automation, Control, and Intelligent Systems, pp. 444–449 (2020)
2. Xu, W., Liu, T., Li, Y.: Kinematics, dynamics, and control of a cable-driven hyper-redundant manipulator. IEEE/ASME Trans. Mechatron. **23**(4), 1693–1704 (2018)
3. Armada, D.: Snaking around in a nuclear jungle. Ind. Robot Int. J. **32**, 120–127 (2013)
4. Buckingham, R., Graham, A.: Dexterous manipulators for nuclear inspection and maintenance case study. In: The International Conference on Applied Robotics for the Power Industry, pp. 1–6 (2010)
5. Buckingham, R.: Snake arm robots. Ind. Robot. **29**, 242–245 (2002)
6. Liu, T., Xu, W., Yang, T., Li, Y.: A hybrid active and passive cable-driven segmented redundant manipulator: design, kinematics, and planning. IEEE/ASME Trans. Mechatron. **26**(2), 930–942 (2021)
7. Hwang, M., Kwon, D.: K-flex: a flexible robotic platform for scar-free endoscopic surgery. Int. J. Med. Robot. Comput. Assist. Surg. **16**(2), e2078 (2020)
8. Walker, I.D., Choset, H., Chirikjian, G.S.: Snake-like and continuum robots. In: Siciliano, B., Khatib, O. (eds.) Springer Handbook of Robotics, pp. 481–498. Springer, Cham (2016). https://doi.org/10.1007/978-3-319-32552-1_20
9. Cui, X., Chen, W., Yang, G., Jin, Y.: Closed-loop control for a cable-driven parallel manipulator with joint angle feedback. In: 2013 IEEE/ASME International Conference on Advanced Intelligent Mechatronics, Wollongong, NSW, Australia, pp. 625–630 (2013)
10. Thuruthel, T.G., Falotico, E., Renda, F., Laschi, C.: Model-based reinforcement learning for closed-loop dynamic control of soft robotic manipulators. IEEE Trans. Robot. **35**(1), 124–134 (2019)
11. Cao, Z., Zhang, D., Zhou, M.: Direction control and adaptive path-following of 3-D snake-like robot motion. IEEE Trans. Cybern. **52**(10), 10980–10987 (2022)
12. Mochiyama, S., Hikihara, T.: Experimental implementation of power packet density modulation to close-loop control of manipulator. In: International Symposium on Power Electronics, Electrical Drives, Automation and Motion (SPEEDAM), Amalfi, Italy, pp. 762–767 (2018)

13. Potkonjak, V., et al.: The puller-follower control of compliant and noncompliant antagonistic tendon drives in robotic systems. Int. J. Adv. Robot. Syst. **8**(5), 143–155 (2011)

14. Wu, B., Zeng, L., Zheng, Y., Zhang, S., Zhu, X., Xu, K.: A closed-loop controller for cable-driven hyper-redundant manipulator with joint angle sensors. In: IEEE International Conference on Robotics and Biomimetics (ROBIO), pp. 2433–2438 (2019)

15. Yuan, H., Zhou, L., Xu, W.: A comprehensive static model of cable driven multi-section continuum robots considering friction effect. Mech. Mach. Theory **135**, 130–149 (2019)

Autonomous Exploration for Mobile Robot in Three Dimensional Multi-layer Space

Yusheng Yang⬤, Jinghan Zhang, Wei Qian, Hao Geng, and Yangmin Xie(✉)

Shanghai Key Laboratory of Intelligent Manufacturing and Robotics,
School of Mechatronic Engineering and Automation, Shanghai University,
Shangda Road 99, Shanghai 200444, China
`xieym@shu.edu.cn`

Abstract. Autonomous exploration of unknown environments is the basis for mobile robots in applications like rescue and industrial inspection. The critical capability for autonomous exploration is the determination of the next exploration point. In this paper, we proposed an autonomous exploration strategy for 3D multi-layer environments. The ML-SKiMap structure is presented to store and retrieve the map with the layer information, and the stability and obstacle collision situation are analyzed to check the traversability of each voxel in ML-SKiMap. Furthermore, a cost function in terms of exploration information entropy, layer weight, and navigation cost is adopted to evaluate the exploration performance, and the optimal next exploration point is selected with minimum exploration cost. The experiments in simulation and practice demonstrate that the proposed method can explore multi-layer environments effectively.

Keywords: Multi-layer Environment · Traversability · Exploration Information Entropy

1 Introduction

Autonomous exploration is one of the critical capabilities of mobile robots. It refers to the robot's ability to autonomously identify boundary areas according to the known map, and further expand unknown areas along the boundary until the environment is fully explored or the specified task is completed. Autonomous exploration plays an essential role in the fields of emergency rescue, battlefield inspection, planet exploration, etc. For example, Tung Dang et al. [1] presented a graph-based autonomous exploration algorithm for the underground mine rescue task by using aerial robots. Chao Cao et al. [2,3] presented a hierarchicalexploration framework for complex three-dimensional (3D) environments,

---

Sponsored by Natural Science Foundation of Shanghai, Grant No. 20ZR1419100.

© The Author(s), under exclusive license to Springer Nature Singapore Pte Ltd. 2023
H. Yang et al. (Eds.): ICIRA 2023, LNAI 14274, pp. 254–266, 2023.
https://doi.org/10.1007/978-981-99-6501-4_22

such as the Nuclear Plant. The indoor environment like the office is explored by Wenchao Gao et al. [4] with a mobile robot.

In the process of autonomous exploration, environmental information is unknown in the beginning. Conventional exploration methods always assumed that the environment only contains a single layer, and represents the map as a 2D grid map or the 3D map with one layer. For instance, Reinis Cimurs et al. [5] represented the unknown environment as the 2D grid map. A 3D occupancy grid map is adopted by Ryota Uomi et al. [6] to describe the unexplored environment. However, the environment with multi-layer properties is often occurred in real life, such as multi-story parking lots, buildings, etc. In the multi-layer environment, the traditional exploration strategy, which didn't contain layer information, would drive the mobile robot to search around between different layers, which decreases the exploration efficiency greatly.

To overcome the above problem of robot motion redundancy in the exploration process, an autonomous exploration strategy for a multi-layer 3D environment is presented in this paper. The critical for autonomous exploration is to decide the mobile robot's subsequent exploration point based on the explored map. The exploration point should locate near the boundary of the explored region to facilitate the potential search. Furthermore, the mobile robot should be able to capture as much follow-up environmental information as possible at the exploration point, under the premise of exploration safety. On the basis of satisfying the above requirements, the proposed exploration strategy mainly contains two steps. First, the proposed strategy calculated the traversability of the explored map to ensure searching safety and the map can be categorized as accessible region, dangerous region, and unknown region. Then the exploration point is evaluated and determined from the accessible region in terms of potential exploration information entropy, layer weight, and navigation cost. Repeating these two steps until the map is explored completely or the specified task is achieved. The main contributions of this paper include the following:

1. An traversability analysis strategy for a multi-layer 3D environment is proposed to guarantee the searching safety for robot autonomous exploration.
2. An exploration point selection strategy for a multi-layer 3D environment is proposed according to the information of potential exploration entropy, layer information, and traveling cost.

The remaining context of the paper is organized as follows. In Sect. 2 a brief literature review about autonomous exploration is introduced. The detail of the proposed exploration strategy is given in Sect. 3. To evaluate the effectiveness of the proposed method, the experimental results and discussion are presented in Sect. 4. The paper ends with a short conclusion in Sect. 5.

2 Related Work

The critical for mobile robot autonomous exploration is how to determine the next exploration point from the explored region. According to different search principles, the present exploration strategy can be separated into frontier-based strategy and learning-based strategy.

The frontier-based exploration method is first presented by Brian Yamauchi [7] in 1977. In the 2D environmental map, the frontier area is defined as the junction of known and unknown regions [8]. Researchers believe that the unknown environment can only be observed in these frontier areas. Therefore, many strategies are presented to identify the optimal exploration point. Brian Yamauchi [7] proposed that the closest point to the starting position among the candidate boundary points can be selected as the next exploration point. However, only considering the distance factor when exploring is not reasonable especially when the environment is cluttered. Andreas Bricher et al. [9] presented the exploration point selection method according to the search information entropy. By predicting in advance the scanning area that will be increased at each candidate point, the next exploration point is selected with the largest potential scanning area. Based on prior environmental information, an exploration strategy is introduced by Daniel Perea Strom et al. [10] by predicting the structure information that may exist in the unknown environment. And the frontier point that has more environmental gain is selected accordingly. A cost function is proposed by Wenchao Gao et al. [4] to evaluate the exploration performance of candidate frontier points, which takes into account the size of the frontier point set, the navigation distance, and the turning cost. The best exploration point is decided with the best performance value. Samaahita S Belavadi et al. [11] adopted the K-means clustering method to divide the boundary points and only left the center of each point cluster as the final candidate point for exploration. However, the number of clusters needs to be set for this algorithm, which limits its applications in practice, especially when the environment is full of complex features. Garen Haddeler et al. [12] presented a 3D exploration method applied to the wheeled-legged robot. They first performed the passability analysis on uneven terrain according to the roughness, slope angle and segmentation step, and construct the passability map. Then determining the exploration point based on the gravity boundary analysis of the robot's current posture and the desired posture. Hyungseok Kim et al. [13] proposed a framework for autonomous exploration by exploiting the 2D map segmentation and geometric information between frontiers and mobile robot. For large-scale environment, Junlong Huang et al. [14] presented a fast preprocessing algorithm to improve path generation frequency during autonomous exploration.

With the development of artificial intelligence in recent years, deep learning methods have been used by researchers for autonomous exploration. By constructing the heatmap for the existing environment, Dimitrios I.Koutras et al. [15] proposed a reinforcement learning-based exploration method to pick the optimal exploration point. Reinis Cimurs et al. [5] presented a TD3 network structure that considers the motion strategy and global navigation evaluation metrics, and the corresponding trained model is used to compute the target point for subsequent exploration. Rakesh Shrestha et al. [16] separated the map regions into obstacles, free space, and unknown space, and took them as three channels of the image. Taking that image as the input for the deep neural network, the optimal rectangular candidate areas can be output directly. Although the deep neural network can obtain the next exploration point directly, the prediction process always presents a disadvantage in terms of computational overhead and efficiency over traditional frontier-based methods.

The aforementioned exploration strategies usually address the mobile robot exploration problem in the structured 2D flat ground environment. For complex 3D environments, the exploration is always conducted by the unmanned aerial vehicle (UAV) instead of the mobile robot [1, 17, 18]. Few studies have researched the 3D autonomous exploration problem for mobile robots, especially the multi-layer 3D environment. However, in real life, many target search and localization tasks need to be conducted in a complex multi-layer 3D environment, and the optimal exploration point needs to be given for the mobile robot. Therefore, a multi-layer autonomous exploration strategy is presented in this paper to address the above problem.

3   Methodology

Fig. 1. The procedure of the proposed exploration point selection strategy.

Figure 1 illustrates the procedure of the proposed method, which contains two main steps. First, the traversability of the explored map is analyzed, Then the potential exploration point set is generated and evaluated with the proposed criterion. The eventual exploration point is selected with the optimal evaluation metrics.

3.1   Traversability Analysis

In this work, the map is represented as the point cloud format and denoted as P. To accelerate the data processing efficiency, an improved SkiMap [19] is presented to store and retrieve the point cloud information, which is called multi-layer SKiMap (ML-SKiMap). ML-SKiMap is a voxelized point cloud representation. Compared with the SKiMap, which has three layers, one extra layer is added to ML-SKiMap to store the environmental layer information, as shown in Fig. 2a. Specifically, the point cloud is layered according to their z-axis values, and the point cloud that locates at the approximate height is divided into the same layer.

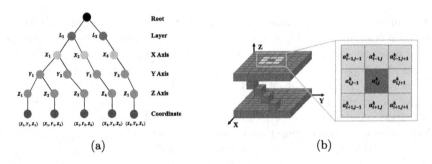

Fig. 2. (a) The structure of ML-SKiMap. (b) The traversability map of ML-SKiMap.

With the ML-SKiMap, the traversability map is generated by analyzing the traversability for each voxel. As shown in Fig. 2b, $a_{i,j}^k$ represents the voxel in ML-SKiMap, where i, j are the indexes in the x-axis and y-axis respectively, and k means the layer information. The traversability of $a_{i,j}^k$ is denoted as $F_{i,j}^k$ and represents the difficulty of a mobile robot moving from eight surrounding voxels to the current position.

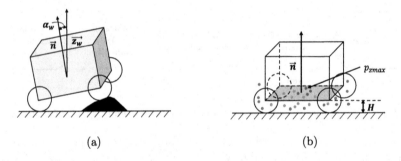

Fig. 3. (a) The robot is regarded as instability when its tilt angle is too large. (b) The robot is considered to be in a collision situation when there are point clouds that exceed the height of the chassis.

Even though many factors impact the robot's access traversability, the platform stability and the obstacle collision situations are the crucial factors [20], and are used for traversability evaluation for each ML-SKiMap voxel. As depicted in Fig. 3a, the robot is considered unstable when the angle α_w between the normal vector $\boldsymbol{n}$ of the robot chassis plane and the z-axis positive direction $\vec{z_w}$ is greater than the stability threshold α_{max}. Otherwise, the robot is stable. The obstacle collision is determined by checking where the highest position p_{zmax} of the point clouds within the voxel exceeds the height H of the robot chassis. Accordingly, the traversability is computed as follows:

$$F_{i,j}^k = \begin{cases} F_{unknown} & P_{i,j}^k = \emptyset \\ F_{danger} & \alpha_w \geq \alpha_{max} \text{ or } p_{zmax} \geq H \\ tan(\alpha_w) & \alpha_w < \alpha_{max} \text{ and } p_{zmax} < H \end{cases} \qquad (1)$$

$F_{unknown}$ means that no point cloud $P_{i,j}^k$ exist in the corresponding voxel. F_{danger} represents that the voxel is dangerous for the mobile robot. Traversing the ML-SKiMap voxels and calculating the corresponding traversability. Eventually, the ML-SKiMap can be separated into unknown regions, dangerous regions, and accessible regions.

3.2   Exploration Point Identification

For exploration safety, the exploration point needs to be located inside the accessible regions. Initially, the candidate exploration points are recognized from the accessible regions. Then an exploration evaluation cost function is presented to identify the final exploration point among candidate points.

Exploration Point Candidates. To maximize exploration efficiency, the exploration point is preferred to lie near the frontier. Therefore, the frontier points are identified and denoted as C_{bou}. Since there may be a large number of frontier points, a candidate point deletion strategy is proposed. First, an improved K-means algorithm is adopted to cluster frontier points [20] based on distance. Secondly, setting a candidate filtering radius r_f, and iterating through candidate points in C_{bou}. If there are dangerous points or unknown points inside the filtering radius of the current point, this point is regarded as a potentially dangerous exploration point and is deleted from C_{bou}, as shown in Fig. 4a. Finally, the filtered point set is regarded as the potential exploration point set C_{cp}.

Exploration Point Evaluation. To determine the optimal exploration point for the multi-layer 3D environment, three aspects are evaluated for comparison in this work, which are the exploration information entropy, multi-layer weight, and the navigation cost.

The exploration information entropy means the area of potential exploration region. Since the unknown environment is not captured yet, the area of potential exploration region can not be obtained. In this work, the number of frontier points is used to represent the potential exploration region. As illustrated in Fig. 4b, an information gain radius r_g is set, and the number of frontier points N_c inside the circle is adopted to describe the corresponding point's exploration information entropy.

Considering the uncertain number of layers in the environment, the exploration efficiency would decrease significantly if the mobile robot explores alternately between different layers. Therefore, the multi-layer weight k_c is adopted to guarantee that voxels on the same layer would be searched in high priority.

Specifically, k_c is calculated as the difference between the voxel's layer index and the lowest layer index in the ML-SKiMap. With the multi-layer weight, each layer is preferred to be searched completely before exploring another layer.

Even though for the same layer, there may be several exploration candidate points. For calculation efficiency, The Euclidean distance from the current position to each candidate is calculated as the navigation cost T_c. Smaller T_c means that the mobile robot can explore the environment efficiently.

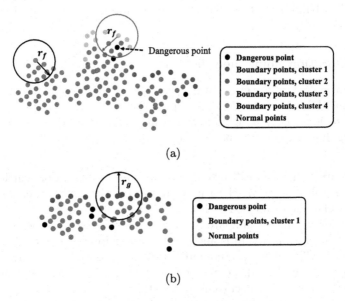

(a)

(b)

Fig. 4. (a) The candidate point is deleted if there are dangerous points inside the radius of this point. (b) With the information gain radius r_g, the number of frontier points inside the circle is adopted to describe the corresponding point's exploration information entropy.

Combined above factors, the evaluation cost for the exploration candidate is given as:

$$E(c) = k_1 \cdot T_c^{k_c - 1} + k_2 \cdot \frac{N_{C_{cp}}}{N_c} \tag{2}$$

where k_1 and k_2 are the coefficients to balance evaluation terms. $N_{C_{cp}}$ represents the size of C_{cp}. Traversing every point c in C_{cp}, the point with minimum cost value is regarded as the optimal exploration point.

4   Experiments and Discussion

The proposed autonomous exploration strategy was verified in both simulation and real-world experiments with a self-built mobile robot. As depicted in Fig. 5,

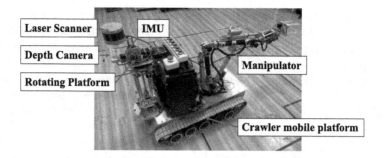

Fig. 5. The mobile robot used in the experiment.

the self-built mobile robot consists of a laser scanner (Velodyne VLP-16) that is mounted on a rotating platform, thus the system could capture dense point clouds. One depth camera (Real Scene D455) is used for image capturing. To improve localization accuracy, an IMU sensor (FSS-IMU618) is used as well. The proposed algorithm is built in the framework of ROS melodic, and runs on a laptop (EVOC GROUP, EC3-1821) with an Intel Core I7-6600U CPU.

During the experiment, the mobile robot is deployed at the starting point of the environment to be explored. The dense map is reconstructed based on the laser scanning system at this point, and the next exploration point is calculated based on the proposed strategy. Then the mobile robot would navigate to the next exploration point. Repeating the above procedure until the environment is scanned completely or the specified task is finished. Noted that the laser scanning system doesn't work during the movement phase, the scanning is only conducted at the exploration point.

4.1   Simulation Experiment

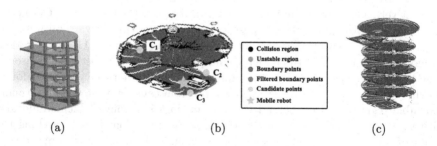

Fig. 6. (a) The multi-layer parking lots in simulation. (b) The result of autonomous exploration for one layer. (c) The eventual point cloud after exploration.

To demonstrate the feasibility of the proposed method, a simulated 3D multi-layer parking lot is built for exploration as shown in Fig. 6a. Figure 6b gives the traversability analysis result of the first two layers of the environment in detail. The recognized unstable regions are colored green and the regions that are in collision with the robot are colored black. It's obvious that most collision regions are close to unstable regions. There are also some collision regions that are close to the map's boundary (color fig online Fig. 6b). One possible reason is that the edge of the road in the parking lot always has curbstones, which may exceed the height of the robot's chassis. By clustering boundary points and filtering outliers, three clusters are extracted eventually, and the optimal exploration point is selected with minimum evaluation cost in those clusters. Specifically, the evaluation costs for three candidate exploration points are 27.869, 6.735, and 4.283 respectively, and C_3 is selected as the optimal exploration point for the next search. The overall reconstruction of the simulated environment is given in Fig. 6c.

4.2 Real-World Experiment

Figure 7a shows the progress of mobile robot autonomous exploration in a real-world underground parking lot. The size of the parking lot is about $10\,\text{m} \times 70\,\text{m} \times 10\,\text{m}$, and it has two layers, which satisfies the multi-layer requirement for evaluation. Three toy babies are placed in the environment as the exploration targets, and the task would stop when all of them are recognized.

As depicted in Fig. 7a, twenty-one exploration points are generated with the proposed method, and the eventual point cloud map is shown in Fig. 7b. According to the movement route of the mobile robot, it can be observed that the mobile robot always proceeds in the direction that maximizes the exploration information entropy. Taking the 13th exploration point as an example (Fig. 8a), the first layer (ground) environment has been explored completely, most candidate exploration points locate in the direction of underground searching. Combining the navigation cost and the exploration information entropy, the next exploration point is selected as the farthest frontier point along the moving direction.

The three target toy babies are recognized in 1_{th}, 8_{th}, and 21_{th} exploration respectively, as illustrated in Fig. 8b. After recognizing the first target, the mobile robot moves through the narrow passage and keeps moving forward until finding the second target baby. The moving direction changes at the 11_{th} exploration, where is the entrance of the underground parking lot. The most likely reason is due to the fact that a greater exploration information entropy could be found in the direction of downwards. Another possible cause is that there are many unstable regions located behind the 11_{th} exploration point, which would also drive the mobile robot to move in the opposite direction. Keep searching the slope of the parking lot, the exploration task ends when the third target object was found in 21th exploration.

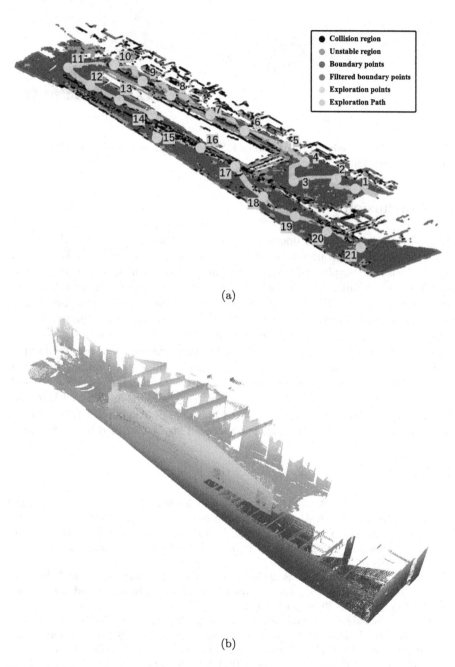

(a)

(b)

Fig. 7. (a) The exploration procedure in the real-world environment. (b) The 3D point cloud model after exploration.

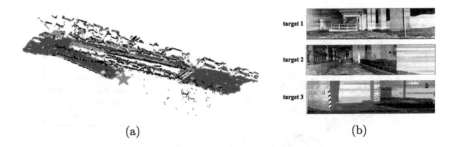

(a)   (b)

Fig. 8. (a) The procedure of calculating 13th exploration point. (b) The three recognized target toy babies.

5   Conclusion

This paper proposed an autonomous exploration strategy for the mobile robot in a multi-layer 3D environment, which contains two primary modules: traversability analysis and exploration point evaluation. By storing the map as ML-SKiMap, the stability and obstacle collision situation are adopted to determine whether the voxel in ML-SKiMap is accessible, and the map can be separated into unknown regions, dangerous regions, and accessible regions accordingly. The cost function that combines the influence of exploration entropy, multi-layer weight, and navigation cost is proposed to evaluate the performance of potential exploration points inside accessible regions. The effectiveness of the proposed method was verified in both simulation and real-world experiments. Further research directions can be carried out on facilitating traversability analysis with semantic information based on deep learning methods. Additionally, how to conduct multi-layer exploration with multi robots could also be studied in the future.

References

1. Dang, T., et al.: Autonomous search for underground mine rescue using aerial robots. In: 2020 IEEE Aerospace Conference, pp. 1–8. IEEE (2020)
2. Cao, C., Zhu, H., Choset, H., Zhang, J.: Tare: a hierarchical framework for efficiently exploring complex 3D environments. In: Robotics: Science and Systems, vol. 5 (2021)
3. Cao, C., et al.: Autonomous exploration development environment and the planning algorithms. In: 2022 International Conference on Robotics and Automation (ICRA), pp. 8921–8928. IEEE (2022)
4. Gao, W., Booker, M., Adiwahono, A., Yuan, M., Wang, J., Yun, Y.W.: An improved frontier-based approach for autonomous exploration. In: 2018 15th International Conference on Control, Automation, Robotics and Vision (ICARCV), pp. 292–297 (2018). https://doi.org/10.1109/ICARCV.2018.8581245
5. Cimurs, R., Suh, I.H., Lee, J.H.: Goal-driven autonomous exploration through deep reinforcement learning. IEEE Robot. Autom. Lett. **7**(2), 730–737 (2021)

6. Uomi, R., Yorozu, A., Ohya, A.: Autonomous exploration for 3D mapping using a mobile manipulator robot with an RGB-D camera. In: Petrovic, I., Menegatti, E., Marković, I. (eds.) IAS 2022. LNNS, vol. 577, pp. 441–454. Springer, Cham (2023). https://doi.org/10.1007/978-3-031-22216-0_30

7. Yamauchi, B.: A frontier-based approach for autonomous exploration. In: Proceedings 1997 IEEE International Symposium on Computational Intelligence in Robotics and Automation CIRA 1997, Monterey, CA, USA. Towards New Computational Principles for Robotics and Automation, pp. 146–151. IEEE Computer Society Press (1997). https://doi.org/10.1109/CIRA.1997.613851

8. Senarathne, P., Wang, D.: Towards autonomous 3D exploration using surface frontiers. In: 2016 IEEE International Symposium on Safety, Security, and Rescue Robotics (SSRR), pp. 34–41. IEEE (2016)

9. Bircher, A., Kamel, M., Alexis, K., Oleynikova, H., Siegwart, R.: Receding horizon "next-best-view" planner for 3D exploration. In: 2016 IEEE International Conference on Robotics and Automation (ICRA), pp. 1462–1468. IEEE (2016)

10. Perea Ström, D., Bogoslavskyi, I., Stachniss, C.: Robust exploration and homing for autonomous robots. Robot. Auton. Syst. **90**, 125–135 (2017). https://doi.org/10.1016/j.robot.2016.08.015

11. Belavadi, S.S., Beri, R., Malik, V.: Frontier exploration technique for 3D autonomous SLAM using k-means based divisive clustering. In: 2017 Asia Modelling Symposium (AMS), Kota Kinabalu, pp. 95–100. IEEE (2017). https://doi.org/10.1109/AMS.2017.23

12. Haddeler, G., Chan, J., You, Y., Verma, S., Adiwahono, A.H., Meng Chew, C.: Explore bravely: wheeled-legged robots traverse in unknown rough environment. In: 2020 IEEE/RSJ International Conference on Intelligent Robots and Systems (IROS), Las Vegas, NV, USA, pp. 7521–7526. IEEE (2020). https://doi.org/10.1109/IROS45743.2020.9341610

13. Kim, H., Kim, H., Lee, S., Lee, H.: Autonomous exploration in a cluttered environment for a mobile robot with 2D-map segmentation and object detection. IEEE Robot. Autom. Lett. **7**(3), 6343–6350 (2022)

14. Huang, J., et al.: FAEL: fast autonomous exploration for large-scale environments with a mobile robot. IEEE Robot. Autom. Lett. **8**(3), 1667–1674 (2023)

15. Koutras, D.I., Kapoutsis, A.C., Amanatiadis, A.A., Kosmatopoulos, E.B.: Marsexplorer: exploration of unknown terrains via deep reinforcement learning and procedurally generated environments. Electronics **10**(22), 2751 (2021)

16. Shrestha, R., Tian, F.P., Feng, W., Tan, P., Vaughan, R.: Learned map prediction for enhanced mobile robot exploration. In: 2019 International Conference on Robotics and Automation (ICRA), Montreal, QC, Canada, pp. 1197–1204. IEEE (2019). https://doi.org/10.1109/ICRA.2019.8793769

17. Batinović, A., Petrović, T., Ivanovic, A., Petric, F., Bogdan, S.: A multi-resolution frontier-based planner for autonomous 3D exploration. IEEE Robot. Autom. Lett. **6**(3), 4528–4535 (2021). https://doi.org/10.1109/LRA.2021.3068923

18. Dang, T., Mascarich, F., Khattak, S., Papachristos, C., Alexis, K.: Graph-based path planning for autonomous robotic exploration in subterranean environments. In: 2019 IEEE/RSJ International Conference on Intelligent Robots and Systems (IROS), pp. 3105–3112. IEEE (2019)

19. De Gregorio, D., Di Stefano, L.: Skimap: an efficient mapping framework for robot navigation. In: 2017 IEEE International Conference on Robotics and Automation (ICRA), pp. 2569–2576. IEEE (2017)

20. Tang, Y., Cai, J., Chen, M., Yan, X., Xie, Y.: An autonomous exploration algorithm using environment-robot interacted traversability analysis. In: 2019 IEEE/RSJ International Conference on Intelligent Robots and Systems (IROS), pp. 4885–4890. IEEE (2019)

Model Predictive Control-Based Pursuit-Evasion Games for Unmanned Surface Vessel

Yan Peng[1], Tingke Mo[2], Ding Zheng[2], Qun Deng[2], Jinduo Wang[2], Dong Qu[1,3], and Yangmin Xie[2(✉)]

[1] Institute of Artificial Intelligence, Shanghai University, Shanghai 200444, China
[2] School of Mechatronic Engineering and Automation, Shanghai University, Shanghai 200444, China
xieym@shu.edu.cn
[3] Shanghai Artificial Intelligence Laboratory, Shanghai, China

Abstract. In response to the issue of close-range adversarial pursuit-evasion involving unmanned surface vessel (USV), this paper proposes a model predictive control-based algorithm for USV pursuit-evasion games. Firstly, considering the inherent variability among USV systems, the paper employs identification experiments by collecting data from the USV' movements to obtain a more accurate kinematic model. Secondly, specific criteria are established to determine successful pursuit or evasion, taking into account the requirements of speed and safety. Considering the kinematic capabilities and attack angles of the USV, a Particle Swarm Optimization (PSO) algorithm is employed to dynamically select suitable velocities and headings for executing tactical maneuvers during pursuit and evasion scenarios. Moreover, to minimize errors between the USV subsystems and mitigate the impact of external factors, the identification model is integrated with the mechanism model to construct a comprehensive pursuit-evasion model, thereby improving the overall accuracy and reliability of the model. Finally, through simulation experiments, the proposed pursuit-evasion method is thoroughly validated in terms of its feasibility and effectiveness.

Keywords: pursuit-evasion games · model predictive control · USV · PSO

1 Introduction

USV, as exemplars of intelligent unmanned systems and combat platforms in maritime environments, possess distinctive characteristics such as compact size, cost-effectiveness, superior stealth, high maneuverability, global navigation capability, and all-weather operability [1]. They have the potential to play a significant role in various domains, including environmental surveying, maritime rescue operations, intelligence reconnaissance, port defense, and patrol surveillance [2, 3].

Within the context of collaborative USV operations, pursuit-evasion games theory plays a vital role as it not only serves as the foundation for intelligent military applications but also holds the key to enhancing the precision, efficiency, and intelligence level of unmanned maritime operations. Therefore, the study of pursuit and evasion

© The Author(s), under exclusive license to Springer Nature Singapore Pte Ltd. 2023
H. Yang et al. (Eds.): ICIRA 2023, LNAI 14274, pp. 267–278, 2023.
https://doi.org/10.1007/978-981-99-6501-4_23

techniques for USV holds significant importance and military value in strengthening national defense capabilities and advancing the development of a maritime power [4].

Deng proposed a collaborative pursuit-defense strategy that enables multiple defenders to protect a designated area from attacks by attackers while simultaneously attempting to capture the attackers outside the protected zone [5]. Wang extensively investigated the optimized deployment of a swarm of unmanned aerial vehicles for cooperative interception missions in a confined region, focusing specifically on the linear interception strategy that considers the interception distance [6]. M. Sani introduced a novel game-theoretic approach using limited information model predictive control (MPC) for pursuit-evasion games with non-holonomic mobile robots, where players can measure only the opponent's current position [7]. Moreover, M. Sani explored pursuit-evasion games of non-holonomic mobile robots by leveraging game theory principles and MPC algorithms [8]. In their work [9], Yamaguchi introduced a distributed controller incorporating feedback mechanisms. In Ref. [10], scholars proposed a distributed pursuit algorithm that allows pursuers to encircle and approach the evader who is moving at a higher speed.

The above research findings indicate that scholars both domestically and internationally have made certain advancements in the field of adversarial pursuit-evasion involving USV. However, these efforts are still in their early stages, characterized by disparities between the established models and real-world scenarios. For instance, an unrealistic assumption prevails that the evader is considered captured if the distance between the pursuer and the evader falls below a certain threshold. In light of this, this paper presents a novel model predictive control-based algorithm for USV adversarial pursuit-evasion. On one hand, this algorithm takes into account the mutual attack region and kinematic capabilities of the USV. On the other hand, it employs an identification-mechanism model, which considers the influences of the motion control system and the actuation system. By integrating the identification model with the mechanism model, the algorithm effectively addresses uncertainties and model errors, thereby improving the overall accuracy and reliability of the model.

1.1 Configuration of Pursuit and Evasion Scenario

In the scenario of a cluster of USV engaged in naval warfare, there is a safe zone and a combat zone, along with multiple USV. The red and blue USV are randomly distributed within the combat zone, which is a circular area with a radius of R. It is assumed that both red and blue USV are equipped with a certain number of weapons and possess identical destructive capabilities, with their attack range simplified as the sector depicted in Fig. 1. Within the opponent's sector, the life of a USV gradually diminishes over time until it is ultimately destroyed. The objective of the red side is to eliminate the blue USV before they manage to escape the combat zone, while the blue side aims to evade the attacks launched by the red side and swiftly reach the safe zone. The focus is primarily on close-range confrontations within the combat zone. This study's pursuit and evasion process is conducted within a simulated marine environment utilizing the Unity3D simulator, with both sides obtaining the USV' state information through detection devices.

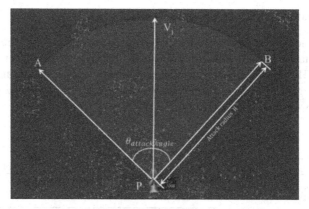

Fig. 1. Illustrates the attack range of unmanned surface vessel.

2 MPC Pursuit-Evasion Framework Design

2.1 Model Predictive Control Algorithm

Model Predictive Control (MPC) is an advanced process control algorithm that employs a model to forecast the future behavior of a system within a control framework. It optimizes the controller based on these predictions, thereby facilitating effective control over the system. Compared to conventional control methods like Linear Quadratic Regulator (LQR) and Proportional-Integral-Derivative (PID), MPC offers numerous advantages. It excels in addressing complex control problems characterized by nonlinearity, multivariable systems, and finite constraints. Additionally, MPC takes into account the anticipated states of the system, allowing for proactive control strategies [11] (Fig. 2).

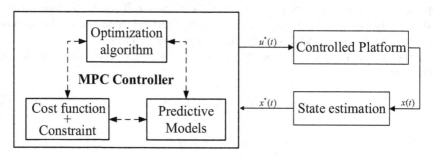

Fig. 2. Principle of Model Predictive Control

In this research, we have developed an enhanced MPC controller specifically designed for the pursuit and evasion tasks in a 1v1 engagement scenario involving USV. The proposed controller enables USV to execute agile tactical maneuvers during close-quarters combat situations, thereby facilitating effective engagement strategies encompassing pursuit and evasion actions.

2.2 Identification of USV Dynamics Model

The identification model is derived by analyzing and estimating the parameters based on motion data from USV, effectively capturing the dynamic behavior exhibited by these vessels. This model takes into account nonlinearity, time variation, and uncertainty factors, utilizing observed data. Researchers have recently incorporated the identification model into USV hull modeling [15].

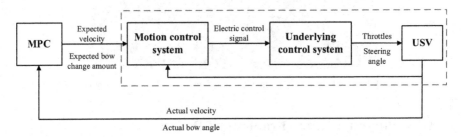

Fig. 3. Block Diagram of USV Control System

The identification model described in this paper is represented using state-space equations. To facilitate the implementation of MPC, the process employs differential equations described as Eq. (1), while measurements are represented in a time-discrete form.

$$\begin{cases} \dot{x}(t) = Ax(t) + Bu(t) + Ke(t) \\ y(t) = Cx(t) + Du(t) + e(t) \end{cases} \tag{1}$$

In Eq. (1), $x(t)$ represents the state vector, $u(t)$ represents the input vector, $y(t)$ represents the observation vector, A denotes the state matrix, B denotes the input matrix, C denotes the observation matrix, D represents the direct transition matrix, K represents the disturbance matrix, and cc signifies the state estimation error.

Experimental Input $u(t)$ and Output $y(t)$ of USV Dynamics Model Identification are as follows:

$$u(t) = \left(v_{hope}(t), \theta_{hope}(t) - \theta_{real}(t) \right)^T \tag{2}$$

$$y(t) = \left(v_{predict}(t), \theta_{predict}(t) - \theta_{real}(t) \right)^T \tag{3}$$

In Eq. (2, 3), $v_{hope}(t)$ represents the desired velocity, $\theta_{hope}(t)$ represents the desired heading angle, $\theta_{real}(t)$ represents the actual heading angle, $v_{predict}(t)$ represents the predicted velocity, and $\theta_{predict}(t)$ represents the predicted heading angle.

The dynamic model of USV obtained from the identification experiments includes the motion control system and actuation system. The experiments only require analyzing the input-output response relationship of the red-boxed section in Fig. 3. This includes factors that address the interaction between USV subsystems and mitigate the impact of external factors, such as wind and wave disturbances.

2.3 USV Pursuit-Evasion Model

Establish a coordinate system as shown in Fig. 4, where A and B represent our own vessel and the enemy vessel, respectively. Their velocities are denoted by V_A and V_B, and their current positions are $(x_A(t), y_A(t))$ and $(x_B(t), y_B(t))$, respectively. In the relative space, the reference direction is set to be true north. θ_A represents the heading angle of our own vessel relative to true north, while θ_B represents the heading angle of the enemy vessel relative to true north. R and q respectively represent the relative distance $R(t) = \sqrt{(x_A(t) - x_B(t))^2 + (y_A(t) - y_B(t))^2}$ and line-of-sight angle, $q \in (-\pi, \pi]$.

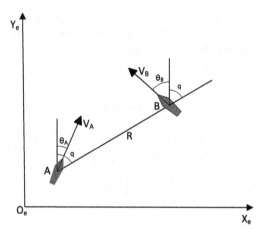

Fig. 4. Geometric Diagram of USV 1-on-1 Pursuit-Evasion

The relative motion relationship of USV is as follows:

$$\dot{R} = V_B \cos(\theta_B - q) - V_A \cos(\theta_A - q) \tag{4}$$

$$\dot{q} = \frac{1}{R}\left[V_B \sin(\theta_B - q) - V_A \sin(\theta_A - q)\right] \tag{5}$$

In Eq. (4, 5), $\dot{R}$ and $\dot{q}$ represent the derivatives of the relative distance R and line-of-sight angle q, respectively. The system state equation is established as follows:

$$\dot{\zeta}(t) = Bu_2(t) + d(t) = By_1(t) + d(t) \tag{6}$$

In Eq. (6), $\xi = (R, q)^T$, the control variable of our vessel is denoted by $u_2 = (v_{real}, \theta_{real})^T$, $d(t)$ representing disturbances, the state-space expression can be derived as follows:

$$\begin{pmatrix} \dot{R} \\ \dot{q} \end{pmatrix} = \begin{pmatrix} -\cos(\theta_{real} - x_4) & 0 \\ -\frac{\sin(\theta_{real} - x_4)}{R} & 0 \end{pmatrix} \begin{pmatrix} v_{real} \\ \theta_{real} \end{pmatrix} + \begin{pmatrix} V_B \cos(\theta_B - x_4) \\ \frac{V_B \sin(\theta_B - x_4)}{R} \end{pmatrix} \tag{7}$$

To integrate and discretize the model, the control variable sequence $u = \left[v_{hope}(k), \theta_{hope}(k), v_{hope}(k+1), \theta_{hope}(k+1), \cdots, v_{hope}(k+N), \theta_{hope}(k+N)\right]^T$ is generated by the PSO algorithm [12], where N represents the prediction horizon in MPC. Subsequently, the control variable $u = [v_{hope}(k), \theta_{hope}(k)]^T$ corresponding to the first frame in this sequence is substituted into the derived unmanned vessel dynamic model, as shown in Eq. (8):

$$
\begin{cases}
\begin{pmatrix} x_1(k) \\ x_2(k) \end{pmatrix} = A \begin{pmatrix} x_1(k-1) \\ x_2(k-1) \end{pmatrix} + B \begin{pmatrix} v_{hope}(k) \\ \theta_{hope}(k) - \theta_{real}(k-1) \end{pmatrix} + Ke(t) \\
\begin{pmatrix} v_{real}(k) \\ \Delta\theta_{real}(k) \end{pmatrix} = C \begin{pmatrix} x_1(k) \\ x_2(k) \end{pmatrix} + D \begin{pmatrix} v_{hope}(k) \\ \theta_{hope}(k) - \theta_{real}(k-1) \end{pmatrix} + e(t)
\end{cases}
\tag{8}
$$

In Eq. (8), $x_1(k)$ and $x_2(k)$ represent the predicted velocity and the angular deviation between the predicted yaw angle and the actual yaw angle at the Kth step of the identification mode. The predicted yaw angle is calculated using Eq. (9).

$$
\theta_{real}(k) = \theta_{real}(k-1) + \Delta\theta_{real}(k)
\tag{9}
$$

Finally, the discretized pursuit-evasion model is given by Eq. (10).

$$
\begin{pmatrix} R(k) \\ q(k) \end{pmatrix} = \begin{pmatrix} R(k-1) \\ q(k-1) \end{pmatrix} + \begin{pmatrix} -\cos(\theta_{real}(k-1) - q(k-1)) & 0 \\ -\frac{\sin(\theta_{real}(k-1)-q(k-1))}{R(k-1)} & 0 \end{pmatrix} \begin{pmatrix} v_{real}(k-1) \\ \theta_{real}(k-1) \end{pmatrix} \Delta t
$$
$$
+ \begin{pmatrix} V_T(k-1)\cos(\theta_T(k-1) - q(k-1)) \\ \frac{V_T(k-1)\sin(\theta_T(k-1)-q(k-1))}{R(k-1)} \end{pmatrix} \Delta t
\tag{10}
$$

Following the aforementioned procedure, the control input of the second frame, denoted as $u = [v_{hope}(k+1), \theta_{hope}(k+1)]^T$, is applied to the USV dynamics model, resulting in the output $k = k+1$. By completing this iteration, the predicted future state of the USV for the desired number of steps can be obtained by applying the corresponding control sequence.

2.4 Constructing the Cost Function

In the scenario of close-range maritime unmanned vessel confrontation, various factors such as speed, distance, and attack zone of the unmanned vessel need to be considered. It is crucial to effectively attack the enemy and protect the allied forces. Therefore, an evaluation system can be constructed based on these factors, transforming the close-range maritime unmanned vessel confrontation problem into a numerical optimization problem subject to certain constraints. The specific construction of the cost function is as follows.

Pursuit Cost Function
In the pursuit process, our vessel should approach the target vessel while positioning itself between the target vessel and our mother vessel to prevent the target vessel from attacking our mother vessel [13]. In this context, $R_i(t)$ represents the distance between our vessel and the target vessel, $q_i(t)$ represents the line-of-sight angle between our vessel and the target vessel, $\gamma_i(t)$ represents the line-of-sight angle between our vessel and our

mother vessel, i represents the step index in the predictive control, and α_1^p represents the weight coefficient.

$$J_1^p = \alpha_1^p R_i(t)^2 - (q_i(t) - \gamma_i(t))^2 \tag{11}$$

When the heading angle of our vessel approaches the line-of-sight angle, it allows the enemy vessel to be within the attack angle in front of our vessel. Therefore, the cost function for the attack angle is designed as Eq. (12). Where, α_2^p represents the weight coefficient.

$$J_2^p = \begin{cases} \alpha_2^p |\tan(\theta_A(t) - q_i(t))|, & \theta_A(t) - q_i(t) \in \left[-\frac{\pi}{4}, \frac{\pi}{4}\right] \\ \infty, & other \end{cases} \tag{12}$$

During the process of approaching the enemy vessel, it is necessary to avoid the attack zone of the enemy vessel in order to achieve self-protection. Where, α_3^p represents the weight coefficient.

$$J_3^p = \alpha_3^p e^{|(\theta_B(t) - q_i(t))|}, \theta_B(t) - q_i(t) \in (-\pi, \pi] \tag{13}$$

Therefore, the overall pursuit cost function is defined as follows:

$$J_{pursuit} = \frac{1}{N} \sum_{i=1}^{N} (J_1^p + J_2^p + J_3^p) \tag{14}$$

In Eq. (14), N represents the prediction horizon, where i is an integer between 0 and N. Additionally, considering the motion dynamics and collision avoidance of the unmanned vessel, the algorithm should satisfy the constraints defined in Eq. (15).

$$\begin{cases} u_{min} \leq u \leq u_{max} \\ \Delta u_{min} \leq \Delta u(k+1) \leq \Delta u_{max} \\ R > R_{collision} \end{cases} \tag{15}$$

Evasion Cost Function

During the evasion process, our vessel needs to move away from the enemy vessel. Therefore, we design the distance function with the following formula (16). Here, $R_i(t)$ represents the distance between our vessel and the enemy vessel, and α_1^e is the weight coefficient. The cost value is inversely proportional to the square of the distance, meaning that the farther the distance, the smaller the cost value.

$$J_1^e = -\alpha_1^e R_i(t)^2 \tag{16}$$

During the evasion process, our vessel should avoid being within the attack angle of the enemy vessel to ensure its own safety. Considering the line-of-sight angle of the enemy vessel, the escape cost function is designed as shown in Eq. (17). Here, α_2^e represents the weight coefficient. $q_e(t)$ denotes the line-of-sight angle of the enemy vessel relative to our vessel, $q_e(t) = q_i(t) + \pi$.

$$J_2^e = -\alpha_2^e e^{(\theta_A(t) - q_e(t))}, \theta_A - q_e(t) \in (-\pi, \pi] \tag{17}$$

Therefore, the final escape cost function is given by Eq. (18) [14], where N represents the prediction horizon, and i is an integer ranging from 0 to N, satisfying the constraints defined in Eq. (15).

$$J_{\text{escape}} = \frac{1}{N} \sum_{i=1}^{N} (J_1^e + J_2^e) \tag{18}$$

3 Simulation Experiments

3.1 USV Simulation System

A gaming platform for USV has been developed using the Unity-3D framework to meet the requirements of pursuit and evasion games. The platform accurately simulates the kinematic model of USV, specifically the "Jinghai-7500" USV at Shanghai University. The simulator incorporates realistic environmental disturbances such as wind, waves, and currents. It provides dedicated interfaces for implementing game algorithms, allowing for extensive experimentation and validation of pursuit and evasion strategies. The validated algorithms can be seamlessly transferred for deployment on actual USV systems in the future (Fig. 5 and Table 1).

(a) Jinhai-7500   (b) simulator

Fig. 5. USV and Simulator

Table 1. Configuration of USV and adversarial environment

Attack Angle	Attack distance	Health points	MPC prediction horizon	Maximum acceleration	Maximum angular acceleration	Wind and wave levels	endurance with Maximum speed
90°	150 m	500	10	0.6 m/s^2	6°/s	3	10 min

3.2 Pursuit and Evasion Simulation Experiments

Pursuit Simulation Experiments

Testing an MPC-based USV adversarial pursuit strategy was conducted on an USV simulator. The experiment began by initializing the positions of the adversary and pursuer vessels as shown in Fig. 6(a). The red vessel was designated as the pursuing vessel representing our side, while the blue vessel represented the escaping adversary. The initial distance between the adversary and pursuer was set at 600m, with a maximum speed of 16m/s for both vessels. The red pursuing vessel was controlled using the pursuit strategy designed in this study, with the weighting coefficients of the strategy determined through debugging to find the optimal combination, denoted as $[\alpha_1, \alpha_2, \alpha_3] = [0.1, 10, 10]$. The escaping adversary unmanned vessel employs the Artificial Potential Field Method for its escape.

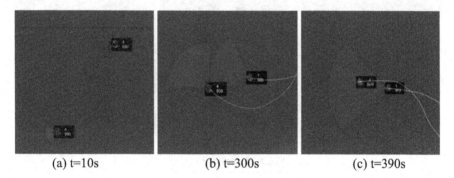

(a) t=10s   (b) t=300s   (c) t=390s

Fig. 6. Pursuit Process

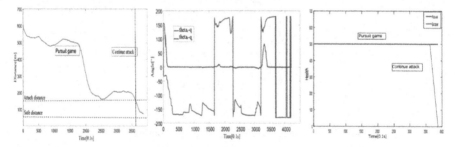

Fig. 7. Distance, angle and health change during pursuit

In the process of pursuit or evasion, if the escaping vessel is successfully destroyed by the pursuing vessel within the designated duration of the game, the pursuit is considered successful, while the escape is deemed unsuccessful. From Fig. 6 and 7, it can be observed that our vessel can approach the adversary's vessel from a safe angle. After the approach, our vessel maintains a safe distance and angle to continuously attack the adversary.

Evasion Simulation Experiments
Figure 8(a) illustrates the positions of the two vessels in the escape scenario. The red adversary pursuit vessel utilizes the Artificial Potential Field Method for pursuit, while the blue escaping vessel is controlled using the proposed escape algorithm. The initial distance, maximum speed, duration, and prediction step size of the pursuit-evasion game remain consistent with the pursuit scenario. The weight coefficients are set as $[\alpha_1, \alpha_2] = [1, 0.1]$.

As shown in Fig. 8(b), the pursuing adversary vessel immediately steers towards our escaping vessel upon detecting its presence. Meanwhile, our vessel begins to escape in the opposite direction, away from the adversary's vessel, during which it is not subjected to any attacks from the pursuing adversary vessel (Fig. 9).

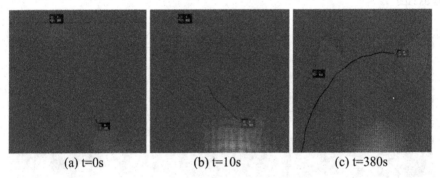

(a) t=0s   (b) t=10s   (c) t=380s

Fig. 8. Evasion Process

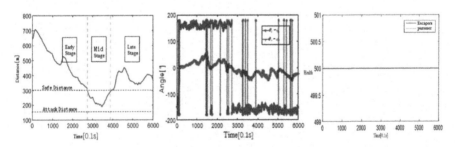

Fig. 9. Distance, angle and health change during escape

The distances, attack angles, and angles of being attacked for both the pursuer and the adversary vessels during the pursuit and evasion process are illustrated in Fig. 8. Although there is a decreasing trend in the distance between the two vessels, it remains above the safety threshold. The line-of-sight angle also stays within the safe range, meeting the requirements for a successful evasion mission.

4 Conclusion

An adversarial pursuit and evasion algorithm based on MPC was designed for the USV pursuit and evasion game scenario. The algorithm incorporates an identification-based mechanistic model to reduce the influence of external disturbances, thereby improving the real-time performance and robustness of the algorithm. Considering the kinematic performance and attack angles of the USV, the algorithm utilizes model predictions of future states, combined with the PSO algorithm and a cost function, to select appropriate speed and heading angles for executing pursuit and evasion tactical maneuvers. The USV model in the simulation environment closely resembles a real USV, facilitating the future application of the algorithm in actual USV experiments. Finally, the feasibility and effectiveness of the proposed pursuit and evasion method were validated through simulation experiments.

Acknowledgments. This work was supported by program of shanghai academic research leader (Grant No. 20XD1421700).

References

1. Tanakitkorn, K.: A review of unmanned surface vehicle development. Marit. Technol. Res. 1(1), 2–8 (2019)
2. On the real-time receding horizon control in harbor defense [EB/OL], 4 April 2023. https://ieeexplore.ieee.org/document/7171889/
3. Peng, Z., Wang, J., Wang, D., et al.: An overview of recent advances in coordinated control of multiple autonomous surface vehicles. IEEE Trans. Industr. Inf. 17(2), 732–745 (2020)
4. Wu, G., Xu, T., Sun, Y., et al.: Review of multiple unmanned surface vessels collaborative search and hunting based on swarm intelligence. Int. J. Adv. Rob. Syst. 19(2), 17298806221091884 (2022)
5. Deng, Z., Kong, Z.: Multi-agent cooperative pursuit-defense strategy against one single attacker. IEEE Rob. Autom. Lett. 5(4), 5772–5778 (2020). https://doi.org/10.1109/LRA.2020.3010740
6. Wang, C., Wu, A., Hou, Y., et al.: Optimal deployment of swarm positions in cooperative interception of multiple UAV swarms. Digit. Commun. Netw. (2022)
7. Sani, M., Robu, B., Hably, A.: Limited information model predictive control for pursuit-evasion games. In: 2021 60th IEEE Conference on Decision and Control (CDC), Austin, TX, USA, pp. 265–270 (2021). https://doi.org/10.1109/CDC45484.2021.9683016
8. Sani, M., Robu, B., Hably, A.: Pursuit-evasion games based on game-theoretic and model predictive control algorithms. In: 2021 International Conference on Control, Automation and Diagnosis (ICCAD), Grenoble, France, pp. 1–6 (2021). https://doi.org/10.1109/ICCAD52417.2021.9638775
9. Lopez, V.G., Lewis, F.L., Wan, Y., et al.: Solutions for multiagent pursuit-evasion games on communication graphs: finite-time capture and asymptotic behaviors. IEEE Trans. Autom. Control 65(5), 1911–1923 (2019)
10. Fang, X., Wang, C., Xie, L., et al.: Cooperative pursuit with multi-pursuer and one faster free-moving evader. IEEE Trans. Cybern. 52(3), 1405–1414 (2020)
11. Manoharan, A., et al.: NMPC based approach for cooperative target defence. In: 2019 American Control Conference (ACC), Philadelphia, PA, USA, pp. 5292–5297 (2019). https://doi.org/10.23919/ACC.2019.8815386

12. Wang, X., Feng, K., Wang, G., et al.: Local path optimization method for unmanned ship based on particle swarm acceleration calculation and dynamic optimal control. Appl. Ocean Res. **110**, 102588 (2021)
13. Qu, X., Gan, W., Song, D., et al.: Pursuit-evasion game strategy of USV based on deep reinforcement learning in complex multi-obstacle environment. Ocean Eng. **273**, 114016 (2023)
14. Lin, B., Qiao, L., Jia, Z., et al.: Control strategies for target-attacker-defender games of USVs. In: 2021 6th International Conference on Automation, Control and Robotics Engineering (CACRE), pp. 191–198. IEEE (2021)
15. Yao, M., Xiufeng, Z., Yunong, C.L Parameter identification of ship mathematical model based on modified grey wolf algorithm [J/OL]. J. Harbin Eng. Univ., 1–9. http://kns.cnki.net/kcms/detail/23.1390.U.20230509.1028.002.html

Accelerated Informed RRT*: Fast and Asymptotically Path Planning Method Combined with RRT*-Connect and APF

Zhixin Tu[1,2], Wenbing Zhuang[1,2], Yuquan Leng[1,2],
and Chenglong Fu[1,2(✉)]

[1] Department of Mechanical and Energy Engineering, Southern University of Science
and Technology, Shenzhen 518055, China
fucl@sustech.edu.com
[2] Shenzhen Key Laboratory of Biomimetic Robotics and Intelligent Systems and
Guangdong Provincial Key Laboratory of Human-Augmentation and Rehabilitation
Robotics in Universities, Southern University of Science and Technology,
Shenzhen 518055, China

Abstract. In recent years, path planning algorithms have played a crucial role in addressing complex navigation problems in various domains,
including robotics, autonomous vehicles, and virtual simulations. This
abstract introduces a improved path planning algorithm called Informed
RRT*-connect based on APF, which combines the strengths of the fast
bidirectional rapidly-exploring random tree (RRT-connect) algorithm
and the informed RRT* algorithm. The proposed algorithm aims to
efficiently find collision-free paths with less iterations and time while
minimizing the path length.
Unlike traditional RRT-based algorithms, Informed RRT*-connect based
on Artificial Potential Fields (APF) incorporates a bidirectional connection and rewiring of a new sampling point to explore the search space.
This enables the algorithm to connect both the start and goal nodes more
effectively and quickly to find a initial solution, reducing the search time
and provide a better initial heuristics sapling for the next optimal steps.
Furthermore, Informed RRT*-connect introduces an informed sampling
strategy that biases the sampling towards areas of the configuration space
likely to yield better paths. This approach significantly reduces the exploration time to find a path and enhances the ability to discover optimal
paths efficiently.
To evaluate the effectiveness of the Informed RRT*-connect algorithm,
we conducted the simulation experiments on two different experiment

Z. Tu and W. Zhuang—Contribute equally to this work. This work was supported in
part by the National Natural Science Foundation of China [Grant U1913205, 52175272],
in part by the Science, Technology, and Innovation Commission of Shenzhen Municipality [Grant: ZDSYS20200811143601004, JCYJ20220530114809021], and in part by
the Stable Support Plan Program of Shenzhen Natural Science Fund under Grant
20200925174640002.

© The Author(s), under exclusive license to Springer Nature Singapore Pte Ltd. 2023
H. Yang et al. (Eds.): ICIRA 2023, LNAI 14274, pp. 279–292, 2023.
https://doi.org/10.1007/978-981-99-6501-4_24

protocol. The results demonstrate that our approach outperforms existing state-of-the-art algorithms in terms of both planning efficiency and solution optimality.

Keywords: Path planning · RRT-connect · RRT* · Artificial Potential Fields (APF)

1   Introduction

The path planning problem [3] is a common and fundamental problem in the navigation and motion control of robotics, vehicles, and other mobile devices. Path planning aims to find a feasible and good path for agents in their complex interaction environment. To date, many methods have been proposed to solve the problem of path planning. Traditional approaches include potential field methods such as Artificial Potential Fields (APF) [8], which generate the path according to the attractive and repulsive forces that assumed to be generated by the goal point and obstacles. These field based methods often suffer from local optimal and lack guarantees for finding the global optimal path. Recently, researchers have explored grid-based methods that discretize the environment into a grid map and use graph-based search algorithms like A* [11] and D* [1] to find the optimal path if the path exists. While grid-based methods provide optimality guarantees, they often struggle with high-dimensional spaces, suffer from the curse of dimension, and face challenges in handling complex obstacles with irregular shapes.

Sampling-based path planning methods have emerged as a popular and effective approach to address the complexities of path planning in a wide range of domains. These methods rely on randomly sampling the configuration space to construct a graph representation of the environment, enabling the discovery of feasible paths. One prominent family of sampling-based algorithms is the rapidly-exploring random tree (RRT) algorithm and its variants, which have demonstrated remarkable success in generating collision-free paths. However, existing RRT-based algorithms often struggle to balance the trade-off between finding optimal paths and maintaining computational efficiency. One famous variants algorithm is called RRT-connect [4,7,12], which is the extension of the original RRT, focuses on connecting the start node and the goal node at the same time by two separated trees. RRT-connect can find a feasible path very quickly and saving the memory, but the resulting paths are often not the shortest. An asymptotically optimal sampling-based path planning algorithm is RRT* [5,9], which addresses the optimality drawback of RRT. RRT* refining the tree structure by rechoose the parent node of the new sampling node and rewire the tree around a distance to help reduce the redundant node. However, the drawback of RRT* is that it may be slow to converge towards an optimal solution within a limited number of iterations. In [2], Jonathan *et al.* proposed a method that utilizes the current path length and the distance between the start and goal points to generate ellipses as heuristic sampling regions to improve the performance of the

RRT* algorithm. This method significantly enhances the quality of the generated paths. However, due to the characteristics of RRT*, the algorithm requires a considerable amount of time to search for a feasible initial solution, resulting in sub-optimal optimization efficiency. Therefore, finding an optimal path within a short period of time is a prominent challenge in current path planning methods.

In this paper, we introduce a improved sampling-based path planning algorithm called Informed RRT*-connect based on APF, which combines the strengths of the RRT-connect algorithm and the optimal RRT* algorithm to address this challenge effectively. Moreover, the APF method utilizes obstacle information to guide the sampling function, allowing the sampled points to selectively deviate from obstacles while getting closer to the target point, which aims to further reduce the number of ineffective sampling attempts. Informed RRT*-connect based on APF could accelerate the process of Informed RRT* iteratively finding the optimal solution and can make up for the shortcomings of RRT-connect that cannot guarantee asymptotic optimality. Specifically, the proposed method first utilizes RRT-connect to quickly obtain a feasible path. While conducting sampling in RRT-connect, the path is optimized through the parent node re-selection and rewiring functions in RRT*. Subsequently, the initially obtained solution serves as the base solution for Informed RRT* optimization, where heuristic sampling is employed to rapidly converge the optimal path length. It is important to note that the APF method considers obstacle information as a priori for sampling bias throughout the entire planning process, thereby significantly enhancing the performance of the algorithm.

2 Preliminaries

2.1 Path Planning Problem Definition

The planning problem is defined similarly to [2,10]. Let $\chi \in \mathbb{R}^n$ be the state space, and the free space and the obstacle space are denoted as χ_{free} and χ_{obs}. Let x_{start} be the starting state and x_{goal} be the goal state. The path planning problem is to find a path $\sigma[0,T]$ from the starting state x_{start} to the goal state x_{goal} in the given space χ, denoted as

$$\sigma[0,T] \to \chi_{\text{free}}, \quad \sigma(0) = x_{\text{start}} \quad \text{and} \quad \sigma(T) = x_{goal}. \tag{1}$$

Assume α is the whole set of the feasible paths, then the optimal path σ^* with the minimum path length can be defined as

$$\sigma^* = \arg\min_{\sigma \in \alpha} \|\sigma\|$$
$$\text{s.t. } \sigma(0) = x_{\text{start}}$$
$$\sigma(T) = x_{\text{goal}} \tag{2}$$
$$\sigma(t) \in \chi_{\text{free}}(t) \quad \forall t \in [0,T].$$

where $\|\cdot\|$ is the calculator of the path length using Euclidean distance, T is the time taken for the entire path planning.

2.2 Informed RRT*

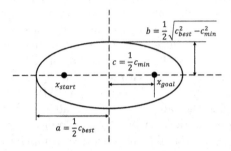

Fig. 1. The heuristic sampling set of Informed RRT* [2]. The x_{start} and x_{goal} are the focal points. a represents the semi-major axis length of the ellipse, and b represents the semi-minor axis length of the ellipse, and c represents the half length of the focal, respectively. c_{best} and c_{min} are the current path length and the theoretical shortest path length, respectively.

The informed RRT* algorithm [2,6] follows the following steps to find a feasible path and try to improve the path with the current solution. Informed RRT* primarily improves the performance of RRT* by generating an elliptical region based on the current feasible solution length and the theoretical shortest distance between the start and goal points. This region is used as a heuristic for RRT* sampling, aiming to enhance the efficiency and effectiveness of the algorithm. The informed ellipse sampling set can be expressed as the standard equation denoted by

$$\frac{x^2}{a^2} + \frac{y^2}{b^2} = 1, \tag{3}$$

where a represents the semi-major axis length of the ellipse, and b represents the semi-minor axis length of the ellipse, as shown in Fig. 1. As the length of the discovered path continues to decrease, the corresponding ellipse sampling region becomes smaller. Consequently, the sampling region is further constrained to areas that have the potential to improve the path length. Through iterative iterations, Informed RRT* can converge towards a path that is close to optimal more rapidly than RRT*.

However, the Informed RRT* algorithm is the same as RRT* because when an initial path is not found, the elliptical sampling region can be considered infinite. This drawback is a notable limitation of Informed RRT*. It entails a significant time cost associated with searching for an initial path for optimization. Furthermore, due to the inherent randomness of RRT*, there is a possibility of obtaining a low-quality initial solution. Consequently, a substantial portion of the algorithm's execution time may be spent without achieving substantial improvements in path optimization.

3   Informed RRT*-Connect Based on APF

In this section, an accelerated Informed RRT* algorithm combined with RRT-connect and APF method is proposed to improve the Informed RRT*. The overall framework of the proposed algorithm is illustrated in Fig. 2. Its main idea is to utilize prior information about obstacles to generate a virtual potential field as a sampling bias. Additionally, it leverages the characteristics of RRT-connect, which uses bidirectional greedy connections, to rapidly find a high-quality initial solution. This approach accelerates the path optimization process of Informed RRT*. The algorithm is mainly divided into three parts: 1) APF Biased Sampling, 2) RRT*-connect (Initial path finding), 3) Informed RRT* with better initial solution (Informed heuristic sampling path optimization).

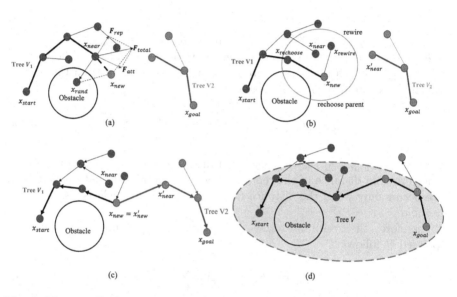

Fig. 2. The overall schematic diagram of the Informed RRT*-connect algorithm based on APF. (a) Illustration of the sampling bias guided by APF. Orange node x_{rand} is the biased sampling point guided by the APF and x_{rand} is the original sampling point. (b) Illustration of the parent node re-selection and node rewiring in RRT*-connect. The blue circle is the optimized node ranges with the rewire radius. x_{rechoose} and x_{rewire} are the selected optimized nodes. (c) Illustration of the generation of the initial path in RRT*-connect. The direction of the arrows inside the figure represents the parent-child relationships, pointing from a node to its parent node. (d) Illustration of the integration of bidirectional trees and the elliptical heuristic sampling based on the initial path. (Color figure online)

3.1   APF Biased Sampling

RRT-connect and Informed RRT* algorithm does not effectively utilize obstacle information, which can lead to low efficiency in sampling and path planning.

Therefore, it will consume a significant amount of time sampling on obstacles or in infeasible areas, especially when there are a large number of obstacles. To solve this problem, the APF method [13] is introduced into the whole sampling process, and an adaptive attractive potential field is set up at the target point, and an adaptive repulsive potential field is set up at the obstacle. Under the influence of the attractive and repulsive potential fields, newly sampled points will be biased, being pushed away from obstacles and towards the direction closer to the goal point.

The principle of APF is shown in Fig. 2(a). Assume the new sampling point is x_{rand} and x_{near} is the nearest point of the x_{rand} in the tree V_1. $\boldsymbol{F}_{\mathrm{att}}$ is the adaptive attractive force generate by x_{goal} to x_{near}, which is proportional to the distance from the nearest point to the goal point,

$$\boldsymbol{F}_{\mathrm{att}}(x_{\mathrm{near}}) = k\rho(x_{\mathrm{near}}, x_{\mathrm{goal}}), \tag{4}$$

where $\rho(x_{\mathrm{near}}, x_{\mathrm{goal}}$ is the Euclidean distance from x_{near} to x_{goal}.

$\boldsymbol{F}_{\mathrm{rep,i}}$ is the adaptive repulsion force generate by the obstacle i in the environment to x_{near}, which is inversely proportional to the distance from the nearest point to the contour of each the obstacles,

$$\boldsymbol{F}_{\mathrm{rep,i}}(x_{\mathrm{near}}) = \begin{cases} \beta\left(\frac{1}{d} - \frac{1}{\rho_0}\right)^2, & d < \rho_0 \\ 0, & d \geq \rho_0 \end{cases} \tag{5}$$

where $d = \rho(x_{\mathrm{near}}, x_{\mathrm{obs}})$ is the Euclidean distance from x_{near} to obstacle i. ρ_0 is the threshold distance of the repulsion force, which means that the repulsion force occurs only when the distance from x_{near} to the obstacle is less than the threshold.

Therefore, the resultant force F_{total} experienced at point x_{near} can be expressed as follows:

$$\boldsymbol{F}_{\mathrm{total}}(x_{\mathrm{rear}}) = \boldsymbol{F}_{\mathrm{att}}(x_{\mathrm{near}}) + \sum_{i}^{n} \boldsymbol{F}_{\mathrm{rep,i}}(x_{\mathrm{near}}) \tag{6}$$

where n is the total number of the obstacles in the environment.

Under the guidance of APF, the newly sampled point x_{rand} will undergo a certain displacement in the direction of the resultant force, resulting in a new biased sampling point, denoted as x_{new}. Specifically, this is achieved by synthesizing the unit vector between x_{rand} and x_{near} with the unit vector of the resultant force F_{total}. The point is then offset along this synthesized vector along the synthesized vector direction by a distance equal to the magnitude of the vector multiplied by a half of the step size ϵ, which can be calculated by

$$x_{\mathrm{new}} = x_{\mathrm{near}} + \frac{\varepsilon}{2}\left(\frac{x_{\mathrm{rand}} - x_{\mathrm{near}}}{|x_{\mathrm{rand}} - x_{\mathrm{near}}|} + \frac{\boldsymbol{F}_{\mathrm{total}}(x_{\mathrm{near}})}{|\boldsymbol{F}_{\mathrm{total}}(x_{\mathrm{near}})|}\right) \tag{7}$$

where ϵ is the step size that is a parameter of the algorithm; $\frac{x_{\mathrm{rand}} - x_{\mathrm{near}}}{|x_{\mathrm{rand}} - x_{\mathrm{near}}|}$ is the unit vector from x_{near} to the x_{rand} and $\frac{F_{\mathrm{total}}(x_{\mathrm{near}})}{|F_{\mathrm{total}}(x_{\mathrm{near}})|}$ is the unit vector in the total force direction, respectively.

The biased sampling guided by APF allows for better utilization of obstacle information in the map, reducing the number of invalid samples and greatly improving the efficiency of the sampling process. As shown in Fig. 2(a), when a new sampling point falls within an obstacle, the influence of APF enables the point to be biased towards the area outside the obstacle. This makes the sampling process effective and partially addresses the issue of low sampling efficiency in sample-based path planning algorithms. The APF-biased sampling function is shown in Algorithm 1.

Algorithm 1. $APF\_biased(x_{rand}, x_{near}, x_{goal}, x_{obs})$

1: $F_{attract} \leftarrow Calculate\_attract(x_{near}, x_{goal})$;
2: **for** Obs in x_{obs} **do**
3:     $F_{repulsion} += Calculate\_repusion(x_{near}, Obs)$;
4: $F_{total} = F_{attract} + F_{repulsion}$;
5: $Delta = 0.5 * \varepsilon * F_{total}/norm(F_{total})$;
6: $x_{new} = x_{rand} + Delta$;
7: **return** x_{new}

3.2   RRT*-Connect Fast Solution Initialization

To address the issue of lengthy computation time in finding feasible paths using the RRT algorithm and to allocate more time for improving path quality, we have combined the optimization node approach of RRT* with the fast feasibility searching capability of RRT-connect. This integration has resulted in the development of the RRT*-connect method. This method enables the rapid finding of feasible paths with higher quality, which can then serve as the starting point for optimization in Informed RRT*.

As shown in Fig. 2(b), RRT*-connect follows a similar approach to RRT-connect, where two trees V_1 and V_2, are grown outward from the start and goal points, respectively, to quickly connect the two trees and obtain a feasible path. Moreover, we have incorporated the optimization node technique from RRT* by introducing parent node re-selection and rewiring. These steps are utilized to optimize the parent node relationships between the sampled nodes and their neighboring nodes. Specifically, once the sampling point x_{new} is determined, a search is conducted within a designated rewire radius to locate nearby nodes. These nodes are then evaluated as potential parent nodes for x_{new}. The evaluation involves comparing the path length from x_{new} to the start point, selecting the node $x_{rechoose}$ that results in the shortest path be the parent node of x_{new}. Subsequently, rewire process is to assigned the x_{new} as the parent node for the nodes found within the rewire radius, and their path length changes are examined. Among these nodes, the node x_{rewire} with the shortest path length, after rewiring its parent node to x_{new}, is selected.

Algorithm 2. *RRT star_connect* (x_{start}, x_{goal})

1:   $V_1 \leftarrow \{x_{start}\}; E_1 \leftarrow \emptyset; G_1 \leftarrow (V_1, E_1)$
2:   $V_2 \leftarrow \{x_{goal}\}; E_2 \leftarrow \emptyset; G_2 \leftarrow (V_2, E_2)$;
3:   $i \leftarrow 0$;
4:   **while** $i < N$ **do**
5:     $x_{rand} \leftarrow Sample(i); i \leftarrow i + 1$;
6:     $x_{nearest} \leftarrow Nearst(G_1, x_{rand}))$;
7:     $x_{rand} \leftarrow Steer(x_{nearest}, x_{rand})$;
8:     $x_{new} \leftarrow APF\_biased(x_{rand}, x_{nearest}, x_{goal})$;
9:     **if** $ObstacleFree(x_{nearst}, x_{new})$ **then**
10:      $x_{neighbor} \leftarrow Neighbor(V_1, x_{new})$
11:      $V_1 \leftarrow V_1 \cup x_{new}$;
12:      $E_1 \leftarrow E_1 \cup (x_{nearest}, x_{new})$;
13:      $Choose\_parent(x_{new}, x_{neighbor})$
14:      $Rewire(x_{new}, x_{neighbor})$
15:      $x'_{nearest} \leftarrow Nearst(G_2, x_{new}))$;
16:      $x'_{new} \leftarrow Steer(x'_{nearest}, x_{new}))$;
17:      **if** $ObstacleFree(x'_{nearest}, x'_{new})$ **then**
18:       $V_2 \leftarrow V_2 \cup x'_{new}$;
19:       $E_2 \leftarrow E_2 \cup (x'_{nearest}, x'_{new})$;
20:       **while** NOT $x'_{new} = x_{new}$ **do**
21:        $x''_{new} \leftarrow Steer(x''_{new}, x'_{new}))$;
22:        **if** $ObstacleFree(x''_{new}, x'_{new})$ **then**
23:         $V_2 \leftarrow V_2 \cup x''_{new}$;
24:         $E_2 \leftarrow E_2 \cup (x_{nearest}, x'_{new})$;
25:         $x'_{new} \leftarrow x''_{new}$
26:        **else**
27:         **break**;
28:      **if** $x'_{new} = x_{new}$ **then**
29:       **return** (G_a, G_b) .
30:     **if** $|V_2| < |V_1|$ **then**
31:      $Swap(G_a, G_b)$

After the optimization steps are performed, the node x'_{near} in tree V_2, which is closest to x_{new}, is extended towards x_{new}. The extension continues until the extended node x'_{new} and x_{new} coincide, indicating a successful connection between the two trees. At this point, a better initial solution can be obtained by combining the tree V_1 and V_2, as shown in Fig. 2(c). The proposed RRT*-connect with APF-biased sampling can be shown in Algorithm 2. Line 8, 13, and 14 is the improved part of the original RRT-connect algorithm.

3.3 Informed RRT* Optimization

After RRT*-connect completes the initial path finding, the nodes in the V_1 and V_2 trees have been connected together, but since the two trees are connected from the target point to the new sampling nodes. The parent relationship of nodes in V_2 needs to be reversed to match the V_1 to merge to a new tree V, as shown in Fig. 2(d).

Finally, an corresponding ellipse is generated according to the length of the generated initial path and the distance between the start point and the end point to guide the sampling range of RRT* in the path optimization process. Then the size of the ellipse is further reduced according to the optimized path length to further reduce the sampling range and converge to the optimal path.

The whole process of the algorithm is shown in Algorithm 3. Line 5, 6, 7, 8, and 14 is the improved content of the Informed RRT*.

4   Simulation Results and Discussion

In this section, simulation was conducted to fully verify the effectiveness of the proposed algorithm compared to different existing RRT path planning algorithms. The simulation is divided into two parts: 1) Simulation with fixed iterations. This part is to compare the average path length and the successful rate of finding the path with a fixed number of iterations. 2) Simulation with fixed path length. This part is to compare the average time and the average iterations consumed to find a fixed length of path with the three different algorithm.

4.1   Simulation with Fixed Iterations

In the first simulation, two maps with rectangular and circle obstacles is used to test the performance of four different algorithms, include Informed RRT*-connect based on APF, Informed RRT*, RRT*, RRT, and RRT-connect, under a fixed number of iterations. Specifically, we will compare the success rate of finding paths (for RRT-connect and RRT) and the path lengths obtained by the other three optimization algorithms.

The start point and end point are located in the lower left corner and upper right corner of the map, as shown in the Fig. 3. In the tow maps, the maximum number of iterations N of the five algorithms is set to 1000 and 2000, and the step size is set to 1. By running the algorithms 500 times in a loop, the corresponding evaluation metric are calculated for comparison. The specific results are shown in Table 1 and Table 2.

We can see from both Table 1 and Table 2 that Informed RRT*-connect based on APF has successfully found the path in all the iterations, which is the highest among the other algorithms. The length of the path found by Informed RRT*-connect is shortest, compared with the same asymptotically optimal RRT* and Informed RRT*. Specifically, compared to Informed RRT*, although it can eventually find a nearly optimal path, due to the acceleration of RRT*-connect in finding the initial solution, the overall planning time is around 4% shorter than Informed RRT*. It is worth noting that due to the introduction of rewire and APF sampling methods, Informed RRT*-Connect based on APF outperforms RRT-connect in finding the initial path, with an average reduction of about 18%

in iteration count. In the two maps, the average initial path length found by RRT*-Connect based on APF is 67.696 and 70.754, respectively, which is also shorter than the average path length 69.076 and 76.162 found by RRT-connect.

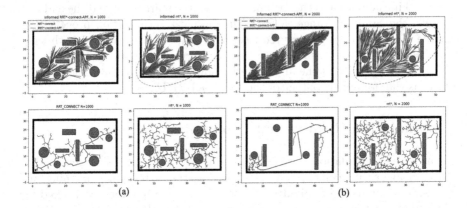

Fig. 3. Comparative illustration of the algorithm results from the first set of simulation experiments. The four images, from left to right and top to bottom, depict the path planning results of Informed RRT*-connect based on APF, Informed RRT*, RRT-connect, and RRT algorithms, respectively. The blue point is the starting point x_{start} and the red point is the goal point x_{goal}, respectively. In the first plot of each simulation, the blue line is the initial solution found by RRT*-connect, and the red line is the final optimal path. (a) The results in Map A. Map A is a 50*30 two-dimensional map, consisting of four rectangles and four circles evenly distributed. (b) The results in Map B. Map B is a 50*30 two-dimensional map, consisting of three rectangles and three circles. (Color figure online)

Table 1. The Performance Comparison in Map A (N = 1000)

	Ave time	Ave path length	Iter for finding path	Success rate
RRT	0.1119	70.534	619.11	0.702
RRT*	0.3996	69.135	-	0.674
RRT-connect	0.0483	69.076	354.18	0.978
IRRT*	3.800	57.051	-	0.682
IRRT*-connect-APF	3.951	56.260	291.60	1.000

Table 2. The Performance Comparison in Map B (N = 2000)

	Ave time	Ave path length	Iter for finding path	Success rate
RRT	0.1274	77.124	1039.98	0.911
RRT*	1.1225	73.940	-	0.932
RRT-connect	0.0592	76.162	773.42	0.992
IRRT*	8.6232	58.102	-	0.960
IRRT*-connect-APF	7.9003	55.930	638.90	1.000

4.2   Simulation with Fixed Path Length

The second simulation was conducted on five randomly generated $30 * 50$ maps with circle obstacles. The criteria for generating these maps included the presence of 25 circular obstacles, ensuring that the distance between any two obstacles was not less than 1 unit. The radius of the obstacles ranged from 1 to 5 units. The size of each map was set to 50 units in width and 30 units in height. To prevent any overlap between the randomly generated obstacles and the starting and ending points, the coordinates of the obstacles were constrained within the range $([4, 46], [4, 26])$. The coordinates of the starting point were $(2, 2)$, and the coordinates of the ending point were $(48, 28)$. The five random maps can be seen in Fig. 4.

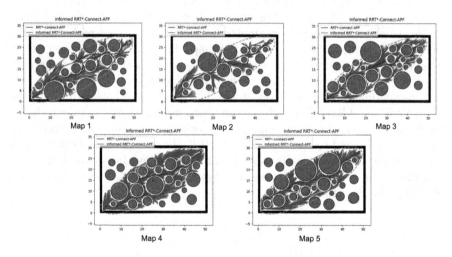

Fig. 4. Path planning results of Informed RRT*-connect based on APF on five randomly generated test maps, with the blue dots representing the start points x_{start} and the red dots representing the goal points x_{goal}. (Color figure online)

In the random maps, the start and target points are fixed, thus the theoretical shortest distance of the path can be calculated as 52.839. Due to the presence

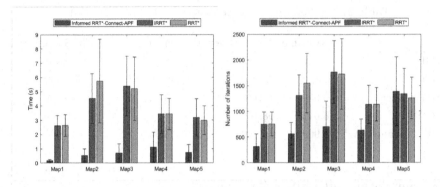

Fig. 5. Comparison of the time and iteration count required by the three algorithms to find the optimal path on five different test maps.

of obstacles, the feasible path length will increase. The path is considered to be optimal when its length is less than 110% of the theoretical shortest length, i.e. 55.480. Once an optimal path is found, the algorithm terminates, and the running time and number of iterations required are recorded. In Simulation 2, all three algorithms will be iterated 100 times on each random map.

The average runtime and iteration count of the three algorithms on each map are compared in Fig. 5. From the results, it can be observed that across all five random maps, the proposed Informed RRT*-Connect based on APF algorithm can find the optimal path in less than 1 s, while RRT* and Informed RRT* require at least 3 to 4 times more time to find the same optimal path. Regarding the iteration count, on four out of the five maps, Informed RRT*-Connect based on APF has fewer iterations compared to the other two algorithms, approximately 50% of the iteration count of the other algorithms.

The experimental results demonstrate that the proposed algorithm, utilizing the acceleration of RRT-Connect and the bias sampling of APF, can quickly find a better quality initial path, enabling rapid convergence in subsequent optimization steps. Compared to RRT* and Informed RRT*, we speculate that the main reason for the improvement is that the proposed algorithm reduces the sampling time spent in obstacle regions and globally invalid areas, thus significantly enhancing the algorithm's performance.

Algorithm 3. *Informed RRTstar_connect based on APF*

1: $V \leftarrow \emptyset$
2: $E \leftarrow \emptyset$
3: $X_{\text{soln}} \leftarrow 0$
4: $T \leftarrow (V, E)$
5: $(G_a, G_b) = RRTstar\_connect(x_{start}, x_{goal})$
6: $V \leftarrow V_1 \cup Reverse(V_2)$
7: $C_{best} = Cost(V[-1])$
8: $x_{\text{soln}} \leftarrow x_{\text{soln}} \cup \{V[-1]\}$
9: **for** iteration = 1 to N **do**
10:　　$C_{\text{best}} \leftarrow \min_{x \in x_{\text{soln}}}(\text{Cost})$
11:　　$x_{\text{rand}} \leftarrow \text{Sample}(x_{\text{start}}, x_{\text{goal}}, C_{\text{best}})$
12:　　$x_{\text{nearest}} \leftarrow \text{Nearest}(V, x_{\text{rand}})$
13:　　$x_{\text{rand}} \leftarrow \text{Steer}(x_{\text{nearest}}, x_{\text{rand}})$
14:　　$x_{new} \leftarrow APF\_biased(x_{rand}, x_{nearest}, x_{goal})$;
15:　　**if** CollisionFree$(x_{\text{nearest}}, x_{\text{new}})$ **then**
16:　　　　$V \leftarrow V \cup \{x_{\text{new}}\}$
17:　　　　$x_{\text{near}} \leftarrow \text{Near}(V, x_{\text{new}}, r_{\text{RRT*}})$
18:　　　　$x_{\text{min}} \leftarrow x_{\text{nearest}}$
19:　　　　$C_{\text{min}} \leftarrow \text{Cost}(x_{\text{min}}) + c \cdot \text{Line}(x_{\text{nearest}}, x_{\text{new}})$
20:　　　　**for** $V_{\text{near}} \in x_{\text{near}}$ **do**
21:　　　　　　$C_{\text{new}} \leftarrow \text{Cost}(x_{\text{near}}) + c \cdot \text{Line}(x_{\text{near}}, x_{\text{new}})$
22:　　　　　　**if** $C_{\text{new}} < C_{\text{min}}$ **then**
23:　　　　　　　　**if** CollisionFree$(x_{\text{near}}, x_{\text{new}})$ **then**
24:　　　　　　　　　　$x_{\text{min}} \leftarrow x_{\text{near}}$
25:　　　　　　　　　　$C_{\text{min}} \leftarrow C_{\text{new}}$
26:　　　　$E \leftarrow E \cup \{(x_{\text{min}}, x_{\text{new}})\}$
27:　　　　**for** $V_{\text{near}} \in \text{Near}(V, x_{\text{new}}, T_{\text{RRT*}})$ **do**
28:　　　　　　$C_{\text{near}} \leftarrow \text{Cost}(x_{\text{near}})$
29:　　　　　　$C_{\text{new}} \leftarrow \text{Cost}(x_{\text{new}}) + c \cdot \text{Line}(x_{\text{new}}, x_{\text{near}})$
30:　　　　　　**if** $C_{\text{new}} < C_{\text{near}}$ **then**
31:　　　　　　　　**if** CollisionFree$(x_{\text{new}}, x_{\text{near}})$ **then**
32:　　　　　　　　　　$x_{\text{parent}} \leftarrow \text{Parent}(x_{\text{near}})$
33:　　　　　　　　　　$E \leftarrow E \cup \{(x_{\text{parent}}, x_{\text{near}})\}$
34:　　　　　　　　　　$E \leftarrow E \cup \{(x_{\text{new}}, x_{\text{near}})\}$
35:　　　　**if** InGoalRegion(x_{new}) **then**
36:　　　　　　$x_{\text{soln}} \leftarrow x_{\text{soln}} \cup \{x_{\text{new}}\}$
37: **return** T

5　Conclusion and Future Work

In this paper, we proposed a accelerated Informed RRT* algorithm to find the optimal path in a fast way. The proposed algorithm, through the utilization of bidirectional connection and sampling bias, achieves rapid identification of the optimal path. The results from two distinct sets of simulation experiments demonstrate a significant improvement of the proposed method compared to RRT* and Informed RRT* under fixed iteration count and fixed path length conditions. This underscores the importance of effectively utilizing obstacle information and minimizing unnecessary sampling in sampling-based path planning algorithms, as it leads to substantial enhancements in both time optimality and length optimality of the generated paths.

The future work includes evaluating the algorithm's performance in the presence of dynamic obstacles and deploying the algorithm on physical robot hardware systems and testing its effectiveness.

References

1. Ferguson, D., Stentz, A.: Using interpolation to improve path planning: the field D* algorithm. J. Field Robot. **23**(2), 79–101 (2006)
2. Gammell, J.D., Srinivasa, S.S., Barfoot, T.D.: Informed RRT: optimal sampling-based path planning focused via direct sampling of an admissible ellipsoidal heuristic. In: 2014 IEEE/RSJ International Conference on Intelligent Robots and Systems, pp. 2997–3004. IEEE (2014)
3. Gasparetto, A., Boscariol, P., Lanzutti, A., Vidoni, R.: Path planning and trajectory planning algorithms: a general overview. In: Motion and Operation Planning of Robotic Systems: Background and Practical Approaches, pp. 3–27 (2015)
4. Kang, J.G., Lim, D.W., Choi, Y.S., Jang, W.J., Jung, J.W.: Improved RRT-connect algorithm based on triangular inequality for robot path planning. Sensors **21**(2), 333 (2021)
5. Karaman, S., Frazzoli, E.: Sampling-based algorithms for optimal motion planning. Int. J. Robot. Res. **30**(7), 846–894 (2011)
6. Kim, M.C., Song, J.B.: Informed RRT* with improved converging rate by adopting wrapping procedure. Intel. Serv. Robot. **11**, 53–60 (2018)
7. Kuffner, J.J., LaValle, S.M.: RRT-connect: an efficient approach to single-query path planning. In: Proceedings 2000 ICRA. Millennium Conference. IEEE International Conference on Robotics and Automation. Symposia Proceedings (Cat. No. 00CH37065), vol. 2, pp. 995–1001. IEEE (2000)
8. Lee, M.C., Park, M.G.: Artificial potential field based path planning for mobile robots using a virtual obstacle concept. In: Proceedings 2003 IEEE/ASME International Conference on Advanced Intelligent Mechatronics (AIM 2003), vol. 2, pp. 735–740. IEEE (2003)
9. Solovey, K., Janson, L., Schmerling, E., Frazzoli, E., Pavone, M.: Revisiting the asymptotic optimality of RRT. In: 2020 IEEE International Conference on Robotics and Automation (ICRA), pp. 2189–2195. IEEE (2020)
10. Wang, J., Chi, W., Li, C., Wang, C., Meng, M.Q.H.: Neural RRT*: learning-based optimal path planning. IEEE Trans. Autom. Sci. Eng. **17**(4), 1748–1758 (2020). https://doi.org/10.1109/TASE.2020.2976560
11. Warren, C.W.: Fast path planning using modified A* method. In: [1993] Proceedings IEEE International Conference on Robotics and Automation, pp. 662–667. IEEE (1993)
12. Xinggang, W., Cong, G., Yibo, L.: Variable probability based bidirectional RRT algorithm for UAV path planning. In: The 26th Chinese control and decision conference (2014 CCDC), pp. 2217–2222. IEEE (2014)
13. Xinyu, W., Xiaojuan, L., Yong, G., Jiadong, S., Rui, W.: Bidirectional potential guided RRT* for motion planning. IEEE Access **7**, 95046–95057 (2019)

Intelligent Inspection Robotics

Design and Practice of Space Station Manipulator Inspecting for Berthing Manned Spacecraft

Dongyu Liu[✉], Linhou Bai, Wei Wang, Changchun Liang, and Pengfei Xin

Beijing Institute of Spacecraft System Engineering, Beijing 100094, China
liudongyu2004@yeah.net

Abstract. Design and simulation of space station manipulator inspection mission for berthing manned spacecraft during the assembly and construction of the Tiangong space station is presented in this paper. The system model and simulation verification platform are established by using OpenInventor and VC++ joint programming. A design method of spacecraft on-orbit inspection outside the cabin using space manipulator is proposed. This method realizes decoupling design of space station platform tracking, telemetry, command (TT&C), field of view of extravehicular sensor and manipulator motion through degree of freedom decomposition, and realizes rapid design of extravehicular inspection mission. Through on-orbit flight verification, this method effectively ensures the reliable implementation of the mission and accumulates experience and technical basis for the stable operation of Tiangong space station.

Keywords: Space Station · Space Manipulator · On-orbit Servicing · Systemic Simulation

1 Introduction

The extravehicular structure and equipment of large manned spacecraft are in a harsh space environment for long-term flight on orbit. They need to experience cold and heat alternation, small space debris impact and attachment for a long time, which will adversely affect the normal operation of extravehicular equipment. Some key parts, such as the return capsule of manned spacecraft, are directly related to the life safety of astronauts. Generally, routine state confirmation is also needed before return. By using the hand-eye camera of the space manipulator to carry out regular or irregular inspections for key equipment or suspicious parts, the state information of the outer surface of the cabin can be obtained, and the ground flight control personnel can be assisted to understand the health status of the spacecraft on orbit.

The Columbia space shuttle was launched on the STS-107 mission in 2003. During the launch, a piece of thermal insulation tile of the space shuttle fell off the spacecraft, resulting in the fracture of the necessary thermal protection system during the reentry, which caused the crash of the space shuttle. The Shuttle Remote Manipulator System

© The Author(s), under exclusive license to Springer Nature Singapore Pte Ltd. 2023
H. Yang et al. (Eds.): ICIRA 2023, LNAI 14274, pp. 295–304, 2023.
https://doi.org/10.1007/978-981-99-6501-4_25

(SRMS) of the space shuttle Columbia was added new mission requirements due to the crash of the Shuttle Columbia. Based on this, NASA developed the Orbiter Boom Sensor System (OBSS), a 50-foot extended rod sensor system, which is compatible with SRMS and provides the ability to inspect and repair the space shuttle thermal protection system. Before the subsequent space shuttle re-entry, SRMS and OBSS are used for joint inspection, as shown in Fig. 1 [1, 2].

Fig. 1. SRMS and OBSS checking space shuttle thermal protection structure.

Drawing on the successful experience of the inspection of key parts before return of space shuttle, China's Tiangong space station has considered the task and functional requirements in the early stage of design and development. The manipulator system has the ability to inspect the key parts of the manned spacecraft. After confirming the safety of key parts, the manned spacecraft is allowed to deorbit and return [3, 4].

Large solar arrays, attitude measurement sensors, relay antennas and other equipment are arranged outside the space station cabin. The inspection movement of the space manipulator may have a coupling effect on the energy, control and communication of the spacecraft platform. How to decouple the motion and inspection tasks of the manipulator from the normal operation of the platform, not only to ensure the stable operation of the platform, but also to ensure that the manipulator completes the inspection tasks, has become the key to system design.

In this paper, the design and on-orbit implementation of the inspection mission of manipulator before the return of manned spacecraft during the construction of the space station are introduced. Design method and procedure of spacecraft on-orbit inspection outside cabin using space manipulator are proposed. This method realizes decoupling design of space station platform TT&C, field of view of extravehicular sensor and manipulator motion through degree of freedom decomposition, and realizes rapid design of inspection mission. Through on-orbit flight verification, this method effectively ensures the reliable implementation of the mission and accumulates experience and technical basis for the stable operation of Tiangong space station.

2 Mission Scheme

During the construction of the space station, the complex docked the manned spacecraft in the radial direction and the cargo spacecraft in the backward direction, in an inertial flight attitude. The core cabin is equipped with a 7-DOF manipulator. Its operating radius is 10 m.

More than ten days before the return of the manned spacecraft, the task of photographing and inspecting the surface state of the return capsule of the manned spacecraft by using the manipulator is carried out. The main requirements are: ①The surface state is photographed statically from four angles of the return capsule. ②The movement and inspection process of the manipulator should have enough safe distance from the manned spacecraft and the space station.

The inspection of manned spacecraft by manipulator mainly includes three stages: initial state setting, inspection task implementation and state recovery. ①The initial state setting section mainly completes the power setting of each equipment of the space station, and the manipulator moves to the vicinity of the manned spacecraft return capsule. ② The manipulator moves to each inspection observation position of the manned spacecraft return capsule, and photographs the inspection position in the sunshine area. ③It mainly completes the power outage and long-term flight state recovery of the space station equipment.

The manipulator first moves to the observation preparation configuration, and then performs four multi-joint movements in a point-to-point mode as shown in Fig. 2. The hand-eye camera of the manipulator is used to complete the staring shooting of the four quadrants of the manned spacecraft return capsule. After collecting and confirming the state information outside the capsule, the manipulator moves back to the initial configuration of the task [5].

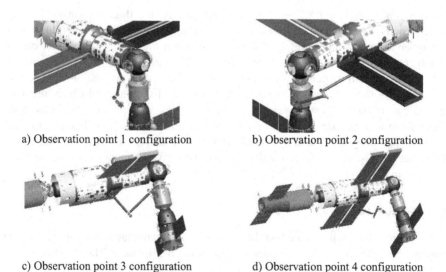

a) Observation point 1 configuration   b) Observation point 2 configuration

c) Observation point 3 configuration   d) Observation point 4 configuration

Fig. 2. Space station manipulator inspecting for berthing manned spacecraft.

3   System Modeling and Simulation

After clarifying the target position of the inspection task, the selection requirements of the manipulator camera and the observation distance of the manipulator camera from the target position can be determined according to the resolution of the inspection observation. In the three-dimensional modeling software, the three-dimensional model of the camera field angle is used for preliminary assembly, and the homogeneous transformation matrix of the end effector coordinate system of the manipulator in the geometric coordinate system of the spacecraft body is extracted in the software as the initial input condition for the path planning of the manipulator [6].

The task planning and path planning of the manipulator inspection are carried out. The task planning mainly focuses on the synthesis of each inspection position, the order of the inspection object or position, and the constraint analysis of the spacecraft solar array angle. The path planning is mainly aimed at the reasonable design of the trajectory between the current inspection position and the next inspection position.

In order to confirm the safe distance between the manipulator and the cabin and the solar arrays during the inspection movement of the manipulator, the inspection field of view of the manipulator, and the occlusion of the manipulator movement on the TT&C and the field of view of the extravehicular sensor, based on the three-dimensional model and the kinematics equation of the manipulator, this paper carries out the analysis of the safe distance during the movement of the manipulator, the analysis of the inspection field of view of the manipulator, the analysis of the TT&C link occlusion and the sensor field of view to verify the system scheme, improve the efficiency of the system design and ensure the reliability of the task.

3.1   System Modeling

Using OpenInventor and VC + + joint programming, the three-dimensional model of each part is established and assembled. After setting the color, unit, illumination and other features of the model, it is converted into a file format (*.iv) that can be read by OpenInventor. According to the parent-child relationship of the space station + manipulator system model shown in Fig. 3a, the space station complex is divided into three categories: moving parts, sensor field of view and fixed parts, which are the fixed module part of the space station complex, the base of the manipulator, the joints of the manipulator and its connecting link parts, the star sensor of each module and its field of view, each relay antenna and its field of view, and each solar array. The sub-model integrates the system in VC + + software, and the software human machine interface is shown in Fig. 3b.

3.2   Collision Detection

Collision detection is performed on the motion of the manipulator in each cycle in the loop program that reads the path planning file of the manipulator. The collision detection SoCollisionManager class function is used to detect the collision of the manipulator motion process. The function uses the Oriented Bounding Box(OBB)-based three-dimensional graphics collision detection bounding box as shown in Fig. 4. A bounding

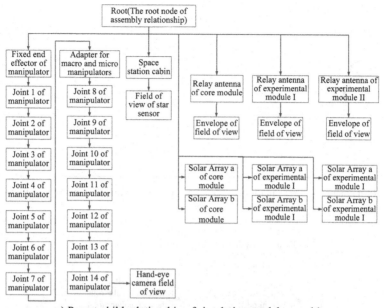

a) Parent-child relationship of simulation model assembly.

b) Space station manipulator inspection simulation software.

Fig. 3. Simulation model and software assembly parent-child relationship.

box is created at each node in the simulation software scene. The position and orientation of the bounding box of each dynamic node are given in real time through the forward kinematics calculation of the manipulator, and the position and orientation of the bounding box are changed in real time. The collision detection between the bounding box and the space station module and the solar arrays during the motion of the manipulator is realized. The program flow is shown in Fig. 5.

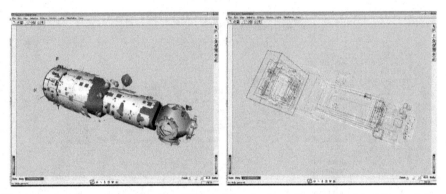

Fig. 4. Refinement and segmentation of 3D models using bounding box models (core module as an example).

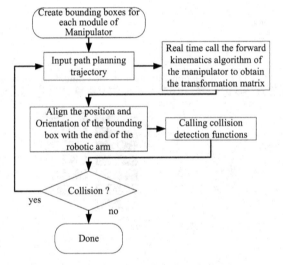

Fig. 5. Flow chart of collision detection program.

3.3 Field of View (FOV) Simulation

The OpenInventor package function SoPerspectiveCamera class is used to simulate the field of view of the hand-eye camera of the manipulator. The process is shown in Fig. 6. Firstly, the angle and depth of field of view of the camera are set according to the camera parameters, and then the simulation parameters are set according to the external parameters of the camera installed at the end of the manipulator. Finally, the camera field of view node is used as a child node of the end of the manipulator to move with the simulation motion of the manipulator in the program. When the manipulator moves in place, the camera switching program is called to simulate and confirm the field of view of the camera at the end of the manipulator.

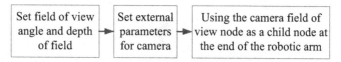

Fig. 6. Flow chart of field of view simulation settings.

3.4 Occlusion Simulation

According to the Beijing time of the flight mission planning, the tracking simulation of the X / Y angle of the relay antenna terminal is first performed, and the simulation output of the X / Y angle are set to the angle sequence with the Beijing time (.txt file). Using the idea of degree of freedom decomposition, the manipulator motion planning file (.txt file) and the relay terminal X / Y angle sequence file are aligned according to Beijing time, and then substituted into the field of view occlusion simulation software for simulation.

The simulation results are shown in Fig. 7a. For flight events with TT&C link occlusion, the flight event arrangement is re-adjusted to avoid them, so as to ensure the smooth flow of the space-ground TT&C link during the flight mission.

In the simulation software, the field of view of the sensor is set to the enable state, and the manipulator motion planning file (.txt file) is substituted into the software, and then the occlusion analysis of the sensor field of view is carried out, as shown in Fig. 7b. The occlusion analysis of the sensor mainly clarifies the occlusion time range of the manipulator inspection movement to the field of view of the extravehicular Guidance Navigation Control sensors. Usually, the sensor is redundantly configured. The short-term occlusion of the manipulator for a certain sensor will not have a subversive impact on the overall scheme. After the analysis of this step, only the task planning of the manipulator is needed to avoid the occlusion during the TT&C link initial building.

4 On-orbit Implementation

During the construction of the space station, the manipulator was used to inspect the surface state of the manned spacecraft 's return capsule before the manned spacecraft returned. The trajectory of the manipulator inspection is shown in Fig. 8. The simulation and the actual effect of on-orbit inspection are shown in Fig. 9. Through the system modeling and simulation method described in this paper, the TT&C link is smooth, the system attitude control of Tiangong space station is stable, the manipulator is accurate in the target inspection position, and the image is clear.

a) Influence analysis of manipulator motion on relay antenna tracking.

b) Influence analysis of manipulator motion on the field of view of star sensors.

Fig. 7. Occlusion simulation.

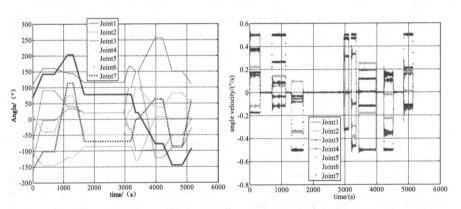

Fig. 8. Motion trajectory of manipulator inspection.

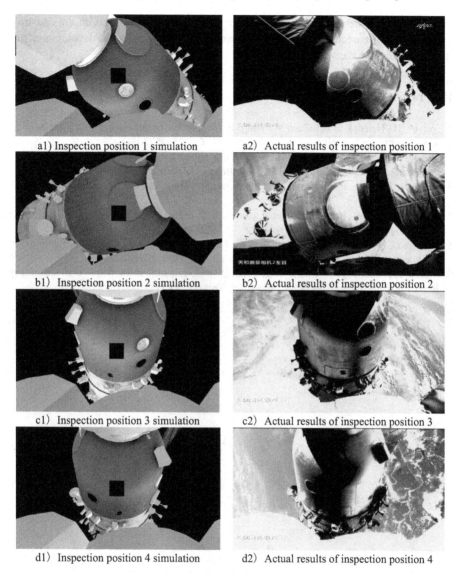

a1) Inspection position 1 simulation   a2) Actual results of inspection position 1

b1) Inspection position 2 simulation   b2) Actual results of inspection position 2

c1) Inspection position 3 simulation   c2) Actual results of inspection position 3

d1) Inspection position 4 simulation   d2) Actual results of inspection position 4

Fig. 9. Field of view simulation and actual observation results of manipulator inspection.

5   Conclusion

In the design process of space station manipulator inspecting manned spacecraft, the system modeling and simulation method based on VC + + is used to improve the efficiency of system design and simulation verification. The three-dimensional model display, manipulator path planning and design verification, safety distance simulation, and manipulator inspection field simulation are integrated to improve the efficiency of design verification for manipulator inspection tasks. The correctness of the method is verified by on-orbit implementation, which ensures the reliability of the space station construction task, and also accumulates experience and technical basis for the development and stable operation of the space station.

References

1. Wayne, H., Helen, L., Gail, C., et al.: Wings in orbit: scientific and engineering legacies of the space shuttle, pp.268. NASA/SP-2010–3409. JSC-CN-21695 (2011)
2. Jorgensen, G., Bains, E.: SRMS history, evolution and lessons learned. In: AIAA SPACE 2011 Conference and Exposition, pp. 1–23. Long Beach, California, USA (2011)
3. Jianping, Z.: Chinese space station project overall vision. Manned Spaceflight **19**(2), 1–10 (2013)
4. Xiang, W., Wei, W.: Key technical characteristics of the Tiangong spacestation. Scientia Sinica Technologica **51**(11), 1–12 (2021)
5. Chengwei, H., Sheng, G., Minghua, X., et al.: Key technologies of the China space station core module manipulator. Scientia Sinica Technologica **52**, 1299–1331 (2022)
6. Wenfu, X., Xiaodong, D., Chengjiang, W., et al.: Determination method of overall technology index for space manipulator. Chin. Space Sci. Technol. **33**(1), 53–60 (2013)

Research on Chain Detection of Coke Oven Inspection Robot in Complex Environment

Yuhan Ma[1,2]([✉])[iD], LingLing Chen[2], Lijuan Ji[3], Bin Zuo[2], and Bei Liu[2]

[1] China Academy of Machinery Science and Technology Group,
Beijing 100037, China
mayuhan_123@126.com

[2] Machinery Technology Development Co. Ltd., Beijing 100037, China

[3] Yanqihu Fundamental Manufacturing Technology Research Institute (Beijing) Co.,
Ltd., Beijing 100037, China

Abstract. This article designs a mobile robot applied to the inspection task of coke oven basement, and conducts in-depth analysis on the anomaly detection of the chain in the basement. Because of the absence of fault samples, the detection accuracy of normal state chains should be improved. When no detection target appears in the image, it is considered as an abnormal chain state. In addition, using environmental information to add features to the chain can improve the recognition accuracy of the normal working state of the chain. In order to avoid over-fitting of the model, light changes are used to enrich the content of the dataset, while reducing the dependence of the model on external added features. After experimental comparison, Mobilenet-v3-large is finally selected as the backbone network of YOLO-V3 algorithm. This model has been successfully deployed in the coke oven inspection robot detection system, which can detect normal working chains in complex environment. The accuracy rate reaches 99%.

Keywords: Inspection robot · Coke oven · Chain detection · YOLO-V3

1 Introduction

The coking industry is a process industry that converts coal into metallurgical fuel and chemical raw materials. The coke oven heating equipment transports and regulates the gas and air used for heating to the coke oven, as well as discharges the waste gas after combustion [9]. The environment of the coke oven basement is relatively complex, with a large number of ventilation equipment and staggered pipelines. The ambient temperature is maintained above 40 °C all year round, and the air is filled with coal dust and coal powder. The work area has severe electromagnetic interference and unstable ambient light.

National key research and development program (2020YFB1313300).

© The Author(s), under exclusive license to Springer Nature Singapore Pte Ltd. 2023
H. Yang et al. (Eds.): ICIRA 2023, LNAI 14274, pp. 305–316, 2023.
https://doi.org/10.1007/978-981-99-6501-4_26

In such a complex environment, the inspection work of coke oven basement is mostly done manually. The coke oven belongs to the first level explosion-proof zone, which poses risks such as gas leakage and explosion. Patrol personnel need to carry a carbon monoxide alarm and handheld infrared temperature measuring equipment to enter the basement together. Due to the heavy workload of inspection tasks and significant potential hazards in the work environment, manual inspections bear enormous security risks [3].

With the development of artificial intelligence and mobile robot technology, how to improve the intelligent level of inspection has become a focus of research for many scholars and enterprises. Compared to traditional manual methods, inspection robots can not only adapt to harsher and more dangerous working environments, but also utilize the powerful learning ability of artificial intelligence to improve the accuracy and efficiency of inspection tasks.

Our team has designed and manufactured a rail-type intelligent mobile robot for the inspection task of coke oven basement. In addition, in-depth research was conducted on anomaly detection of pull rod chains based on practical application scenarios. Further, by comparing the performance of YOLO-V3 algorithm with three different backbone network structures, the optimal model is selected to deploy to the inspection robot. Finally, the experiment proved that the model can effectively detect anomalies in the chain.

2   Inspection Robot

2.1   Overview of the Inspection Robots

By analyzing the current research status at home and abroad in recent years, it was found that the type design and development methods of intelligent inspection robots have become more mature. However, the on-site adaptability and ontology construction of robots for specific engineering environments still need to be improved [17]. This article designs and manufactures a coke oven basement inspection robot tailored to the actual production environment, and deploys an algorithm based on YOLO-V3 for chain anomaly detection.

The rail-type inspection robot can only inspect along a fixed route and lacks flexibility in movement. The aerial guide rail can fully utilize the upper space in the environment, but in the turning and climbing sections of the robot, it poses a huge challenge to the track, the robot's steering ability, pan tilt control ability, and battery loss. Wheeled inspection robots have high requirements for the ground, requiring timely obstacle avoidance and re planning of inspection routes. The underground passage of coke oven is long and narrow, the task route of the wheeled inspection robot may conflict with workers. The prominent exhaust gas exchange device can easily block the perspective from the ground. Based on practical considerations, the rail-type inspection robot is more suitable for working in the complex environment of the coke oven basement.

Due to significant safety hazards such as gas leakage in coke oven basement, only intrinsically safe robots can enter the working area. Sparks are strictly prohibited when the robot is moving. All modules of the robot need to undergo explosion-proof treatment, including mechanical structure and internal electrical control components. The inspection robot designed by our team is shown in the following Fig. 1.

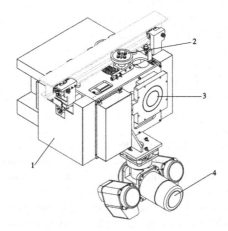

Fig. 1. Schematic diagram of inspection robot (1. Robot body 2. Walking device 3. Wireless charging device 4. Dual mode pan-tilt)

2.2   The Functions of Inspection Robots

The explosion-proof intelligent rail-type inspection robot in coke oven basement should include the following functions:

1) Move autonomously along the track. The basement of coke oven is designed with corresponding I-beam track according to different inspection tasks. The robot moves forward or backward along the tracks, and can complete U-shaped turns and climbs if necessary.

2) Command receiving and sending. The inspection robot sends inspection tasks remotely through the console software, and triggers a photo taking command through the RFID radio frequency tag on the I-beam track. The pan-tilt receives instructions for photo taking and storage, and the data is returned to the server through the gigabit network.

3) Wireless charging. Charging uses advanced magnetic field induction charging, with no contact throughout the entire process to avoid sparks. The charging points are set at both ends of the track, and the robot can replenish the battery nearby when the inspection task is completed. Due to the intrinsic safety design of the inspection robot, its weight is much higher than that of ordinary rail-type robots, and the capacity, power, and temperature of the battery need to meet the actual requirements of engineering.

4) Dual mode pan-tilt photography and temperature measurement. The inspection robot is equipped with a visible light and infrared binocular platform for

360° observation without dead angles. A 2 million pixels visible light camera collects images and returns them to the server for detection algorithms to diagnose equipment faults and provide the location of the faulty equipment. Due to the unstable ambient light in coke oven basement, the pan-tilt needs to turn on and off the fill light according to different illumination. Infrared camera can achieve real-time temperature measurement and shooting images in 384×288 pixels, and provide alarm information for device fire.

5) Intelligent detection. Deployment of inspection robots based on deep learning detection model, which detects the working status of the equipment by processing the information returned by the pan-tilt. The detection result will be returned to the server to compare with the standard state of the gas exchange process, and the server will evaluate the abnormal phenomenon and give an alarm.

6) Gas detection. The inspection robot carries various gas sensors to monitor dangerous gases such as carbon monoxide and sulfur dioxide in real-time. If there is an abnormal gas concentration in the environment, it will give an alarm in a timely manner.

7) Wireless communication. The coke oven chamber is approximately 150 m long and 15 m wide, with numerous and widely distributed support columns and U-shaped track layout. Therefore, a 5.8G explosion-proof wireless communication scheme with high bandwidth and low delay is adopted, which can seamlessly transmit commands and data in electromagnetic interference environments.

8) L1 control. The L1 control(Level one automation control) of the robot adopts the S7-1200 master-slave distributed design, and the Siemens S7 communication protocol is used between the master station PLC and the inspection robot. The internal drivers and sensor network of the robot adopt the mainstream Profinet communication method. The main station PLC is interconnected with the scheduling system and the main production line interface.

9) Pedestrian detection. During an inspection process, the inspection robot moves along the aerial track to take photos. Due to the narrow passage in coke oven basement, the robot detects pedestrians entering the path ahead and needs to stop urgently and issue an alarm.

3   Pull Rod Chain Detection

The basement of coke oven changes the air flow rate in the flue by controlling the opening and closing of the air port cover plate of the waste gas exchange device and the lifting of the weight rod, thereby affecting the adequacy of gas combustion. Therefore, ensuring the accurate opening or closing status of the cover plate and the lifting status of the weight rod in the standard task process has become a key step in maintaining the quality of coke production. Every 20 min, the pull rod at the top of the waste gas exchange device is driven by a guide chain to the cover plate and the weight rod, switching between the inlet and outlet states in the furnace. The pull rod is connected at the corner of the working area with a roller chain.

The interval of roller chain repair or replacement is set according to the operating hours provided by the manufacturer. But due to different service conditions, the fixed interval may not be completely suitable for the roller chain [15]. The gas exchange in the coke oven is frequent, and the strong pulling force acts on the pull rod chain for a long time, which makes the roller chain more likely to be dislodged, broken, and disconnected from the sprocket. If the pull rod is disconnected from the power equipment, the gas exchange process will be interrupted. This may lead to a decrease in coke quality or shutdown of coke ovens, even serious gas leakage and explosion. Therefore, using inspection robots to regularly check the working status of the chain has played a very positive role in safety production and reducing accident losses.

3.1 Difficulties in Chain Detection

Due to the complex environment of coke oven basement, there are following difficulties in rod chain detection based on inspection robots.

Firstly, interference from surface attachments, just like Fig. 2. In order to reduce the friction coefficient of the roller chain, a large amount of semi-solid lubricant is coated on the surface of the pull rod chain. Irregularly distributed lubricants come into contact with coal dust and coal powder in the environment for a long time, forming black blocky stains that adhere to the surface of the chain, making it hard to collect regular target features.

Secondly, the guardrail blocks the chain. To prevent chain breakage and personal injury, it is necessary to add guardrails at a close distance outside the chain to achieve the effect of enclosing the chain. The large area of occlusion further increases the difficulty for mobile robots to detect from the outside.

Thirdly, the anomaly sample is missing. Frequent manual inspections in coke oven and regular replacement of pull rod chains greatly avoid accidents such as chain breakage and detachment, making it difficult to obtain negative samples in this environment.

(a)   (b)

Fig. 2. Attachment of tie rod chain in coke oven basement

3.2 Solution

Add Features. Color identification is frequently used in industrial production, such as yellow and black warning lines, red and green safety areas, etc. The coke oven equipment has been exposed to coal dust and coal powder for a long time, so the surface color of the equipment tends to be similar to the background. Therefore, using bright warning colors to mark the chain has become an intuitive idea. As shown in Fig. 3, a grille guardrail with yellow and black warning colors is used to surround the pull rod chain, and the grille minimizes the area obstructing the chain. Furthermore, the grille adds features to the chain from the outside.

Fig. 3. Yellow and black warning color grille and pull rod chain (Color figure online)

Supervised Learning Based on Normal Samples. Supervised learning uses the known information to train the optimal model according to the label of the dataset [4]. When facing unlabeled data, the model can automatically obtain the relationship between input and output. The possible faults of the pull rod chain in the actual production of the coke oven basement include chain detachment, out of stock, and breakage. The only way to deal with different faults is to replace them. The model does not need to learn the types of faults, only needs to focus on whether abnormal events occur. Therefore, this paper selects the supervised learning algorithm based on normal samples to detect the working state of the coke oven basement chain. The model should learn as many features as possible from normal chain samples. When there is no normal chain in the image, it is defined as an abnormality. The detection system stores the images without detection results separately and alerts the staff.

4   YOLO-V3 Based Detection Algorithm

The one stage [1] algorithm YOLO-V3 [11] has been validated over time and through numerous projects around the world. This algorithm obtains feature maps of three scales through tensor concatenation and FPN(feature pyramid network [10]) idea. Therefore, it is possible to detect targets of different scales, large, medium, and small, which can meet most of the detection needs in industrial production.

YOLO-V3 algorithm provides more backbone network options to meet different detection requirements. Since this dataset only has normal samples of a single target, the detection algorithm should focus on finding the detection target in complex backgrounds. This paper compares the feature extraction ability of Darknet53 and Mobilenet series backbone networks for normal chains, and selects the optimal model for the state detection of the coke oven basement chain according to the actual demand.

4.1   Darknet53

As shown in Fig. 4, the Darknet53 [11] in YOLO-V3 connects BN layer [8], Leaky-relu [16] activation function and residual module [5] after the convolution layer. The BN layer regularization the output of the convolution layer to accelerate the training process of the neural network and improve its accuracy. The Leaky-relu function can effectively prevent the gradient from disappearing. The residual block is used to deepen the number of network layers and improve the feature extraction ability.

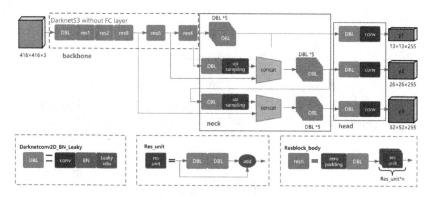

Fig. 4. YOLO-V3 network structure (Darknet53)

4.2   Mobilenet-v1

Mobilenet-v1 replaces the standard convolutional layer in the VGG [12] network with a deep separable convolutional layer [7]. The deep separable convolution layer splits the convolution into a single channel form. Firstly, without changing the depth of the input feature image, convolution operations are performed on each channel to obtain output features that match the number of channels in the input feature map. Then use 1×1 convolutional kernel to elevates the output features to the dimension of the input image. As shown in Table 1, M-v1 calculated fewer parameters compared to VGG16 and GoogleNet [13], but achieved almost the same accuracy.

Table 1. Comparison of Data Volume between Mobilenet and Other Models

Models	Image Net Accuracy	Million Mult-Adds	Million Parameters
VGG16	71.5%	15300	138
GoogleNet	69.8%	1550	6.8
Mobilenet-v1	70.6%	569	4.2

4.3 Mobilenet-v3-Large

The architecture of the Mobilenet-v3-large network is based on MnasNet [14] and uses the h-swish activation function instead of the ReLU function [6], as shown in Eq. 3, v3's detection accuracy and real-time performance are higher than those of Mobilenet-v1. The h-swish function use Eq. 2 to replace sigmoid function in Eq. 1. It has no upper bound, lower bound, smooth and non-monotonic characteristics. H-Swish can be embedded in mobile devices at a lower cost than functions with the same activation effect.

$$f(x) = x \cdot sigmoid(\beta x) \tag{1}$$

Table 2. Experimental Platform

	RAM	CPU	GPU	System
Model training	16 GB	Intel i7-12700	Nvidia-3060	Ubuntu20 x86-64 GNU/Linux
Model deployment	16 GB	Intel i7-12700	Nvidia-1660Ti	Windows 11

$$\frac{ReLU6(x+3)}{6} \tag{2}$$

$$h - swish(x) = x\frac{ReLU6(x+3)}{6} \tag{3}$$

In this paper, YOLO-V3 algorithm of three different backbone networks. Darknet53, Mobilenet-v1 and Mobilenet-v3-large are selected to train the positive samples of coke oven chamber pull rod chain. Then compare the performance of the model to obtain the optimal solution.

5 Experiment

According to practical needs, two servers were used for model training and model deployment in this experiment, and the device information is shown in Table 2.

5.1 Dataset

The robot is shown as Fig. 5. The rail-type inspection robot vertically collects images of 8 chains through the guardrail grille, and regards the colored grille mesh as the chain feature. Because the movement track and presentation state of the chain are relatively single, a large number of similar training data are easy to lead to over-fitting of the model. To improve the generalization of the model, data pruning should be performed on the model and complex environmental information should be fully utilized. For example, taking photos under different environmental lighting not only reduces the interference of lighting on detection accuracy, but also enhances the changes in the dataset image.

Collect data from multiple angles under different lighting conditions such as daytime, nighttime, and flashing red warning lights [2]. The timing of taking photos is set before, during, and after the chain movement, which enhances the richness of the dataset. Furthermore, in order to prevent the model from over fitting and reduce the dependence on external features, the original chain without grid is added to the data set. The addition of the original chain enhances the extraction ability of the model for roller chain features.

This dataset contains 694 chain images, including 347 during the day and 347 at night. Among them, there are 50 original chain images, accounting for approximately 7.2%.

Fig. 5. Robot in the coke oven

Table 3. Training and deployment data in different backbone network models

	IoU = 0.5@mAP*	Loss	RAM	InferSpeed(GPU)	InferSpeed(CPU)
Darknet53	0.98897	2.010	1.5 GB	0.06 ms	0.11 ms
Mobilenet-v1	0.98727	2.367	0.7 GB	0.08 ms	0.02 ms
Mobilenet-v3-large	0.99975	2.045	0.7 GB	0.08 ms	0.02 ms

*The binary mAP indicator with only positive samples is no different from AP

5.2 Model Training and Deployment

Using YOLO-V3 algorithm with the backbone network of Darknet53, Mobilenet-v1 and Mobilenet-v3-large to train the dataset. Then test and evaluate the models. Model inference test used 20 sheets 1920×1080 pixel chain image. Due to the small proportion of target pixels in the input image and the detection type being 1, the detection time for a single image is in the nanosecond level. For ease of presentation, the model inference time in Table 3 is the sum of 20 images, measured in milliseconds.

It is easy to see from Table 3 and Fig. 6 that the mAP (Mean Average Precision) of the Darknet53 backbone network fluctuated significantly at the initial stage of training. After multiple weight updates, it gradually converges. There is almost no difference in the mAP of the three backbone networks. However, in actual production, RAM usage is a more noteworthy issue. Working with multiple software at the same time can lead to high RAM usage, resulting in issues such as screen lag and program flicker. Under almost the same precision, YOLO-V3 model based on Mobilenet backbone network occupies less RAM on the server and has faster detection speed.

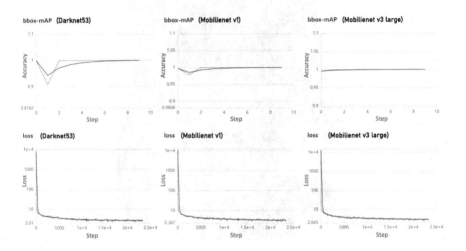

Fig. 6. Comparison of three backbone networks mAP and Loss

In terms of detection speed, there is a significant difference in inference using GPU or CPU. In the GPU inference process, Darknet53 has faster speed. While in the CPU inference process, Mobilenet has better performance. Analyzing the underlying reasons, although deep separable convolution reduces the number of parameters calculated by the model, it deepens the number of layers in the convolution layer. GPU is a computing platform for parallel processing of large-scale data, and the computation of each layer of neural networks is considered parallel processing. Therefore, the dominant factor in total inference time is the number of network layers. The CPU calculates data serially, and the inference time is positively correlated with the amount of computation. It can be intuitively seen that Mobilenet is suitable for deployment on mobile devices based on CPU inference, and performs well on the inspection robot platform in this article.

The YOLO-V3 model using Mobilenet-v1 and Mobilenet-v3-large backbone networks occupies the same RAM on the server. Mobilenet-v1 has higher detection speed, but is lower than Mobilenet-v3-large in detection accuracy and loss value. After actual testing, Mobilenet-v3-large detection speed can fully meet the requirements of patrol tasks, so Mobilenet-v3-large with higher accuracy is selected as the backbone network of YOLO-V3.

5.3   Model Reliability Testing

During the model training process, yellow and black warning color grids are used as chain features. A certain proportion of the original chain image is added to the data set to reduce the dependence of the model on the grid and prevent overfitting. To verify the reliability of the model, the original chain image, empty yellow black grid, and the "chain+grid" actual scene image proposed in this article were used for testing. The average scores of the four image detection methods are shown in Table 4.

Table 4. Model Reliability Testing

	Chain	Grid	Chain+Grid	Environment
Average Scores	0.819	0.373	0.973	0.127

Table 4 shows YOLO-V3 model with Mobilenet-v3-large as the backbone network has far lower recognition score for grid and non grid environment than chain detection score. Prove that the model can filter out empty grids and environmental interference by increasing the score threshold. After using the grid as a feature, the model's detection score for the chain was 0.154 higher than the original chain detection score, proving that adding grid features externally can effectively improve the chain recognition rate in normal working conditions.

6   Conclusion

This article designs and briefly introduces a mobile robot applied to the inspection task of coke oven basement, and conducts in-depth analysis on the abnormal detection of the pull rod chain. The functions of inspection robots involved and how to use complex environments to enhance the features of detection targets provide certain ideas for scholars engaged in coke oven basement inspection work. The discussion of lightweight models also provides some inspiration for the development of embedded inspection robots in the future. The selection of backbone network focuses on the actual needs, and the optimal model is selected based on coking production and server hardware performance. Finally, experiments prove that YOLO-V3 model with Mobilenet-v3-large as the backbone network can effectively detect the normal working state of the chain.

References

1. Aksoy, T., Halici, U.: Analysis of visual reasoning on one-stage object detection (2022)
2. Carlevaris-Bianco, N., Ushani, A.K., Eustice, R.M.: University of Michigan North campus long-term vision and lidar dataset. Int. J. Robot. Res. **35**(9), 1023–1035 (2015)
3. Diying, S., Chuncai, Z.: Application of inspection robot in cock oven. Technology-Wind (000-013) (2022)
4. Al Hasan, M.: Link prediction using supervised learning. In: Proceedings of SDM Workshop on Link Analysis Counterterrorism & Security (2005)
5. He, K., Zhang, X., Ren, S., Sun, J.: Deep residual learning for image recognition. IEEE (2016)
6. Howard, A., et al.: Searching for mobilenetv3. In: 2019 IEEE/CVF International Conference on Computer Vision (ICCV) (2020)
7. Howard, A.G., et al.: Mobilenets: efficient convolutional neural networks for mobile vision applications (2017)
8. Ioffe, S., Szegedy, C.: Batch normalization: accelerating deep network training by reducing internal covariate shift. JMLR.org (2015)
9. Jianwen, L., Hong, W., Kai, T., Dongming, D., Nan, Z., Yang, D.: Research on intelligent inspection system for coke oven ventilation equipment. Clean Coal Technol. (S02), 027 (2021)
10. Lin, T.Y., Dollar, P., Girshick, R., He, K., Hariharan, B., Belongie, S.: Feature pyramid networks for object detection. IEEE Computer Society (2017)
11. Redmon, J., Farhadi, A.: Yolov3: an incremental improvement. arXiv e-prints (2018)
12. Simonyan, K., Zisserman, A.: Very deep convolutional networks for large-scale image recognition. Computer Science (2014)
13. Szegedy, C., Liu, W., Jia, Y., Sermanet, P., Rabinovich, A.: Going deeper with convolutions. IEEE Computer Society (2014)
14. Tan, M., et al.: MnasNet: platform-aware neural architecture search for mobile (2018)
15. Tikai, J., Hao, M., Yaoguo, H.: Research on condition detection of roller chain based on wavelet packet decomposition and decision tree. Mod. Inf. Technol. **3**(13), 3 (2019)
16. Xu, B., Wang, N., Chen, T., Li, M.: Empirical evaluation of rectified activations in convolutional network. Computer Science (2015)
17. Yongli, L., Feiyan, W.: Research status of inspection robots at home and abroad. Technol. Innov. Appl. **12**(30), 66–68 (2022)

Powerline Detection and Accurate Localization Method Based on the Depth Image

Hai Li[1], Zhan Li[1,2(✉)], Tong Wu[1], Fulin Song[1], Jiayu Liu[1], and Zonglin Li[1]

[1] The Research Institute of Intelligent Control and Systems,
Harbin Institute of Technology, Harbin, China
`zhanli@hit.edu.cn`
[2] Department of Mathematics and Theories, Peng Cheng Laboratory,
No. 2, Xingke 1st Street, Nanshan, Shenzhen, China

Abstract. In recent years, various types of aerial work robots have been developed for the inspection and maintenance of the powerline. In this regard, the aerial manipulator system (AMS) has shown broad application potential because it combines the advantages of the UAVs and the manipulator. However, it is full of challenges for the AMS to perform close-range aerial interactive operations on the powerline, which requires stable and accurate detection and positioning information of the powerline. Therefore, a powerline detection and accurate localization method based on the depth image is proposed. Firstly, the depth image is converted into a grayscale image through background filtering and a designed special mapping operator. Then, detect the edges of the powerline in the grayscale image and identify different powerlines. Finally, the Kalman filter is used to track the position of the powerline and obtain the accurate localization information. The experimental results show that the proposed method can stably detect and accurately locate the powerline, which can provide stable and reliable relative position information for close-range aerial interactive operations.

Keywords: Powerline detection · Accurate localization · Kalman filter · Depth image

1 Introduction

The regular inspection and maintenance of the powerline is an important measure to ensure the safe and stable operation of the power system [1]. At present, this work is mainly carried out by maintenance personnel wearing professional equipments to climb on the powerline for operation, which is inefficient and dangerous. Compared with the traditional manual method, the AMS has the advantages of good flexibility, high efficiency and safety. Therefore, the AMS has been developed and applied to the powerline inspection and maintenance operations in recent years. Powerline detection and location is an important

© The Author(s), under exclusive license to Springer Nature Singapore Pte Ltd. 2023
H. Yang et al. (Eds.): ICIRA 2023, LNAI 14274, pp. 317–328, 2023.
https://doi.org/10.1007/978-981-99-6501-4_27

function of the system. In order to ensure the safe and effective aerial operations of the AMS, it is necessary to detect the powerline and determine their relative position.

In common interactive tasks [2] such as garbage cleaning and component replacement of the powerline, the AMS usually need to carry a specific end-effector to approach the powerline for aerial operations. When operating at close range, without stable detection and accurate location information, the AMS could easily collide with the powerline, which will damage the powerline and cause the AMS to crash. However, most of the existing powerline detection and location methods can only meet the needs of the UAVs cruising near the powerline, and their positioning accuracy cannot meet the operation requirements of the AMS. Therefore, it is necessary to research a stable detection and accurate localization method of the powerline for aerial operations.

The strong electromagnetic field near the powerline may cause strong interference to the IMU, magnetic compass and satellite navigation system [3], while the visual image technology will not be affected by the above interference. As a result, visual image technology is the better choice to realize the detection and location of the powerline. The main challenge encountered by the image-based powerline detection and localization methods is how to stably detect the powerline in complex background environment. The powerline is usually in outdoor environment, where the horizon, the sun and the outline of buildings will all affect the detection performance of the algorithm. In addition, the limited computing resources of the onboard computer also limit the deployment of the learning-based detection methods such as deep convolutional networks on the platforms [4]. The depth camera can better deal with the above two problems. Firstly, the depth background outputted by the depth camera in the high-altitude operation environment is very clean and almost only the powerline feature are preserved. Secondly, the depth camera directly outputs the depth information in the field of view, which does not require additional algorithms and also has low requirements for platform computing power.

To make up for the shortcomings of the existing methods, this paper proposes a powerline detection and accurate localization method based on the depth image. This method can stably detect the powerline and provide accurate and reliable relative position information for the AMS during close-range interactive operations, and is lightweight enough to be deployed on an onboard computer.

2   Related Works

The powerline detection and location methods based on visual image technology can be divided into three categories according to their technical routes. Firstly, in traditional image processing, researchers usually use a variety of techniques to reduce background noise and enhance powerline features, and then utilize Hough transform, Radon transform and the Line Segment Detector (LSD) and their improvements [5–10] to detect the powerline. For example, in [5], the authors developed a pulse-coupled neural network filter to remove background noise in images, and then used knowledge-based line clustering to refine the powerlines detected by the hough transform. In [6], an improved Radon transform, the Cluster Radon Transform (CRT), was proposed for extracting powerline features from satellite images. These methods rely on certain prior information and the detection effect is easily affected by the complex operating backgrounds, so they cannot meet the needs of close-range aerial operation tasks.

Secondly, with the popularity of the deep learning-based image processing methods, some learning-based line segment detection methods [11–14] and learning-based powerline extraction networks [15–20] were proposed for the powerline detection and segmentation. In [12], the authors proposed the first deep network for joint line segment detection and description by introducing a new dynamic programming-based line matching method and showed how to self-supervise this network for line segment detection. In [15], in order to produce powerline guidance information during the powerline automatic inspection, the authors proposed an end-to-end convolutional neural network to detect powerline with different pixel widths and orientations. Other different learning-based powerline extraction networks were proposed to achieve powerline detection and segmentation in [16,18,20]. These learning-based methods can effectively detect powerline in long-distance detection scenarios such as powerline inspection. However, their generalization performance are poor, which make them difficult to be applied to the close aerial operation scenarios. Moreover, these learning-based methods require high computing power and are difficult to deploy on the AMS with limited computing resources.

Thirdly, the above method can only obtain the position information of the powerline in the image, but cannot directly obtain the actual position information. For this reason, the powerline detection and localization methods based on the binocular stereo vision [4,21–23] were proposed. In [23], the authors used a cross-area based robust matching algorithm to obtain depth information and matched the powerline edges based on morphology and Mini-Census transform. In [4], a special feature extraction operator and the corresponding density-based feature recognition algorithm were designed to detect multi-scale powerlines, and a depth estimation method based on binocular vision was proposed. The detection stability of these methods is limited in the complex background, resulting in their positioning accuracy and detection stability can not meet the requirements of the close-range aerial operations.

3 Detection and Localization Method

3.1 Depth Filtering and Inverse Normalization Mapping

At present, the farthest distance measured by some depth cameras can reach more than ten meters. However, the actual working distance of the AMS is often within three meters. The depth information beyond this range is useless for aerial operations of the AMS. Therefore, after obtaining the depth image collected by the depth camera, the algorithm first carries out standardized filtering according to the set working distance threshold. At this time, all the depth values outside the threshold will be normalized to the background depth to filter out most of the background noise. If the depth of a point in the depth image plane is $P_{(i,j,\ \text{depth}\ )}$ and the set background depth threshold is P_{max}, the standardized filtering formula can be expressed as:

$$P_{(i,j,\ \text{depth}\ )} = \begin{cases} P_{(i,j,\ \text{depth}\ )} & P_{(i,j,\ \text{depth}\ )} < P_{max} \\ P_{max} & P_{(i,j,\ \text{depth}\ )} \geq P_{max} \end{cases} \tag{1}$$

Subsequently, in order to facilitate the extraction and detection of powerline features, the filtered depth image $P_{(i,j,\ \text{depth}\ )}$ is inversely normalized and mapped into a gray image $P_{(i,j,\ \text{gray}\ )}$ with reference to the following formula:

$$P_{(i,j,\ \text{gray}\ )} = 255 - \varepsilon \times P_{(i,j,\ \text{depth}\ )} \tag{2}$$

where $\varepsilon = 255/P_{\text{max}}$ is the inversely normalized factor.

After inverse normalization, the part of the powerline with small depth will be displayed in the gray image with high brightness, which is more conducive to the detection of the powerline. At this time, the gray image still contains a lot of measurement noise. Therefore, a series of image processing operations are carried out to reduce the image noise: The black cracks and noises in the powerline are eliminated by closed operation, so that the powerline tends to a single body. Using open operation to eliminate high brightness burr and make the edge of powerline as smooth as possible. If the powerline is thin, expansion operation is needed to connect breakpoints and thicken it. It should be noted that when the AMS is operated near the powerline, the powerline is always approximately horizontal in the perspective of the horizontally installed depth camera in a stable state. That is, we prefer to blur and eliminate the noise in the horizontal direction and connect the breakpoints, while retaining and strengthening the horizontal edge (abrupt change) information distributed in the vertical direction. As a result, in the above image operation, we use a flatter convolution kernel to highlight the linear characteristics of the powerline in the horizontal direction. So far, we have obtained a gray image with clear characteristics of the powerlines.

3.2   Edge Detection and Powerline Detection

On the basis of the above obtained grayscale image, the detection of the edge features of the powerline is performed. The step of powerline detection is to use canny algorithm to extract the edge pixels of the powerline in the image and map the gray image into a binary image, and then perform Hough transform to match the edge of the powerline that conforms to the straight line characteristics.

Canny is a classical edge detection algorithm with high accuracy and simple calculation. The edge detection algorithm is mainly divided into four steps. The first step is to perform median filtering and Gaussian filtering on the above gray image to eliminate burrs. The second step is to calculate the gradient by using sobel operator. If $\mathbf{S}_x$ and $\mathbf{S}_y$ are gradient calculation masks in two directions respectively, and $\mathbf{H}(i,j)$ (the central pixel is C) is the calculated image, then the

---

Algorithm 1: Powerline detection and accurate localization

1: **Parameters:** Flattened convolution kernel C = getStructuringElement(MORPH_RECT, Size(9, 3)), Mapping operator ε, Measuring distance ρ, Pixel ordinate y, Horizontal included angle of powerline θ, Depth image P_{depth}, Depth threshold P_{max};
    Input: Depth image P_{depth};
    Output: Position of the powerline relative to the AMS $\mathbf{P_s}$;

2: **begin:**
    for $P_{(i,j,\ depth)}$ *in* P_{depth} **do**
      if $P_{(i,j,\ depth)} \geq P_{max}$ **then**
        | $P_{(i,j,\ depth)} = P_{max}$;
      else
        | $P_{(i,j,\ depth)} = P_{(i,j,\ depth)}$;
      end
    $P_{(i,j,\ gray)} = 255 - \varepsilon \times P_{(i,j,\ depth)}$;
    end
    P_{mid} =medianBlur(P_{gray});
    P_{morp} =morphologyEx(P_{mid}, C);
    P_{canny} =Canny(P_{morp});
    Lines =HoughLinesP(P_{canny} ,lines);
    for L_i *in* Lines **do**
      Remove_outlier($P_{(m,n,\ depth)}$ in L_i);
      ρ_i =Mean($P_{(m,n,\ depth)}$ in L_i);
      L_i = extend L_i ;
      y_i = The ordinate of midpoint(L_i);
      θ_i =Horizontal included angle of L_i ;
    end
    for L_i, L_j *in* Lines **do**
      if $y_i \approx y_j$ *and* $\rho_i \approx \rho_j$ **then**
        | Combine L_i and L_j;
      end
    end
3: **output** $\mathbf{P_s}$

---

image gradient calculation is calculated by (3) (4):

$$G_x = \sum_{m=0}\sum_{n=0}\left(\mathbf{S_x}(m,n) * \mathbf{H}(i-m, j-n)\right) \tag{3}$$

$$G_y = \sum_{m=0}\sum_{n=0}\left(\mathbf{S_y}(m,n) * \mathbf{H}(i-m, j-n)\right) \tag{4}$$

where $\mathbf{G}_x$ and $\mathbf{G}_y$ respectively represent the gradient in two directions, and i, j denote the matrix size of the calculated image. Then the total gradient amplitude $\mathbf{G}_C$ and gradient direction θ_c at C are calculated by (5) and (6).

$$G_c = \sqrt{G_x^2 + G_y^2} \tag{5}$$

$$\theta_c = \arctan\left(G_x/G_y\right) \tag{6}$$

The third step of the algorithm is to suppress non-maximum data. Each pixel is searched along its gradient direction. If the gradient amplitude of adjacent pixels in the gradient direction is greater than that of the pixel, the possibility that the point is an edge is directly ruled out.

Finally, two lag thresholds maxVal and minVal are designed. Pixels with gradient amplitude greater than maxVal are directly identified as image edges, and pixels with gradient amplitude less than minVal are directly discarded. However, pixels with gradient amplitude between two thresholds are considered as edge pixels if they are adjacent to the identified edge pixels, otherwise they are not considered as edge pixels.

Because the total length of the powerline is very long, the edge in the field of view of the camera can always be regarded as two parallel straight lines. Therefore, we use hough transform to match the edges of powerlines that meet the characteristics of straight lines. Any straight line passing through a certain point(x, y) in the pixel plane can be expressed in polar coordinates as follows:

$$\varphi = x \cos \beta + y \sin \beta \tag{7}$$

For any straight line in the plane, we can always determine the unique $L(\varphi, \beta)$ corresponding to it. Therefore, (7) can be used to determine whether a point is on a straight line. If there are enough points on a straight line, then we can think that these pixels constitute a straight line. In order to improve the speed of calculation, the algorithm matches straight lines in the pixel plane by random sampling, and gives the coordinates of the starting point and ending point of the matched straight line segment.

Theoretically, the upper and lower edges of the powerline will be extracted into two line segments by hough change, and the same edge of the same power-line may also be extracted into several line segments. Therefore, it is necessary to classify the line segments of the same power line together and distinguish different power lines. Still consider the situation that the power line is approximately horizontal in the steady state. At this time, the attributes associated with each line segment and the power line are: the pixel position in the vertical direction, the corresponding measurement depth and the small included angle between the line segment and the horizontal direction.

Hough transform will directly return the two endpoints of each line segment, so we can easily calculate the small angle between each line segment and the horizontal direction and the vertical position of the line segment. We extend the two ends of the line segment to make its endpoint fall on the image boundary, and the vertical position is determined by the pixel coordinates of the middle point of the extended line segment. The depth of each line segment needs to be obtained as follows: firstly, a parallelogram region mask with a vertical height of 20 pixels is created with the line segment as the center line; Then, the depth value of the corresponding pixel in the region without filtering is extracted, and the depth greater than the background depth threshold and the invalid depth with the depth value of 0 are eliminated; Next, the outliers are eliminated; Finally, the depth of the first two-thirds of the depth value of the point set from small to large is averaged as the corresponding depth of the line segment to ensure that the depth we obtain is closer to the actual distance from the front surface of the powerline to the camera.

After obtaining the attributes of such multiple line segments. We classify the line segments with close vertical position, close average depth value and close horizontal included angle into the same powerline, fit multiple line segments into two long line segments across the pixel plane, calculate their vertical positions, and average the depths of their sub-line segments to obtain the final position of the powerline. Finally, we get the position representation of the powerline in pixel coordinates (y, ρ, θ). Where y is the vertical pixel coordinate of the power line, ρ is the average measurement depth from the powerline to the camera, and θ is the included angle between the powerline and the horizontal direction.

3.3   Position Calculation Based on the Kalman Filter

The position of powerline can be tracked by the Kalman filter. If coordinate transformation is used to calculate the actual position of powerlines in the air, it is necessary to establish at least six-dimensional state space equations. In order to compress the matrix dimension in calculation, the state equation can be directly established for the three components in the previous section. Then the following discrete state space equation can be established:

$$
\begin{cases} x(k+1) = x(k) + w(k) \\ z(k) = x(k) + v(k) \end{cases} \tag{8}
$$

where $x = [y, \rho, \theta]^{\mathrm{T}}$ is the state quantity of the position. w and v are 3*1 gaussian white noise matrix, which are process noise and measurement noise respectively.

On this basis, the discrete recursion of Kalman filter is realized. One-step prediction formula is:

$$
\begin{cases} \hat{x}_{k/k-1} = \hat{x}_{k-1} \\ P_{k/k-1} = P_{k-1} + Q \end{cases} \tag{9}
$$

where $\hat{x}_{k/k-1}$ is the predicted value, $P_{k/k-1}$ is the prediction error covariance matrix and Q is the process covariance matrix.

Further, we carry out measurement correction:

$$
\begin{cases} K_k = P_{k/k-1} / \left(P_{k/k-1} + R \right) \\ \hat{x}_k = \hat{x}_{k/k-1} + K_k \left(z_k - \hat{x}_{k/k-1} \right) \\ P_k = \left(I - K_k \right) P_{k/k-1} \end{cases} \tag{10}
$$

where K_k is the Kalman gain. R is the measurement covariance matrix, which can be obtained by measurement and calculation in the static state of the ground. $\hat{x}_{k/k-1}$ is the measurement correction value.

Next, we use coordinate transformation to calculate the relative position between the power line and the UAV. The observation model of the camera on the powerline is shown in Fig. 1, in which M is the midpoint of the powerline in the field of view. M' is the projected pixel point of M point on the powerline in the pixel plane. Because the power line is very long, we take the midpoint M of the power line in the field of vision as the calculation object. The calculation formula is as follows:

$$\begin{cases} \mathbf{X}_c = \rho \mathbf{K}^{-1}\mathbf{u} \\ \begin{bmatrix} \mathbf{X}_s \\ 1 \end{bmatrix} = \mathbf{T}_{sc}^{-1}\begin{bmatrix} \mathbf{X}_c \\ 1 \end{bmatrix} \\ \mathbf{p}_s = \mathbf{R}_{cs}\mathbf{p}_c \end{cases} \tag{11}$$

where $\mathbf{u}$ is the pixel coordinate of the midpoint of the power line on the image plane. $\mathbf{K}$ is the camera internal parameter matrix. ρ is the distance from the power line to the camera after Kalman filtering. $\mathbf{X}_c$ is the position coordinate of point M on the powerline in camera coordinate system. $\mathbf{T}_{sc}^{-1}$ is the transformation matrix from the AMS coordinate system to the camera coordinate system. $\mathbf{X}_s$ is the coordinate of point M on the powerline in the AMS coordinate system. $\mathbf{p}_c$ is the powerline attitude in camera coordinate system. $\mathbf{p}_s$ is the powerline attitude in the AMS coordinate system, and $\mathbf{R}_{cs}$ is the rotation matrix from camera coordinate system to the AMS coordinate system.

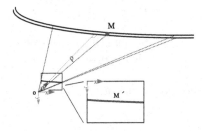

Fig. 1. Model of the powerline observed by camera

So far, the overall process of the proposed algorithm is shown in Algorithm 1, which can provide reliable and accurate relative position and attitude information for the close-range aerial interactive operations on the powerline.

4   Experiments

For the application scenario of the close-range aerial interactive operations of the AMS, the key indicators are the stability of detection and the accuracy of positioning at close range. For this reason, we use D435i camera as the depth image acquisition equipment and install it on the AMS to carry out the ground static state and aerial movement state tests. The Intel-NUC with the core of 8th i7cpu is adopted as the onboard computer to run the proposed algorithm in real time. During the test, the frame rate of depth image acquisition is 30 fps.

We tested the positioning accuracy in an indoor scene with Optitrack indoor positioning system. Optitrack is an indoor positioning detection system with positioning accuracy up to millimeter level. During our test, the relative position between the AMS and the powerline outputted by Optitrack is taken as the true value on the ground, and compared with the positioning results detected by the proposed algorithm. In order to facilitate the calculation of the relative position, we establish a coordinate system with a point on the powerline as the coordinate origin, the vertical upward direction as the positive direction of Y axis and the horizontal left direction as the positive direction of X axis. The AMS does three degree-of-freedom motion in the plane of XY axis. The overall test scenario is shown in Fig. 2.

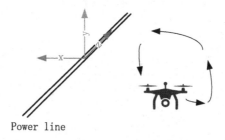

Power line

Fig. 2. Indoor test

After testing, the algorithm can stably detect the powerline and locate its position within a certain distance. The process is shown in the Fig. 3, in which the original depth image outputted by the depth camera is in the upper left, the depth grayscale image processed by inverse normalization filtering algorithm and image morphological filtering is in the upper right, the detected image edge is in the lower left, and the detected powerline is in the lower right. We map it into the color image to judge whether the detection of power lines is effective or not.

Fig. 3. Indoor test results

As shown in Fig. 4a to Fig. 4d, in the experiment, we test the positioning accuracy of the AMS when it is stationary (Fig. 4a), moving along the X axis (Fig. 4b), moving along the Y axis (Fig. 4c) and moving freely in the XY plane (Fig. 4d). Because the powerline along the Z axis runs through the whole camera field of vision and the basic posture of the AMS facing the powerline remains unchanged, the influence of the position along the Z axis on the experimental positioning can be ignored. In the test, we can ignore the slight influence of the movement in the Z axis direction and other axial rotation movements on the experimental results, and only observe the positioning accuracy in the X axis, Y axis direction and XY plane. The final test results are shown in Table 1. From the experimental results, it can be found that the algorithm has good positioning

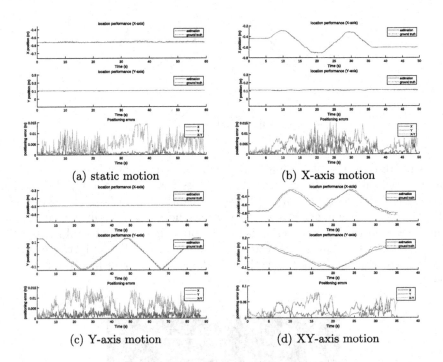

(a) static motion   (b) X-axis motion

(c) Y-axis motion   (d) XY-axis motion

Fig. 4. Powerline positioning result

Table 1. Positioning accuracy of different motions

System motion	Root mean square error (RMSE)		
	X axis	Y axis	composite error
static	0.00618 m	0.00119 m	0.00629 m
X-axis motion	0.00464 m	0.00411 m	0.00620 m
Y-axis motion	0.00198 m	0.00723 m	0.00749 m
X-Y 2-dof motion	0.03561 m	0.01389 m	0.03823 m

results in all kinds of movements of the AMS. When the camera is stationary or moving along X axis and Y axis, the positioning accuracy of the algorithm can reach sub-centimeter level. Even in the case of severe movement, the positioning accuracy can be kept at centimeter level.

5   Conclusion

In order to realize the stable detection and accurate localization of the powerline in the scenario of close-range aerial interactive operations, a powerline detection and accurate localization method based on the depth image is proposed in this paper. Firstly, the depth image is transformed into a grayscale image by filtering and inversely normalized mapping. Then, the edges of powerline in the image are detected and the edges are classified into different depths to identify different powerlines. Finally, the position of the powerlines is tracked by the Kalman filter. Experiments demonstrate that the proposed method can stably detect the powerline and provide accurate and reliable relative position information for the close-range aerial interactive operations of the AMS.

Acknowledgments. This work was supported by the National Natural Science Foundation of China (Grant No. 62273122).

References

1. Song, Y., Wang, H., Zhang, J.: A vision-based broken strand detection method for a power-line maintenance robot. IEEE Trans. Power Delivery **29**(5), 2154–2161 (2014)
2. Stuhne, D., et al.: Design of a wireless drone recharging station and a special robot end effector for installation on a power line. IEEE Access **10**, 88719–88737 (2022)
3. Suarez, A., Salmoral, R., Zarco-Periñan, P.J., Ollero, A.: Experimental evaluation of aerial manipulation robot in contact with 15 kv power line: shielded and long reach configurations. IEEE Access **9**, 94573–94585 (2021)
4. Li, Z., et al.: Vision-based autonomous landing of a hybrid robot on a powerline. IEEE Trans. Instrum. Meas. **72**, 1–11 (2022)
5. Li, Z., Liu, Y., Hayward, R., Zhang, J., Cai, J.: Knowledge-based power line detection for UAV surveillance and inspection systems. In: 2008 23rd International Conference Image and Vision Computing New Zealand, pp. 1–6. IEEE (2008)
6. Chen, Y., Li, Y., Zhang, H., Tong, L., Cao, Y., Xue, Z.: Automatic power line extraction from high resolution remote sensing imagery based on an improved radon transform. Pattern Recogn. **49**, 174–186 (2016)
7. Cao, W., Zhu, L., Han, J., Wang, T., Du, Y.: High voltage transmission line detection for UAV based routing inspection. In: 2013 IEEE/ASME International Conference on Advanced Intelligent Mechatronics, pp. 554–558. IEEE (2013)
8. Sarabandi, K., Park, M.: Extraction of power line maps from millimeter-wave polarimetric SAR images. IEEE Trans. Antennas Propag. **48**(12), 1802–1809 (2000)
9. Yan, G., Li, C., Zhou, G., Zhang, W., Li, X.: Automatic extraction of power lines from aerial images. IEEE Geosci. Remote Sens. Lett. **4**(3), 387–391 (2007)

10. Zhang, J., Liu, L., Wang, B., Chen, X., Wang, Q., Zheng, T.: High speed automatic power line detection and tracking for a UAV-based inspection. In: 2012 International Conference on Industrial Control and Electronics Engineering, pp. 266–269. IEEE (2012)

11. Gu, G., Ko, B., Go, S., Lee, S.H., Lee, J., Shin, M.: Towards light-weight and real-time line segment detection. In: Proceedings of the AAAI Conference on Artificial Intelligence, vol. 36, pp. 726–734 (2022)

12. Pautrat, R., Lin, J.T., Larsson, V., Oswald, M.R., Pollefeys, M.: Sold2: self-supervised occlusion-aware line description and detection. In: Proceedings of the IEEE/CVF Conference on Computer Vision and Pattern Recognition, pp. 11368–11378 (2021)

13. Liu, Z., et al.: B-spline wavelet neural network-based adaptive control for linear motor-driven systems via a novel gradient descent algorithm. IEEE Trans. Ind. Electron. (2023)

14. Xu, Y., Xu, W., Cheung, D., Tu, Z.: Line segment detection using transformers without edges. In: Proceedings of the IEEE/CVF Conference on Computer Vision and Pattern Recognition, pp. 4257–4266 (2021)

15. Xu, C., Li, Q., Zhou, Q., Zhang, S., Yu, D., Ma, Y.: Power line-guided automatic electric transmission line inspection system. IEEE Trans. Instrum. Meas. **71**, 1–18 (2022)

16. Chang, W., Yang, G., Li, E., Liang, Z.: Toward a cluttered environment for learning-based multi-scale overhead ground wire recognition. Neural Process. Lett. **48**, 1789–1800 (2018)

17. Gao, H., An, H., Lin, W., Yu, X., Qiu, J.: Trajectory tracking of variable centroid objects based on fusion of vision and force perception. IEEE Trans. Cybern. (2023)

18. Gao, Z., Yang, G., Li, E., Liang, Z., Guo, R.: Efficient parallel branch network with multi-scale feature fusion for real-time overhead power line segmentation. IEEE Sens. J. **21**(10), 12220–12227 (2021)

19. Liu, B., Li, J., Yang, Y., Zhou, Z.: Controller design for quad-rotor UAV based on variable aggregation model predictive control. Flight Control Detect. **4**(3), 1–7 (2021)

20. Liu, B., Huang, J., Lin, S., Yang, Y., Qi, Y.: Improved YOLOX-S abnormal condition detection for power transmission line corridors. In: 2021 IEEE 3rd International Conference on Power Data Science (ICPDS), pp. 13–16. IEEE (2021)

21. Ma, Q.: The research on binocular ranging technology for transmission lines based on two-dimensional line matching. In: 2020 IEEE Conference on Telecommunications, Optics and Computer Science (TOCS), pp. 98–103. IEEE (2020)

22. Mao, T., et al.: Development of power transmission line defects diagnosis system for UAV inspection based on binocular depth imaging technology. In: 2019 2nd International Conference on Electrical Materials and Power Equipment (ICEMPE), pp. 478–481. IEEE (2019)

23. Zhou, X., Zheng, X., Ou, K.: Power line detect system based on stereo vision and FPGA. In: 2017 2nd International Conference on Image, Vision and Computing (ICIVC), pp. 715–719. IEEE (2017)

Dexterity of Concentric Magnetic Continuum Robot with Multiple Stiffness

Na Li[1,2,3], Daojing Lin[1,2,3], Junfeng Wu[1,2,3], Quan Gan[1,2,3], and Niandong Jiao[1,2(✉)]

[1] State Key Laboratory of Robotics, Shenyang Institute of Automation, Chinese Academy of Sciences, Shenyang 110016, China
ndjiao@sia.cn
[2] Institutes for Robotics and Intelligent Manufacturing, Chinese Academy of Sciences, Shenyang 110016, China
[3] University of Chinese Academy of Sciences, Beijing 100049, China

Abstract. With the advancement of minimally invasive surgery, research pertaining to miniature continuum robots is progressively gaining momentum. In contrast to non-magnetic continuum robots, magnetic continuum robots (MCRs) exhibit a simple structure and dexterous operation characteristics, as they can be remotely and wirelessly controlled through magnetic manipulation. Dexterity serves as a vital parameter in evaluating MCRs. Nevertheless, conventional MCRs encounter limited dexterity and controllability issues due to their soft bodies. To enhance the dexterity of MCRs, we propose a novel concentric magnetic continuum robot (C-MCR), comprising a magnetic catheter and magnetic guidewire in a concentric combination. The substantial discrepancy in stiffness between the catheter and the guidewire facilitates the C-MCR to operate in four working modes, resulting in superior dexterity. Within this study, we evaluated the dexterity of the C-MCR utilizing a homemade eight-coil electromagnetic system. The experimental findings demonstrate that the C-MCR exhibits better dexterity, simplified operation, minimal risk, and promising prospects for clinical applications.

Keywords: Continuum Robot · Stiffness Control · Magnetic Control

1 Introduction

Minimally invasive surgery (MIS) has flourished in the last decade or so, particularly in areas such as neurosurgery and cardiac surgery. This surge can be attributed to the considerable reduction in postoperative pain and recovery time [1–4]. To address the goal of minimizing the extent and quantity of traumatic incisions, the adoption of continuum robots in MIS has been steadily growing [5, 6]. By incorporating magnetic miniature continuum robots (MCRs) into surgical procedures, surgeons are able to accomplish more with less exertion, as these robots can actively traverse intricate pathways under remote control [7, 8].

Non-magnetic continuum robots, such as those utilizing pneumatic control, concentric tube mechanisms, or tendon control, are constrained by the limitations of their

© The Author(s), under exclusive license to Springer Nature Singapore Pte Ltd. 2023
H. Yang et al. (Eds.): ICIRA 2023, LNAI 14274, pp. 329–338, 2023.
https://doi.org/10.1007/978-981-99-6501-4_28

control methods, resulting in restricted actuation capabilities. Consequently, this limitation poses operational inconveniences [9]. In stark contrast, magnetic control offers the advantage of remote manipulation for continuum robots. By employing magnetic control, a continuum robot can not only possess compact dimensions but also exhibit exceptional precision in its control.

The dexterity of magnetic miniature continuum robots (MCRs) holds significant importance as an indicator of their capabilities. A higher level of dexterity enables MCRs to navigate through more intricate cavities, thus providing enhanced operational convenience for surgeons. To enhance the dexterity of MCRs, researchers have explored various approaches. For instance, incorporating uniform ferromagnetic particles and hydrogel coatings on MCRs enables omnidirectional steering and self-lubrication, facilitating greater maneuverability [10, 11]. Another strategy involves employing opposite-magnetized magnets to induce active deformation in multi-mode MCRs, thereby improving their dexterity [12–14]. Additionally, the utilization of thermally variable stiffness materials for achieving section control of catheter stiffness opens up new possibilities [15–18].

To enhance the dexterity of MCRs, we have introduced a novel concept called the concentric magnetic continuum robot (C-MCR) [19]. The C-MCR primarily comprises a magnetic catheter and magnetic guidewire in a concentric combination. By taking advantage of their significant stiffness disparity and relatively independent properties, the C-MCR exhibits four distinct working modes and allows large curvature bending. This paper concentrates on the comprehensive evaluation of the dexterity exhibited by the four working modes of the C-MCR, accompanied by an in-depth analysis and discussion of the experimental results.

2 Design and Methodology

2.1 Design

A stable magnetic navigation system serves as the foundation for driving MCRs. In our study, we have built an eight-coil electromagnetic system that can provide a reliable magnetic field for the C-MCR (shown in Fig. 1a). The system mainly comprises eight programmable DC powers, eight coils with corresponding cooling brasses, a camera, and a workstation. Its internal spherical workspace measures approximately 300 mm in diameter, generating a magnetic field of approximately 120 mT at the sphere's centre. To enhance the dexterity of the MCRs, we have integrated a nickel–titanium alloy guidewire with a hollow rubber catheter, both of which have been equipped with custom axially magnetized hollow cylindrical N52 neodymium magnets at their front end, as illustrated in Fig. 1b.

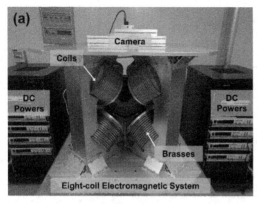
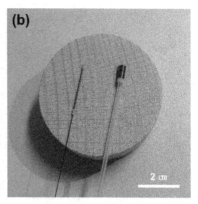

Fig. 1. (**a**) Physical diagram of the eight-coil electromagnetic system. (**b**) Physical view of the magnetic guidewire (left) and magnetic catheter (right).

2.2 Four Working Modes

The C-MCR exhibits four distinct working modes: Single Catheter (SC), Single Guidewire (SG), Guidewire Inside Catheter (GIC), and Guidewire Through Catheter (GTC). These modes are made possible by the significant stiffness difference between the magnetic catheter and the magnetic guidewire, as well as their independent characteristics. In the forthcoming experimental section, we will conduct tests to assess the dexterity of each working mode and subsequently analyze the results obtained (Fig. 2).

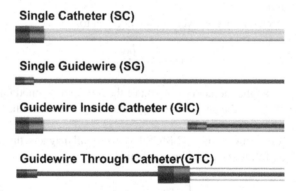

Fig. 2. Diagram of the four working modes

2.3 Deflection Model

The C-MCR is deflected towards the direction of the magnetic field under the influence of the deflecting magnetic field. The steady state is reached when the C-MCR is subjected to a magnetic torque $\|t_m\| \in R^3$ equal to the recovery torque $\|t_r\| \in R^3$ [20], as shown in Fig. 3.

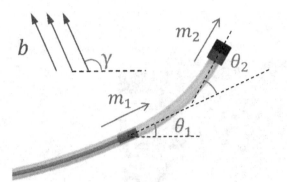

Fig. 3. Schematic diagram of the deflection model

The magnetic torque applied to the C-MCR in the deflection plane is equal to

$$\|t_m\| = \|m\|\|b\|\sin(\gamma - \theta) \tag{1}$$

where m denotes the magnetic moment of the magnet, θ denotes the deflection angle of the magnet, $b \in R^3$ represents the deflected magnetic field as shown in Eq. (2), and γ is the pitch angle of b.

$$b = A_m\left[\sin\gamma \ \cos\alpha \ \sin\gamma \ \sin\alpha \ \cos\gamma\right]^T \tag{2}$$

where A_m denotes the magnitude of the magnetic field and α represents the yaw angle of the magnetic field.

C-MCR is subjected to the recovery moment equal to

$$\|t_r\| = \frac{EI_A\theta}{L_C} \tag{3}$$

where I_A and E denote the moment of inertia of the area and the modulus of elasticity, and L_C is the length from the end of the magnet to the point where the bending of the segment occurs.

Since the GIC operating mode of C-MCR has two small magnets, the overall balance is reached when the following equation is satisfied.

$$\begin{cases} \|t_{m1}\| = \|t_{r1}\| \\ \|t_{m2}\| = \|t_{r2}\| \end{cases} \tag{4}$$

3 Experiments and Results

Conventional MCRs often suffer from limited dexterity due to their excessive softness, which poses challenges for surgeons during operations, despite being remotely drivable. To address this issue, we have developed the C-MCR, which incorporates a concentric arrangement of a magnetic catheter and a magnetic guidewire, allowing for controllable stiffness. This straightforward detachable structure enables the C-MCR to offer four distinct working modes (SC, SG, GIC, GTC). During practical usage, these working modes can be easily switched as needed, depending on the specific requirements of the application scenario. Dexterity, as a crucial measure of MCR performance, is analyzed in this subsection through experimental evaluations conducted on a 3D-printed model simulating a blood vessel.

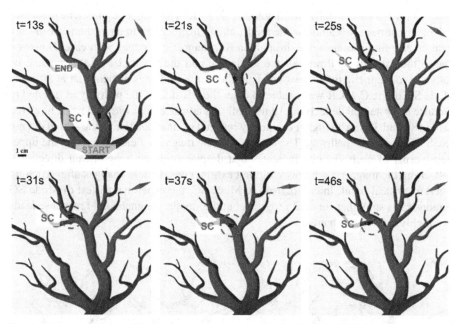

Fig. 4. Dexterity of Mode SC. During the experiment, Mode SC of the C-MCR passes through a section of the channel. The insets show the relative pose of the C-MCR to each key moment.

3.1 Dexterity of Mode SC

Mode SC represents a mode with only one magnetic catheter, which is a common configuration seen in conventional MCRs. The rubber body of the catheter provides dexterity for bending but faces challenges in advancing through minor obstacles. Nevertheless, the internal hollow cavity of the catheter enables the delivery of drugs, lasers, and other procedures such as soft tissue sampling, rendering it highly valuable in clinical applications. In this subsection, we aimed to navigate Mode SC of the C-MCR from a predetermined starting point to an endpoint within a vascular-like model using the eight-coil electromagnetic system. As depicted in Fig. 4, although it ultimately reached the endpoint at 46 s, it encountered wall collisions at three instances (25 s, 31 s, and 37 s), resulting in the inability to move forward and necessitating retreat and subsequent retries to reach the endpoint. Through the experimental test, we have a certain knowledge of the dexterity of Mode SC. In this working mode, the C-MCR exhibits sensitivity to variations in the magnetic field, with its small front-end magnet responding effectively to such changes. However, due to its soft body, it can only perform small curvature bending, and when encountering even minor obstacles, it becomes unable to pass through. Thus, its progress is reliant on persistent attempts to reach the desired endpoint.

3.2   Dexterity of Mode SG

Mode SG is a mode with only one magnetic guidewire. The magnetic guidewire possesses a diameter of merely 0.3mm, while the front-end magnet has an outer diameter of only 0.6mm, enabling it to navigate through narrow magnetic conduits with ease. However, due to the excessive stiffness of the guidewire and the small size of the magnet, its response to magnetic field variations is limited. In Fig. 5, it is evident that at 10 s, the Mode SG of the C-MCR was unable to enter the left side of the pathway as it failed to produce a substantial deflection. Additionally, its advancement was somewhat hindered in the 18 s and 33 s. Although it eventually reached its final position in the 40 s, it did not reach the end of the pathway. The direction of the magnetic field depicted in the upper right corner of each vignette indicates that despite applying a significant directional deflection, the magnetic guidewire did not exhibit considerable changes after reaching a certain critical point. In comparison to Mode SC, the experimental test of Mode SG demonstrates smoother forward progress, but the smaller magnetic field response leads to a highly limited reach area.

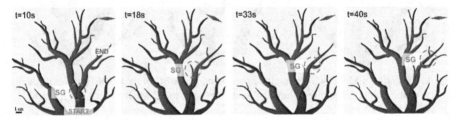

Fig. 5. Dexterity of Mode SG. During the experiment, Mode SG of the C-MCR passes through a section of the channel. The insets show the relative pose of the C-MCR to each key moment.

3.3   Dexterity of Mode GIC

Mode GIC refers to the configuration where the magnetic guidewire is placed inside the magnetic catheter, building upon Mode SC. Previous experiments have demonstrated that a single magnetic conduit allows for significant curvature bending, while a single magnetic guidewire enables smooth advancement. By combining the magnetic catheter and the guidewire, a complementary effect is achieved. In our experiments, we deliberately chose the same starting and ending points for Mode GIC as in Mode SC to investigate whether the dexterity of the C-MCR is enhanced under Mode GIC. As depicted in Fig. 6, Mode GIC successfully reached the endpoint at 23 s without the need for retreat, even when faced with minor obstacles that couldn't be overcome. It is worth noting that the distance between the magnetic catheter and the magnetic guidewire is adjustable, as exemplified by the smooth forward movement at 12 s through distance control. The experimental results clearly indicate that Mode GIC exhibits superior dexterity compared to Mode SC. This improvement can be attributed to the significant stiffness difference between the guidewire and the catheter, with the flexibility of the MCR being regulated by controlling the distance between them. Mode GIC represents the most common and classical working mode of the C-MCR, demonstrating excellent performance when traversing channels.

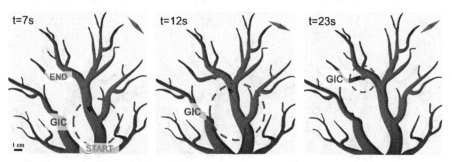

Fig. 6. Dexterity of Mode GIC. During the experiment, the Mode GIC of the C-MCR passes through a section of the channel. The insets show the relative pose of the C-MCR to each key moment.

3.4 Dexterity of Mode GTC

Mode GTC is a configuration derived from Mode GIC, where the magnetic guidewire passes through the magnetic catheter. To preserve the internal working cavity of the catheter for tasks like drug delivery or soft tissue sampling, we selected a magnetic catheter with a 2 mm outer diameter and a small front-end magnet with a 1 mm outer diameter. The overall size of the catheter is slightly larger for some small vessels. While Mode GIC can bypass minor obstructions, it is unable to address obstacles such as thrombosis. In Mode GTC, the magnetic guidewire passing through the magnetic catheter effectively navigates and unblocks small vessels. As illustrated in Fig. 7, the magnetic guidewire successfully reached the end of the smaller cavity at 64 s. In addition to this, compared to Mode SG, the response of both the magnetic catheter and the magnetic guidewire to the magnetic field is superimposed. For instance, at 11 s, the C-MCR traverses the left pathway with the assistance of the external catheter. It should be noted that using this mode alone may present certain problems. For example, at 28 s, the rigid magnetic guidewire becomes stuck and unable to progress. However, during actual usage, a single mode is not employed exclusively. Surgeons familiar with the C-MCR can proficiently judge and switch between working modes as needed.

3.5 Comparison of Four Working Modes

Based on the outcomes of the aforementioned experimental tests, we have succinctly outlined the merits and demerits of the four operational modalities, as delineated in

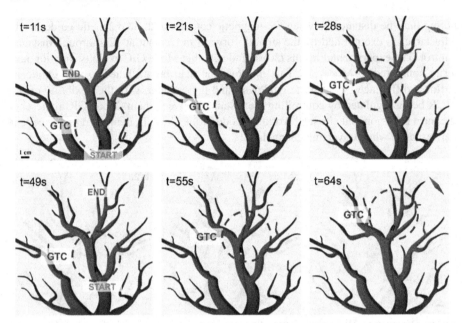

Fig. 7. Dexterity of Mode GTC. During the experiment, the Mode GTC of the C-MCR passes through a section of the channel. The insets show the relative pose of the C-MCR to each key moment.

Table 1. Mode SC exhibits sensitive responsiveness to magnetic fields and achieves minor curvatures deftly, albeit exhibiting a propensity for stagnation when confronted with minor obstructions and necessitating greater dexterity in operation. Mode SG allows for smooth advancement unaffected by supple impediments, yet its responsiveness to magnetic fields is insensitive, severely restricting its spatial reach. Mode GIC represents the quintessential operating mode of C-MCR, enabling large curvature bending at any position with remarkable dexterity and controllability, but it remains unable to access diminutive vessels due to inherent size limitations. Mode GTC not only attains access to narrow areas but also effectively resolves obstructions such as blood clots; however, as an independent mode, GTC encounters limitations in its spatial reach and necessitates amalgamation with other modes. These four working modalities exhibit distinct strengths and weaknesses; however, in practical scenarios, surgeons possess the capability to seamlessly switch between modes, mitigating the deficiencies and rendering them highly applicable.

Table 1. Comparison of the four working modes.

Working mode	Advantages	Disadvantages
Mode SC	Sensitive to magnetic field changes; Complete delivery of drugs, soft tissue sampling and so on	Small curvature bending; Advancement hindered; Larger size
Mode SG	Advancement unhindered; Smaller size	Insensitive to magnetic field changes; Limited work scope
Mode GIC	Large curvature bending; High dexterity	Access to larger cavities only
Mode GTC	Access to narrow cavities; Protecting blood vessels	Less Dexterity

4 Discussion and Conclusion

This paper focuses primarily on evaluating the dexterity of the C-MCR, which is an MCR we have developed through the concentric integration of a magnetic catheter and a magnetic guidewire [19]. Traditional MCRs often encounter challenges related to poor controllability and limited dexterity due to their soft bodies. To address these issues, we propose a solution by incorporating controllable stiffness. The combination of a magnetic catheter, which exhibits sensitivity to magnetic field variations, and a magnetic guidewire, which enables smooth advancement, enhances the overall dexterity of the MCR. Additionally, the independent nature of the magnetic catheter and magnetic guidewire allows for not only controllable stiffness at any position of the C-MCR but also the availability of four distinct working modes. Using an eight-coil electromagnetic system, we conducted experiments to assess the dexterity of each of the four working modes of the C-MCR. Subsequently, we analyzed the obtained results to gain insights into the performance and capabilities of the C-MCR.

Although we have analyzed the dexterity of C-MCR based on our previous studies, our research on it still is ongoing and requires further exploration. To enhance its practicality, our future research endeavours will involve integrating camera, ultrasound, and CT technologies to enable closed-loop control of the C-MCR. Additionally, we aim to incorporate functionalized designs tailored to specific diseases, leveraging the existing structure as a foundation. It is important to note that animal experiments will be crucial in order to ultimately apply the C-MCR in a clinical setting. We have confidence in the potential of the C-MCR and remain committed to advancing our research in this field.

Acknowledgement. This work was supported by the CAS Project for Young Scientists in Basic Research (Grant No. YSBR-036), the National Natural Science Foundation of China (Grant Nos. 62273331, 61925307, 62127811, 61821005), and the CAS/SAFEA International Partnership Program for Creative Research Teams.

References

1. Jinxing, L.: Micro/nanorobots for biomedicine: delivery, surgery, sensing, and detoxification. Sci. Robot. **2**(4), 6431 (2017)
2. Menaker, S.A., Shah, S.S., Snelling, B.M., Sur, S., Starke, R.M., Peterson, E.C.: Current applications and future perspectives of robotics in cerebrovascular and endovascular neurosurgery. J. NeuroIntervent. Surg. **10**(1), 78–82 (2018)
3. Valentina, V.: Emerging robotic platforms for minimally invasive surgery. IEEE Rev. Biomed. Eng. **6**, 111–126 (2013)
4. Mayank, G.: Neurointerventional robotics: challenges and opportunities. Clin. Neuroradiol. **30**(2), 203–208 (2020)
5. Mark, R.: Soft robotics in minimally invasive surgery. Soft Robot. **6**(4), 423–443 (2019)
6. Matteo, C.: Biomedical applications of soft robotics. Nat. Rev. Mater. **3**(6), 143–153 (2018)
7. Yang, G.-Z.: The grand challenges of science robotics. Sci. Robot. **3**(14), 7650 (2018)
8. Jessica, B.-K.: Continuum robots for medical applications: a survey. IEEE Trans. Robot. **31**(6), 1261–1280 (2015)
9. Matteo, R.: Continuum robots: an overview. Adv. Intell. Syst. **5** (2023) https://doi.org/10.1002/aisy.202200367
10. Yoonho, K.: Ferromagnetic soft continuum robots. Sci. Robot. **4**(33), 7329 (2019)
11. Yoonho, K.: Telerobotic neurovascular interventions with magnetic manipulation. Sci. Robot. **7**(65), 9907 (2022)
12. Daojing, L.: A magnetic continuum robot with multi-mode control using opposite-magnetized magnets. IEEE Robot. Autom. Lett. **6**(2), 2485–2492 (2021)
13. Daojing, L.: Kinematic analysis of multi-section opposite magnetic catheter robots with solution multiplicity. IEEE Trans. Autom. Sci. Eng. Lett. 1–12 (2022)
14. Daojing, L.: Position and orientation control of multisection magnetic soft microcatheters. IEEEASME Trans. Mechatron. **28**(2), 907–918 (2023)
15. Mattmann, M.: Thermoset shape memory polymer variable stiffness 4D robotic catheters. Adv. Sci. **9**(1), 2103277 (2022)
16. Jonas, L.: A Submillimeter Continuous Variable Stiffness Catheter for Compliance Control. Adv. Sci. **8**(18), 2101290 (2021)
17. Yegor, P.: A variable stiffness magnetic catheter made of a conductive phase-change polymer for minimally invasive surgery. Adv. Funct. Mater. **32**(20), 2107662 (2022)
18. Christophe, C.: Magnetic continuum device with variable stiffness for minimally invasive surgery. Adv. Intell. Syst. **2**(6), 1900086 (2020)
19. Na, L.: Novel concentric magnetic continuum robot with multiple stiffness modes for potential delivery of nanomedicine. Magnetochemistry. **9**(5), 5 (2023)
20. Tiantian, X., Jiangfan, Y., Yan, X., Choi, H., Zhang, L.: Magnetic actuation based motion control for microrobots: an overview. Micromachines **6**(9), 1346–1364 (2015)

Efficient and Accurate Detector with Global Feature Aggregation for Steel Surface Defect Detection

Kefei Qian, Zhiwen Wang, and Lai Zou[✉]

State Key Laboratory of Mechanical Transmission, Chongqing University, No. 174 Shazhengjie, Shahpingba, Chongqing 400044, China
zoulai@cqu.edu.cn

Abstract. Object detection-based steel surface defect detection is a typical application of deep learning technology in the industry, which performs better than traditional detection methods. However, simply using popular networks and porting high-performance modules does not yield the desired effect on steel due to the vastly different datasets. In response to the problems of large-scale variation, inconspicuous features, and substantial background interference of steel surface defects, we propose a lightweight global feature aggregation and redistribution (GFAR) module that significantly improves detection accuracy while ensuring efficiency. Our method uses yolov5m as the baseline network and embeds the proposed module at the neck: adaptive aggregation of feature maps in a parameter-free manner, output in the same and opposite manner after feature refinement and refusion with the feature maps of the PAFPN branch. The proposed network is extensively experimentally validated on the steel surface defect datasets NEU-DET and GC10-DET, and the results show that our method achieves a relatively competitive level of accuracy while ensuring the detection speed.

Keywords: deep learning · defect detection · feature aggregation · YOLO v5

1 Introduction

Due to limitations in production levels and storage conditions, various types of defects are inevitably formed on the surface of the steel. These defects not only affect the appearance but also easily lead to a decline in the quality and performance of the steel. Therefore, efficiently and accurately detecting these defects is extremely important to improve product quality and enhance production levels. Influenced by many factors such as impacts, corrosion, foreign objects, and others, the surface of the steel is prone to various defects, such as scratches, folds, and inclusions. These defects are diverse in type, vary in size, are low in contrast, and are subject to intense background interference, which poses enormous challenges to industrial automated defect detection.

The traditional defect detection method relies on experienced inspectors, but this manual inspection method has a heavy workload, subjective detection results, and poor labor stability and consistency. In recent years, machine vision-based inspection methods

© The Author(s), under exclusive license to Springer Nature Singapore Pte Ltd. 2023
H. Yang et al. (Eds.): ICIRA 2023, LNAI 14274, pp. 339–350, 2023.
https://doi.org/10.1007/978-981-99-6501-4_29

have gradually been widely used in industry. Early vision-based methods mainly obtained two-dimensional feature information through laser scanning [1], spectral analysis [2], and other methods, then processed it using image processing techniques (such as Hough transform [3] and Canny edge detection [4]) or used classifiers (such as SVM [5] and its variants [6, 7]) to detect surface defects. This detection method can have high detection accuracy for specific defects. However, it is difficult to achieve complete modeling and migration of defect features, could be more reusable, and needs to be more effective in detecting minor defects.

With the rapid development of deep learning and computer vision, object detection-based methods have made many breakthroughs in steel surface defect detection. Wang et al. [8] combined the improved ResNet50 and the enhanced Faster RCNN for the classification and localization of defects in images. He et al. [9] developed a steel surface defect detector combining multilayer features based on ResNet and RPN, which achieved a very advanced performance then. However, the networks mentioned above are two-stage networks based on region proposals with large spatial complexity. In contrast, one-stage networks have been more widely used in industrial defect detection due to their detection speed advantage with real-time potential. Cui et al. [10] designed a feature retention module and a skip-densely connected module in SSD to enable the network to learn defective features with rich information. Yu et al. [11] processed feature maps with different resolutions in different ways and fully interacted with each other to obtain faster convergence and higher detection accuracy. Guo et al. [12] introduced the TRANS structure in yolov5 and combined it with features with global information to enhance the detector's ability to dynamically adjust to targets at different scales. Cheng et al. [13] introduced a channel attenuation mechanism and an adaptive spatial feature fusion module in RetinaNet to effectively fuse shallow and deep features while reducing information loss. These single-stage detectors have excellent performance on NEU-DET defect datasets, but they still have limitations in feature fusion and resistance to background interference.

Conventional feature fusion methods only transfer feature information between adjacent size feature maps, which somewhat dilutes the semantic and detail information in deep and shallow feature maps. Steel surface defects are highly variable in size, inconspicuous in character, and have substantial background interference, so we need to minimize defect information loss and highlight defect areas in the background. To address these issues, we improved the SPP structure and introduced the global feature aggregation and redistribution module (GFAR) structure into the neck to enhance the information interaction of multi-scale features. The Global Position Attention Module (GPAM) is embedded into the GFAR to make the network focus more on the defective parts of the image to reduce background interference.

2 Methodology

2.1 Overall Structure

Our method is performed using YOLOv5 [14] as the baseline network. This single-stage detection network integrates many of the best results from recent academia for more flexible deployment and higher detection accuracy and speed. We combine the proposed

GFAR in the neck of yolov5. The overall structure of our proposed network is shown in Fig. 1.

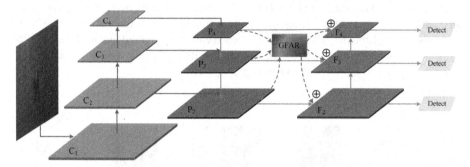

Fig. 1. Overall structure of the proposed network

The network first extracts multi-scale, high-quality features from the input image using the backbone network CSPDarkNet53. After a series of downsampling and residual processing, three sets of feature maps, C_2, C_3, and C_4, are obtained, where the subscript represents the number of downsampling times. After feature propagation from top to bottom using FPN, feature maps with multi-scale information, P_2, P_3, and P_4, are obtained. The network then bifurcates into two branches that run in parallel. The first branch follows the same process as PAFPN, that is, it learns and processes features in parallel at multiple scales through operations such as lateral connections, context-aware feature selection, and feature aggregation. In the other branch, the GFAR module performs feature aggregation for P_2, P_3, P_4 in a weighted parameter-free manner, which is redistributed to the output of the previous branch in the same and opposite manner after refinement and attention enhancement, as described in detail in Sect. 2.2.

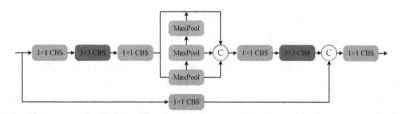

Fig. 2. Structure of SPPFCSPC module

In addition, we introduced Cross Stage Partial Connection to the original spatial pyramid pooling structure, which is called SPPFCSPC and shown in Fig. 2. SPPFCSPC divides the feature map into two parts for processing. Typical convolutions process one part to preserve the global information of the feature map. In contrast, the other part is processed by SPPF to achieve feature fusion across different receptive fields. Finally, the results are concatenated and convolved to adjust the number of channels. This method combines the advantages of SPPF and SPPCSPC, obtaining better feature representation capabilities.

2.2 Global Feature Aggregation and Redistribution

The neck network of YOLOv5 only strengthens the interaction between adjacent feature maps without considering the global feature information distribution and the differences in contribution to the output features from input features of different resolutions. Therefore, inspired by Libra RCNN [15] and combined with the weighted fusion idea of BiFPN [16], we propose a global feature aggregation and redistribution (GFAR) module. The overall structure of GFAR is shown in Fig. 3.

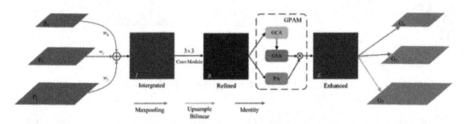

Fig. 3. Overall workflow of proposed GFAR

The Process of Aggregation and Redistribution. In the GFAR module, we employ a parameter-free approach for feature aggregation. The objects to be aggregated are three sets of feature maps, P_2, P_3, and P_4, generated by FPN, where the subscript denotes the number of downsampling operations, and the feature depth gradually increases. We transform P_2 and P_4 to the same scale as P_3 for balanced feature fusion. Generally, we set a balance feature layer P_i and transform other feature maps to this scale. The transformation process can be expressed as:

$$P_{k'} = \begin{cases} Upsample(P_k, \ bilinear) \ if \ k > i \\ Identity(P_k) \ if \ k = i \\ Maxpool(P_k) \ if \ k < i \end{cases} \qquad (1)$$

where $P_k' \in \mathbb{R}^{C \times H \times W}$ denotes feature maps generated by transforming FPN's k-th level feature map to a new dimension and scale corresponding to the selected balance feature level i. Bilinear downsampling and max pooling are parameter-free transformation methods that introduce minimal additional computational overhead. Then, we add learnable coefficients to each P_k' to achieve weighted aggregation, and the final aggregated feature map $I \in \mathbb{R}^{C \times H \times W}$ can be expressed as:

$$I = \sum_{k=k_{min}}^{k_{max}} w_k P_{k'} \qquad (2)$$

Although the aggregated feature map I contain richer semantic and detailed information, it also has more noise information and the aliasing effect caused by upsampling. Therefore, further processing is needed to refine the aggregated feature map. We adopt a 3×3 convolution to further enhance its discriminability. Subsequently, a global positional attention mechanism is employed to enhance the features and highlight the regions of interest. The specific process can be represented by the following formula:

$$R = Conv_{3\times3}(I)$$
$$E = GPAM(R)$$
(3)

where $R, E \in \mathbb{R}^{C\times H\times W}$ denote the refined and enhanced feature maps, respectively. $GPAM(\cdot)$ represents the global position attention mechanism.

Finally, we transform the enhanced feature maps back to the original multi-scale dimensions and add them to the same-dimensional feature maps generated by PAFPN to enhance the original features. In the reallocation process, we employ the identical and opposite parameter-free transformation methods used in the aggregation process. The specific process can be represented by the following formula:

$$G_k = \begin{cases} Upsample(E, \ bilinear) \ if \ k < i \\ Identity(E) \ if \ k = i \\ Maxpool(E) \ if \ k > i \end{cases}$$
(4)

$$F_k = G_k + PAN(P_k)$$
(5)

where G_k denotes the multi-scale feature maps generated by the redistribution of the enhanced feature map E, F_k denotes the feature map of the original PAFPN after being enhanced by GFAR.

The Global Positional Attention Mechanism. Given the considerable variation in the shape and the relatively insignificant defect features of steel surface defects, it is significant to introduce an attention mechanism to highlight the defect region. We propose a GPAM to make the network pays more attention to the information that is more important for the current task. The Global meaning is that the attention mechanism generates a weight map of the same shape as the input.

The detailed structure diagram of GPAM is shown in Fig. 4. For a given feature map $F \in \mathbb{R}^{C\times H\times W}$, the enhanced feature map $F' \in \mathbb{R}^{C\times H\times W}$ generated by GPAM can be expressed as:

$$F' = GPAM(F) = M(F) \otimes P(F)$$
(6)

where $\otimes$ denotes element-wise multiplication, $M(\cdot)$ and $P(\cdot)$ represents global attention mechanism and position attention mechanism respectively. $M(\cdot)$ consists of two sub-modules of sequentially connected global channel attention $M_C(\cdot)$ and global spatial attention $M_S(\cdot)$.

Global Channel Attention (GCA). To better explore the channel relationships in the channel branches while reducing information loss in space, we use 3D permutation to integrate spatial information into one dimension. Then, we use a multi-layer perceptron (MLP) with hidden layers to amplify the spatial channel dependencies across dimensions. To save computational costs, the hidden layer of the MLP is set to $\mathbb{R}^{HW\times C/r}$, where

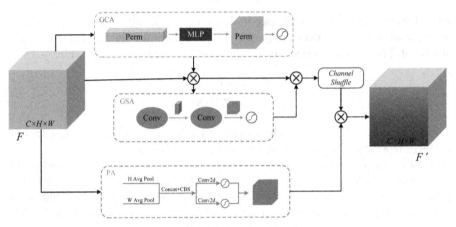

Fig. 4. Overall Structure of GPAM

r is the reduction ratio. Finally, we use the activation function to model the output nonlinearly and generate a global channel attention map $M_C(F) \in \mathbb{R}^{C \times H \times W}$, which can be represented by the following formula:

$$M_C(F) = \sigma(Perm(MLP(Perm(F)))) \tag{7}$$

where σ denotes the sigmoid function, and $Perm\,(\cdot)$ represents a 3D permutation.

Global Spatial Attention (GSA). We use the relationship between feature spaces to generate a spatial attention map to highlight or restrain features at different positions in the spatial domain. To focus on spatial features, we use a 7x7 convolution layer for spatial feature fusion of the original features. We also use a hidden layer with a reduction ratio of r, similar to a 3D MLP, where the fully connected operation is replaced with convolution. The global spatial attention map $M_S(F) \in \mathbb{R}^{C \times H \times W}$ can be expressed as:

$$M_S(F) = \sigma(Conv(Conv(F))) \tag{8}$$

where $Conv(\cdot)$ represents 7×7 2d convolution. Two convolutions with different numbers of input and output channels.

Positional Attention (PA). The convolution and permutation operations involved in the above steps may cause misalignments in positional information. Therefore, we add a branch to capture directional awareness and position-sensitive information about the original feature map. Here, we draw inspiration from the basic idea of position information encoding in CA [18], which has advanced performance in existing techniques for focusing on position information. We decompose global pooling into two parallel one-dimensional feature encoding processes to stimulate the attention module to ascertain long-range spatial dependencies with precise positional information and mitigate information loss caused by 2D pooling. Specifically, for a given input feature $F \in \mathbb{R}$

$C \times H \times W$, we aggregate the feature maps separately from the width and height directions into two distinct position-aware feature maps. Thus, the corresponding outputs on height h and width w on the c-th channel are:

$$z_c^h(h) = \frac{1}{W} \sum_{0 \le i \le W} x_c(h, i) \tag{9}$$

$$z_c^w(w) = \frac{1}{H} \sum_{0 \le j \le H} x_c(j, w) \tag{10}$$

This parallel transformation enables the attention module to capture long-range spatial dependencies along one spatial direction while obtaining precise positional information along the other. Next, we will fully utilize the acquired positional information and broadcast it to the global feature for further processing. First, we concatenate the position-aware feature maps generated by Eq. 9 and Eq. 10 along the spatial dimension, and feed the resulting feature map into a 1×1 convolutional module, yielding:

$$f = F_1([z^H, z^W]) \tag{11}$$

$$F_1(X) = \zeta(BN(Conv_{1 \times 1}(X))) \tag{12}$$

where ζ denotes the SiLU activation function, BN $(\cdot)$ represents batch normalization operation, $[\cdot, \cdot]$ represents concatenate operation, $f \in \mathbb{R}^{C/r \times (H+W)}$ denotes the generated intermediate feature map, and r denotes reduction ratio. Next, along the channel dimension, we partition f into two identically shaped tensors $f_s \in \mathbb{R}^{C/r \times (H \times W)/2}$, one of which represents the position information in the height f_h and the other represents the position information in the width f_w after 3D permutation. We transform them with 1×1 convolution to recover the number of channels to the same as the original input feature map, and output $g_h \in \mathbb{R}^{C \times H \times 1}$, $g_w \in \mathbb{R}^{C \times 1 \times W}$ can be expressed as:

$$g_h = \sigma(F_h(f_h)) \tag{13}$$

$$g_w = \sigma(F_w(f_w)) \tag{14}$$

where σ denotes the same sigmoid function as in Eq. 7. We unfold g_h and g_w, yielding the final positional feature map $P_F \in \mathbb{R}^{C \times H \times W}$:

$$P_F = g_h \times g_w \tag{15}$$

In summary, GPAM not only minimizes information loss and applies attention in a global perspective to input features but also captures long-range spatial dependencies and precise positional information, enabling the attention mechanism to more accurately locate the exact position of the object of interest, thus helping the entire model to better identify defects.

3 Experiments

3.1 Data Set and Experimental Setup

This section evaluates our method on two representative datasets of steel surface defects NEU-DET and GC10-DET with SOTA comparisons and ablation studies. NEU-DET [9] is a surface defect dataset for hot-rolled strip steel that contains six types of defects, including crease (Cr), inclusion (In), patches (Pa), pitted spot (Ps), rolled-in scale (Rs), and scratch (Sc). The dataset consists of 1800 grayscale images with an original resolution of 200×200, with 300 samples of each of the six typical surface defect types. In the experiment, we randomly split the dataset into training and test sets in a 7:3 ratio. GC10-DET [19] is a steel plate surface defect dataset collected from real industry, containing ten types of surface defects, including crease (Cr), crescent gap (Cg), inclusion (In), oil spot (Os), punching hole (Ph), rolled pit (Rp), scratch (Ss), waist folding (Wf), water spot (Ws) and welding line (Wl). The original dataset contains many mislabeled and misclassified samples. After data cleaning, the dataset contains 2294 grayscale images with an original resolution of 2048×1000. We randomly divided the dataset into training and test sets in an 8:2 ratio.

All experiments were performed on the Pytorch 1.8.0 deep learning framework. The graphics processing unit was a Nvidia GeForce RTX 3060 with 12GB memory, and the central processing unit was an Intel i5-11400F. In addition, we used CUDA 11.1 as the parallel computing platform and implemented high-performance GPU acceleration on cuDNN 8.4.0 deep neural network acceleration library. In the hyperparameter setting, the initial learning rate was set to 1×10^{-3}, and the cosine annealing algorithm was used for dynamic adjustment of the learning rate. We used the first 3 epochs to warm up the model and set the momentum to 0.937 to accelerate SGD convergence in relevant directions and suppress oscillation. The batch size was set to 16, and the epoch was formed to 200. As the input size of the network should be a multiple of 32, for NEU-DET, the input image resolution was adjusted to 256×256, and for GC10-DET, the input image resolution was adjusted to 512×512.

3.2 Ablation Experiment

To verify each proposed module's effectiveness and overall performance on the baseline network model, we conducted an ablation experiment by sequentially adding each module we proposed to the baseline network. The experimental results are shown in Tables 1 and 2, respectively. We measure the detection accuracy of the model in terms of the average precision (AP) of each category and the mean average precision (mAP) of all categories and evaluate the detection efficiency of the model in terms of the number of frames per second (FPS). As can be seen from the table, compared to the baseline, our method improves 4.1% and 4.4% mAP, respectively. The AP of each category has also reached nearly-optimal levels, with only a marginal decrease in detection speed. As we sequentially added the proposed sub-modules, each category's mAP and AP values exhibited an increasing trend. This suggests that each proposed module has a positive impact on the network.

Table 1. Results of ablation experiments on the NEU-DET dataset

Architecture	Cr	In	Pa	Ps	Rs	Sr	mAP(%)	FPS
Baseline	38.2	78.6	91.8	74.6	63.4	96.0	73.8	70
+SPPFCSPC	43.3	80.5	90.6	78.3	62.8	95.5	75.2	67
+GFAR	49.2	79.2	91.9	83.8	71.5	91.7	77.9	63

Table 2. Results of ablation experiments on the GC10-DET dataset

Architecture	Cr	Cg	In	Os	Ph	Rp	Ss	Wf	Ws	Wl	mAP(%)	FPS
Baseline	68.7	98.2	60.8	76.1	97.7	60.3	82.8	51.5	78.6	92.8	77.2	63
+SPPFCSPC	67.7	98.8	61.4	75.4	97.3	73.8	81.3	56.0	82.7	94.5	78.9	59
+GFAR	70.7	98.6	67.2	75.8	97.1	76.6	85.8	62.6	81.4	94.1	81.6	54

Feature Fusion Method. We compared the GFAR neck network with popular, high-performance neck networks to validate its competitiveness in similar feature fusion networks. In addition to the PAFPN utilized by the baseline network, we choose BiFPN and Balanced FPN as representatives of weighted fusion strategy and multi-scale fusion strategy, respectively, for the ablation experiment. It can be seen from Table 3 that our proposed GFAR module has the best performance in terms of accuracy and a negligible decrease in detection speed. BiFPN also exhibits a decent performance improvement but with a more significant reduction in detection speed. The detection accuracy level of Balanced FPN is essentially the same as the baseline, while the detection speed increases slightly. The experiments demonstrate that the GFAR module achieves outstanding competitive detection accuracy and speed performance.

Table 3. Comparison with feature fusion networks

Architecture	NEU-DET		GC10-DET		Param(M)
	mAP (%)	FPS	mAP (%)	FPS	
PAFPN(Baseline)	75.2	67	78.9	59	35.3
PAFPN + GFAR	**77.9**	63	**81.6**	54	37.6
BiFPN	76.0	57	80.2	48	39.4
Balanced FPN	75.3	**69**	78.9	**60**	**35.1**

Attentional Mechanisms. To better understand the contribution of GPAM in GFAR, we conducted ablation experiments on the attention module in GFAR. We set up four control groups for GPAM, including the absence of an attention module (None), CBAM, GAM, and CA. A classic channel spatial joint attention mechanism (CBAM), a global dimension-crossing interactive attention mechanism (GAM) that focuses on the whole, and a coordinate attention mechanism (CA) were set as the control group for ablation experiments. We replaced the attention mechanisms in GFAR with each of these mechanisms respectively and tracked performance changes. In addition, to explore the contribution of attention modules to GFAR, we set an additional control group that did not add any attention mechanisms.

Table 4. Comparison of GFAR with different attention mechanisms

	None	CBAM	GAM	CA	GPAM
mAP_{NEU} (%)	75.9	76.1	76.6	77.1	**77.9**
mAP_{GC10} (%)	79.8	80.2	81.0	80.9	**81.6**

Table 4 shows that the GFAR without the attention module achieved only a slight improvement in mAP. After adding attention mechanisms in GFAR, the detection accuracy was further improved to varying degrees. Among them, CBAM showed a mAP improvement of only 0.2% and 0.3%, compared with GFAR without attention. This demonstrates that excessive global pooling can lead to undesirable information loss for industrial defects with less apparent features. GAM and CA showed a more significant mAP improvement, increasing by 0.7%, 1.2%, and 1.2%, 1.1%, respectively. GPAM improved the mAP by 2.0% and 1.8% respectively, achieving the best performance. This suggests that combining original position attention adjustment with global attention is well-suited for industrial defect detection tasks.

3.3   Comparison with SOTA Networks

To further verify the effectiveness of the proposed method, we compared our network with representative one-stage and two-stage SOTA detectors. All SOTA networks were implemented based on mmdetection [20], and the comparison results are shown in Table 5. Our method achieved a competitive level of performance on the NEU-DET dataset. Regarding detection speed, our network maintained the efficiency level of YOLO v5, outperforming most detectors, especially two-stage detectors. Regarding detection accuracy, our method reached the state-of-the-art level, second only to DDN and DCC-CenterNet. On the GC10-DET dataset, our approach demonstrated even more significant advantages, achieving the best performance in terms of accuracy and speed. The experimental results indicate that the proposed GFAR module can significantly improve the detection capability of surface defects on steel while its structure does not bring too much additional computational burden.

Table 5. Comparison with state-of-the-art methods

Method	Backbone	NEU-DET		GC10-DET	
		mAP(%)	FPS	mAP(%)	FPS
Two-stage:					
Faster RCNN	ResNet-50	74.1	14	67.5	18
Cascade RCNN	ResNet-50	73.3	12	72.1	14
Libra RCNN	ResNet-50	77.1	12	67.1	18
TridentNet	ResNet-50	77.0	11	63.2	20
DDN [9]	ResNet-50	82.3	11	–	–
One-stage:					
YOLO v3	DarkNet-53	72.0	34	51.2	25
RetinaNet	ResNet-50	68.4	40	71.6	19
VFNet	ResNet-50	74.1	34	74.6	17
YOLO v7	CSPDarkNet-53	74.2	62	71.8	46
FCOS	ResNet-50	73.9	40	70.6	35
EDDN [19]	VGG16	72.4	37	65.1	30
DCC-CenterNet [21]	ResNet-50	79.4	51	61.9	31
Our method	CSPDarkNet-53	77.9	63	81.6	54

4 Conclusions

This paper proposes a defect detection framework based on yolov5 for automatically detecting multi-class defects on steel surfaces with large size changes and strong background interference. In this framework, SPPF is replaced with SPPFCSPC, which combines the residual structure in the spatial pyramid structure to achieve higher precision in the fusion of global and local information. A global feature aggregation and redistribution module (GFAR) is embedded in the baseline neck network to endow the feature map with richer and more accurate feature representation capability. In GFAR, we introduce a global position attention mechanism that highlights defect features in a minimally information-lossy way. Experiments on the NEU-DET and GC10-DET datasets demonstrate that our method has advanced detection performance. Our method achieved 77.9% mAP and 63 FPS on the NEU-DET dataset, and 81.6% mAP and 54 FPS on the GC10-DET dataset, outperforming most SOTA networks and defect detectors. However, there is much room for improvement in our method. In the future, we will continue to improve the network, for example, by optimizing the detection of difficult samples, distinguishing classification and regression tasks in the detection head, etc.

References

1. Zhang, J., Qin, X., Yuan, J., Wang, X., Zeng, Y.: The extraction method of laser ultrasonic defect signal based on EEMD. Optics Commun. **484**, 126570 (2021)

2. Wang, H., Zhang, J., Tian, Y., Chen, H., Sun, H., Liu, K.: A simple guidance template-based defect detection method for strip steel surfaces. IEEE Trans. Industr. Inf. **15**, 2798–2809 (2019)
3. Baucher, B., Chaudhary, A.B., Babu, S.S., Chakraborty, S.: Defect characterization through automated laser track trace identification in slm processes using laser profilometer data. J. Mater. Eng. Perform. **28**, 717–727 (2019)
4. Mei, H., Jiang, H., Yin, F., Wang, L., Farzaneh, M.: Terahertz imaging method for composite insulator defects based on edge detection algorithm. IEEE Trans. Instrum. Meas. **70**, 1–10 (2021)
5. Gómez-Sirvent, J.L., de la Rosa, F.L., Sánchez-Reolid, R., Fernández-Caballero, A., Morales, R.: Optimal feature selection for defect classification in semiconductor wafers. IEEE Trans. Semicond. Manuf. **35**, 324–331 (2022)
6. Wang, X., Yan, Z., Zeng, Y., Liu, X., Peng, X., Yuan, H.: Research on correlation factor analysis and prediction method of overhead transmission line defect state based on association rule mining and RBF-SVM. Energy Rep. **7**, 359–368 (2021)
7. Xu, C., Li, L., Li, J., Wen, C.: Surface defects detection and identification of lithium battery pole piece based on multi-feature fusion and PSO-SVM. IEEE Access **9**, 85232–85239 (2021)
8. Wang, S., Xia, X., Ye, L., Yang, B.: Automatic detection and classification of steel surface defect using deep convolutional neural networks. Metals - Open Access Metall. J. **11**, 388 (2021)
9. He, Y., Song, K., Meng, Q., Yan, Y.: An end-to-end steel surface defect detection approach via fusing multiple hierarchical features. IEEE Trans. Instrum. Meas. **69**, 1493–1504 (2020)
10. Cui, L., Jiang, X., Xu, M., Li, W., Lv, P., Zhou, B.: SDDNet: a fast and accurate network for surface defect detection. IEEE Trans. Instrum. Meas. **70**, 1–13 (2021)
11. Yu, X., Lyu, W., Zhou, D., Wang, C., Xu, W.: ES-Net: efficient scale-aware network for tiny defect detection. IEEE Trans. Instrum. Meas. **71**, 1–14 (2022)
12. Guo, Z., Wang, C., Yang, G., Huang, Z., Li, G.: MSFT-YOLO: improved YOLOv5 based on transformer for detecting defects of steel surface. Sensors **22**(9), 3467 (2022)
13. Cheng, X., Yu, J.: RetinaNet with difference channel attention and adaptively spatial feature fusion for steel surface defect detection. IEEE Trans. Instrum. Meas. **70**, 1–11 (2022)
14. Jocher, G.: YOLOv5 by Ultralytics (2020). https://doi.org/10.5281/zenodo.3908559
15. Pang, J., Chen, K., Shi, J., Feng, H., Ouyang, W., Lin, D.: Libra R-CNN: towards balanced learning for object detection. In: 2019 IEEE/CVF Conference on Computer Vision and Pattern Recognition (CVPR) (2020)
16. Tan, M., Pang, R., Le, Q.V.: EfficientDet: scalable and efficient object detection. In: 2020 IEEE/CVF Conference on Computer Vision and Pattern Recognition (CVPR), pp. 10778–87 (2020)
17. Woo, S., Park, J., Lee, J.-Y., Kweon, I.S.: CBAM: Convolutional Block Attention Module. In: Ferrari, V., Hebert, M., Sminchisescu, C., Weiss, Y. (eds.) Computer Vision – ECCV 2018: 15th European Conference, Munich, Germany, September 8–14, 2018, Proceedings, Part VII, pp. 3–19. Springer International Publishing, Cham (2018). https://doi.org/10.1007/978-3-030-01234-2_1
18. Hou, Q., Zhou, D., Feng, J.: Coordinate attention for efficient mobile network design. In: 2021 IEEE/CVF Conference on Computer Vision and Pattern Recognition (CVPR), pp. 13708–13717 (2021)
19. Lv, X., Duan, F., Jiang, J.-j, Fu, X., Gan, L.: Deep metallic surface defect detection: the new benchmark and detection network. Sensors **20**(6), 1562 (2020)
20. MMDetection contributors. OpenMMLab detection toolbox and benchmark (2018)
21. Tian, R., Jia, M.: DCC-CenterNet: a rapid detection method for steel surface defects. Measurement **187**, 110211 (2022)

A Novel Radius Measurement Method for Vertical Oil Tank Based on Laser Tracking and Wall-Climbing Robot

Hongfei Zu[1]([✉]), Junjun Ma[1], Cunjun Li[2], Xianlei Chen[2], Haolei Shi[2], Xuwen Chen[3], Xiang Zhang[3], and Zhangwei Chen[4]

[1] School of Mechanical Engineering, Zhejiang Sci-Tech University, Hangzhou 310018, China
zuhongfei@zstu.edu.cn
[2] Zhoushan Institute of Calibration and Testing for Qualitative and Technical Supervision, Zhoushan 316012, China
[3] Zhejiang Premax Co. Ltd., Ningbo 315048, China
[4] State Key Laboratory of Fluid Power and Mechatronic Systems, Zhejiang University, Hangzhou 310058, China

Abstract. In order to address the issue of low efficiency and poor accuracy in measuring the radius of large vertical oil tanks, a novel measurement method based on the combination of laser tracking and wall-climbing robot was proposed in this manuscript. To solve the problem of light interruption during the laser tracking measurement process, an active spherically mounted retroreflector (SMR) device that can automatically align the laser was designed. A wall-climbing robot equipped with the active target and temperature sensor was developed to crawl on the tank wall and collect four-dimensional point cloud data. And a self-written program based on the PCL point cloud processing library was adopted to fit and calculate the tank plate radius. Furthermore, multiple measurements were carried out on a vertical oil tank with a capacity of 1000 m^3, and the average radius error was only 1.39 mm, which strongly verified the repeatability and feasibility of the method proposed in this manuscript. This method provides a more effective and accurate method for measuring the radius of oil tanks, and it is foreseeable that it will be a good supplement to existing methods.

Keywords: Vertical Oil Tank · Radius Measurement · Wall-climbing Robot · Laser Tracking · Circle Fitting

1 Introduction

Vertical metal storage tanks are the main storage equipment for oil and gas transportation in the petrochemical industry and is also an important measuring tool for trade settlement. The accuracy of the capacity detection and calibration of the vertical metal storage tank is not only directly related to the enterprise management, cost accounting, and economic benefits, but also related to national foreign trade interests and national measurement reputation [1]. After long-term service, the wall of the vertical oil tank may experience

© The Author(s), under exclusive license to Springer Nature Singapore Pte Ltd. 2023
H. Yang et al. (Eds.): ICIRA 2023, LNAI 14274, pp. 351–363, 2023.
https://doi.org/10.1007/978-981-99-6501-4_30

radial deformation, causing a deviation between the actual radius and the nominal radius, which affects the accuracy of volume measurement. Therefore, vertical oil tanks must be regularly tested for their capacities to ensure the precision of measurement. Currently, the capacity measurement of vertical storage tanks mainly adopts geometric measurement methods such as the strapping method, water injection method, and optical baseline method as shown in the "Chinese Metrology Regulation: Vertical metal tank capacity" (JJG168–2018) [2]. However, there are some problems with these methods, such as low precision in detection results, high manual detection costs, long detection cycle that affects the production process.

In recent years, with the rapid development of photoelectric measurement technology, many new capacity measurement methods for vertical metal tanks have been proposed. Wang *et al.* studied an automatic tank volume measurement system based on 3D laser scanning, which first installed a 3D laser scanner at the bottom of the oil tank to scan the interior wall of the oil tank to obtain a 3D point cloud. Then, the point clouds at the 1/4 and 3/4 heights of each layer of the oil tank's circumferential plates were selected, and the radius of the oil tank was calculated by using the Direct Iterative Method (DIM) [3]. Hao *et al.* established a capacity measurement system for a large vertical energy storage tank based on photoelectric measurement technology and total station scanning technology. The horizontal cross-sectional area was calculated through the point cloud data of the tank obtained by the total station. After that, integration was performed along the vertical height direction to calculate the volume corresponding to different liquid level heights [4]. Mohammed Abdullah Al Rashed used a climbing robot equipped with ultrasonic devices for non-destructive testing of large and complex geometry structures [5].

The existing measurement methods, such as strapping method, are with the drawbacks of heavy workload and low measurement efficiency. The total station method improves the efficiency to some extent but is only able to collect points on the measured baseline, which has a limited number of measurement points, and the degree of automation needs to be further improved. The 3D scanning method has low single-point accuracy, which increases the difficulty in point cloud processing and decreases the accuracy of radius fitting, though it increases point cloud density. The laser tracking method has high accuracy but requires manual deployment of the spherically mounted retroreflector (SMR), which incurs high costs and workload [6]. Furthermore, existing methods can only measure geometric parameters of oil tanks, lacking the ability to simultaneously measure other environmental parameters such as tank temperature, which leads to measurement deviations in tank volume under different temperature. In this manuscript, a novel vertical oil tank measurement method based on a laser tracking device and a wall-climbing robot equipped with a laser SMR and a temperature sensor was proposed. This method successfully achieved high-precision laser tracking measurement without the need for manual SMR deployment, while also possessing the ability to measure tank wall temperature. In addition, the feasibility and effectiveness of this method in measuring the capacity of large vertical storage tanks were verified through multiple measurements and comparison with traditional methods.

2 Measurement System Implementation

2.1 Problem Description

Vertical oil tanks are typically constructed by welding several cylindrical rings together [7]. After long-term usage, these rings will undergo varying degrees of radial deformation, so the radius of each ring layer needs to be measured separately during tank inspection. In order to efficiently and accurately complete this task, the following urgent issues must be addressed:

(1) In order to make the measurement process more efficient, an automatic SMR movement device should be adopted instead of the manual way.
(2) In order to ensure the continuity and comprehensiveness of measurement, SMR should be able to automatically align with the laser tracker, even when the angle between them is large.
(3) The measuring system should be able to provide real-time temperature measurement of the tank, so as to facilitate subsequent volume compensation.
(4) A fast and accurate point cloud fitting algorithm is needed to calculate the measurement radius.

To address the above issues, a more comprehensive measurement system with the following configurations was proposed: First, a negative pressure suction-type wall-climbing robot was adopted to realize automatic wall-climbing operations. Next, an active SMR device was designed to automatically align with the laser tracker and measure the tank temperature. The laser tracker was located at a fixed position on the ground, while the active SMR device was installed on the wall climbing robot. The system captured 4D point cloud data (X, Y, Z, T, where T represents the temperature) on the tank surface as the robot crawled. Finally, a point cloud fitting algorithm was developed using the PCL point cloud processing library to calculate the radius of the ring.

2.2 Wall-Climbing Robot

The wall-climbing robots usually used for oil tank measurement mainly include magnetically suction-type robots and negative-pressure suction-type robots, as shown in Fig. 1. The magnetically suction-type robot uses a magnetic suction crawler to attach the entire measuring device to the tank wall, and the magnetic crawler is driven by a chain wheel to climb along the tank wall. In contrast, the negative-pressure suction-type robot is fixed to the tank wall through an air suction system based on a vacuum suction mechanism, achieving non-contact suction between the device and the tank wall, which effectively solves the problem of damage to the wall by the magnetic suction type robot. In addition, the negative-pressure suction-type robot provides faster crawling speed as well as stronger turning ability and environmental adaptability. The maximum load of the robot used in this research is 2kg, which is large enough for the active SMR device.

2.3 Design of Active SMR Device

During the measurement process of a laser tracker, a significant angular deviation between the orientation of the SMR and the emitted laser may lead to signal loss, resulting in invalid measurements.

Fig. 1. Wall-climbing robots: magnetically suction-type robot (left), and negative-pressure suction-type robot (right).

To address this issue, an active SMR device that integrates a temperature measurement module was designed, which can automatically track laser and measure temperature during movement. The device comprises a SMR holder, a stepper motor positioned below the holder, a gyroscope located beneath the stepper motor, a WiFi communication module adjacent to the gyroscope, and an infrared temperature sensor, as shown in Fig. 2. As the SMR moves relative to the laser tracker, the active SMR device receives real-time horizontal angular deviations through WiFi. When the active SMR device rotates, the gyroscope would detect the angle. Subsequently, the motor controls the rotation of the SMR and automatically aligns it with the laser tracker.

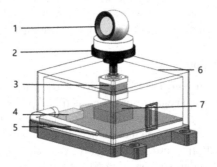

Fig. 2. Structure Diagram of the Active SMR Device: 1-SMR, 2-SMR Holder, 3-Stepper Motor, 4-WiFi Communication Module, 5-Antenna, 6-Casing, 7-Gyroscope.

The specific control methods are as follows:

(1) The temperature sensor communicates with the processing module of the active SMR device via RS485 bus based on the Modbus protocol. The temperature is transmitted to the upper computer through the WiFi module. The upper computer combines the target position information (X, Y, Z) from the laser tracker and the tank wall temperature information (T) from the temperature sensor to form a four-dimensional point cloud data (X, Y, Z, T).

(2) The active SMR device obtains the current spatial position of the SMR and the horizontal angle deviation γ_i between the SMR and the laser tracker from the upper computer via the WiFi module. At the same time, it reads the current horizontal rotation angle δ_i of the target from the gyroscope located below the SMR holder.

(3) Next, the active SMR device receives the horizontal angle deviation γ_{i+1} and the self-horizontal rotation angle δ_{i+1} at the next moment, as shown in Fig. 3. By comparing the angular deviation between the SMR and the tracker and the self-horizontal rotation angle of the target at the next moment, the deviation angle θ between the SMR and the laser can be obtained.

(4) Finally, the deviation angle θ will be converted into the corresponding pulses of the stepper motor to control the SMR reversely rotate θ to achieve automatic alignment of SMR.

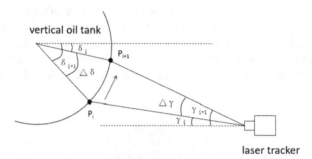

Fig. 3. The deviation angle between SMR and laser tracker.

The relationship between various angles in Fig. 3 is shown in (1):

$$\begin{cases} \Delta\gamma = \gamma_{i+1} - \gamma_i \\ \Delta\delta = |\delta_{i+1} - \delta_i| \\ \theta = \Delta\gamma + \Delta\delta \end{cases} \tag{1}$$

To ensure accurate measurement of the horizontal angle, the active SMR device should be horizontally installed on the climbing robot, with the Z-axis of the gyroscope perpendicular to the ground. Furthermore, to ensure precise temperature measurement, the temperature sensor should be oriented perpendicular to the tank wall and installed on one side of the robot, as shown in Fig. 4.

2.4 Performance Test of Active SMR Device

To verify the effectiveness of the active SMR device, the performance tests using an indoor oil tank wall model was conducted first. The active SMR device was installed on the climbing robot, and the robot was controlled to move horizontally along the oil tank wall model, as shown in Fig. 5. The number of light interruptions that occurred during the movement of the SMR was recorded. This experiment was aimed to evaluate the

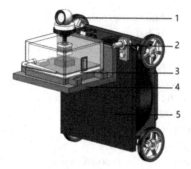

Fig. 4. Installation Diagram of Active SMR Device: 1-SMR, 2-Temperature Sensor, 3-Active SMR Device, 4-Fixed frame, 5-Wall-climbing Robot.

performance of the active SMR device in practical applications.During the experiment, three light interruptions occurred when the active SMR device was not used, while only one light interruption occurred when the active SMR device was used.

The results demonstrate that the active SMR device exhibits excellent automatic light alignment performance during movement, which reduce the number of light interruptions from 3 to 1.

Fig. 5. Performance Test of Active SMR Device.

3   Radius Measurement

3.1   Point Cloud Acquisition

To measure the radius of the first ring plate of the oil tank, two methods, namely, internal measurement and external measurement, were employed in this study. For the internal measurement, the tracking device was installed at the central position inside the oil tank, while the climbing robot adhered to the inner side of the tank wall and completed one round of measurement by crawling horizontally along the tank wall (Fig. 6).

For the external measurement, the laser tracker was set at a distant location from the oil tank to obtain a larger field of view. The climbing robot adhered to the outer side

Fig. 6. Picture of device layout for internal measurement.

of the tank wall and crawled horizontally along the tank wall, capturing the point cloud data for one-third of the circumference of the ring plate (Fig. 7).

Fig. 7. Picture of device layout for external Measurement.

To accurately measure the radius of the first layer of the oil tank's ring plate, three measurements on both the inner and outer sides were conducted. Each of the inner measurements captured the complete point cloud of the whole ring plate, as shown in Fig. 8, while each of the outer measurements captured the point cloud of 1/3 of the ring plate, as shown in Fig. 9. The point cloud data consists of the X, Y, and Z coordinates of each measurement point, along with their corresponding temperature values, T. Through these measurements, the detailed geometric information of the ring plate and its temperature distribution can be obtained.

3.2 Point Cloud Preprocessing

During the horizontal crawling motion of the climbing robot along the circumference, there is an unavoidable sliding effect in the Z-axis direction due to the influence of gravity. Therefore, after obtaining the point cloud data of the tank's circumferential plates, it is necessary to project the point cloud to a specified height before further performing point

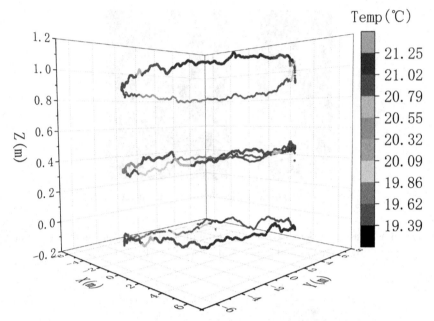

Fig. 8. Point cloud of internal measurement.

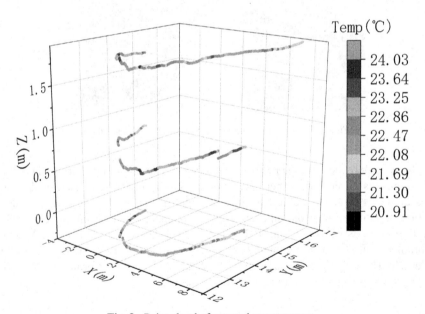

Fig. 9. Point cloud of external measurement.

cloud fitting. As shown in Fig. 10, the red lines represent the original point cloud data, while the blue ones represent the projected data. This processing step eliminates the height differences caused by sliding and ensures the consistency and accuracy of the point cloud.

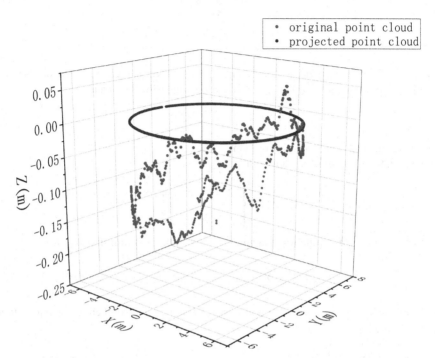

Fig. 10. Original point cloud data (red) and the projected data (blue).(Color figure online)

3.3 Point Cloud Fitting

In this study, the weighted least squares method was adopted to fit the point clouds of each layer of the oil tank's circular plates. The traditional least squares method is widely used, however, it assigns equal weights to all points in the point cloud to be fitted, which would lead to significant error of outlier points on the fitting results. To address this issue, the Iteratively Reweighted Least Squares (IRLS) method was employed as an improvement to the traditional least squares method. In the IRLS approach, different weights were introduced for each point, and the greater the deviation from the circular model, the smaller the weight. The following are the implementation steps of this method:

(1) Construct the general equation of a circle and use the standard least squares method to fit the center (X_c, Y_c) and radius r_c:

$$x^2 + y^2 + ax + by + c = 0 \tag{2}$$

$$x_c = -\frac{a}{2}$$

$$y_c = -\frac{b}{2}$$

$$r_c = \frac{\sqrt{a^2 + b^2 - 4c}}{2}$$

(2) Iterate through the point cloud of a circular plate layer and calculate the deviation δ of each point from the fitted circle to compute the trimming factor τ:

$$\tau = \frac{\text{media}(|\delta_i|)}{0.6745} \tag{3}$$

where media() represents the median of a set.

(3) Calculate the weight for each point:

$$w(\delta) = \begin{cases} (1 - (\frac{\delta}{\tau})^2)^2, & |\delta| \leq \tau \\ 0, & |\delta| > \tau \end{cases} \tag{4}$$

(4) Construct the error function dist and solve for a, b, c to minimize dist:

$$\text{dist} = \sum_{i=1}^{n} w_i(x^2 + y^2 + ax + by + c)^2 \tag{5}$$

(5) Take partial derivatives of dist with respect to a, b, c and set them to zero to obtain the following equation:

$$\begin{bmatrix} \sum_{i=1}^{n} w_i x_i^2 & \sum_{i=1}^{n} w_i x_i y_i & \sum_{i=1}^{n} w_i x_i \\ \sum_{i=1}^{n} w_i x_i y_i & \sum_{i=1}^{n} w_i y_i^2 & \sum_{i=1}^{n} w_i y_i \\ \sum_{i=1}^{n} w_i x_i & \sum_{i=1}^{n} w_i y_i & n \end{bmatrix} \begin{bmatrix} a \\ b \\ c \end{bmatrix} = - \begin{bmatrix} \sum_{i=1}^{n} (w_i x_i^3 + w_i x_i y_i^2) \\ \sum_{i=1}^{n} (w_i x_i^2 y_i + w_i y_i^3) \\ \sum_{i=1}^{n} (w_i x_i^2 + w_i y_i^2) \end{bmatrix} \tag{6}$$

(6) Repeat steps (2) to (5) until the change in radius value is smaller than a threshold, then consider the current radius as the fitted value.

3.4 Result of Point Cloud Fitting

The fitting point cloud of the tank is obtained by fitting the point cloud of the three measurements, as shown in Fig. 11.

4 Analysis of Measurement Results

The fitting results of the internal point cloud of the oil tank are shown in Table 1. The measurement error of the proposed method is calculated based on the total station measurement value of 5987.425 mm. The average radius of the internal measurements is 5988.66 mm, with an average measurement error of 1.238 mm and a relative error of 0.21‰. The close proximity between the measurement results and the reference value indicates a relatively high level of accuracy in the measurements.

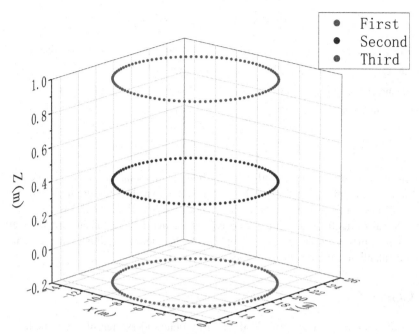

Fig. 11. Fitting point cloud of oil tank.

Table 1. Results of the Internal measurement.

Internal measurement	Results of radius(mm)	Measurement error(mm)	Relative error(‰)
First measurement	5988.26	0.835	0.14
Second measurement	5989.35	1.925	0.32
Third measurement	5988.38	0.955	0.16
Average	5988.66	1.238	0.21

And the fitting results of the external point cloud of the oil tank are shown in Table 2. The measurement error of the proposed method is calculated based on the total station measurement value of 5992.6 mm. The average radius of the external measurements is 5993.99 mm, with an average measurement error of 1.39 mm and a relative error of 0.23‰. It also demonstrates a high level of measurement accuracy for the external measurements.

The experimental results demonstrate that the repeatability of internal measurements in the oil tank is higher than the accuracy of external measurements. This is mainly because the point cloud collected from internal measurements is evenly distributed on the tank's ring plate, while the point cloud collected from external measurements is concentrated on a 1/3 arc of the ring plate. As a result, the fitting error in the external measurements is larger than that in the internal measurements.

Table 2. External measurement.

External measurement	Results of radius(mm)	Measurement error(mm)	Relative error(‰)
First measurement	5991.11	−1.49	0.25
Second measurement	5994.04	1.44	0.24
Third measurement	5996.81	4.21	0.70
Average	5993.99	1.39	0.23

The measurement errors of both measurement methods satisfy the requirement specified in the national standard JJG-128, which states that the measurement uncertainty for vertical oil tank volume measurement should be less than 3‰. This confirms the feasibility and effectiveness of the proposed method in this study. Therefore, the method presented in this work can be widely applied in the field of radius measurement and volume calculation for vertical oil tanks.

5   Conclusion

This study proposes a new vertical oil tank ring plate radius measurement method that combines climbing robots and laser tracking systems, which significantly reduces manual workload and improving the safety and efficiency of oil tank measurement. The laser tracking system enables fast and accurate measurement of the spatial coordinates of laser target spheres, while the wall-climbing robot replaces the manual process of point placement on the tank wall. The use of an active SMR device ensures the continuity of the measurement point cloud and enables the measurement of tank temperature, providing data support for subsequent temperature corrections. This method exhibits characteristics of scientific efficiency and high automation. In this study, the proposed method was employed to measure the annular plates of a vertical oil tank with a capacity of 1000 m^3. The experimental measurement results show an average absolute error of 1.39 mm and a relative error of 0.23‰, indicating good repeatability and feasibility and high accuracy of this method. The measurement method presented in this manuscript combines high-precision optoelectronic measurement equipment with a highly automated climbing robot, which is a novel, fast, and high-precision approach for tank measurement and inspection.

Acknowledgment. This work was supported by the "National Key R&D Program of China" (No.: 2022YFF0606003) and "Eaglet planning cultivation project of Zhejiang Administration for Market Regulation" (No.: CY2022231).

References

1. Shizhong,T., Zhi, X., Changhai, L., et al.: Research on the innovative examination method of vertical tank capacity. In: 2009 International Conference on Measuring Technology and Mechatronics Automation (2009)

2. JJG168–2018: Chinese Metrology Regulation: Vertical Metal Tank Capacity. China Metrology Press, Beijing (2018)
3. Jintao, W., Ziyong, L., Long, Z., et al.: Precise measurement of liquid petroleum tank volume based on data cloud analysis. In: 6th International Symposium on Precision Engineering Measurement and Instrumentation (2010)
4. Hao, H., Shi, H., Yi, P., et al.: Research on volume metrology method of large vertical energy storage tank based on internal electro-optical distance-ranging method. In: 2017 International Conference on Optical Instruments and Technology (2017)
5. Rashed, M.A.A., Sattar, T.P.: Inexpensive spatial position system for the automation of inspection with mobile robots. Ind. Robot Int. J. **41**(6), 508–517 (2014)
6. Yonggang, G., Jing, H., Yi, J., et al.: A smart car for the surface shape measurement of large antenna based on laser tracker. In: Modern Technologies in Space- and Ground-based Telescopes and Instrumentation II (2012)
7. Hao, H., Li, C., Chen, X., et al.: Volume measurement system of large vertical energy storage tank based on optoelectronic measurement technology. In: 2019 International Conference on Optical Instruments and Technology (2019)
8. ISO7507–1: Liquid measurement-Calibration of vertical cylindrical tanks-Part1: Strapping method. Academic, Switzerland (2003)
9. Zhang, Z.: A new measurement method of three-dimensional laser scanning for the volume of railway tank car (container). Measurement **170**, 108454 (2021)
10. Li, J., Wu, J., Tu, C., Wang, X.: Spatial positioning robotic system for autonomous inspection of LPG tanks. Ind. Robot. **50**(1), 70–83 (2023)

Kinetostatic and Cable-Hole Friction Modeling for Cable-Driven Continuum Robots

Zheshuai Yang[1], Laihao Yang[1(✉)], Yu Sun[1], Xuefeng Chen[1], Guangrong Teng[2], and Miaoqing Yang[2]

[1] School of Mechanical Engineering, Xi'an Jiaotong University, No. 28, Xianning West Road, Xi'an 710049, China
yzs12138@stu.xjtu.edu.cn, {yanglaihao,yu.sun,chenxf}@xjtu.edu.cn
[2] AECC Sichuan Gas Turbine Establishment, Chengdu 610500, Sichuan, China

Abstract. As one of the novel bionic robots, cable-driven continuum robot (CDCR) has a talent for compliance and dexterity in operations of narrow environments. However, due to its hyper-redundant structure, it is challenging to establish a precise model to estimate its morphology. Especially the cable-hole friction modeling for such a CDCR, which plays an essential role in its morphology estimate. In this study, we first establish the kinetostatics of the CDCR based on previous work. And then, we deduce two cable-hole friction models based on the Coulomb friction theory and the Capstan friction model, respectively. Finally, experimental validation is performed to verify the effectiveness of the proposed algorithm. The results indicate that the proposed kinetostatics with the two friction models can precisely characterize the morphology of the CDCR. The average morphology estimate errors of them are 5.05 mm and 4.79 mm, accounting for 2.63% and 2.49% of the manipulator length.

Keywords: Cable-driven Continuum robots (CDCRs) · Kinetostatics · Cable-hole Friction Model

1 Introduction

As novel bionic robots inspired by snakes, elephants, and other natural biologies, cable-driven continuum robots (CDCRs) have increasingly attracted attention in the last two decades to the talent of compliance and dexterity [1, 2]. Compared with conventional rigid-link robots, CDCRs can provide better accessibility and operation in uncertain environments by compliantly changing their shape, and have been potentially employed in biomedical surgery [3, 4], nuclear industry [5], and aerospace field [6–8].

Due to their hyper-redundant manipulator that is composed of multiple joints in series, it is essential to establish a precise model to describe their morphology. Kinematics based on the classical piecewise constant curvature theory (PCCT) is widely utilized to implement this, where each section is assumed to be a constant arc [9, 10]. However, this section-based kinematics suffers from the defect of low modeling accuracy since the curvature of each joint within the section is different actually. To address this, kinetostatic

© The Author(s), under exclusive license to Springer Nature Singapore Pte Ltd. 2023
H. Yang et al. (Eds.): ICIRA 2023, LNAI 14274, pp. 364–370, 2023.
https://doi.org/10.1007/978-981-99-6501-4_31

and static models are hence proposed to calculate the bending angle of each joint [7, 11, 12]. By concatenating these joint curvatures, the morphology of the CDCR can be described by the joint-based kinematics, which outperforms the classical one in terms of modeling accuracy.

When it comes to kinetostatics or statics, they are often deduced based on the material mechanics theory (such as Kirchhoff elastic rod theory and Euler-Bernoulli beam theory) to characterize the deformation of compliant mechanisms [7, 13]. As one of the essential parts, cable-hole friction has been reported frequently in previous research. For example, some studies ignore the friction effect and propose frictionless models under small deflection approximation [14, 15]. Most static models are established based on a constant friction coefficient, which may neglect the influence of deflection configuration on cable-hole friction [12, 16]. Considering this, some variable friction models are investigated to compensate for this [7, 17]. Therefore, the cable-hole friction needs to be further explored for such a cable-driven manipulator.

In this paper, a kinetostatic model of the TDCR is established based on previous work. Subsequently, two cable-hole friction models of the kinetostatics are deduced and compared. Furthermore, an experimental setup is constructed to verify the effectiveness of the proposed algorithm. The morphology of the CDCR is measured by the Fiber Bragg Grating (FBG) sensor with a high measurement accuracy (1% of the sensing length).

The remainder of this paper is organized as follows. Section 2 deduces the kinetostatics with two different cable-hole friction models. In Sect. 3, the experimental validation is performed. The last section summarizes the whole paper and gives the conclusions.

2 Modeling

In this section, a kinetostatics with two cable-hole friction models is deduced based on the previous work.

2.1 Kinetostatics of the CDCR

Based on the previous work [18], a continuum robot using twin-pivot compliant joints is constructed. The kinetostatics is established based on the Euler-Bernoulli beam theory, which can be expressed as follows.

$$
\begin{cases}
\mathbf{F}_{D_{i-1}}^{O_{i-1}} = \mathbf{F}_{D_i C}^{O_{i-1}} + \mathbf{G}_{D_i}^{O_{i-1}} + \mathbf{G}_{\mathrm{Rod}_i}^{O_{i-1}} + \displaystyle\sum_{j=4s-3}^{4K} \mathbf{G}_{J_i C_j}^{O_{i-1}} + \mathbf{F}_{EX_i}^{O_{i-1}} + \mathbf{F}_{D_i}^{O_{i-1}} \\[4mm]
\mathbf{M}_{D_{i-1}}^{O_{i-1}} = \mathbf{M}_{D_i C}^{O_{i-1}} + \mathbf{M}_{G_{D_i}}^{O_{i-1}} + \mathbf{M}_{\mathrm{Rod}_i}^{O_{i-1}} + \displaystyle\sum_{j=4s-3}^{4K} \mathbf{M}_{J_i C_j}^{O_{i-1}} + \mathbf{M}_{EX_i}^{O_{i-1}} + \mathbf{M}_{\mathbf{F}_{EX_i}}^{O_{i-1}} + \mathbf{M}_{D_i}^{O_{i-1}} + \mathbf{M}_{\mathbf{F}_{D_i}}^{O_{i-1}}
\end{cases}
\tag{1}
$$

where $\mathbf{F}_{D_{i-1}}^{O_{i-1}}$ and $\mathbf{M}_{D_{i-1}}^{O_{i-1}}$ are the lumped force and moment applied on the $(i-1)^{th}$ disk. $\mathbf{F}_{D_i C}^{O_{i-1}}$ and $\mathbf{M}_{D_i C}^{O_{i-1}}$ are the are respectively the actuating forces applied to the ith disk and the moments generated by $\mathbf{F}_{D_i C}^{O_{i-1}}$. $\mathbf{G}_{D_i}^{O_{i-1}}$, $\mathbf{G}_{\mathrm{Rod}_i}^{O_{i-1}}$, and $\mathbf{G}_{J_i C_j}^{O_{i-1}}$ are gravities of disk, compliant backbones, and driving cables, respectively. $\mathbf{F}_{EX_i}^{O_{i-1}}$ and $\mathbf{M}_{EX_i}^{O_{i-1}}$ are the external force and moment. $\mathbf{M}_{\mathbf{F}_{EX_i}}^{O_{i-1}}$ and $\mathbf{M}_{\mathbf{F}_{D_i}}^{O_{i-1}}$ are the moment of $\mathbf{F}_{EX_i}^{O_{i-1}}$ and $\mathbf{F}_{D_i}^{O_{i-1}}$ relative to point O_{i-1}, respectively. The above forces and moments are expressed within the coordinate frame $\{O_{i-1}\}$. The bending moment of the ith joint can be formulated as follows:

$$\mathbf{M}_{Ela_i}^{O_{i-1}} = [0\ 0\ 2 \times \tfrac{\beta_i}{L} \cdot E \cdot I\ 0]^T \tag{2}$$

where E is Young's modulus. I is the moment of inertia of the compliant backbone. L is the length of the compliant backbone. β_i is the bending angle of the ith joint. Thus, the kinetostatic equilibrium equation can be established by Newton-Euler formula, which can be written as:

$$\mathbf{F}_i(\beta_{1 \times N}) = \mathbf{M}_{O_{i-1}}^{O_{i-1}} - \mathbf{M}_{Ela_i}^{O_{i-1}} = 0 \tag{3}$$

where N is the number of joints. These recursive equations need to be calculated by numerical solutions due to their non-linearity.

2.2 Cable-hole Friction Modeling

This subsection focusses on the cable-hole friction modeling of the proposed kinetostatics. We deduce two cable-hole friction models based on the Coulomb friction theory and the Capstan friction model, respectively [2].

Cable-hole Friction Model I. The first model is established based on the Coulomb friction theory, where the friction coefficient is assumed to be a function of the bending angle. The friction coefficient is measured in the next section.

Benefitting from our hollow-carved design [see Fig. 1], the contact area and the uncertainty of cable-hole friction are significantly reduced, making it possible to model the cable-hole friction behavior on two sides of the disk separately. Thus, the frictional force at the ith disk along j^{th} cable can be obtained by the sum of two parts:

$$f_{D_i C_j} = \mu_{i,1} \cdot \left\| \mathbf{N}_{D_i C_j,1}^{O_i} \right\| + \mu_{i,2} \cdot \left\| \mathbf{N}_{D_i C_j,2}^{O_i} \right\| \tag{4}$$

where $\mu_{i,1}$ and $\mu_{i,2}$ are the friction coefficients of the ith disk, which will be measured in Sect. 3. $\mathbf{N}_{D_i C_j,1}^{O_i}$ and $\mathbf{N}_{D_i C_j,2}^{O_i}$ are the pressure generated by the jth cable.

Cable-hole Friction Model II. Another model is deduced based on the Capstan friction model, where the friction coefficient is a constant value. Based on the infinitesimal method, the frictional force can be given by:

$$f_{D_i C_j} = F_{J_i C_j} \cdot e^{\pm \frac{1}{2}(\beta_i + \beta_{i+1})} - F_{J_i C_j} \tag{5}$$

where $F_{J_i C_j}$ is the tension of the ith joint. ± 1 represents the direction of the friction. Up to now, the two cable-hole friction models have been formulated, and we will estimate their validity in the following section.

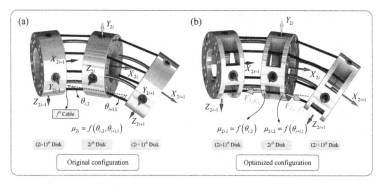

Fig. 1. Optimization of the segment: (a) Original configuration. (b) Optimized configuration.

3   Experimental Validation

In this section, the effectiveness of our algorithm is validated through a few groups of experiments.

3.1   Friction Coefficient Experiment

As illustrated in Fig. 2, an experimental setup is established, and twenty sets of experiments are performed at different bending angles (i.e., 1°, 3°, 5°, 7°, and 9°) and payloads (i.e., 303.5g, 353.5g, 403.5g, and 503.5g) to measure the friction coefficient. The results are shown in Fig. 3, which lays the foundation for the following morphology experiments.

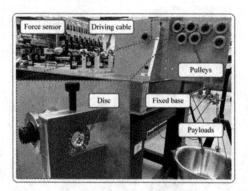

Fig. 2. Experimental setup for friction coefficient.

3.2   Morphology Experiment

To compare and verify the effectiveness of the proposed two cable-hole friction models, an experimental platform with a single-section continuum robot is constructed, as shown in Fig. 4. The purpose of this experiment is to evaluate the validity of the two friction

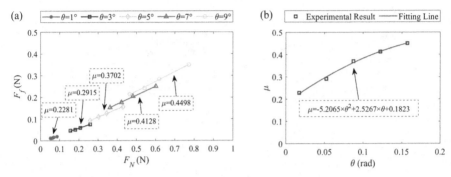

Fig. 3. Results of friction coefficient: (a) Twenty sets of experimental results. (b) Variable friction coefficient.

models by comparing the morphology estimate error of the CDCR, which is measured by the FBG sensor. We performed this experiment under two different force configurations, which is implemented by hanging payloads. Note that the friction coefficient in friction model II is 0.1823. The results are illustrated in Fig. 5. Note that the FBG result is represented by black line, the results of friction model I and II are represented by grey cylinder and colorful cylinder, respectively. It can be clearly observed that both of the two friction models achieve good results, and the average morphology estimate error of them are 5.05 mm (model I) and 4.79 mm (model II), accounting for 2.63% and 2.49% of the manipulator length (i.e., 192 mm). The results suggest that the friction model II outperforms the former in terms of modeling accuracy.

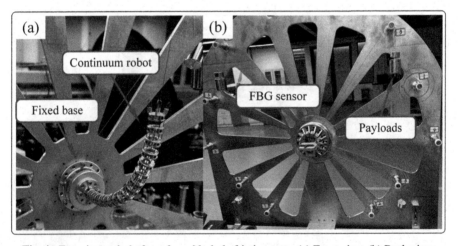

Fig. 4. Experimental platform for cable-hole friction tests: (a) Front view. (b) Back view.

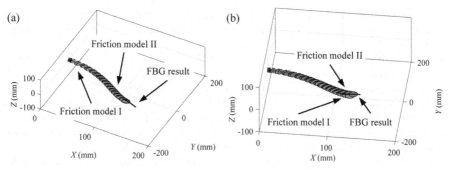

Fig. 5. Experimental platform for cable-hole friction tests: (a) Force configuration I. (b) Force configuration II.

4 Conclusion

This paper proposes and compares a kinetostatics with two cable-hole friction models. First and foremost, a kinetostatics is established based on the joint-based PCCT to calculate the bending angles of each joint. And then, two cable-hole friction models are deduced based on the Coulomb friction theory and the Capstan friction model to explore the friction modeling of the kinetostatics. Finally, the experimental validation is performed to verify the effectiveness of the proposed algorithm. The results suggest that the kinetostatics with the two friction models can precisely characterize the morphology of the CDCR.

Acknowledgment. This work is supported by National Natural Science Foundation of China (No. 52105117, No. 52105118, and No. 92060302).

References

1. Liu, T., Yang, T., Xu, W., et al.: Efficient inverse kinematics and planning of a hybrid active and passive cable-driven segmented manipulator. IEEE Trans. Syst. Man Cybern. Syst. **52**(7), 4233–4246 (2022)
2. Li, S., Hao, G.: Current trends and prospects in compliant continuum robots: a survey. Actuators **10**(7), 145 (2021)
3. Gao, A., Liu, N., Shen, M., et al.: Laser-profiled continuum robot with integrated tension sensing for simultaneous shape and tip force estimation. Soft Rob. **7**(4), 421–443 (2020)
4. Nwafor, C.J., Girerd, C., Laurent, G.J., Morimoto, T.K., Rabenorosoa, K.: Design and fabrication of concentric tube robots: a survey. IEEE Trans. Robot. **39**(4), 2510–2528 (2023). https://doi.org/10.1109/TRO.2023.3255512
5. Qin, G., Cheng, Y., Pan, H., et al.: Systematic design of snake arm maintainer in nuclear industry. Fusion Eng. Des. **176**, 113049 (2022)
6. Tang, C., Du, B., Jiang, S., Qi, S., Dong, X., Liu, X.-J., Zhao, H.: A pipeline inspection robot for navigating tubular environments in the sub-centimeter scale. Sci. Robot. **7**(66), eabm8597 (2022). https://doi.org/10.1126/scirobotics.abm8597

7. Wang, M., Dong, X., Ba, W., et al.: Design, modelling and validation of a novel extra slender continuum robot for in-situ inspection and repair in aeroengine. Robot. Comput. Integr. Manuf. **67**, 102054 (2021)
8. Peng, J., Wu, H., Liu, T., Yu, Y.: Workspace, stiffness analysis and design optimization of coupled active-passive multilink cable-driven space robots for on-orbit services. Chin. J. Aeronaut. **36**(2), 402–416 (2023). https://doi.org/10.1016/j.cja.2022.03.001
9. Dong, X., Raffles, M., Cobos-Guzman, S., et al.: A novel continuum robot using twin-pivot compliant joints: design, modeling, and validation. J. Mech. Robot. **8**(2), 021010 (2016)
10. Rao, P., Peyron, Q., Lilge, S., et al.: How to model tendon-driven continuum robots and benchmark modelling performance. Front. Robot. AI **7**, 630245 (2021)
11. Wu, K., Zheng, G.: A comprehensive static modeling methodology via beam theory for compliant mechanisms. Mech. Mach. Theory **169**, 104598 (2022)
12. Yuan, H., Zhou, L., Xu, W.: A comprehensive static model of cable-driven multi-section continuum robots considering friction effect. Mech. Mach. Theory **135**, 130–149 (2019)
13. Chen, G., Ma, F., Hao, G., et al.: Modeling large deflections of initially curved beams in compliant mechanisms using chained beam constraint model. J. Mech. Robot. **11**(1), 011002 (2019)
14. Rucker, D.C., Jones, B.A., Webster, R.J., III.: A geometrically exact model for externally loaded concentric-tube continuum robots. IEEE Trans. Rob. **26**(5), 769–780 (2010)
15. Rucker, D.C., Webster Iii, R.J.: statics and dynamics of continuum robots with general tendon routing and external loading. IEEE Trans. Rob. **27**(6), 1033–1044 (2011)
16. Boyer, F., Lebastard, V., Candelier, F., et al.: Statics and dynamics of continuum robots based on cosserat rods and optimal control theories. IEEE Trans. Robot. **39**, 1–19 (2022)
17. Li, W., Xi, H., Yan, L., et al.: Force sensing and compliance control for a cable-driven redundant manipulator. IEEE/ASME Trans. Mech. **2023**, 1–12 (2023). https://doi.org/10.1109/TMECH.2023.3263922
18. Yang, Z., Yang, L., Xu, L., Chen, X., Guo, Y., Liu, J., Sun, Y.: A continuum robot with twin-pivot structure: the kinematics and shape estimation. In: Liu, X.-J., Nie, Z., Yu, J., Xie, F., Song, R. (eds.) Intelligent Robotics and Applications. LNCS(LNAI), vol. 13013, pp. 466–475. Springer, Cham (2021). https://doi.org/10.1007/978-3-030-89095-7_45

Measurement and Application of Industrial Robot Jitter

Jie Li[1], Haiming Ma[1], Xiang Zhang[2], Xianhuan Wu[2], Zhangwei Chen[3(✉)],
Xueying Li[1], Naisheng Li[1], and Zhiyong Cheng[1]

[1] Foshan Nanhai Institute of Quality and Technical Testing Supervision, Foshan 528200, China
[2] Premax Technologies (Zhejiang) Co. Ltd., Ningbo 315048, China
[3] State Key Laboratory of Fluid Power and Mechatronic Systems, Zhejiang University, Hangzhou 310058, China
chenzw@zju.edu.cn

Abstract. Industrial robots are widely used in automobile and auto parts manufacturing, mechanical processing industry, electronic and electrical industry, rubber and plastic industry and many other critical areas. The jitter of robots during the operation process may lead to the severe decline in important parameters such as positioning accuracy and trajectory accuracy, which is destructive for fine work such as welding, laser cutting, grinding, and polishing. The jitter characteristic is an important indicator for evaluating the comprehensive performance of industrial robots, and it is an urgent issue to be solved.

Keywords: Industrial Robot · Jitter Frequency · Jitter Amplitude · Modal Frequency

1 Introduction

Industrial robots are with rotating joints similar to human arms and palms [1] that are able to complete various difficult movements and tasks. Driven by Industry 4.0 technology, industrial robots are entering all fields of life in China's manufacturing industry, replacing more and more industrial workers. Since 2013, China has been a big consumer of industrial robots [2]. Benefiting from strong market demand, the scale of domestic robot industry has maintained a rapid growth state over the past decade. However, in this growing group of industrial robots, foreign brands account for over 80% of the market share, and the main reason for this disparity is that the performance and reliability of domestic industrial robots are inferior to foreign brands [3].

During robot motion, the end of the robot is prone to jitter. This leads to a large gap between the actual motion performance of the robot and the desired high precision motion performance. Jitter can seriously affect production quality and efficiency. Jitter measurement and analysis of industrial robots are widely used in various aspects such as the research and development, production, and application of industrial robots. In the process of robot development, jitter analysis can be used to identify the locations, sources, degrees, and patterns that cause jitter [4], and then propose optimization methods and

© The Author(s), under exclusive license to Springer Nature Singapore Pte Ltd. 2023
H. Yang et al. (Eds.): ICIRA 2023, LNAI 14274, pp. 371–380, 2023.
https://doi.org/10.1007/978-981-99-6501-4_32

measures. Jitter is one of the main factors affecting the accuracy degradation of in-service industrial robots, and its measurement and analysis research are of great significance for both scientific research and engineering applications. It can promote the development of our robots.

2 Testing Method

2.1 Basic Principle

The measurement and analysis of industrial robot jitter includes robot jitter data measurement and modal testing [4], as well as analysis of influencing factors based on big data of jitter and modal.

1) Obtaining jitter data (such as displacement, acceleration, frequency response, etc.) of the end and various joints of the robot during operation [4, 5].
2) Obtaining the modal characteristics of the robot (natural frequency, modal information, damping ratio, etc.) [6].

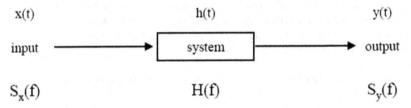

Fig. 1. Vibration transmission process of the robots.

The vibration transmission process of the robot is shown Fig. 1. The vibration is generated by excitation sources such as motors and reducers, passes through the vibration transmission system, and finally outputs at the end of the robot [7].

2.2 Testing Scheme

This manuscript proposes a testing method and sensor layout scheme for the overall jitter of robots [7, 8], as shown in Fig. 2. This method adopts accelerometers, charge amplifiers, and dynamic signal analyzers to build the testing platform [7].

2.3 Testing Procedure

The specific testing procedure can be divided into the following steps:

1) Preliminary evaluation test

Control the robot to perform multi-joint movement and measure the intensity of end and axis jitter during the operation, which is quantitatively described by parameters such as displacement, acceleration, and frequency [7, 9].

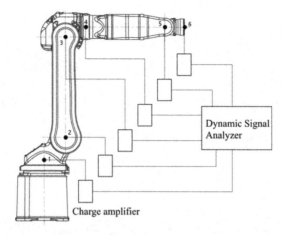

Fig. 2. Sensor layout scheme of the testing system.

2) Single joint motion measurement

On the basis of assessment testing, determine the analysis object and conduct uniaxial motion and testing. Measure the jitter data near the target joint and the end of the robot [9].

3) Modal testing

Arrange the accelerometers on the robot according to the design plan, use an exciter/hammer to excite the robot, and obtain the modal parameters of the robot, such as the natural frequency [10].

4) Data acquisition and analysis

Identify the factors related to end jitter by comprehensively analyzing the jitter data during multi-joint and single joint movements [11, 12].

3   Results and Discussion

Based on the above testing system and process, a six-axis robot was tested, and the specific results are as follows.

3.1   Preliminary Evaluation Test

The results of preliminary evaluation test are as follows, among which Fig. 3 shows the test results of six joint comprehensive motion, Fig. 4 exhibits its frequency domain results, indicating that the peak jitter in this test is 0.2 g, and Fig. 5 presents the time-domain test results in one cycle, showing that the main frequencies of the robot's jitter are 7.5 Hz, 15 Hz, and 30 Hz, respectively.

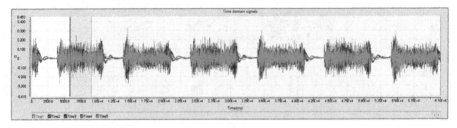

Fig. 3. Result of six joint comprehensive motion.

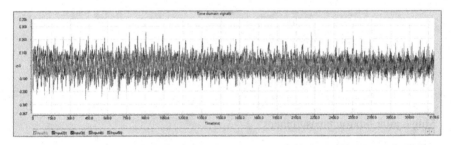

Fig. 4. Preliminary evaluation test result in frequency domain.

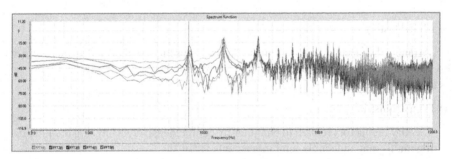

Fig. 5. Preliminary evaluation test result in time domain, one cycle.

3.2 Test Results When only the First Axis Moves

The test results when only the first axis moves are as follows, among which Fig. 6 shows the result of entire measurement process, Fig. 7 exhibits its frequency domain results, indicating that the peak jitter in this test is 0.09 g, and Fig. 8 presents the time-domain test results in one cycle, showing that the main frequencies of the robot's jitter are 7.5 Hz and 15 Hz, respectively.

3.3 Test Results When only the Second Axis Moves

The test results when only the second axis moves are as follows, among which Fig. 9 shows the result of entire measurement process, Fig. 10 exhibits its frequency domain results, indicating that the peak jitter in this test is also 0.09 g, and Fig. 11 presents the

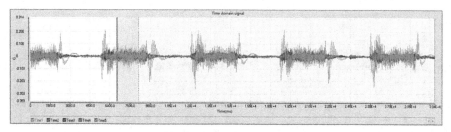

Fig. 6. Result when only the first axis moves.

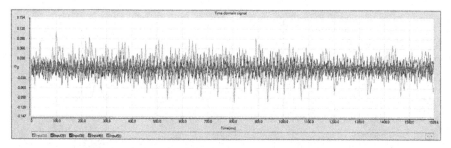

Fig. 7. Result in frequency domain when only the first axis moves.

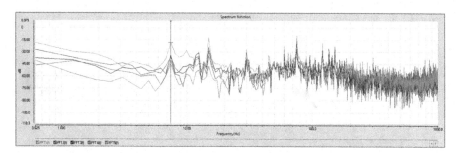

Fig. 8. Result in time domain when only the first axis moves, one cycle.

time-domain test results in one cycle, showing that the main frequencies of the robot's jitter are 7.5 Hz and 15 Hz, respectively, which is similar to the results when only the first axis moves.

3.4 Test Results When only the Third Axis Moves

The test results when only the third axis moves are as follows, among which Fig. 12 shows the result of entire measurement process, Fig. 13 exhibits its frequency domain results, indicating that the peak jitter in this test is 0.12 g, and Fig. 14 presents the time-domain test results in one cycle, showing that the main frequencies of the robot's jitter are 7.5 Hz and 30 Hz, respectively.

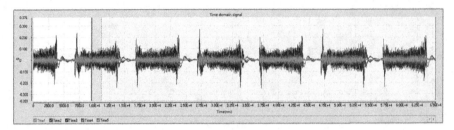

Fig. 9. Result when only the second axis moves.

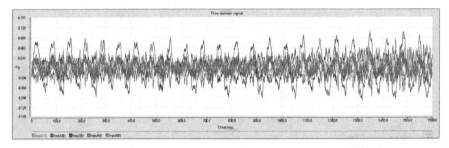

Fig. 10. Result in frequency domain when only the second axis moves.

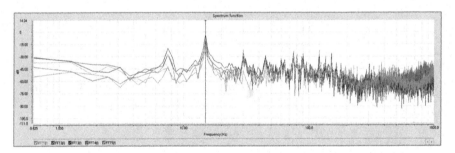

Fig. 11. Result in time domain when only the second axis moves, one cycle.

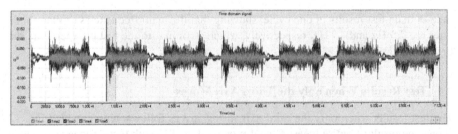

Fig. 12. Result when only the third axis moves.

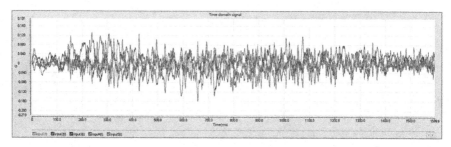

Fig. 13. Result in frequency domain when only the third axis moves.

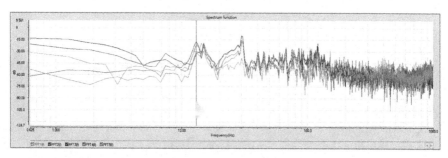

Fig. 14. Result in time domain when only the third axis moves, one cycle.

3.5 Test Results When only the Fourth Axis Moves

The test results when only the fourth axis moves are as follows, among which Fig. 15 shows the result of entire measurement process, Fig. 16 exhibits its frequency domain results, indicating that the peak jitter in this test is 0.08 g, and Fig. 17 presents the time-domain test results in one cycle, showing that the main frequency of the robot's jitter are 15 Hz.

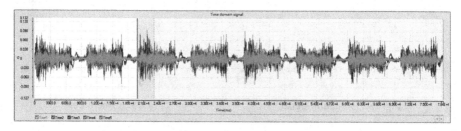

Fig. 15. Result when only the fourth axis moves.

3.6 Modal Testing

After the above tests, the modal testing was conducted through the force hammer method, which can help to confirm whether the robot jitter was caused by resonance. Figures 18,

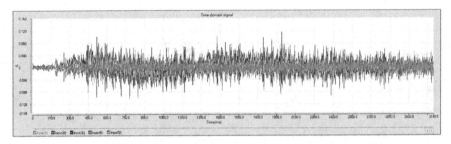

Fig. 16. Result in frequency domain when only the fourth axis moves.

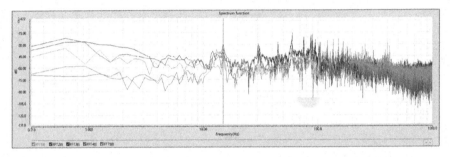

Fig. 17. Result in time domain when only the third axis moves, one cycle.

19, 20, 21 show the excitation signal, coherence, self-power spectrum and frequency response respectively. From the frequency response of the robot, its first and second resonant frequencies are 13.75 Hz and 27.5 Hz respectively.

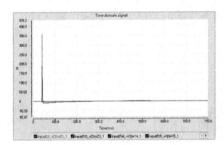

Fig. 18. Excitation signal.

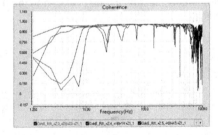

Fig. 19. Coherence.

3.7 Summary and Analysis

Integrating and analyzing the test results of the robot during motion and the modal test under force hammer excitation, as shown in Table 1, can preliminarily determine the source of the robot's end shaking [7, 10]. The first and second order natural frequencies of the robot are 13.75 Hz and 27.5 Hz, respectively, which are very close to the two main frequencies 15 Hz and 30 Hz in the jitter test. This indicates that one possible reason

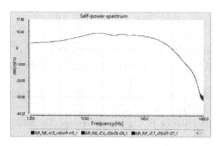

Fig. 20. Self-power spectrum.

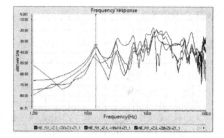

Fig. 21. Frequency response.

for the end jitter of the robot is the motion frequencies of the first, second, third, and fourth axes, that is, the motion of the motor and reducer, are very close to the natural frequencies of the robot. Another thing that can be seen is that when only the third axis moves, the jitter amplitude was higher, indicating that the movement of the third axis has a greater impact on the end jitter of the robot.

Table 1. Jitter measurement modal testing data records.

Mode of operation	Velocity	Jitter frequency (Hz)	Jitter amplitude (g)
Six axes	15% about 0.3 m/s	7.5, 15, 30	± 0.2
First axis	15% about 0.3 m/s	7.5, 15	± 0.09
Second axis		7.5, 15	± 0.09
Third axis		7.5, 30	± 0.12
Fourth axis		15	± 0.08
Modal testing	Force hammer method	The first two orders natural frequencies: 13.75 Hz, 27.5 Hz	/

4   Conclusions

This work designs and builds a robot jitter testing and analysis platform, and tests a six axis robot accordingly. Preliminary evaluation testing (with all axes moving), independent motion testing of each axis, and modal testing and analysis were conducted in sequence. Through jitter testing and model analysis [11], the source of end jitter of the robot has been preliminarily determined [12], which can provide a basis for further design optimization of the robot.

Acknowledgment. This work was supported by the "2022 Foshan Science and Technology Innovation Project" (No.:2220001005535) and "Ningbo High tech Zone 2021 Major Science and Technology Special Project (Major Technological Innovation Project)" (No.: 2021DCX050012).

References

1. GB/T 12642-2013: Industrial robots-performance criteria and related test methods (2013)
2. Huinong, H., Liansheng, H.: Progress of industrial robot performance testing. J. China Jiliang Univ. **28**(2), 134–140 (2017)
3. Maolin, W., Benwang, L., Yue, G., Yujiao, Y.: Experimental study on the influence mechanism of industrial robot performance Machine Tool & Hydraulics, 2020.8.15 (2018)
4. Zu, H., Chen, Z., Fan, K., Zhang, X.: Industrial Robot Performance Testing Technology. Zhejiang University Press (2019)
5. Utsuno, H., Isomura, K., Matsuhisa, H.: Acceleration and deceleration pattern to suppress residual vibration of the robot arm. The Japan Society of Mechanical Engineers. In: The Proceedings of the Dynamics & Design Conference. Japan: The Japan Society of Mechanical Engineers, 2010, pp. 371–379 (2010)
6. Gao, Z.H., Bian, Y.S.: Resonance analysis of manipulators with flexible link and flexible joint. Adv. Mater. Res. **2012**(383–390), 2868–2874 (2012)
7. Chen, Y., Fan, K., Tan, J.: Research on end jitter of industrial six-axis robot. Lab. Res. Explor. **38**(12), 44–47 (2019) https://doi.org/10.3969/j.issn.1006-7167.2019.12.011
8. Kuric, I., Tlach, V., Císar, M., Ságová, Z., Zajačko, I.: Examination of industrial robot performance parameters utilizing machine tool diagnostic methods. Int. J. Adv. Rob. Syst. (2020)
9. Gourishankar, M., Ruby, M., Shubham, S.: Real-time vibration analysis of a robotic arm designed for CT image guided diagnostic procedures. In: Kumar, M., Pandey, R.K., Kumar, V. (eds.) Advances in Interdisciplinary Engineering, pp. 163–171. Springer, Singapore (2019)
10. Tao, W., Zhang, M., Liu, M.: Residual vibration analysis and suppression for SCARA robot arm in semiconductor manufacturing. In: IEEE. 2006 IEEE/RSJ International Conference on Intelligent Robots and Systems, Piscataway, pp. 5153–5158. IEEE (2007)
11. Liang, D., Song, Y., Qi, Y.: Efficient modeling and integrated control for tracking and vibration of a lightweight parallel manipulator including servo motor dynamics. Mech. Syst. Signal Process. **153**, 107502 (2021)
12. Hearne, J.: Posture Dependent Vibration Resistance of Serial Robot Manipulators to Applied Oscillating Loads. University of Waterloo (2010)

Attitude Control of Flapping-Wing Micro Air Vehicles Based on Hyperbolic Tangent Function Sliding Mode Control

Xiao Liu[1,3,4], Weijun Wang[1,2,3,4], Wei Feng[1,2,3,4(✉)], Shijie Wang[1,3,4],
Xincheng Wang[1,4], and Yunxiao Cheng[1,3]

[1] Shenzhen Institute of Advanced Technology, Chinese Academy of Sciences, Shenzhen, China
{xiao.liu1,wei.feng,sj.wang,xc.wang,yx.cheng}@siat.ac.cn,
wj.wang@giat.ac.cn
[2] University of Chinese Academy of Sciences, Beijing, China
[3] International Joint Research Center for Robotics and Intelligent Construction,
Guangdong, China
[4] Guangdong Provincial Key Lab of Robotics and Intelligent System, Shenzhen Institutes
of Advanced Technology, Chinese Academy of Sciences, Shenzhen, China

Abstract. The flying animals in nature mainly include insects, birds, and bats, which have formed flexible flight wings and control systems through natural evolution. Compared with fixed wing and rotor wing vehicle, flapping wing micro air vehicle (FMAV) have higher maneuverability during flight, but the implementation of different motion attitudes requires effective control of flight attitudes.

FMAV is a typical non-constant aerodynamic system, and it is difficult to establish an accurate analytical or semi-analytical mechanical model, which poses certain technical challenges to the systematic design of control laws. Sliding mode control (SMC) is a typical and special nonlinear control, which has good control effect and robustness for uncertain nonlinear systems such as unmanned aerial vehicle (UAV), spacecraft, FMAV, etc. and can solve various disturbances and model uncertainty brought by external complex environment. However, the traditional Sliding mode control has the problem of chattering, so the hyperbolic tangent function is introduced to replace the discontinuous switching function, Then, an attitude control of FMAV based on hyperbolic tangent function Sliding mode control is established to complete the target attitude tracking control.

Keywords: Flapping wing micro air vehicle · Sliding mode control · Attitude control

1 Introduction

Through a long process of evolution of nature's superiority and inferiority, flying animals have developed flexible flight wings and control systems. Nowadays, the flight of birds, insects and bats in nature is basically flapping wing flight. Flapping wing micro air vehicle (FMAV) has fully integrated lift, propulsion and control functions in the flutter

© The Author(s), under exclusive license to Springer Nature Singapore Pte Ltd. 2023
H. Yang et al. (Eds.): ICIRA 2023, LNAI 14274, pp. 381–393, 2023.
https://doi.org/10.1007/978-981-99-6501-4_33

wing system, which can fly long distances with little energy. Compared with traditional fixed wing and rotary wing aircraft, FMAV is characterized by small size, high stability, high maneuverability, low noise, etc. [1]. Where maneuverable and flexible flight attitude control is crucial.

Due to the enormous advantages of flapping wing flight, European and American are competing to carry out research on flapping wing bionic vehicles, and more and more advanced technologies are being introduced into the position and attitude research of FMAV [2]. The main model-based controllers in the control strategy of FMAV [3] mainly include feedforward control [4], boundary control [5], predictive control [6], etc. Due to the controller being designed after model linearization, it is difficult for the controller to achieve the expected effect. FMAV is an uncertain high-order system, and building an accurate numerical model with all the characteristics is a difficult task. Therefore, researchers have subsequently proposed many model-free solutions: model-free control, model-free passive control [7], and model-free adaptive/intelligent control. Among them, model free active control mainly includes PID control [8–10], active (passive) position feedback [11], linear speed feedback [12], fractional derivative control [13], Singular perturbation control [14]. Model free adaptive/intelligent control mainly includes: Sliding mode control [15], adaptive control [16], neural network control [17], fuzzy control [18], etc. [19] proposed a full form dynamic linearized model free adaptive control scheme (FFDL-MFAC) to address the difficulties in controller design caused by the nonlinear, time-varying, and strong coupling characteristics of micro air vehicles, achieving pitch control of the controlled aircraft. [20] proposed a closed-loop Active Disturbance Rejection Control (ADRC) strategy to stabilize attitude during flapping, transition, and gliding flight. In flap glide flight mode, ADRC can track the target pitch signal better than the PID controller. [21] proposed a neural dynamics model based on neural dynamics methods to achieve attitude tracking control of FMAV, enabling the error to converge to zero in a short period of time. [22] proposed a multi axis adaptive controller with a reference generator, which uses a backstepping design method for attitude and altitude control, providing an idea for maintaining stable flight. [23] developed a self-tuning sliding mode control strategy to perform robust and adaptive tracking control for an uncertain coaxial octocopter unmanned aerial vehicle (COUAV) with actuator failure.

In recent years, the research on sliding mode control algorithms based on hyperbolic tangent functions has flourished, and has been applied to electric power, fuel cell UAV power systems [24], rolling missiles [25], industrial robots [26] and quadcopter micro-aircraft [27, 28]. Compared with these systems, the construction of flapping wing aircraft models is more complicated, and it is difficult to establish accurate analytical or semi-analytical mechanical models, which usually only can be used by numerical modeling and analysis methods, which puts forward certain technical challenges for the systematic design of flapping wing aircraft control laws. Among many advanced control methods, Sliding Mode Control (SMC) is a nonlinear control, which has strong robustness to disturbances and unmodeled dynamics. It is especially suitable for uncertain nonlinear systems such as FMAV. The mass of FMAV is relatively small, very sensitive to environmentally unstable airflow interference, requiring the control system to have strong anti-interference performance, the use of SMC method can reduce the handling of unknown or uncertain model systems, and can well suppress external disturbance to obtain the required performance. However, SMC will cause chattering in the process of logic switching, resulting in system instability and energy consumption. Therefore, based on the traditional SMC, this paper introduces the hyperbolic tangent function and establishes a flapping wing vehicle attitude control based on the hyperbolic tangent function SMC to achieve attitude tracking and real-time adjustment in the flight.

2 System Modeling of Flapping Wing Micro Air Vehicle

FMAV relies on changing the flapping frequency, flapping angle, twisting angle, and swinging angle of the wings. The forces and moments generated by aerodynamics act on the body, causing changes in the speed, position, and flight attitude of the aircraft. It can achieve hovering, takeoff, and inverted flight, and has the advantages of rotor and fixed wing aircraft.

The basic coordinate systems of FMAV include inertial coordinate system and airframe coordinate system, etc. The inertial coordinate system is a coordinate system with the Earth as the reference object, labeled OXYZ. The Z-axis is perpendicular to the horizontal plane and the upward direction is positive. The inertial coordinate system is shown in Fig. 1, which is very convenient for describing the position and attitude of flapping wing aircraft. The origin o of the airframe coordinate system (labeled oxyz) is the center of mass of the vehicle, with the vehicle itself as the reference object, and the positive direction of the x-axis is along the head direction, pointing forward. The y-axis is perpendicular to the xz-plane, following the right-hand rule. The airframe coordinate system is shown in Fig. 1. The airframe coordinate system is a dynamic coordinate system, and when the attitude of the aircraft changes, it also changes accordingly. Its Euler angle relative to the inertial coordinate system is the overall attitude angle, is used both to describe the relationship with the inertial coordinate system and to describe the attitude change of the vehicle.

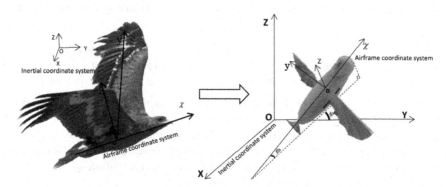

Fig. 1. Schematic diagram of the coordinate system for FMAV

As shown in Fig. 2 (a), the angle between the oxy plane of the FMAV's airframe coordinate system and the horizontal plane OXY is the roll angle γ, which is positive if it is rotated clockwise. As shown in Fig. 2 (b), the angle between the x-axis of the FMAV and the horizontal plane OXY is the pitch angle φ, and if the x-axis deviates upwards, it is a positive value. As shown in Fig. 2 (c), the angle between the projection of the x-axis on the horizontal plane OXY and the X-axis is the yaw angle ψ, if the x-axis deviates to the right, it is a positive value.

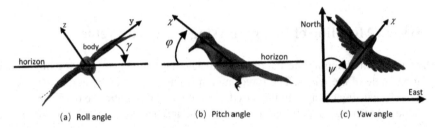

(a) Roll angle   (b) Pitch angle   (c) Yaw angle

Fig. 2. Schematic diagram of Euler angle for FMAV

The attitude of FMAV in the inertial coordinate system can be represented by Euler angle, which includes yaw angle, pitch angle, and roll angle. The airframe coordinate system can coincide with the inertial coordinate system through rotation and translation. According to the Euler rotation theorem, the conversion between the inertial coordinate system and the airframe coordinate system can be obtained as shown in Eq. (1).

$$
\begin{bmatrix} x \\ y \\ z \end{bmatrix} = L(\gamma)L(\varphi)L(\psi) \begin{bmatrix} X \\ Y \\ Z \end{bmatrix} = L(\gamma\ \varphi\ \psi) \begin{bmatrix} X \\ Y \\ Z \end{bmatrix} \tag{1}
$$

$$
= \begin{bmatrix} 1 & 0 & 0 \\ 0 & \cos\gamma & \sin\gamma \\ 0 & -\sin\gamma & \cos\gamma \end{bmatrix} \begin{bmatrix} \cos\varphi & \sin\varphi & 0 \\ -\sin\varphi & \cos\varphi & 0 \\ 0 & 0 & 1 \end{bmatrix} \begin{bmatrix} \cos\psi & 0 & -\sin\psi \\ 0 & 1 & 0 \\ \sin\psi & 0 & \cos\psi \end{bmatrix} \begin{bmatrix} X \\ Y \\ Z \end{bmatrix}
$$

where Eq. (2) is the conversion matrix from the inertial coordinate system to the airframe coordinate system

$$
L(\gamma\ \varphi\ \psi) = \begin{bmatrix} \cos\varphi\cos\psi & \sin\varphi & -\cos\varphi\sin\psi \\ -\sin\varphi\cos\psi\cos\gamma + \sin\psi\sin\gamma & \cos\varphi\cos\gamma & \sin\varphi\sin\psi\cos\gamma + \cos\psi\sin\gamma \\ \sin\varphi\cos\psi\sin\gamma + \sin\psi\cos\gamma & -\cos\varphi\sin\gamma & \sin\varphi\sin\psi\sin\gamma + \cos\psi\cos\gamma \end{bmatrix} \tag{2}
$$

Assuming FMAV is in a hovering state, without considering the motion of ascending, descending, advancing, or retreating, and from the coordinate system, it can be seen that o is the center of mass of the vehicle, oxyz is the airframe coordinate system of the vehicle, and OXYZ is the inertial coordinate system of the vehicle. The attitude angular velocity dynamic equation of an aircraft rotating around the center of mass in the airframe coordinate system is determined by the following Eq. (3):

$$
J\dot{\omega} = F_M - \Omega J\omega - mg + d \tag{3}
$$

where $J \in R^{3\times3}$ is the moment of inertia matrix of the aircraft rotating around the center of mass in the airframe coordinate system, $\omega = [\omega_x\ \omega_y\ \omega_z]^T$ is the angular velocity around the airframe coordinate system, $F_M = [F_x\ F_y\ F_z]$ is the dynamic moment defined in the airframe coordinate system to overcome gravity and to provide the rotational torque of the FMAV, generated by the continuous flapping of wings against the air. $d = [d_x\ d_y\ d_z]^T$ represents the uncertainty and external disturbance torque of the FMAV model.

The matrices J, Ω are defined as follows:

$$J = \left\{ \begin{matrix} J_{xx} & -J_{xy} & -J_{xz} \\ -J_{yx} & J_{yy} & -J_{yz} \\ -J_{zx} & -J_{zy} & J_{zz} \end{matrix} \right\}, \Omega = \left\{ \begin{matrix} 0 & -\omega_z & -\omega_y \\ \omega_z & 0 & -\omega_x \\ -\omega_y & \omega_x & 0 \end{matrix} \right\} \tag{4}$$

When the attitude of the FMAV rotates around the center of mass in the order of pitch, yaw, and roll, the attitude dynamics equation is as follows:

$$\dot{\theta} = R(\theta)\omega \tag{5}$$

where $\theta = [\gamma\ \psi\ \varphi]^T$ is the Euler angle of the vehicle, γ is the roll angle, ψ is the yaw angle, φ is the pitch angle. The $R(\theta)$ matrix is determined by Eq. (6).

$$R(\theta) = \begin{pmatrix} 1 & \tan\psi \sin\gamma & \tan\psi \cos\gamma \\ 0 & \cos\gamma & -\sin\gamma \\ 0 & \frac{\sin\gamma}{\cos\psi} & \frac{\cos\gamma}{\cos\psi} \end{pmatrix} \tag{6}$$

Assuming the ideal attitude angle is $\theta_c = \begin{bmatrix} \gamma_c & \psi_c & \varphi_c \end{bmatrix}^T$, the attitude dynamics equation of FMAV is:

$$\begin{cases} J\dot{\omega} = F_M - \Omega J\omega - mg + d \\ \dot{\theta} = R(\theta)\omega \\ y = \theta \end{cases} \tag{7}$$

And then there is:

$$\ddot{\theta} = \dot{R}(\theta)\omega + R(\theta)\dot{\omega} \tag{8}$$

That is:

$$\dot{\omega} = R^{-1}(\theta)(\ddot{\theta} - \dot{R}(\theta)\omega) \tag{9}$$

From Eq. (3) and Eq. (9), we have:

$$JR^{-1}(\theta)(\ddot{\theta} - \dot{R}(\theta)\omega) = F_M - \Omega J\omega - mg + d \tag{10}$$

That is:

$$\ddot{\theta} = \dot{R}(\theta)\omega + J^{-1}R(\theta)(F_M - \Omega J\omega - mg + d) \tag{11}$$

Therefore, the attitude angle θ can be changed by designing the rotational dynamic moment F_M.

3   Design of Control Law for FMAV

3.1   Design of Traditional Sliding Mode Control Law

For the attitude dynamics model Eq. (7), let the deviation of the attitude angle command be $\theta_e = \theta_c - \theta$, and design the sliding surface as follows [29]:

$$s = c_1\theta_e + \dot{\theta}_e \tag{12}$$

where $c_1 = diag\{c_{11}, c_{12}, c_{13}\} \succ 0$ is the gain matrix. Define the Lyapunov function as:

$$V = \frac{1}{2}s^2 \tag{13}$$

Then,

$$\dot{s} = c_1\dot{\theta}_e + \ddot{\theta}_e = c_1\dot{\theta}_e + \ddot{\theta}_c - \ddot{\theta} \tag{14}$$

$$\dot{s} = c_1\dot{\theta}_e + \ddot{\theta}_c - (\dot{R}(\theta)\omega + J^{-1}R(\theta)(F_M - \Omega J\omega - mg + d)) \tag{15}$$

By using the upper bound of d and Eq. (13), the control law can be designed as:

$$F_M = \Omega J\omega + JR^{-1}(\theta)(\text{sgn}(s)D + c_1\dot{\theta}_e + \ddot{\theta}_c - \dot{R}(\theta)\omega) + mg \tag{16}$$

Substituting the control law (16) into $\dot{s}$, we get:

$$\dot{s} = -\text{sgn}(s)D - J^{-1}R(\theta)d \tag{17}$$

Taking $\left\| J^{-1}R(\theta)d \right\| \leq D$, then:

$$\dot{V} = s^T\dot{s} = -\left\| s^T \right\|D - s^T R(\theta)J^{-1}d \leq 0 \tag{18}$$

When $\dot{V} \equiv 0$, $s \equiv 0$, according to the LaSalle invariance principle, the closed-loop system tends to stabilize, and when $t \to \infty$, $s \to 0$. When the disturbance dt is large, we should ensure a sufficiently large upper bound of disturbance to maintain a certain degree of robustness [30], but a large upper bound D for inducing the chattering phenomenon.

3.2   Design of Sliding Mode Control Law for FMAV Based on Hyperbolic Tangent Function

Compared with the traditional Sliding Mode Control, the use of continuous smooth hyperbolic tangent function can avoid the turning angle when switching by approximate fitting, thus reducing the chattering problem of the system control quantity. The attitude dynamics model for FMAV in Eq. (7), $\ominus$ is the attitude Euler angle, F_M is the torque input, J is the moment of inertia, and d is the uncertain disturbance term, $|d(t)| \leq D$. Definition $\theta_e = \theta_c - \theta$, $\dot{\theta}_e = \dot{\theta}_c - \dot{\theta}$, Where θ_c is the target attitude angle, and θ_e is the attitude angle error [31].

The sliding mode function is designed as shown in Eq. (19), where c must be greater than 0 [32].

$$s = c\theta_e + \dot{\theta}_e \tag{19}$$

Define the Lyapunov function as:

$$V = \frac{1}{2}s^2 \tag{20}$$

Then,

$$\dot{s} = c\dot{\theta}_e + \ddot{\theta}_e = c\dot{\theta}_e + \ddot{\theta}_c - \ddot{\theta}$$

$$= c\dot{\theta}_e + \ddot{\theta}_c - \left(\dot{R}(\theta)\omega + J^{-1}R(\theta)(F_M - \Omega J\omega - mg + d)\right)^{\cdot}$$

And,

$s\dot{s} = s\left(c\dot{\theta}_e + \ddot{\theta}_c - \left(\dot{R}(\theta)\omega + J^{-1}R(\theta)(F_M - \Omega J\omega - mg + d)\right)\right).$

To make $s\dot{s} \leq 0$, a control law of Eq. (21) is designed using a hyperbolic tangent function.

$$F_M = J^{-1}R(\theta)\left(-\dot{R}(\theta)\omega + \ddot{\theta}_c + c\dot{\theta}_e + \eta s\right) + \Omega J\omega + mg - D\tanh(\frac{s}{\varepsilon}) \tag{21}$$

According to $0 \leq |x| - x\tanh(\frac{x}{\varepsilon}) \leq \mu\varepsilon$, $\mu = 0.2785$, for any $x \in R$, there exists a constant $\varepsilon > 0$, thus obtaining: $|s| - s\tanh(\frac{s}{\varepsilon}) \leq \mu\varepsilon$.

Then, $D|s| - Ds\tanh(\frac{s}{\varepsilon}) \leq D\mu\varepsilon$. Secondly, it can be obtained that:

$$-Ds\tanh(\frac{s}{\varepsilon}) \leq -D|s| + D\mu\varepsilon \tag{22}$$

Then,

$$s\dot{s} = s\left(c\dot{\theta}_e + \ddot{\theta}_c - \left(\dot{R}(\theta)\omega + J^{-1}R(\theta)(F_M - \Omega J\omega - mg + d)\right)\right)$$

$$= s\left(c\dot{\theta}_e + \ddot{\theta}_c - \left(\dot{R}(\theta)\omega + J^{-1}R(\theta)(JR^{-1}(\theta)(-\dot{R}(\theta)\omega + \ddot{\theta}_c + c\dot{\theta}_e + \eta s) + d - D\tanh(\frac{s}{\varepsilon}))\right)\right)$$

$$= s\left(-\eta s - J^{-1}R(\theta)d - J^{-1}R(\theta)D\tanh(\frac{s}{\varepsilon})\right)$$

$$= -\eta s^2 - J^{-1}R(\theta)sd - J^{-1}R(\theta)sD\tanh(\frac{s}{\varepsilon})$$

$$\leq -\eta s^2 - J^{-1}R(\theta)sd - J^{-1}R(\theta)(D|s| + D\mu\varepsilon)$$

$$\leq -\eta s^2 - J^{-1}R(\theta)D\mu\varepsilon = -2\eta V - a \tag{23}$$

where a $= J^{-1}R(\theta)D\mu\varepsilon$, b $= -2\eta(t - t_0)$.

The solution of the inequality $\dot{V} \leq -2\eta V - a$ is:

$$V(t) \leq e^b V(t_0) - ae^{-2\eta t}\int_{t_0}^t e^{2\eta\tau}d\tau$$

$$= e^b V(t_0) - \frac{a}{2\eta}(1 - e^b)$$

$$= e^{-2\eta(t-t_0)} V(t_0) - \frac{D\mu\varepsilon}{2\eta JR(\theta)}(1 - e^{-2\eta(t-t_0)}) \qquad (24)$$

That is,

$$\lim_{t\to\infty} V(t) \le \frac{D\mu\varepsilon}{2\eta R(\theta)J}$$

where the absolute value of $R(\theta)$ is a finite value not greater than 1. The asymptotic convergence of $V(t)$ is determined by D, η and ε. The larger η, the smaller ε and the smaller D, the smaller the convergence accuracy.

4 Simulation Analysis

Simulation experiments are conducted according to the attitude dynamics model Eq. (7) of the FMAV, and a MATLAB simulation model is established to simulate the entire process of adjusting the attitude of the flapping wing vehicle to achieve the target attitude. In the whole system (see Fig. 3), the "Target angle" module serves as the input for the target attitude Euler angle θ_c, and the "angle-F" module is the angular dynamics system, which adjusts the output torque F_M based on the angle deviation. The "Real angle" module provides real-time attitude Euler angles. The simulation design is carried out according to the traditional control law and the hyperbolic tangent function Sliding mode control law.

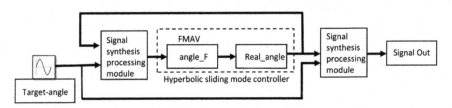

Fig. 3. Simulation diagram of attitude control system of FMAV

Design a control flowchart based on the attitude adjustment process of FMAV (see Fig. 4). Design a control flowchart based on the attitude adjustment process of FMAV (see Fig. 4). Firstly, set the controller parameters, select appropriate values for c, D, η and ε, and then compare the real-time attitude values feedback with the ideal attitude values of the target to calculate the relative error. Secondly, the control output torque is calculated based on the hyperbolic sliding mode control law to eliminate the error until it converges to 0.

Through Simulink simulation, the changes of attitude angle and moments of FMAV based on traditional Sliding mode control law during attitude adjustment are shown in Fig. 5 and Fig. 6. The target angles are set to $\theta_c = [\sin t, \sin t, \sin t]^T$, the initial states are set to $\begin{bmatrix} -1 & 0.7 & -0.4 \end{bmatrix}^T$, take c = 0.5, η = 0.5, D = 50, ε = 0.02, and the disturbance $d(t) = 50\sin t$.

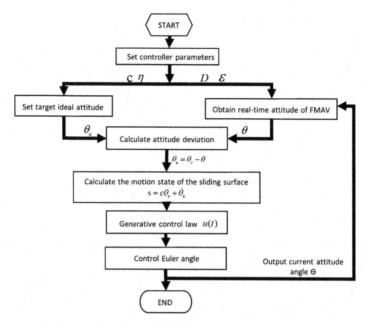

Fig. 4. Attitude control flow chart of FMAV based on hyperbolic sliding mode control

From the target attitude and real-time attitude tracking in Fig. 5, it can be seen that using traditional sliding mode variable structure control can effectively track and reach the ideal target attitude in about 6 s–9 s. But the real-time output torque adjustment changes in Fig. 6 shows a regional periodic oscillation phenomenon. Due to the discontinuity of traditional switching functions, when the system state moves near the switching surface, the continuous switching of the control structure will cause the system state to frequently enter and exit the switching surface, resulting in chattering phenomenon.

Based on the control model of FMAV, the changes of attitude angle and torque in the attitude adjustment process based on the hyperbolic tangent function Sliding mode control law are shown in Fig. 7 and Fig. 8. The target angles are set to $\theta_c =$ [cost, cost, cost]^T, the initial states are set to $\begin{bmatrix} 0 & 1.2 & -0.3 \end{bmatrix}^T$, take $c = 0.5$, $\eta = 0.5$, $D = 50$, $\varepsilon = 0.02$, and the disturbance $d(t) = 50 \sin t$.

According to the comparison between the target attitude and real-time attitude in Fig. 7, the hyperbolic tangent function Sliding mode control is used to make the initial attitude reach the specified target ideal attitude in about 3.5 s–6 s. Compared with Fig. 5 and Fig. 7, the attitude adjustment speed of the SMC based on the Hyperbolic functions is about 3s faster than that of the traditional SMC, but the difference between the two is not significant, indicating that the SMC based on the Hyperbolic functions also has a fast attitude adjustment response speed. As can be seen from Fig. 8, the change of real-time output torque adjustment is more moderate, and the continuous smooth hyperbolic tangent function softens the output of the controller and effectively reduces chattering in the sliding mode control [33]. The FMAV has good robustness and improves the stability of attitude adjustment.

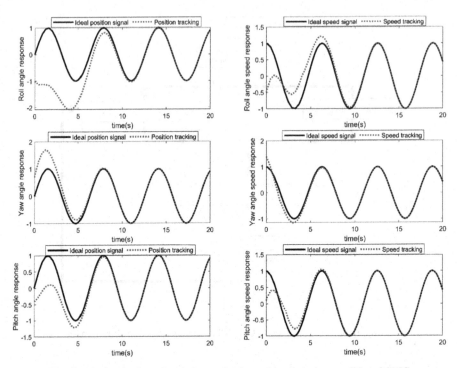

Fig. 5. Ideal attitude and real-time attitude tracking based on traditional SMC

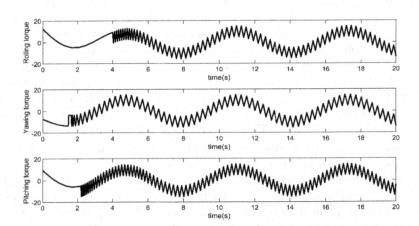

Fig. 6. Real time torque output adjustment change of traditional Sliding mode control law

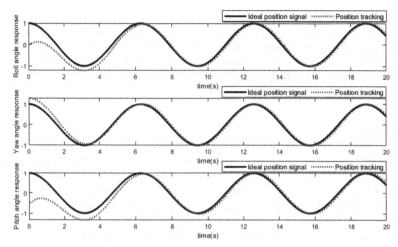

Fig. 7. Ideal attitude and real-time attitude tracking of hyperbolic tangent function Sliding mode control

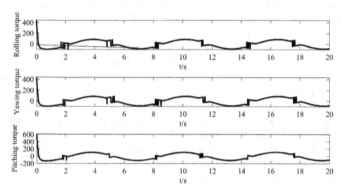

Fig. 8. Real time torque output adjustment changes of hyperbolic tangent function Sliding mode control law

5 Conclusion

This paper takes FMAV as the research object, establishes the attitude control model of FMAV, makes corresponding improvement in the control switching function of the traditional Sliding mode control method, and design of a sliding mode control based on hyperbolic tangent function for flight attitude control of FMAV. The hyperbolic tangent function is used to replace the switching function in the traditional Sliding mode control, so that the system state is kept on the switching surface to achieve stability. Finally, the simulations were carried out separately in MATLAB software, which not only realize the superiority of tracking performance, but also illustrate that the continuous and smooth characteristics of hyperbolic tangent function can effectively reduce chattering in FMAV control based on sliding mode control.

Acknowledgment. This work was supported in part by the Guangdong Provincial Key Laboratory of Construction Robotics and Intelligent Construction (2022KSYS013), in part by the CAS Science and Technology Service Network Plan (STS) - Dongguan Special Project (Grant No. 20211600200062), in part by the Science and Technology Cooperation Project of Chinese Academy of Sciences in Hubei Province Construction 2023.

References

1. Song, F., Yan, Y., Sun, J.: Review of insect-inspired wing micro air vehicle. Arthropod Struct. Dev., 101225 (2022)
2. Ma, D., Jin, L., Fu, D., Xiao, X., Liu, M.: On position and attitude control of flapping wing micro-aerial vehicle. In: Han, M., Qin, S., Zhang, N. (eds.) ISNN 2020. LNCS, vol. 12557, pp. 207–216. Springer, Cham (2020). https://doi.org/10.1007/978-3-030-64221-1_18
3. Tong, S., Weiping, Z., Jiawang, M., Zihao, C.: Research progress on control of bioinspired flapping-wing micro air vehicles. In: 2019 IEEE International Conference on Unmanned Systems (ICUS), Beijing, China, pp. 842–847 (2019)
4. Steltz, E., Avadhanula, S., Fearing, R.S.: High lift force with 275 Hz wing beat in MFI. In: 2007 IEEE/RSJ International Conference on Intelligent Robots and Systems. IEEE (2007)
5. Jones, K.D., et al.: Bio-inspired design of flapping-wing micro air vehicles. Aeronaut. J. **109**(1098), 385–393 (2005)
6. Kamel, M., Burri, M., Siegwart, R.: Linear vs nonlinear MPC for trajectory tracking applied to rotary wing micro aerial vehicles. IFAC-PapersOnLine **50**(1), 3463–3469 (2017)
7. Liu, L.-Y., Yuan, K.: Noncollocated passivity-based PD control of a single-link flexible manipulator. Robotica **21**(2), 117–135 (2003)
8. Percin, M., et al.: Force generation and wing deformation characteristics of a flapping wing micro air vehicle 'DelFly II' in hovering flight. Bioinspir. Biomim. **11**(3), 036014 (2016)
9. Farrell Helbling, E., Wood, R.J.: A review of propulsion power and control architectures for insect-scale flapping-wing vehicles. Appl. Mech. Rev. **70**(1), 010801 (2018)
10. Ma, K.Y., Chirarattananon, P., Wood, R.J.: Design and fabrication of an insect-scale flying robot for control autonomy. In: 2015 IEEE/RSJ International Conference on Intelligent Robots and Systems (IROS). IEEE (2015)
11. Ahmed, B., Pota, H.R.: Dynamic compensation for control of a rotary wing UAV using positive position feedback. J. Intell. Rob. Syst. **61**(1–4), 43–56 (2011)
12. Shen, S., Michael, N., Kumar, V.: Autonomous multifloor indoor navigation with a computationally constrained MAV. In: 2011 IEEE International Conference on Robotics and Automation. IEEE (2011)
13. Bagley, R.L.: Applications of generalized derivatives to viscoelasticity. Air Force Materials Lab Wright-Patterson Afb Oh (1979)
14. James, E.C.: Lifting-line theory for an unsteady wing as a singular perturbation problem. J. Fluid Mech. **70**(4), 753–771 (1975)
15. Ming, P.U., et al.: Recursive terminal sliding mode control of higher-order nonlinear system with mismatched uncertainties. Acta Automatica Sinica **38**(11), 1777–1793 (2012)
16. Zhang, W., Liu, J., Hu, G.: Stability analysis of robust multiple model adaptive control systems. Acta Automatica Sinica **41**(1), 113–121 (2015)
17. He, W., et al.: Adaptive neural network control of a flapping wing micro aerial vehicle with disturbance observer. IEEE Trans. Cybern. **47**(10), 3452–3465 (2017)
18. Ferdaus, Md.M., et al.: Development of c-means clustering based adaptive fuzzy controller for a flapping wing micro air vehicle. J. Artif. Intell. Soft Comput. Res. **9**(2), 99–109 (2019)

19. Wang, T., Jin, S., Hou, Z.: Model free adaptive pitch control of a flapping wing micro aerial vehicle with input saturation. In: 2020 IEEE 9th Data Driven Control and Learning Systems Conference (DDCLS), Liuzhou, China, pp. 627–632 (2020)
20. Dejene, L.A.: Dynamic modelling and control of flapping wing micro air vehicle for flap-glide flight mode. Int. J. Eng. Manuf. **12**(5), 22 (2022)
21. Liu, M., Ma, D., Li, S.: Neural dynamics for adaptive attitude tracking control of a flapping wing micro aerial vehicle. Neurocomputing **456**, 364–372 (2021). Neural dynamics for adaptive attitude tracking control of a flapping wing micro aerial vehicle
22. Mou, J., Zhang, W., Wu, C., et al.: Adaptive control of flapping-wing micro aerial vehicle with coupled dynamics and unknown model parameters. Appl. Sci. **12**(18), 9104 (2022)
23. Xiong, J.J., Guo, N.H., Mao, J., et al.: Self-tuning sliding mode control for an uncertain coaxial octorotor UAV. IEEE Trans. Syst. Man Cybern. Syst. (2022)
24. Guo, L., Huangfu, Y., Ma, R.: A novel high-order sliding mode observer based on tanh-function for a fuel cell UAV power system with uncertain disturbance. In: 2019 IEEE Industry Applications Society Annual Meeting, pp. 1–7. IEEE (2019)
25. Siyu, H., Xugang, W., Yin, Z.: Sliding-mode control for a rolling-missile with input constraints. J. Syst. Eng. Electron. **31**(5), 1041–1050 (2020)
26. 郑银湖,宋永胜,邓静.基于双曲正切函数的工业机器人滑模控制算法分析. 现代信息科技**4**(22), 119–122 (2020)
27. Noordin, A., Mohd Basri, M.A., Mohamed, Z., Mat Lazim, I.: Position and attitude control of quadrotor mav using sliding mode control with tanh function. In: Khairuddin, I.M., et al. (eds.) Enabling Industry 4.0 through Advances in Mechatronics. LNEE, vol. 900 pp. 193–204. Springer, Singapore (2022). https://doi.org/10.1007/978-981-19-2095-0_18
28. Noordin, A., Basri, M.A.M., Mohamed, Z.: Sliding mode control with tanh function for quadrotor UAV altitude and attitude stabilization. In: Bahari, M.S., Harun, A., Zainal Abidin, Z., Hamidon, R., Zakaria, S. (eds.) Intelligent Manufacturing and Mechatronics. LNME, pp. 471–491. Springer, Singapore (2021). https://doi.org/10.1007/978-981-16-0866-7_41
29. Wang, J., Zhu, H., Zhang, C., et al.: Adaptive hyperbolic tangent sliding-mode control for building structural vibration systems for uncertain earthquakes. IEEE Access **6**, 74728–74736 (2018)
30. Hu, Z., Hu, W., Wang, Z., et al.: Global sliding mode control based on a hyperbolic tangent function for matrix rectifier. J. Power Electron. **17**(4), 991–1003 (2017)
31. Shi, Z., Deng, C., Zhang, S., et al.: Hyperbolic tangent function-based finite-time sliding mode control for spacecraft rendezvous maneuver without chattering. IEEE Access **8**, 60838–60849 (2020)
32. Leśniewski, P., Bartoszewicz, A.: Hyperbolic tangent based switching reaching law for discrete time sliding mode control of dynamical systems. In: 2015 International Workshop on Recent Advances in Sliding Modes (RASM), pp. 1–6. IEEE (2015)
33. Zhu, D., Zhang, W., Liu, C., et al.: Fractional-order hyperbolic tangent sliding mode control for chaotic oscillation in power system. Math. Probl. Eng., 1–10 (2021)

L-EfficientUNet: Lightweight End-to-End Monocular Depth Estimation for Mobile Robots

Xiangyu Liu[1]([✉]), Junyan Chen[1], Yan Zhou[1,2], Yuexia Zhou[1], Jinhai Wang[1], Xiaoquan Ou[1], and Haotian Lei[1]

[1] Foshan University, Foshan, China
lxy3371@163.com
[2] South China University of Technology, Guangzhou, China

Abstract. In order to solve the problems of monocular depth estimation based on deep learning, such as the amount of computation and parameters of deep network architecture is too large and difficult to be applied in engineering equipment, a lightweight end-to-end monocular depth estimation model is proposed. Firstly, an improved feature extraction module is designed based on migration learning, and the effects of scaling the model's depth, width, and input image resolution on the model's accuracy and computational resources are also considered. An optimized combination of model expansion is used to ensure the model's accuracy and save computational resources simultaneously. Secondly, the fusion loss function is designed to fully consider the characteristics between the predicted value and the real value of the image, reduce the storage requirements and computational complexity of the model, and maintain the accuracy of the model in the reasoning phase. The experimental results on the NYU Depth-V2 dataset show that the proposed method has an average accuracy improvement of 0.086 with a threshold ratio of 1.25, and an average structural similarity improvement of 0.006 in depth maps. The method in this paper uses only 5.9M parametric quantities and 4.4G multiplicative computations, which are 16.982M and 20.544G lower than the comparative literatures. The method in this paper can be deployed on the mobile robot with Raspberry Pi 4 4 GB and achieve an inference speed of 5 Hz, which is 2.86 times faster than the comparative literatures.

Keywords: Depth Estimation · Monocular · Lightweight · End-to-end

1 Introduction

Depth estimation is one of the key technologies in the fields of autonomous driving environment detection [1], human-computer interaction [2], augmented reality [3], and mobile robot navigation [4, 5]. The commonly used sensors are LIDAR [6], TOF (Time of Flight) camera, RGB camera, etc. LIDAR and TOF cameras can be used to achieve accurate depth measurements in specific situations depending on their technical characteristics. The study of depth estimation based on monocular images still has promising applications. Firstly, 3D reconstruction based on visual scenes has a large demand in

© The Author(s), under exclusive license to Springer Nature Singapore Pte Ltd. 2023
H. Yang et al. (Eds.): ICIRA 2023, LNAI 14274, pp. 394–408, 2023.
https://doi.org/10.1007/978-981-99-6501-4_34

several areas of industry; Second, LIDAR sensors are difficult to measure the depth of highly reflective objects [7] and cause the phenomenon of "ghosting", while LIDAR sensors may also generate the phenomenon of "interference between pairs" [8], while RGB camera sensors do not have this problem; Third, the cost of LiDAR and TOF cameras is relatively high, and RGB image sensors are more popular in practical application scenarios because of their cheaper and lighter characteristics.

The monocular depth estimation task is based on the training model to fit the end-to-end mapping relationship between RGB images and depth images and to directly predict the pixel-by-pixel depth map of the actual scene images from the trained model. Studies have been conducted using Convolutional Neural Networks (CNN) and transfer learning [9] to accelerate the solution of deep prediction problems. More researchers are now using more complex neural network architectures [10] to improve the accuracy of deep predictive inference. The neural network architecture aims to predict depth from a single RGB image through supervised learning. However, this approach's computational demands, requiring multiple GPUs or specialized server hardware, prevent its suitability for offline applications or low-power devices such as industrial cameras, drones, and privacy-focused personal devices.

In this work, we introduce an improved migration learning-based feature extraction module, which takes into account the effects on both model accuracy and computational resources. Additionally, a fusion loss function is proposed to consider the characteristics between predicted and true image values, reducing storage requirements and computational complexity during inference while maintaining model accuracy. Combining lightweight and energy-efficient networks with encoder-decoder architecture design [11], compared with existing methods, this method performs depth estimation for indoor scenes, reducing parameter and computational complexity exponentially while improving inference speed and ensuring accuracy. The indoor scene depth predicted by this method is more reasonable and suitable for deployment on low-power embedded devices. Therefore, the method proposed in this article has high practical application value.

2 Related Work

How to estimate the depth of pixels accurately and reasonably in an RGB image is a fundamental topic in scene reconstruction in the field of computer vision. Early work on predicting depth based on a single RGB image usually used traditional machine learning methods of manual image feature finding and probabilistic modeling. Saxena et al. [12] and Liu et al. [13] used Markov random fields to model the depth of individual points of an image and the relationship between the depths of different points, Daniel et al. [14] used the stochastic Hough transform to estimate the planar parameters. Traditional depth estimation methods based on machine learning are mainly based on visual feature extraction and geometric relationship modeling to infer depth information in images. However, these methods tend to perform poorly for scenes with complex textures, lighting changes, occlusions, and perspective changes.

With the development of deep learning techniques and the performance of graphics image processing devices, Convolution Neural Network (CNN) is unique in the field of computer vision due to its efficient image feature extraction and representation capabilities. Depth estimation techniques use convolutional neural networks to predict the relationship between RGB images and depth information. In recent years, many CNN-based image depth estimation algorithms have achieved good results.

Eigen et al. [15] firstly used the CNN of two modules to predict the depth, one for the overall prediction result and the other for local optimization details. Liu et al. [16] combined CNN with a conditional random field to perform depth estimation on image chunks after segmenting the image using superpixels, and used pairs of superpixels output to the conditional random field to obtain the probability of depth. However, this approach is complex and inefficient in structure, and an end-to-end model is needed to solve this problem. The literature [17] converts the depth regression prediction problem into a depth classification problem by obtaining a score map for depth classification through a fully convolutional network, and the classified score map is paired with the original map to obtain the final depth map through a fully connected conditional random field. The depth map obtained by this type of method has low resolution and requires linear interpolation to obtain the depth map corresponding to the original input map size, and this method also reduces the accuracy of depth estimation.

As more powerful models of deep convolutional neural networks are introduced, these models are also applied to image depth prediction work. Without using conditional random fields or other optimization methods, Laina et al. [18] used only residual neural networks for end-to-end training and generated dense depth maps based on the encoder-decoder architecture of ResNet, achieving better depth estimation performance with fewer parameters and less training time compared to other literature. The literature [19] demonstrated through ablation experiments that using a loss function based on size-invariant image gradients has an excellent performance in multiple-depth prediction datasets. Skip Connections structure is widely used in several image tasks, such as semantic segmentation [20] and image recovery [21], etc. Such structures are used in encoder-decoder networks, such as U-Net [11]. This network structure can recover the resolution degradation due to downsampling when combined with the feature extraction capability and feature analysis capability of the encoder-decoder structure for image features to obtain better prediction results. In summary, this paper uses various U-Net-based variants for experiments on various backbone networks. In this paper, we propose a lightweight end-to-end monocular depth estimation neural network for indoor scenes. By combining a lightweight, energy-efficient network and encoder-decoder architecture design with an improved migratory learning-based feature extraction module design and fusion loss function design, the number of parameters and computation are reduced exponentially while the inference speed is increased while ensuring accuracy.

3   Methodology

3.1   Model Architecture

Depth estimation based on monocular images means that the neural network used for depth prediction infers a depth map of the environment by learning spatial or optical features of RGB images, such as the shape, texture, boundary, or area between the object and the environment, and other characteristics. A mapping framework is designed for depth estimation, which can be expressed as Eq. (1)

$$f_{de} : R(u, v) \rightarrow D(u, v) \tag{1}$$

where I denotes the RGB image input, D denotes the corresponding depth map, (u, v) represents the pixel coordinates of the image, and f_{de} represents the mapping relationship.

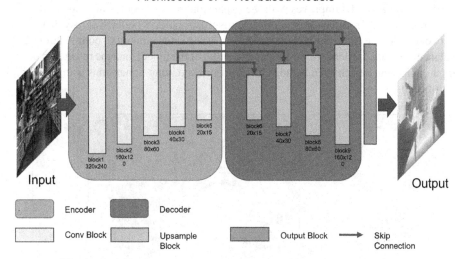

Fig. 1. Convolutional Neural Network with encoder-decoder architecture

The lightweight end-to-end monocular depth estimation neural network proposed in this paper is shown in Fig. 1. The network structure in this paper consists of two parts: encoder and decoder. The encoder aims to maximize the extraction of key features in the input image by mapping high-dimensional data into a low-dimensional space. The various layers of the encoder represent feature information at different scales of the image, which can be used by the decoder to restore the original image. The role of the decoder is to reconvert the features that have been mapped to the low-dimensional space by the encoder into the original high-dimensional data, thus enabling image reconstruction or restoration. The decoder gradually restores the details and structure of the image by decoding the output of the encoder through inverse operations. The decoder uses the feature information stored in the encoder to convert the low-dimensional representation into an output image that matches the dimensions of the input image. The hierarchical structure of the decoder is the opposite of the encoder hierarchy, gradually increasing the size and complexity of the feature map to restore the details and content of the original image. Through the cooperative work of the encoder and decoder, an effective mapping relationship can be established between the low-dimensional feature representation and the high-dimensional image for depth map generation.

The encoder part of some studies uses classical image classification networks, such as VGG [22], ResNet [23] and DenseNet [24] etc., these network structures have relatively high accuracy, but their number of parameters and computation is too large, which makes it difficult to realize the deployment in low-power embedded devices and practical offline work scenario applications. Therefore, to enable real-time inference on embedded devices, this paper selects EfficientNet-B0 [25] which combines inference speed and accuracy as the encoder backbone network. The idea of EfficientNet-B0 is to scale the depth of the model, the width of the model, and the resolution of the input image to achieve the impact on the accuracy of the model and the computational resources. EfficientNet-B0 uses an optimized combination of model expansion to ensure that the accuracy of the model improves with the expansion of the model, while saving the use of computational resources, making EfficientNet-B0 achieves better accuracy than other networks with the same amount of parameters or the same amount of computation. The balance between the depth of the model, the width of the model, and the resolution of the input image can be achieved by adjusting the corresponding dimensions using a simple set of ratios.

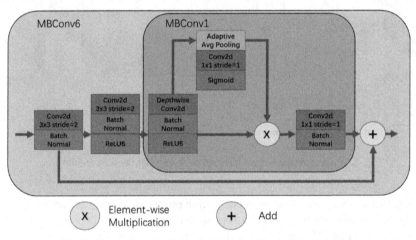

Fig. 2. Structure of the improved EfficientNet MBConv module

EfficientNet-B0 consists mainly of the MBConv module, an inversion bottleneck referencing MobileNet [26], which features the use of Depthwise separable convolutional layers, and the structure is shown in Fig. 2. The EfficientNet-B0 network structure has two main features: 1) the use of the residual module of ResNet and the Squeeze-and-Excitation [27] modules to solve the gradient vanishing and channel attention problems, respectively. 2) The activation function for convolution computation in this network uses the Swish activation function, which is different from the ReLU activation function used by MobileNet. However, the Swish activation function is highly complex and not conducive to quantization. Quantization refers to converting the representation of parameters in a model from floating point numbers to lower precision data types, such as integers or fixed points. Quantification aims to reduce the storage complexity and computational complexity of the model while maintaining the accuracy of the model in the inference phase. In conjunction with the literature EfficientNet-Lite [28], the loss of model accuracy during quantization is mitigated when the ReLU6 activation function restricts the output to [0, 6]. Therefore, in this paper, the Swish activation function in the EfficientNet network is replaced with the ReLU6 activation function. During the training process, in order to ensure the uniformity of variables, the main guideline of this paper to transform each backbone model feature network as an encoder into a U-Net model is to treat the features before each down-sampling module as jump-connected features in the backbone feature network, and the spatial dimensions of each jump-connected feature are kept as 1/4, 1/8, 1/16, 1/32 of the original dimensions, respectively.

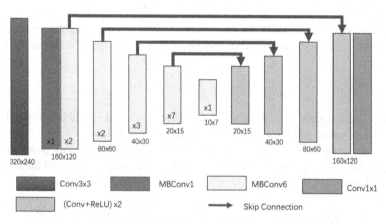

Fig. 3. EfficientUNet structure diagram

The work of the decoder is to reduce the low-dimensional features from the encoder into predicted values layer by layer, which is generally done by inverse pooling, deconvolution, and upsampling. Our decoder is a simple quadratic linear interpolation upsampling to ensure that there is no loss of performance in upsampling. The feature size after each upsampling is twice the original size, i.e., equal to the length and width of the feature in the corresponding layer of the encoder. Only one convolutional layer is set to adjust the features after upsampling. To achieve a lightweight network structure and further improve the speed of the decoder, this article proposes a redundant upsampling removal method in the decoder process to reduce the number of upsampling. The resolution of the output image has the following relationship which is defined as Eq. (2):

$$\hat{r} = 2^{\frac{up}{down}} \times r \qquad (2)$$

where, r, $\hat{r}$ are the input resolution and output resolution, and up, down are the times of upsampling and downsampling, respectively. As shown in Fig. 3, it can be seen that the length and width dimensions of the output image are half of those of the input image. The method can achieve a fast decoder, and in the training process, the number of output channels of each layer of the decoder is fixed in this paper, respectively [512, 256, 128, 64].

3.2 Loss Function

A well-designed loss function plays a crucial role in the fitting and convergence of neural networks. This paper proposes various loss functions that consider the disparity between the predicted depth and the ground truth, the gradient difference between the predicted and true depth, and the structural similarity (SSIM) of their gradients. These loss functions are then combined comprehensively to serve as the network's optimization objective, ensuring constrained and multi-level fitting optimization of the neural network for more accurate, perceptually sound, and reasonable depth maps.

1) The loss function is commonly used in the current research literature, which make the distance between the predicted and true values of the image depth as the loss:

$$l_1 = \frac{1}{p} \sum_{i=1}^{p} |y_i - \hat{y}_i| \tag{3}$$

where y_i denotes the pixel point of the predicted value, and $\hat{y}_i$ denotes the pixel points of the true value, and p means the sum of image pixel points.

2) To improve the model's perception for image depth gradient, this paper make he distance between the image gradient of the depth prediction value and the true value as the loss:

$$l_{gradient} = \frac{1}{p} \sum_{i=1}^{m} \sum_{j=1}^{n} \left| \left(y_{ij} - y_{i(j+1)} \right) - \left(\hat{y}_{ij} - \hat{y}_{i(j+1)} \right) \right|$$
$$+ \left| \left(y_{ij} - y_{(i+1)j} \right) - \left(\hat{y}_{ij} - \hat{y}_{(i+1)j} \right) \right| \tag{4}$$

where m, n denote the length and width of the image.

3) To better measure the rationality of predicted depth maps, this paper make the structure between the image gradient of the depth predicted value and the true value similarity (SSIM) as a loss function:

$$l_{SSIM} = 1 - SSIM(y, \hat{y}) \tag{5}$$

$$SSIM(x, y) = \frac{(2\mu_x \mu_y + c_1)(2\sigma_{xy} + c_2)}{(\mu_x^2 + \mu_{2y} + c_1)(\sigma_x^2 + \sigma_y^2 + c_2)} \tag{6}$$

where, μ_x, μ_y denote the average value of x and y respectively. σ_x^2, σ_y^2 denotes the variance of x and y. σ_{xy} denotes the covariance of x and y. $c_1 = (k_1 L)^2$, and $c_2 = (k_2 L)^2$ are constants, L denotes the range of pixel values, and $k_1 = 0.01$, $k_2 = 0.03$.

In summary, the fractional loss functions used in this paper can be divided into l_1, $l_{gradient}$ and l_{SSIM}, The combined loss function is specifically defined as:

$$l = \varphi(\alpha_1 l_1 + \alpha_2 l_{gradient}) + \alpha_3 l_{SSIM} \tag{7}$$

where φ denotes the weight constants of the network at different training stages. α_1, α_2, α_3 denotes the weight constants of each sub-loss function.

4 Experiments

This section presents the experimental validation details of the method in this paper, as well as the comparison with the current mainstream algorithms on the NYU Depth V2 dataset. Finally, the effectiveness of the proposed method was verified through ablation experiments.

4.1 Dataset

In this paper, the NYU Depth V2 dataset [29] is used for training and performance validation of the proposed method. The dataset consists of video sequences based on RGB images and depth images captured by Microsoft Kinect devices, with an effective depth interval of 0–10 m, specifically including about 407k RGB and depth image pairs in 464 indoor scenes. In this paper, the dataset is divided by scene based on the official division provided, separating the training set and the test set, with the training set containing 249 scenes and the test set containing 215 scenes. In this paper, the downsampled image is converted from the original 640×480 to 320×240 by linear interpolation method, and the depth map label is downsampled to 160×120 to fit the output size.

Multiple studies [15, 30, 31] have confirmed that data enhancement helps to improve accuracy and avoid overfitting. Therefore, in this paper, the following data enhancement methods are used and applied to image samples in an online manner: 1) Horizontal flip with probability 0.5; 2) Random switching of RGB channels with a probability of 0.25; 3) Random brightness, contrast and saturation adjustment with a range of $[-0.2, 0.2]$, with a probability of 0.5.

4.2 Experimental Details

The experiments in this paper use the PyTorch framework for deep neural network training. The computing platform is equipped with the following hardware devices: CPU: Intel Xeon Platinum 8338C; GPU: NVIDIA RTX3080Ti 12 GB. The system environment is Ubuntu 20.04.

The encoders of the proposed model in this paper are used separately in ImageNet [32] pre-trained EfficientNet-B0, VGG-16, ResNet-101,and DenseNet-169 (which are called EfficientUNet-B0, VGGUNet-16, ResUNet-101 and DenseUNet-169 in this paper, respectively). The initialization method of decoder weights uses Kaiming Normalization [33]. The optimizer used throughout the training period is the Adam optimizer with the initial learning rate set to 0.0001 and the learning rate multiplied by 0.1 for every 5 epochs elapsed and the optimizer parameters $\beta_1 = 0.9$, and $\beta_2 = 0.999$, and a total of 20 epochs are trained. The batch size is set to 16 during the experiment. The super-entry settings in the loss function are $\varphi = 1, \alpha_1 = 1, \alpha_2 = 1, \alpha_3 = 1/2$.

4.3 Evaluation Indicators

To measure the accuracy and rationality of the image depth prediction value, referring to the work of [16], this paper uses 6 measurement indicators for model performance verification.

1) log10 Mean Absolute Error (MAE), which is defined as:

$$MAE(y, \hat{y}) = \frac{1}{n} \sum_{i=1}^{p} |\log_{10} y_i - \log_{10} \hat{y}_i| \qquad (8)$$

2) Root Mean Square Error (RMSE), which is defined as:

$$RMSE(y, \hat{y}) = \sqrt{\frac{1}{n} \sum_{i=1}^{n} (y_i - \hat{y}_i)^2} \qquad (9)$$

3) Mean Absolute Percentage Error (MAPE), which is defined as:

$$MAPE(y, \hat{y}) = \frac{1}{n} \sum_{i=1}^{p} \frac{|y_i - \hat{y}_i|}{y_i} \qquad (10)$$

4) Threshold Accuracy (TA), which is defined as:

$$TA(y, \hat{y}) = \frac{1}{n} \sum_{i=1}^{n} \max\left(\frac{y_i}{\hat{y}_i}, \frac{\hat{y}_i}{y_i}\right) < thr \in [1.25^1, 1.25^2, 1.25^3] \qquad (11)$$

5) Mean Structure Similarity Index Measure (SSIM): $SSIM(y, \hat{y})$
6) Edge F1-Score (Edge(I)). The Sobel operator is used to detect the edges of the depth map, and the F1 score is used to compare the edge prediction of the model with the real edges. Different thresholds represent capturing different degrees of edges.

$$G_x = \begin{bmatrix} -1 & 0 & 1 \\ -2 & 0 & 2 \\ -1 & 0 & 1 \end{bmatrix}, G_y = \begin{bmatrix} -1 & -2 & -1 \\ 0 & 0 & 0 \\ 1 & 2 & 1 \end{bmatrix} \qquad (12)$$

$$Edge(I) = \begin{cases} 1 \text{ if} \sqrt{(G_x * I)^2 + (G_y * I)^2} > thr \in [0.25, 0.50, 1.00] \\ 0 \text{ otherwise} \end{cases} \qquad (13)$$

where y_i denotes the pixel point of the predicted value, and $\hat{y}_i$ denotes the pixel point of the true value.

4.4 Experimental Results

To prove the effectiveness and advancement of the method in this paper, the method in this paper is compared with related methods in recent years in terms of neural network performance and neural network parameters on the NYU Depth V2 dataset, and the method in this paper is deployed on a low-power embedded device Raspberry Pi 4 4 GB to realize the depth estimation of mobile robots in real indoor scenes.

The following Table 1 gives the performance comparison results of the neural network models. From Table 1, the method in this paper outperforms other neural network models in three performance metrics: MAE, TA and SSIM. The lead of MAE and TA means that the method in this paper outperforms other neural network models in a small error range. The lead in SSIM that the depth map for image depth prediction using this method is more consistent with the human visual system. It is also observed that the results of Edge(I) lie in the suboptimal position, which means that this paper's method is slightly behind DenseUNet-169 in the depth prediction of the front and back views.

Table 1. Neural network model performance comparison: ↓ means lower is better, ↑ means higher is better. Bolded numbers indicate the optimal results, and underlining indicates the suboptimal results. The models are sorted in ascending order from left to right in terms of balanced overall metrics.

Method	Metric							
	Eigen et al. [31]	Laina et al. [18]	Fast Depth [34]	Rudolph et al. [35]	VGG UNet-16	Res UNet-101	Dense UNet-169	Efficient UNet-B0 (ours)
MAE↓	–	0.065	0.067	**0.060**	0.073	0.077	0.064	<u>0.063</u>
RMSE↓	0.907	0.621	0.576	0.514	0.411	**0.311**	<u>0.313</u>	0.336
MAPE↓	0.215	0.152	0.165	0.144	0.175	**0.128**	<u>0.133</u>	0.152
SSIM↑	–	–	–	–	0.958	<u>0.963</u>	0.959	**0.966**
δ_1↑	0.611	0.749	0.777	<u>0.812</u>	0.736	0.721	0.793	**0.835**
δ_2↑	0.887	0.934	0.949	<u>0.958</u>	0.939	0.930	0.950	**0.966**
δ_3↑	0.971	0.985	0.987	<u>0.989</u>	0.985	0.981	0.986	**0.991**
$F1_{0.25}$↑	–	–	–	–	0.660	0.912	**0.975**	<u>0.939</u>
$F1_{0.50}$↑	–	–	–	–	0.657	0.965	**0.993**	<u>0.971</u>
$F1_{1.00}$↑	–	–	–	–	0.603	0.964	**0.998**	<u>0.989</u>

Table 2. Comparison of neural network model parameters: number of parameters, multiplicative computation and number of frames per second predicted in Raspberry Pi 4 4 GB. Bolded numbers indicate the optimal structure, and underlining indicates suboptimal results. The models are sorted in ascending order from left to right by balanced overall metrics.

	Eigen et al.[31]	Laina et al. [14]	Fast Depth [31]	Rudolph et al. [32]	VGG UNet-16	Res UNet-101	Dense UNet-169	Efficient UNet-B0 (ours)
Param↓	–	28.5M	**3.9M**	5.8M	18.6M	62.9M	26.4M	<u>5.8M</u>
MACs↓	8.4G	–	**1.2G**	6.0G	34.1G	26.9G	21.4G	<u>4.4G</u>
FPS ↑	–	–	–	–	1.76	2.24	<u>2.83</u>	**5.03**

To verify the feasibility of the method in this paper for offline, low-power device application scenarios, the proposed method is deployed in a small mobile robot device loaded with a Raspberry Pi 4 4 GB, as shown in Fig. 4. This paper compares three aspects, namely the number of parameters, the multiplicative computation, and the number of predicted frames per second, as shown in Table 2. From the Table 2, the method in this paper has a great speed and storage advantage over other neural network models, and the number of parameters and multiplication computation of this paper decreases by 77.8% and 79.4%, compared with the advanced DenseUNet-169. The running speed in a small mobile robotic device loaded with Raspberry Pi 4 4 GB is improved by 77.4% to 5 Hz compared to DenseUNet-169. However, we also note that the decrease in computation and number of parameters is not linearly related to the actual computation speed, which is related to the design of the backbone neural network EfficientNet. EfficientNet uses the Depthwise convolution operation, which increases the number of memory accesses and increases the computation time of the neural network, but this operation saves the overhead of parameters. In summary, the operation speed of the method in this paper is still the fastest among all the studies that participated in the comparison.

Fig. 4. The mobile robot with Raspberry Pi 4 4GBand indoor environment prediction

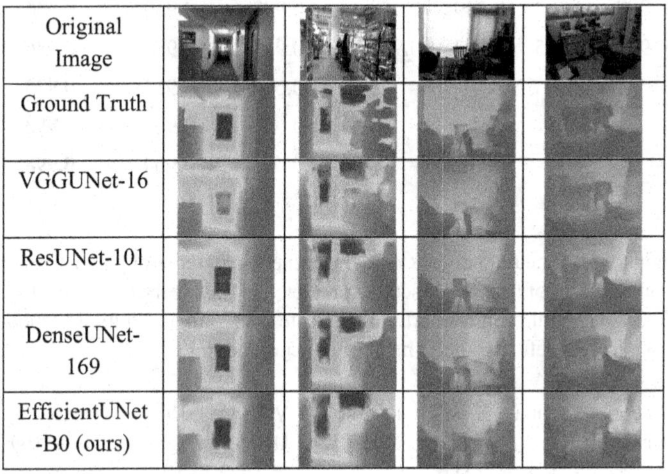

Original Image				
Ground Truth				
VGGUNet-16				
ResUNet-101				
DenseUNet-169				
EfficientUNet-B0 (ours)				

Fig. 5. Comparison of 4 images from different models. From the first to the last row: the input RGB original image, depth map label, VGGUNet-16, ResUNet-101, DenseUNet-169, and EfficientUNet-B0, respectively.

The depth map of the image prediction performed by the method in this paper and other neural network models are shown in Fig. 5. From the Fig. 5, it can be seen more clearly that the effect of different backbone networks on the depth prediction performance is very different. The method in this paper benefits from the better network structure of the selected backbone network EfficientUNet, which has more accurate depth prediction results for distant views than other neural network models and does not easily ignore foreground items of smaller size. However, for the depth prediction of detailed object structures, as seen from the Edge F1 scores and comparison plots, the method in this paper is more difficult to identify the distance to the depth between the edges of objects compared to the DenseUNet-169. The VGGUNet-16 tends to ignore the depth relationship in the foreground of small objects and cannot predict the foreground region of small objects correctly. This phenomenon may be due to the fact that VGGUNet-16 fails to capture the information in terms of the depth relationship of small objects well when learning image features. This makes the items in the VGGUNet-16 depth prediction map appear transparent or blurred in the comparison map.

For the feasibility of loss function design, we used different loss function combinations to conduct ablation experiments on the training of EfficientUNet-B0, and the results are shown in Table 3. We find that the loss function based on image gradient can improve the pixel level measurement index (MAE, RMSE, MAPE, Accuracy) better because the loss function of image gradient can help the model to learn edge and detail information better in the process of optimization. The structural similarity loss function takes more into account the structural information of the depth estimation results, which can help the model to better maintain the structural consistency of the image, especially in the edge region, so the structural similarity loss function can better improve the structural metrics (SSIM and Edge (I)).

Table 3. Loss function ablation experiment: bold numbers indicate the optimal results, and underscores indicate the suboptimal results.

Loss	Metric			
	L1+ Grad+ SSIM	L1+ Grad	L1+ SSIM	L1
MAE↓	**0.0634**	0.0636	0.0647	0.0641
RMSE↓	**0.3356**	0.3765	0.4598	0.3807
MAPE↓	**0.1519**	0.1530	0.1555	0.1534
SSIM↑	**0.9658**	0.8842	0.9067	0.8771
$\delta < 1.25^1$↑	**0.8354**	0.7974	0.7893	0.7950
$\delta < 1.25^2$↑	**0.9657**	0.9528	0.9511	0.9518
$\delta < 1.25^3$↑	**0.9905**	0.9863	0.9865	0.9863
F1 0.25↑	**0.9388**	0.6220	0.6919	0.6210
F1 0.50↑	**0.9714**	0.7005	0.8052	0.7005
F1 1.00↑	**0.9894**	0.7396	0.8920	0.7372

5   Conclusion

In this paper, a lightweight monocular depth estimation model EfficientNet-B0 is proposed for low-power embedded device application scenarios. The method uses EfficientNet as the backbone network, improves the existing depth estimation methods, and further optimizes the backbone network according to practical requirements. The overall network of the method in this paper is trained in an end-to-end manner without any post-processing optimization. In this paper, experimental validation is performed using the

NYU Depth V2 dataset and measured using various performance metrics. EfficientNet-B0 consumes less number of parameters and computation and improves the inference speed while obtaining similar accuracy compared to other advanced networks. Through practical scenario application experiments, it is demonstrated that the network model proposed in this paper can be deployed on embedded systems and the inference speed reaches 5 Hz on Raspberry Pi 4 4 GB, thus, the EfficientUNet proposed in this paper is deployed on embedded devices to better achieve real-time monocular depth estimation with limited storage conditions. In the future, on the one hand, research will continue to reduce the number of network model parameters and the amount of multiplication and addition calculation. On the other hand, research will be carried out to improve the accuracy and reasoning speed of the network model, which is conducive to quantification, and transfer learning technology will be used for higher quality training to obtain a better depth estimation model.

Acknowledgement. This work is supported by the National Natural Science Foundation of China (No. 61972091), Natural Science Foundation of Guangdong Province of China (No. 2022A1515010101, No. 2021A1515012639), the Key Research Projects of Ordinary Universities in Guangdong Province (No. 2019KZDXM007, No. 2020ZDZX3049), the Scientific and Technological Innovation Project of Foshan City (No. 2020001003285), National Natural Science Foundation of China under Grant (No. 32171909, No. 51705365) and Featured Innovation Project of Foshan Education Bureau (No. 2022DZXX06).

References

1. Chen, X., Kundu, K., Zhang, Z., Ma, H., Fidler, S., Urtasun, R.: Monocular 3D object detection for autonomous driving. In: Proceedings of the IEEE Conference on Computer Vision and Pattern Recognition, pp. 2147–2156 (2016)
2. Ren, Z., Meng, J., Yuan, J.: Depth camera based hand gesture recognition and its applications in human-computer-interaction. In: 2011 8th International Conference on Information, Communications & Signal Processing, pp. 1–5 (2011)
3. Bai, H., Gao, L., El-Sana, J., Billinghurst, M.: Free-hand interaction for handheld augmented reality using an RGB-depth camera. In: SIGGRAPH Asia 2013 Symposium on Mobile Graphics and Interactive Applications, SA 2013, pp. 1–4. Association for Computing Machinery, New York (2013)
4. Kong, Y., Fu, Y., Song, R.: Traversability analysis for quadruped robots navigation in outdoor environment. In: Liu, XJ., Nie, Z., Yu, J., Xie, F., Song, R. (eds.) ICIRA 2021. LNCS, vol. 13014, pp. 246–254. Springer, Cham (2021). https://doi.org/10.1007/978-3-030-89098-8_23
5. Li, Y., Xiao, N., Huo, X., Wu, X.: Knowledge-enhanced scene context embedding for object-oriented navigation of autonomous robots. In: Liu, H., et al. (eds.) ICIRA 2022. LNCS, vol. 13455, pp. 3–12. Springer, Cham (2022). https://doi.org/10.1007/978-3-031-13844-7_1
6. Zhang, Z.: Microsoft kinect sensor and its effect. IEEE MultiMedia **19**(2), 4–10 (2012)
7. Yang, S.-W., Wang, C.-C.: On solving mirror reflection in LIDAR sensing. IEEE/ASME Trans. Mech. **16**(2), 255–265 (2011)
8. Li, Y., Ibanez-Guzman, J.: Lidar for autonomous driving.: the principles, challenges, and trends for automotive Lidar and perception systems. IEEE Signal Process. Mag. **37**(4), 50–61 (2020)

9. Alhashim, I., Wonka, P.: High quality monocular depth estimation via transfer learning. arXiv, March 10 (2019)
10. Hu, Y., Wang, Z., Chen, J., Wang, W.: Context dual-branch attention network for depth completion of transparent object. In: Liu, H., et al. (eds.) ICIRA 2022. LNCS, vol. 13458, pp. 604–614. Springer, Cham (2022). https://doi.org/10.1007/978-3-031-13841-6_54
11. Ronneberger, O., Fischer, P., Brox, T.: U-Net: convolutional networks for biomedical image segmentation. arXiv, May 18 (2015)
12. Saxena, A., Chung, S., Ng, A.: Learning depth from single monocular images. In: Advances in Neural Information Processing Systems. MIT Press (2005)
13. Liu, B., Gould, S., Koller, D.: Single image depth estimation from predicted semantic labels. In: 2010 IEEE Computer Society Conference on Computer Vision and Pattern Recognition, pp. 1253–1260 (2010)
14. Dube, D., Zell, A.: Real-time plane extraction from depth images with the randomized hough transform. In: 2011 IEEE International Conference on Computer Vision Workshops (ICCV Workshops), pp. 1084–1091 (2011)
15. Eigen, D., Puhrsch, C., Fergus, R.: Depth map prediction from a single image using a multi-scale deep network. In: Advances in Neural Information Processing Systems, Curran Associates (2014)
16. Liu, F., Shen, C., Lin, G.: Deep convolutional neural fields for depth estimation from a single image. In: Proceedings of the IEEE Conference on Computer Vision and Pattern Recognition, pp. 5162–5170 (2015)
17. Cao, Y., Wu, Z., Shen, C.: Estimating depth from monocular images as classification using deep fully convolutional residual networks. IEEE Trans. Circuits Syst. Video Technol. **28**(11), 3174–3182 (2018)
18. Laina, I., Rupprecht, C., Belagiannis, V., Tombari, F., Navab, N.: Deeper depth prediction with fully convolutional residual networks. In: 2016 Fourth International Conference on 3D Vision (3DV), pp. 239–248 (2016)
19. Ummenhofer, B., et al.: DeMoN.: depth and motion network for learning monocular stereo. In: Proceedings of the IEEE Conference on Computer Vision and Pattern Recognition, pp. 5038–5047 (2017)
20. Jiang, J., Zheng, L., Luo, F., Zhang, Z.: RedNet: residual encoder-decoder network for indoor RGB-D semantic segmentation, 06 August 2018
21. Mao, X., Shen, C., Yang, Y.-B.: Image restoration using very deep convolutional encoder-decoder networks with symmetric skip connections. In: Neural Information Processing Systems, Curran Associates (2016)
22. Simonyan, K., Zisserman, A.: Very deep convolutional networks for large-scale image recognition, 10 April 2015
23. He, K., Zhang, X., Ren, S., Sun, J.: Deep residual learning for image recognition, 10 December 2015
24. Huang, G., Liu, Z., van der Maaten, L., Weinberger, K.Q.: Densely connected convolutional networks, 28 January 2018
25. Tan, M., Le, Q.V.: EfficientNet: rethinking model scaling for convolutional neural networks, 11 September (2020)
26. Howard, A.G., et al.: MobileNets: efficient convolutional neural networks for mobile vision applications, 16 April 2017
27. Hu, J., Shen, L., Albanie, S., Sun, G., Wu, E.: Squeeze-and-excitation networks, 16 May 2019
28. Higher accuracy on vision models with EfficientNet-Lite. https://blog.tensorflow.org/2020/03/higher-accuracy-on-vision-models-with-efficientnet-lite.html. Accessed 03 Jan 2023
29. Silberman, N., Hoiem, D., Kohli, P., Fergus, R.: Indoor segmentation and support inference from RGBD images. In: Fitzgibbon, A., Lazebnik, S., Perona, P., Sato, Y., Schmid, C. (eds.)

ECCV 2012. LNCS, vol. 7576, pp. 746–760. Springer, Heidelberg (2012). https://doi.org/10.1007/978-3-642-33715-4_54

30. Ma, F., Karaman, S.: Sparse-to-dense: depth prediction from sparse depth samples and a single image. In: 2018 IEEE International Conference on Robotics and Automation (ICRA), pp. 4796–4803 (2018)

31. Eigen, D., Fergus, R.: Predicting depth, surface normals and semantic labels with a common multi-scale convolutional architecture. In: Proceedings of the IEEE International Conference on Computer Vision, pp. 2650–2658 (2015)

32. Russakovsky, O., et al.: ImageNet large scale visual recognition challenge, 29 January 2015

33. He, K., Zhang, X., Ren, S., Sun, J.: Delving deep into rectifiers: surpassing human-level performance on ImageNet classification, 06 February 2015

34. Wofk, D., Ma, F., Yang, T.-J., Karaman, S., Sze, V.: FastDepth: fast monocular depth estimation on embedded systems. In: 2019 International Conference on Robotics and Automation (ICRA), pp. 6101–6108 (2019)

35. Rudolph, M., Dawoud, Y., Güldenring, R., Nalpantidis, L., Belagiannis, V.: Lightweight monocular depth estimation through guided decoding. In: 2022 International Conference on Robotics and Automation (ICRA), pp. 2344–2350 (2022)

Integrated Device for Controllable Droplet Generation and Detection on Open Array Chip

Zijian Zhou[1], Jie Wang[2], Yuxin Li[1], Jia Zhou[3], and Lin Du[1,3(✉)]

[1] School of Mechanical Engineering, University of Shanghai for Science and Technology,
Shanghai 200433, China
dulin@usst.edu.cn
[2] School of Optical-Electrical and Computer Engineering, University of Shanghai for Science
and Technology, Shanghai 200433, China
[3] State Key Laboratory of ASIC and System, School of Microelectronics, Fudan University,
Shanghai 200433, China

Abstract. The open array chip is an incredibly valuable tool for analyzing single molecule levels. Its efficiency, speed, compatibility, and precision make it an essential part of this process. However, efficient sample addition has become a significant challenge in the development of open array chips due to the coupling of the solid-liquid interface and the need for high-precision control. To address this challenge, we have developed an integrated adding sample device using technology of generates and detects controllable droplets array based on an open array chip with a biomimetic structure. This device combines a microfluidic chip, image detection, and smear speed regulation. We have studied the factors that affect the efficiency of sample loading, such as the number, speed and fluctuation of smears, and microwell size. The experiments have shown that the open array chip with the microwell's diameter of 350 μm can generate arrays of ~470/cm^2 ~8 nL droplets, significantly reducing controlled speed fluctuation errors by 7.24% and volume fluctuation errors by 24% compared to traditional manual ways. The device has also displayed excellent performance on chips with microwell diameters of 120, 350, 700, and 1300 μm, respectively, with a notable first-time success rate of up to 91% on chips with microwell diameters of 120 μm.

Keywords: MEMS · Microfluidics Chip · Feedback Control · Adding Sample · Biomimetic Structure

1 Introduction

Preparing biological samples into large quantities of homogeneous droplets in a rapid and efficient manner has numerous advantages for detection and analysis. Microfluidic chips offer high throughput, low pollution, low cost, and require small dosages. Combining them with groundbreaking chemistry and biology solutions can greatly enhance their efficacy, especially in the fields of molecular biology and biomedicine. The dispersion formation of a large number of droplets has attracted more and more attention from researchers and is widely used in high-throughput reactors such as high-throughput

© The Author(s), under exclusive license to Springer Nature Singapore Pte Ltd. 2023
H. Yang et al. (Eds.): ICIRA 2023, LNAI 14274, pp. 409–419, 2023.
https://doi.org/10.1007/978-981-99-6501-4_35

cell screening [1], high-throughput single-cell sequencing [2, 3], cell and enzyme isolation [4, 5]. In contrast to the continuous flow mode, the preparation of droplet arrays by performing surface modulation and physical or chemical treatment of the surface to achieve droplet arrays has been an important aspect of droplet preparation [6–9]. With the increasing maturity of microfabrication techniques and the study of physical structures, microstructures have been heavily studied and applied to the fabrication of droplet arrays, such as pneumatic microvalves [10, 11], sliding chips [8], high-density structure arrays [12, 13], etc. Through the research, under some specific conditions, droplet whole array can be achieved without chemical treatment, but by some special surface structure for droplet array, droplet array with chamber can not only avoid contamination due to chemical modification [14], but also avoid the problem of efficiency reduction due to chemical modification failure, and also provide a solution for cross contamination, and the special surface structure provides a practical detection better microfluidic platform. Most current methods replace the air in the microwells with liquid to achieve droplet arrays, such as expelling air through vacuum technology and feeding liquid into the microwells [15]. However, for large-scale droplet arrays, the way of simplicity, efficiency, low cost, and ease of adding samples are gradually attracting researchers' attention facing the challenge of coupling the solid-liquid interface and the need for high-precision control.

By utilizing an open array chip with an open design and a hydrophobic surface [16–18], it is possible to convert an aqueous solution into an array of droplets without the need for an external pressure device or an additional liquid phase. This process will be facilitated by a precise smear mechanism that will guide the liquid into forming the droplet array. In this paper, we developed an integrated device for the controlled generation and detection of droplets, where a controller and a miniature guide are used for the fabrication of droplet arrays. The microscope platform and the smear device are integrated to create a controlled droplet generation and detection device using an automatic spiking device and a microscope system to observe the droplet state more clearly. As shown in Fig. 1a, the signal is transmitted from the controller to the driver, who then accepts it and controls the movement of the stepper motor. The stepper motor connects the screw and the table, allowing the chip to move back and forth. This movement is observed in real-time through the microscope system, which sends the processed image through the charge-coupled device (CCD) to the monitor. The droplet array can be viewed on the monitor, and the speed is adjusted using feedback. The device for control and detection is illustrated in Fig. 1b, displaying the workflow diagram. It carries out the control and detection of the droplet array through a cycle. The controller is used to move the chip, producing the droplet array. The processing of the droplet array on the chip is transmitted to the display by the charge-coupled element (CCD). The data is then analyzed through the display. If the droplet array produces a non-additive effect, a second application is made, or the application speed is changed. When the droplet array has a good effect, the chip is removed, and subsequent experiments are carried out. We investigated the number of smearing times and smearing speed using an integrated device for controlled droplet generation and detection, and further confirmed the effectiveness of preparing droplet arrays using a controlled smearing device for preparing droplet arrays on bionic structure chips.

a

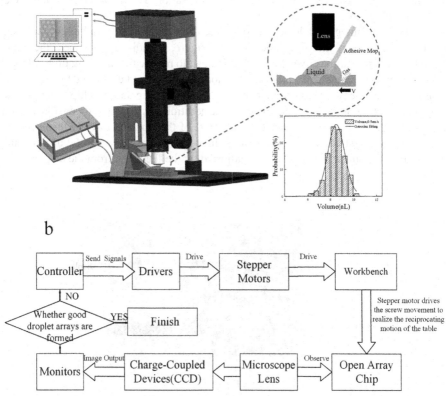

b

Fig. 1. a. Schematic diagram of integrated adding sample device. b. Workflow diagram of controlled and detection of droplet array with the open array chip

2 Materials of Integrated Device

2.1 Hardware

The integrated device for controlled droplet generation and detection mainly consists of two parts, as shown in Fig. 2a, mainly including the smear device and the microscope system. The smear device is used to realize the droplet array of the bionic chip, which can realize different speed adjustments and mode selection, and the microscope system is used to observe the state of the droplet in real-time. The smear device mainly consists of the controller, driver, stepper motor, and viscous dragging board. The controller and driver, as key components, control the speed as well as the mode of smear, and four modes of selection can be performed, which can realize automatic round trip, forward and reverse pointing, single departure and single round trip functions, and the controller and driver are shown in Fig. 2c. The microscope system selected model TD-4KH, the microscope system is embedded system, HDMI real-time output connected to high-definition HDMI display, can be real-time measurement, photo and video, image comparison and other functions through the embedded measurement system, is used to detect the droplets generated by the smear for observation. The microscope system CCD is shown in Fig. 2b.

We build the integrated device of controlled droplet generation and detection based on the microscope platform, as shown in the figure, by adjusting the bed, the angle between the chip and the coverslip can be changed to realize the dragging of droplets at different angles; the speed of smear and the mode of smear can be adjusted by the control board to realize the relative movement between the coverslip and the chip to realize the dragging function of the liquid to complete the addition of samples and generate a good array of droplets. In the smearing stage, the state of the smear is directly displayed by the microscope system, the droplet state is directly observed through the display, and the speed of the smear device is further adjusted by the feedback from the display.

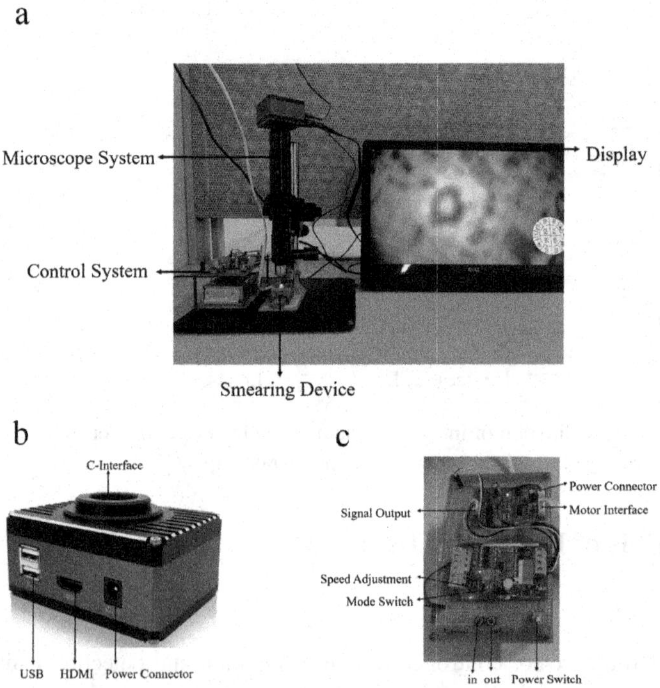

Fig. 2. Integrated device for controlled droplet generation and detection. (a. Physical drawing of the integrated droplet generation and detection device. b. Charge-coupled components(CCD) physical diagram. c. Control system physical diagram.)

2.2 Smear and Assembly Process

The plasma process treats microfluidic chips and glass for bonding to prevent stress bending of the chip due to high temperature during bioassay. The chip is coated as well as observed and detected using an integrated device for controlled droplet generation and detection. The coating process observes the droplet state through the microscope system and adjusts the coating speed in time. The device can effectively improve the efficiency of coating and avoid unnecessary contamination and waste through timely feedback. The smaller the droplet, the larger the specific surface area and the faster the energy transfer, so small droplets are easy to evaporate in the air, so preventing evaporation of mineral oil droplets (M8410, Merck KGaA, MO) is necessary to be coated by coverslips (10212424 C, CITOGLAS, China) to reduce excessive evaporation of droplets. Therefore, the smearing operation should not be performed for a long time and the droplet array should be covered with mineral oil immediately after generation (Fig. 3).

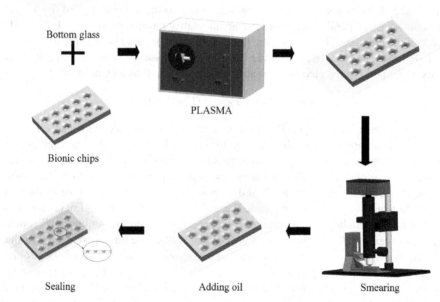

Fig. 3. The process of integrated device for controllable droplet generation and detection

3   Mechanism of Integrated Device

During the smear process, we adjust the speed according to the feedback from the microscope system. We use the bionic chip as the coordinate system, record the initial value, start the smear and time up the device to the bionic chip for droplet array, reach a specific position, stop the time, and perform speed calculation for speed control purposes. The speed control mechanism is shown in Fig. 4a. In the process of smearing, the bed drives the chip for reciprocating motion to realize the process of smearing, at this stage, the position of the drops at the end is unchanged and always in the same position, therefore, it is possible to achieve real-time observation of the formation of the whole column of drops using the microscope head, we connect the monitor through the microscope system to observe the generation of drops at a certain speed in real time for speed feedback, and when the generation of drops at a certain speed When the effect is poor, fine-tuning is performed using the control system. In this cycle, we can observe the droplet formation in real time and adjust the speed, thus improving the coating efficiency.

When smearing under this surface structure, the liquid exhibits low surface wettability by replacing air in the small pores leaving an array of droplets, which is mainly due to the following reasons, the chip has a series of micropores with inclined walls that provide surface energy differences for the liquid during the liquid picture, which can generate forward momentum for the droplets in this environment, thus allowing the liquid to replace air and enter under surface tension in the small holes [19, 20]. Second, during the operation of the coating device, the chip can be considered as a stationary body, and by generating relative motion with a viscous drag plate that is attracted to the liquid, the phenomenon of Couette flow occurs due to the laminar flow of the viscous fluid between two parallel flat plates that are in relative motion, as shown in Fig. 4b. The force of the pressure difference on the liquid is F_p. And the drag plate shear force is F_{s1}. The stationary body generates a shear force of F_B because of the presence of the fixed body, the liquid is subjected to shear and surface tension, thus leaving droplets.

$$F_{s1} + F_{s2} + F_p = \sigma(1 + cos\,\theta_s) \tag{1}$$

where θ_s is the contact angle. However, this equilibrium is unstable because F_{s1} and surface tension are unavoidable. The equilibrium of forces is broken and the droplet advances because of the change in force, thus the contact line will continue to advance. Therefore, the contact perturbation line enters the micropore, and as the droplet advances F_p increases, the boundary of the liquid creeps. Finally, the wettable state of the chip surface gradually changes to a wettable Wenzel state. The equilibrium Eq. (1) also tells us that both the indispensable external energy input F_{s1} and the "equivalent" contact angle between the PDMS surface and the oblique wall of the micropore can be further transformed into the wettable immersion state during the fabrication of the droplet. As in the results reported by other scientists [21–25], once the chip surface is in the wettable warm state, it is difficult to return to the superhydrophobic Casey state, even if the drag plate provides the driving pressure within the fluid. The equilibrium equation is also unsustainable when the fluid has attached to the micropores. Therefore, a small movement of the backward angular contact line will result in a continuous thinning of the meniscus in the drag direction next to the micropore. The result of this analysis is that the contact line does not have a stable position on the sidewall of the pore to rupture the meniscus, thus leaving a liquid droplet.

4   Results and Discussions

We use an integrated device for controlled droplet generation and detection to investigate the relationship between the number of coating times and the preparation success rate and to study the stability of droplet arrays prepared by bionic structures. We used four bionic

a

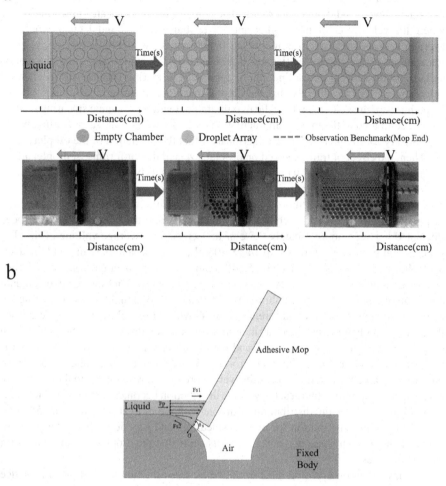

Fig. 4. Mechanism of an integrated device for controlled droplet generation and detection. (a. Solving for the application velocity. b. Schematic diagram of an open array chip implementing a droplet array.)

chips with similar structures and different sizes for experiments and measurements to improve the controllability of the droplet arrays. Four bionic microporous chips with different sizes were used to measure the real-time nature of each smear. The bottom dimensions of the bionic chips 1 to 4 micropores were 120, 350, 700, and 1300 μm, respectively, with a depth of 100 μm. After all the micropores were filled with droplets, 2–3 drops of mineral oil (M8410, Merck KGaA, MO) were added to the surface of the chips to reduce excessive evaporation of droplets. We used a slide with a width of 26 mm as a viscous dragging plate and could complete 1.3 cm^2 and 2.6 cm^2 per second at v = 0.5 cm/s and v = 1 cm/s, respectively, and for four different micropores, v = 1 cm/s was equivalent to about 3200, 1200, 400, and 150 wells could be coated, respectively.

We performed 15 velocity analyses of 0.5 cm/s and 1 cm/s measurements from the integrated device and manual operation. The velocity fluctuations are shown in Fig. 5a, where the velocity is slightly higher and lower than 0.5 cm/s and 1 cm/s, where the average velocity of 15 measurements are 0.4986 cm/s and 0.9952 cm/s. The average fluctuations of the two velocities are 0.28% and 0.48%, which are small fluctuation values and their effect on trailing can be ignored. Comparing manual and mechanical smearing, we can see directly that the mutual machine smearing greatly improves the smoothness of the velocity, where the maximum fluctuation of manual smearing reaches 29.5%, compared to the maximum fluctuation of 2.44% of mechanical smearing, which is necessary for manual smearing to seriously affect the formation of the droplet array.

Then, the effect of trailing speed on droplet size and the uniformity of droplet arrays was investigated using a 350 μm diameter micropore that is being used by us as an example. We studied droplet generation using three levels of manual application, machine control at 0.5 cm/s and 1 cm/s. As shown in Fig. 5b, the three smearing modes corresponding to 0.5 cm/s and 1 cm/s and manual smearing, the manual smearing speed fluctuated between approximately 0.5 cm/ to 1 cm/s. The average volume of droplets generated at pore size 350 μm chip was 8.408 nL, 7.943 nL and 6.39 nL, and the average volume of 0.5 cm/s increased by 5.54% compared to the average volume of 1 cm/s and 24% compared to the average volume of manual smear, and the relative standard deviation of generated droplet volumes was 8.39%, 9.12%, and 33.4%. Contrasting the results generated at the three different speeds shown in Figs. 5b–d, we can clearly see that manual application produces a small and very uneven droplet array volume, which is not conducive to subsequent tests, and therefore machine replacement of manual is necessary. In contrast to machine control at 0.5 cm/s and 1 cm/s, better results were produced at 0.5 cm/s and the test results were more in line with the normal distribution. Consequently, at high velocities, the volume distribution becomes scattered and less uniform. Figure 5c gives the distribution of droplet volume ratio at 0.5 cm/s, Fig. 5d gives the liquid volume distribution for manual smearing, and Fig. 5e gives scatter plots for 0.5 cm/s and manual smearing, and the results show that the droplets are more uniform and fluctuate less at 0.5 cm/s.

Our investigation explored the correlation between the number of times the device was used and the fill rate. We conducted the study on four open chips with the same rate of application. In Fig. 6a, the results showed that the fill rates of micropores with 120 μm, 350 μm, 700 μm, and 1300 μm diameters were 91.12%, 82.97%, 56.66%, and 21.66%, respectively, after the first application. We found that the two open chips with diameters of 120 μm and 350 μm achieved a 100% fill rate with two smears while the two chips with diameters of 700 μm and 1300 μm needed four smears to achieve the same. The fill effect is shown in Fig. 6b. The data indicated that the efficiency of smearing declines as the size of the micro vias increases when using the same device speed. Furthermore, we investigated the relationship between the same-size micropore and the fill rate when using different methods. The findings indicated that for a 350 μm diameter micropore, the fill rate was 82.97% for machine application and 31.91% for manual application after one application. Two applications of machine application resulted in a 100% fill rate while manual application required four applications to achieve the same. Our experiments showed that the micropore diameter size and application method are crucial factors that

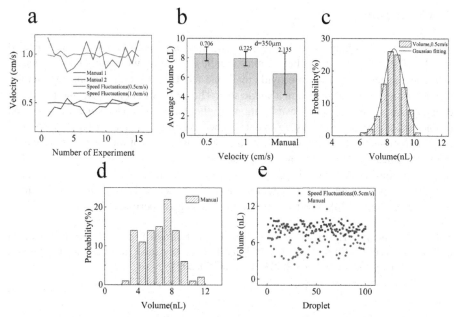

Fig. 5. Influencing factors of droplet array fabrication process (a. Speed fluctuations of the integrated device for controlled droplet generation and detection and manual addition of samples. b. The average volume and deviation of droplets generated by different speeds and manual feeds during device spiking. c. Statistical distribution of liquid volume at 0.5 cm/s for device spiking. d. Statistical distribution of droplet volume at manual spiking. e. Distribution of liquid volume generated at 0.5 cm/s for device spiking and manual feeding.)

affect the chip's fill rate. Machine application is more efficient for droplet arrays than manual application, and smaller diameter micropores are recommended.

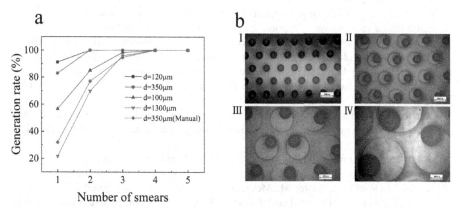

Fig. 6. a. Effect of number of smears and smear method on filling rate of droplet arrays. b. Physical view of droplet array state

5 Conclusion

We have created an innovative device that generates and detects droplets in a controlled manner. The device utilizes a bionic microfluidic chip along with a microscope system and smear speed regulation to provide real-time feedback for adjustments and enables droplet arrays to be performed in a single step. This greatly enhances the automation of droplet arrays. We conducted investigations on the impact of device smearing speed on droplet arrays, the effect of varying smear numbers on filling rates for different pore sizes, and fluctuations in device speed. Our results demonstrated that the device significantly improved smearing efficiency and droplet uniformity compared to manual addition. The bionic structure of the chip also facilitates changes in the infiltration state of aqueous solutions on the surface, thereby reducing the need for chemical modification techniques. Practical validation of the device was obtained through experimental results.

Acknowledgements. This work was supported by the National Science Foundation of China under Grant No. 62104148 and No. 61874033, and the State Key Laboratory of ASIC and Systems, Fudan University under Grant No. 2021KF001 and No. 2021MS001.

Conflict of Interests. The authors declare no conflict of interest.

References

1. Du, G., Fang, Q., den Toonder, J.M.J.: Microfluidics for cell-based high throughput screening platforms—a review. Anal. Chim. Acta **903**, 36–50 (2016)
2. Zhou, W.M., et al.: Microfluidics applications for high-throughput single cell sequencing. J. Nanobiotechnol. **19**(1), 312 (2021)
3. Klein, A.M., et al.: Droplet barcoding for single-cell transcriptomics applied to embryonic stem cells. Cell **161**, 1187–1201 (2015)
4. Cui, X., et al.: A fluorescent microbead-based microfluidic immunoassay chip for immune cell cytokine secretion quantification. Lab Chip **18**(3), 522–531 (2018)
5. Källberg, J., Xiao, W., Van Assche, D., Baret, J., Taly, V.: Frontiers in single cell analysis: multimodal technologies and their clinical perspectives. Lab Chip **22**, 243–2422 (2022)
6. Xu, J.G., Huang, M.S., Wang, H.F., Fang, Q.: Forming a large-scale droplet array in a microcage array chip for high-throughput screening. Anal. Chem. **91**(16), 10757–10763 (2019)
7. Yin, K., et al.: Femtosecond laser thermal accumulation-triggered micro-/nanostructures with patternable and controllable wettability towards liquid manipulating. Nanomicro Lett. **14**(1), 97 (2022)
8. Wu, D., et al.: 3D microfluidic cloth-based analytical devices on a single piece of cloth by one-step laser hydrophilicity modification. Lab Chip **21**(24), 4805–4813 (2021)
9. Rezaei, M., Radfar, P., Winter, M., McClements, L., Thierry, B., Warkiani, M.E.: Simple-to-operate approach for single cell analysis using a hydrophobic surface and nanosized droplets. Anal. Chem. **93**(10), 4584–4592 (2021)
10. Zhou, Y., et al.: Single-cell sorting using integrated pneumatic valve droplet microfluidic chip. Talanta **253**, 124044 (2023)

11. Easley, C.J., et al.: A fully integrated microfluidic genetic analysis system with sample-in-answer-out capability. Proc. Natl. Acad. Sci. U.S.A. **103**, 19272–19277 (2006)
12. Dangla, R., Kayi, S.C., Baroud, C.N.: Droplet microfluidics driven by gradients of confinement. Proc. Natl. Acad. Sci. U.S.A. **110**, 853–858 (2013)
13. He, Y., Lu, Z., Fan, H., Zhang, T.: A photofabricated honeycomb micropillar array for loss-free trapping of microfluidic droplets and application to digital PCR. Lab Chip **21**, 3933–3941 (2021)
14. Lin, H.Y., et al.: Highly efficient self-assembly of metallacages and their supramolecular catalysis behaviors in microdroplets. Angew. Chem. Int. Ed. Engl. **23**, e202301900 (2023)
15. Gao, Y., et al.: An enzyme-loaded metal-organic framework-assisted microfluidic platform enables single-cell metabolite analysis. Angew. Chem. Int. Ed. Engl. **5**, e202302000 (2023)
16. Du, L., Liu, H., Zhou, J.: Picoliter droplet array based on bioinspired microholes for in situ single-cell analysis. Microsyst. Nanoeng. **6**, 33 (2020)
17. Du, L., Riaud, A., Zhou, J.: Smearing observation of picoliter droplets pinning on bio-inspired negative lotus leaf replicas. IEEE Trans. Nanotechnol. **19**, 102–106 (2020)
18. Du, L., Wei, Y., Riaud, A., Zhou, J.: Anti-lotus leaf effect: smearing millions of picoliter droplets on bio-inspired artificial lotus leaf. In: IEEE 19th International Conference on Nanotechnology (IEEE-NANO), Macao, China, pp. 223–226 (2019)
19. Rong, N., Chen, K., Shao, J., Ouyang, Q., Luo, C.: A 3D scalable chamber-array chip for digital LAMP. Anal. Chem. **95**(20), 7830–7838 (2023)
20. Lin, D., et al.: One-step fabrication of droplet arrays using a biomimetic structural chip. ACS Appl. Mater. Interfaces **15**(13), 17413–17420 (2023)
21. Liu, M., Wang, S., Jiang, L.: Nature-inspired superwettability systems. Nat. Rev. Mater. **2**, 17036 (2017)
22. Ren, W.: Wetting transition on patterned surfaces: transition states and energy barriers. Langmuir **30**, 2879–2885 (2014)
23. Xin, B., Hao, J.: Reversibly switchable wettability. Chem. Soc. Rev. **39**, 769–782 (2010)
24. Xue, Y., Chu, S., Lv, P., Duan, H.: Importance of hierarchical structures in wetting stability on submersed superhydrophobic surfaces. Langmuir **28**, 9440–9450 (2012)
25. Yoshimitsu, Z., Nakajima, A., Watanabe, T., Hashimoto, K.: Effects of surface structure on the hydrophobicity and sliding behavior of water droplets. Langmuir **18**, 5818–5822 (2002)

Robotics in Sustainable Manufacturing for Carbon Neutrality

Research on Energy Consumption Prediction of Pump Truck Based on LSTM-Transformer

Kuiliang Liu, Guiqin Li$^{(\boxtimes)}$, Yicong Shen, Haoju Song, Xin Xiong, and Bin He

Shanghai Key Laboratory of Intelligent Manufacturing and Robotics, Shanghai University, Shanghai, China
leeching@shu.edu.cn

Abstract. The Transformer model based on Attention mechanism has the ability of highly parallel computing and capturing the dependency between data, providing a new means for time series prediction. However, while Transformer abandons convolution and recursive deduction in exchange for data association capture capability, it also produces data fragmentation problem. In order to overcome the difficulty of obtaining long time series feature data caused by the above reasons, this paper proposes an improved Attention model based on the fragment cycle mechanism, which can improve the computational efficiency and expand the learning range of long time series feature data. On the other hand, in order to improve the accuracy of information location after the learning range is expanded, this paper locates the information location based on the Long Short Time Memory (LSTM) coding method. The result of data analysis shows that the improved Transformer model based on LSTM has high accuracy for the prediction of pump truck energy consumption data in real environment. The comparison and analysis with the prediction results of LSTM and Transformer models prove the superiority of the method proposed in this paper, and provide a new method for the prediction of pump truck energy consumption.

Keywords: Energy consumption prediction · Transformer · LSTM · Fragment cycle mechanism · Pump Truck

1 Introduction

Energy prediction for pump trucks is one of the important tasks in the implementation of energy saving strategies for pump trucks, and is an important prerequisite for achieving energy saving, emission reduction and environmental protection. So accurate and fast energy prediction can help pump trucks to adjust their own operating status and working parameters in time, and also greatly reduce mechanical work energy consumption and improve operating efficiency.

The current methods for predicting energy consumption can be divided into traditional methods, and deep learning methods. The traditional includes regression models, etc., which require high stability for the original sequence and cannot handle non-linear relationships and large data [1]. Li Hui et al. [2] optimized the parameters of Recurrent Neural Network (RNN) by particle swarm algorithm, and the experimental results

© The Author(s), under exclusive license to Springer Nature Singapore Pte Ltd. 2023
H. Yang et al. (Eds.): ICIRA 2023, LNAI 14274, pp. 423–433, 2023.
https://doi.org/10.1007/978-981-99-6501-4_36

showed that the improved Particle Swarm Optimization (PSO)-RNN model had significant improvement in the accuracy of electricity load prediction. Long Short Term Memory (LSTM) is an improved version of RNN that can better learn to remember information from historical data over longer time spans [3]. Marino et al. [4] investigated a sequence to sequence (seq2seq) model based on long and short term neural networks, using the UCI The results showed that the seq2seq- LSTM prediction model performed well on different temporal granularity datasets. The Attention Mechanism, which was first applied to machine translation, can assign different weights to the hidden layer units of a neural network to enable the hidden layer to focus on more critical information, and this idea has been borrowed by many scholars for time series prediction [5]. Xu L [6] proposed a Transformer-based multi-layer attention mechanism model for predicting the short-term energy consumption of buildings and demonstrated the effectiveness of the model in an experiment. A local neighborhood set is dynamically generated for each location based on the current state. However, when Transformer handles some long-range correlated sequence prediction work [7], it needs to use a large amount of computational resources, so when using Transformer for training, the sequence needs to be segmented into a certain length and encoded with the same location, which causes information weakening between different segments of the data [8], making its long-range feature capture capability. At the same time, when using word vectors, the information of the words can be largely preserved if the word vectors are varied linearly. However, location encoding does not have such variability, so simply adding location encoding to a word vector cannot represent location information well.

This paper therefore proposes a method for predicting energy consumption based on a long short-term memory neural network, the LSTM- Transformer [9]. Firstly, the information weakening problem caused by Transformer segmented data is solved by a circularly expanding self-attentive mechanism [10]. Secondly, this paper proposes an LSTM-based location coding, which solves the problem of lack of global information linkage of the training data under the condition of large data training by the traditional positive-cosine absolute coding method. In contrast, LSTM position coding ensures the complete validity of the features [11], preserves the relative position information of the sequences and reflects the global characteristics. Although it has more parameters and a somewhat more complex model, it offers higher performance in the face of large amounts of data compared to the slightly faster convergence rate of GRU [12].

2 Theoretical Foundations

2.1 Modeling of LSTM

The LSTM is modeled for processing sequential data, it introduces a gate mechanism to control the flow and loss of features [13], and the LSTM structure is shown in Fig. 1.

The core parts of the internal structure of the LSTM are four parts: the forgetting gate, the input gate, the memory cell and the output gate. The forgetting gate f_t serves to discard the information that is not needed in the computation and subsequently decides which information in the memory cell C_t of the previous moment is forgotten; the input gate i_t will decide which information is retained in the output of the new input and the LSTM of the previous moment; the memory cell is used to save and pass the state

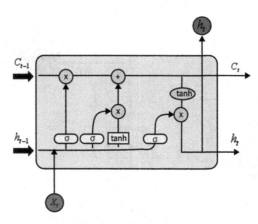

Fig. 1. LSTM structure

information of the current LSTM to the LSTM of the next moment; the output gate o_t takes the state of the cell after the selection of the input gate, the forgetting gate and the input gate together as the signal output of the current moment.

$$f_t = \sigma(W_f \bullet [x_t, h_{t-1}] + b_f)$$
$$i_t = \sigma(W_i \bullet [x_t, h_{t-1}] + b_i)$$
$$\tilde{C}_t = \tanh(W_c \bullet [x_t, h_{t-1}] + b_c) \tag{1}$$
$$C_t = f_t \bullet C_{t-1} + i_t \bullet \tilde{C}_t$$
$$o_t = \sigma(W_o \bullet [x_t, h_{t-1}] + b_o)$$

where σ is the sigmoid-activation formula, x_t is the input at moment t. h_t is the information at the previous moment. W_f, W_t, W_c, W_o are the weight parameters. b_f, b_i, b_c, b_0 are the bias parameters, and $\tilde{C}$ refers to the temporary memory cells at the current moment.

2.2 The Transformer Modeling

The Transformer is modeled as a novel machine translation model that does not use RNN methods and modules, but instead pioneers the attention mechanism as the core construct of its codec.

The overall structure of the Transformer model is shown in Fig. 2.

As in Fig. 2, the Transformer is an Encoder-Decoder structure; each layer in the Encoder consists of two sub-layers, a multi-headed self-attentive mechanism layer and a feed-forward linking layer, with an additional normalization processing layer between each of the sub-layers.

Meanwhile, each layer of Decoder consists of three sub-layers. Unlike the Encoder layer, the masking of values after moment t is required in order to avoid the influence of the real data after the current moment t on the prediction.

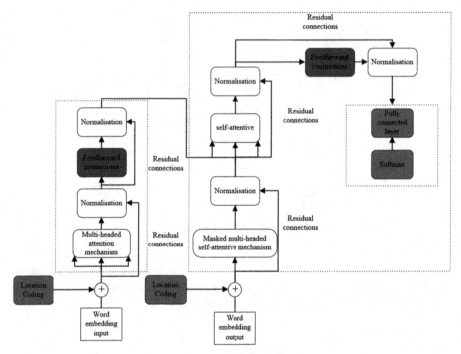

Fig. 2. Transformer structure

In the self-attentive mechanism model, the sequence of inputs is assumed to be $X = [x_1, ..., x_k]$ and the sequence of outputs is $H = [h_1, ..., h_k]$. The individual inputs are then mirrored into different spaces, resulting in three vectors, the query vector Q, the key vector K and the value vector V, respectively.

$$Q = W_Q X \in R^{D_k \times N} \tag{2}$$

$$K = W_k X \in R^{D_k \times N} \tag{3}$$

$$V = W_v X \in R^{D_k \times N} \tag{4}$$

where the input time series $X \in R^{D_k \times N}$, d_{mol} represents being at a particular moment in time, and d_t indicates how many sequence vectors are input, where W_q, W_k, W_v are the corresponding training parameters.

The output is H, calculated as follows:

$$H = Att(Q, K, V) = Vsoftmax(\frac{K^T Q}{\sqrt{D_k}}) \tag{5}$$

In this case, the normalisation calculation is performed using the normalised exponential function (softmax). And by dividing by $\sqrt{D_k}$ a to handle the occurrence of events that fall into a region of very small gradients.

In contrast, the multi-headed self-attentive mechanism [11] means that on a template that initially uses a single attention, we separately perform several different attention pooling and stitch their outputs together to produce a combined output, which is the multi-headed attention mechanism.

$$M_{head}(X_T) = W_{head}[H_1, ..., ..., H_n] \tag{6}$$

where W_{head} is the linear mapping matrix and $M_{head}(X_T)$ corresponds to the final distribution of the input X.

3 LSTM-Transformer Energy Consumption Prediction Based on Fragment Loop Mechanism

We propose in this paper an LSTM-Transformer energy consumption model based on a fragmented cyclic mechanism. The model takes as input a combination of attributes affecting the energy consumption of a pump truck [10] into a time series. A total of 31 operating conditions are set up by adjusting the three parameters of displacement, pressure and speed. The pressure and flow rate of the main pump outlet and the pressure of the main cylinder are measured under each of these 31 conditions.

In summary, the data input in this paper consists of the following characteristics: pressure in the large and small chambers of the left main cylinder, pressure in the large and small chambers of the right main cylinder, pressure in the oscillating cylinder, pressure in the pilot valve, pressure and flow rate at the P1 and P2 ports of the main pump, pressure at the outlet of the constant pressure and dosing pumps, as well as torque load factor, instantaneous fuel consumption, speed and other data collected via the CAN data bus. The data is sampled in 1 s steps and the time series is fed into the model using a sliding window. To speed up the training, normalised coding of each continuous variable is required.

An input layer, encoder, decoder and output layer are included in the energy consumption prediction model.

Firstly, in the input layer, the embedding of the energy consumption data and external features as $X = [\cdots, X_t, \cdots]$ is encoded in position by the LSTM method and the embedding is performed in X_t^0 summation manner to obtain a as the input side data of the encoder.

$$X_t^0 = X_t + W_{tt}LSTM(X_t) \tag{7}$$

The structure of the input layer is shown in Fig. 3:

Secondly, a sliding window mechanism is used in this paper to remove the results of encoder calculations cached in previous time slices and input them for subsequent calculations in order to do reuse of the previous state. The sliding window mechanism here is based on the fragment as the basic unit. The arrows in the diagram indicate the actual source of the currently computed fragment. The red arrows represent memory units from the previous layer, while the black arrows represent fragments from the same location on the previous layer (Fig. 4).

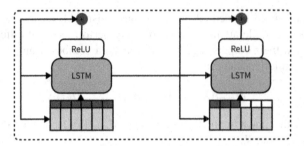

Fig. 3. Input layer structure

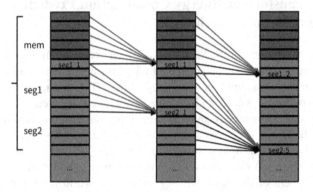

Fig. 4. Fragment cycle mechanism

At the same time, the higher the layer, the larger the expansion factor will be. Such an expansion mechanism will make the effective window size grow exponentially with the depth of the layer, by which a larger field of view can be obtained, and the learning field of view is calculated as.

$$A_e(X) = Concat(X_{T-(n_b-i)e}) \tag{8}$$

e is the expansion factor, n_b is the number of branches, X is the input sequence and Concat is the splicing function.

By splicing the sequences at level $l-1$ in the multi-headed self-attentive with the above formula, the attention at level l can be calculated to be

$$\tilde{X}_t^{l-1} = Concat(\{X_{T-ie}^{l-1} \mid 0 \le i \le n_b-1, i \in Z\}) \tag{9}$$

$$[Q_t^l; K_t^l; V_t^l] = [W_q X_t^{l-1}; W_k \tilde{X}_t^{l-1}; W_v \tilde{X}_t^{l-1}] \tag{10}$$

$$h = att((K^l, V^l), Q^l) \tag{11}$$

The structure of the decoding layer is shown in Fig. 5:

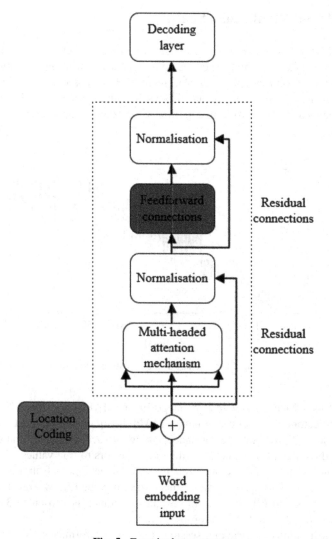

Fig. 5. Encoder layer structure

The model is optimized during the model training phase by using Adam's adaptive moment estimation method. The loss function uses Mean Square Error (MSE) to calculate the error between the prediction and the true value.

$$loss = \frac{1}{n} \sum (y_t - \hat{y}_t)^2 \tag{12}$$

where n is the number of samples, y_t is the actual value of energy consumption at moment t and $\hat{y}$ is the predicted value of energy consumption at moment t.

4   Calculation Results and Analysis

All the data was obtained from the data set in the data collection test bench built by the field pump truck. The data was collected under various working conditions such as 30 displacement 1100 rpm and 50 displacement 1100 rpm as the background, 20% of which was taken as the validation set and 80% as the training set, and the 30 displacement 1100 rpm data was used as working condition 1 for example, and the fuel consumption rate is shown in Fig. 6.

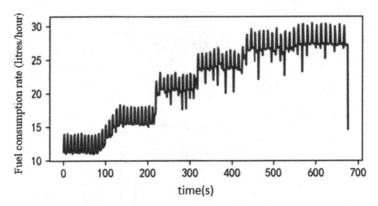

Fig. 6. Change chart of fuel consumption rate

The test uses Mean Absolute Percentage Error (MAPE) and Mean Square Error (MSE) as indicators of model performance, MAPE being one of the most popular indicators for assessing prediction performance, taking into account the full range of errors between predicted and true values, and the ratio of errors to true values. The MSE, on the other hand, is more effective in correcting for large deviations from the value.

In order to consider the speed and results of training, the LSTM-Transformer coder and decoder are set to 6 layers and the expansion branch is chosen to 3 in order to consider the correlation of the data for long sequences.

As the most intuitive metric in assessing predictive performance, this paper reflects the training efficiency in terms of MSE, as shown in Fig. 7. In the figure, it is found that the Transformer is trained very quickly and the MSE has dropped below 5 after 15,000 training cycles based on a very large amount of data. Although the initial training fluctuations are relatively large, this is due to the LSTM having to encode for the global position while filling the expansion cells to make the curve drop more smoothly.

In order to visually compare the effectiveness of the LSTM-Transformer model for energy consumption prediction, this paper focuses on the Transformer, LSTM as a control model, and tests the data with a displacement of 30 and 800 rpm as an example. The experimental results of the recorded models are shown in the table.

From Table 1, we can learn that the prediction accuracy of LSTM-Transformer is better than the other methods, and its MAPE is reduced by 0.226% and 1.008% respectively compared to the other two methods. MSE is reduced by 4.497 and 7.532

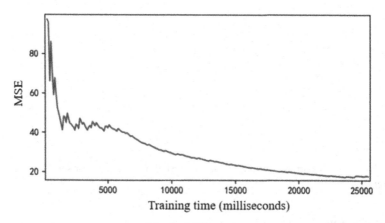

Fig. 7. MSE trends

compared to the other two methods, and the training time is significantly faster by comparing the Transformer method. This demonstrates that the methods described in this paper significantly reduce the training and prediction time while improving accuracy through LSTM and circular expansion mechanisms. Figure 8 shows a comparison of the energy consumption prediction curves for the same operating conditions for each method and a partial comparison of the test set of the energy consumption prediction curves for the same operating conditions for each method.

Table 1. Comparison of predictions by different methods

Methods	MAPE/%	MSE	MAE	Training time/s	Predicted time/s
LSTM-Transformer	1.135	17.901	2.9982	167	833
Transformer	1.362	22.398	4.3550	213	861
LSTM	2.143	25.433	5.2170	459	1866

The red solid line in the figure is the prediction result of the LSTM-Transformer method, the blue dotted line is the Transformer prediction result, the yellow solid line is the LSTM prediction result, and the purple solid line is the real value. The LSTM-Transformer method has the highest prediction error, followed by Transformer, and the LSTM-Transformer method has the highest agreement with the actual measurement results, which is due to the fact that this paper uses a fragment loop mechanism to effectively enhance the attentional field of view and improve the coherence of the location coding, thus significantly improving the prediction accuracy is significantly improved.

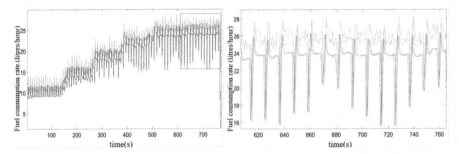

Fig. 8. Comparison Chart of Forecast by Different Methods and Comparison Chart of Test Set Prediction

5 Conclusion

An LSTM-Transformer-based method is proposed in this paper for predicting the energy consumption of pump trucks, firstly by optimizing the long sequence data set processing method, which is not available in the traditional Transformer, to improve the attentional field of the model, and then by improving the position information of the sequence through LSTM. The experimental results demonstrate that the loop expansion mechanism can effectively capture long sequence features in multiple dimensions, which can significantly improve the prediction accuracy while shortening the training time. At the same time, the multi-headed self-attentive mechanism we adopt can capture features targeted to different types of data.

Compared with other data prediction methods, the Transformer model still suffers from problems such as top-level gradient disappearance, and further optimization of the Transformer may be required in the future to improve the stability and convergence of the model in terms of local feature capture, loss of location information and gradient disappearance.

Acknowledgement. This research is partly supported by the National Key Research & Development Program of China (grant No. 2020YFB1709902).

References

1. Kang, C., Xia, Q., Liu, M., Xiang, N.: Special problems of regression analysis applied to load forecasting. Power Syst. Autom. (10), 38–41+49 (1998)
2. Hui, L., Jun, W.: The short-term load forecast based on the PSO-RNN. Softw. Guide **16**(11), 125–128 (2017)
3. Gao, Y., Jiang, G., Qin, X., Wang, Z.: LSTM-based algorithm for mobile object location prediction. Comput. Sci. Explor. **13**(01), 23–34 (2019)
4. Marino, D.L., Amarasinghe, K., Manic, M.: Deep neural network based energy load forecasting for buildings. In: IECON 2016 - 42nd Annual Conference of the IEEE Industrial Electronics Society, pp. 7046–7051 (2016)
5. Vaswani, A., Shazeer, N., Parmar, N., et al.: Attention is all you need. In: 31 Conference on Neural Information Processing Systems (NIPS), December 48, A, pp. 5998-6008 (2017)

6. Xu, L., Zhang, S., Yang, Q.: A multi-level attention mechanism for short-term building energy consumption forecasting using transformer. Buildings **03**, 151–156 (2021)
7. Zhang, C.H., Luo, W., Lin, K.Z.: Grid merge unit level forecasting based on time series analysis. J. Data Acquis. Process. **37**(05), 1169–1178 (2022)
8. Wang, J., Li, X., Jia, H., et al.: Predicting stock market volatility from candlestick charts: a multiple attention mechanism graph neural network approach. Math. Probl. Eng. **2022** (2022)
9. Zeng, Y., Zeng, F., Wang, C., Liu, L., Cai, Y.: Research on energy-saving control method of concrete pump truck. Eng. Mach. **41**(04), 20–24+98 (2010)
10. Zhang, C., Wang, W., Du, Y.H., et al.: Group recommendation algorithm combining context information and self attention mechanism. Appl. Res. Comput. **40**(02), 498–503 (2023)
11. Lim, B., Arik, S.O., Loeff, N., et al.: Temporal fusion transformers for interpretable multi-horizon time series forecasting. Int. J. Forecast. **37**, 1748–1764 (2021)
12. Hu, Y., Xiao, F.: Network self attention for forecasting time series. Appl. Soft Comput. **124**, 109092 (2022)
13. Luong, M.T., Pham, H., Manning, C.D.: Effective approaches to attention-based neural machine translation. arXiv preprint arXiv:1508.04025 (2015)

Magnetically Controllable Liquid Metal Droplet Robots

Peiran Zhao[1], Liang Yan[1,2,3,4(✉)], Xiaoshan Gao[1], and Suwan Bu[1]

[1] School of Automation Science and Electrical Engineering, Beihang University,
Beijing 100191, China
lyan1991@gmail.com
[2] Ningbo Institute of Technology, Beihang University, Ningbo 315800, China
[3] Tianmushan Laboratory, Hangzhou 310023, China
[4] Science and Technology on Aircraft Control Laboratory, Beihang University, Beijing 100191,
China

Abstract. Magnetically actuated miniature robots exhibit great potential in lab-on-a-chip and biomedical applications. However, the existing soft robots made from elastomers have limited functionality and are unable to operate in very narrow environments such as channels much smaller than their size due to their limited deformability. Herein, a magnetically actuated millirobot based on liquid metal is proposed to address the above problems. The droplet robot is fabricated by mixing iron particles and a gallium-indium droplet. The static analysis of the robot is conducted, and the dynamic equation is established. The control strategy is analyzed, the experimental setup is designed, and related experiments are conducted. In the experiments, the droplet robot demonstrates remarkable flexibility and softness when navigating freely in narrow channels, allowing it to easily pass through confined spaces much smaller than its size. The demonstrated capabilities of the droplet present a promising potential for its application in lab-on-a-chip or biomedical devices.

Keywords: Soft robots · Millirobots · Liquid metal · Magnetic control

1 Introduction

Miniature soft robots have received much attention and arise the interest of researchers in recent years due to their outstanding performance such as the ability to navigate in confined and narrow spaces [1, 2]. Various actuation methods have been employed for the movement of miniature robots, including electrical [3, 4], chemical [5, 6], and optical [7, 8] methods. However, magnetically actuation is particularly effective for miniature robots due to its non-invasive ability to enable movement and operation in non-transparent and constrained spaces. Therefore, they have wide applications, for example, acting as pumps or valves in microfluidic chips [9], appealing for lab-on-a-chip [10], and biomedical devices [11, 12]. At present, rigid robots are limited in their functionalities, for they cannot work in spaces smaller than themselves. On the other hand, although soft robots made from elastomer can deform and access unreachable

© The Author(s), under exclusive license to Springer Nature Singapore Pte Ltd. 2023

H. Yang et al. (Eds.): ICIRA 2023, LNAI 14274, pp. 434–442, 2023.
https://doi.org/10.1007/978-981-99-6501-4_37

regions, their deformability is limited, making it difficult for them to adapt to more working environments. For instance, when navigating through narrow and constrained channels that are much smaller than the robot's size, these robots may fail to maneuver effectively due to their limited deformability and predesigned shapes. This issue poses a significant challenge to their practical applications. Furthermore, rigid robots and soft robots made from elastomer cannot achieve self-healing once they are injured or split for cooperative motions. This limitation can further restrict their potential applications. In other words, when rigid robots and soft robots made from elastomer encounter damage during operation, they cannot repair themselves, which could lead to permanent malfunctioning or even complete failure. This drawback is particularly concerning for applications where robots must perform continuous and prolonged tasks without human intervention, such as in medical procedures or environmental monitoring.

In this work, a magnetically actuated millirobot based on liquid metal is proposed to address the above problems. Based on our previous work [13], more detailed theoretical analysis of the robot are carried out. The static analysis of the droplet robot is conducted, the forces exerted on the robot are analyzed, and the dynamic equation is established. Based on theoretical analysis, the magnetically actuated control strategy is analyzed. The experimental setup is designed to realize the control strategy, and experiments are conducted to explore the relationship between the lag distance and the air gap and demonstrate the outstanding performance of the droplet robot in navigating in narrow and confined channels. The results show the impressive capabilities of droplet robots.

2   Mechanism and Methodology

2.1   Static Analysis of the Droplet Robot

The droplet robots cannot keep their spherical shape and will deform when they contact a flat surface due to their flexibility and fluidity, as shown in Fig. 1a. Consider a droplet robot with a constant volume of V on a flat solid substrate. It is evident that the liquid-air interface of the drop loses its spherical shape under gravity and can be represented by an oblate spheroid, which is formed by rotating an ellipse [14]

$$(y - \alpha R)^2 + \alpha^3 x^2 = \alpha^2 R^2 \tag{1}$$

around the y-axis. Where αR and $R/\sqrt{\alpha}$ are the hemi-axes of the ellipse and dimensionless parameter α is in the interval $(0, 1)$. The internal pressure P of the droplet robot can be obtained by the Young-Laplace equation

$$P = P_0 + \frac{2\gamma_{lv}}{R} \tag{2}$$

where P_0 is the atmospheric pressure, γ_{lv} is the surface tension of the liquid-air surface, and R is the radius of the droplet robot. Since there is no other external force, the pressure at the bottom of the droplet on the contact surface is equal to the gravity

$$\begin{cases} \Delta P \cdot \pi l^2 = \rho g V \\ \Delta P = \frac{2\gamma_{lv}}{R} \end{cases} \tag{3}$$

The oblate spheroid droplet robot forms a contact angle between the robot surface and the contact surface because of the deformation of the droplet robot. The contact angle θ can be expressed by Young's equation

$$\cos \theta = \frac{\gamma_{sv} - \gamma_{sl}}{\gamma_{lv}} \tag{4}$$

where γ_{sv} is the surface tension of the solid-air surface and γ_{sl} is the surface tension of the solid-liquid surface. In addition, the contact angle of a droplet on the solid substrate can be analyzed by the energy method, and the contact angle can be calculated by [14]

$$\begin{cases} \cos \theta = \frac{\beta - 1}{h(\alpha, \beta)} \\ h(\alpha, \beta) = \sqrt{1 - (1 - \alpha^3)\beta(2 - \beta)} \\ \beta = \frac{b}{R} \end{cases} \tag{5}$$

where dimensionless parameter β is less than 1. The droplet robot is hydrophobic when the contact angle is higher than 90°. The contact angle of the droplet robot in this work is measured at about 120°, thereby the droplet robot is hydrophobic.

2.2 Kinetics Analysis of the Droplet Robot

Figure 1b shows the forces exerted on the droplet robot, including the magnetic force F_m, the resistance of the contact angle change F_c, the viscous resistance F_f, the normal force N, and gravity G. The dominant driving force of the droplet robot is the magnetic force F_m, which arises from the effect of the magnetic forces exerted on all iron particles contained within the droplet. The strength and gradient of the magnetic field are key factors influencing F_m. Specifically, the volume force f_m associated with F_m can be mathematically represented as follow

$$f_m = \frac{\mu_0}{2} \nabla(\chi_m H^2) \tag{6}$$

where $\mu_0 = 4\pi \times 10^{-7}$ H/m is the vacuum permeability, χ_m is the magnetic susceptibility of the droplet robot, and H represents the magnetic field strength. The relationship between F_m and f_m satisfies $F_m = \int f_m dV$. F_m is the main driving force, and the motion direction is always the same as the horizontal component of F_m.

When a droplet attains equilibrium, the front and rear angles of the droplet robot are equal. However, when there is a rapid change in the velocity of the droplet robot, its front and rear contact angles are different, leading to the hysteresis of contact angle. This phenomenon is similar to droplet motion on lotus leaves [15]. The resistance of the contact angle change F_c can be expressed as

$$F_c = 2R\gamma_{lv}(\cos \theta_1 - \cos \theta_2) \tag{7}$$

where θ_1 and θ_2 are the front and rear contact angles, respectively. Droplet robots generally move at a slow velocity (mm/s), thereby F_c is generally ignored.

The viscous resistance F_f is the force on an object in viscous laminar flow, and it is the main resistance on the droplet robot. At low Reynolds numbers, F_f can be expressed by the Stokes formula

$$F_f = 6\pi \eta v R \tag{8}$$

where η is the dynamic viscosity, and v is the velocity of the droplet robot. There is a correction factor (0.54) for the hydrophobic droplets with large three-phase contact angles [16].

Droplet robots are also affected by G and N. In a two-dimensional plane, the resultant force of G and N is zero. Furthermore, interfacial tension force exists on the droplet surface, and it can affect the motion flexibility and deformation. The higher the interfacial tension force is, the more challenging it is for the droplet robot to deform and the nimbler the robot moves. The interfacial tension force can be expressed as follows [17]

$$f_s = -\gamma_{lv}\kappa N_u D(d) \tag{9}$$

where κ is the average radius of curvature, N_u is the normal vector of the liquid surface, and $D(d)$ is the incremental function which can be expressed as

$$D(d) = \begin{cases} \frac{1+\cos(\pi d/\varepsilon)}{2\varepsilon} & |d| < \varepsilon \\ 0 & else \end{cases} \tag{10}$$

where d is the distance from the point to the interface and ε is a given tiny value. When the absolute value of d is smaller than ε, then it can be inferred that the point locates within the boundary of the interface. Conversely, the point locates outside the boundary of the interface.

The droplet robot motion can be described by the continuity equation and Navier-Stokes equation. These fundamental equations serve as the governing equations

$$\begin{cases} \frac{\partial \rho}{\partial t} + \nabla \cdot (\rho u) = 0 \\ \rho \frac{\partial u}{\partial t} + \rho u \cdot \nabla u = -\nabla p + \eta \nabla^2 u + f_m + f_s \end{cases} \tag{11}$$

where ρ is density, u is velocity, and p is pressure. The continuity equation concisely describes the conservation of mass, while the Navier-Stokes equation describes the conservation of momentum in the fluid. The influence of inertial forces on the droplet shape can be neglected due to the low velocity of the droplet robot. Consequently, the dynamic equations can be also expressed as

$$m\frac{dv}{dt} = F_m + F_c + F_f \tag{12}$$

where m is the quality of the robot. Figure 1a shows the relationship between V and R satisfies the following equation

$$V = \frac{\pi R^3}{3}(2 - \beta)^2(1 + \beta) \tag{13}$$

Differentiating both sides of the above equation for volume, the simplified equation is the universal dynamic equation

$$\rho g \frac{dv}{dt} = \frac{\mu_0}{2} \nabla(\chi_m H^2) + \frac{6\eta v}{R^2(2-\beta)^2(1+\beta)} \tag{14}$$

Therefore, H is the only parameter that needs to be changed to control the motion of the droplet robot.

2.3 Control Strategy of the Droplet Robot

A cylindrical permanent magnet is used to produce the actuating magnetic field. The magnetic field can be calculated as

$$H_m = \frac{B_r}{4\pi\mu_0} \int_{-h}^{0} \int_{0}^{2\pi} \frac{\begin{bmatrix} i & j & k \\ -r\sin\theta & r\cos\theta & 0 \\ x-r\cos\theta & y-r\sin\theta & z-z_0 \end{bmatrix}}{K_m} d\theta dz_0 \tag{15}$$

where B_r is the remanence of the magnet, h is the height of the magnet, x, y, and z are the coordinate of the robot in the coordinate system in Fig. 1c, r is the radius of the cylindrical magnet, and K_m can be expressed as follows

$$K_m = [x^2 + y^2 + r^2 + (z-z_0)^2 - 2xr\cos\theta - 2yr\sin\theta]^{3/2} \tag{16}$$

The permanent is installed on a coordinate robot or a robotic arm as an end-effector. Therefore, the actuating magnetic field can move with the coordinate robot or robotic arm. As shown in Fig. 1d, the coordinate of the origin of the magnetic field coordinate system in the absolute coordinate system is (x_m, y_m, z_m), and the coordinate of the droplet robot is (x_d, y_d, z_d). The coordinate of the droplet robot in the magnetic field coordinate system can be expressed as

$$\begin{cases} x = x_d - x_m \\ y = y_d - y_m \\ z = z_d - z_m \end{cases} \tag{17}$$

Combing Eqs. 14–17, the governing equation of the droplet robot can be expressed as follows

$$\begin{cases} \rho g \frac{dv}{dt} = \frac{\mu_0}{2} \nabla(\chi_m H^2) + \frac{6\eta v}{R^2(2-\beta)^2(1+\beta)} \\ H_x = \frac{B_r}{4\pi\mu_0} \int_{-h}^{0} \int_{0}^{2\pi} \frac{(z_d - z_m - z_0)r\cos\theta}{K_m} d\theta dz_0 \\ H_y = \frac{B_r}{4\pi\mu_0} \int_{-h}^{0} \int_{0}^{2\pi} \frac{(z_0 - z_d + z_m)r\sin\theta}{K_m} d\theta dz_0 \\ H_z = \frac{B_r}{4\pi\mu_0} \int_{-h}^{0} \int_{0}^{2\pi} \frac{-(y_d - y_m - r\sin\theta)r\sin\theta - (x_d - x_m - r\cos\theta)r\cos\theta}{K_m} d\theta dz_0 \\ K_m = [(x_d - x_m)^2 + (y_d - y_m)^2 + r^2 + (z_d - z_m - z_0)^2 \\ \quad - 2(x_d - x_m)r\cos\theta - 2(y_d - y_m)r\sin\theta]^{3/2} \end{cases} \tag{18}$$

Therefore, the position of the droplet robot (x_d, y_d, z_d) can be obtained by solving Eq. 18 with the input parameter (x_m, y_m, z_m).

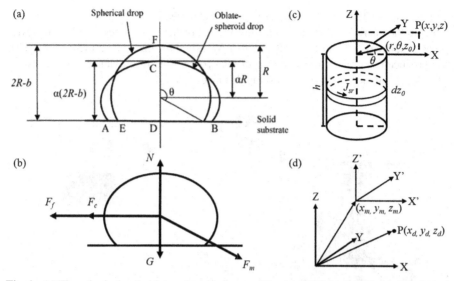

Fig. 1. (a) The spherical and oblate-spheroid shapes of the droplet deposited on a solid substrate [14]. (b) Force analysis diagram of the droplet robot. (c) The parameters schematic of the cylindrical magnet. (d) The relationship between the two coordinate systems.

3   Experiments

3.1   The Experimental Setup

The workbench is capable of producing four degrees of freedom (DOF) motions, three of which are translations (in the X, Y, and Z directions), and one is a rotation (as shown in Fig. 2a). The X and Y translational DOF determine the position of the droplet robot, while the Z translational DOF determines the distance between the surface of the permanent magnet and the droplet robot, and the rotational DOF determines the direction of the permanent magnet. The workbench is controlled by an Arduino Mega 2560, and the MCU receives the signal from a computer to execute the predetermined path. With regards to power consumption, the system's maximum power usage is approximately 45 W; typically, 15–30 W is required for regular operation. The rated voltage of the workbench is 12 V, and it is powered by a DC power supply. A Gauss meter with a probe is utilized to measure the magnetic flux density.

3.2   Hysteresis Analysis of Droplet Robots

There is a lag distance between the droplet robot and the magnet due to the forces analyzed in Sect. 2.2 (Fig. 2b). The lag distance is an important factor to evaluate motion accuracy. The smaller the lag distance, the more consistent the droplet robot trajectory is with the desired one. Therefore, the lag distance should be controlled as small as possible. The air gap ΔR is the most important factor influencing the lag distance. The relationship between the lag distance and ΔR is analyzed and the result is shown in Fig. 2c. The curve declines gradually at the beginning and bottoms out at 3.15 mm with a lag distance of 1.30 mm. Specifically, when ΔR increases, F_m and N decrease, which results in the decrease of resistance. Thus, the lag distance becomes smaller. However, the lag distance rises from 1.30 to 3.25 when ΔR is in the range of 3.15 to 5 mm, because F_m is reduced too much to actuate the droplet robot effectively. Hence, 1.3 mm is the optimum size to achieve the smallest lag distance.

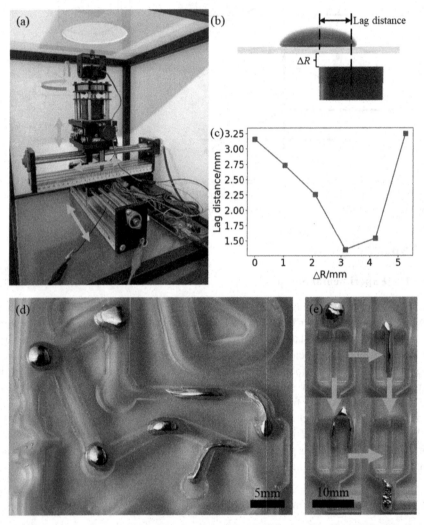

Fig. 2. (a) The experimental setup. (b) Schematic diagram of the lag distance and the air gap ΔR. (c) The relationship between the lag distance and ΔR. (d) The droplet robot navigates freely and flexibly in the small model with different channels. (e) Two ways for the droplet robot to pass through the multi-channel.

3.3 Motion in Narrow Channels

One of the primary advantages of the droplet robot is its unique ability to passively adapt to confined spaces due to its inherent softness and flexibility. Unlike most rigid or traditional soft robots, the droplet robot can navigate narrow channels and tight spaces without causing damage to its surroundings. To understand the mobility and flexibility of the droplet robot in such scenarios better, a small testing model with various channels was designed to provide different motion environments, as depicted in Fig. 2d. This figure shows various ways that the droplet robot can navigate through narrow channels, effectively demonstrating the softness and flexibility of the droplet robot.

Figure 2e provides two distinct ways for the droplet robot to pass through narrow multi-channel structures. The top right figure depicts a scenario where the robot squeezes directly through a single channel. However, it is worth noting that larger-sized droplet robots may not be able to pass through similarly-sized channels easily and may even cause breakage. Alternatively, the droplet robot can split itself and pass through two narrow channels simultaneously. This splitting process can be achieved by directly hitting the channel wall, and this method allows for immediate splitting and achieves smooth and efficient motions. Figures 2d and 2e highlight the softness and flexibility of the droplet robot. Overall, the droplet robot's ability to move freely within narrow spaces while remaining undamaged is a clear advantage over traditional robotic systems, showcasing the potential to revolutionize various industries and applications.

4 Conclusion

In this work, a magnetically actuated millirobot based on liquid metal is reported, which is realized by encapsulating iron particles within a gallium-indium droplet. Through this mixing process, the magnetism of the gallium-indium droplet is significantly augmented without incurring undue alteration to its intrinsic characteristics. The droplet robot exhibits remarkable capabilities that surpass those previously observed in conventional elastomer-based soft robots. The enhanced flexibility and adaptability of the droplet robot are attributed to the liquid nature of gallium-indium alloy, as well as the inherent magnetism of the iron particles. Consequently, these features enable the droplet robot to perform a diverse range of complex functions with ease and precision. These demonstrated capabilities provide more possibilities for applications in biomedical devices.

Acknowledgments. This research was funded by the National Natural Science Foundation of China (NSFC) under grants 52130505, 52205044, and 51875013, the China Postdoctoral Science Foundation under grant 2022M720351, the Ningbo key scientific and technological project under grant 2022Z040, the National Key R&D Program under grant 2022YFE0113700, the Aeronautical Science Foundation of China (ASFC) under grant 20200007051002, and Fundamental Research Funds for the Central Universities.

References

1. Kim, Y., Zhao, X.: Magnetic soft materials and robots. Chem. Rev. **122**, 5317–5364 (2022). https://doi.org/10.1021/acs.chemrev.1c00481

2. Sitti, M.: Miniature soft robots — road to the clinic. Nat. Rev. Mater. **3**, 74–75 (2018). https://doi.org/10.1038/s41578-018-0001-3

3. Gupta, B., Goudeau, B., Garrigue, P., Kuhn, A.: Bipolar conducting polymer crawlers based on triple symmetry breaking. Adv. Funct. Mater. **28**, 1705825 (2018). https://doi.org/10.1002/adfm.201705825

4. Yang, C., et al.: Hydrogel walkers with electro-driven motility for cargo transport. Sci. Rep. **5**, 13622 (2015). https://doi.org/10.1038/srep13622

5. Tang, S., et al.: Enzyme-powered Janus platelet cell robots for active and targeted drug delivery. Sci. Robot. **5**, eaba6137 (2020). https://doi.org/10.1126/scirobotics.aba6137

6. Li, A., Li, H., Li, Z., Zhao, Z., Li, K., Li, M., Song, Y.: Programmable droplet manipulation by a magnetic-actuated robot. Sci. Adv. **6**, eaay5808 (2020). https://doi.org/10.1126/sciadv.aay5808

7. Shahsavan, H., et al.: Bioinspired underwater locomotion of light-driven liquid crystal gels. Proc. Natl. Acad. Sci. **117**, 5125–5133 (2020). https://doi.org/10.1073/pnas.1917952117

8. Palagi, S., et al.: Structured light enables biomimetic swimming and versatile locomotion of photoresponsive soft microrobots. Nat. Mater. **15**, 647–653 (2016). https://doi.org/10.1038/nmat4569

9. Yang, R.-J., Hou, H.-H., Wang, Y.-N., Fu, L.-M.: Micro-magnetofluidics in microfluidic systems: a review. Sens. Actuators B Chem. **224**, 1–15 (2016). https://doi.org/10.1016/j.snb.2015.10.053

10. Xue, R., et al.: Small universal mechanical module driven by a liquid metal droplet. Lab Chip **21**, 2771–2780 (2021). https://doi.org/10.1039/D1LC00206F

11. Dupont, P.E., et al.: A decade retrospective of medical robotics research from 2010 to 2020. Sci. Robot. **6**, eabi8017 (2021). https://doi.org/10.1126/scirobotics.abi8017

12. Ahmed, R., Ilami, M., Bant, J., Beigzadeh, B., Marvi, H.: A shapeshifting ferrofluidic robot. Soft Robot. **8**, 687–698 (2021). https://doi.org/10.1089/soro.2019.0184

13. Zhao, P., Yan, L., Gao, X.: Magnetic liquid metal droplet robot with multifunction and high output force in Milli-Newton. Soft Rob. (2023). https://doi.org/10.1089/soro.2022.0183

14. Whyman, G., Bormashenko, E.: Oblate spheroid model for calculation of the shape and contact angles of heavy droplets. J. Colloid Interface Sci. **331**, 174–177 (2009). https://doi.org/10.1016/j.jcis.2008.11.040

15. Zhao, Y.: Surface and Interface Mechanics. Science Press, Beijing (2012)

16. Petkov, J.T., Denkov, N.D., Danov, K.D., Velev, O.D., Aust, R., Durst, F.: Measurement of the drag coefficient of spherical particles attached to fluid interfaces. J. Colloid Interface Sci. **172**, 147–154 (1995). https://doi.org/10.1006/jcis.1995.1237

17. Liu, J., Tan, S.-H., Yap, Y.F., Ng, M.Y., Nguyen, N.-T.: Numerical and experimental investigations of the formation process of ferrofluid droplets. Microfluid. Nanofluid. **11**, 177–187 (2011). https://doi.org/10.1007/s10404-011-0784-7

Comparative Carbon Footprint and Environmental Impacts of $LiFePO_4$ - $LiCo_xNi_yMn_{(1-x-y)}O_2$ Hybrid Batteries Manufacturing

Quanwei Chen[1], Xin Lai[1(✉)] , Junjie Chen[1], Shuai Yao[1], Guan Wang[1], Yi Guo[2], Xuebing Han[2], and Yuejiu Zheng[1]

[1] School of Mechanical Engineering, University of Shanghai for Science and Technology, Shanghai 200093, China
`laixin@usst.edu.cn`
[2] State Key Laboratory of Automotive Safety and Energy, Tsinghua University, Beijing 100084, China

Abstract. Although the electrification of the transportation sector is crucial to mitigating climate change and the energy crisis, understanding the carbon footprint and environmental impact of the manufacturing process for the power batteries used in electric vehicles is limited. The carbon footprint and environmental impacts of the manufacturing process of $LiCo_xNi_yMn_{(1-x-y)}O_2$ (NCM), $LiFePO_4$ (LFP), and $LiFePO_4$ - $LiCo_xNi_yMn_{(1-x-y)}O_2$ (LFP-NCM) batteries are quantified and compared based on life cycle assessment method. The results show that NCM batteries have the highest carbon footprint (96.2 kg CO2-eq/kWh) among the batteries studied. The carbon footprint of the cathode material and assembly process accounts for more than 60.0% of the NCM manufacturing process. LFP-NCM batteries can reduce the carbon footprint by 3.4% compared to NCM while improving economic efficiency and safety. The mineral resource scarcity of NCM is 12.6% and 75.5% higher than that of LFP-NCM and LFP batteries, respectively. The LFP batteries significantly impact freshwater eutrophication and human carcinogenic toxicity. The environmental impacts of the manufacturing processes of NCM and LFP batteries can be better balanced by LFP-NCM batteries. This study provides a reference for optimizing battery manufacturing processes and promoting low-carbon and sustainable development in the transportation industry.

Keywords: Hybrid battery · $LiCo_xNi_yMn_{(1-x-y)}O_2$ · $LiFePO_4$ · Carbon footprint · Environmental impacts

1 Introduction

Transportation significantly contributes to climate change and energy consumption, with its greenhouse gas (GHG) emissions accounting for about a quarter of total energy emissions [1]. Electric vehicles (EVs) produce zero greenhouse gas and pollutant emissions

© The Author(s), under exclusive license to Springer Nature Singapore Pte Ltd. 2023
H. Yang et al. (Eds.): ICIRA 2023, LNAI 14274, pp. 443–453, 2023.
https://doi.org/10.1007/978-981-99-6501-4_38

during use, while also not consuming fossil fuels. Replacing fossil-fueled vehicles with EVs is critical to decarbonizing transportation and mitigating the energy crisis [2, 3]. Current EVs are exclusively powered by lithium-ion batteries (LIBs) due to their high energy density, long lifespan, and low weight [4]. The global shipment of LIBs in 2021 was 562.4 GWh, and it is estimated that the LIBs demand for EVs will reach 740 GWh by 2030 [5, 6]. The Chinese government's proposed strategy to reach a "carbon peak" by 2030 and achieve "carbon neutrality" by 2060 represents a significant contribution to the worldwide effort towards reducing greenhouse gas emissions and promoting a low-carbon economy. With the sharp increase in battery production and sales, the carbon footprint and environmental impacts of the LIBs manufacturing process have attracted widespread attention from governments, enterprises, and consumers.

Life cycle assessment (LCA) is a standardized method for systematically quantifying the environmental aspects and impacts of a product, system, or service throughout its life cycle [3, 7] and arousing the interest of many scholars in quantitatively studying the environmental impacts of battery manufacturing processes. Current LCA studies on battery manufacturing mainly focus on the following areas: (1) Carbon footprint and environmental impacts assessment of different LIBs manufacturing processes. The carbon emissions during the production phase of $LiCo_xNi_yMn(1-x-y)O_2$ (NCM) batteries are 91.21 kg CO2-eq/kWh, with the production of the cathode being the primary source of carbon footprint in battery manufacturing [2]. However, the energy consumption during the $LiFePO_4$ (LFP) [8], lithium-sulfur [9], and lithium-oxygen batteries [10] manufacturing process is lower, resulting in less carbon footprint and environmental impact because these batteries do not contain high-priced metal elements such as nickel, cobalt, and manganese in the cathode material. (2) Comparative assessment of carbon footprint and environmental impacts of batteries with different material systems. LIBs have a lower carbon footprint and environmental impact than lead-acid and nickel-cadmium batteries [11, 12]. At the same time, the carbon footprint of LIBs during the assembly stage is significantly lower than that of nickel-metal hydride batteries. And the environmental impacts caused by energy consumption during manufacturing are also lower [13].

A battery of different types of batteries connected in series or parallel is called a hybrid battery. By complementing the advantages and disadvantages of different types of batteries, it aims to reduce costs, extend service life, and improve safety [14]. And it has attracted widespread attention in the industry. However, there is almost no assessment of the carbon footprint and environmental impacts of manufacturing such hybrid batteries. In this study, the manufacturing process of LIBs is modeled by the LCA method. And the carbon footprint and environmental impacts of the manufacturing processes of $LiFePO_4$ - $LiCo_xNi_yMn(1-x-y)O_2$ (LFP-NCM), NCM, and LFP batteries are compared. The key processes and materials affecting the LIBs manufacturing process's carbon footprint and environmental indicators are identified. This study provides a reference for process optimization for battery manufacturers from an environmental perspective and promotes the low-carbon and sustainable development of the battery and transportation industries.

2 Methods and Modeling

The carbon footprint and environmental impacts of LIBs manufacturing are modeled and analyzed by the LCA method in this study. As an assessment tool, LCA is mainly used to assess and account for a product or service's energy consumption and environmental impact throughout its life cycle, from cradle to grave [15]. LCA consists of four stages: goal and scope definition, inventory analysis, impact assessment, and interpretation [16, 17]. Inventory analysis is the core of LCA and involves compiling and evaluating the inputs, outputs, and potential environmental impacts during the life cycle of a product or service.

2.1 Goal and Scope Definition

The present LCA study aims to investigate the carbon footprint and environmental impacts in the manufacturing of LIBs. This study provides a basis for formulating related policies and promotes improving LIBs' manufacturing technology. Meanwhile, driving the development of carbon neutrality and the circular economy in the transportation industry. A quantitative comparison is made of the carbon footprint and multiple environmental indicators while manufacturing NCM, LFP, and LFP-NCM batteries. And the key processes and materials affecting the environmental indicators in the battery manufacturing process are identified. In this study, the system boundary of the life cycle of LIBs manufacturing is displayed in Fig. 1. The baseline geographical boundary is limited to China, and the inventory parameters of materials and energy inputs in the manufacturing process reflect the average level of China's industry. The manufacturing of LIBs is a "cradle-to-gate" process, including extracting and processing raw materials, manufacturing components, and assembling batteries. The carbon footprint and environmental impacts of manufacturing stages for different batteries are compared and analyzed within the same boundary scope.

The functional unit is the basic unit of LCA analysis, determining the comparison benchmark and the accuracy of the evaluation results for a product or service. The functional unit provides the basis for quantifying and comparing different products and stages [18]. In this study, the functional unit is defined as the nominal capacity of 1 kWh LIBs, emphasizing the environmental burden brought by actual output. Data collected during the LIBs manufacturing stage are all converted into functional units for the calculation to ensure quantitative assessment and cross-comparability of different batteries.

2.2 Life Cycle Inventory Analysis

NCM and LFP Batteries Manufacturing

As depicted in Fig. 1, battery manufacturing is a complex process that primarily involves extracting and processing raw materials, manufacturing electrodes, and other components, and assembling the battery [2]. The difference between NCM and LFP batteries is reflected in the different materials used for the cathode. The cathode materials of the NCM batteries include lithium, nickel, cobalt, and manganese. Which usually require stages such as exploration, development, ore selection, and mining. Lithium materials

Fig. 1. The system boundary of the life cycle of LIBs manufacturing.

mainly come from pegmatite and brine, nickel mainly comes from laterite nickel ore and sulfide nickel ore, and cobalt mainly comes from sedimentary cobalt-manganese ore [19]. Metals such as nickel, cobalt, and manganese are mixed with lithium salts in a particular ratio and then precipitated and heat-treated to produce precursor materials. The cathode material of the LFP batteries includes elements such as phosphorus, iron, and lithium. Iron powder, oxidants, and PH-regulating reagents are mixed proportionately to obtain an initial iron phosphate product. Then, iron phosphate and lithium salt are dispersed and ground together. After granulation and drying, they are sintered at high temperatures to obtain LFP batteries cathode materials [20].

The anode materials of both NCM and LFP batteries are artificial graphite. It's made from materials such as petroleum coke and asphalt through high-temperature graphitization and carbonization. The function of the separator is to prevent contact between the cathode and anode and short circuits between ions. Typically consisting of polypropylene and polyethylene [15]. The electrolyte of LIBs is usually lithium hexafluorophosphate (LiPF6), made by mixing lithium carbonate, fluorides, and phosphates. LiPF6 is heated and mixed with organic solvents (such as ethylene carbonate and ethyl methyl carbonate) under certain conditions to make the electrolyte [21]. In the battery assembly phase, active materials, conductive agents, and binders are mixed and coated on a foil body, then baked, rolled, and cut. The cathode, anode, and separator are stacked together after drying and injection, encapsulated, formed, and sorted. Then, undergo inspection to ensure the battery's safety, reliability, and stability. To ensure that battery performance is not negatively impacted by temperature and humidity, the stacking, injecting, forming, and sorting need to be carried out in a drying room. The data utilized in this study was obtained from previous research [6, 22].

Hybrid Batteries

In traditional hybrid systems, LIBs were usually directly paralleled with supercapacitors or other power electronic devices to form parallel systems [23, 24]. As shown in Fig. 2, the subject of this study is a hybrid battery configuration that can be flexibly adjusted according to actual application scenarios. In Fig. 2(a), NCM and LFP batteries are connected in series in a 1:1 ratio, aiming to effectively reduce the risk of thermal propagation by leveraging the thermal stability of the LFP battery. In Fig. 2(b), the number ratio of NCM to LFP in series is x:1. Some battery cells in the NCM battery pack are replaced with cheaper LFP cells. This new configuration can better reconcile the cost and energy density of the battery. In Fig. 2(c), only one NCM battery is used, aiming to achieve state estimation of LFP batteries based on reducing costs and improving safety by using the NCM battery, which is easy to estimate the state. This study selects the battery configuration in Fig. 2(b), based on the battery pack of the world's leading battery manufacturer, with a series number ratio of NCM to LFP of 5:1. To assess the carbon footprint and environmental impacts of LFP-NCM batteries production.

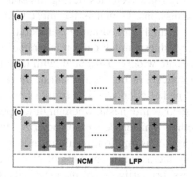

Fig. 2. Configuration of LFP-NCM hybrid batteries.

3 Environmental Impact Assessment

The carbon footprint and environmental impacts of LIBs manufacturing are modeled and calculated by SimaPro. The LCA tool has a rich database and multiple evaluation methods to provide reliable scientific data analysis and reporting [25]. And the environmental impact assessment is performed by the method of ReCiPe 2016. This method offers a combined impact and damage approach from the perspective of midpoint and endpoint categories [6]. One of the key advantages of the ReCiPe 2016 method is its comprehensiveness, as it covers a wide range of environmental impacts and is based on the latest scientific research [22]. In this study, four midpoint indicators are applied to compute the environmental impacts of LIBs manufacturing, including terrestrial acidification (TAC), freshwater eutrophication (FEU), human carcinogenic toxicity (HCT), and mineral resource scarcity (MRS). GHG emissions are one of the leading causes of global climate change, and human activities and industrial development will increase emissions [26]. In addition, mining raw materials, production, and use of batteries will cause resource and energy consumption. In this study, the IPCC 2013 GWP 100a and calculative energy demand (CED) indicators are used to study the carbon footprint and energy demand of LIBs manufacturing.

4   Results and Discussion

4.1   Comparison of Carbon Footprint

The comparison results of the carbon footprint at different LIBs manufacturing stages are presented in Fig. 3. The carbon footprint of manufacturing for NCM, LFP-NCM, and LFP are 96.2, 92.9, and 76.6 kg CO_2 eq/kWh, respectively. The carbon footprint contributed by the cathode materials of the NCM batteries accounts for 32.8%. The contribution to the carbon footprint of the NCM batteries comes from the upstream processes related to the extraction and ore selection of nickel, cobalt, and lithium. More than 50% of the world's lithium resources are concentrated in Australia. The primary energy consumption caused by mining machinery and transport vehicles during mineral extraction is significant, resulting in high carbon emissions. Cobalt is the most valuable battery component, with two-thirds of the global supply mined in the Democratic Republic of Congo [27]. Due to technological backwardness, much carbon is emitted during cobalt extraction. International nickel reserves are widely distributed, with lateritic nickel ore accounting for 60% of global terrestrial nickel resources and sulfide nickel ore accounting for 40% [28]. The global supply of nickel mainly comes from a few countries with nickel and coal resource advantages, such as Indonesia, where high-temperature pyrometallurgical smelting is the primary method. This process is characterized by high temperatures, low yields, and high fossil energy consumption, resulting in many carbon emissions. The carbon emissions caused by the assembly process of NCM account for 27.7% of the entire manufacturing process, primarily due to the electricity and thermal energy used in the battery assembly process. The power structure in China is dominated by thermal power. The consumption of fossil energy in the coal-burning power generation process is the main factor for the high carbon footprint of NCM manufacturing.

As shown in Fig. 3, the carbon footprint of LFP battery manufacturing is 20.4% lower than that of NCM. The carbon emissions caused by cathode materials account for 22.5% of the entire battery manufacturing process. The extraction and preparation processes of raw materials like lithium, phosphate, and ferric hydroxide will generate a certain amount of carbon emissions. Meanwhile, producing materials such as phosphoric acid, iron, and ammonia is also an indirect factor causing high carbon emissions from the cathode materials of LFP batteries. The chemical synthesis process of LFP battery cathode materials (including mixed sintering, ball milling, and impregnation) also consumes much energy, such as electricity and natural gas. In addition, the carbon emissions of aluminum manufacturing account for 37.7% of the carbon emissions of LFP battery manufacturing. The primary raw material of aluminum is bauxite, and the mining and processing process consumes much fossil energy, such as coal and natural gas. Moreover, the production of aluminum products in China involves electrolytic smelting, which consumes much electricity dominated by thermal power. It is also one of the reasons for the high proportion of carbon footprint in the manufacturing process of LFP batteries. Because the ratio of NCM batteries to LFP-NCM batteries is higher, this leads to a 17.5% increase in the overall carbon footprint compared to LFP batteries. Further increasing the proportion of LFP batteries in LFP-NCM hybrid batteries can reduce the carbon footprint but will lose a specific energy density. Replacing fossil fuels with renewable energy, further improving energy utilization efficiency, and improving the process of cathode materials and battery manufacturing will effectively reduce the carbon footprint of battery manufacturing.

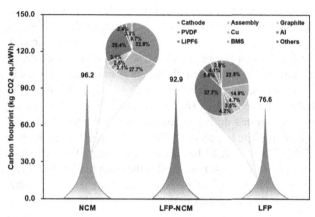

Fig. 3. Carbon footprint of different LIBs in the manufacturing stage. PVDF (Polyvinylidene difluoride), LiPF6 (Lithium hexafluorophosphate), and BMS (Battery management system).

4.2 Comparison of Environmental Impacts

The comparison results of five environmental impacts during manufacturing processes for different batteries are depicted in Fig. 4. The mining and processing of raw materials, the chemical synthesis of battery components, battery assembly, and packaging and transportation processes require a large amount of electricity, thermal energy, and fossil energy, etc. The most considerable difference in CED among the three types of batteries is only 4.4%, and the NCM batteries dominate in terms of CED. The energy consumption produced during the mining and processing metal elements such as nickel, cobalt, and manganese is higher than the phosphorus and iron elements in LFP. The degree to which LFP-NCM batteries can reduce CED compared to NCM batteries is very limited. The main reason is the combination of NCM batteries containing elements such as nickel, cobalt, and manganese. Simultaneously, the impact of the manufacturing of NCM batteries in terms of MRS is 12.6% and 75.5% higher than that of LFP-NCM and LFP batteries, respectively. The reason for the difference stems from the cathode materials. The precursor of the NCM batteries cathode ($Ni_xCo_yMn_{(1-x-y)}(OH)_2$) contains metal elements such as nickel, manganese, and cobalt. Their reserves and mining volumes are lower, and the potential for resource depletion is more significant. In addition, the impact of NCM batteries on TAC is 8.4% and 50.4% higher than that of LFP-NCM and LFP batteries, respectively. The precursor of the NCM battery will use metal sulfates such as $NiSO_4$, $CoSO_4$, and $MnSO_4$ and highly acidic compounds in the manufacturing process, significantly affecting soil acidity.

As presented in Fig. 4, the impacts of LFP batteries are significantly higher than the other two types of batteries in terms of HCT and FEU. In HCT, LFP-NCM and NCM batteries are 31.6% and 38.0% lower than LFP batteries. On the one hand, a large amount of copper and aluminum foil is used as substrates for electrode materials in cathode and anode collectors. The mining and manufacturing process of copper and aluminum resources generates many inhalable particulates and harmful gases (such as sulfur dioxide and nitrogen oxides), causing severe effects on human health. On the other hand, the processing and manufacturing of nickel and cobalt in NCM batteries cathode materials will produce many toxic heavy metals. The phosphorus in LFP batteries will have significant amounts of poisonous gases, wastewater, and waste materials during production. In addition, the toxicity of phosphate is substantial. It's the main reason the HCT value of LFP batteries is higher than the other two types of batteries. The LFP-NCM batteries can better balance the high HCT caused by LFP batteries, thereby reducing the impact of pollutants emitted during manufacturing on human health while improving safety and the economy. The impact of LFP batteries on FEU is 25.8% and 30.9% higher than that of LFP-NCM and NCM batteries, respectively. The eutrophication of water caused by the production of phosphoric acid is the main reason for the high FEU of LFP batteries. However, LFP-NCM batteries can reduce the use of LFP batteries through battery combinations, thereby reducing the impact on FEU.

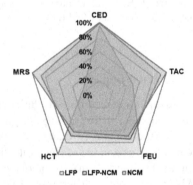

Fig. 4. Comparison of the environmental impacts for different LIBs manufacturing.

5   Conclusion

The manufacturing of LIBs is constantly challenged by environmental and resource sustainability, which will affect the stability of battery supply and the progress of net zero carbon emissions in the transportation industry. Based on the LCA method, this study built the life cycle models of the manufacturing processes for three types of LIBs. The carbon footprint and various environmental indicators in the manufacturing processes of different batteries are calculated and analyzed, and the environmental hotspots in the battery manufacturing process are identified. The main conclusions are as follows:

(1) The carbon footprint of manufacturing stages for NCM, LFP-NCM, and LFP batteries are 96.2, 92.9, and 76.6 kg CO2 eq/kWh, respectively. Among them, the carbon footprint of the cathode material and assembly process of NCM batteries in the manufacturing process account for 32.8% and 27.7%, respectively. The carbon footprint impact caused by aluminum in LFP batteries is 15.2% higher than that of the cathode material. And the carbon footprint of LFP-NCM batteries is 3.4% lower than that of NCM batteries.

(2) The NCM batteries dominate CED, MRS, and TAC. And NCM batteries are 12.6% and 75.5% higher than LFP-NCM and LFP batteries in terms of MRS. The impact of LFP batteries in terms of HCT and FEU is higher than the other two types of batteries. LFP-NCM batteries can better balance the environmental impact caused by the manufacturing process of NCM and LFP batteries while improving safety and the economy.

Acknowledgment. This research is supported National Natural Science Foundation of China (NSFC) under Grant numbers 51977131, 52277222, and 52277223.

References

1. Zhang, C., Zhao, X., Sacchi, R., You, F.: Trade-off between critical metal requirement and transportation decarbonization in automotive electrification. Nat. Commun. **14**(1) (2023). https://doi.org/10.1038/s41467-023-37373-4
2. Chen, Q., et al.: Investigating carbon foot-print and carbon reduction potential using a cradle-to-cradle LCA approach on lithium-ion batteries for electric vehicles in China. J. Clean. Prod. **369**, 133342 (2022). https://doi.org/10.1016/j.jclepro.2022.133342
3. Lai, X., et al.: Critical review of life cycle assessment of lithium-ion batteries for electric vehicles: a lifespan perspective. eTransportation (2022). https://doi.org/10.1016/j.etran.2022.100169
4. Lai, X., et al.: Turning waste into wealth: a systematic review on echelon utilization and material recycling of retired lithium-ion batteries. Energy Storage Materials **40**, 96–123 (2021). https://doi.org/10.1016/j.ensm.2021.05.010
5. Lin, B., Wu, W.: The impact of electric vehicle penetration: a recursive dynamic CGE analysis of China. Energy Econ. **94**, 105086 (2021). https://doi.org/10.1016/j.eneco.2020.105086
6. Chen, Q., et al.: Evaluating environmental impacts of different hydrometallurgical recycling technologies of the retired NCM batteries from electric vehicles in China. Available at SSRN 4303305. https://doi.org/10.1016/j.seppur.2023.123277
7. Yuan, C., et al.: Water-based manufacturing of lithium-ion battery for life cycle impact mitigation. CIRP Ann. Manuf. Technol. **70**(1), 25–28 (2021). https://doi.org/10.1016/j.cirp.2021.04.038
8. Feng, T., Guo, W., Li, Q., Meng, Z., Liang, W.: Life cycle assessment of lithium nickel cobalt manganese oxide batteries and lithium iron phosphate batteries for electric vehicles in China. J. Energy Storage **52**, 104767 (2022). https://doi.org/10.1016/j.est.2022.104767

9. Lopez, S., Akizu-Gardoki, O., Lizundia, E.: Comparative life cycle assessment of high-performance lithium-sulfur battery cathodes. J. Clean. Prod. **282**, 124528 (2021). https://doi.org/10.1016/j.jclepro.2020.124528

10. Wang, F., Deng, Y., Yuan, C.: Life cycle assessment of lithium oxygen battery for electric vehicles. J. Clean. Prod. **264**, 121339 (2020). https://doi.org/10.1016/j.jclepro.2020.121339

11. Hammond, G.P., Hazeldine, T.: Indicative energy technology assessment of advanced rechargeable batteries. Appl. Energy **138**, 559–571 (2015). https://doi.org/10.1016/j.apenergy.2014.10.037

12. Yang, J., Gu, F., Guo, J.F.: Environmental feasibility of secondary use of electric vehicle lithium-ion batteries in communication base stations. Resour. Conserv. Recycl. **156**, 104713 (2020). https://doi.org/10.1016/j.resconrec.2020.104713

13. Liang, Y., et al.: Life cycle assessment of lithium-ion batteries for greenhouse gas emissions. Resour. Conserv. Recycl. **117**, 285–293 (2017). https://doi.org/10.1016/j.resconrec.2016.08.028

14. Wang, G., Jin, B., Wang, M., Sun, Y., Zheng, Y., Su, T.: State of charge estimation for "LiFePO4 - LiCoxNiyMn1-x-yO2" hybrid battery pack. J. Energy Storage **65**, 107345 (2023). https://doi.org/10.1016/j.est.2023.107345

15. Lai, X., et al.: Investigating greenhouse gas emissions and environmental impacts from the production of lithium-ion batteries in China. J. Clean. Prod. **372**, 133756 (2022). https://doi.org/10.1016/j.jclepro.2022.133756

16. Li, P., Xia, X., Guo, J.: A review of the life cycle carbon footprint of electric vehicle batteries. Sep. Purif. Technol. **296**, 121389 (2022). https://doi.org/10.1016/j.seppur.2022.121389

17. Kallitsis, E., Korre, A., Kelsall, G.H.: Life cycle assessment of recycling options for automotive li-ion battery packs. J. Clean. Prod. **371**, 133636 (2022). https://doi.org/10.1016/j.jclepro.2022.133636

18. Wu, H., Hu, Y., Yu, Y., Huang, K., Wang, L.: The environmental footprint of electric vehicle battery packs during the production and use phases with different functional units. Int. J. Life Cycle Assess. **26**(1), 97–113 (2020). https://doi.org/10.1007/s11367-020-01836-3

19. Lai, X., Chen, Q., Gu, H., Han, X., Zheng, Y.: Life cycle assessment of lithium-ion batteries for carbon-peaking and carbon-neutrality: framework, methods, and progress. J. Mech. Eng. **58**(22), 3–18 (2022). https://doi.org/10.3901/JME.2022.22.003

20. Porzio, J., Scown, C.D.: Life-Cycle assessment considerations for batteries and battery materials. Adv. Energy Mater., 2100771 (2021). https://doi.org/10.1002/aenm.202100771

21. Yu, A., Wei, Y., Chen, W., Peng, N., Peng, L.: Life cycle environmental impacts and carbon emissions: a case study of electric and gasoline vehicles in China. Transp. Res. **65**(DEC.), 409–420 (2018). https://doi.org/10.1016/j.trd.2018.09.009

22. Chen, Q., et al.: Investigating the environmental impacts of different direct material recycling and battery remanufacturing technologies on two types of retired lithium-ion batteries from electric vehicles in China. Sep. Purif. Technol. **308**, 122966 (2023). https://doi.org/10.1016/j.seppur.2022.122966

23. Lai, X., Zhou, L., Zhu, Z., Zheng, Y., Sun, T., Shen, K.: Experimental investigation on the characteristics of coulombic efficiency of lithium-ion batteries considering different influencing factors. Energy **274**, 127408 (2023). https://doi.org/10.1016/j.energy.2023.127408

24. Lai, X., Wang, S., Wang, H., Zheng, Y., Feng, X.: Investigation of thermal runaway propagation characteristics of lithium-ion battery modules under different trigger modes. Int. J. Heat Mass Transf. **171**(2021), 121080 (2021). https://doi.org/10.1016/j.ijheatmasstransfer.2021.121080

25. Pre-sustainability. SimaPro | LCA software for informed change-makers. https://simapro.com/. Accessed 12 May 2023

26. Degen, F., Schuette, M.: Life cycle assessment of the energy consumption and GHG emissions of state-of-the-art automotive battery cell production. J. Cleaner Prod. (Jan.1), 330 (2022). https://doi.org/10.1016/j.jclepro.2021.129798

27. Baars, J., Domenech, T., Bleischwitz, R., Melin, H., Heidrich, O.: Circular economy strategies for electric vehicle batteries reduce reliance on raw materials. Nat. Sustain. 4 (2021). https://doi.org/10.1038/s41893-020-00607-0

28. Weimer, L., Braun, T., Hemdt, A.V.: Design of a systematic value chain for lithium-ion batteries from the raw material perspective. Resour. Policy 64 (2019). https://doi.org/10.1016/j.resourpol.2019.101473

Wiring Simulation of Electric Control Cabinet Based on Industrial Robot

Chaoyue Zhao[1], Yida Liu[2], and Zongxing Lu[1,2(✉)]

[1] School of Mechanical Engineering and Automation, Fuzhou University, No. 2 Xueyuan Road, Fuzhou 350116, Fujian, People's Republic of China
luzongxing@fzu.edu.cn
[2] School of Advanced Manufacturing, Fuzhou University, Shuicheng Road, Jinjiang 362251, Fujian, People's Republic of China

Abstract. Cabinet wiring is a crucial process in the field of electrical engineering. Traditional wiring methods are labor-intensive, time-consuming, and prone to safety hazards. Consequently, robot wiring technology has emerged as a promising solution. This paper investigates how to simulate the cabinet wiring robot using Robot Studio software. The rise of robot wiring technology has brought about novel automation solutions to the field of electrical engineering, improving work efficiency and reducing safety risks. In this automated wiring process, we achieve cabinet automation through the control of upper and lower computers and validate the wiring effectiveness and feasibility of the robot through simulation. During the simulation process, we analyze the relevant parameters of setting reasonable robot offline programming to achieve optimal automation wiring results. This paper aims to provide a novel solution for cabinet wiring work and promote the development and application of automation technology in electrical engineering.

Keywords: Cabinet Wiring · Simulation · Industrial Robot · Automatic Wiring harness · Feasibility Wiring

1 Introduce

With the widespread use of electrical cabinets in modern factories, their production and manufacturing face some problems. Due to the limitations of manual assembly processes, automation options for electrical cabinets are relatively limited, and wiring processes are time-consuming and highly repetitive, accounting for 50% of the total assembly time [1]. Therefore, wire harness assembly work is considered a relevant opportunity for improving human assembly work's occupational health. Musculoskeletal disorders account for 61% of permanent work disability, all of which are issues related to industrial workers' skeletal, muscular, and joint problems [2]. The domestic electrical cabinet industry uses nail plate wiring diagrams for prefabricated wire harnesses. Still, their hand-drawn accuracy is low, and they require repeated modifications and validations, which are time-consuming and unsuitable for small-batch and multi-variety products [3, 4]. Modern factories use robots as production automation equipment in large quantities

© The Author(s), under exclusive license to Springer Nature Singapore Pte Ltd. 2023
H. Yang et al. (Eds.): ICIRA 2023, LNAI 14274, pp. 454–462, 2023.
https://doi.org/10.1007/978-981-99-6501-4_39

to improve production efficiency and safety. Robots can effectively reduce the manu-facturing cost of industrial products and improve the standardization and accuracy of production. Robots can perform repetitive and dangerous tasks, reducing the ergonomic risk level of workers [5]. Offline programming, using mature computer graphics and image algorithms, can complete the programming of complex robot paths, which aligns with the industrial robots' development trend [6]. Compared with online programming, offline programming has many advantages, such as reducing the downtime of produc-tion robots, improving programming flexibility, pre-checking programs, and improving productivity and safety [7].

As early as the 1980s, Germany's Stuttgart Fraunhofer IPA began researching automation solutions, including installation board configuration, connector housing posi-tioning, and wiring problems [8]. Over time, the industry's interest in applying robots to factory floors has grown. Many robot manufacturers, such as KUKA, ABB, and Rethink Robotics, have also developed collaborative robots [2]. These robots have built-in sen-sors that can detect external forces and stop or return to a parking position in the event of incidental contact or collision. The advantages of robot replication accuracy, flexibil-ity, and the ability to perform repetitive work, combined with human capabilities, have opened a new era in manufacturing [9].

The Averex robot developed by Kiesling in Germany, combined with EPLAN soft-ware, can automatically prepare wiring terminals, and lead wires into pipes, and connect them to various components, but the robot uses a dedicated machine tool design method, which is expensive and bulky. The SYNDY wiring robot developed by Italy's System Robot Automation company is specifically designed for connecting wires in electrical cabinets. Still, its end effector is relatively large, and challenging to complete high-density electrical cabinet wiring tasks [10]. Jiang et al. [11] used multiple robotic arms to assemble wire harnesses in deformable part assembly automatically. The additional robotic arms are expected to help with wire arrangement, re-grasping, and other opera-tions by expanding the workspace with three Mitsubishi PA10 robotic arms. In China, Professor Yu Zhenglin's team at Changchun University of Science and Technology proposed a comprehensive wiring system for electrical cabinets, using a UR10 robot for kinematic analysis and the ant colony algorithm for wiring path planning and used ROBODK software to simulate and verify the feasibility of the wiring robot [12, 13]. Shenyang Xinsong Robotics has developed a robot to automatically assemble automo-tive wire harnesses, which can automate automotive wire harness wiring and save time and workload from manual wiring [12]. In addition, Wang Hailing et al. proposed an intelligent wiring robot platform, which uses three servo motors to achieve movement in the X, Y, and Z axes and designed a mechanism to process and insert wire harnesses. The development of these robots provides strong technical support for wire harness automation [14].

There are few fully integrated automation solution using a collaborative robot in the wire harness assembly process as of today in the scientific literature [15]. To construct an automatic wire harness assembly system, the development of a method that can automatically generate wiring robot programs is indispensable. Therefore, this paper presents an approach that simulates robot motion for cable routing. Combining robot technology with offline programming software avoids the laborious process of robot teaching. Additionally, generating robot control code based on cable routing information from 3D software enables adaptable solutions for various cable routing situations, thus providing a more comprehensive range of possibilities for applying industrial robots.

2 Establishment of Robot Simulation Platform

2.1 Robot Automatic Wiring Framework

Offline programming and simulation are essential parts of industrial robot production, and the selection of offline programming software significantly impacts the program's correctness and stability. In this paper, we have adopted ABB RobotStudio software for secondary development to ensure compatibility between the software and robot hardware. ABB robots use the RAPID programming language, which has complex program structures, complete instruction functions, and rich operands. It is one of the most functional programming languages in industrial robots. The RAPID program consists of program data and job programs. The program needs to be declared at the beginning, followed by the programming of the program path. After the program is written, the module needs to be uploaded to the robot. If there is an exception in the program, RobotStudio will provide error feedback, and the program needs to be modified. After confirming that the robot program uploaded has no syntax errors, the simulation function of RobotStudio is used to simulate the robot's motion path. The robot program can be adjusted or regenerated based on the simulation results. Finally, the upper computer is used to monitor the 6-axis angle and torque of the robot to determine whether the robot will exhibit non-ideal behavior, thereby ensuring production efficiency and safety (Fig. 1).

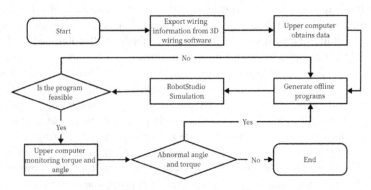

Fig. 1. Wiring process simulation flowchart

2.2 Cabinet Wiring Harness Trajectory

This article presents a method for utilizing 3D wiring software to generate wiring diagrams and export path points automatically. The method also considers changing the path direction by 90° when wiring in a groove or nail plate. The exported path file includes path coordinates and robot posture parameters. The posture parameter determines whether the robot's end posture needs to be changed. Specifically, when the parameter is set to "0", the robot end posture remains unchanged; when set to "1", the robot end posture rotates clockwise by 90°; when set to "-1", the robot end posture rotates counterclockwise by 90°. These details can assist robots in performing wiring more efficiently (Fig. 2).

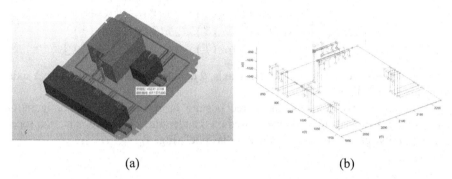

(a)   (b)

Fig. 2. Path Map (a) Three-dimensional wiring diagram. (b) Path verification of Matlab.

In wiring scenarios, the path may turn a full circle, causing the robot's end posture to accumulate a rotation of 360°, exceeding the motion range of the robot's six axes. In order to avoid this issue, it is necessary to determine whether the path turns a full circle when generating the trail and create an identification symbol on the path information to record the number of times the robot's end posture must change. Finally, a Txt file containing the path information is exported (Fig. 3).

Fig. 3. Path information obtained from 3D software

2.3 Simulation of Robot Interactive Control

This article explores the secondary development of ABB robots using the PC SDK in the Microsoft Visual Studio platform. This development enables the transmission of robot programs from RobotStudio to the robot through an upper computer. The upper computer reads path information from a (.txt) file and generates the robot's running program. As the tool posture of the ABB robot is defined in quaternion form, the program must declare target position data by first converting Euler angles to quaternions at the beginning of the program. The conversion formula can be found in Eq. (1).

$$
q = \begin{bmatrix} q1 \\ q2 \\ q3 \\ q4 \end{bmatrix} = \begin{bmatrix} \cos\left(\frac{\varphi}{2}\right)\cos\left(\frac{\theta}{2}\right)\cos\left(\frac{\Psi}{2}\right) + \sin\left(\frac{\varphi}{2}\right)\sin\left(\frac{\theta}{2}\right)\sin\left(\frac{\Psi}{2}\right) \\ \sin\left(\frac{\varphi}{2}\right)\cos\left(\frac{\theta}{2}\right)\cos\left(\frac{\Psi}{2}\right) - \cos\left(\frac{\varphi}{2}\right)\sin\left(\frac{\theta}{2}\right)\sin\left(\frac{\Psi}{2}\right) \\ \cos\left(\frac{\varphi}{2}\right)\sin\left(\frac{\theta}{2}\right)\cos\left(\frac{\Psi}{2}\right) + \sin\left(\frac{\varphi}{2}\right)\cos\left(\frac{\theta}{2}\right)\sin\left(\frac{\Psi}{2}\right) \\ \cos\left(\frac{\varphi}{2}\right)\cos\left(\frac{\theta}{2}\right)\sin\left(\frac{\Psi}{2}\right) - \sin\left(\frac{\varphi}{2}\right)\sin\left(\frac{\theta}{2}\right)\cos\left(\frac{\Psi}{2}\right) \end{bmatrix} \tag{1}
$$

where φ denotes the Euler angle of the X-axis, θ denotes the Euler angle of the Y-axis, Ψ denotes the Euler angle of the Z-axis.

To ensure that the robot is in the correct posture during operation, the configuration data of the robot needs to be defined based on the identifier. The robot's motion speed is temporarily set to "v1000", and the zone is "fine" (Fig. 4).

Fig. 4. Upper computer-generated path interface

After generating the program code on the upper computer, save it as a (. Mod) file, transfer it to the robot in RobotStudio through the upper computer, and display the robot's wiring trajectory on the simulation interface of RobotStudio (Fig. 5).

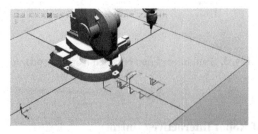

Fig. 5. Path Map for Robot Simulation

3   Results and Discussion

During the robot wiring process, each joint of the robot rotates and is subjected to different loads, resulting in varying torques. After completing the basic simulation, real-time monitoring of the robot's six-axis angle and torque during the operation was carried out using an upper computer to detect anomalies. The path with the maximum change in the six-axis angle was selected for monitoring. The upper computer obtained real-time data through a timer to monitor the angle and torque changes of each joint of the robot and optimize the robot's parameters based on the results (shown in Fig. 6). The simulation demonstrated that the range of motion for each of the robot's six axes did not exceed the joint range of motion during offline programming.

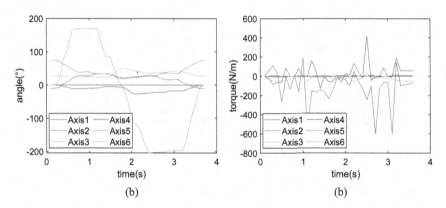

Fig. 6.   Robot 6-axis angle and torque change (a) Angle (b) Torque

By analyzing the robot's joint torque changes, we can observe that the second joint experiences the most significant torque change. This is because the second joint needs to move up and down continuously during robot wiring, resulting in a significant amount of torque. To reduce the robot's torque changes and improve its efficiency during wiring, optimizing the robot's parameters is necessary.

Initially, it was considered that the robot's speed may be too high, resulting in excessive torque changes. Thus, torque changes were monitored at different rates. As shown in Fig. 7, as the movement speed decreased, the fluctuation amplitude of the robot's torque became gentler. In Fig. 8, due to the decrease in rate, the robot's average torque of axes 1 and 2 significantly decreased, but the running time was greatly increased. Therefore, after offline programming, an appropriate motion speed should be selected to minimize the impact of the robot's significant torque changes without affecting the robot's efficiency. As a result, v100 was used as the running speed of the robot.

In the previous section, it was mentioned that the in-place interval of the robot was set to "fine". However, when the robot transitions through a circular arc, it may result in a decrease in torque variation. Therefore, the impact of different in-place intervals on torque should be monitored when the speed is set to v100.

It can be observed that when the speed is set to v100, some peak values of torque with partial mutations exist. As mentioned earlier, the robot's in-place interval was "fine".

To determine whether the robot's torque changes could be reduced using arc transition paths, we monitored the effects of different zones on torque when the speed was set to v100.

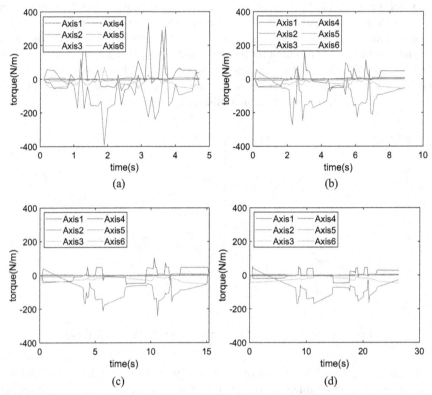

Fig. 7. Torque at different speeds. (a) Speed v500 torque change. (b) Speed v200 torque change. (c) Speed v100 torque change. (d) Speed v50 torque change.

Based on the results shown in Fig. 9,the addition of zone leads to a slight reduction in peak torque values but has little effect on the average torque. Moreover, a significant decrease in the maximum negative torque of the 2nd axis was observed after the z30 in-place interval. Choosing a more significant in-place gap is not advisable, considering the possibility of collisions. To ensure that the robot does not produce substantial torque changes and without affecting the robot's performance, a comprehensive comparison suggests that setting the speed to v100 and the in-place interval to z30 is the optimal parameter choice for robot wiring.

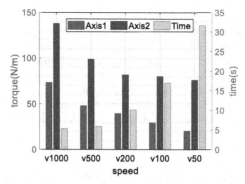

Fig. 8. Average torque and time at different speeds

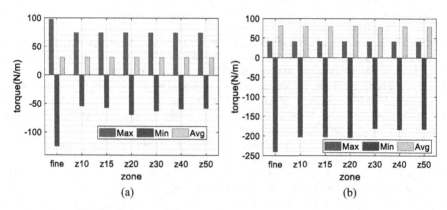

(a)   (b)

Fig. 9. Torque variation in different zone. (a) Axis1. (b) Axis2.

4 Conclusion

Based on the Robot Studio software for robot wiring, simulation and analysis of joint torque changes can lead to the production of more reliable offline programming code for robot wiring. We present a robot control scheme for automated wire harness production, which improves the efficiency and safety of electrical cabinet wiring. Further research will involve the inclusion of the end effector in the wiring simulation process and will conduct collision testing in accordance with the wiring environment. The advancement of robot wiring technology presents a vast potential for achieving automated and intelligent wiring processes, which can revolutionize smart manufacturing. With the increasing demand for automation in the production industry, robot wiring technology is expected to have extensive applications.

References

1. Spies, S., Bartelt, M., Kuhlenkötter, B.: Wiring of control cabinets using a distributed control within a robot-based production cell. In: 2019 19th International Conference on Advanced Robotics (ICAR), pp. 332–337. IEEE, Belo Horizonte, Brasil (2019)

2. El Zaatari, S., Marei, M., Li, W., et al.: Cobot programming for collaborative industrial tasks: an overview. Robot. Auton. Syst. **116**, 162–180 (2019)
3. Liu, C., Hong, W., Tang, X., Zhai, W.: Three-dimensional wiring design and intelligent wiring platform prefabricated electrical cabinet wiring harness. China High-Tech **02**, 25–26 (2022)
4. Heisler, P., Utsch, D., Kuhn, M., et al.: Optimization of wire harness assembly using human–robot-collaboration. Procedia CIRP **97**, 260–265 (2021)
5. Navas-Reascos, G.E., Romero, D., Rodriguez, C.A., et al.: Wire harness assembly process supported by a collaborative robot: a case study focus on ergonomics. Robotics **11**(6), 131(2022)
6. Wei, Z., Song, Z., Guo, R.: Review on commercial systems for off-line programming of robot. Mach. Build. Autom. **45**(06), 180–183 (2016)
7. Pan, Z., Polden, J., Larkin, N., et al.: Recent progress on programming methods for industrial robots. Robot. Comput.-Integr. Manuf. **28**(2), 87–94 (2012)
8. Trommnau, J., Kühnle, J., Siegert, J., et al.: Overview of the state of the art in the production process of automotive wire harnesses, current research and future trends. Procedia CIRP **81**, 387–392 (2019)
9. Yumbla, F., Abeyabas, M., Luong, T., et al.: Preliminary connector recognition system based on image processing for wire harness assembly tasks. In: 2020 20th International Conference on Control, Automation and Systems (ICCAS), pp.1146–1150. IEEE, Busan, Korea (2020)
10. Li, X., Zheng, S., Wang, K.: Visual servo of integrated wiring machine for electric control cabinet. Mod Electron. Tech. **45**(21), 117–121 (2022)
11. Jiang, X., Koo, K., Kikuchi, K., et al.: Robotized assembly of a wire harness in a car production line. Adv. Robot. **25**(3–4), 473–489 (2011)
12. Chai, J.: Research on trajectory planning and offline programming for wiring harness robots. M.E. thesis, Changchun University of Science and Technology (2018)
13. Sun, C.: Research on the integrated wiring system of electric control cabinet robot. M.E. thesis, Changchun University of Science and Technology (2018)
14. Wang, H., Zhou, L., et al.: Design and research of intelligent wiring robot system. Hunan Electric Power **41**(05), 78–80 (2021)
15. Navas-Reascos, G.E., Romero, D., Stahre, J., et al.: Wire harness assembly process supported by collaborative robots: Literat. Rev. Call R&D. Robotics 11(3), 65 (2022)

Intelligent Identification Approach of Vibratory Roller Working Stages Based on Multi-dimensional Convolutional Neural Network

Haoju Song[1], Guiqin Li[1(✉)], Zijie He[1], Xin Xiong[1], Bin He[1], and Peter Mitrouchev[2]

[1] Shanghai Key Laboratory of Intelligent Manufacturing and Robotics, School of Mechatronic Engineering and Automation, Shanghai University, Shanghai 200444, China
leeching@shu.edu.cn
[2] G-SCOP, University Grenoble Alpes, 38030 Grenoble, France

Abstract. A multi-dimensional classification model based on convolutional neural networks (MDC-CNN) is proposed to realize the intelligent identification for the working stages of vibratory rollers. The approach achieves multi-dimensional classification by five parallel classifiers, and combines the information from multiple classifiers by voting mechanism to obtain the final recognition result. A learning rate decay mechanism is also used to avoid overfitting of the model. Furthermore, a data acquisition system is constructed to collect the working characteristic parameters of the roller, and the excitation force of vibration wheel is calculated according to the collected vibration signal. The pressure signals of vibrating pump and driving pump, as well as the excitation force of vibration wheel are used as inputs to the model. The experimental results show that the identification accuracy with excitation force is improved by about 2% compared to that without excitation force, and the identification accuracy of MDC-CNN is about 6.3% higher than that of the CNN, reaching 97.3%, verifying its effectiveness.

Keywords: Vibratory roller · Working-stages identification · Excitation force · Convolutional neural network

1 Introduction

As an important equipment for paving engineering based on vibration principle, vibratory rollers are widely used for filling and compaction in large-scale engineering projects such as railways, highways, airports, and ports [1]. A significant amount of research has been conducted on dynamic response [2], evaluation system for compaction quality [3], dynamic responses of excitation system [4], and path tracking control [5]. The compaction performance of the vibratory roller has been greatly improved. However, according to recent research, the research on reducing energy consumption in rollers is still insufficient, which cannot meet the requirements of low-carbon design.

© The Author(s), under exclusive license to Springer Nature Singapore Pte Ltd. 2023
H. Yang et al. (Eds.): ICIRA 2023, LNAI 14274, pp. 463–475, 2023.
https://doi.org/10.1007/978-981-99-6501-4_40

During the operation of the rollers, most fully hydraulic vibratory rollers can achieve the highest and constant engine speed during steady operation, which means that the output power and specific fuel consumption are constant. However, in the actual operation process, the power required by the actuators of vibratory roller is different at different working stages, and the power is wasted for stages with less power consumption. Therefore, it is essential to establish an intelligent identification approach for the roller working stages, this will enable the staged power matching for energy saving and consumption reduction.

Computer vision-based working stage identification approach is one of the methods for working stage recognition of construction machinery, and there have been many researches [6–10]. However, there may be issues such as feature viewpoint occlusion, excessive light or darkness in complex working environments, and the appearance and pose of construction machinery may vary in different working scenes. Therefore, it is difficult to explain the whole dynamic operating stage by studying only part of the postures, and the recognition accuracy will be limited [11, 12]. For vibrator rollers, the different operating stages are mainly manifested at different vibration frequencies, which cannot be distinguished by vision-based methods.

Another method of working stages identification is multi-sensor data fusion [13, 14]. This method identifies the working stages through characteristic data collected by sensors deployed on construction machinery, such as engine speed, flow rate, and pressure in the hydraulic system. Ahn [15] applied accelerometers to the acquisition of equipment status parameter information to classify the equipment state into idle, working, and engine-off states. Hou [16] focused on a low-cost and efficient sensor configuration to achieve intelligent identification of operation data for loader working stages. Shi [17] put forward an intelligent identification method for excavator working cycle stages based on the main pump pressure waveform. Through the intelligent calibration system, the support vector machine (LIBSVM) model achieved an accuracy of 93.82%. Shi [18] investigated a work stage recognition method based on the operating handle control signals, which overcome the effect of hydraulic system response delay on recognition results, and verified its classification accuracy of 93.21% by a long short-term memory (LSTM) classifier.

A multi-dimensional classification method based on CNN (MDC-CNN) is proposed to achieve end-to-end intelligent recognition for the working stages of vibratory roller. In this method, the pressure signals of the vibrating pump and the driving pump, and the excitation force of the vibrating wheel are taken as inputs. A multi-dimension classifier with five classifiers is fused by a voting mechanism to improve the generalization ability of roller work identification and avoid overfitting.

The rest of this paper is organized as follows. In Sect. 2, the research framework of the proposed vibratory roller work cycle recognition approach is described. Section 3 presents the data preparation and work cycle division process, and Sect. 4 builds a multi-dimensional classification approach based on CNN. Experimental results and analysis are given in Sect. 5. Finally, the conclusion and future work are drawn in Sect. 6.

2   Research framework

The mapping relationship between the working cycle stages and the working characteristic parameters is analyzed, and an end-to-end intelligent identification approach for the working stages of vibratory roller based on MDC-CNN is proposed, as shown in Fig. 1. The six processed are included: (1) signal acquisition: The characteristic parameters during the operation of the roller are collected. (2) stage division: The five working stages of the roller, such as idle, walking, small vibration mode, big vibration mode, site transfer, are accurately divided based on the collected waveform. (3) model establish: The MDC-CNN identification apprach is built, the relevant parameters and model structure is determined. (4) identification experiments: The working stage identification experiments of the roller is carried out based on the MDC-CNN approach. (5) Results output: The identification results of the MDC-CNN are output. (6) Performance evaluation: The performance of MDC-CNN is comprehensively evaluated by confusion matrix and other performance indicators.

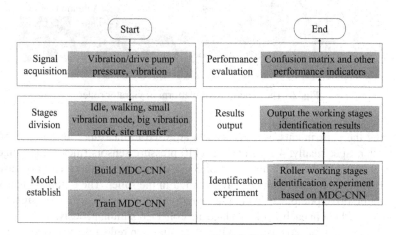

Fig.1. The operation flow of MDC-CNN approach.

3   Data preparation and stage division

3.1   Data collection

A single steel wheel full hydraulic vibratory roller from XCMG is used to collect real vehicle data, and the characteristics signals of various working stages are obtained. The roller is composed of hydraulic system, power system, transmission system, electrical control system and mechanical structure. Three pumps, namely, hydraulic drive pump, hydraulic vibration pump and hydraulic steering pump, are connected in series by a coupling to the same engine torque output shaft to achieve the same speed rotation. The direction of the oil at the outlet of the variable pump changes with the direction of the swash plate, thus enabling thr motor output shaft to switch between forward/reverse steering, that is, dual frequency. The vibration force is mainly generated by the rotation of the eccentric block in the vibrating wheel and is transmitted to the vibrating wheel, which in turn is in contact with the ground, so that the compacted ground surface is subjected to greater impact and the particles in the soil become more compact.

Fig. 2. The experimental platform of vibrator roller

During the experiments, various sensors are used to measure the state parameters of the roller. Specifically, 4 Hydrotech PR110 pressure sensors (measuring range: 0–600 bar, accuracy: 0.5% F.S.), and 1 Dytran 3333A2 triaxial vibration sensor (measuring range: ± 50g, accuracy: 100mV/g) are installed in the roller. The output signals from the hydraulic drive pump, the hydraulic vibration pump and the vibration signal from the vibrating wheel in each working stage are collected simultaneously.

In addition, in order to ensure that the test results can reflect the working characteristics of the roller in each working stage and to avoid adverse effects caused by personal operating habits, an operator with no less than 3 years working experience is selected to carry out the data acquisition, and the data acquisition process is shown in Fig. 2.

3.2   The calculation of excitation force

The vibration mode of roller is essentially generated by the rotation of the eccentric block in the vibration wheel. The eccentric block creates an excitation force and transmits it to the vibration wheel. The vibration wheel then makes contact with the ground, causing an even greater impact on the compacted soil particles and making them more compact. In the large vibration mode, the gravity of the eccentric block is located at 0 degrees relative to the vibration axis, and the mass is superimposed.

It is characterized by low frequency and high amplitude when vibrating. In the small vibration mode, the gravity of the two eccentric blocks are located at 180 degrees relative to the vibration axis, and the mass is offset, high frequency and low amplitude are generated during the vibration. Therefore, different vibration modes produce different excitation forces, which can serve as important features for identifying the vibration modes.

$$F_0 = Me\omega^2 = Me4\pi^2 f_0^2 \tag{1}$$

where M is the mass of the eccentric block (kg), e is the eccentricity (m), ω is the angular frequency, and f_0 is the excitation frequency.

The excitation frequencies of the eccentric blocks are extracted to obtain accurate excitation forces. The Fast Fourier Transform (FFT) is used to extract the excitation frequency characteristics of the eccentric block in the vibration mode of the roller, as shown in Fig. 3.

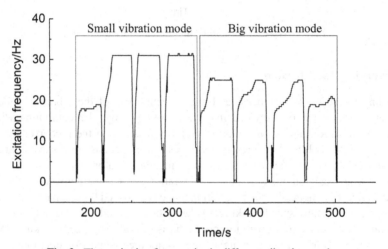

Fig. 3. The excitation frequencies in different vibration modes.

According to the technical specifications of the vibratory roller, it is known that the eccentric moment of the vibration wheel in the small vibration mode is $M_s e_s = 7.79 kg \cdot m$ and the vibration wheel in the large vibration mode is $M_b e_b = 15.12 kg \cdot m$. The excitation frequency f_0 extracted by FFT, and the eccentric moment of the vibration wheel are added to calculate the excitation force by Eq. (1). The magnitude of the excitation force is shown in Fig. 4. It can be seen that the excitation force of the roller is obviously different under different vibration modes. Hence, the excitation force obtained in this study is used as an important feature for identifying the vibration modes of the roller.

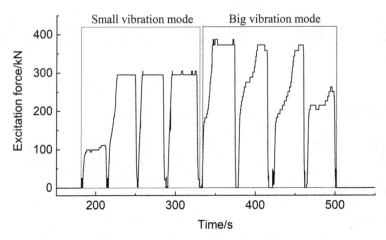

Fig. 4. The excitation force in different vibration modes.

3.3 Working stage division

According to the working process and the collected data of the vibratory roller, the complete working cycle is divided into five working stages by combining with the pressure time series data of the actuator vibration motor and the precursor motor, as shown in Fig. 5. (1) Idle, the vibratory roller has started but has not started compaction operation, and it is in a stationary state. (2) Working, the vibratory roller is traveling at the speed of the compaction operation, and the vibration mode is not activated at this stage. (3) Small vibration mode, the small vibration mode is activated for compaction operation on the basis of walking speed working. (4) Big vibration mode, the big vibration mode is activated for compaction operation on the basis of walking speed working. (5) Site transfer, the site is transferred at a higher speed after the compaction operation.

In the idle stage, the pressure of the vibratory pump and vibration acceleration are at a small value as the vibratory roller is neither walking nor vibrating. During the walking stage, the pressure of the precursor motor and drive pump increases rapidly, while the pressure of the vibration motor and vibration acceleration are still at a small value. In small vibration stage, the vibration mode must be activated when walking, the pressures of drive pump and precursor motor pressures are similar to those in the walking stage, while the vibration pump pressure and vibration acceleration increase significantly. The difference between the big vibration stage and the small vibration stage is that the vibration acceleration values are higher. The vibration mode is not turned on in the site transfer stage. Unlike the walking stage, the vehicle speed is obviously faster, so the pressure of the drive pump and precursor motor are obviously higher than that in the walking stage.

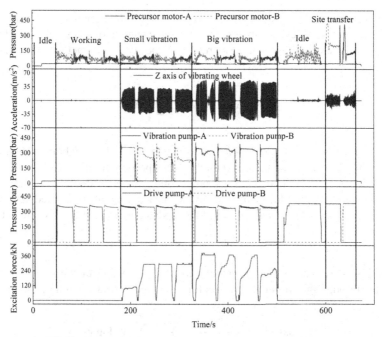

Fig.5. The working stage division diagram of vibratory roller.

4 Multi-dimensional classification approach based on CNN

Traditional CNN ecentually achieve data classification by combining multiple convolution and pooling layers. However, the phenomenon of overfitting may occur when there is only one fully connected classifier. Although the learning rate is manually set to a more suitable value, the overfitting phenmenon still cannot be avoided and affects the generalization ability of the model. Moreover, once the structure and initial parameters of the full connected layer are not properly optimized, the classification results will be seriously affected and the training model will be rendered meaningless.

Inspired by random forest and bagging [19], MDC-CNN is proposed to solve the problems in traditional CNN. The output after feature extraction is divided into five parallel branches, which are respectively transmitted to five parallel classifiers for classification calculation. Each classifier outputs the probability distribution of the labels by Softmax function, and five classification results are obtained respectively. Finally, the final classification results of the model is selected through the voting mechanism.

On the one hand, the MDC-CNN consists of multiple fully connected classifiers and multiple voting operations, so this model can effectively avoid overfitting phenomenon and improve generalization ability. On the other hand, a decay mechanism of learning rate η is added to the model, making it a parameter that needs to be continuously learned and updated. Through the optimization of the above two aspects, MDC-CNN achieves improved classification performance.

The MDC-CNN improves the accuracy and generalization performance of the model in classification tasks by setting up several different classifiers. The classification results of each classifier are fused using the relative majority voting method to obtain the final classification result. If several labels receive the same number of votes and are the highest, one of them is selected randomly. The relative majority voting method is expressed as follows:

$$V(x) = y_{\underset{j}{\arg\max}} \sum_{i=1}^{T} y_i^j(x) \tag{2}$$

where $y_i^j(x)$ represents the prediction label of the model on the i-th branch classifier.

A slightly larger learning rate is initially set to speed up training. As the weights are updated closer to the optimal value, a small learning rate is desirable. So a learning rate decay mechanism is introduced into the model. The learning rate is updated in an orderly manner and a coefficient is set $\gamma = 0.95$. The updated learning rate lr is calculated as:

$$lr_{i+1} = \gamma \cdot lr_i \tag{3}$$

The loss between the output value and the target value of the trained model is calculated through the cross entropy loss function, and the calculation method is:

$$Loss = -\frac{1}{batch\_size} \sum_{j=1}^{batch\_size} \sum_{i=1}^{n} y_{ji} \log \hat{y}_{ji} \tag{4}$$

where $batch\_size$ is the batch size of the initial dataset, n is the number of classification categories, y_{ji} is the real label of the i-th sample in the j-th batch, $\hat{y}_{ji}$ is the output of the top-level classifier, that is, the prediction label.

Since the MDC-CNN builds five classifiers, each classifier has a classification loss. The total classification loss is the sum of the classification losses of each branch:

$$Loss_{MDC-CNN} = \sum_{i=1}^{5} Loss_{Ci} \tag{5}$$

where $Loss_{Ci}$ represents the loss of the fully connected layer classifier of the i-th branch.

The CNN and MDC-CNN models used in this study as shown in Fig. 6. The structure of the five classifiers before parallel concatenation is the same as that of the traditional CNN model, and the feature matrix with 128 features is obtained after pooling. The feature matrix is customized into sub-feature matrices with 8, 8, 16, 32, and 64 features, which are then transmitted to the five parallel classifiers. Each classifier outputs a probability distribution of five labels and the final classification result is obtained by the relative majority voting mechanism. The multi-dimensional sub-feature matrix and diversified fully connected layer classifiers facilitate the diversity of classification results.

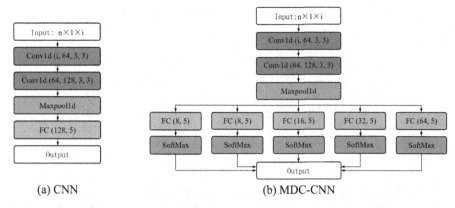

(a) CNN   (b) MDC-CNN

Fig. 6. The structure diagram of CNN and MDC-CNN model

5 Experiment results and discussion

The MDC-CNN method is implemented by PyCharm, and all programs run on computers with the following configurations: AMD Ryzen7 4800U @ 1.8GHz processor, 16GB memory. The model is comprehensively evaluated and compared by accuracy, recall, precision and F1-score:

$$Accuracy = \frac{num(\hat{y}_T)}{num(y)} \qquad (6)$$

$$Recall_i = \frac{num(\hat{y}_{Ti})}{num(y_i)} \qquad (7)$$

$$Precision_i = \frac{num(\hat{y}_{Ti})}{num(\hat{y}_i)} \qquad (8)$$

$$F1 - score_i = \frac{2 \cdot Recall_i \cdot Precision_i}{Recall_i + Precision_i} \qquad (9)$$

where $num(y)$ is the total number of samples, $num(\hat{y}_T)$ means that the predicted labels are equal to the number of true labels, $num(\hat{y}_{Ti})$ is the correct number of predicted labels i, $num(y_i)$ is the number of true labels i, $num(\hat{y}_i)$ is the number of predictions as label i.

The dataset obtained in Sect. 3.1 is used, which contains 50000 data samples, and each sample contains 5 characteristics such as driving pump pressure, vibrating pump pressure and exciting force. The initial data set is divided into training set and test set in the ratio of 8:2 to ensure the training effect to the greatest extent. To verify the effect of the excitation force on the accuracy of the vibratory roller working stages identification, the identification accuracy of the K-Nearest Neighbors (KNN), Decision Tree (DT), CNN and MDC-CNN are compared with the initial data set containing the excitation force features and the initial data set without the excitation force features, respectively. The results are shown in the Table 1.

As can be seen from Table 1, the identification accuracy with the excitation force is higher than that without the excitation force for all five models. The results show that

Table 1. The accuracy comparison of different approach.

Approach	Accuracy	
	Without the excitation force	With the excitation force
KNN	90.1%	92.1%
DT	93.5%	95.1%
CNN	88.6%	91.0%
MDC-CNN	95.2%	97.3%

the excitation force can effectively improve the accuracy of the identification models for the working phase of the vibratory roller. Among them, the recognition accuracy of the MDC-CNN is improved by about 2%.

The comparison results of CNN and MDC-CNN identification accuracy curves are shown in the Fig. 7. It can be seen that the recognition accuracy of MDC-CNN is significantly improved compared with that of traditional CNN, whether in training set or test set. The MDC-CNN eliminates the great fluctuation on the recognition accuracy curve of the traditional CNN, which indicates that the stability of MDC-CNN has been significantly improved.

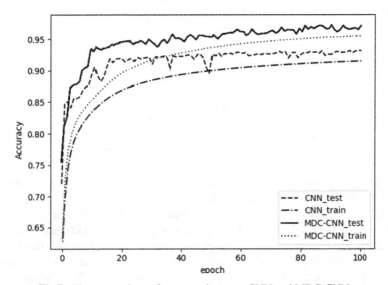

Fig.7. The comparison of accuracy between CNN and MDC-CNN.

Furthermore, the evaluation indicators of the two models are compared. After training the models 100 times, the indicators are recorded in Table 2. The results show that the MDC-CNN model outperforms the CNN model in the four indexes. The accuracy of MDC-CNN model is approximately 6.3% higher than that of the traditional CNN.

Table 2. Comparison of traditional CNN and MDC-CNN model.

Model	Accuracy	Recall	Precision	F1-score
CNN	90.97%	94.51%	94.46%	94.48%
MDC-CNN	97.33%	98.88%	98.92%	98.90%

Comparing the identification accuracy of the two models at each working stage, it can be seen from Table 3 that when using the traditional CNN, the difference in identification accuracy at each working stage is relatively large, with a maximum of 95.86% and a minimum of 87.68%, In the MDC-CNN, the accuracy is more balanced, with a difference of about 3% between the maximum and minimum. Meanwhile, compared with the traditional CNN, the recognition results of MDC-CNN showed a significant improvement, with the smallest increase by about 3.4% and the largest increase by about 8.6%.

Table 3. Comparison of identification accuracy at different working stages.

Working stage	Accuracy	
	CNN	MDC-CNN
Idle	90.50%	96.30%
Working	95.86%	99.25%
Small vibration	87.68%	96.24%
Big vibration	91.60%	97.08%
Site transfer	89.20%	97.80%

The confusion matrix of the two models is shown in Fig. 8, it can be seen that each label has more prediction errors in CNN classification results, and the classification error of each label is significantly reduced in MDC-CNN.

Misidentification still exists in the identification results, which are mainly reflected in the following aspects: parts of working stage 0 are wrongly identified as working stages 2 and 3. Parts of working stage 1 are incorrectly identified as working stages 0 and 4. Work stage 2 is wrongly recognized as stage 0 and 1. Part of working stage 3 are incorrectly identified as working stage 1 and parts of working stage 4 are wrongly identified as working stage 1.

The reasons for misidentification can be attributed to: (1) Working stage switching. When the operator switches between the working stages of walking at working speed, small vibration mode, large vibration mode and site transfer, the vibratory roller needs to be stopped briefly to change gear, resulting in inaccurate identification. (2) The data characteristics of the working stages are similar. The data characteristics of the site transfer stage are somewhat similar to those of working speed walking, leading to identification errors.

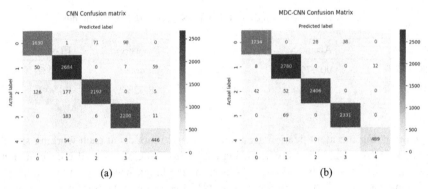

Fig. 8. Confusion matrix diagram of identification results, (a) CNN, (b) MDC-CNN

6   Conclusion

An end-to-end intelligent identification approach of vibratory roller working stages based on MDC-CNN is proposed. The approach takes the vibration pump, driving pump, and the excitation force as inputs. Multi-dimensional classification is achieved by implementing five parallel classifiers. The information from multiple classifiers is also combined using a voting mechanism to achieve intelligent identification for the working stages of the roller. This approach effectively improves the classification accuracy and enhances the generalization ability of the model. In addition, the experimental results of the vibratory roller working stages show that the identification accuracy of MDC-CNN reaches 97.33%, which is 6.3% higher than that of CNN, demonstrating its effectiveness.

Acknowledgments. This research was supported by the National Key Research & Development Program of China (2020YFB1709902).

References

1. Liu, D., Chen, J., Li, S.: Collaborative operation and real-time control of roller fleet for asphalt pavement compaction. Autom. Constr. **98**, 16–29 (2019)
2. Wan, Y., Jia, J.: Nonlinear dynamics of asphalt–screed interaction during compaction: application to improving paving density. Constr. Build. Mater. **202**, 363–373 (2019)
3. Wang, X., et al.: Automated monitoring and evaluation of highway subgrade compaction quality using artificial neural networks. Autom. Constr. **145**, 104663 (2023)
4. Shen, P., Lin, S.: Mathematic modeling and chaotic identification for practice construction in vibratory compacting. J. Vib. Eng. Technol. **6**(1), 1–13 (2018)
5. Guan, S., et al.: Dynamic hyperparameter tuning-based path tracking control for robotic rollers working on earth-rock dam under complex construction conditions. Autom. Constr. **143**, 104576 (2022)
6. Golparvar-Fard, M., Heydarian, A., Niebles, J.C.: Vision-based action recognition of earth-moving equipment using spatio-temporal features and support vector machine classifiers. Adv. Eng. Inform. **27**(4), 652–663 (2013)

7. Gong, J., Caldas, C.H., Gordon, C.: Learning and classifying actions of construction workers and equipment using Bag-of-Video-Feature-Words and Bayesian network models. Adv. Eng. Inform. **25**(4), 771–782 (2011)
8. Yang, J., Vela, P.: Vision-Based tower crane tracking for understanding construction activity. J. Comput. Civil. Eng. **28**(1), 103–112 (2014)
9. Fang, W., el al.: Automated detection of workers and heavy equipment on construction sites: a convolutional neural network approach. Adv. Eng. Inform. **37**, 139–149 (2018)
10. Soltani, M.M., Zhu, Z., Hammad, A.: Framework for location data fusion and pose estimation of excavators using stereo vision. J. Comput. Civil. Eng. **32**(6), 04018045 (2018)
11. Soltani, M.M., Zhu, Z., Hammad, A.: Skeleton estimation of excavator by detecting its parts. Autom. Constr. **82**, 1–15 (2017)
12. Kim, J., Chi, S., Seo, J.: Interaction analysis for vision-based activity identification of earthmoving excavators and dump trucks. Autom. Constr. **87**, 297–308 (2018)
13. Zhou, H., Zhao, P.Y., Chen, Y.L.: Fuzzy logic control for a hydraulic hybrid excavator based on torque prediction and genetic algorithm optimization. P. I. Mech. Eng. D-J. Aut. **232**(8), 983–994 (2017)
14. Akhavian, R., Behzadan, A.H.: Smartphone-based construction workers' activity recognition and classification. Autom. Constr. **71**, 198–209 (2016)
15. Ahn, C.R., Lee, S., Peña-Mora, F.: Application of low-cost accelerometers for measuring the operational efficiency of a construction equipment fleet. J. Comput. Civil. Eng. **29**(2), 04014042 (2015)
16. Hou, L., et al.: Feature-based sensor configuration and working-stage recognition of wheel loader. Autom. Constr. **141**, 104401 (2022)
17. Shi, Y., Xia, Y., Zhang, Y., Yao, Z.: Intelligent identification for working-cycle stages of excavator based on main pump pressure. Autom. Constr. **109**, 102991 (2020)
18. Shi, Y., et al.: Working stage identification of excavators based on control signals of operating handles. Autom. Constr. **130**, 103873 (2021)
19. Qin, Y., et al.: Multiscale transfer voting mechanism: a new strategy for domain adaption. IEEE. T. Ind. Inform. **17**(10), 7103–7113 (2021)

Research Status and Application Prospects of Magnetically Driven Micro- and Nanorobots

Xu Du[1], Pengfei Ren[1], Junqiang Zheng[2,3](✉), and Zichong Zhang[1]

[1] School of Mechanical Engineering, Zhejiang Sci-Tech University, 310018 Hangzhou, People's Republic of China
duxu@zstu.edu.cn

[2] School of Mechanical Engineering, Hangzhou Dianzi University, 310018 Hangzhou, People's Republic of China
zhengjunqiang@hdu.edu.cn

[3] School of Mechanical Engineering, Hefei University of Technology, 230009 Hefei, People's Republic of China

Abstract. Micro- and nanorobots can effectively convert different energies into kinetic energy, and have been widely concerned by people for a long time. In recent years, magnetically driven micro- and nanorobots have become a research hotspot due to their excellent controllability and motion performance in complex environments. Micro- and nanorobots have the characteristics of wireless magnetically drive and control, and can adapt well to small and enclosed environments in vitro and in vivo. They have shown great potential in various fields such as biomedical, electronic, and environmental applications. This article first reviews the research progress of magnetically driven micro- and nanorobots both domestically and internationally in recent years, summarizes the exterior structure design, manufacturing methods, magnetic drive system selection and motion control methods of magnetically driven micro- and nanorobots, and then introduces the application research of magnetically driven micro- and nanorobots in the biomedical field. Finally, the problems and prospects of magnetically driven micro/nano robots are pointed out.

Keywords: Magnetic · nanorobots · Magnetically drive · Application research

1 Introduction

Micro- and nanorobots can obtain energy from surrounding media [1], or utilize external energy sources such as light [2], ultrasound [3], electric or magnetic fields [4], or a combination of these energy sources [5], and effectively convert energy into kinetic energy. For a long time, micro- and nanorobots have been widely concerned because of their good application prospects in drug delivery, sensing, environmental remediation and small object manipulation [6].

In recent years, with the development of new intelligent materials and intelligent structures, various types of magnetically driven micro- and nanorobots have come to people's attention. Magnetically drive has unique medical application potential in opaque

© The Author(s), under exclusive license to Springer Nature Singapore Pte Ltd. 2023
H. Yang et al. (Eds.): ICIRA 2023, LNAI 14274, pp. 476–492, 2023.
https://doi.org/10.1007/978-981-99-6501-4_41

tissues with high penetration depth. Magnetically driven micro- and nanorobots can achieve non-destructive remote regulation in organisms by utilizing a certain strength of magnetic field, which can adapt to different liquid environments and have strong controllability. This has sparked a widespread research boom in the biomedical field. At the same time, magnetically drive can quickly and accurately drive a single or a group of micro- and nanorobots in different complex environments [7–10], and in recent years, it has also shown broad application prospects in the fields of electronics and environmental applications. In order to promote the further development and application of magnetically driven micro- and nanorobots, researchers have developed different magnetic drive systems based on magnetically driven micro- and nanorobots designed using different exterior structures and manufacturing methods. They can customize the design workspace and multiple degrees of freedom, and use corresponding motion control methods to control the robot. This article will first outline the appearance and structure design, manufacturing methods, magnetic drive system and motion control methods selection of magnetically driven micro- and nanorobots, analyze and compare their technical characteristics. Then, summarize the application prospects of magnetically driven micro- and nanorobots in the biomedical field. Finally, the existing problems in the research of magnetically driven micro- and nanorobots are pointed out and future research prospects are proposed.

2 Appearance and Structure Design

The innovative design inspiration of the appearance and structure of magnetically driven micro- and nanorobots mostly comes from nature. At present, the appearance design of common magnetically driven micro- and nanorobots is mainly based on the basic geometric shape and bionic structure shape. This section will introduce in detail the special structure and composition design of the magnetically driven micro- and nanorobots based on the specific appearance in combination with the characteristics of various appearance designs.

2.1 Basic Geometric Shape

As shown in Fig. 1, the shape design of magnetically driven micro- and nanorobots based on basic geometry mainly includes spherical [11], ellipsoidal [12], cylindrical [13], membrane [14], U-shaped [15], cubic [16], tubular [17], capsule [18].

2.2 Bionic Structure Shape

As shown in Fig. 2, the shape design of magnetically driven micro- and nanorobots based on basic bionic structure mainly includes worm type [19], spiral type [20], starfish/snowflake type [21], origami type [22], multi legged type (lateral flagella) [23], octopus like type [24].

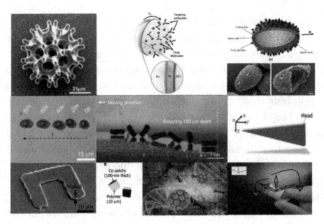

Fig. 1. Magnetic driven micro- and nanorobots based on basic geometry [11–18]

Fig. 2. Magnetic driven micro- and nanorobots based on basic bionic structure [19–24]

2.3 Combined Shape and Multiple Motion Modes

Based on the expansion of people's application requirements and the continuous deepening of research, micro- and nanorobots with various combined shapes and multiple motion modes are also gradually developed successfully, such as:

In 2016, Huang and his colleagues [25] developed a bio-inspired soft micro robot with rapid self-folding formation by adding magnetic nanoparticles to thermal responsive hydrogel soft materials. This kind of robot has complex body structure, reconfigurable body shape and controllable movement ability (as shown in (Fig. 3 (a)). This type of robot is composed of a non-expandable support hydrogel layer and an expandable thermal responsive N-isopropylacrylamide (NIPAAm) hydrogel layer, on which polyethylene glycol diacrylate (PEGDA) is selectively patterned. The self-folding shape of the monolayer or bilayer hydrogel of the micro robot and the magnetization axis of the final structure can be determined in advance through the alignment of the added magnetic particles during the fabrication. In addition, the micro robot with thermal responsive hydrogel material can also realize refolding and shape switching by near-infrared light (NIR) heating.

In 2018, Kim et al. [19] designed a software robot with programmable ferromagnetic domain magnetic moment that can be produced by 3D printing technology. In this method, the elastomer composite containing ferromagnetic particles is used as the ink for 3D printing (as shown in Fig. 3 (b)). During printing, a programmable magnetic field is applied at the nozzle to reorient the particles along the applied magnetic field, so that the printed filaments have patterned magnetic poles. The programmable magnetization pattern soft robot can show complex shape changes under the external driving magnetic field, and derive a variety of functions, including reconfigurable soft micro robot, soft robot that can jump, and soft robot that can crawl, roll, capture fast moving objects and transmit drug dose.

In 2018, Hu et al. [26] embedded the hard magnetic particles (NdFeB) into the flexible polymer silicon elastomer to produce a magnetoelastic rectangular thin plate soft micro robot. Through further magnetization process, the soft robot was specially magnetized and programmed to have a single wavelength harmonic magnetization profile along the body axis. The robot can be controlled by the external time-varying driving magnetic field to produce different motion modes, such as swimming and climbing the liquid meniscus inside and on the surface of the liquid, rolling, walking and jumping over obstacles on the solid surface, crawling in narrow tunnels, and even moving reversibly between different liquid and solid terrains, and switching between different motion modes (as shown in Fig. 3 (c)).

In 2019, Xie et al. [27] proposed a strategy of using alternating magnetic field to program hematite colloidal particles into liquid, chain, vortex and ribbon micro-obovate clusters, and realized rapid and reversible conversion between them (as shown in Fig. 3 (d)). Using the proposed discrete particle simulation method, the generation mechanism of these four populations and the "cross pool" movement of chain and vortex communities were studied. The scheme has good operability, and the particles can move in any direction through programmed magnetic field control. This strategy can achieve rapid switching between community forms, so it has high environmental adaptability.

In 2019, Xu and his colleagues [28] proposed a method to accurately program the discrete three-dimensional magnetization pattern of planar flexible composites embedded with hard magnetic particles at the sub millimeter scale (as shown in Fig. 3 (e)). This method is based on UV lithography technology. By controlling the redirection of magnetic particles and selective exposure to UV light, the magnetization geometric coding of magnetic particles in planar flexible composites is realized. A number of planar flexible micro robots with different sizes, geometric shapes and magnetization profiles designed by this method can be directly and automatically fabricated by 3D printing system, making it possible for planar micro robots with arbitrary magnetic torque distribution, such as high-order, multi axis bending, large angle bending, etc.

In 2019, Cui et al. [29] further promoted the production boundary of magnetic soft micro robot with programmable magnetic moment, and proposed an electron beam lithography technology. Based on this method, micro robot with the size of only a few microns and rewritable magnetic moment can be manufactured (as shown in Fig. 3 (f)). This work uses single domain cobalt nano magnetic materials with line-of-sight type, i.e. nano magnetism materials with a transverse size ranging from 100nm to 500nm. This means that they still have stable residual magnetization after being separated from the external magnetization field, and have adjustable magnetic anisotropy at room temperature. In addition, a miniature "bird" shaped robot has been constructed in this work, and it can perform complex behaviors, including "slap", "hover", "turn" and "side-slip".

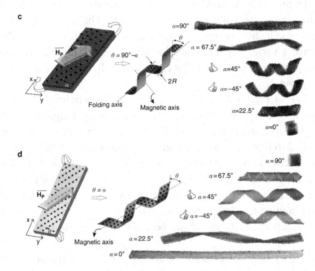

(a) Soft micro robot with programmable body shape [25]

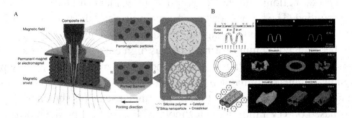

(b) Soft robot with programmable magnetic moment of ferromagnetic domain [19]

Fig. 3. The combined shape and multiple motion modes of micro- and nanorobots

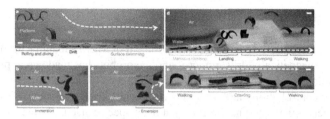

(c) Soft micro robot with multiple motion modes [26]

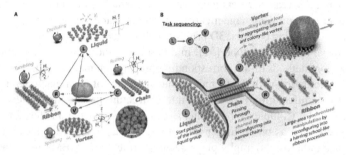

(d) Multi motion modes of magnetic nano-particles [27]

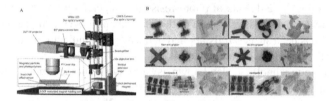

(e) Magnetic soft robot with precisely programmable discrete 3D magnetization pattern [28]

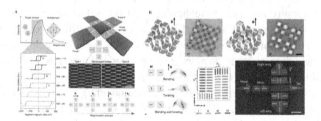

(f) Deformable micro robot capable of rewriting magnetization direction on nanometer scale [29]

Fig. 3. (*continued*)

3 Manufacturing Methods

In recent years, with the continuous development of MEMS manufacturing technology, the field of magnetically driven micro- and nanorobots has made great progress. However, in order to meet the design needs of magnetically driven micro- and nanorobots with better controllability and motion performance, how to efficiently and rapidly prepare magnetic micro- and nanorobots that meet specific needs for magnetic micro- and nanorobots with special appearance, structure and composition is an urgent problem to be solved. For this reason, researchers have also carried out a lot of researches. Methods commonly used to prepare magnetically driven micro- and nanorobots Mainly including: MEMS manufacturing process, 3D printing technology [7], 4D printing technology [30] and biological template method [31]. In this section, the applicable material types and the realization methods of the corresponding preparation methods will be introduced in detail in combination with the technical characteristics of each manufacturing method.

MEMS manufacturing process is a micro structure processing process down to the nanometer scale. Complex three-dimensional shapes are manufactured through basic process steps such as photo-lithography, thin film deposition, sputtering and etching. Among them, photo-lithography plays a leading role in the MEMS manufacturing process. This technology is to transfer the graphics produced on the photo-lithography mask to the surface of the substrate. Its graphics resolution, overlay accuracy, photo-resist side-wall morphology, the defects of photo-resist and the etching resistance of photo-resist directly affect the success or failure of the subsequent process. At present, lithography technology has been successfully applied in the micro manufacturing process to prepare magnetically driven micro- and nanorobots.

3D printing technology, also known as "additive manufacturing", originated in the 1970s. It is an advanced manufacturing process for manufacturing parts or products through layer-by-layer accumulation. At present, 3D printing technologies that have been successfully used to prepare magnetically driven micro- and nanorobots mainly include 3D direct writing printing technology (DW) based on magnetic composite ink, stereo lithography appearance technology (SLA), selective laser melting (SLM) and laser metal deposition technology (LMD) according to different mechanisms.

4D printing technology is the combination of 3D printing technology and intelligent materials, which means that the physical properties and functions of 3D objects processed by 3D printing can change with time under specific environment and excitation (such as electricity, light, magnetism, water, heat, sound, etc.), that is, a time variable is added on the basis of traditional 3D printing, which can print more complex autonomous deformation structures. The structure, shape and size of the magnetic response structure printed by 4D can change with time under magnetic excitation, and can be controlled under the action of a constant magnetic field.

Biological template method is a new method and way to prepare materials with special structure by using natural biological structure. The biological template can realize the morphological diversity and functional diversity of synthetic inorganic materials, and also meet the requirements of environmental protection for materials. At present, researchers have prepared magnetic driven micro- and nanorobots with various functions by using biological template method.

In 2012, the Nelson Institute for robotics and intelligent systems described a technology for manufacturing tubular and helical magnetic microstructures using diacetyl phospholipid as a template[32]. These structures are able to move using externally generated magnetic fields and magnetic field gradients. It is proved that the direction of motion of the tubular structure can be determined by using the external magnetic field, and the tubular structure can move along the main axis by using the magnetic field gradient. In 2019, Faher et al. used Spirulina as a biological template to prepare a magnetic spiral micro robot [33]. By immersing Spirulina in nano-Fe_3O_4 dispersion, the surface of Spirulina can adsorb Fe_3O_4 nanoparticles, so that Spirulina can be driven in a rotating magnetic field. Due to the biological characteristics of spirulina, this robot can perform fluorescence imaging without any surface modification, and the fluorescence imaging experiment was carried out in mice. In 2020, the team of Zhejiang University successfully improved the hypoxic microenvironment of tumor and effectively realized tumor diagnosis and treatment under the guidance of magnetic resonance, fluorescence or photoacoustic three-mode medical image navigation by using microalgae as a living scaffold and "putting on" a magnetic coating coat (Fe_3O_4 nanoparticles) and targeted delivery to tumor tissue with the help of alternating magnetic field [34].

4 Magnetic Drive System and Motion Control Methods Selection

In order to realize the precise control of magnetically driven micro- and nanorobots in different and complex environments, researchers have developed corresponding magnetic drive systems and motion control methods such as open-loop pre-programming control and closed-loop path tracking control based on magnetic drive. In particular, various magnetic drive systems can customize the design workspace and multiple degrees of freedom for micro- and nanorobots. This section will combine the technical characteristics of various magnetic drive systems and motion control methods, and introduce their applications and corresponding implementation methods in micro- and nanorobots in detail.

4.1 Magnetic Drive System

At present, the common driving magnetic fields of the magnetic drive system mainly include: rotating field, oscillating field and gradient field. Different types of magnetic fields can be obtained by designing permanent magnets and electromagnetic coils. Especially for electromagnets, the direction, intensity and frequency of the external magnetic field can be adjusted by adjusting the current intensity, frequency, phase and switching mode of the electromagnetic coil that provides the external magnetic field, so that controllable magnetic force or magnetic torque can be applied to the micro nano robot to provide power and multi degree of freedom motion control for driving various micro nano robots.

In 1995, McNeil [35] designed a magnetic stereotactic system, which is composed of three pairs of orthogonal coils to form a "helmet" structure to control the magnetic field of the whole head. However, this design cannot achieve full torque and force control. In 2006, Yesin et al. [36] used the combination of uniform magnetic field generated by

Helmholtz coil pair and magnetic gradient generated by Maxwell coil pair to control the elliptical micro robot. This system has two degrees of freedom. In 2010, Kummer designed an electromagnetic system called OctoMag[37], which consists of eight electromagnets with five degrees of freedom (as shown in Fig. 4a). In recent years, many researchers have used three pairs of orthogonal Helmholtz coils to generate a uniform rotating magnetic field in the working space, and the three pairs of orthogonal Helmholtz coils allow rotation controlled by three degrees of freedom[38] (as shown in Fig. 4b). Many other researchers [39] use rotating manipulator to control the movement of permanent magnet (as shown in Fig. 4c).

(a) OctoMag system [37]   (b) 3D Helmholtz coil system [38]   (c) Manipulator drive permanent magnet [39]

Fig. 4. Rotating magnetic fields

As shown in Fig. 5 (a), in 2021, Zheng et al. [40] designed an ionic shape-morphing micro-robotic end effectors, which consists of 8 electromagnetic coils and can achieve high magnetic field gradient. The eight-axis coil magnetic field can generate magnetic field gradients in any direction in space, so the robot can move in any direction. For the micro robot driven by magnetic torque, it generally needs different axis uniform magnetic field to realize the arbitrary motion of the robot in space. The magnetic drive system used in reference consists of four pairs of orthogonal Helmholtz coils. If the robot is driven only on a two-dimensional plane, only two pairs of Helmholtz coils are needed. As shown in **Fig. 5** (b), in 2010, the two-axis Helmholtz coil with large size designed by Park [41] can provide a two-dimensional uniform magnetic field. Magnetic gradient coil and magnetic uniform coil can also be combined to provide multi-functional driving mode. Then Park et al. [42] designed a two-axis coil system, including two pairs of Helmholtz coils and two pairs of Maxwell coils, which can generate two-axis uniform magnetic field and gradient magnetic field respectively. In addition to circular and square coils, saddle coils can also be used to generate uniform and gradient magnetic fields. As shown in Fig. 5 (c), in 2010, the coil system developed by Jeon et al. [43] includes a pair of Helmholtz coils, a pair of Maxwell coils, a pair of gradient saddle coils and a pair of uniform saddle coils. Compared with the traditional circular coil system, this kind of coil system has a more compact structure, greatly reduces the occupied space, is conducive to the human body lying flat in the coil, and provides a feasible control platform for the micro robot navigation in the human blood vessels.

(a) Eight-axis coil system generating gradient magnetic field [40]   (b) Two axis Helmholtz coil [41]

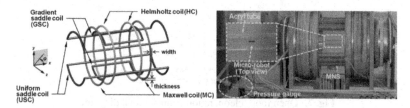

(c) Coil system with saddle coil [43]

Fig. 5. Gradient magnetic field

4.2 Motion Control Methods Selection

The motion control method of magnetically driven micro- and nano robot includes open-loop control and closed-loop control. According to the different control principles, the open-loop control method can be divided into pre-programming control and open-loop teleoperation control. The closed-loop control method can be divided into point-to-point position control for holonomic constraint mobile micro- and nanorobots and speed independent path tracking control for nonholonomic constraint mobile micro- and nanorobots.

Figure 6 shows the pre-programming control block diagram of the micro- and nanorobots. In order to realize the pre-programming open-loop control of the magnetically driven micro- and nanorobots, researchers first need to estimate the control information. In the pre-programming open-loop control method based on magnetic drive, because there is no feedback in the control process, the micro robot will deviate from the reference trajectory or path under the action of environmental noise or boundary effect. Reference path following means following the virtual robot in a time-dependent manner, and reference path following means following the time-independent trajectory. In the pre-programming control method, the motion error of micro- and nanorobots can sometimes be corrected automatically by means of external environmental conditions rather than control methods.

Figure 7 shows the open-loop teleoperation control block diagram of the micro- and nanorobots. In the open-loop teleoperation control method based on magnetic drive, the user only sends motion commands without any mechanical force feedback, and the visual feedback can be returned to the operator without any tracking and calculation of the robot position.

In the motion process based on this control method, the robot corrects the deviation in a non-automatic way, so this method is mostly applied to the targeted drug delivery tasks that do not require a lot of repetitive work, and is not suitable for industrial operations that require high precision and high repeatability, such as the robot micro assembly process.

Fig. 6. Pre-programming control block diagram

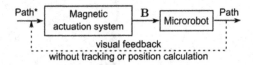

Fig. 7. Open loop teleoperation control block diagram

Under the disturbance caused by thermal noise or the drift caused by boundary effect, it is possible for the micro- and nanorobots to achieve accurate motion by using closed-loop control. Due to the high sensitivity of the micro system to environmental variables and the high-speed characteristics on the micro scale, the micro- and nanorobots needs a robust and efficient control system, and it is difficult to design sensors on the body because of the small scale. Therefore, a fast external sensing method is needed to locate the robot, such as vision. Figure 8 shows the closed-loop positioning control block diagram of holonomic constraint micro- and nanorobots. This point-to-point closed-loop position control method is widely used in holonomic constraint mobile micro- and nanorobots.

For nonholonomic constraint mobile micro- and nanorobots, such as spiral Swimming Micro Robot, simple PID controller can't be applied in the position of micro robot, because nonholonomic constraint system is a mechanical system with constraint on speed, and speed is not differentiable for position constraint. Figure 9 shows the plane path following control block diagram, and the control process uses two controllers. The controller I is used to minimize the horizontal error, and can deduce the target direction of the spiral Swimming Micro Robot. The controller II is a P controller based on the directional error of the spiral Swimming Micro Robot in three-dimensional space, which can give the target driving magnetic field. Another nonholonomic constraint mobile micro nano robot is the rolling magnetic robot, which can generate positive velocity on the surface under the rolling motion driven by the rotating magnetic field.

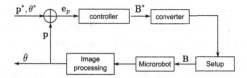

Fig. 8. Control block diagram of holonomic constrained micro- nanorobots

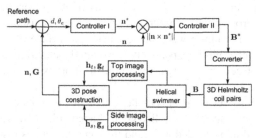

Fig. 9. Planar path following control block diagram of nonholonomic constrained spiral swimming robot

5 Application Prospect of Magnetically Driven Micro- and Nanorobots

The realization of magnetically driven micro- and nanorobots not only makes it possible to drive micro- and nanorobots wirelessly, but also endows the micro- and nanorobots with incentive response behavior. The micro- and nanorobots with specific appearance and structure manufactured by special manufacturing method can actively realize the transformation of shape and structure under the excitation of external magnetic field. This technology will have a wide application prospect. This section will mainly introduce the application research of magnetically driven micro- and nanorobots in biomedical field. Biomedical field is a highly demanding field for wireless magnetically micro- and nanorobots. The micro- and nanorobots has achieved good controllability in opaque tissues with high penetration depth, can carry out non-invasive remote control in organisms, and can also adapt to different liquid environments such as blood and tissue fluid. This technology provides a new technical scheme for the field of minimally invasive medicine. Therefore, magnetically driven micro nano robots show great potential and practical value in the biomedical field.

In 2015, Nelson Institute of robotics and intelligent systems [44] demonstrated for the first time that ABF loaded with plasmid DNA (pDNA) in vitro successfully delivered wireless targeting and single-cell genes to human embryonic kidney (HEK293) cells. ABF contains p-type DNA fatty expression enzyme to produce functional ABF. f-ABF is wirelessly guided by a low-intensity rotating magnetic field and transmits the loaded pDNA to the target cells. The target cells of f-ABF were successfully transfected with pDNA and expressed the encoded protein. These f-ABF can also be used for gene delivery in vivo and other applications, such as sensors, actuators, and cell biology.

In 2016, researchers from MIT Artificial Intelligence Laboratory CSAIL, Sheffield University and Tokyo Institute of technology jointly developed an edible miniature foldable robot [45]. The micro robot is made of pig large intestine and permanent magnet. It can be used for direct swallowing so that the button battery can be removed without surgery. In addition, the robot can perform other visceral operations, such as repairing the inner wall of the intestinal tract. The core of the robot is the permanent magnet on the robot and the controllable electromagnetic field around it.

In 2019, D.Sun et al. [46] of the City University of Hong Kong designed a magnetically driven spiny porous spherical micro robot, which can be used to carry cells in vivo. A layer of nickel and titanium were sputtered on the surface of the robot to provide magnetic and biocompatibility respectively. Through the electromagnetic drive system, the robot loaded with cells can navigate in zebrafish embryos, and the experiment of cell release is carried out in nude mice.

In 2019, Wu Dong, et al. [47]. Of the University of science and technology of China prepared a magnetically controlled cone-shaped hollow micro screw robot using modulated structured light, loaded nano and micron scale goods inside and outside the cone-shaped spiral structure respectively, and completed the transplantation of neural stem cells in vitro. Compared with the straight micro screw, the forward swimming ability of the cone-shaped micro screw was increased by 50%, and the lateral drift was reduced by 70%.

In 2020, the Max Planck Institute for intelligent systems in Germany [48] prepared a spherical micro robot on a single layer of pre-dried silica particles. The micro robot is essentially a glass particle, half of which is coated with a layer of nickel and gold film, and the other half carries drug molecules and antibodies that recognize cancer cells. The robot moves along the blood vessel wall in a rolling manner. When the magnetic force is large enough, it can drag the robot against the current to make it move "upstream" in the blood.

In 2020, the team of Zhejiang University [34] successfully improved the hypoxic micro-environment of tumor and effectively realized tumor diagnosis and treatment under the guidance of magnetic resonance, fluorescence or photo-acoustic three-mode medical image navigation by using micro-algae as a living scaffold and "putting on" a magnetic coating coat (Fe3O4 nanoparticles) and targeted delivery to tumor tissue with the help of alternating magnetic field (Fig. 10).

6   Conclusion and Prospect

Magnetically driven micro- and nanorobots have broad application prospects in biomedical applications, such as disease diagnosis and treatment, targeted delivery, non-invasive surgery and other biomedical fields due to their flexible movement, accurate targeting, drug transportation and other capabilities. However, at this stage, most of the relevant researches on magnetically driven micro- and nanorobots are focused on in vitro, and more expected functions for in vivo therapeutic applications are still very challenging. That is to say, the application of magnetically driven micro- and nanorobots is in the initial stage, and there are still some challenges in the application of these devices in the actual scene. In the current research, with the progress of micro and nano processing technology, the preparation methods of magnetically driven micro- and nanorobots are more

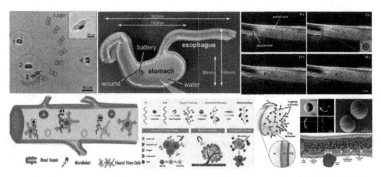

Fig. 10. Application prospect of magnetically driven micro- nanorobots in biomedical field [34] [44–48]

and more abundant. Based on the processing characteristics and application occasions of materials, a variety of processing methods are used together, and a variety of micro robots are prepared on a variety of scales. From the perspective of movement mode, it not only simulates the movement mode of micro-organisms in nature, but also has received extensive attention on the new movement mechanism, which greatly enriches the movement form of robots. According to different applications, the magnetic field drive system of micro robot is also varied, including the drive system compatible with the existing magnetic platform and the drive system for complex motion control and navigation.

According to the above literature, it can be found that some materials with excellent performance have no application in the field of micro robot due to the lack of processing means, which greatly limits the application scope of materials. Therefore, it is of great significance for the development of magnetically driven soft micro robot to overcome the difficulties of material processing, study the processing methods of materials and give full play to the excellent performance of materials. In order to meet the design needs, the micromachining and manufacturing technology that can produce the corresponding magnetically driven soft micro robot in a low-cost, large-scale and environmentally friendly way still needs to be continuously developed. The response characteristics of the micro- and nanorobots under the magnetic field are not only related to the external excitation magnetic field, but also related to its inherent magnetization characteristics. The existing magnetization technologies mainly include the following three types: unidirectional magnetization, winding magnetization and 3D printing assisted magnetization. The first two magnetization modes are single, while the last one can show a variety of magnetization modes, but the process is complex and requires high equipment. In addition, it can be seen that the magnetic field control system and real-time information feedback are very important. The multi degree of freedom, efficient and accurate motion control needs the continuous development of closed-loop control system, biological imaging and other technologies.

Magnetic control software micro robot has a wide range of potential applications in the biomedical field. However, the real application still faces many scientific and technological challenges. The corresponding research is still in its infancy, and the movement behavior and mechanism need to be studied. The development space of accurate and fast intelligent control methods is huge, and playing its full potential faces many unknown and challenges. Therefore, in the future, the magnetic control software micro robot based on the magnetic field driving system will develop in a more intelligent direction, and will have the characteristics of high mobility, deformable structure, sustainable operation, precise control and so on, which is expected to realize the cluster intelligent cooperation between robots.

Acknowledgement. This work was Supported by the Fundamental Research Funds for the Provincial Universities of Zhejiang [grant number GK209907299001-011], the National Natural Science Foundation of China [grant number 52005142).

References

1. Sitti, M., Wiersma, D.S.: Pros and cons: magnetic versus optical microrobots. Adv. Mater. **32**(20), e1906766 (2020). https://doi.org/10.1002/adma.201906766
2. Huang, C., Lv, J., Tian, X., Wang, Y., Yu, Y., Liu, J.: Miniaturized swimming soft robot with complex movement actuated and controlled by remote light signals. Sci. Rep. **5**(1), 17414 (2015). https://doi.org/10.1038/srep17414
3. Chen, X.Z., et al.: Small-scale machines driven by external power sources. Adv. Mater. (Deerfield Beach, Fla.) **30**(15), e1705061 (2018)
4. Steager, E.B., Sakar, M.S., Magee, C., Kennedy, M., Cowley, A., Kumar, V.: Automated biomanipulation of single cells using magnetic microrobots. Int. J. Rob. Res. **32**(3), 346–359 (2013)
5. Katuri, J., Ma, X., Stanton, M.M., Sánchez, S.: Designing micro- and nanoswimmers for specific applications. Acc. Chem. Res. **50**(1), 2–11 (2017)
6. Tottori, S., Zhang, L., Qiu, F., Krawczyk, K.K., Franco-Obregón, A., Nelson, B.J.: Magnetic helical micromachines: fabrication, controlled swimming, and cargo transport. Adv. Mater. (Deerfield Beach Fla.) **24**(6), 811–816 (2012)
7. Shao, G., Ware, H.O.T., Huang, J., Hai, R., Li, L., Sun, C.: 3D printed magnetically-actuating micro-gripper operates in air and water. Addit. Manuf. **38**, 101834 (2021)
8. Tang, J., Yao, C., Gu, Z., Jung, S., Luo, D., Yang, D.: Super-soft and super-elastic DNA robot with magnetically driven navigational locomotion for cell delivery in confined space. Angewandte Chemie (Int. ed. in English.) **59**(6), 2490–2495 (2020)
9. Wang, L., Meng, Z., Chen, Y., Zheng, Y.: Engineering, magnetic, micro/nanorobots for versatile biomedical applications. Adv. Intell. Syst. **3**, 2000267 (2021)
10. Koleoso, M., Feng, X., Xue, Y., Li, Q., Munshi, T., Chen, X.: Micro/nanoscale magnetic robots for biomedical applications. Mater. Today Bio. **8**, 100085 (2020)
11. Li, J., et al.: Development of a magnetic microrobot for carrying and delivering targeted cells. Sci. Robot. **3**, 8829 (2018)
12. Khalil, I.S.M., Dijkslag, H.C., Abelmann, L., Misra, S.: MagnetoSperm: a microrobot that navigates using weak magnetic fields. Appl. Phys. Lett. **104**(22), 223701 (2014)
13. Won, S., Kim, S., Park, J.E., et al.: On-demand orbital maneuver of multiple soft robots via hierarchical magnetomotility. Nat. Commun. **10**, 4751 (2019)
14. Huang, C., Xu, T., Liu, J., Manamanchaiyaporn, L., Wu, X.: Visual servoing of miniature magnetic film swimming robots for 3-D arbitrary path following. IEEE Robot. Autom. Lett. **4**(4), 4185–4191 (2019)
15. Kim, H., Ali, J., Cheang, U.K., Jeong, J., Kim, J.S., Kim, M.J.: Micro manipulation using magnetic microrobots. J. Bionic Eng. **13**(4), 515–524 (2016)

16. Han, K., et al.: Sequence-encoded colloidal origami and microbot assemblies from patchy magnetic cubes. Sci. Adv. **329**, e1701108 (2017)
17. Yang, L., et al.: Targeted single-cell therapeutics with magnetic tubular micromotor by one-step exposure of structured femtosecond optical vortices. Adv. Funct. Mater. **29**, 1905745 (2019)
18. Hu, H., Yang, X., Song, L., Wei, W., Peng, G., Feng, L.: High position accuracy and 5 degree freedom magnetic driven capsule robot. In: 2019 WRC Symposium on Advanced Robotics and Automation (WRC SARA), Beijing, China, pp. 19–24 (2019)
19. Kim, Y., Yuk, H., Zhao, R., et al.: Printing ferromagnetic domains for untethered fast-transforming soft materials. Nature **558**, 274–279 (2018)
20. Yan, X., et al.: Multifunctional biohybrid magnetite microrobots for imaging-guided therapy. Sci. Robot. **2**(12), eaaq1155 (2017). https://doi.org/10.1126/scirobotics.aaq1155
21. Go, G., Nguyen, V.D., Jin, Z., et al.: A thermo-electromagnetically actuated microrobot for the targeted transport of therapeutic agents. Int. J. Control Autom. Syst. **16**, 1341–1354 (2018)
22. Miyashita, S., Guitron, S., Ludersdorfer, M., Sung, C.R., Rus, D.: An untethered miniature origami robot that self-folds, walks, swims, and degrades. In: 2015 IEEE International Conference on Robotics and Automation (ICRA), Seattle, WA, USA, pp. 1490–1496 (2015)
23. Zhang, L., Huang, H., Chen, L., Li, X., Li, Y., Huang, J.: A magnetically controlled micro-robot with multiple side flagella. In: 2017 IEEE 12th International Conference on Nano/Micro Engineered and Molecular Systems (NEMS), Los Angeles, CA, USA, pp. 544–549 (2017)
24. Du, X., et al.: Reconfiguration, camouflage, and color-shifting for bioinspired adaptive hydrogel-based millirobots. Adv. Funct. Mater. **30**, 1909202 (2020)
25. Huang, H.W., Sakar, M., Petruska, A., et al.: Soft micromachines with programmable motility and morphology. Nat Commun **7**, 12263 (2016)
26. Hu, W., Lum, G., Mastrangeli, M., et al.: Small-scale soft-bodied robot with multimodal locomotion. Nature **554**, 81–85 (2018)
27. Hui, X., et al.: Reconfigurable magnetic microrobot swarm: multimode transformation, locomotion, and manipulation. Sci. Robot. **4**, eaav8006 (2019)
28. Xu, T., et al.: Millimeter-scale flexible robots with programmable three-dimensional magne-tization and motions. Sci. Robot. **4**, eaav4494 (2019)
29. Cui, J., Huang, T.Y., Luo, Z., et al.: Nanomagnetic encoding of shape-morphing microma-chines. Nature **575**, 164–168 (2019)
30. Adam, G., Benouhiba, A., Rabenorosoa, K., Clévy, C., Cappelleri, D.J.: 4D printing: enabling technology for microrobotics applications. Adv. Intell. Syst. **3**, 2000216 (2021)
31. Yang, L., Zhang, Y., Wang, Q., Chan, K.-F., Zhang, L.: Automated control of magnetic spore-based microrobot using fluorescence imaging for targeted delivery with cellular resolution. IEEE Trans. Autom. Sci. Eng. **17**(1), 490–501 (2020)
32. Schuerle, S., Pané, S., Pellicer, E., Sort, J., Baró, M.D., Nelson, B.J.: Helical and tubular lipid microstructures that are electroless-coated with CoNiReP for wireless magnetic manipulation. Small **8**, 1498–1502 (2012)
33. Mushtaq, F., Chen, X.Z., Staufert, S., et al.: On-the-fly catalytic degradation of organic pollu-tants using magneto-photoresponsive bacteria-templated microcleaners. J. Mater. Chem. A. **7**, 24847–24856 (2023)
34. Zhong, D., Li, W., Qi, Y., He, J., Zhou, M.: Photosynthetic biohybrid nanoswimmers system to alleviate tumor hypoxia for FL/PA/MR imaging-guided enhanced radio-photodynamic synergetic therapy. Adv. Funct. Mater. **30**, 1910395 (2020)
35. McNeil, R.G., et al.: Characteristics of an improved magnetic-implant guidance system. I.E.E.E. Trans. Biomed. Eng. **42**(8), 802–808 (1995)
36. Yesin, K.B., Vollmers, K., Nelson, B.J.: Modeling and control of untethered biomicrorobots in a fluidic environment using electromagnetic fields. Int. J. Robot. Res. **25**(5–6), 527–536 (2006)

37. Kummer, M.P., Abbott, J.J., Kratochvil, B.E., Borer, R., Sengul, A., Nelson, B.J.: OctoMag: an electromagnetic system for 5-DOF wireless micromanipulation. IEEE Trans. Rob. **26**(6), 1006–1017 (2010)

38. Mahoney, A.W., Sarrazin, J.C., Bamberg, E., Abbott, J.J.: Velocity control with gravity compensation for magnetic helical microswimmers. Adv. Robot. **25**(8), 1007–1028 (2011)

39. Mahoney, A.W., Cowan, D.L., Miller, K.M., Abbott, J.J.: Control of untethered magnetically actuated tools using a rotating permanent magnet in any position. In: 2012 IEEE International Conference on Robotics and Automation, Saint Paul, MN, USA, pp. 3375–3380 (2012)

40. Zheng, Z., Wang, H., Dong, L., et al.: Ionic shape-morphing microrobotic end-effectors for environmentally adaptive targeting, releasing, and sampling. Nat. Commun. **12**, 411 (2021)

41. Byun, D., Choi, J., Cha, K., Park, J., Park, S.: Swimming microrobot actuated by two pairs of Helmholtz coils system. Mechatronics **21**(1), 357–364 (2011)

42. Choi, H., Choi, J., Jang, G., et al.: Two-dimensional actuation of a microrobot with a stationary two-pair coil system. Smart Mater. Struct **18**(5), 055007 (2009)

43. Jeon, S.M., Jang, G.H., Choi, J.H., Park, S.H., Park, J.O.: Precise manipulation of a microrobot in the pulsatile flow of human blood vessels using magnetic navigation system. J. Appl. Phys. **109**(7), 07B316 (2011)

44. Qiu, F., Nelson, B.J.: Magnetic helical micro- and nanorobots: toward their biomedical applications. Engineering **1**(1), 021–026 (2015)

45. Miyashita, S., Guitron, S., Yoshida, K., Li, S., Damian, D.D., Rus, D.: Ingestible, controllable, and degradable origami robot for patching stomach wounds. In: 2016 IEEE International Conference on Robotics and Automation (ICRA), Stockholm, pp. 909–916 (2016)

46. Li, D., Dong, D., Lam, W., Xing, L., Wei, T., Sun, D.: Automated in Vivo navigation of magnetic-driven microrobots using OCT imaging feedback. I.E.E.E. Trans. Biomed. Eng. **67**(8), 2349–2358 (2020)

47. Xin, C., et al.: Conical hollow microhelices with superior swimming capabilities for targeted cargo delivery. Adv Mater. **31**(25), e1808226 (2019)

48. Alapan, Y., Bozuyuk, U., Erkoc, P., Karacakol, A.C., Sitti, M.: Multifunctional surface micro-rollers for targeted cargo delivery in physiological blood flow. Sci. Robot. **5**(42), eaba5726 (2020). https://doi.org/10.1126/scirobotics.aba5726

A Novel Transfer Learning Method for Robot Bearing Fault Diagnosis Based on Deep Convolutional Residual Wasserstein Adversarial Network

Bing Pan[1,2], Xin Xiong[3], Hailiang Hu[4], Jun He[1,2(✉)], and Shixi Yang[1,2]

[1] The State Key Laboratory of Fluid Power and Mechatronic Systems, School of Mechanical Engineering, Zhejiang University, Hangzhou, China
{22025213,hjshenhua,yangsx}@zju.edu.cn
[2] The Key Laboratory of Advanced Manufacturing Technology of Zhejiang Province, School of Mechanical Engineering, Zhejiang University, Hangzhou, China
[3] Shanghai Key Laboratory of Intelligent Manufacturing and Robotics, Shanghai University, Shanghai 200444, China
xxiong@shu.edu.cn
[4] Hangzhou Steam Turbine Power Group Co., Ltd., Hangzhou, China
hhll@htc.cn

Abstract. In the process of robot bearing fault diagnosis based on data-driven, transfer learning is an effective method to solve the lack of labeled data, and data distribution difference between source domain data and target domain data will lead to domain drifts under variable working conditions. In this paper, a robot bearing fault diagnosis method based on deep convolutional residual Wasserstein adversarial network (DCRWAN) is proposed to reduce domain offsets and improve the robot bearing fault diagnosis accuracy. In the proposed method, a deep convolutional residual network is constructed to extract the transferable features of source domain and target domain. Then, a domain discrimination module is constructed and the domain adversarial training is carried out to minimize the distribution discrepancy of cross-domain by the Wasserstein loss function. At the same time, a domain distribution discrepancy metrics module is applied to estimate the difference of features distribution between two domains, and further fine-tuning the network parameters to obtain domain-invariant and class-separable features for the classification. The average accuracy of the two transfer tasks using this method is 95.65% and 93.75%, respectively, and the results show that the method effectively reduces the domain differences caused by varying working conditions and improves the fault diagnosis accuracy of robot bearings under variable working conditions.

Keywords: Robot Bearing · Fault Diagnosis · Transfer Learning · Wasserstein Adversarial Network

© The Author(s), under exclusive license to Springer Nature Singapore Pte Ltd. 2023
H. Yang et al. (Eds.): ICIRA 2023, LNAI 14274, pp. 493–505, 2023.
https://doi.org/10.1007/978-981-99-6501-4_42

1 Introduction

Robots play an important role in modern production and life. Bearing is an important part of the flexible rotation of the robotic arm. Its faults can lead to unexpected interruption of manufacture and huge economic losses, sometimes even personal injury [1, 2]. However, research on robot bearing fault diagnosis is still rare. The detection and diagnosis of its faults is of great significance in modern society.

Intelligent fault diagnosis methods, which can effectively analyze massive data and automatically provide accurate diagnosis results without too much expert knowledge, have been widely applied to identify robot bearing faults [3]. Particularly, deep learning has attracted more and more attention in the field of intelligent fault diagnosis with its powerful feature learning and nonlinear mapping capabilities [4]. Deep learning models such as autoencoder (AE) [5], convolutional neural network (CNN) [6] and deep belief network (DBN) [7] have presented numerous achievements in fault diagnosis domain. In general, the prerequisites for the robot bearing fault diagnosis using deep learning methods mainly include two parts: (1) there are enough training samples with labels to train the reliable intelligent diagnosis model; (2) the training samples and test samples have similar feature distribution. However, these two prerequisites are difficult to satisfied in engineering scenarios. With the advancement of technology, the quality of the bearings used in robots has improved significantly, which makes robot bearings fault events rare. Therefore, it is very difficult to collect and label the fault data of the robot bearings. In addition, robot bearing data is often collected under different operating conditions or even different robots, and it is difficult to collect enough data from the same sample distribution. These become a huge challenge for the application of intelligent fault diagnosis [8].

Transfer learning has recently proved its ability to solve the above problems, which learn the transferable knowledge from one domain and transfer it to another domain to minimize the distribution discrepancy of cross-domain samples [9]. At present, feature-based transfer learning methods have become a research hotspot due to its excellent robustness for the tasks with serious distribution discrepancy of cross-domain [10, 11]. The feature-based transfer learning methods map the source domain and target domain into a common feature space and then extract transferable features with similar distribution. Chen et al. [12] proposed a residual deep subdomain adaptation network for the fault diagnosis of bearing across multiple domains. Yang et al. [13] proposed a feature-based transfer neural network to identify the health states of locomotive bearing with the help of diagnosis knowledge from laboratory bearing. Wen et al. [14] utilized a three-layer sparse auto-encoder to extract transferable feature. Li et al. [15] proposed an intelligent fault diagnosis method for bearing based on deep distance metric learning.

In recent years, feature-based combined with domain adversarial network has been increasingly applied in the field of fault diagnosis, which the adversarial learning between source domain and target domain is performed to minimize the distribution discrepancy of cross-domain samples [16]. Han et al. [17] proposed a hybrid model combining CNN and domain adversarial network for solving the problem of fault diagnosis with extremely limited fault data in practical applications. Liu et al. [18] proposed an adversarial discriminative domain adaptation transfer learning network for gas turbine rotor fault diagnosis. Li et al. [19] proposed a deep convolutional domain adversarial network for rolling bearings fault diagnosis. Satisfactory fault diagnosis results were obtained by the above method.

Based on the inspiration of the above researches, this paper introduces a domain discrimination module and a domain distribution discrepancy metrics module into the deep convolution residual neural network, and proposes a novel transfer learning method based on deep convolutional residual Wasserstein adversarial network (DCRWAN) for robot bearing fault diagnosis under variable working conditions and different machines. The main contributions of this paper are summarized as follows:

(1) Aiming at the large distribution discrepancy between labeled samples and unknown state samples in engineering scenarios, a transfer learning method based on DCR-WAN is proposed, which adds a domain discrimination module and a domain discrepancy metrics module after the feature extraction module in parallel.
(2) In the feature extraction module, a deep convolutional neural network with two residual blocks is applied, and the global average pooling layer is applied to replace the fully connected layer to reduce excessive parameters in the network.
(3) In the domain discrimination module, the adversarial loss function replaces the Jensen-Shannon (JS) divergence with the Wasserstein distance. In the domain discrepancy metrics module, the difference of feature distribution between two domains is estimated by multi-Kernel maximum mean discrepancy (MK-MMD).

The rest of this paper is organized as follows. In Sect. 2, we describe the theoretical model of DCRWAN and its components. Section 3 introduces the robot bearing fault diagnosis process based on DCRWAN. The case study and comparative analysis are presented in Sect. 4. Finally, conclusions are given in Sect. 5.

2 Proposed Model

Consider a transfer learning task from source domain with labeled samples to target domain with unlabeled samples. Specifically, we set $D_s = \left(x_i^s, y_i^s\right)_{i=1}^{n_s}$ as source domain, $x_i^s \in X^s$ is the source domain sample, $y_i^s \in Y^s$ is the label corresponding to each sample and n_s is the number of samples. Similarly, the target domain with unlabeled samples can be defined as $D_t = \left(x_j^t\right)_{j=1}^{n_t}$. Since the working conditions of the source domain and target domain are different, the marginal probability distribution of these two domains is also different, i.e., $P(X^s) \neq P(X^t)$. The purpose of transfer learning is to learn the diagnostic knowledge of target domain with the help of knowledge from source domain.

This paper proposes a novel transfer learning method based on DCRWAN for robot bearing fault diagnosis. The structure of the proposed DCRWAN is shown in Fig. 1, which consists of a deep residual feature extractor module, a domain discrimination module, a distribution discrepancy metrics module and a classification module. The deep residual feature extractor module is used to extract the high-level features of input data. The domain discrimination module uses the Wasserstein distance to estimate the distribution distance between the source domain and target domain. The distribution discrepancy metrics module uses MK-MMD to estimate the difference in feature distribution between two domains and further fine-tuning the feature extraction module. The classification module achieves fault classification of the samples in two domains. Each module's detail is described in the next subsection.

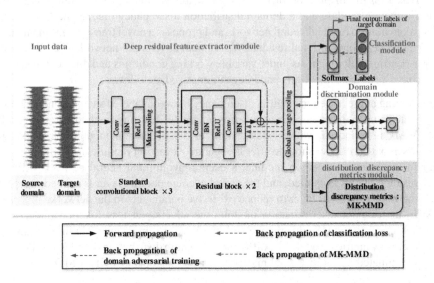

Fig. 1. The structure of proposed DCRWAN.

2.1 Deep Residual Feature Extractor Module

The deep residual feature extractor module consists of three standard convolutional blocks, two residual blocks and a global average pooling layer. For each standard convolutional block, the input data is first proceeded by a convolutional layer, which can be defined as:

$$x_i^{conv,l} = f_{\mathrm{ReLU}}\left(\omega^l * x_i^{input,l} + b^l\right) \tag{1}$$

where $x_i^{conv,l}$ is the output value after convolution operation in the lth standard convolutional block, $x_i^{input,l}$ is the input of the convolutional layer, ω^l is the weight vector of the convolution kernel, b^l is the bias and f_{ReLU} represents the activation function of rectified linear unit (ReLU). For the first standard convolutional block, $x_i^{input,1}$ is equal to the raw cross-domain samples x_i^D.

The batch normalization (BN) and max pooling are applied to speed up convergence and improve the generalization ability, then the features extracted by a standard convolutional block can be defined as:

$$y_i^{conv,l} = max\left(x_i^{conv,l}, s\right) \tag{2}$$

where s is the size of the pooling kernel.

The stacking of network structure may lead to gradient divergence and gradient disappearance during training [20]. Residual network is helpful to solve this problem, which constructs a skip connection between the input and output [21]. In this paper, two residual blocks are added behind the standard convolutional blocks. Each residual block includes two convolutional layers, which can be defined as:

$$x_i^{rb,l} = f_{ReLU}\left[f_{rb}^l\left(x_i^{rb,l-1}\right) + x_i^{rb,l-1}\right] \quad (3)$$

where f_{rb}^l is the residual mapping function of the lth residual block, and $x_i^{rb,0} = y_i^{conv,2}$.

Then, a global average pooling layer is applied to replace the traditional full-connected layers after the residual blocks.

2.2 Domain Discrimination Module

The domain discrimination module is added behind the deep residual feature extractor module to minimize the distribution discrepancy of cross-domain through adversarial learning. In this paper, the structure of domain discrimination module is similar to generative adversarial network (GAN) [22]. However, we replace the generator with the above deep residual feature extractor. The optimization objective function to train discriminator $D(\cdot)$ and feature extractor $F(\cdot)$ is shown as:

$$L(F, D) = \min_F \max_D E_{x \sim P_s}\left[\log D(F(x))\right] + E_{x \sim P_t}\left[\log(1 - D(F(x)))\right] \quad (4)$$

where P_s and P_t are the probability density function of the source domain and target domain samples respectively.

Commonly, the JS divergence is used to estimate the distribution discrepancy. This paper replaces JS divergence with Wasserstein distance. The advantage of Wasserstein distance is that it can measure the distance of two distributions even if these two distributions do not overlap, thus providing a meaningful gradient [23]. The expression of Wasserstein distance is shown as:

$$W(P_s, P_t) = \inf_{\gamma \in \Omega(P_s, P_t)} E_{(x,y)} \gamma x - y \quad (5)$$

where $\Omega(P_s, P_t)$ is the set of joint probability distribution γ with P_s and P_t as the marginal distribution. Then, the optimization objective function to train discriminator $D(\cdot)$ and feature extractor $F(\cdot)$ can be written as:

$$L(F, D) = \min_F \max_{f_D} E_{x \sim P_s}\left[f_D(F(x))\right] + E_{x \sim P_t}\left[f_D(F(x))\right] \quad (6)$$

where $f_D(\cdot)$ means a domain discriminator whose output layer lacks the activation function.

2.3 Distribution Discrepancy Metrics Module

The distribution discrepancy metrics module is added behind the deep residual feature extractor module to further reduce the features distance between two domains and fine-tuning the network parameters. The maximum mean discrepancy (MMD) has been widely used to estimate the distribution discrepancy of two datasets, which can be expressed as [24]:

$$MMD(X, Y) = \left[\frac{1}{m^2} \sum_{i=1}^{m} \sum_{j=1}^{m} k(x_i, x_j) + \frac{1}{n^2} \sum_{i=1}^{n} \sum_{j=1}^{n} k(y_i, y_j) - \frac{2}{mn} \sum_{i=1}^{m} \sum_{j=1}^{n} k(x_i, y_j) \right]^{1/2} \quad (7)$$

where $k(\cdot, \cdot)$ is the kernel function.

MK-MMD assumes that the optimal kernel function can be obtained by the linear combination of multiple kernel functions, which can avoid the difficulty of MMD in selecting kernel function and achieve better domain adaptation [25]. The combination of kernel functions K can be expressed as [26]:

$$K \in \left\{ k = \sum_{u=1}^{m} \beta_u k_u, \sum_{u=1}^{m} \beta_u = 1, \beta_u \geq 0, \forall u \right\} \quad (8)$$

where β_u is the weight coefficient of the corresponding kernel function. Then the MK-MMD becomes:

$$MK - MMD(X, Y) = \sum_{u=1}^{m} \beta_u MMD_{k_u}(X, Y) \quad (9)$$

2.4 Optimization Objective Function

Based on the function of each module, the optimization objective function of the DCR-WAN is consist of three parts. The first part is to minimize the cross-entropy loss of the source domain samples in the supervised pre-training process of the deep residual feature extractor module, the second part is to maximize the Wasserstein loss between two domains during the adversarial learning in the domain discrimination module, and the third part is to minimize the MK-MMD between two domains in the distribution discrepancy metrics module.

The features output from the deep residual feature extractor module are processed by the Softmax function in the classification module to predict the health states. The cross-entropy loss of the source domain samples with labels can be expressed as:

$$L_c = -\frac{1}{n_s} \sum_{i=1}^{n_s} \sum_{j=1}^{k} I(y_i^s = j) \log P_j(x_i^s) \quad (10)$$

where x_i^s is the source domain sample, y_i^s is the label corresponding to each sample, n_s is the number of samples, k is the number of categories, $I(\cdot)$ is the indicator function and $P_j(x_i^s)$ represents the predict probability that the sample x_i^s belongs to category j.

According to (5), the Wasserstein loss used to train the domain discriminator can be expressed as:

$$L_{wd} = \frac{1}{n_s} \sum\nolimits_{i=1}^{n_s} f_D\big(F\big(x_i^s\big)\big) - \frac{1}{n_t} \sum\nolimits_{j=1}^{n_t} f_D\big(F\big(x_j^t\big)\big) \tag{11}$$

where $f_D(\cdot)$ means a domain discriminator.

According to (9), the MK-MMD loss function that used to reduce the distribution discrepancy of extracted features between two domains can be expressed as:

$$L_{MK-MMD} = MK - MMD\big(F\big(X^s\big), F\big(X^t\big)\big) \tag{12}$$

where $F(X^s)$ and $F(X^t)$ are respectively the learned features of two domains in the deep residual feature extractor module.

Therefore, the final optimization objective function of DCRWAN is shown as:

$$L = \min_{\theta_f, \theta_c, \theta_d} \{L_c + \beta L_{MK-MMD} - \alpha L_{wd}\} \tag{13}$$

where θ_f, θ_c and θ_d are the parameters of the deep residual feature extractor module, the classification module and the domain discrimination module respectively, β and α represent the tradeoff parameters.

3 The Training Process

The training process of DCRWAN mainly includes four steps, which is detailed as follows:

Step 1: the raw robot bearing data in the source domain and target domain are normalized and divided into a certain number of samples respectively, then these samples are input into the deep residual feature extractor module of DCRWAN and the high-level features of two domains are extracted simultaneously;

Step 2: the high-level features of source domain are input into the classification module to obtain the corresponding predict labels, then the actual labels are introduced to achieve supervised pre-training of deep residual feature extractor module based on L_c;

Step 3: the high-level features of two domains are input into the domain discrimination module to get the Wasserstein loss function L_{wd} and the distribution discrepancy metrics module to get the MK-MMD loss function L_{MK-MMD} respectively, then the random gradient descent algorithm is used to optimize the parameters of network until the stop condition is reached.

Step 4: the test samples in target domain are input into the well-trained DCRWAN to predict the categories.

Specifically, the training process of DCRWAN is detailed in Table 1.

Table 1. The training process of DCRWAN.

Input: source domain samples $(x_i^s, y_i^s)_{i=1}^{n_s}$, target domain samples $(x_j^t)_{j=1}^{n_t}$, batch size m, tradeoff parameters β and α, learning rate ε, total iteration number N_p.

Output: diagnosis results of target domain samples $(y_j^t)_{j=1}^{n_t}$.

---

1.   Initialize the network parameters θ_f, θ_c and θ_d randomly.
2.   While the total iteration number has not reached
3.   For iteration number $n = 1,2,\cdots,N_p$
4.   Randomly select a sample batch from the source domain and target domain
5.   Obtain the high-level features of two domains though forward propagation
6.   Update $\theta_c \leftarrow \theta_c - \varepsilon\nabla_{\theta_c}(L_c(X^s,Y^s))$
7.   Update $\theta_d \leftarrow \theta_d + \varepsilon\nabla_{\theta_d}(L_{wd}(X^s,X^t))$
8.   Update $\theta_f \leftarrow \theta_f - \varepsilon\nabla_{\theta_f}(L_c(X^s,Y^s) + \beta L_{MK\text{-}MMD}(X^s,X^t) - \alpha L_{wd}(X^s,X^t))$
9.   End
10. Output diagnosis results of target domain samples $(y_j^t)_{j=1}^{n_t}$

---

4 Experimental Results

4.1 Dataset Construction

In order to verify the effectiveness of the proposed method, a robot bearing fault simulation test bench is built to collect experimental data and two public datasets are used for verification. Dataset A is collected from test bench (LAB). As shown in Fig. 2, the test bench mainly includes motor, converter, acceleration, test bearing, health bearing and data acquisition system. The health states of the test bearings include normal (N), inner ring fault (IF), outer ring fault (OF), and ball fault (BF). Dataset B is the bearing dataset of Case Western Reserve University (CWRU) in the United States, and Dataset C is the public dataset provided by Jiangnan University (JNU).

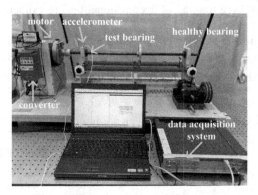

Fig. 2. The test bench.

In this paper, 800 normal samples and 400 samples for each fault state are randomly selected to form an unbalanced dataset, each containing 512 sampling points. The details of the dataset are shown in Table 2.

Table 2. The details of datasets.

Datasets	Data source	Health states	Number of samples	Work conditions
A	LAB	N/IF/OF/BF	800/400/400/400	2100 rpm
B	CWRU	N/IF/OF/BF	800/400/400/400	1797 rpm
C	JNU	N/IF/OF/BF	800/400/400/400	600 rpm

In the experiment, we create two transfer tasks: B→A and C→A. Datasets B and C are the source domains that provide transferable knowledge, and dataset A is target domain, and the ratio of the number of training samples and test samples is 8:2. For the above transfer tasks, we use the learning rate of $0.01/(1 + 10 \times \theta)^{0.75}$, where θ changes linearly from 0 to 1 with the training process, the α and β are $2/(1 + \exp(-10 \times \theta)) - 1$, the training number is 100, and the batch size is 64.

4.2 Analysis of Experimental Results

The confusion matrix of the proposed method of the two transfer tasks in this paper is shown in Fig. 3. The results show that the proposed method can well identify the four health states of bearings, the classification accuracy is more than 95%. The classification accuracy of each working condition under these two transfer tasks is very high, which means that the proposed DCRWAN obtains superior transfer performance in robot bearing fault diagnosis.

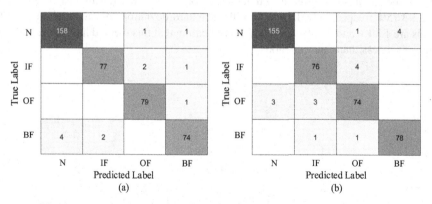

Fig. 3. The confusion matrix of the proposed method: (a) B→A, (b) C→A

In order to verify the superiority of the proposed method, five typical transfer learning methods are used to compare and analyze: transfer component analysis (TCA), joint distribution adaptation (JDA), deep Coral (D-CORAL) [27], deep domain confusion (DDC) [28] and domain adversarial neural network (DANN) [29]. As a baseline for comparison, all methods use deep convolutional residual network as feature extractors. In order to guarantee the reliability of the experimental results, 10 experiments were performed for each method. The diagnostic results of the two transfer tasks by different methods are shown in Table 3.

Table 3. Comparison of diagnostic results of two transfer tasks.

Methods	Accuracy (%)	
	B → A	C → A
TCA	24.55 ± 4.38	27.45 ± 4.53
JDA	26.25 ± 5.68	28.45 ± 5.37
D-CORAL	58.61 ± 8.47	54.00 ± 6.18
DDC	65.14 ± 5.96	68.35 ± 4.05
DANN	76.45 ± 3.20	75.10 ± 3.20
DCRWAN	95.65 ± 1.89	93.75 ± 2.28

Experimental results show that the diagnostic accuracy of the traditional transfer learning method based on TCA and JDA is less than 30%, which cannot be applied to cross-machine fault diagnosis. The domain adaptation method based on D-CORAL and DDC leads to the overfitting to the source domain and poor performance on the target domain. The DANN method improves the diagnostic accuracy through adversarial training, but the diagnostic accuracy is still less than 80%. The proposed method can extract domain invariant and class separable features for fault classification. As shown in Fig. 4, the diagnostic results show that the accuracy of the two transfer tasks are 95.65% and 93.75%, respectively. In addition, the standard deviations of this method after 10 trials are 1.89% and 2.28%, respectively, indicating that this method has higher stability and robustness than other methods.

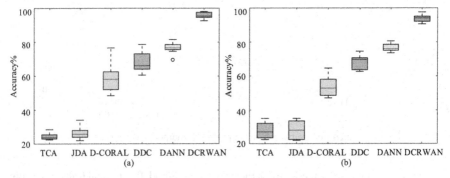

Fig. 4. Box plots of the proposed method: (a) B→A, (b) C→A

In order to better verify the effectiveness of the method, The feature extracted from the global average pooling layer is taken as output, and the high-dimensional features of different methods are reduced and visualized by t-distributed Stochastic Neighbor Embedding (t-SNE). Taking the transfer task B→A as an example, the visualization results of classification results of different methods are shown in Fig. 5. The methods of D-CORAL and DDC overlap in different categories and do not correctly classify target domains. The classification boundary of the DANN method is not clear. The DCRWAN method proposed in this paper can effectively aggregate the features of the same category and separate the features of different categories, which can achieve accurate classification of different fault types.

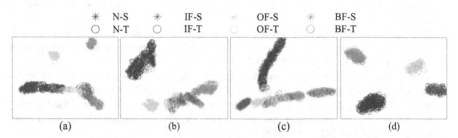

Fig. 5. The visualization of classification results of different methods (a) D-CORAL, (b) DDC, (c) DANN, (d) DCRWAN

5 Conclusion

In this paper, a novel robot bearing fault diagnosis method based on DCRWAN is proposed to realize robot bearing fault diagnosis under variable working conditions and different machines. The results are summarized as follows:

(1) In the proposed method, a deep convolutional residual network is constructed to extract transferable features of source domain and target domain simultaneously. The network has the advantage of avoiding gradient divergence and gradient disappearance during training. Besides, the global average pooling layer is applied to reduce excessive parameters in the network and improve the training efficiency.
(2) A domain discrimination module and a domain discrepancy metrics module are innovatively constructed to achieve domain adaption. These two modules help to effectively extract domain-invariant and class-separable features for the classification.
(3) Two transfer tasks are used to verify the effectiveness of the proposed method. The two public datasets are set as the source domain, and the dataset collected by the robot bearing fault simulation test bench is set as the target domain. Based on the comparison results, the proposed method is superior to the traditional transfer learning method under variable working conditions and different machines.

References

1. Alobaidy, M.A., Abdul-Jabbar, D.J.M.: Faults diagnosis in robot systems: a review. Al-Rafidain Eng. J. **25**(2), 164–175 (2020)
2. Lu, N., Yin, T.: Transferable common feature space mining for fault diagnosis with imbalanced data. Mech. Syst. Signal Process. **156**, 107645 (2021)
3. He, J., Yang, S., Papatheou, E.: Investigation of a multi-sensor data fusion technique for the fault diagnosis of gearboxes. Proc. Inst. Mech. Eng. C J. Mech. Eng. Sci. **233**(13), 4764–4775 (2019)
4. Lei, Y., Yang, B., Jiang, X.: Applications of machine learning to machine fault diagnosis: a review and roadmap. Mech. Syst. Signal Process. **138**, 106587 (2020)
5. Li, X., Li, X., Ma, H.: Deep representation clustering-based fault diagnosis method with unsupervised data applied to rotating machinery. Mech. Syst. Signal Process. **143**, 106825 (2020)
6. Zhang, L., Lv, Y., Huang, W.: Bearing fault diagnosis under various operation conditions using synchrosqueezing transform and improved two-dimensional convolutional neural network. Meas. Sci. Technol. **33**(8), 085002 (2022)
7. Gao, S., Xu, L., Zhang, Y.: Rolling bearing fault diagnosis based on intelligent optimized self-adaptive deep belief network. Meas. Sci. Technol. **31**(5), 055009 (2020)
8. Su, H., Yang, X., Xiang, L.: A novel method based on deep transfer unsupervised learning network for bearing fault diagnosis under variable working condition of unequal quantity. Knowl. Based Syst. **242**, 108381 (2022)
9. Li, C., Zhang, S., Qin, Y.: A systematic review of deep transfer learning for machinery fault diagnosis. Neurocomputing **407**, 121–135 (2020)
10. Yang, B., Lee, C.G., Lei, Y.: Deep partial transfer learning network: a method to selectively transfer diagnostic knowledge across related machines. Mech. Syst. Signal Process. **156**, 107618 (2021)
11. Yang, B., Xu, S., Lei, Y.: Multi-source transfer learning network to complement knowledge for intelligent diagnosis of machines with unseen faults. Mech. Syst. Signal Process. **162**, 108095 (2022)
12. Chen, Z., Wu, J., Deng, C.: Residual deep subdomain adaptation network: a new method for intelligent fault diagnosis of bearings across multiple domains. Mech. Mach. Theory **169**, 104635 (2022)
13. Yang, B., Lei, Y., Jia, F.: An intelligent fault diagnosis approach based on transfer learning from laboratory bearings to locomotive bearings. Mech. Syst. Signal Process. **122**, 692–706 (2019)
14. Wen, L., Gao, L., Li, X.: A new deep transfer learning based on sparse auto-encoder for fault diagnosis. IEEE Trans. Syst. Man Cybern. Syst. **49**(1), 136–144 (2017)
15. Li, X., Zhang, W., Ding, Q.: A robust intelligent fault diagnosis method for rolling element bearings based on deep distance metric learning. Neurocomputing **310**, 77–95 (2018)
16. Li, X., Zhang, W., Ding, Q.: Cross-domain fault diagnosis of rolling element bearings using deep generative neural networks. IEEE Trans. Industr. Electron. **66**(7), 5525–5534 (2018)
17. Han, T., Liu, C., Wu, R.: Deep transfer learning with limited data for machinery fault diagnosis. Appl. Soft Comput. **103**, 107150 (2021)
18. Liu, S., Wang, H., Tang, J.: Research on fault diagnosis of gas turbine rotor based on adversarial discriminative domain adaption transfer learning. Measurement **196**, 111174 (2022)
19. Li, F., Tang, T., Tang, B.: Deep convolution domain-adversarial transfer learning for fault diagnosis of rolling bearings. Measurement **169**, 108339 (2021)
20. Wang, G., Zhang, M., Xiang, L.: A multi-branch convolutional transfer learning diagnostic method for bearings under diverse working conditions and devices. Measurement **182**, 109627 (2021)

21. Shafiq, M., Gu, Z.: Deep residual learning for image recognition: a survey. Appl. Sci. **12**(18), 8972 (2022)
22. Goodfellow, I., Pouget-Abadie, J., Mirza, M.: Generative adversarial networks. Commun. ACM **63**(11), 139–144 (2020)
23. Li, Y., Zou, W., Jiang, L.: Fault diagnosis of rotating machinery based on combination of Wasserstein generative adversarial networks and long short term memory fully convolutional network. Measurement **191**, 110826 (2022)
24. Gretton, A., Borgwardt, K.M., Rasch, M.J.: A kernel two-sample test. J. Mach. Learn. Res. **13**(1), 723–773 (2012)
25. Pei, X., Su, S., Jiang, L.: Research on rolling bearing fault diagnosis method based on generative adversarial and transfer learning. Processes **10**(8), 1443 (2022)
26. Gretton A., Sejdinovic D., Strathmann H.: Optimal kernel choice for large-scale two-sample tests. Adv. Neural Inform. Process. Syst. **25** (2012)
27. Li, X., Zhang, Z., Gao, L.: A new semi-supervised fault diagnosis method via deep coral and transfer component analysis. IEEE Trans. Emerg. Top. Comput. Intell. **6**(3), 690–699 (2021)
28. Tzeng, E., Hoffman, J., Zhang, N.: Deep domain confusion: Maximizing for domain invariance. arXiv preprint arXiv 1412, 3474 (2014)
29. Mao, W., Liu, Y., Ding, L.: A new structured domain adversarial neural network for transfer fault diagnosis of rolling bearings under different working conditions. IEEE Trans. Instrum. Meas. **70**, 1–13 (2020)

Design and Implementation of a Multifunctional Screw Disassembly Workstation

Shengmin Zhang[1], Yisheng Zhang[1], Zhigang Wang[2], Hengwei Zhang[1], Kai Gu[1], Yanlong Peng[1], and Ming Chen[1](✉)

[1] School of Mechanical Engineering, Shanghai Jiaotong University, Shanghai, China
mingchen@sjtu.edu.cn
[2] Intel Labs China, Beijing, China

Abstract. The rapid growth of the electric vehicle industry has created a significant demand for the recycling of end-of-life electric vehicle batteries (EOL-EVB). Manual disassembly methods suffer from low efficiency, highlighting the urgent need for intelligent disassembly solutions for electric vehicle batteries. A major challenge in intelligent disassembly is dealing with uncertainty, especially when it comes to the disassembly of screws, which vary in shape, size, and rust level. To address this challenge, we present a multifunctional screw disassembly workstation specifically designed for the disassembly of screws, which constitutes a substantial portion of the EOL-EVB disassembly process. The workstation incorporates an automated sleeve replacement device that can seamlessly replace and disassemble sleeves during disassembly. Additionally, we propose a screw-type recognition method based on attributes, enabling the identification of various screw attributes to determine appropriate disassembly methods. This method exhibits scalability and requires only a small amount of data. By expanding the capabilities of our previous Neurosymbolic TAMP (Task and Motion Planning) work, we can support multiple types of screw disassembly and integrate it into the overall process of EOL-EVB disassembly, significantly reducing repetitive tasks such as screw disassembly during the disassembly process. Experimental results demonstrate the effectiveness of the workstation in disassembling multiple types of screws within a realistic disassembly environment.

Keywords: EOL-EVB · automatic disassembly · sleeve replacement device · recognition · attributes · NeuroSymbolic TAMP

1 Introduction

The disassembly of end-of-life electric vehicle batteries (EOL-EVB) presents an opportunity for resource reuse and recycling, which can help reduce the demand for new resources, environmental pollution, and resource waste. Additionally, recycling rare metals and other valuable materials from EOL-EVB can provide necessary raw materials for manufacturing new batteries. According to a report by Deloitte - a market research and consulting firm - the global electric vehicle battery recycling market is expected to grow from 5.5 billion yuan in 2021 to 299.7 billion yuan in 2028, with a compound annual growth rate of 55.92% [1]. This suggests a promising future for the recycling of

© The Author(s), under exclusive license to Springer Nature Singapore Pte Ltd. 2023
H. Yang et al. (Eds.): ICIRA 2023, LNAI 14274, pp. 506–519, 2023.
https://doi.org/10.1007/978-981-99-6501-4_43

discarded electric vehicle batteries. With the increasing number of electric vehicles, the recycling and reuse of EOL-EVB will become an increasingly important issue.

Currently, manual disassembly is the primary method for disassembling EOL-EVB [2]. The main reason is that EOL-EVBs come in various brands, models, and specifications, which require different processing methods depending on the specific situation. Furthermore, the use process of EOL-EVB can cause significant changes, further increasing the uncertainty during the disassembly process. Even the simple task of disassembling screws can be challenging due to uncertainty. If the EOL-EVB has undergone deformation, the screw's position cannot be determined based on the existing battery model. If the EOL-EVB had been repaired before being scrapped, the screw type might have been changed. Similar issues exist, and they represent significant obstacles to achieving automated disassembly using robots. Some existing research has developed customized systems. Due to a lack of autonomy, they are only suitable for static environments (clean, non-deformable, and specific types of batteries) [3,4].

In the field of intelligent disassembly, the existing methods proposed mainly focus on task planning, Among them, one research [5,6] is based on a cognitive robot system to realize the disassembly of products, The system is equipped with four cognitive functions: reasoning, execution monitoring, learning, and revision. Another research [7] proposed an intelligent disassembly system based on intelligent vision, which incorporates image processing, machine learning, close loop control, multi-agent, and disassembly planning. Munir merdan et al. Proposed an ontology based automatic disassembly system [8], which couples the ontology with visual information to dynamically determine the disassembly action of the robot to achieve more flexible action. However, these methods often can not meet higher requirements for the accuracy of disassembly and can not complete the disassembly of small objects (such as screws).

In the past, there were also many studies on accurate positioning and disassembly, Such as adjusting the posture of an object using tactile feedback to achieve a desired nesting task [9,10], Another study [11] uses the moment probability function to match the object surface and the finger surface through the object point cloud map to achieve accurate grasping, Alireza rastegarpanah et al. [12] determine the position and attitude of objects through model-based feature matching, but these methods do not apply to small objects and flexible end effectors. In addition, Li Xinyu et al. [13] utilized Faster R-CNN (high-performance deep learning algorithm) and innovative Rotating Edge Similarity (RES) algorithm to achieve high-precision positioning and classification of screws, but due to the long computational time, it is not suitable for actual disassembly tasks. Some studies [14–16] use target recognition based on grayscale values and contours to detect screws or use grayscale maps, depth maps, and HSV values to detect screws. These methods have improved the positioning accuracy of screws to a certain extent, but they cannot accurately classify various attributes such as the shape and rust of screws, and cannot be effectively applied in actual disassembly tasks.

The peak of EOL-EVB disposal is imminent, and automated disassembly of EOL-EVB is urgently needed. In our previous work, we successfully completed the continuous disassembly of a single screw in the battery pack using the framework of Neurosymbolic TAMP, introducing neural predicates and action primitives [17,18]. In this paper, we focus on the task of screw disassembly, which accounts for 40% of the disassembly work [19,20], and design a multi-functional screw disassembly workstation. This workstation has customized end effectors and sleeve replacement devices, enabling it to disassemble various types of screws at the mechanism level. In addition, force feedback devices and visual perception modules provide multimodal sensing capabilities for workstations and propose attribute based screw-type recognition methods. Additionally, force feedback devices and visual perception modules provides the workstation with multi-modal sensing capabilities. Most importantly, we establish a neural-symbolic planning system that significantly enhances the robot's intelligence, ensuring efficient and accurate completion of the screw disassembly task.

In summary, this paper introduces three key innovative contributions: 1. Expansion of NeuroSymbolic TAMP: Building upon the original NeuroSymbolic Task and Motion Planning (TAMP) framework, this study extends its capabilities to support multiple types of screws. This advancement significantly broadens the potential applications of this method in battery disassembly and related processes.

2. Development of a Reliable Screw Replacement Mechanism: A novel screw replacement mechanism has been designed and implemented, ensuring continuous and stable operation. This mechanism holds promise for application in various screw-related tasks beyond the scope of this study.

3. Attribute-based Screw Type Recognition Method: A screw-type recognition method based on attributes is proposed, which exhibits scalability and requires minimal data. The effectiveness of this method will be further evaluated in subsequent research and development, specifically for industrial part recognition tasks.

Overall, these innovations contribute to advancing intelligent disassembly processes, expanding the capabilities of existing frameworks, and providing practical solutions for screw-related tasks in battery disassembly and beyond.

2   Screw Disassembly Workstation

This workstation aims to achieve rapid disassembly of various types of screws through autonomous motion planning and manipulation of robots to improve work efficiency. The main structure of the workstation is divided into a task planning layer, a multimodal sensing layer, and a mechanical structure layer. Figure 1 shows the main structure of the workstation. This workstation supports disassembling screws of various shapes and specifications. The operator only needs to place the parts to be disassembled on the workstation, and the system will automatically carry out disassembly planning; The visual perception module installed on the robot will automatically find the position of the screws and classify them; In order to adapt to various types of screws, the workstation is equipped with various types of disassemblers. When the workstation finds that the types of screws do not match, it will automatically replace the corresponding disassembler to ensure smooth disassembly; The robot is equipped with a force feedback device that can adjust the splicing action based on the shape of the screw and the force feedback of the current splicing situation, thereby achieving more accurate disassembly operations. For some severely corroded screws, conventional disassembly methods may not be effective. This workstation can perform special treatments based on the situation of the screws, such as using a power saw or milling cutter for destructive disassembly or using methods such as electrolytic rust removal, to facilitate disassembly.

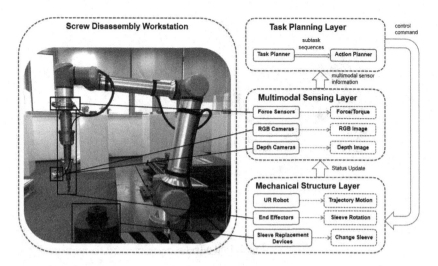

Fig. 1. The main structure of the workstation: 1) task planning layer. 2) multimodal sensing layer. 3) mechanical structure layer.

In summary, this workstation has the characteristics of intelligence and efficiency, which can adapt to various types of screw disassembly, and can perform fine processing for different situations.

2.1 Task Planning Layer

The task planning layer includes a task planner and an action planner. The task planner obtains disassembly environment information through multimodal perception, generates subtask execution sequences based on the current disassembly environment and disassembly tasks, and corrects subsequent subtask execution sequences based on the real-time disassembly environment during the subtask execution process, improving the efficiency and success rate of disassembly; The action planner generates a robot action trajectory based on the generated subtasks and combines multimodal perceptual information to drive the robot to execute.

2.2 Multimodal Sensing Layer

The multimodal sensing layer consists of a variety of sensors, including RGB cameras, depth cameras, and force sensors. The RGB camera and depth camera are Realsense D435, which are installed on the end effector and can obtain RGB image information and depth image information of the area in front of the end effector during robot movement; The six-dimensional pose of the target in three-dimensional space relative to the robot base coordinates is obtained by fusing multiple image information obtained in real-time, providing a basis for subsequent task planning and action planning. The force sensor uses ATI multi-axis force/torque sensors, which can measure and output forces and torque at various coordinates in the Cartesian rectangular coordinate system; Real-time detection of the forces and torque applied to the end effector during the robot's movement corrects the robot's movement and better realizes the disassembly action.

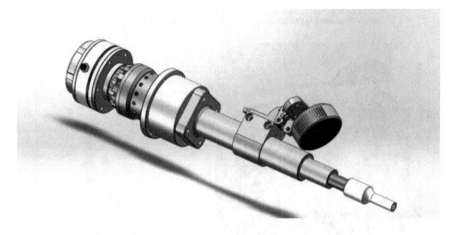

Fig. 2. End effector.

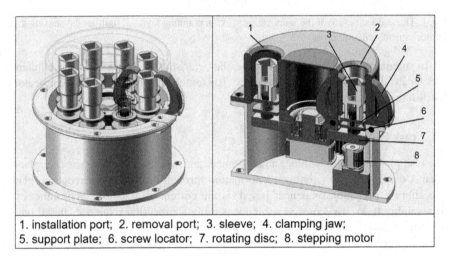

1. installation port; 2. removal port; 3. sleeve; 4. clamping jaw;
5. support plate; 6. screw locator; 7. rotating disc; 8. stepping motor

Fig. 3. Sleeve replacement devices.

2.3 Mechanical Structure Layer

The mechanical structure layer mainly includes end effectors and sleeve replacement devices. The main mechanical structure is shown in Fig. 2 and Fig. 3. The end effector is a screw disassembler driven by a motor to drive the sleeve rod and sleeve to rotate to complete the screw disassembly; The sleeve rod is connected to the main body of the disassembler by a spring, providing passive flexibility in the vertical direction for the end effectors. At the same time, the sleeve rod is flexibly connected to provide passive flexibility in the horizontal direction for the socket connection. These designs reduce the accuracy requirements required for the end effectors during the screw socket connection process.

In order to adapt to various screw disassembly tasks, it is necessary to design a sleeve replacement device for the workstation, which is mainly composed of a rotating disc carrying multiple sleeves, a stepping motor, a clamping jaw, and a housing. There is a sleeve removal position and a sleeve installation position on the housing. The motor drives the sleeve disk to rotate the required sleeve to the desired position. When it is necessary to remove the sleeve, insert the end effectors with the sleeve into the sleeve removal position. Press to make the left and right clamping jaws tightly grasp the sleeve to fix it, and lift the end effectors to separate the sleeve rod from the end effectors; When a new sleeve needs to be installed later, insert the end effectors into the sleeve mounting position, and press to connect the end effectors to the sleeve to complete the installation of the new sleeve.

When it is necessary to disassemble severely rusted screws, it is not possible to use sleeve rotation for disassembly. At this time, a milling cutter disassembler needs to be designed to grind the rusted screws flat and complete the disassembly.

When it is necessary to disassemble screws without a suitable disassembly sleeve, it is not possible to disassemble them. Instead, a power saw disassembler needs to be designed to cut a groove in the screw and then use a slotted screw sleeve for disassembly.

3   Disassembly Implementation Details

3.1   Task Planning

NeuroSymbolic TAMP. The advantages of NeuroSymbolic TAMP lie in its interpretability, learnability, and extensibility. By introducing neural predicates, the system can abstract and represent the features of small fastener disassembly. At the same time, the continuous optimization and expansion of action primitives also enable the system to adapt to more complex disassembly tasks.

When applied to screw disassembly, the system can sense the disassembly environment through multimodal sensors, and use NeuroSymbolic to abstract information such as the position, shape, and characteristics of screws into understandable symbolic forms, thereby avoiding the use of complex methods to identify screw features. By generating action primitive sequences that conform to logical reasoning, the system can directly drive the robot to complete the disassembly task. The training and enhancement of neural predicates and the expansion and optimization of action primitives enable the system to better adapt to different types of screws, thereby improving the accuracy and efficiency of disassembly. In previous work, the advantages of NeuroSymbolic TAMP in disassembling small fasteners in unstructured environments have also been verified [17].

Neural Predicates and Action Primitives. In previous work, two neural predicates, "target_aim()" and "target_clear()", was defined to determine whether the end effector is consistent with the position and posture of the target object and whether there are obstacles around or above the target object. At the same time, eight action primitives are defined, including "Approach", "Mate", "Push", "Insert", "Fumble", "Search", "Re insert", and "Disassemble". This intelligent disassembly system can achieve continuous and stable disassembly of a single type of screw, but in reality, there are many

Table 1. Description of Disassembly Primitives

Primitive	Pre-condition	Result	Function Description
Recognize	1. The sleeve is aligned with the screw; 2. There are no obstacles near the screw.	1. The system has completed screw type identification; 2. The system completes the identification of the degree of screw corrosion; 3. The screw type matches the sleeve type. 4. There is matching sleeve in the sleeve replacement device	This primitive identifies the type, specification, and degree of corrosion of the screw currently being disassembled. Determine if there is a matching sleeve in the sleeve replacement device.
Change	1. The system has completed screw type identification; 2. The screw type does not match the sleeve type; 3. There is a matching sleeve in the sleeve replacement device.	1. The screw type matches the sleeve type.	This primitive drives the robotic arm to replace a sleeve that matches the current screw shape and specification.
Cut	1. The system has completed screw type identification; 2. There is no matching sleeve in the sleeve replacement device.	1. The screw type changed to a flat-head screw.	This primitive cuts screws without matching sleeves into slotted screws.
Mill	1. The system has completed the identification of the degree of screw corrosion; 2. The target screw is severely rusted.	1. The screw disassembly is completed.	This primitive grind the severely rusted screws flat.

Table 2. Description of Predicates

Predicate	Function Description
target_match(senor)	This neural predicate means that the shape and specification of the current screw can be disassembled using the currently equipped sleeve.
exist_sleeve(senor)	This neural predicate means that there is a matching disassembly sleeve for the current screw.
target_rust(senor)	This neural predicate means that the degree of rust on the screw is very severe.

types of screws in disassembly work, with different shapes and sizes. A disassembly workbench that can only disassemble a single screw cannot be extended to a real disassembly operation. To solve this problem, We have added the neural predicate "target_ match()", "exist_sleeve()" and "target_rust()" to determine whether the current target screw matches the currently assembled disassembler, whether there is a matching sleeve, and whether there is excessive rust. Four action primitives, "Recognize", "Change", "Cut" and "Mill", are newly defined to identify the feature type of the current target screw, drive the robot to automatically replace the disassembler when the disassembler and target screw types are inconsistent, cut screws without matching sleeves and grind down severely rusted screws.

The definition of its action primitive is shown in the following Table 1.

The implementation of the action primitive "Recognize" is to move the end effector to a position 20 mm directly above the target screw, acquire the RGB image captured by the camera at the current position, and input it into the YOLO network. The YOLO network is a screw position recognition network whose main functions are to obtain the center position of the positioning frame, the size of the positioning frame, and the captured screw image of the target screw. Then input the captured screw image into the VAE network to determine the shape attributes of the current target screw, and combine the size of the positioning frame to obtain the size of the screw to comprehensively determine the specific model of the screw. Compare the type of the target screw with the sleeve type on the current end effector: If the type matches, set "target_match()" to True; If the types do not match, set "target_match()" to False (Table 2).

Implementation of the "Change" Primitive. When executing the action primitive "Change", we need to input the current end effector position, current sleeve type, and target sleeve type. In order to allow the end effector to be vertically inserted into the sleeve replacement device, two pre-replacement positions have been set, which are located 20 mm above the sleeve installation and removal port. Firstly, place the current sleeve back into the sleeve replacement device, drive the stepping motor to rotate the rotating disc and move the current sleeve placement position below the removal port, move the end effector from its initial position to the pre-replacement position at the removal port, and insert it vertically downwards into the removal port. At this time, the sleeve contacts the screw locator and compresses the spring in the end effector, Drive the end effector motor to rotate slightly so that the notch under the sleeve matches the shape of the screw locator. The spring in the end effector is released and pressed down on the sleeve and support plate (supported by a spring between the support plate and the rotating disc). The support plate presses down on the lower part of the clamping claw, causing the clamping claw to tighten in the middle and make contact with the upper part of the sleeve. At this time, move the end effector upwards to remove the current sleeve; The next step is to install the target sleeve. Drive the stepping motor to rotate the rotating disc and move the target sleeve below the installation port, move the end effector to the pre-replacement position at the installation port, and vertically insert it into the installation port. At this time, the empty rod contacts and compresses the target sleeve, causing the spring in the end effector to compress. driving the end effector motor to rotate slightly to fit the shape of the gap on the rod and sleeve, The spring release in the end effector compresses and installs the sleeve onto the end effector, and then moves back to the initial position to complete an automatic replacement of the sleeve. Update the current casing type in the planner and set "target_match()" to True.

Execution Flow Chart. Firstly, when obtaining a rough positioning position of the screw to be disassembled, the execution action primitive "Approach" moves to the vicinity above the screw; When there are obstacles around the target screw, execute the action primitive "Push" to clear the obstacles; When the end effector is not aligned with the target screw, execute the action primitive "Mate" to align it; When there are no obstacles around the target screw and the end effector is aligned with the target screw, the execution action primitive "Recognize" identifies the current screw type and spec-

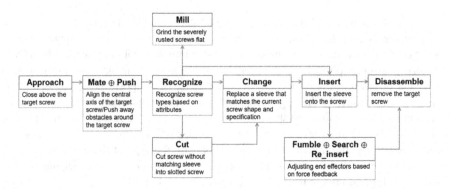

Fig. 4. Execution Flow Chart.

ification; When the screw type and specification do not match the sleeve, execute the action primitive "Change" to replace the appropriate sleeve; When the screw type and specification match the sleeve, execute the action primitive "Insert"; According to the force feedback data during the sleeve connection, select and execute some or all of the action primitives "Fumble", "Search", and "Re_insert" until the screw socket connection is successful. Execute the action primitive "Disassemble" to remove the current screw and proceed with the disassembly of the next screw. When the target screw does not have a matching sleeve during the disassembly process, execute the action primitives "Cut" to turn it into a This primitive cuts screws without matching sleeves into slotted screw and use a slotted screw sleeve for disassembly. When the target screw is severely rusted during the disassembly process, execute the action primitives "Mill" to grind it flat.

The flow diagram is shown in the Fig. 4.

3.2 Screw Type Recognition Based on Attribute

In contrast to conventional detection methods that directly rely on types of object detection, our approach utilizes a series of classifiers to categorize the various attributes of screws. For instance, we classified screws into four categories based on the degree of rust, ranging from "no rust" to "severe rust". Additionally, we employed shape-based classification, distinguishing "outer hexagonal", "inner hexagonal" and so on. This methodology offers several significant advantages:

1. Sufficient availability of training data: During the training phase of the object detection network, we found it advantageous to group all screws together and consider them as a single class. However, when training for attribute classification, we organized screws with similar attributes into distinct groups. This approach eliminated the need to partition the limited data into numerous small classes for training purposes. Importantly, our investigation revealed that subdividing the data into smaller classes would not meet our requirements within the dataset.
2. Combination of multiple attributes: By combining different attributes, we were able to infer and identify screws that were not originally present in the dataset. This capability demonstrates the versatility and robustness of our approach, enabling it

to handle screw types that were not encountered during the initial data collection phase.

VAE Recognition Algorithm. Our system uses VAE to classify attributes for several reasons: 1 Subsequent experiments have shown that VAE performs best in our dataset; 2. VAE facilitates the expansion of attributes in the future. For example, the degree of corrosion can be divided into no rust and severe rust. If future treatment methods require recognition of mild and moderate rust, we can generate a new classification method by defining the distance from the existing two categories without retraining this attribute.

The VAE network is an unsupervised learning network, which obtains an encoder and a decoder through training and can encode pictures into feature vectors containing their various attributes and restore them through the decoder. VAE networks can be trained with a small amount of data, and can effectively extract target attribute information such as shape, color, and state from images. Therefore, VAE networks are very suitable for classifying various small fasteners such as screws in unstructured scenes.

The conventional VAE loss function is defined as:

$$L(x) = E_{q(z|x)}[\log p(x|z)] + \beta \cdot D_{KL}(q(z|x)\|p(z)) \tag{1}$$

but this loss function only focuses on the pixels of a single image and cannot effectively distinguish images with different characteristics. On this basis, we use pairs of images during training and add the relationship between images in the loss function [21]:

$$L(x_1, x_2) = (L(x_1) + L(x_2))/2 + aH(x_1, x_2) \tag{2}$$

$$H(x_1, x_2) = \begin{cases} \max(0, d_m - \|z_1 - z_2\|_1) & similar(x_1, x_2) \\ \|z_1 - z_2\|_1 & different(x_1, x_2) \end{cases} \tag{3}$$

where H is the feature difference between images and its weight is adjusted by the coefficient a. The hyper-parameter d_m describes the spread distance margin of the potential vector so that z_1 and z_2 are distributed in different regions in the potential space. This allows the VAE network to make the encoding vectors of images with the same attributes closer and images with different attributes further during training, which is more conducive to our judgment of target attributes.

Identification of Screw Types. Collect screw image data on the battery pack in advance, use a VAE encoder to convert it into a feature vector, cluster the screws with the same shape attributes, and calculate the average vector. After obtaining the image information of the target screw to be disassembled, it is input into the VAE encoder to obtain its feature vector. By comparing the feature vector of the target screw with the average vector of screws with different shape attributes, the closest one is the geometric shape attribute of the current target screw. Similarly, the screw status attribute can be determined. Finally, based on the size of the YOLO positioning bracket and the relative coordinate relationship between the camera and the screw, the specifications of the screw can be comprehensively determined to determine the specific model of the screw. Multiple types of screws in a real disassembly environment are shown in Fig. 5.

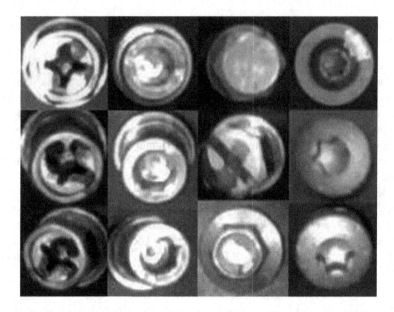

Fig. 5. Multiple types of screws in a real disassembly environment.

3.3 Force Feedback Adjustment of Different Screws

In our previous work, we added action primitives "Fumble", "Search", and "Re_insert" to successfully implement force feedback correction if a particular type of screw cannot be successfully inserted during disassembly. But when using different disassembly sleeves to disassemble different screws, due to the different shapes and specifications of the screws, using a single force feedback correction model cannot effectively correct the deviation of the sleeve connection during the disassembly process. Therefore, we train different force feedback models based on the shapes and specifications of different screws, and change them to "Fumble (bolt_type)", "Search (bolt_type)" and "Re_insert (bolt_type)" based on the original action primitive, select an appropriate force feedback model based on the judgment of the screw type during disassembly and invoke action primitives to correct the splicing process.

4 Experimental Verification

4.1 Accuracy and Speed of VAE Judgment

In a simulation environment, we conducted experiments on four different shapes of screws (outer hexagonal screw, inner hexagonal screw, cross screw, and star screw) with varying degrees of rust (no rust, mild rust, moderate rust, and severe rust). The trained VAE screw classification network achieved a success rate of 97.75% in identifying specific shapes of screws during actual disassembly, At the same time, the accuracy of identifying the degree of corrosion of screws has reached 100%; At the same time, we use classical image classification networks to train four classification networks for screw

Table 3. Success Rate of Classical Image Classification Network Detection

	shape(4class)	rust(4class)	shape&rust(16class)
VGG-16	94.84%	98.48%	89.28%
ResNet	87.87%	100%	73.7%
Mobilevit	84.84%	91.18%	89.79%
Densenet	88.18%	99.74%	82.39%
VAE	97.75%	100%	—

shape and rust degree, while training sixteen classification networks for screw shape and rust degree, with classification accuracy shown in the Table 3. In a real machine environment, the trained VAE screw classification network achieved a success rate of 100% in identifying specific screw shapes during the actual disassembly process.

Compared to classical image classification networks, VAE networks have higher classification accuracy and can perform well even in smaller datasets. Previously, we used YOLO to directly detect and classify screw types, but it was difficult for YOLO to classify multiple features of screws, and it required recalibration when adding new feature types, resulting in a large workload. In contrast, using VAE networks can complete training using smaller datasets and easily collect training data during the disassembly process without excessive processing.

4.2 Success Rate of Continuous Disassembly of Multiple Screws

In the simulation environment, in the disassembly experiment of six different types of screws (M8 outer hexagon screw, M10 outer hexagon screw, M12 outer hexagon screw, inner hexagon screw, cross screw, and star screw), the recognition success rate of specific screw shape was 97.75%, and the sleeve replacement success rate was 100%. The overall continuous disassembly success rate was 97.75%. In the actual machine disassembly experiment, in the disassembly experiment of five different types of screws (M8 outer hexagon screw, M10 outer hexagon screw, M13 outer hexagon screw, M10 outer hexagon cross screw, M13 outer hexagon cross screw), the recognition success rate of the specific screw shape was 100%, and the sleeve replacement success rate was 100%. The overall continuous disassembly success rate was 100%. Related experimental videos can be found on the website https://sites.google.com/view/disassembly-real.

5   Conclusions

In order to solve the problem of screw disassembly for robots in industrial disassembly tasks, we have designed a multifunctional screw disassembly workstation. Expanding its functionality on the existing NeuroSymbolic TAMP, workstations can autonomously plan and execute action primitives based on their perception of the current environment to complete the disassembly of various screws. A sleeve replacement device has been designed to achieve automatic sleeve replacement, which can stably achieve sleeve replacement during disassembly. When identifying screws, a screw type recognition method based on attributes has been proposed, which only requires a small amount of data and has scalability. Through experiments, we have verified that the system can recognize various screw shapes, specifications, and degrees of rusting in a simulation environment, achieving a disassembly success rate of 97.75%. Complete the identification of multiple real screw shapes and specifications in a real machine environment and achieve a 100% success rate in disassembly. However, in the real environment, the number of severely rusted screws is scarce, making it difficult to conduct experiments on them. Therefore, there is no identification of screw rust attributes and destructive disassembly experiments conducted in the real environment.

In the future, we will add more types of disassembly sleeves to complete the identification and disassembly of more types of screws and conduct destructive disassembly experiments on unmatched sleeves and severely corroded screws. The work of locating screws and obtaining screw images completed by YOLO can be completed using Segment-Anything [22], which does not require specialized training to achieve good segmentation results and fewer recognition errors. Increase mobile platforms to expand robot workspace and achieve global disassembly.

References

1. Chris Lu, N.K.: China lithium industry Deloitte POV 3.0: sustainable future of lithium recycle. Deloitte Consulting China, Technical report 6 (2022)
2. Harper, G., et al.: Recycling lithium-ion batteries from electric vehicles. Nature **575**(7781), 75–86 (2019)
3. Chen, H., Shen, J.: A degradation-based sorting method for lithium-ion battery reuse. PLoS One **12** (2017)
4. Scrosati, B., Garche, J., Sun, Y.-K.: 20 - recycling lithium batteries. In: Scrosati, B., Garche, J., Tillmetz, W. (eds.) Advances in Battery Technologies for Electric Vehicles. Woodhead Publishing Series in Energy, pp. 503–516. Woodhead Publishing (2015)
5. Vongbunyong, S., Kara, S., Pagnucco, M.: Application of cognitive robotics in disassembly of products. CIRP Ann. **62**(1), 31–34 (2013)
6. Vongbunyong, S., Kara, S., Pagnucco, M.: Learning and revision in cognitive robotics disassembly automation. Robot. Comput.-Integr. Manuf. **34**, 79–94 (2015)
7. Weyrich, M., Wang, Y.: Architecture design of a vision-based intelligent system for automated disassembly of e-waste with a case study of traction batteries. In: 2013 IEEE 18th Conference on Emerging Technologies & Factory Automation (ETFA), pp. 1–8. IEEE (2013)
8. Merdan, M., Lepuschitz, W., Meurer, T., Vincze, M.: Towards ontology-based automated disassembly systems. In: 36th Annual Conference on IEEE Industrial Electronics Society, IECON 2010, pp. 1392–1397. IEEE (2010)
9. Kim, S., Rodriguez, A.: Active extrinsic contact sensing: application to general peg-in-hole insertion. In: 2022 International Conference on Robotics and Automation (ICRA), pp. 10 241–10 247. IEEE (2022)
10. Ma, D., Dong, S., Rodriguez, A.: Extrinsic contact sensing with relative-motion tracking from distributed tactile measurements. In: 2021 IEEE International Conference on Robotics and Automation (ICRA), pp. 11 262–11 268. IEEE (2021)

11. Adjigble, M., Marturi, N., Ortenzi, V., Rajasekaran, V., Corke, P., Stolkin, R.: Model-free and learning-free grasping by local contact moment matching. In: 2018 IEEE/RSJ International Conference on Intelligent Robots and Systems (IROS), pp. 2933–2940. IEEE (2018)
12. Rastegarpanah, A., Gonzalez, H.C., Stolkin, R.: Semi-autonomous behaviour tree-based framework for sorting electric vehicle batteries components. Robotics **10**(2), 82 (2021)
13. Li, X., et al.: Accurate screw detection method based on faster R-CNN and rotation edge similarity for automatic screw disassembly. Int. J. Comput. Integr. Manuf. **34**(11), 1177–1195 (2021)
14. Büker, U., et al.: Vision-based control of an autonomous disassembly station. Robot. Auton. Syst. **35**(3–4), 179–189 (2001)
15. Bdiwi, M., Rashid, A., Putz, M.: Autonomous disassembly of electric vehicle motors based on robot cognition. In: IEEE International Conference on Robotics and Automation (ICRA), pp. 2500–2505. IEEE (2016)
16. Bdiwi, M., Rashid, A., Pfeifer, M., Putz, M.: Disassembly of unknown models of electrical vehicle motors using innovative human robot cooperation. In: Proceedings of the Companion of the 2017 ACM/IEEE International Conference on Human-Robot Interaction, pp. 85–86 (2017)
17. Zhang, H., Yang, H., Wang, H., Wang, Z., Zhang, S., Chen, M.: Autonomous electric vehicle battery disassembly based on neurosymbolic computing. In: Arai, K. (ed.) Intelligent Systems and Applications, pp. 443–457. Springer, Cham (2023). https://doi.org/10.1007/978-3-031-16078-3_30
18. d'Avila Garcez, A., Lamb, L.C.: Neurosymbolic AI: the 3rd wave. arXiv e-prints, pp. arXiv-2012 (2020)
19. Li, R., et al.: Unfastening of hexagonal headed screws by a collaborative robot. IEEE Trans. Autom. Sci. Eng. **17**(3), 1455–1468 (2020)
20. Wegener, K., Andrew, S., Raatz, A., Dröder, K., Herrmann, C.: Disassembly of electric vehicle batteries using the example of the Audi Q5 hybrid system. Procedia CIRP **23**, 155–160 (2014). 5th CATS 2014 - CIRP Conference on Assembly Technologies and Systems
21. Du, Y., et al.: Learning symbolic operators: a neurosymbolic solution for autonomous disassembly of electric vehicle battery. arXiv preprint arXiv:2206.03027 (2022)
22. Kirillov, A., et al.: Segment anything. arXiv preprint arXiv:2304.02643 (2023)

Inverse Kinematics Solver Based on Evolutionary Algorithm and Gradient Descent for Free-Floating Space Robot

Hongwen Zhang[1], Yongxing Tang[2], and Zhanxia Zhu[2]([✉])

[1] Zhejiang Lab, Hangzhou 310000, Zhejiang, China
[2] School of Astronautics, Northwestern Polytechnical University,
Xi'an 710072, Shanxi, China
zhuzhanxia@nwpu.edu.cn

Abstract. This paper investigates the inverse kinematics (IK) problem of free-floating space robot (FFSR) and proposes an IK solver called IK Solver Based on Evolutionary Algorithm and Gradient Descent for FFSR (EA&GD-Based IK Solver for FFSR). The IK problem for FFSR aims to find a configuration satisfying: the end-effector (EE) reaches a specific pose; the base attitude angle in this configuration is as close as possible to its nominal value. This IK solver includes the initial value module and the gradient descent module. The first module uses evolutionary algorithm to get an initial configuration, where the base attitude angle is set to its nominal value, and EE pose corresponding to this configuration is very close to the goal EE pose. The second module uses the initial configuration as initial value and obtains the gradient by projecting the EE pose error using the pseudo-inverse of the Generalized Jacobian Matrix (GJM). It can further reduce the EE pose error in the first module and obtain a configuration as a solution to the IK problem. As the EE pose corresponding to the initial configuration is very close to goal EE pose, the second module will not bring too much change in the base attitude. Therefore, the base attitude angle of the configuration obtained by the second module is very close to the nominal base attitude angle.

Keywords: Free-Floating Space Robot · Inverse Kinematics · Evolutionary Algorithm · Gradient Descent

1 Introduction

A space robot typically consists of a base satellite and a manipulator. FFSR disables the base satellite's position and attitude controllers, providing advantages like fuel savings and extending lifespan, making it widely used in on-orbit services [1]. Motion planning is a key technique for FFSR to execute tasks. For motion planning of a manipulator, a major challenge is IK problem, which requires determining a configuration that satisfies certain constraints [2,3].

Lots of existing methods for the IK problem focus on fixed-base manipulators and can be classified into 3 types [2]. **The first type** obtains the analytical solution to the IK problem by analyzing the structure of the manipulator's

© The Author(s), under exclusive license to Springer Nature Singapore Pte Ltd. 2023
H. Yang et al. (Eds.): ICIRA 2023, LNAI 14274, pp. 520–532, 2023.
https://doi.org/10.1007/978-981-99-6501-4_44

kinematic equations [2]. Many manipulators with special mechanical structures and less than 6 degrees of freedom (DOFs) have analytical solutions for the IK problem [3,4]. For manipulators with more than 6 DOFs, IKfast [2] splits the IK problem into two parts: a) the redundant DOFs above 6 are numerically discretized; b) the remaining 6 DOFs are solved in closed form. **The second type** views the IK problem as a root-finding problem for polynomial equations and addresses the root-finding issue using the Bertini or homotopy continuation methods [5]. However, it cannot handle the inequality constraints. **The third type** models the IK problem as a nonlinear optimization problem and uses gradient-based techniques [6,7] or evolutionary algorithms (EA) [8] to solve this problem. The gradient descet is sensitive to initial value and suffers from local minimum. EA is not affected by local minimum. However, since the orientation and position of EE have different and properties, for example, the position can take very large values while the range of attitude angle is limited [8]. It is difficult to construct a fitness function that completely eliminates the difference between position and attitude, but constructing a suitable fitness function is critical for the convergence of EA.

Compared to fixed-base manipulator, the IK problem of FFSR is highly complex. The fixed-base manipulator's configuration comprises its joint angles, but FFSR's configuration includes both the base attitude angles and the manipulator's joint angles. Furthermore, the disturbance of the base attitude needs to be as small as possible due to the requirements of ground communication and solar panel orientation, etc. This makes the kinematic constraints for FFSR more complex. The kinematic constraints for a fixed-base manipulator involve EE reaching a specific goal pose [2]. However, the constraints for FFSR require not only the EE to achieve a goal pose but also the base attitude angle as close as possible to the nominal base attitude angle. [9] pointed out that by using "virtual manipulator (VM)" [10] to establish FFSR's motion equations, IK problem of FFSR can be transformed into IK problem of a fixed-base manipulator. However, [9] did not provide a specific IK solver. In fact, unlike the kinematic equations for a fixed-base manipulator, the VM model includes the dynamic parameters of FFSR, so it is difficult to obtain an analytical solution based on VM model.

This paper proposes a new IK solver named EA&GD-Based IK Solver for FFSR, which combines the strengths of both EA and gradient descent. This IK Solver consists of the initial value module based on EA and the gradient descent module based on the GJM. **The initial value module** uses EA to obtain an initial configuration, where the base attitude angle is set to the nominal base attitude angle. However, since it is difficult to design a suitable fitness function, there still exists an error between the EE pose corresponding to this initial configuration and the goal EE pose, even though they are very close to each other. The initial value module provides **the gradient descent module** with an initial value that is very close to the goal EE pose, which avoids the sensitivity to initial values of the gradient-based method. Furthermore, the gradient descent module can further eliminate the EE pose error in the initial value module. Also, since the EE pose corresponding to the initial configuration is very close to the goal EE pose, the gradient descent module will not significantly alter the base attitude. Therefore, the base attitude angle of the configuration obtained by the gradient descent module is very close to the nominal base attitude angle.

2   Motion Equations for FFSR

This paper focuses on the single-arm FFSR, as shown in Fig. 1, which consists of $n+1$ rigid bodies. These rigid bodies include the base satellite and n links of the manipulator, represented as B_0 and $B_1, B_2, \cdots, B_n$, respectively. The FFSR also has n rotating joints, denoted by $J_1, J_2, \cdots, J_n$, respectively, which connect adjacent rigid bodies. Table 1 provides definitions for some important symbols used in this paper, while definitions for others can be found in [1,9].

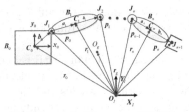 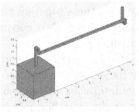

(a) Schematic Diagram of FFSR.   (b) FFSR in 3-D Space.

Fig. 1. Schematic Diagram of FFSR and FFSR in 3-D Space.

2.1   Motion Equations in Position Form

As shown in Table 1, attitude transformation matrix $^I R_e$ is a function of q. $^I R_e$ and $\boldsymbol{\Psi}_e$ are two different representations of EE's orientation. Therefore, without considering singularities and other situations, $\boldsymbol{\Psi}_e$ is also a function of q:

$$\boldsymbol{\Psi}_e = \boldsymbol{f}_{e\Psi}(\boldsymbol{q}) \tag{1}$$

Figure 1 shows that the centroid position vector of B_i $(i = 1, 2, \cdots, n)$ is:

$$\boldsymbol{r}_i = \boldsymbol{r}_0 + \boldsymbol{b}_0 + \sum_{j=1}^{i-1}(\boldsymbol{a}_j + \boldsymbol{b}_j) + \boldsymbol{a}_i \tag{2}$$

And the position vector of EE can be calculated as:

$$\boldsymbol{p}_e = \boldsymbol{r}_0 + \boldsymbol{b}_0 + \sum_{j=1}^{n}(\boldsymbol{a}_j + \boldsymbol{b}_j) \tag{3}$$

The conservation of FFSR's linear momentum is a holonomic constraint, and can be integrated into a position form: $M\boldsymbol{r}_g = m_0\boldsymbol{r}_0 + \sum_{i=1}^{n}(m_i\boldsymbol{r}_i)$. By adding Eq. (2) to this equation, we can derive the following result:

$$\boldsymbol{r}_0 = \boldsymbol{r}_g - \sum_{i=1}^{n}(m_i\boldsymbol{r}_{0i})/M \tag{4}$$

Table 1. Some Important Symbols Used in This Paper

Symbols	Definitions
θ_i	$i^{th}(i = 1, 2, \cdots, n)$ joint angle of the manipulator
Θ	$\Theta = [\theta_1, \theta_2, \cdots, \theta_n]^T$, the joint angle vector
Ψ_0	$\Psi_0 = [\alpha_0, \beta_0, \gamma_0]^T$, the Euler angles describing the base orientation with respect to the inertial coordinate system (ICS), with a rotation sequence of "$z - y - x$"
q	$q = [\Psi_0^T, \Theta^T]^T$, the configuration of FFSR
$^{i-1}R_i$	$^{i-1}R_i = f1_i(\theta_i)$, $i = 1, 2, \cdots, n$, the attitude transformation matrix (ATM) from the fixed coordinate system(FCS) of B_i to the FCS of B_{i-1}
$^{I}R_0$	$^{I}R_0 = f2(\Psi_0)$, ATM from FCS of the base satellite to ICS
$^{I}R_i$	$^{I}R_i = {}^{I}R_0{}^0R_1 \cdots {}^{i-1}R_i = f3_i(\Psi_0, \theta_1, \cdots, \theta_i)$, ATM from FCS of B_i to ICS
$^{I}R_e$	$^{I}R_e = {}^{I}R_0{}^0R_1 \cdots {}^{n-1}R_n = f_{eR}(\Psi_0, \Theta) = f_{eR}(q)$, ATM from FCS of EE to ICS
Ψ_e	$\Psi_e = [\alpha_e, \beta_e, \gamma_e]^T$, the Euler angles describing the EE attitude with respect to ICS
r_0	the position vector of base satellite's centroid
v_0, ω_0	linear velocity and angular velocity of base satellite
r_g	the position vector of FFSR's centroid
m_i	mass of B_i, $i = 0, 1, 2, \cdots, n$, and $M = \sum_{i=0}^{n}(m_i)$ is the mass of FFSR

in which $r_{0i} = b_0 + \sum_{j=1}^{i-1}(a_j + b_j)$ represents the position vector of each link's centroid with respect to the base satellite's centroid. By putting Eq. (4) into Eq. (3), we obtain the following formula to compute p_e:

$$p_e = r_g - \sum_{i=1}^{n}(m_i r_{0i})/M + b_0 + \sum_{j=1}^{n}(a_j + b_j) = f_{ep}(q) \tag{5}$$

Finally, we can get the equation to calculate EE pose x_e:

$$x_e = \begin{bmatrix} p_e \\ \Psi_e \end{bmatrix} = \begin{bmatrix} f_{ep}(q) \\ f_{e\Psi}(q) \end{bmatrix} = f_e(q) \tag{6}$$

2.2 Equations of Motion in Velocity Form

FFSR's momentum (including linear momentum P, angular momentum L) is:

$$\begin{bmatrix} P \\ L \end{bmatrix} = \begin{bmatrix} ME & M\tilde{r}_{og}^T \\ M\tilde{r}_{og} & H_\omega \end{bmatrix} \begin{bmatrix} v_0 \\ \omega_0 \end{bmatrix} + \begin{bmatrix} J_{T\omega} \\ H_{\omega\psi} \end{bmatrix} \dot{\Theta} = H_b \begin{bmatrix} v_0 \\ \omega_0 \end{bmatrix} + H_m \dot{\Theta} \tag{7}$$

Reference [9] provides definitions for $\tilde{r}_{og}$, H_ω, etc. FFSR's momentum is conserved, assuming an initial momentum of $\mathbf{0}$ for it, then we can get v_0 and ω_0:

$$\begin{bmatrix} v_0 \\ \omega_0 \end{bmatrix} = -(H_b)^{-1}H_m\dot{\Theta} = J_{b\Theta}\dot{\Theta} = \begin{bmatrix} J_{bv} \\ J_{b\omega} \end{bmatrix} \dot{\Theta} \tag{8}$$

ω_0 is represented as $^b\omega_0$ in the fixed coordinate system of the base satellite, and the relationship between $^b\omega_0$ and $\dot{\Psi}_0$ can be expressed as follows [9]:

$$^b\omega_0 = N_0\dot{\Psi}_0 \tag{9}$$

of which: $\boldsymbol{N}_0 = \begin{bmatrix} 1 & \tan(\beta_0) * \sin(\alpha_0) & \tan(\beta_0) * \cos(\alpha_0) \\ 0 & \cos(\alpha_0) & -\cos(\alpha_0) \\ 0 & \sin(\alpha_0)/\sin(\beta_0) & \cos(\alpha_0)/\cos(\beta_0) \end{bmatrix}$. Considering Eq. (8) and Eq. (9), we can get:

$$\dot{\boldsymbol{\Psi}}_0 = \boldsymbol{N}_0^{-1}(^b\boldsymbol{\omega}_0) = \boldsymbol{N}_0^{-1}(^I\boldsymbol{R}_0)^{-1}\boldsymbol{\omega}_0 = \boldsymbol{N}_0^{-1}(^I\boldsymbol{R}_0)^{-1}\boldsymbol{J}_{b\omega}\dot{\boldsymbol{\Theta}} = \boldsymbol{J}_{b\Psi}\dot{\boldsymbol{\Theta}} \tag{10}$$

Figure 1 illustrates how to obtain EE's linear and angular velocities based on the speed transfer between rigid bodies:

$$\begin{bmatrix} \boldsymbol{v}_e \\ \boldsymbol{\omega}_e \end{bmatrix} = \boldsymbol{J}_b \begin{bmatrix} \boldsymbol{v}_0 \\ \boldsymbol{\omega}_0 \end{bmatrix} + \boldsymbol{J}_m \dot{\boldsymbol{\Theta}} \tag{11}$$

By substituting Eq. (8) into Eq. (11), we can get:

$$\begin{bmatrix} \boldsymbol{v}_e \\ \boldsymbol{\omega}_e \end{bmatrix} = (\boldsymbol{J}_b \boldsymbol{J}_{b\Theta} + \boldsymbol{J}_m)\dot{\boldsymbol{\Theta}} = \boldsymbol{J}_g \dot{\boldsymbol{\Theta}} \tag{12}$$

where $\boldsymbol{J}_g = \boldsymbol{J}_b \boldsymbol{J}_{b\Theta} + \boldsymbol{J}_m$ is the Generalized Jacobian Matrix (GJM).

3   EA&GD-Based IK Solver for FFSR

The IK problem of FFSR is defined as follows: A goal EE pose of FFSR is given as $\boldsymbol{x}_e^d = [(\boldsymbol{p}_e^d)^T, (\boldsymbol{\Psi}_e^d)^T]^T$, and an IK solver should find a configuration $\boldsymbol{q}^{ik} = [(\boldsymbol{\Psi}_0^{ik})^T, (\boldsymbol{\Theta}^{ik})^T]^T$ that satisfies the following requirements:

(1) The EE pose corresponding to $\boldsymbol{q}^{ik}$ equals $\boldsymbol{x}_e^d$: $\boldsymbol{x}_e^{ik} = \boldsymbol{f}_e(\boldsymbol{q}^{ik}), \boldsymbol{x}_e^{ik} = \boldsymbol{x}_e^d$.
(2) The base attitude angle $\boldsymbol{\Psi}_0^{ik}$ in $\boldsymbol{q}^{ik}$ should be as close as possible to the nominal base attitude angle $\boldsymbol{\Psi}_0^{nom}$.

We proposes EA&GD-Based IK Solver for FFSR which includes: the initial value module based on EA and the gradient descent module based on GJM.

(1) The 1th module aims to find a configuration $\boldsymbol{q}^{Ini} = [(\boldsymbol{\Psi}_0^{Ini})^T, (\boldsymbol{\Theta}^{Ini})^T]^T$ that satisfies $\boldsymbol{\Psi}_0^{Ini} = \boldsymbol{\Psi}_0^{nom}$, while letting $\boldsymbol{x}_e^{Ini} = \boldsymbol{f}_e(\boldsymbol{q}^{Ini})$ is very close to $\boldsymbol{x}_e^d$.
(2) The 2nd module uses $\boldsymbol{q}^{Ini}$ obtained by the 1th module as initial value, and performs gradient descent to further reduce the EE pose error in the 1th module, resulting in a solution $\boldsymbol{q}^{ik}$ for the IK problem. The gradient is obtained by projecting the EE pose error using the pseudo-inverse of GJM ($\boldsymbol{J}g$).

The EE pose $\boldsymbol{x}_e^{Ini}$ corresponding to $\boldsymbol{q}^{Ini}$ is very close to $\boldsymbol{x}_e^d$. Therefore, although the gradient is generated based on GJM (the gradient generated in this way can disturb the base attitude), the gradient descent will not bring too much change in the base attitude. Furthermore, $\boldsymbol{\Psi}_0^{Ini}$ in $\boldsymbol{q}^{Ini}$ is equal to $\boldsymbol{\Psi}_0^{nom}$, so $\boldsymbol{\Psi}_0^{ik}$ in $\boldsymbol{q}^{ik}$ obtained by the gradient descent module will be very close to $\boldsymbol{\Psi}_0^{nom}$.

3.1   Initial Value Module Based on Evolutionary Algorithm

The initial value module aims to find a joint angle vector $\boldsymbol{\Theta}^{Ini}$ that satisfies: (1) Its value satisfies the joint angle restrictions: $\boldsymbol{\Theta}^{min} \leq \boldsymbol{\Theta}^{Ini} \leq \boldsymbol{\Theta}^{max}$; (2) The EE pose $\boldsymbol{x}_e^{Ini}$ corresponding to $\boldsymbol{\Theta}^{Ini}$ is very close to $\boldsymbol{x}_e^d$ when $\boldsymbol{\Psi}_0^{Ini} = \boldsymbol{\Psi}_0^{nom}$. The initial value module can be formulated as a optimization problem:

$$
\begin{aligned}
& minimize \quad f(\boldsymbol{q}, \boldsymbol{x}_e^d) = f(\boldsymbol{\Psi}_0, \boldsymbol{\Theta}, \boldsymbol{x}_e^d) \\
& subjetc\ to \quad \begin{array}{c} \boldsymbol{\Theta}^{min} \leq \boldsymbol{\Theta} \leq \boldsymbol{\Theta}^{max} \\ \boldsymbol{\Psi}_0 = \boldsymbol{\Psi}_0^{nom} \end{array}
\end{aligned}
\tag{13}
$$

In this problem, $\boldsymbol{\Theta}$ of $\boldsymbol{q} = [(\boldsymbol{\Psi}_0)^T, (\boldsymbol{\Theta})^T]^T$ is selected as the variables to be optimized, and $\boldsymbol{\Psi}_0$ is set to be equal to $\boldsymbol{\Psi}_0^{nom}$. $f(\boldsymbol{q}, \boldsymbol{x}_e^d)$ is the fitness function used to measure the difference between two different EE poses (the EE pose corresponding to $\boldsymbol{q}$ and $\boldsymbol{x}_e^d$). Choosing a suitable fitness function is critical for evolutionary optimization. The dimensions and value ranges of position and attitude are different, so when designing the fitness function, it is necessary to use techniques such as weighting and scaling to unify them.

Fitness Function. This article adopts the fitness function proposed in [8]:

$$
f(\boldsymbol{q}, \boldsymbol{x}_e^d) = D(\boldsymbol{x}_e, \boldsymbol{x}_e^d) = D_p(\boldsymbol{p}_e, \boldsymbol{p}_e^d) + D_\Psi(\boldsymbol{\Psi}_e, \boldsymbol{\Psi}_e^d)
\tag{14}
$$

Here, $f(\boldsymbol{q}, \boldsymbol{x}_e^d)$ is used to evaluate the difference between $\boldsymbol{x}_e$ and $\boldsymbol{x}_e^d$, of which:

$$
\boldsymbol{x}_e = [(\boldsymbol{p}_e)^T, (\boldsymbol{\Psi}_e)^T]^T = \boldsymbol{f}_e(\boldsymbol{q}) = \boldsymbol{f}_e(\boldsymbol{\Theta}, \boldsymbol{\Psi}_0) = \boldsymbol{f}_e(\boldsymbol{\Theta}, \boldsymbol{\Psi}_0^{nom})
\tag{15}
$$

In Eq. (14), $D_p(\boldsymbol{p}_e, \boldsymbol{p}_e^d)$ and $D_\Psi(\boldsymbol{\Psi}_e, \boldsymbol{\Psi}_e^d)$ represent the position metric and the attitude metric, respectively. $D_p(\boldsymbol{p}_e, \boldsymbol{p}_e^d)$ can be calculated as:

$$
D_p(\boldsymbol{p}_e, \boldsymbol{p}_e^d) = \pi d / \sqrt{(L + d)(\lambda + d)}
\tag{16}
$$

L is the maximum distance that EE can have relative to FFSR's centroid; λ is the distance between EE and the root of the manipulator's first link when the joint angle vector is $\boldsymbol{\Theta}$; d is the Euclidean distance between $\boldsymbol{p}_e$ and $\boldsymbol{p}_e^d$: $d = \|\boldsymbol{p}_e, \boldsymbol{p}_e^d\|$. $D_\Psi(\boldsymbol{\Psi}_e, \boldsymbol{\Psi}_e^d)$ is the Euclidean distance between $\boldsymbol{\Psi}_e$ and $\boldsymbol{\Psi}_e^d$:

$$
D_\Psi(\boldsymbol{\Psi}_e, \boldsymbol{\Psi}_e^d) = \|\boldsymbol{\Psi}_e, \boldsymbol{\Psi}_e^d\|
\tag{17}
$$

It should be noted that it is impossible to design a fitness function that completely eliminates the difference between position and attitude. Therefore, when using evolutionary algorithms to solve this optimization problem, it is difficult for the fitness function to converge to zero, which means that there may still be a certain amount of error between $\boldsymbol{x}_e$ and $\boldsymbol{x}_e^d$ after running the evolutionary algorithm. However, the evolutionary algorithm can find a joint angle $\boldsymbol{\Theta}^{Ini}$ that makes $\boldsymbol{x}_e^{Ini}$ very close to $\boldsymbol{x}_e^d$ when $\boldsymbol{\Psi}_0^{Ini} = \boldsymbol{\Psi}_0^{nom}$.

3.2   Gradient Descent Module Based on GJM

Gradient descent module takes q^{Ini} as the initial value and involves an iterative process that generates a new configuration q^{new} at each iteration. The pseudo-inverse of J_g is used to map the EE pose error to the joint angular velocity space at each iteration, producing a joint angular velocity $\dot{\Theta}$ (i.e. the gradient) that can reduce Δx_e. The iteration continues until $\Delta x_e = x_e^d - f_e(q^{new})$ satisfies the precision requirement. The specific steps of the gradient descent module are illustrated in Algorithm 1, and are described as follows. First, the gradient descent is initialized with q^{Ini} (Algorithm 1, line 1), and Δx_e is initialized to a large value (Algorithm 1, line 2). Then, the iterative process of gradient descent continues until Δx_e is small enough to satisfy the precision requirement (Algorithm 1, line 3, where δ is a very small value set according to the precision requirement). For each iteration:

Algorithm 1: GJM_GradientDescent(q^{Ini},x_e^d)

---

1   $q^{now} \leftarrow q^{Ini}$;
2   $\Delta x_e = inf$;
3   **while** $\Delta x_e > \delta$ **do**
4   $\quad$ $(J_{b\Psi},J_g) \leftarrow$ JacobianMatrix(q^{now}) ;
5   $\quad$ $x_e^{now} \leftarrow f_e(q^{now}), \quad \Delta x_e \leftarrow x_e^d - x_e^{now}$;
6   $\quad$ $\dot{\Theta}^{now} \leftarrow (J_g)^+ \Delta x_e$;
7   $\quad$ $\dot{\Psi}_b^{now} \leftarrow J_{b\Psi}\dot{\Theta}^{now}, \quad \dot{q}^{now} = [(\dot{\Psi}_b^{now})^T, (\dot{\Theta}^{now})^T]^T$;
8   $\quad$ $q^{now} \leftarrow q^{now} + \dot{q}^{now} * \Delta t$;
9   **return** q^{now};

Step A. Calculate the Jacobian matrices $J_{b\Psi}$ and J_g (Algorithm 1, line 4), as well as the EE pose x_e^{now}, when $q = q^{now}$. Then, compute the error between x_e^d and x_e^{now} (Algorithm 1, line 5).

Step B. Generate joint angular velocity vector $\dot{\Theta}^{now}$ (i.e. the gradient) that can reduce Δx_e by using $(J_g)^+$ to project Δx_e (Algorithm 1, line 6). Then, use $J_{b\Psi}$ to multiply $\dot{\Theta}^{now}$ to obtain $\dot{\Psi}_b^{now}$ (Algorithm 1, line 7).

Step C. Integrate to update the configuration(Algorithm 1, line 8).

Return the final obtained configuration q^{now} as the solution q^{ik} when the iteration is completed. It should be noted that the joint angular velocity (the gradient) is obtained by projecting the EE pose error using the pseudo-inverse of GJM, which can cause disturbance to the base attitude (Eq. (10)). Therefore, there is a certain difference between the nominal base attitude angle Ψ_0^{nom} and Ψ_0^{ik} in the final obtained configuration q^{ik}. However, since the EE pose corresponding to q^{Ini} is very close to x_e^d, the above difference is not significant. Some scholars have proposed the "reaction null-space" strategy for FFSR [11]. This strategy generates gradients within the null-space of $J_{b\Psi}$, that is, line 6 of Algorithm 1 generates $\dot{\Theta}^{now}$ as follows.

$$\dot{q}^{now} = Null(J_{b\Psi})\zeta$$
$$\zeta = (J_g Null(J_{b\Psi}))^+ \Delta x_e$$
$$Null(J_{b\Psi}) = E_{n \times n} - J_{b\Psi}^+ J_{b\Psi} \tag{18}$$

Theoretically, this strategy could achieve non-disturbance of the base attitude. However, the DOFs in the joint space of the FFSR are usually limited to only 6 or 7, resulting in the null-space of $J_{b\Psi}$ having only 3 or 4 DOFs. Therefore, the "reaction null-space" strategy is unable to converge the EE pose error.

Table 2. Dynamic Parameters for FFSR

Rigid Body	mass(kg)	Moment of Inertia(kg · m^2)		
		I_{xx}	I_{yy}	I_{zz}
Base	900	6000	12000	8000
Link1	20	20	20	30
Link2	20	20	20	30
Link3	40	1	40	40
Link4	40	1	40	40
Link5	20	20	20	30
Link6	20	20	20	30
Link7	40	10	8	4

4 Numerical Simulation

The numerical simulation consists of 2 parts: The 1th part uses the evolutionary algorithm-based IK Solver (EA-Based IK Solver) to solve FFSR's IK problem, while the 2nd part uses the gradient descent-based IK solver (GD-Based IK Solver). The 1th part adops Particle Swarm Optimization (PSO), and includes 3 cases: setting the goal EE position only, setting the goal EE orientation only, and setting both goal EE position and orientation. The 2nd part sets both the goal EE pose and orientation, and includes 2 cases: Using an arbitrary configuration as the initial value, and using the result obtained from the first part as the initial value (i.e. EA&GD-Based IK Solver for FFSR). A FFSR with a base satellite and a 7-joint manipulator is chosen for the simulation. FFSR's dynamic parameters are displayed in Table 2, while the D-H parameters of FFSR's manipulator are shown in Table 3. Figure 1(b) shows the FFSR in 3-D space when the joint angle and base attitude angle are both $\mathbf{0}$. In all cases, the nominal base attitude is $\mathbf{\Psi}_0^{nom} = [0, 0, 0]°$, and the centroid of FFSR is $r_g = [0, 0, 0]m$.

Table 3. D-H Parameters of the Manipulator

i	1	2	3	4	5	6	7
$a_{i-1}(m)$	0	0	0	4	4	0	0
$\alpha_{i-1}(°)$	0	90	90	0	0	90	90
$d_i(m)$	2.5	0.35	0.35	0	0.35	0.35	1.2
$\theta_i(°)$	600	20	20	40	40	20	20

4.1   Simulation of EA-Based IK Solver for FFSR

Case 1: EA-Based IK Solver for Setting the Goal EE Position Only.
The goal EE position is $p_e^d = [4, 2, 1]m$. The optimization problem is constructed using the method in Sect. 3.1 with the L_∞ norm which measures the distance between 2 different positions as fitness function. After 27 iterations of PSO, the fitness function converged to 0, and the change in fitness function is shown in Fig. 2(a). We obtained $\Theta^{Ini} = [66.7, -14.1, -26.4, 125.7, -46.2, 72.1, 28.8]^\circ$ that satisfied $f_{ep}(\Psi_0^{nom}, \Theta^{Ini}) = p_e^d$.

Case 2: EA-Based IK Solver for Setting the Goal EE Attitude Only. The goal EE attitude is $\Psi_e^d = [60, 70, 80]^\circ$. The optimization problem is also constructed using the method in Sect. 3.1 with the L_∞ norm which can measure the distance between two different attitudes as the fitness function. After 32 iterations of PSO, the fitness function converged to 0, and we obtained $\Theta^{Ini} = [23.4, -66.9, 6.8, 53.4, 140.2, -14.1, -143.6]^\circ$ that satisfied $f_{e\Psi}(\Psi_0^{nom}, \Theta^{Ini}) = \Psi_e^d$. The change in fitness function with respect to the number of iterations is shown in Fig. 2(b).

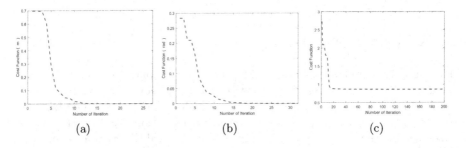

$\qquad\qquad$ (a) $\qquad\qquad\qquad\qquad\qquad$ (b) $\qquad\qquad\qquad\qquad\qquad$ (c)

Fig. 2. Simulation Results of EA-Based IK Solver for FFSR.

Case 3: EA-Based IK Solver for Setting Both Goal EE Position and Goal EE Attitude. The goal EE position is $p_e^d = [4, 2, 1]m$, and the goal EE attitude is $\Psi_e^d = [60, 70, 80]^\circ$. The optimization problem is constructed using the method in Sect. 3.1 and we adopt the fitness function proposed in [8]. The change in fitness function is shown in Fig. 2(c). The fitness function eventually converges to a relatively small value, but fails to converge to 0. We obtained joint angles $\Theta^{Ini} = [68.8, -12.1, -28.9, 126.5, -39.1, 75.4, 27.0]^\circ$ that satisfied $f_{ep}(\Psi_0^{nom}, \Theta^I) = p_e^d$, and $\Delta\Psi_e = \Psi_e^d - f_{e\Psi}(\Psi_0^{nom}, \Theta^{Ini}) = [-3.1, -1.6, 2.9]^\circ$.

According to the results, we can see that in comparison to the first and second cases, in the third case, PSO fails to find joint angles that allow the EE pose of FFSR to perfectly match the target EE pose even after numerous iterations. This is because the orientation and position of the EE have different dimensions and properties. Constructing a fitness function that completely eliminates the difference between position and attitude is extremely challenging.

4.2   Simulation of GD-Based IK Solver for FFSR

This subsection includes 4 simulation examples, and the goal EE position and goal EE attitude for them are the same as that of case 3 in Sect. 4.1. Examples 1 and 2 select the initial value arbitrarily, while examples 3 and 4 use the results from case 3 in Sect. 4.1 as the initial value. Furthermore, in examples 1 and 3, gradient descent is performed in the entire joint angular velocity space (Algorithm 1, line 6), while in examples 2 and 4, gradient descent is performed within the null-space of $J_{b\Psi}$ (Eq. (18)). It should be noted that example 3 refers to the EA&GD-Based IK Solver for FFSR proposed in this paper.

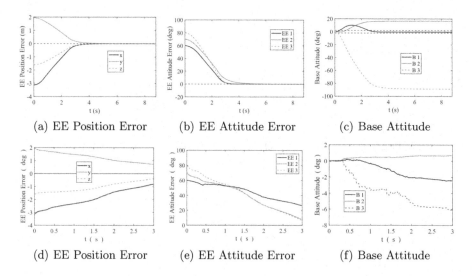

(a) EE Position Error   (b) EE Attitude Error   (c) Base Attitude

(d) EE Position Error   (e) EE Attitude Error   (f) Base Attitude

Fig. 3. Simulation Results of Examples 1 & 2 for GD-Based IK Solver for FFSR.

Using an Arbitrary Value as the Initial Value. Without loss of generality, the initial value (i.e. initial configuration q^{Ini}) is set as: $\Psi_b^{Ini} = [0,0,0]^\circ$, $\Theta^{Ini} = [0,0,0,0,0,0,0]^\circ$. The results of example 1 are shown in Fig. 3(a), (b) and (c), and we can see that performing gradient descent in the entire joint angular velocity space yields a configuration q^{ik} that satisfies: $f_e(q^{ik}) = x_e^d$. However, due to the significant difference between the EE pose corresponding to q^{Ini} and x_e^d, the gradient descent could result in significant changes in the base attitude (i.e. there is a significant difference between Ψ_0^{ik} of the obtained q^{ik} and Ψ_0^{nom}). On the other hand, the results of example 2 are shown in Fig. 3(c), (d) and (e), and we can see that performing gradient descent within the null-space of $J_{b\Psi}$ can result in small changes in the base attitude, but it is unable to make the EE pose error converge.

Using the Result from EA-Based IK Solver as the Initial Value. Taking the results from case 3 of in Sect. 4.1 as initial value (i.e. initial configuration

q^{Ini}): $\boldsymbol{\Psi}_b^{Ini} = [0,0,0]°$, $\boldsymbol{\Theta}^{Ini} = [68.8, -12.1, -28.9, 126.5, -39.1, 75.4, 27.0]°$. The results of example 3 are shown in Fig. 4(a), (b) and (c), and we can see that using the result from the EA-Based IK Solver as the initial value, and performing gradient descent in the entire joint angular velocity space, can yield a configuration q^{ik} that satisfies: $\boldsymbol{f}_e(q^{ik}) = \boldsymbol{x}_e^d$. Besides, due to the EE pose corresponding to q^{Ini} is very close to $\boldsymbol{x}_e^d$, the gradient descent module will not significantly alter the base attitude (i.e. $\boldsymbol{\Psi}_0^{ik}$ of the obtained q^{ik} and $\boldsymbol{\Psi}_0^{nom}$). On the other hand, the results of example 4 are shown in Fig. 3(4), (d) and (e), and we can see that although the EE pose corresponding to q^{Ini} is very close to $\boldsymbol{x}e^d$, performing gradient descent within the null-space of $\boldsymbol{J}_{b\Psi}$ is still unable to make the EE pose error converge.

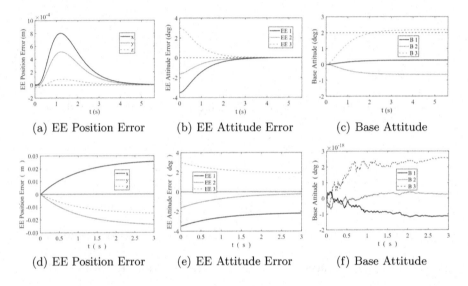

(a) EE Position Error   (b) EE Attitude Error   (c) Base Attitude

(d) EE Position Error   (e) EE Attitude Error   (f) Base Attitude

Fig. 4. Simulation Results of Examples 3 & 4 for GD-Based IK Solver for FFSR.

According to the above results, we can see that for IK problem of FFSR, using EA-Based IK Solver to obtain an initial configuration as the initial value for gradient descent, and generating the gradient based on GJM (i.e., EA&GD-Based IK Solver for FFSR, example 3) is effective. For IK problem in the simulation, the solution (q^{ik}) obtained by EA&GD-Based IK Solver for FFSR is: $\boldsymbol{\Psi}_0^{ik} = [0.26, -0.64, 2.18]°$, $\boldsymbol{\Theta}^{ik} = [66.73, -14.05, -26.42, 125.69, -46.17, 72.11, 28.76]°$. We can see that the difference between the $\boldsymbol{\Psi}_0^{ik}$ in q^{ik} and the nominal base attitude $\boldsymbol{\Psi}_0^{nom}$ is very small.

5   Conclusion

This paper proposes a new IK solver called EA&GD-Based IK Solver for FFSR, which consists of an initial value module based on EA and a gradient descent module. The initial value module uses EA to solve an optimization problem. The optimization problem selects the joint angles of the configuration as the variables to be optimized, sets the base attitude angle to be its nominal value, and constructs a fitness function which reduces the difference between the position and attitude through weighting and scaling. The gradient descent module uses the results from the first module as the initial value and generates the gradient by projecting the EE pose error using the pseudo-inverse of GJM. The gradient descent module can further reduce the EE pose error in the initial value module, and since the EE pose corresponding to the initial value is very close to the goal EE pose, the base attitude will not be significantly altered. When using EA&GD-Based IK Solver for FFSR to solve the IK problem of FFSR, the base attitude angle in the obtained configuration can be very close to the nominal base attitude angle. Simulations were conducted for the IK problem of a FFSR with a 7-DOFs manipulator, and the results verified the effectiveness of the proposed EA&GD-Based IK Solver for FFSR. Besides, the simulation results also validated the rationality of combining EA with gradient descent to solve the IK problem of FFSR, and explained why the "reaction null-space" strategy was not used to generate gradients in the second module.

References

1. Flores-Abad, A., Ma, O., Pham, K., Ulrich, S.: A review of space robotics technologies for on-orbit servicing. Prog. Aerosp. Sci. **68**, 1–26 (2014)
2. Dai, H., Izatt, G., Tedrake, R.: Global inverse kinematics via mixed-integer convex optimization. Int. J. Robot. Res. **38**(12–13), 1420–1441 (2019)
3. Lynch, K.M., Park, F.C.: Modern Robotics. Cambridge University Press, Liberty Plaza (2017)
4. Qiao, S., Liao, Q., Wei, S., Su, H.J.: Inverse kinematic analysis of the general 6R serial manipulators based on double quaternions. Mech. Mach. Theory **45**(2), 193–199 (2010)
5. Varedi, S.M., Daniali, H.M., Ganji, D.D.: Kinematics of an offset 3-UPU translational parallel manipulator by the homotopy continuation method. Nonlinear Anal. Real World Appl. **10**(3), 1767–1774 (2009)
6. Buss, S.R.: Introduction to inverse kinematics with Jacobian transpose, pseudoinverse and damped least squares methods. IEEE J. Robot. Autom. **17**(1–19), 16 (2004)
7. Beeson, P., Ames, B.: TRAC-IK: an open-source library for improved solving of generic inverse kinematics. In: 2015 IEEE-RAS 15th International Conference on Humanoid Robots, Seoul, South Korea, pp. 928–935. IEEE (2015)
8. Starke, S., Hendrich, N., Zhang, J.: A memetic evolutionary algorithm for real-time articulated kinematic motion. In: 2017 IEEE Congress on Evolutionary Computation, Donostia, Spain, pp. 2473–2479. IEEE (2017)
9. Xu, W., Li, C., Wang, X., Liu, Y., Liang, B., Xu, Y.: Study on non-holonomic cartesian path planning of a free-floating space robotic system. Adv. Robot. **23**(1–2), 113–143 (2009)
10. Vafa, Z., Dubowsky, S.: On the dynamics of manipulators in space using the virtual manipulator approach. In: 1987 IEEE International Conference on Robotics and Automation, Raleigh, NC, USA, vol. 4, pp. 579–585. IEEE (1987)

11. Yoshida, K., Nenchev, D.N.: Space robot impact analysis and satellite-base impulse minimization using reaction null-space. In: 1995 IEEE International Conference on Robotics and Automation, Nagoya, Japan, vol. 2, pp. 1271–1277. IEEE (1995)

Potential Energy Recovery of Robotic Extractors for Low Carbon Footprint

Chenyue Zhang, Bin He$^{(\boxtimes)}$, and Guiqin Li

Shanghai Key Laboratory of Intelligent Manufacturing and Robotics, School of Mechatronic Engineering and Automation, Shanghai University, Shanghai 200444, China
mehebin@gmail.com

Abstract. Robotic excavators have long been recognized as significant contributors to the carbon footprint of the construction machinery sector due to their high energy consumption. As global construction projects continue to escalate, there is an urgent need to prioritize energy conservation and environmental protection. This is particularly crucial in the current Chinese context, where the nation is striving to achieve a "carbon peak" and "carbon neutrality" by balancing carbon emissions through removal or offsetting measures. The objective of this research is to develop and study hydraulic energy-saving technologies for robotic excavators, aiming to reduce their carbon footprint and align with carbon neutrality goals. By focusing on the boom descent potential energy recovery technology, the research seeks to harness the energy generated during boom movement and utilize it efficiently, thereby minimizing energy consumption and mitigating environmental impacts. The adoption of this innovative technology holds immense promise for reducing carbon emissions associated with robotic excavators. By recovering and utilizing the potential energy generated during boom descent, the overall energy consumption of the excavators can be significantly reduced, leading to a considerable decrease in their carbon footprint. By integrating low-carbon practices into the manufacturing and operation of construction machinery, this research strives to achieve substantial reductions in carbon emissions and foster a greener future. Through the development and implementation of carbon footprint reduction strategies, the construction machinery industry can actively contribute to China's carbon neutrality objectives and support global efforts towards mitigating climate change.

Keywords: Hydraulic excavator · Boom potential energy · Energy recovery system · Hydraulic accumulator

1 Introduction

As one of the typical engineering machinery, excavation robots are widely used in mechanized construction of mining, transportation, and road construction [1, 2]. Although they have a wide range of applications, the problems of high energy consumption and poor emissions cannot be ignored [3, 4]. The emergence of energy recycling and hybrid

© The Author(s), under exclusive license to Springer Nature Singapore Pte Ltd. 2023
H. Yang et al. (Eds.): ICIRA 2023, LNAI 14274, pp. 533–542, 2023.
https://doi.org/10.1007/978-981-99-6501-4_45

powertrain control provides new ideas for solving the above problems [5–7]. These technologies are also important energy-saving technologies in construction machinery. The former mainly recovers braking energy or released potential energy, which is then reused through energy storage devices. The latter typically uses auxiliary tools from the second power to optimize engine fuel economy.

Low carbon development is a common vision of society, and achieving carbon peak is a key task that countries are striving to promote [8–10]. Faced with this goal, the construction machinery industry, as a major emitter of exhaust emissions, is full of opportunities and challenges. As one of the representative models of construction machinery, the fuel cost of excavation robots during their operation accounts for approximately 25% of the cost within the lifespan of the machine. Therefore, applying energy recovery technology to robotic excavators can not only improve fuel utilization and reduce the increased cost in terms of fuel, but also reduce power loss in the hydraulic oil circuit and faults caused by the hydraulic system's failure to dissipate heat in a timely manner through optimization of the hydraulic system, greatly improving the overall performance and carbon emission performance of the robotic excavator [11].

In the energy efficiency of robotic excavators, the efficiency of the hydraulic system is only 30%, which is the main reason for the high energy consumption and low efficiency of this model [12]. Considering that the excavation robot requires frequent lifting, braking, and falling of its boom during typical construction processes, the boom is the most frequently active key component in this model. During its falling process, most of the gravitational potential energy is converted into thermal energy at the throttle port of the main valve, causing losses [13]. This not only causes energy waste, but also increases the hydraulic oil temperature, thereby reducing the operability of the entire machine and the responsiveness of the hydraulic components. It can be seen that studying the gravity potential energy recovery technology of the robotic excavator boom has important engineering research significance and practical value [14, 15].

Electrohydraulic proportional technology combines the advantages of electrical control and hydraulic control, and its cost is more easily accepted by modern industry compared to electro-hydraulic servo control. However, due to the non-linear and time-varying high-order nature of the electro-hydraulic proportional system, it cannot achieve more effective and accurate control. Proportional Integral Derivative (PID) control has high control accuracy, good robustness, and good dynamic tracking quality, and is currently widely used in engineering [16]. Although PID parameters can be optimized, PID control has a strong dependence on the model, and robotic excavators usually work in complex and ever-changing environments. Therefore, it is difficult to achieve ideal control effects when the system changes solely through PID control. Fuzzy control theory focuses on long-term accumulated operational experience and has strong adaptability to changes in fuzzy parameters of the controlled system. The biggest advantage of the fuzzy PID algorithm is that it does not damage the control effect of the original PID, and the PID parameters are incrementally adjusted according to the established fuzzy control rules based on the tracking error and tracking error change rate of the system. This article studies the simplified model of the electro-hydraulic proportional position system of the robotic excavator's boom, combining fuzzy control with PID control to compensate for the fixed and unchanging control mode of PID three parameters when using PID control alone, making the system have better control performance.

2   Research on Boom Potential Energy Recovery Scheme

During the working process of the excavation robot, the main executing mechanisms such as the boom, bucket, and bucket are frequently lifted and lowered, and due to the large mass of each moving component, the inertia brought by it is also large. Therefore, a large amount of energy is released during startup and shutdown. Using Amesim simulation software to verify the feasibility of the boom potential energy recovery system through simulation is helpful for proposing energy recovery methods for robotic excavators and designing actual boom potential energy recovery devices.

The fuzzy adaptive PID algorithm is mainly composed of a combination of fuzzy controller and PID controller. The fuzzy controller takes error e and error change rate ec as inputs, and uses fuzzy rules to adaptively adjust the parameters Kp, Ki, and Kd of the PID controller, so as to maintain the controlled object in a good dynamic and static stable state. Compared to traditional PID control, fuzzy adaptive PID is more flexible and stable, especially for controlled objects with large time-varying and nonlinear characteristics, and its advantages are more prominent (see Fig. 1).

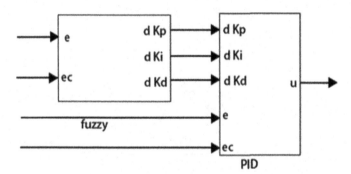

Fig. 1. Fuzzy PID controller simulation model diagram.

3   Mathematical Model of Hydraulic Circuit and Research on Joint Simulation of Boom Position Control

3.1   Mathematical Model of Hydraulic Circuit

Based on the system principle of hydraulic excavator boom potential energy recovery described in the previous chapter, establish mathematical models of various main hydraulic components targeting the boom system of XCMG XE15U excavator (see Fig. 2). This new hydraulic control system uses pressure sensors to collect the upward displacement D1 of the actuator arm, the downward displacement D2 of the arm, the pressure P1 of the large chamber of the upward hydraulic cylinder of the arm, and the pressure P2 of the small chamber of the downward hydraulic cylinder of the arm. After being judged and processed by the upper computer program, control the on-off of directional valves 1, 2, 3, 4, and 5, thereby achieving the purpose of controlling the on-off of hydraulic valves by the control system to achieve the recycling and reuse of boom potential energy. The following Table 1 gives a summary of all excavator parameters.

Table 1. Excavator parameters

Parameters	Value	Unit
discharge coefficient	0.7	/
fuel supply pressure	23	MPa
working area of the small chamber during hydraulic cylinder operation	2099.37	mm^2
working area of the large chamber during hydraulic cylinder operation	3117.24	mm^2
hydraulic cylinder stroke	240	mm
equivalent volume of hydraulic cylinder	503848.63	mm^3
equivalent mass of the load and piston rod	4600	kg

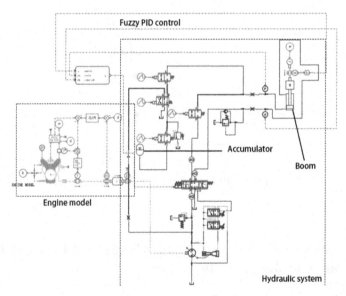

Fig. 2. Simulation Model of Boom Potential Energy Recovery System Based on Accumulator.

To achieve joint simulation, an interface module must be created in AMESim and an S-function module must be created in MATLAB. The interfaces of AMESim and Simulink are channels for data transfer, allowing for the addition of environment variables, compilers, and interface files. The function of the interface module in AMESim is to import the physical model of AMESim into MATLAB. The input end of the interface module is the displacement signal x of the displacement sensor, and the output end is the control signal u of the electro-hydraulic proportional valve calculated through MATLAB.

The function of the S-function module in MATLAB is to run the AMESim physical model. The input end of this module is the control signal u of the electro-hydraulic proportional valve, and the output end is the displacement signal x of the displacement sensor. Realize data exchange between physical models and control systems through the above methods, and complete joint simulation.

3.2 Research on Joint Simulation of Boom Position Control

The fuzzy PID is established in MATLAB (see Fig. 3). In MATLAB, the ToFile module is used to export the simulation results to a file, and a drawing program is written to draw the simulation curve.

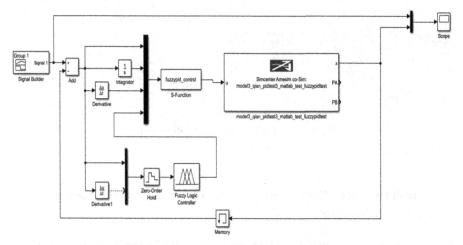

Fig. 3. MATLAB Control Simulation Model.

In response to the characteristics of time delay and multi temporal variability in excavator control, it is necessary to minimize the steady-state error during excavator matching control Δ Kp, Δ Ki and ΔKd. The error of Kd is represented by {NB, NM, NS, ZO, PS, PM, PB}, where NB represents the maximum value of the negative electrode; NM represents negative median; NS represents the minimum negative value; ZO represents zero value; PS represents the small value of the positive electrode; PM represents the median value; PB represents the maximum value of the positive electrode.

The output obtained by fuzzy reasoning is a fuzzy quantity, and the barycenter method widely used in industrial control is selected through the process of defuzzification. This method uses the weighted average method to obtain the decision result for the fuzzy set U.

Set the fuzzy domain, membership function, and input parameters Δ Kp, Δ Ki and ΔKd according to the above requirements. The fuzzy control rule adjustment table of KD adopts the Mammain type inference algorithm and the centroid method to solve the fuzzification, and finally, a schematic diagram of the fuzzy control rules can be obtained.

Fuzzy self-adjusting control monitors the displacement error e and error change rate ec in real time, and provides corresponding correction values for the control parameters according to the relationship between PID control parameters and e, ec, thereby ultimately giving the control signal.

Enter fuzzy in the command window of MATLAB to enter the Fuzzy Logic Toolbox and input fuzzy control rules in the form of if then. Finally, the membership function curves of input and output variables are obtained based on fuzzy rules (see Fig. 4).

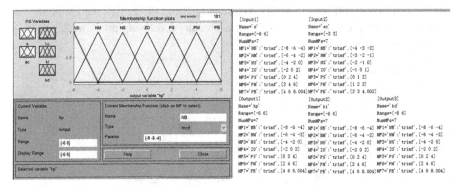

Fig. 4. MATLAB Control Simulation Model.

4   Simulation and Performance Analysis of Potential Energy Recovery System

Based on the measured operating parameters of the actual vehicle, obtain the load and pressure curves of the boom hydraulic cylinder at no load, and modify the simulation model. Take the single machine mechanism of lowering and raising the boom as a working cycle, and set the working cycle to 10 s.

When the boom operates, a pilot controlled directional signal (see Fig. 5) is input to the directional valve. The displacement curve of the follower boom shows that the hydraulic cylinder piston rises at a constant speed and then reaches its maximum stroke; At 2.94 s–7.01 s, during this stage, the hydraulic cylinder piston reaches its maximum and the boom hydraulic cylinder maintains a pressure maintaining state; Afterwards, the directional valve switches, and hydraulic oil is pumped from the hydraulic pump into the rod chamber. Due to the influence of the load gravity on the boom, the hydraulic cylinder piston begins to retract after a brief oscillation. During this period, the hydraulic oil in the rod chamber of the original hydraulic cylinder piston is kept under pressure by the pre charging pressure in the accumulator, and the pressure in the accumulator gradually increases. At the same time, the potential energy generated by the boom lowering is converted into hydraulic energy and stored in the hydraulic accumulator, Increase the pressure inside the accumulator from 94.5 bar of pre inflation pressure to 112.2 bar; The back pressure value of the rodless chamber in the boom hydraulic cylinder increases. Due to the obstruction of pressure in the accumulator, the lowering speed of the boom hydraulic cylinder piston slows down until the boom hydraulic cylinder returns to its initial state.

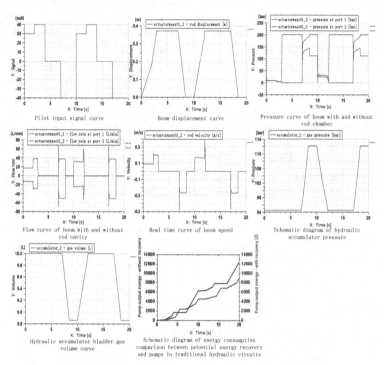

Fig. 5. Real time curve of hydraulic system boom related data and schematic diagram of pump energy consumption comparison between recovery and traditional hydraulic circuits.

According to the simulation results of the potential energy recovery system, it can be seen that during the boom action stage, the starting stage, pressure maintaining stage, and descent stage have relatively smooth speeds, and the overall hydraulic performance is good, which can achieve the purpose of normal operation. This indicates that it is feasible to use a bag type hydraulic accumulator to store the potential energy released by the boom.

The simulated data was sorted out to obtain the energy comparison curve of the variable displacement pump before and after adding the potential energy recovery device.

In a single working cycle, the hydraulic pump in the new circuit consumes a total of 9765.36J of energy, while the hydraulic pump in the traditional circuit consumes a total of 13585.6 J of energy. Compared to the traditional circuit, the new circuit reduces energy consumption by a total of 28.12%. The results show that for every hour of work, approximately 0.38 kg of carbon dioxide emissions are saved.

The circuit using fuzzy PID control reduces energy consumption by 47.92% in total. By comparing the data of the hydraulic circuit with fuzzy adaptive PID control and the hydraulic circuit with classical PID control, significant improvements have been observed in various aspects. The rise, fall, and stability time of the system were notably shortened, and the tracking lag phenomenon was reduced. The number of oscillations was significantly decreased, particularly in the main motion mechanism, ensuring system stability and prolonging component life. Moreover, the pump output energy was further reduced (see Fig. 6). These advancements in energy-saving control have direct implications for carbon neutrality efforts. By reducing energy consumption and improving system efficiency, the hydraulic circuit utilizing fuzzy PID control plays a vital role in achieving carbon neutrality goals. The significant reduction in energy consumption, as evidenced by a 47.92% decrease, contributes to minimizing carbon emissions associated with the operation of robotic excavators. The implementation of energy-saving technologies not only optimizes the performance of hydraulic excavators but also aligns with the broader objective of carbon neutrality. By effectively managing energy utilization and reducing waste, this research contributes to the sustainable development of the construction machinery industry. The integration of fuzzy adaptive PID control techniques promotes energy efficiency, decreases carbon footprints, and supports the transition to a low-carbon and environmentally friendly future.

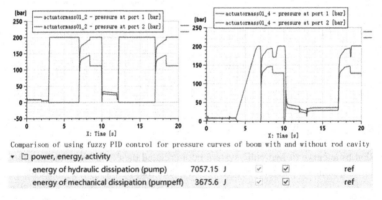

Fig. 6. Comparison of using fuzzy PID control for pressure curves of boom with and without rod cavity and Comparison of pump output energy.

5 Conclusion

In conclusion, this research on the potential energy recovery and utilization scheme for hydraulic excavators addresses the urgent need for energy conservation and environmental protection, particularly in the context of carbon neutrality. The hydraulic system's working principle during the operation cycle of excavators underscores the importance of implementing energy-saving technologies to reduce the carbon footprint. To ensure successful implementation, a comprehensive hydraulic component model has been developed using AMESim and MATLAB, based on the proposed potential energy recovery system. Moreover, fuzzy adaptive PID optimization control has been employed to provide a theoretical framework for efficient energy utilization. This control mechanism optimizes energy-saving performance, thereby further reducing the carbon footprint of hydraulic excavators. Through a quantitative evaluation that compares the power consumption of the prototype with an improved version equipped with an energy reuse system, this research strives to optimize energy-saving performance and make significant contributions to carbon neutrality. The findings of this study contribute to the optimization and advancement of energy-saving technologies in hydraulic excavators, aligning with the goals of carbon neutrality.

Acknowledgments. The work was supported by National Key Research and Development Program of China, (2020YFB1709902), and National Natural Science Foundation of China (No. 52075312).

References

1. Xu, B., Cheng, M.: Motion control of multi-actuator hydraulic systems for mobile machineries: recent advancements and future trends. Front. Mech. Eng. PRC **13**, 151–166 (2018)
2. Huang, J., Song, Z., Wu, J., Guo, H., Qiu, C., Tan, Q.: Parameter adaptive sliding mode force control for aerospace electro-hydraulic load simulator. Aerospace **10**(2), 160 (2023)
3. Wang, H., Wang, Q.: Parameter matching and control of series hybrid hydraulic excavator based on electro-hydraulic composite energy storage. IEEE. Access **8**, 111899–111912 (2020)
4. Yang, J., Liu, B., Zhang, T., Hong, J., Zhang, H.: Application of energy conversion and integration technologies based on electro-hydraulic hybrid power systems: a review. Energ. Convers. Manage. **272**, 116372 (2022)
5. Fu, S., Li, Z., Lin, T., Chen, Q., Ren, H.: A positive flow control system for electric excavators based on variable speed control. Appl. Sci. **10**(14), 4826 (2020)
6. Chen, Q., Cai, S., Li, X., Lin, T.: Power train system control of electric loader based on positive flow system. Appl. Sci. **12**(12), 6032 (2022)
7. Tong, Z., Jiang, Y., Tong, S., Zhang, Q., Wu, J.: Hybrid drivetrain with dual energy regeneration and collaborative control of driving and lifting for construction machinery. Automat. Constr. **150**, 104806 (2023)
8. Li, J., Zhao, J.: Energy recovery for hybrid hydraulic excavators: flywheel-based solutions. Automat. Constr. **125**, 103648 (2021)
9. Zhao, X., Ma, X., Chen, B., Shang, Y., Song, M.: Challenges toward carbon neutrality in China: strategies and countermeasures. Resour. Conserv. Recy. **176**, 105959 (2022)
10. Liu, Z., et al.: Challenges and opportunities for carbon neutrality in China. Nat. Rev. Earth. Env. **3**(2), 141–155 (2022)
11. Chen, Q., Lin, T., Ren, H.: A novel control strategy for an interior permanent magnet synchronous machine of a hybrid hydraulic excavator. IEEE. Access **6**, 3685–3693 (2017)
12. Ge, L., Quan, L., Zhang, X., Dong, Z., Yang, J.: Power matching and energy efficiency improvement of hydraulic excavator driven with speed and displacement variable power source. Chin. J. Mech. Eng-En. **32**, 1–12 (2019)
13. Wang, W., Zhao, J.: Energy-efficient robust control for direct drive and energy recuperation hydraulic servo system. Complexity **2020**, 1–19 (2020)
14. Ge, L., Quan, L., Li, Y., Zhang, X., Yang, J.: A novel hydraulic excavator boom driving system with high efficiency and potential energy regeneration capability. Energ. Convers. Manage. **166**, 308–317 (2018)

15. Guo, W., Zhao, Y., Li, R., Ding, H., Zhang, J.: Active disturbance rejection control of valve-controlled cylinder servo systems based on MATLAB-AMESim Cosimulation. Complexity **2020**, 1–10 (2020)
16. Nguyen, T.H., Do, T.C., Nguyen, V.H., Ahn, K.K.: High tracking control for a new independent metering valve system using velocity-load feedforward and position feedback methods. Appl. Sci. **12**(19), 9827 (2022)

Innovative Design and Performance Evaluation of Robot Mechanisms - II

Design of a Force-Controlled End-Effector with Slender Flexible Beams

Yin Chen[2,3], Genliang Chen[1,2(✉)], Yuchen Chai[2,3], Hao Wang[1,3], and Lingyu Kong[4]

[1] State Key Laboratory of Mechanical Systems and Vibration, Shanghai Jiao Tong University, Shanghai 200240, China
[2] Meta Robotics Institute, Shanghai Jiao Tong University, Shanghai 200240, China
{wanghao,chenyin_sherlock,leungchan,chaiyuchen98}@sjtu.edu.cn
[3] Shanghai Key Laboratory of Digital Manufacturing for Thin-Walled Structures, Shanghai Jiao Tong University, Shanghai 200240, China
[4] Intelligent Robot Research Center, Zhejiang Lab, Hangzhou, China
kongly@zhejianglab.com

Abstract. This paper proposes a force-controlled end-effector with slender flexible beams. On the one hand, it can actively control the deformation of slender flexible beams to output a constant force at the end-effector without using a force sensor. On the other hand, it serves as a passive compliant mechanism utilizing the large deformation characteristic of slender flexible beams to prevent structural damage. The kinetostatic modeling of the force-controlled end-effector has been derived to obtain the relationship between the output force and displacement. To conduct experimental tests, a prototype of the force-controlled end-effector has been fabricated. From the experimental results, it can be seen that the error of the force-controlled end-effector is within 0.5N.

Keywords: End-effector · Kinetostatic modeling · Compliant mechanism

1 Introduction

Robotic systems have been widely used in the industry, and they require interaction with the environment during their applications. The force control of robots is a crucial issue in their applications as it involves the interaction process between the robot and the environment. Force control of robots is involved in various applications such as robotic polishing [1], assembly [2], and human-robot collaboration [3].

Over the last several decades, domestic and foreign scholars have conducted extensive research on force-controlled end-effectors of robots, and have achieved fruitful results. From a principle perspective, force-controlled end-effectors are mainly divided into mechanical, pneumatic, and electric-driven types.

Mechanical force-controlled end-effectors generally use springs to control constant output force. For example, Liu [4] proposed a flexible tool holder for mold

© The Author(s), under exclusive license to Springer Nature Singapore Pte Ltd. 2023
H. Yang et al. (Eds.): ICIRA 2023, LNAI 14274, pp. 545–556, 2023.
https://doi.org/10.1007/978-981-99-6501-4_46

polishing, which uses linear springs to increase the flexibility of the device, that is, changing the contact stiffness to reduce the surface roughness of the mold. However, they have the disadvantage of slow response and low accuracy.

Pneumatic force-controlled end-effectors use pneumatic components such as cylinders and airbags to control the output force by controlling the air pressure. They have good flexibility but suffer from hysteresis. For example, Beom-Sahng Ryuh [5] proposed a single degree of freedom (DOF) force-controlled end-effector using a cylinder for axial compliance control.

Electric-driven force-controlled end-effectors use electric current and magnetic fields to control the output force, with simple mechanisms and fast response capabilities. For example, Abd El Khalick Mohammad and Hong et al. [6] developed a new low-mass force control end-effector for robot polishing. Compared to traditional designs, the design optimized the position, reduced the requirements for the output capacity of the axial compensation device, and also reduced noise and vibration. However, it has the problem of being prone to faults.

There are two types of compliance, including active compliance and passive compliance [7]. Force-controlled end-effectors can also be divided into active and passive types depending on whether additional driving force is required. Active ones involve closed-loop control and are usually implemented through components such as motors and cylinders [8] that have driving capability, which can achieve higher force control accuracy. Passive ones do not have driving components, and their shape is designed according to the characteristics of linear springs and flexible hinges, so that the forces generated when deformed are close. The overall structure is simple and suitable for low-speed and low-precision occasions. Wei, Y et al. [9] propose a bistable mechanism to maintain constant force output.

In recent years, typical force-controlled end-effectors have been dominated by single degree of freedom (DOF) active force-controlled end-effectors using pneumatic and electric drive, with large size and rigid structures. Most force-controlled end-effectors only have the function of active compliance, and lack the ability of passive compliance. The driving components such as motors are easily damaged by impacts.

Therefore, this paper proposes a rope-driven active force-controlled end-effector with slender flexible beams, which can accurately output contact forces parallel to the axis of the robot arm, thereby achieving active constant-force control of robot polishing. At the same time, it also has certain passive compliance function when subjected to external impact.

The paper is organized as follows: Sect. 2 presents the mechanism design and control system of the force-controlled end-effector. Then, the kinetostatic modeling is derived based on a discretization based approach to obtain the relationship between the output force and displacement in Sect. 3. Section 4 presents the experiment of the force-controlled end-effector to validate the accuracy and correctness of kinetostatic modeling and test the force control performance of the end-effector. Finally, conclusions are drawn in Sect. 5.

2 Mechanism Design and Control System

This section mainly introduces the mechanism design and prototype of the force-controlled end-effector, and also explains its control system.

From a structural design perspective, our primary approach involves transforming the rotational motion of the motor through pulleys and ropes into linear motion of the active slider, which controls the deformation of the slender flexible beams to output a constant force.

In terms of control strategy, we primarily use a PID control algorithm to maintain the deformation of the slender flexible beams through data captured by the STM32 integrated laser sensor.

2.1 Mechanism Design

Figure 1(a) shows the overall structure of the end-effector. The rope-driven active force-controlled end-effector is designed with slender flexible beams. It mainly includes the active sliders, guide sliders, output platform, laser sensor, pulleys, motor, active wheel, frame, wire rope and other components.

The motor is fixed to the active wheel by four bolts. The active wheel changes direction via two guide wheels and a fixed pulley. The wire rope is fastened to the active slider with bolts and is tensioned accordingly. The specific structure driven by the wire rope is shown in Fig. 1(b), which ensures even force distribution and has a corresponding wire rope driving device on the symmetrical side.

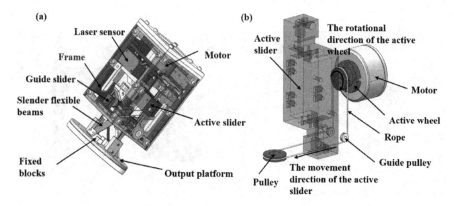

Fig. 1. (a) Overall structure of the end-effector. (b) The specific structure driven by the wire rope.

The guide rails are symmetrically arranged on the frame, and their sliders are connected to the active slider via bolts, ensuring that the active slider can only move axially and balancing the force on the structure. The output platform is fixedly connected to the other two sliders to achieve sliding in the same direction. There are six fixed blocks for slender flexible beams on both the active slider and the output platform. Small connecting blocks and clamping plates are used to connect fixedly the two slender flexible beams, ensuring that the slender flexible beams are not bent in the non-working state. Symmetrically arranged beams provide constant output force and balance torque on both sides.

The laser sensor is connected to the active slider via a 3D printing connecting plate, measuring the distance between the active slider and the output platform. There are limited position devices on the slide rail, allowing the output flange to float within a small range. Several symmetric mounting holes are also provided on the output flange for connecting external instruments.

This device converts the rotational motion of the motor into the movement of the active slider using a wire rope and ensures constant output force through the large deformation characteristics of slender flexible beams.

2.2   Prototype

As Fig. 2 shows, a prototype of the force-controlled end-effector has been fabricated. The maximum radius of the device is 140 mm, the height is 204 mm, and the weight is 1.2 kg. The floating distance of the active slider is 30 mm, and that of the output platform is 15 mm.

The slender flexible beams material chosen is $65Mn$ and $60Si_2Mn$ with an elastic modulus of 197 GPa. The framework and small pulley fixing block are made of aluminum alloy 6061, while the slender flexible beams pressing piece, fixing block, active slider, and end platform are all made using photosensitive resin 3D printing.

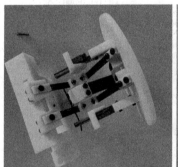

Fig. 2. Prototype of the end-effector

In summary, the combination of slender flexible beams and motor-driven ropes gives the end effector a certain passive compliance ability. When subjected to large impacts, the large deformation characteristics of the slender flexible beams can be used to reduce damage to the structure, providing certain buffering function.

2.3   Control System Design

Due to the design of mechanical structure, the output force of the system is directly generated by the deformation of the slender flexible beams. To control the output force, the shape of slender flexible beams are controlled. The realization in these structures is to control the distance between two ends of the slender flexible beams by the motor. The control system consists of STM32, motor, motor driver, laser sensor. The distance detected by the laser sensor can reflect the deformation of slender flexible beams by generating voltage signal. The voltage signal is collected by STM32. The STM32 calculates the amount of motor motion required to maintain the current shape of the beams according to the obtained information and controls the motor through the motor driver. Therefore, the control of the system can be regarded as the control of the motor position.

Control Strategy of Motor. PID control are used to control the position of motor. PID control employs three modes algorithm, that is proportional, integral and derivative. The proportional term is proportional to the error, but offset could be caused. The integral term is proportional to the amount of time the error is present and is used to eliminate offset, but could cause phase lag. The Derivative is proportional to the rate of change of the error and is often used to avoid overshoot. The control law of PID control is represented as

$$u(t) = K_p(e(t) + \frac{1}{T_i}\int_0^t e(t)dt + \frac{T_d de(t)}{dt}) \tag{1}$$

where $e(t)$ is the system error at time t, K_p, T_i and T_d are proportional gain, integral time and derivative time. To realize PID control in the controller, the control law needs to be dispersed. The formula of System input can be represent as

$$u(k) = k_p(e(k)) + k_i \sum e(k) + k_d(e(k) - e(k-1)) \tag{2}$$

where $e(k)$ is the system error at the kth time, k_p, k_i and k_d are proportional, integral and derivative gain.

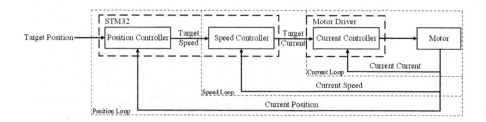

Fig. 3. Control mode

The control method of the position of motor is three-loop control which is often used in motor control. As Fig. 3 shows, three-loop control consists of position loop, speed loop and current loop. For the position loop, the input signal of the position controller is position error, the difference between target position and the motor's current position. For the speed loop, the input signal of the speed controller is speed error, the difference between target speed which is the output of the position controller and current speed of the motor. The output of speed controller is target current and the current loop control method is FOC control between the motor driver and motor. The control signal sent to the motor driver is target current calculated by the control program include position loop and speed loop in STM32. The control frequency of motor set in STM32 is 200 Hz. The motor used in this paper is HT4315, which has an approximate linear relation between output torque and input current.

System Control Strategy. Figure 4 shows the control strategy of the whole system. A target distance is calculated from set target force through the model of slender flexible beams. In every loop, current distance is calculated from the distance information obtained by the laser sensor and makes a difference with target distance to get the distance error. The error is divided by the transmission ratio and added to current position to get target. Current position is changed through PID control and laser sensor changes accordingly, then a new control loop starts.

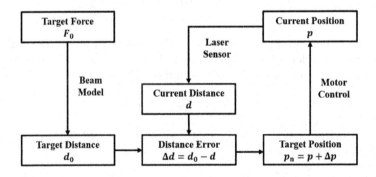

Fig. 4. System Control Strategy

3   Kinetostatics Modeling

This section introduces the kinetostatic modeling of the force-controlled end-effector. As is shown in Sect. 2, force is generated by the deformation of the slender flexible beams. It discretes slender flexible beams into spatial elastic units and equivalent to multiple joints for deformation analysis, according to the approach developed in our prior work [10,11].

3.1 Modeling of Slender Flexible Beams

A spatial elastic unit can be modeled as serial elastic mechanisms with three revolute joints and three prismatic joints whose axes passing through the center of the unit [11]. The revolute joints correspond to the tension or compression of the elastic unit and revolute joints correspond to the bent and twisted of elastic unit. Hence, the structural compliance matrix of each unit with six axes to the form of $\mathbf{C}_\theta = diag(\frac{\delta}{EI_{xx}}, \frac{\delta}{EI_{yy}}, \frac{\delta}{GI_{zz}}, \frac{\delta^3}{3EI_{yy}}, \frac{\delta^3}{3EI_{xx}}, \frac{\delta}{EA})$, with respect to frame in the middle of unit. Where δ is the length of the unit, A represents the area of cross section, I_{xx}, I_{yy} and I_{zz} are the three principal area moments, while E and G are the elastic and shear modulus, respectively. Corresponding stiffness matrix can be wrote as $\mathbf{K}_\theta = \mathbf{C}_\theta^{-1}$.

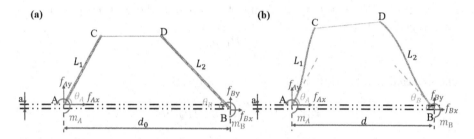

Fig. 5. Modeling of Slender Flexible Beams. (a) The situation without deformation. (b) The situation with deformation.

As is shown in Fig. 5, two slender flexible beams whose length is L_1 and L_2, width is b and thickness is h, is divided into n units, and each unit's joint frame is established at the center of the unit. CD is a rigid connecting component that is connected fixedly to slender flexible beams at points C and D. The length of each unit can be calculated as $\delta = (L_1 + L_2)/n$ and set the pose of beam without bending to the initial state. One end of the first beam (point A) is fixed and the base frame {S} based on point A is set up. The other end of the second beam (point B) is allowed to move along the x-axis of {S}. The distance along x-axis of {S} between points A and B is represented as d, and the acute angles of the beams to the x-axis of {S} are θ_A and θ_B, respectively. The tip frame {T} is set up at point B, whose pose is only related to d. The pose matrix of {T} with respect to {S} can be represented as

$$\mathbf{g}_t(d) = \begin{bmatrix} 1 & 0 & 0 & d \\ 0 & 1 & 0 & -a \\ 0 & 0 & 1 & 0 \\ 0 & 0 & 0 & 1 \end{bmatrix} \tag{3}$$

where a is the distance along y-axis of {S} between point A and B. Due to mechanical constraints, the bending deformation of the slender flexible beams only occur in the plane. Besides, the effect of deformations of revolute joint to the poses of beams are far more than the deformations of prismatic joints due to material properties. Hence, each equivalent unit with six joints is simplified to a unit with only one revolute joint, whose joint stiffness is $k = \frac{EI}{\delta}$. Then, the slender flexible beams can be regarded as a serial robot with n revolute joint, whose axes are parallel withe each other. The ith joint twists without external wrench on beams can be obtained as $\boldsymbol{\xi}_i = [\boldsymbol{\omega}_i^T \ \boldsymbol{v}_i^T]^T$, where $\boldsymbol{\omega}_i = \boldsymbol{e}_z = [0 \ 0 \ 1]^T$ and $\boldsymbol{v}_i = \boldsymbol{r}_i \times \boldsymbol{\omega}_i$, and $\boldsymbol{r}_i$ can be represented as

$$
\boldsymbol{r}_i = \begin{cases} (i - \frac{1}{2})\delta \begin{bmatrix} \cos\theta_A \ \sin\theta_A \ 0 \end{bmatrix}^T, & \boldsymbol{r}_i \in L_1 \\ \begin{bmatrix} d & -a & 0 \end{bmatrix}^T - (n + \frac{1}{2} - i)\delta \begin{bmatrix} \cos\theta_B & -\sin\theta_B & 0 \end{bmatrix}^T, & \boldsymbol{r}_i \in L_2 \end{cases} \tag{4}
$$

A body frame {B} is set up at B-end of the beam, whose initial pose matrix with respect to {S} is

$$
\mathbf{g}_0 = \begin{bmatrix} \mathbf{R}_0 & \boldsymbol{p}_0 \\ O & 1 \end{bmatrix} \tag{5}
$$

The external wrench on point B with respect to {B} is

$$
\boldsymbol{F}_B = [0, 0, m_{Bz}, f_{Bx}, f_{By}, 0]^T \tag{6}
$$

where m_{Bz}, f_{Bx} and f_{By} are the torque and force acting on B Point. To make the formula more concise, m_{Bz}, f_{Bx} and f_{By} are replaced by m_z, f_x and f_y in the following.

3.2   Solution of Slender Flexible Beam from External Force

Calculating the relationship between force and deformation of the slender flexible beam can be considered as a problem of calculating the deformation of the beams with a known x-ward external force f_x. The amounts to be requested include y-ward external force f_y, z-ward torque m_z, the distance along y-axis of {S} between point A and B d, and deflection of each equivalent joint θ_i.

Using the product of exponentials (POE) formula, the geometric constraints of the slender flexible beam can be represented as:

$$
\mathbf{g}(\boldsymbol{\theta}) = \exp(\hat{\boldsymbol{\xi}}_1 \theta_1) \exp(\hat{\boldsymbol{\xi}}_2 \theta_2) \cdots \exp(\hat{\boldsymbol{\xi}}_n \theta_n)\mathbf{g}_0 = \mathbf{g}_t(d) \tag{7}
$$

which means frame {B} coincides with frame {T}. The equilibrium conditions of the slender flexible beam can be represented as:

$$
\mathbf{K}_\theta \boldsymbol{\theta} = \mathbf{J}_\theta^T \boldsymbol{F}_S \tag{8}
$$

which means the static balance of the elastic joints between the restoring torques induced by the deflections and those transmitted from the external wrench. $\mathbf{K}_\theta = \text{diag}(k_1, \cdots, k_n)$ is the diagonal matrix of joint stiffness, whose elements can be calculated as $k_i = k = \frac{EI}{\delta}$ due to the same size of each unit. The Jacobian matrix $\mathbf{J}_\theta = [\boldsymbol{\xi}_1', \cdots, \boldsymbol{\xi}_n']$, where $\boldsymbol{\xi}_i' = Ad_{\exp(\hat{\xi}_1\theta_1)\cdots\exp(\hat{\xi}_{i-1}\theta_{i-1})}\boldsymbol{\xi}_i$ is joint twist in current configuration. $\boldsymbol{F}_S$ is the external wrench with respect to base frame {S} which can be represented as $\boldsymbol{F}_S = \left[Ad_{\mathbf{g}}^T\right]^{-1}\boldsymbol{F}_B$.

To simplify the solution process using gradient descent method, the kinetostatics model of the slender flexible beam satisfies geometric constraints and equilibrium conditions can be represented as:

$$c(x) = \begin{bmatrix} \rho \\ \alpha \\ \tau \end{bmatrix} = \begin{bmatrix} [\mathbf{E}_2 \ \mathbf{O}_{2\times1}](\boldsymbol{p}_B - \boldsymbol{p}_T) \\ \sum_{i=1}^{n}\theta_i \\ \mathbf{K}_\theta\boldsymbol{\theta} - \mathbf{J}_\theta^T\boldsymbol{F}_S \end{bmatrix} \tag{9}$$

where $\boldsymbol{x} = \left[\boldsymbol{\theta}^T, f_y, m_z, d\right]^T$ represents the variables of the problem. ρ and α represent the overlap of the position and orientation of {B} and {T}, respectively. $\mathbf{E}_2$ is a second-order unit matrix and $\mathbf{O}_{2\times1}$ is a zero Matrix. $\boldsymbol{p}_B$ and $\boldsymbol{p}_T$ are the position of {B} and {T}, respectively. The nonlinear algebraic equations (9) have $n+3$ equations with $n+3$ unknown variables and is therefore solvable. Then a closed-form solution of the corresponding gradient with respect to $\boldsymbol{\theta}$, f_y, m_z and d can be derived as

$$\boldsymbol{\nabla} = \begin{bmatrix} \frac{\partial c}{\partial\theta} & \frac{\partial c}{\partial f_y} & \frac{\partial c}{\partial m_z} & \frac{\partial c}{\partial d} \end{bmatrix} = \begin{bmatrix} \frac{\partial\rho}{\partial\theta} & \mathbf{O}_{2\times1} & \mathbf{O}_{2\times1} & \frac{\partial\rho}{\partial d} \\ \frac{\partial\alpha}{\partial\theta} & 0 & 0 & 0 \\ \frac{\partial\tau}{\partial\theta} & \frac{\partial\tau}{\partial f_y} & \frac{\partial\tau}{\partial m_z} & \mathbf{O}_{n\times1} \end{bmatrix} \tag{10}$$

Here, $\frac{\partial\rho}{\partial\theta} = [\mathbf{E}_2 \ \mathbf{O}_{2\times1}]\frac{\partial\boldsymbol{p}_B}{\partial\theta}$, where $\frac{\partial\boldsymbol{p}_B}{\partial\theta} = [-\hat{\boldsymbol{p}}_B \ \mathbf{E}_3]\mathbf{J}_\theta$. It is easy to find that $\frac{\partial\rho}{\partial d} = [-1 \ 0]^T$ and $\frac{\partial\alpha}{\partial\theta} = [1, 1, ..., 1]_{1\times n}$. Meanwhile, $\frac{\partial\tau}{\partial\theta} = \mathbf{K}_\theta - \mathbf{K}_J - \mathbf{K}_F$, where $\mathbf{K}_F = \mathbf{J}_\theta^T\frac{\partial\boldsymbol{F}_S}{\partial\theta} = \mathbf{J}_\theta^T\left[\left[-\hat{\boldsymbol{f}}_B\frac{\partial\boldsymbol{p}_B}{\partial\theta}\right]^T \ \mathbf{O}_{n\times3}\right]^T$. Here, $\mathbf{K}_J$ is a configuration-dependent stiffness item such that

$$\mathbf{K}_J = \boldsymbol{F}_S^T\frac{\partial\mathbf{J}_\theta}{\partial\theta} = \begin{bmatrix} \boldsymbol{F}_S^T\frac{\partial\boldsymbol{\xi}_1'}{\partial\theta_1} & \cdots & \boldsymbol{F}_S^T\frac{\partial\boldsymbol{\xi}_1'}{\partial\theta_n} \\ \vdots & \ddots & \vdots \\ \boldsymbol{F}_S^T\frac{\partial\boldsymbol{\xi}_n'}{\partial\theta_1} & \cdots & \boldsymbol{F}_S^T\frac{\partial\boldsymbol{\xi}_1'}{\partial\theta_n} \end{bmatrix} \tag{11}$$

$$[\mathbf{K}_J]_{i,j} = \begin{cases} \boldsymbol{F}_S^T ad\left(\hat{\boldsymbol{\xi}}_j'\right)\boldsymbol{\xi}_i', & j < i \\ 0, & j \geq i \end{cases} \tag{12}$$

where $ad(\hat{\boldsymbol{\xi}}_i') = Ad_{exp(\hat{\xi}_i')}$. It is easy to find that $\frac{\partial\tau}{\partial f_y} = -\mathbf{J}_\theta^T\frac{\partial\boldsymbol{F}_S}{\partial f_y}$, where $\frac{\partial\boldsymbol{F}_S}{\partial f_y} = [\hat{\boldsymbol{p}}_B^T \ \mathbf{E}_3]^T[0 \ 1 \ 0]^T$. Similarly, $\frac{\partial\tau}{\partial m_z} = -\mathbf{J}_\theta\frac{\partial\boldsymbol{F}_S}{\partial m_z}$ where $\frac{\partial\boldsymbol{F}_S}{\partial m_z} = [0 \ 0 \ 1 \ 0 \ 0 \ 0]^T$.

Then, the problem of kinetostatics analysis of slender flexible beam can be solved efficiently by gradient descent method based on the closed-form gradient. The update theme of the iterative searching process can be represented as

$$\boldsymbol{x}^{(k+1)} = \boldsymbol{x}^{(k)} + \left(\boldsymbol{\nabla}^{(k)}\right)^{-1}\boldsymbol{c}^{(k)} \tag{13}$$

where $x^{(k)}$, $\nabla^{(k)}$ and $c^{(k)}$ are the value of x, ∇ and c in k^{th} step. When the gradient descent method reaches the termination condition, x comes to the value of θ, f_y and m_z under equilibrium condition of slender flexible beams.

4   Experiment Validation

As Fig. 6 shows, an experimental platform was built to measure the relationship between force and deformation, as well as to test the static and dynamic force control performance of the end-effector for force control.

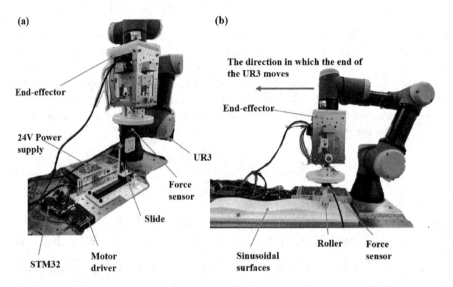

Fig. 6. Experiment Validation. (a) Force and deformation experiment. (b) Force control performance experiment.

4.1   Force and Deformation Experiment

Figure 6(a) shows the setup of the force and deformation experimental platform, where the end-effector is fixed at the end of a UR3 robot, and a force sensor is placed at the lower part of the end-effector. By moving the slide vertically in steps of 1 mm within the range of 0–15 mm, the relationship between force and displacement (d referred in Sect. 3) was measured in five sets to verify the rationality of theoretical calculations.

As Fig. 7(a) shows, the theoretical computation of the force-deformation relationship displays a negligible level of error when compared to experimental measurements. This validates the reliability and accuracy of the modeling of slender flexible beams.

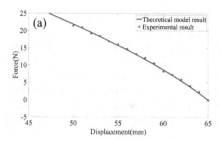 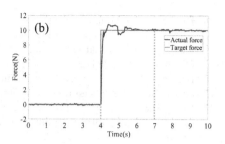

Fig. 7. Experimental result. (a) Experimental result of force-displacement relation. (b) Static and dynamic force control performance.

4.2 Force Control Performance

Figure 6(b) shows the setup of force control performance experimental platform. The force control tracking experiment fixed the end-effector to the end of the UR3 robot, and the end of the UR3 robot walked along a straight line trajectory. The end output force was controlled at 10N, and the reading of the force sensor can be obtained as shown in Fig. 7(b).

At 4 s, the output force is controlled to be 10N while the end of the UR3 remained fixed. From 7 s to 10 s, the UR3 robot end moves horizontally, while using the end-effector to maintain a constant output force of 10N. It can been seen that the end effector had an error of less than 0.5N and exhibited good force holding performance.

5 Conclusion

This article mainly discusses the design and research of an active force-controlled end-effector. Firstly, it introduces the structural design of the end-effector and proposes a method of using slender flexible beams as actuator components for force sensing and control. Then, it describes the design of the control system and kinematic modeling of the force-controlled end-effector. The accuracy of the model has been validated through force-deformation experiments, and the static and dynamic force control performance has been also tested.

Acknowledgement. This research work was supported in part by the Natural Science Foundation of China (NSFC) under the Grants 52022056, and Zhejiang Lab Open Research Project (No. K2022NB0AB03).

References

1. Lin, J., Ran, T., Feng, L.: Research on contact force control in process of aspheric surface polish. Adv. Mater. Res. **621**, 216–22 (2013)
2. Chen, H., Wang, J., Zhang, G., Fuhlbrigge, T.A., Kock, S.: High-precision assembly automation based on robot compliance. Int. J. Adv. Manuf. Technol. **45**, 999–1006 (2009)

3. Huang, S., Koyama, K., Ishikawa, M., Yamakawa, Y.: Human-robot collaboration with force feedback utilizing bimanual coordination. In: Companion of the 2021 ACM/IEEE International Conference on Human-Robot Interaction, HRI 2021, Companion, pp. 234–238. Association for Computing Machinery, New York (2021)

4. Liu, C., Chen, C.C., Huang, J.S.: The polishing of molds and dies using a compliance tool holder mechanism. J. Mater. Process. Technol. **166**(2), 230–236 (2005)

5. Ryuh, B.S., Park, S.M., Pennock, G.R.: An automatic tool changer and integrated software for a robotic die polishing station. Mech. Mach. Theory **41**(4), 415–432 (2006)

6. Mohammad, A.E.K., Hong, J., Wang, D.: Design of a force-controlled end-effector with low-inertia effect for robotic polishing using macro-mini robot approach. Robot. Comput.-Integr. Manuf. **49**, 54–65 (2018)

7. Zeng, G., Hemami, A.: An overview of robot force control. Robotica **15**(5), 473–482 (1997)

8. Cheng, F., Qizhi, Z., Lei, Z., Hongmiao, Z.: Development of the polishing tool system based on the pneumatic force servo. In: 2017 2nd International Conference on Advanced Robotics and Mechatronics (ICARM), pp. 126–131 (2017)

9. Wei, Y., Xu, Q.: Design of a new robot end-effector based on compliant constant-force mechanism. In: 2021 IEEE/RSJ International Conference on Intelligent Robots and Systems (IROS), pp. 7601–7606 (2021)

10. Chen, G., Wang, H., Lin, Z., Lai, X.: The principal axes decomposition of spatial stiffness matrices. IEEE Trans. Rob. **31**(1), 191–207 (2015)

11. Chen, G., Zhang, Z., Wang, H.: A general approach to the large deflection problems of spatial flexible rods using principal axes decomposition of compliance matrices. J. Mech. Robot. **10**(3) (2018)

Development of an Integrated Grapple Chain for a Simultaneous Three-Fingered End-Effector

Jun Wu[1], Yu He[1], He Wang[1], and Shaowei Fan[2(✉)]

[1] School of Mechanical and Electrical Engineering, University of Electronic Science and Technology of China, Chengdu 611731, China
[2] State Key Laboratory of Robotics and System, Harbin Institute of Technology, Harbin 150001, China
fansw@hit.edu.cn

Abstract. This paper presents the development of an integrated grapple chain for a simultaneous three-fingered end-effector. The geometrical constraint with four stages is firstly defined. Then, a grapple finger is presented to fulfill the proposed four stages with an approximately straight line actuation. Then, the actuation chain of linkage is designed by modification, optimization and combination. At last, Simulation indicates that the grapple finger can conduct planar and linear motion, which contributed to restrain the target gradually.

Keywords: Grapple Chain · End-effector · Straight Line Linkage

1 Introduction

In resent year, space robots and spacecraft play increasing key roles in space adventure. The end-effector is one of the most important components of space robots and spacecraft. The mission of the end-effector is to constrain the relative movement between itself and the target. The existing end-effector can be divided into probe-cone type [1], peripheral type [2] and snare type [3]. Because of limited energy and space, different kinematic chains work simultaneously.

The end-effectors with claws have the largest misalignment tolerance. The grapple chain is of great importance for this kind of end-effectors, which consists of grapple finger and actuation chain [4]. With the guideline of reliability and stability, the grapple chain in the field the space application is relatively simpler than those in other applications. Thus, the misalignment tolerance is limited [5]. Therefore, we are motivated to write this paper to share our research.

The paper is organized as following. The geometrical constraint of a simultaneous three-fingered end-effector is described in Sect. 2. Then, Sects. 3 and 4 present the development of the grapple finger and actuation chain, respectively. Section 5 shows the performance of the grapple chain. The results verify the effectiveness of the design. The presented design is summarized in Sect. 6.

© The Author(s), under exclusive license to Springer Nature Singapore Pte Ltd. 2023
H. Yang et al. (Eds.): ICIRA 2023, LNAI 14274, pp. 557–567, 2023.
https://doi.org/10.1007/978-981-99-6501-4_47

2   Constraint Design of the End-Effector

Because the end-effector is developed for orbital payload replacement, large position/orientation misalignment tolerance is a critical character of the end-effector. Geometrical constraint is one of the most important factors which contribute to the misalignment tolerance. In general, geometrical constraint can be classified into caging and immobilizing. Figure 1 shows diagrams of them respectively.

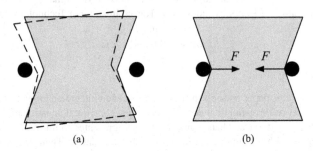

(a)   (b)

Fig. 1. Caging and immobilizing in geometrical constraint

Figure 1(a) shows the diagram of caging. As the target is restrained by obstacles, it cannot escape the enveloping space. However, the target still has the ability of movement in a certain extent [6]. Figure 1(b) shows the diagram of immobilizing. The target is strictly constrained by obstacles [7]. Any movement of the target will break the relationship between the target and obstacles. When designing the geometrical constraint of the end-effector, it is ideal to combine caging and immobilizing. Several serial constraint stages can restrict the relative movement between the target and end-effector gradually. The combination can take the advantages of caging and immobilizing, which contributes to both improving the success rate and enlarging the misalignment tolerance.

We have proposed constraint design of the end-effector as shown in Fig. 2. The constraint design makes up of four stages, which are three claws stage, parallel stage, multiple axle/hole stage and multiple cone/cone stage [8]. The key factors of the end-effector are three axially symmetrical grapple fingers. In the three claws stage, the three fingers move radially. The trilobate grapple interface guides the fingertips to the center area as shown in Fig. 2(a), making the misalignment smaller and smaller. When the fingertips arrive at the center area, they do not move axially any more. The corresponding stage is called parallel stage. The specially designed fingertips present as three parallel circular columns, which interact with the corresponding parallel guide grooves. The remaining multiple axle/hole stage and multiple cone/cone stage are implemented by the geometrical features one the mating faces of the end-effector and interface.

Each of the four constraint stages provides the initial condition for the adjacent stage. The relative misalignment is constrained more and more strict, resulting in ideal connection at last.

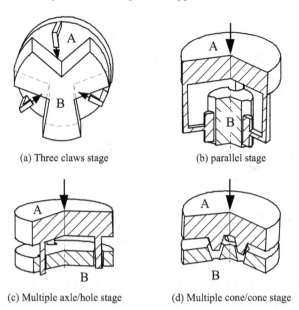

(a) Three claws stage

(b) parallel stage

(c) Multiple axle/hole stage

(d) Multiple cone/cone stage

Fig. 2. Schematic diagrams of four constraint stages

3   Grapple Finger

With the guidance of constraint design, grapple fingers will experience radial contracting and axial dragging. The end-effector on the Orbital Express Capture System has similar requirement [3]. It adopts the solution with the combination of ball screw, planar linkage and cam mechanism, but confronts the weakness of a complex mechanism and large volume.

Under the actuation of linear motion at one revolute joint, the specially designed grapple finger will provide required trajectory by the interaction between guiding slot and guiding post. We design the scheme and its basic motions as shown in Fig. 3. The guiding slot is divided into two segments corresponding to the planar and linear motions of the grapple finger. The interaction between guiding slot and guiding post is achieved with a cam mechanism which is the geometrical closure. With the actuation of joint A and constraint of fixed guiding post B, the grapple finger can conduct planar and linear motion sequentially. The diagrams are shown in Fig. 3(b) and Fig. 3(c) respectively, in which point P is the instantaneous center of the grapple finger.

In the segment of planar motion, the instantaneous center P is determined by directions of point A and point B. Consequently, the direction of fingertip C can be obtained. Firstly, fingertip C has radially contracting velocity. Secondly, fingertip C has relatively large velocity magnitude as the distance between point C and point P is large. The features make the motion of fingertip C extremely appropriate for the proposed geometrical constraint of three claws stage. In the segment of linear motion, the directions of point A and B are the same, which makes the instantaneous center P lie at an infinite distance. As a result, the direction of fingertip C is the same as those of point A and B. Fingertip C conducts axial dragging while keeping constantly radial distance, which makes the

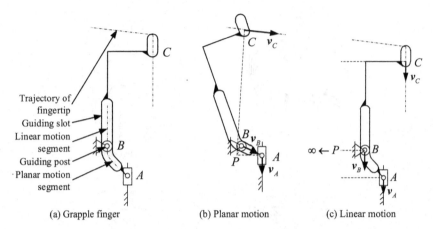

(a) Grapple finger   (b) Planar motion   (c) Linear motion

Fig. 3. Grapple finger and its working process

motion of fingertip C extremely appropriate for the proposed geometrical constraint of parallel stage.

From the previous two stages, fingertip C produces the trajectory as shown in Fig. 3(a). The trajectory in axial dragging segment should be straight line or approximately straight line. The trajectory in radial contracting segment can be either curve or straight line.

4   Actuation Chain

The constraint design of the end-effector and detailed design of the grapple finger bring in the requirement of an actuation with straight line or approximately straight line. Mechanisms with straight trajectory output which are commonly used are ball screw mechanism [3], linkage with straight or approximately straight trajectory [9], gear mechanism [10]. Because linkage mechanism has such advantages as small mass, stable force transition performance and long service life, we adopt the scheme of designing linkage mechanism which can fulfill the moving requirement of the proposed grapple finger. The scheme will be beneficial for reducing the mass and volume of the end-effector.

4.1   Modified Watt's Linkage

Watt invented the first linkage with approximately straight trajectory as shown in Fig. 4. Revolute links AB, BC, CD and fixed link AD form a four-bar linkage. Links AB and CD have the same length. When the center point P of link BC lies in its central position, links AB, CD and link BC are horizontal and vertical, respectively. The complete trajectory of point P is an 8-shaped curve. The segment near the central position is the approximately straight trajectory which can be adopted to actuate other mechanisms.

When applying the Watt's linkage, Crowther made a slight modification. When the center point P lies in its central position, link BC is unnecessary to be vertical [11]. But Crowther's modification still restricted links AB and CD to be horizontal. Inspired by

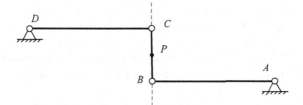

Fig. 4. Watt's linkage

Crowther's idea, we make a bigger modification to the Watt's linkage. When the center point P lies in its central position, link BC is unnecessary to be vertical while links AB and CD are unnecessary to be horizontal. To simplify the analysis process, two fixed joint of modified Watt's linkage are placed one a horizontal line as shown in Fig. 5. When we adopted the same lengths of links as those of Crowther's, the central segment of the coupler curve is an ideal approximately straight line as shown in Fig. 6(a). If the linkage mechanism is rotated clockwise, the coupler curve is a vertical approximately straight line as shown in Fig. 6(b). The rotated angle is one of the factors which determine the behavior of the linkage mechanism.

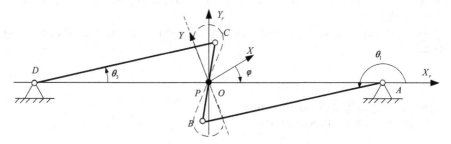

Fig. 5. Diagram of modified Watt's linkage

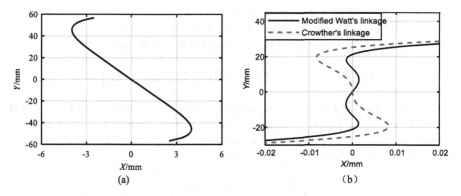

Fig. 6. Coupler curve of modified Watt's linkage

As the coupler curve is an approximately straight line, the deviation between the coupler curve and target line in inevitable. The deviation ratio is defined with the maximal deviation range divided by the stroke of the curve. In Crowther's linkage, the deviation ratio is to $0.016/52 = 3.08 \times 10^{-4}$. In modified Watt's linkage, the rotation of the linkage mechanism makes the maximum deviations at the two sides are equal. The deviation ratio decreases to $0.003/45 = 6.7 \times 10^{-5}$.

It can be seen from Fig. 6(b) that the number of coupler curve intersecting with the target line is five. However, the corresponding numbers in Crowther's modification and original Watt's linage are three and one, respectively. With the increasing of the intersecting number, the deviation ratio becomes smaller and smaller. The purpose of designing modified Watt's linkage is to generate a coupler curve which can intersect with the target line five times. Therefore, condition of generating such coupler curve is the condition of modified Watt's linkage.

In Fig. 5, fixed joint A and D are placed at $(a, 0)$ and $(-a, 0)$. Links AB and CD have the same length as b. The length of link BC is $2c$. The trajectory of coupler point P matches the following function:

$$P_x^2\left(P_x^2 + P_y^2 + P\right)^2 + P_y^2\left(P_x^2 + P_y^2 + Q\right)^2 - RP_y^2 = 0 \tag{1}$$

where $P = c^2 - b^2 - a^2$, $Q = c^2 - b^2 + a^2$, $R = 4c^2a^2$, (P_x, P_y) is the coordinate of coupler point P.

The intersecting points between the coupler curve and target line match the following condition:

$$P_y = kP_x \tag{2}$$

where k is the gradient of the target line.

Combining Eqs. (1) and (2) gives:

$$P_x^2\left(P_x^2 + k^2P_x^2 + P\right)^2 + k^2P_x^2\left(P_x^2 + k^2P_x^2 + Q\right)^2 - Rk^2P_x^2 = 0 \tag{3}$$

It can be observed in Fig. 6 and the condition of modified Watt's linkage that Eq. (3) have five roots, among which zeros is one of the roots. The other roots are two pairs of inverse number. Defining $t = P_x^2$ and $S = k^2$ and rearranging Eq. (3) give:

$$t\left[(1+S)^3t^2 + 2(1+S)(P+SQ)t + P^2 + SQ^2 - SR\right] = 0 \tag{4}$$

Equation (4) should have three roots, among which zero is one of the roots. The other roots are two different positive numbers. The second part at the left of the equation is actually a quadratic polynomial with one variable. The corresponding equation has two roots. So we can get the following inequalities:

$$\begin{cases} S\left[RS + R - (R - Q)^2\right] > 0 \\ P + QS < 0 \\ P^2 + (Q^2 - R)S > 0 \end{cases} \tag{5}$$

where S is the unknown variable.

The solution of (5) should be an interval in the region of positive number. To ensure the solutions of different inequalities have positive intersection range, the parameters should match the following condition:

$$\begin{cases} [-R + (P - Q)^2]/R < -P/Q \\ -P^2/[Q^2 - R] > [-R + (P - Q)^2]/R, Q^2 - R < 0 \\ -P^2/[Q^2 - R] < -P/Q, Q^2 - R > 0 \end{cases} \tag{6}$$

Equation (6) is also the condition of modified Watt's linkage.

4.2 Path Generation of Linkage Mechanism

Frames of modified Watt's linkage are shown in Fig. 5, in which there are two frames: world frame O_{XY} and reference frame $O_{X_rY_r}$. World frame O_{XY} is the working frame of the linkage mechanism whose axis Y is the target straight line. Reference frame $O_{X_rY_r}$ is obtained by clock wisely rotating frame O_{XY} about base point O with angle φ.

The lengths of links AB, BC, CD are defined as r_1, r_2, r_3, respectively. If θ_1 is the input angle, angle θ_3 is decided by the value of angle θ_1. From the vectorial equation $\vec{BC}^2 = (\vec{CD} + \vec{DA} + \vec{AB}) \cdot (\vec{CD} + \vec{DA} + \vec{AB})$, we can get:

$$K_1 \cos\theta_1 - K_2 \cos\theta_3 + K_3 = \cos(\theta_1 - \theta_3) \tag{7}$$

where $K_1 = r_4/r_3, K_2 = r_4/r_1, K_3 = (r_1^2 - r_2^2 + r_3^2 + r_4^2)/(2r_1r_3)$.

By rearranging (7) and the geometrical relationship of linkage, we can get the solution as:

$$\theta_3 = 2\tan^{-1}\left[\left(-R_2 - \sqrt{R_1^2 + R_2^2 - R_3^2}\right)/(R_3 - R_1)\right] \tag{8}$$

where
$R_1 = r_4/r_1 + \cos\theta_1, R_2 = \sin\theta_1, R_3 = -r_4/r_3 \cos\theta_1 - (r_1^2 - r_2^2 + r_3^2 + r_4^2)/(2r_1r_3)$.

When the linkage mechanism is clock wisely rotated with angle φ, we can get the coordinate of coupler point P in frame O_{XY} as (P_x, P_y). The trajectory of coupler point P is an approximately straight line. The relationship between the deviation ratio and the dimensions of the linkage is highly non-linear. Genetic algorithm's basic principle comes from biological evolution phenomenon. It solves optimization problem by random search, which makes it very appropriate for this kind of discontinuous, high-dimensional and non-linear optimization problem.

The objective function is the deviation between coupler points and target trajectory, which is called tracking error. The objective function can be presented as:

$$TE = \sum_{i=1}^{N} \left[\left(P_{dx}^i - P_x^i\right)^2 + \left(P_{dy}^i - P_y^i\right)^2 \right] \tag{9}$$

where $\left[P_{dx}^i \; P_{dy}^i\right]^T, \left[P_x^i \; P_y^i\right]^T$ are the coordinates of the target point and the coupler point, respectively.

Dimension optimization involves finding a proper vector of designing variables $\mathbf{X} = [l_1, l_2, l_3, \varphi, \theta_1^i]$ to get a minimum tracking error. Among the designing variables, l_1, l_2, l_3 are lengths of link AB and CD, link BC and link AD, respectively. φ is the rotation angle between frame $O_{X_r Y_r}$ and O_{XY}, $\theta_1^i (i = 1, 2, \ldots N)$ are sequential input angles. From previous analysis, the constraint conditions lie in the following aspects:

1) The condition of the four-bar linkage
2) The sequence of the input angles
3) The ranges of the design variables
4) The range of the input angle
5) The condition of the 8-shaped coupler curve
6) The condition of the modified Watt's linkage

The modified Watt's linkage is central symmetry. So, target points in the positive direction of axis Y in frame O_{XY} will result in central symmetry coupler curve in the negative direction. The target points are defined as:

$$\{(P_{dx}, P_{dy})\} = \{(0, 15), (0, 10), (0, 5)\} \tag{10}$$

After optimization, we get the coupler curve as shown in Fig. 7, in which Fig. 7(a) shows the curve with larger scale in axis X. The dimension, stroke and maximal deviation range of the linkage are 82.2289, 0.01, 29, respectively.

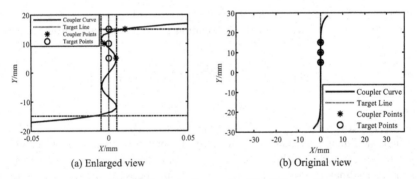

(a) Enlarged view   (b) Original view

Fig. 7. Optimization result of the linkage

Table 1 lists the performance of the mentioned three linkages for comparison. We define another index, stroke ratio, to evaluate the behavior of the coupler curve. The stroke ratio is computed with the stroke of the curve divided by the dimension of the mechanism. We can get the conclusion that the optimization of the modified Watt's linkage can effectively improve the stroke ratio while the reduced dimension has relatively small influence on the deviation ratio. The optimized coupler curve shown in Fig. 6(b) is very close to the target line, which matches the requirement of the actuation chain for grappling.

Table 1. Performance comparison of linkages.

Content	Crowther's linkage	Modified Watt's linkage	Optimized linkage
Stoke(mm)	52	45	29
Deviation range(mm)	0.016	0.003	0.01
Deviation ratio	3.08×10^{-4}	6.7×10^{-5}	3.45×10^{-4}
Dimension(mm)	261.622	261.612	82.2289
Stroke ratio	0.199	0.172	0.353

4.3 Combination of Linkages

We design a combined linkage to reduce the dimension of the mechanism deeply. The principle of the combined linkage is illustrated in Fig. 8. Figure 8(a) is the modified Watt's linkage with the approximate straight curve as shown with the dashed line. Figure 8(b) is the pantograph linkage, in which the trajectory of point A is scaled to point B [12, 13]. By combining the above linkages and removing repeated links, we get a combined linkage as shown in Fig. 8(c). With the combined linkage, we can get an approximate straight trajectory with twice stroke in the same dimension.

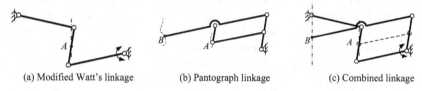

(a) Modified Watt's linkage   (b) Pantograph linkage   (c) Combined linkage

Fig. 8. Principle of combined linkage

5 Performance Validation

In the foregoing description, we have designed a grapple finger and an actuation chain for the end-effector. We conduct the kinematic analysis to check the trajectory of the fingertip. With the kinematics of the combined linkage, we can get the position of the coupler point in the frame of linkage. The interaction between guiding slot and guiding post determines the rotation angle of the finger and the position of the fingertip.

Figure 9(a) shows the trajectory of the fingertip. The grappler finger conducted planar and linear motion sequentially, as shown in state b and a. Figure 9(b) shows the rotation angle in the grappling process. When the angle of the active link was larger than 13°, the grapple finger stayed vertically. It was corresponding to the linear motion in the axial dragging period. When the angle of the active link was smaller than 13°, the grapple finger conducted planar motion in the radial contracting period. When the grapple finger experienced linear motion, the cylinder feature of the fingertip laid the foundation for parallel stage as shown in the state a of Fig. 9(a).

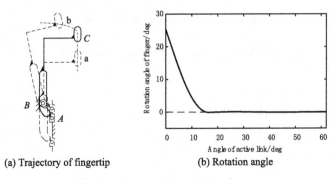

(a) Trajectory of fingertip   (b) Rotation angle

Fig. 9. Grasping process of the finger

6 Conclusion

The development process of an integrated grapple chain for a simultaneous three-fingered end-effector has been proposed in this paper. The geometrical constraint was firstly defined. It was consisted of four stages, which contributed to restricting the relative movement between the target and end-effector gradually. Then, a grapple finger was presented to fulfill the proposed four stages with an approximately straight line actuation. In relevant mechanisms, the linkage mechanism was adopted for such advantages as small mass, stable force transition performance and long service life. The Watt's linkage was modified for larger stroke. Genetic algorithm was adopted for path generation of the linkage mechanism. The proposed linkage was combined with the pantograph linkage to get twice stroke in the same dimension. At last, kinematic chain was analyzed to validate the performance of the grapple chain. Simulation indicated that the grapple finger can conduct planar and linear motion sequentially, which contributed to restrain the target gradually. Our future work will focus on analyzing the performance of the fingertip with the clearance and eccentricity of the revolute joints.

Acknowledgment. This research has been financially supported by State Key Laboratory of Robotics and System (HIT) (Grant No. SKLRS-2023-KF-14).

References

1. Jorgensen, G., Bains, E.: SRMS history, evolution and lessons learned. In: AIAA SPACE 2011 Conference and Exposition, pp. 4–5 (2011)
2. Parma, G.F.: Overview of the Nasa Docking System (Nds) and the International Docking System Standard (Idss). In: AIAA Houston Section Annual Technical Symposium, pp. 1–19 (2011)
3. Stamm, S., Motaghedi, P.: Orbital express capture system: concept to reality. In: Proceedings of SPIE - The International Society for Optical Engineering, pp. 78–91 (2004)
4. Nishida, S.I., Yoshikawa, T.: A new end-effector for on-orbit assembly of a large reflector. In: International Conference on Control, Automation, Robotics and Vision, pp. 1–6 (2007)
5. Han, F., Liu, Y., Sun, K., Liu, H.: Development of the interchangeable devices for space robot system. In: IEEE International Conference on Robotics and Biomimetics, pp. 2055–2061 (2014)

6. Seo, J., Yim, M., Kumar, V.: A theory on grasping objects using effectors with curved contact surfaces and its application to whole-arm grasping. Int. J. Robot. Res. **35**(9), 1–23 (2016)
7. Rimon, E., Burdick, J.W.: Mobility of bodies in contact. I. A 2nd-order mobility index for multiple-finger grasps. robotics and automation. IEEE Trans. **14**(5), 696–708 (1998)
8. Liu, H., Wu, J., Fan, S., Li, Z., Jin, M.: Guideline and design of a six-dimensional constraint gripper. In: IEEE International Conference on Mechatronics and Automation, pp. 1524–1529 (2016)
9. Buśkiewicz, J.: A method for optimal path synthesis of four-link planar mechanisms. Inverse Probl. Sci. Eng. **23**(5), 818–850 (2014)
10. Chironis, N.P., Sclater, N.: Mechanisms and Mechanical Devices Sourcebook. Mcgraw Hill (2003)
11. Bryant, J., Sangwin, C.: How Round Is Your Circle?: Where Engineering and Mathematics Meet. Princeton University Press, Princeton, USA (2008)
12. Elgammal, A.T., Fanni, M., Mohamed, A.M.: Design and analysis of a novel 3d decoupled manipulator based on compliant pantograph for micromanipulation. J. Intell. Rob. Syst. **87**(1), 43–57 (2016)
13. O'Rourke, J.: How to Fold It: The Mathematics of Linkages, Origami, and Polyhedra. Cambridge University Press (2011)

Screw Dynamics of the Upper Limb
of a Humanoid Robot

Han-Lin Sun📱, Dong-Jie Zhao📱, and Jing-Shan Zhao$^{(\boxtimes)}$ 📱

State Key Laboratory of Tribology, Department of Mechanical Engineering,
Tsinghua University, Beijing 100084, China
sunhl22@mails.tsinghua.edu.cn, jingshanzhao@mail.tsinghua.edu.cn

Abstract. In this paper, a new dynamics modeling approach is proposed by using the Newton-Euler equation in screw form. The momentum screw equations of multi-rigid bodies are derived in an absolute coordinate system, which systematically demonstrates the theorem of momentum and the theorem of moment of momentum of a multi-rigid body system in the screw coordinate system. At the same time, this also provides a new approach for the study of velocity screw (twist) and force screw (wrench). The twist is utilized as a variable to associate the screw displacement with the acceleration of the rigid body. On the basis, of the dynamics equation upper limb of a humanoid robot was formed, which was solved by the numerical method. The results show that compared with the common Lagrange equation, the method proposed in this paper requires less mathematical computation and is more convenient for computer programming. In addition, unlike the common Newton-Euler method in Cartesian coordinates, the method proposed by the author has fewer algebraic volumes and fewer computational procedures.

Keywords: Dynamics modeling · Momentum screw · Humanoid robot

1 Introduction

The dynamics of multibody systems is a mechanical problem that studies the relative motion of multiple rigid bodies. In humanoid robots, modeling the human body as a mechanism with joints and links connections has been widely used for dynamics analysis of human motion [1]. The goal is to optimize certain dynamic performance indicators of the robot under constraint conditions during the set motion [2, 3]. In this case, algorithms based on artificial intelligence and neural system simulation are used for robot motion prediction [4]. In addition, an accurate dynamics model can bring less computation for the motion prediction of humanoid robots. The current methods used to solve the prediction of human motion have the common denominator of high computational requirements. This puts forward new requirements for the dynamics modeling of humanoid robots.

Dynamics modeling of humanoid robots is the foundation for accurate control and predictive simulation. The research on the movement of the upper limbs of humanoid robots was directly related to whether humanoid robots can complete specific tasks [5–7]. The Lagrange method built dynamic models based on the energy of the system and

© The Author(s), under exclusive license to Springer Nature Singapore Pte Ltd. 2023
H. Yang et al. (Eds.): ICIRA 2023, LNAI 14274, pp. 568–577, 2023.
https://doi.org/10.1007/978-981-99-6501-4_48

was widely utilized in the dynamics modeling of multibody systems [8, 9]. Additionally, some dynamics modeling methods also were investigated [10–12].

In this paper, we propose a novel method for dynamics modeling of the upper limb of a humanoid robot. The contributions of this paper are as follows: In the screw coordinate system, the twist is used as an independent variable for dynamics modeling, making the Newton-Euler equation applicable to humanoid robots without ignoring any constraints on rigid body joints. Therefore, the derived model is an accurate rigid body dynamics model. The traditional screw theory studies the reciprocity of force screw and velocity screw from the perspective of instantaneous work. Based on the fundamental laws of dynamics, the momentum screw equation in the Plücker coordinate system is derived, which provides a new idea for the analysis of wrench and twist. The change of the momentum screw of the system is equal to the sum of the external force screws of the system. Because the motion of a rigid body is expressed in a unified inertial coordinate system, the inertial forces and Coriolis forces of the rigid body can be uniformly expressed using the momentum screw equation. Dynamics modeling through screws is convenient for computer programming when performing dynamics analysis and calculation of complex multibody systems.

2 Screw Dynamics Equations for a Mechanical System

According to the velocity screw equation of the serial mechanism [13],

$$\xi_i^t = \begin{bmatrix} \omega_i^t(o) \\ v_i^t(o) \end{bmatrix} = \xi_i \omega_i \tag{1}$$

where $i = 1, \cdots, n$, $\xi = \begin{bmatrix} \xi_1 & \xi_2 & \cdots & \xi_n \end{bmatrix}$ and $\omega = \begin{bmatrix} \omega_1 & \omega_2 & \cdots & \omega_n \end{bmatrix}$.

If a coordinate system parallel to the ground absolute coordinate system is established using the centroid of the ith rigid body as the coordinate origin, the velocity screw of the rigid body under the centroid coordinate system is

$$\begin{aligned}
\xi_{A_i}^t(C_i) &= \begin{bmatrix} \omega_{A_i}(o) \\ v_{A_i}(o) \end{bmatrix} \\
&= \begin{bmatrix} \omega_i^t(o) \\ v_i^t(o) \end{bmatrix} + \begin{bmatrix} 0 \\ \omega_i^t(o) \times r_{C_i} \end{bmatrix} \\
&= \begin{bmatrix} \omega_i^t(o) \\ v_i^t(o) + \omega_i^t(o) \times r_{C_i} \end{bmatrix}
\end{aligned} \tag{2}$$

In Cartesian coordinates, to satisfy the geometric constraints of a rigid body system, it is necessary to introduce generalized coordinates to represent the state of the system. As shown in the left sub-image of Fig. 1, taking a rigid body as an object, the Cartesian coordinates of the joints 1 and 2 at both ends of the rigid body are $(x_1 \; y_1 \; z_1)$ and $(x_2 \; y_2 \; z_2)$, respectively. Due to the displacement as a generalized coordinate, using the Cartesian coordinate system to represent the state of the system requires many parameters.

To overcome this difficulty, we introduce the screw coordinate system. As shown in the right subgraph of Fig. 1, the motion state of the link can be represented by the velocity

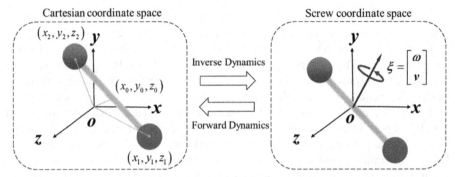

Fig. 1. Two representations of rigid body systems: the left subgraph uses Cartesian coordinates to describe the system state; The right subgraph uses screw coordinates to describe the system state.

screw of the center of mass of the link. The twist includes the linear motion speed and relative rotation angle of the link. At the same time, under Plücker coordinates, the state of a rod can be decoupled through Plücker coordinates: simultaneously describing the rotation and linear movement of a rigid body. If other methods are used for modeling, the length of the link remains unchanged, and it is particularly advantageous to use neural networks for modeling.

It is easy to obtain Newton's equation for a single rigid body is

$$F = \frac{d(mv_C)}{dt} = \frac{dm}{dt}v_C + m\frac{dv_C}{dt} = ma_C \tag{3}$$

Euler's equation for a single rigid body is

$$T = \frac{d(J\omega)}{dt} = \frac{dJ}{dt}\omega + J\frac{d\omega}{dt} = \omega \times J\omega + J\beta \tag{4}$$

where $\omega \times J\omega$ is the inertial torque resulting from Coriolis forces.

When describing the system state using screw coordinates, it can be obtained that

$$\$ = \begin{bmatrix} F_i \\ T_i \end{bmatrix} = \begin{bmatrix} m_i I & 0 \\ 0 & J_i \end{bmatrix}\begin{bmatrix} \dot{v}_i \\ \dot{\omega}_i \end{bmatrix} + \begin{bmatrix} 0 \\ \omega_i \times J_i\omega_i \end{bmatrix} \tag{5}$$

where v_i denotes the linear velocity of the mass center of a link, ω_i denotes the angular velocity of the link, J_i denotes a 3×3 inertia matrix of link i, I is a 3×3 identity matrix.

From Eq. (5), we can obtain

$$\begin{bmatrix} m_i\dot{v}_i \\ J_i\dot{\omega}_i \end{bmatrix} = \begin{bmatrix} F_i \\ T_i \end{bmatrix} + \begin{bmatrix} 0 \\ -\omega_i \times J_i\omega_i \end{bmatrix} \tag{6}$$

where $\boldsymbol{\xi}_i^M = \begin{bmatrix} m_i v_i \\ J_i\omega_i \end{bmatrix}$ and $\left(\$_i^W\right)' = \begin{bmatrix} 0 \\ -\omega_i \times J_i\omega_i \end{bmatrix}$.

The screw dynamics equations can be established for a multi-body system

$$\frac{d}{dt}\left[\sum_{i=1}^{n} \boldsymbol{\xi}_i^M(t)\right] = \sum_{j=1}^{m}\left\{\$_j^W + \left(\$_j^W\right)'\right\} \tag{7}$$

where i represents that the momentum screw is about the ith rigid body, n represents the total number of rigid bodies, j represents the external force screw of the jth rigid body, and m represents the total number of the external forces.

It is worth noting that wrench, twist, and momentum screw are relative to the absolute coordinate system. Thus, the absolute twist of the ith body is $\boldsymbol{\xi}_{iA}^t(o) = \begin{bmatrix} \omega_{iA}(o) \\ v_{iA}(o) \end{bmatrix}$. Twist of the ith body in its Center of Mass Coordinate System is $\boldsymbol{\xi}_{A_i}^t(C_i) = \begin{bmatrix} \omega_{iA}(o) \\ v_{iA}(o) \end{bmatrix} + \begin{bmatrix} 0 \\ \omega_{iA}(o) \times r_{Ci} \end{bmatrix}$.

According to the physical meaning of displacement, velocity, and acceleration, we can obtain that the absolute accelerations of each link are

$$\frac{d\boldsymbol{\xi}_{A_i}^t(C_i)}{dt} = \begin{bmatrix} \frac{d\omega_{iA}(o)}{dt} \\ \frac{d[v_i^t(o)+\omega_i^t(o) \times r_{C_i}]}{dt} \end{bmatrix} \tag{8}$$

and the absolute displacements of each link is

$$\int_0^t \boldsymbol{\xi}_{A_i}^t(C_i)dt = \begin{bmatrix} \int_0^t \omega_{A_i}(o)dt \\ \int_0^t \left[v_{A_i}^t(o) + \omega_{A_i}^t(o) \times r_{C_i} \right]dt \end{bmatrix} \tag{9}$$

Specifically, to describe the dynamic modeling process of a multi-rigid body system, our method mainly includes the following parts:

1. Determine the velocity screw of each rigid body.
2. Represents the screw displacement and absolute acceleration of each rigid body.
3. Convert the force on each rigid body into an acceleration change in screw form.
4. Using a numerical algorithm, calculate the force exerted on each joint by other rigid bodies in the Plücker space.

Figure 2 exhibits the flowchart of screw dynamics equations for a mechanical system.

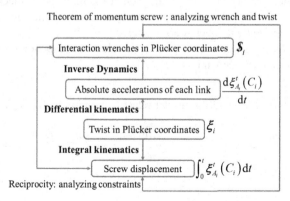

Fig. 2. The flowchart of screw dynamics equations for a mechanical system.

It is worth pointing out that both of the above two vectors ($\frac{\mathrm{d}\xi_{A_i}^t(C_i)}{\mathrm{d}t}$ and $\int_0^t \xi_{A_i}^t(C_i)\mathrm{d}t$) are non-screws. We treat them here as variables. The traditional screw theory analyzes constraints through the reciprocity of two screws. In this paper, we provide a new way to study screws. By introducing such a processing method, describing the motion of a rigid body has better simplicity and systematisms.

3   Screw Dynamics Modeling

The multibody model of a humanoid robot has a tree-like structure as shown in Fig. 3. A fixed coordinate system is connected to the robot's shoulder and has three Degrees of Freedom (DoF).

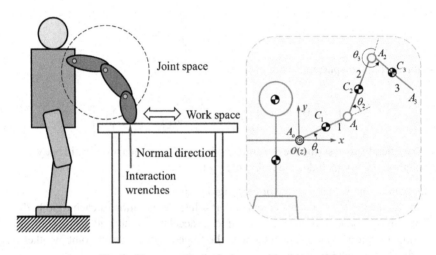

Fig. 3. The upper limb of a humanoid robot model.

Based on the obtained dynamics equation for a multi-body mechanical system, and considering the selected methods for numerically solving the equations, a program capable of solving joint wrenches was developed.

Geometric parameters and initial parameter values, corresponding to the upper limb of a humanoid robot, are shown in Table 1.

Table 1. Geometric and initial parameter values of the upper limb of a humanoid robot.

l_1(mm)	l_2(mm)	l_3(mm)	$\theta_1(0)$ (rad)	$\theta_2(0)$ (rad)	$\theta_3(0)$ (rad)
210	230	160	$\pi/6$	$\pi/3$	$(23\pi)/12$

The coordinates of the centroids C_1, C_2, and C_3 of the kinks 1, 2, and 3 are

$$r_{C_1} = \frac{1}{2}\begin{bmatrix} 0 \\ l_1\cos\theta_1 \\ l_1\sin\theta_1 \end{bmatrix}, r_{C_2} = \begin{bmatrix} 0 \\ l_1\cos\theta_1 \\ l_1\sin\theta_1 \end{bmatrix} + \frac{1}{2}\begin{bmatrix} 0 \\ l_2\cos(\theta_1+\theta_2) \\ l_2\sin(\theta_1+\theta_2) \end{bmatrix}, \text{ and}$$

$$r_{C_3} = \begin{bmatrix} 0 \\ l_1\cos\theta_1 \\ l_1\sin\theta_1 \end{bmatrix} + \begin{bmatrix} 0 \\ l_2\cos(\theta_1+\theta_2) \\ l_2\sin(\theta_1+\theta_2) \end{bmatrix} + \frac{1}{2}\begin{bmatrix} 0 \\ l_3\cos(\theta_1+\theta_2+\theta_3) \\ l_3\sin(\theta_1+\theta_2+\theta_3) \end{bmatrix}$$

The velocity screw of link 1 is

$$\boldsymbol{\xi}_{A_1} = \dot{\theta}_1\begin{bmatrix} 1 & 0 & 0 & 0 & 0 & 0 \end{bmatrix}^T \tag{10}$$

From Eq. (2), it can be seen that the velocity screw in the parallel coordinate system of its center of mass is

$$\boldsymbol{\xi}^t_{A_1}(C_1) = \begin{bmatrix} \boldsymbol{\omega}_{A_1}(o) \\ \boldsymbol{v}_{A_1}(o) \end{bmatrix} + \begin{bmatrix} 0 \\ \boldsymbol{\omega}_{A_1}(o) \times \boldsymbol{r}_{C_1} \end{bmatrix} \tag{11}$$

The velocity screw of link 2 is

$$\boldsymbol{\xi}_{A_2} = \begin{bmatrix} 1 & 1 \\ 0 & 0 \\ 0 & 0 \\ 0 & 0 \\ 0 & -l_1\cos\theta_1 \\ 0 & -l_1\sin\theta_1 \end{bmatrix}\begin{bmatrix} \dot{\theta}_1 \\ \dot{\theta}_2 \end{bmatrix} = \begin{bmatrix} \dot{\theta}_1+\dot{\theta}_2 & 0 & 0 & 0 & -\dot{\theta}_2l_1\cos\theta_1 & -\dot{\theta}_2l_1\sin\theta_1 \end{bmatrix}^T \tag{12}$$

From Eq. (2), it can be seen that the velocity screw in the parallel coordinate system of its center of mass is

$$\boldsymbol{\xi}^t_{A_3}(C_3) = \boldsymbol{\xi}_{A_3} + \begin{bmatrix} 0 \\ \boldsymbol{\omega}_{A_3}(o) \times \boldsymbol{r}_{C_3} \end{bmatrix} \tag{13}$$

According to the speed screw of each link, their accelerations in screw form are obtained. For link 1, the dynamics equation can be established. The force analysis is shown in Fig. 4(a).

$$\begin{cases} F_{A_{1y}} - m_1\dfrac{d\boldsymbol{\xi}^t_{A_1}(C_1)}{dt}(5) - F_{A_{oy}} = 0 \\[2ex] F_{A_{1z}} - m_1\dfrac{d\boldsymbol{\xi}^t_{A_1}(C_1)}{dt}(6) - F_{A_{oz}} - m_1g = 0 \\[2ex] F_{A_{1z}}l_1\cos\theta_1 - F_{A_{1y}}l_1\sin\theta_1 - J_1\dfrac{d\boldsymbol{\xi}^t_{A_1}(C_1)}{dt}(1) \\[2ex] \quad -\dfrac{1}{2}m_1l_1\dfrac{d\boldsymbol{\xi}^t_{A_1}(C_1)}{dt}(6)\cos\theta_1 + \dfrac{1}{2}m_1l_1\dfrac{d\boldsymbol{\xi}^t_{A_1}(C_1)}{dt}(5)\sin\theta_1 \\[2ex] \quad -\dfrac{1}{2}m_1gl_1\cos\theta_1 + T_1 - T_2 = 0 \end{cases} \tag{14}$$

For link 2, the dynamics equation can be established. The force analysis is shown in Fig. 4(b).

$$
\begin{cases}
F_{A2y} - F_{A1y} - m_2 \dfrac{d\boldsymbol{\xi}_{A2}^t(C_2)}{dt}(5) = 0 \\[2mm]
F_{A3z} - m_2 \dfrac{d\boldsymbol{\xi}_{A2}^t(C_2)}{dt}(6) - F_{A2z} - m_2 g = 0 \\[2mm]
F_{A2z} l_2 \cos(\theta_1 + \theta_2) - F_{A2y} l_2 \sin(\theta_1 + \theta_2) - J_2 \dfrac{d\boldsymbol{\xi}_{A2}^t(C_2)}{dt}(1) \\[2mm]
- \dfrac{1}{2} m_2 l_2 \dfrac{d\boldsymbol{\xi}_{A2}^t(C_2)}{dt}(6)\cos(\theta_1 + \theta_2) + \dfrac{1}{2} m_2 l_2 \dfrac{d\boldsymbol{\xi}_{A2}^t(C_2)}{dt}(5)\sin(\theta_1 + \theta_2) \\[2mm]
- \dfrac{1}{2} m_2 g l_2 \cos(\theta_1 + \theta_2) + T_2 - T_3 = 0
\end{cases}
\tag{15}
$$

For link 3, the dynamics equation can be established. The force analysis is shown in Fig. 4(c).

$$
\begin{cases}
F_y - m_3 \dfrac{d\boldsymbol{\xi}_{A3}^t(C_3)}{dt}(5) - F_{A2y} = 0 \\[2mm]
F_z - m_3 \dfrac{d\boldsymbol{\xi}_{A3}^t(C_3)}{dt}(6) - F_{A2z} - m_3 g = 0 \\[2mm]
F_z l_3 \cos(\theta_1 + \theta_2 + \theta_3) - F_y l_3 \sin(\theta_1 + \theta_2 + \theta_3) - J_3 \dfrac{d\boldsymbol{\xi}_{A3}^t(C_3)}{dt}(1) \\[2mm]
- \dfrac{1}{2} m_3 l_3 \dfrac{d\boldsymbol{\xi}_{A3}^t(C_3)}{dt}(6)\cos(\theta_1 + \theta_2 + \theta_3)+ \\[2mm]
\dfrac{1}{2} m_3 l_3 \dfrac{d\boldsymbol{\xi}_{A3}^t(C_3)}{dt}(5)\sin(\theta_1 + \theta_2 + \theta_3) - \dfrac{1}{2} m_3 g l_3 \cos(\theta_1 + \theta_2 + \theta_3) + T_3 = 0
\end{cases}
\tag{16}
$$

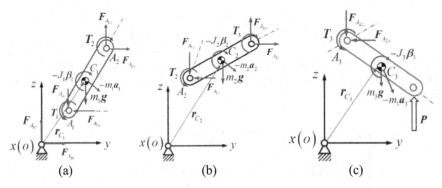

Fig. 4. The force analysis of the upper limb of a humanoid robot model.

Thus, the Newton-Euler equations are established in the screw form of the upper limb of a humanoid robot. In matrix form, we have

$$
Ax = b
\tag{17}
$$

According to linear algebra, the linear Eqs. (17) are solved. The dynamics parameters of the upper limb of a humanoid robot are $m_1 = 158.1$ g, $m_2 = 169.6$ g, and $m_3 = 122.2$ g. The proposed algorithm is programmed, and through numerical calculation, the wrenches curve of each joint is illustrated in Fig. 5. It can be seen that this algorithm solves the joint torques very succinctly.

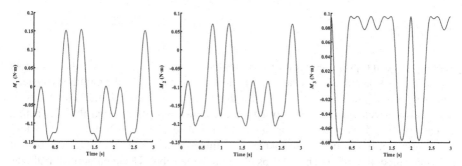

Fig. 5. Wrenches of the joint space.

The wrenches at every joint of the arm are changing cyclically as the robot starts to move from the initial parameters in Table 1.

4   Comparison of the Screw Dynamics with Lagrange Equation

The Lagrange equation is a set of second-order differential equations about the generalized coordinate q_k, where the number of equations is equal to the number of DoFs of the particle system. The generalized coordinates of the upper limb of a humanoid robot are now θ_1, θ_2, and θ_3, the Lagrange equation becomes

$$
\begin{cases}
\dfrac{\mathrm{d}}{\mathrm{d}t}\left(\dfrac{\partial L}{\partial \dot\theta_1}\right) - \dfrac{\partial L}{\partial \theta_1} = M_1 \\[2mm]
\dfrac{\mathrm{d}}{\mathrm{d}t}\left(\dfrac{\partial L}{\partial \dot\theta_2}\right) - \dfrac{\partial L}{\partial \theta_2} = M_2 \\[2mm]
\dfrac{\mathrm{d}}{\mathrm{d}t}\left(\dfrac{\partial L}{\partial \dot\theta_3}\right) - \dfrac{\partial L}{\partial \theta_3} = M_3
\end{cases}
\tag{18}
$$

where M_i ($i = 1, 2, 3$) is the Generalized force. To determine the number of operations of the momentum screw method and Lagrange equation, Eq. (7) and Eq. (18) were used, respectively, as well as related formulas.

From the above analysis, it can be seen that dynamics modeling by using the momentum screw method has simpler algebraic operations. Another advantage of the momentum screw method is that it simplifies the amount of code written. Some key dynamics codes are shorter and can be more easily debugged at runtime. For example, the dynamics modeling based on the Newton-Euler method in the Cartesian coordinate system refers to the Newton equation for the center of mass of a rigid body, and the Euler equation for the rotation relative to the rigid body. Using the momentum screw method, the dynamics modeling of a rigid body can be stated as Eq. (7).

Therefore, a comparison of the two methods indicates that there are fewer operations to describe robot dynamics modeling using the screw dynamics method. At the same time, this method is easy to program. The number of codes is also shorter, making it easier to debug.

5 Conclusions

A new approach is proposed for the dynamics modeling of the upper limb of a humanoid robot. The twist is utilized as a variable to relate the kinematics of the multibody system. The twist is integrated once, and the screw displacement is solved. Differential the twist once and the acceleration in screw form is obtained. In this representation, the force acting on each rigid body is converted into a screw form of acceleration change. The Newton-Euler equation is obtained in the screw coordinate system. On this basis, we conduct dynamics modeling of the upper limbs of a humanoid robot. Using numerical methods, we obtain real-time solutions for joint space. Compared with the Lagrange equation, our method has fewer operations and is easy to program for a solution. Unlike the Newton-Euler method in Cartesian coordinates, our method can have simpler algebraic operations and shorter code.

Acknowledgments. This work was supported in part by the Basic Research Project Group of China under Grant 514010305-301-3, in part by the National Natural Science Foundation of China under Grant 51575291, in part by the National Major Science and Technology Project of China under Grant 2015ZX04002101, in part by the State Key Laboratory of Tribology, Tsinghua University, and part by the 221 Program of Tsinghua University.

References

1. Hicks, J.L., Uchida, T.K., Seth, A., Rajagopal, A., Delp, S.L.: Is my model good enough? best practices for verification and validation of musculoskeletal models and simulations of movement. ASME. J. Biomech. Eng. **137**, 020905 (2015)
2. Manns, P., Sreenivasa, M., Millard, M., Mombaur, K.: Motion optimization and parameter identification for a human and lower back exoskeleton model. IEEE Robot. Autom. Let. **2**, 1564–1570 (2017)
3. Lamas, M., Mouzo, F., Michaud, F., Lugris, U., Cuadrado, J.: Comparison of several muscle modeling alternatives for computationally intensive algorithms in human motion dynamics. Multibody Sys. Dyn. **54**, 415–442 (2022)
4. Liu, X.H., Zheng, X.H., Li, S.P., Chen, X.H., Wang, Z.B.: Improved adaptive neural network control for humanoid robot hand in workspace, Proc. Inst. Mech. Eng. Part C J. Mech. Eng. Sci. **229**, 869–881 (2014)
5. Zhao, J.S., Sun, H.L.: Kinetostatics of a serial robot in screw form. Adv. Mech. Eng. **15**, 1–12 (2023)
6. Qu, J.D., Zhang, F.H., Wang, Y., Fu, Y.L.L: Human-like coordination motion learning for a redundant dual-arm robot. Robot. Comput. Integrat. Manufac. **57** (2019)

7. Shimizu, M.: Analytical inverse kinematics for 5-DOF humanoid manipulator under arbitrarily specified unconstrained orientation of end-effector. Robotica **33**, 1–21 (2015)
8. Paparisabet, M.A., Dehghani, R., Ahmadi, A.R.: Knee and torso kinematics in generation of optimum gait pattern based on human-like motion for a seven-link biped robot. Multibody Sys. Dyn. **47**, 117–136 (2019)
9. Coronel-Escamilla, A., Torres, F., Gómez-Aguilar, J.F., Escobar-Jiménez, R.F., Guerrero-Ramírez, G.V.: On the trajectory tracking control for an SCARA robot manipulator in a fractional model driven by induction motors with PSO tuning. Multibody Sys. Dyn. **43**, 257–277 (2018)
10. Hashemi, E., Khajepour, A.: Kinematic and three-dimensional dynamic modeling of a biped robot. Proc. Inst. Mech. Eng, Part K: J. Multi-body Dyn. **231**, 57–73 (2016)
11. Fang, Y., Wang, S., Cui, D., Bi, Q.S., Yan, C.L.: Multi-body dynamics model of crawler wall-climbing robot. Proc. Inst. Mech. Eng, Part K: J. Multi-body Dyn. **236**, 535–553 (2022)
12. Dimeas, F., Avendaño-Valencia, L.D., Aspragathos, N.: Human - robot collision detection and identification based on fuzzy and time series modelling. Robotica **33**, 1886–1898 (2015)
13. Zhao, J.S., Feng, Z.J., Chu, F.L., Ma, N.: Advanced Theory of Constraint and Motion Analysis for Robot Mechanisms, 1st edn. Academic Press, Florida (2013)

Research on Selective Degradation Strategy of Redundant Degrees of Freedom for Planar 6R Parallel Mechanism

Dong Yang[1] , Yanxu Bi[1] , Ming Han[1]([✉]) , and Tiejun Li[2]([✉])

[1] Hebei University of Technology, Tianjin 300401, China
hanming@hebut.edu.cn

[2] Hebei University of Science and Technology, Shijiazhuang 050091, China
li_tiejun@hebut.edu.cn

Abstract. During specific operational tasks, robots require fewer degrees of freedom than their total degrees of freedom. Therefore, conducting research on selective degradation of redundant degrees of freedom in mechanisms can aid in improving the mechanisms' performance. To address the kinematic performance optimization problem of parallel mechanisms, we propose a selective degradation strategy of redundant degrees of freedom. We take a planar 6R parallel mechanism as an example for research and analysis. We begin our research by establishing the inverse kinematics model of the mechanism and analyzing its workspace. Subsequently, we evaluate the kinematic performance of the mechanism based on the motion/force transmission index and identify its good transmission workspace. What is more, we formulate the degradation rules for the mechanism's redundant degrees of freedom, comparing and analyzing the mechanism's performance before and after selective degradation. Finally, it is verified by experiments that the redundant degree of freedom selective degradation strategy can significantly improve the accuracy of the mechanism. Our findings demonstrate that selective degradation of degrees of freedom is a novel method for enhancing the kinematic performance of parallel mechanisms.

Keywords: Parallel Mechanisms · Motion/Force Transmission Index · Good Transmission Workspace · Performance Optimization

1 Introduction

In comparison to traditional serial robots, parallel mechanisms have significant advantages in overall stiffness, dynamic performance, and bearing capacity. However, due to the challenge presented by direct kinematics [1–3], obtaining inverse kinematics for parallel mechanisms is a relatively easier task. This makes parallel mechanisms a preferred primary functional component in various applications. Xie [4] proposed a six-degree-of-freedom hybrid mechanism for machine tool development. The kinematics of this mechanism were optimized based on the local transmission index (LTI), and geometric design parameters were derived accordingly. Wang [5, 6] designed a parallel mechanism

© The Author(s), under exclusive license to Springer Nature Singapore Pte Ltd. 2023
H. Yang et al. (Eds.): ICIRA 2023, LNAI 14274, pp. 578–589, 2023.
https://doi.org/10.1007/978-981-99-6501-4_49

specifically for ankle rehabilitation purposes. They discussed the multi-objective optimization design problem of the mechanism by evaluating its motion/force transmission efficiency.

When assessing the performance of parallel mechanisms, the local condition number index of the Jacobian matrix is a commonly used metric to evaluate their motion performance [7–9]. However, due to inconsistencies in the dimensions of the Jacobian matrix elements, the local condition number index may lack consistency [10]. Alternatively, the motion/force transmission index is a more reliable measure of the mechanism's ability to transmit internal motion/force. Liu et al. [11] systematically discussed the motion/force transmission characteristics of the parallel mechanism, and defined the LTI by the minimum value method. Therefore, this paper employs the motion/force transmission index as the primary evaluation criterion for assessing parallel mechanism performance.

This paper proposes a novel method for improving the performance of parallel mechanisms. Its main contributions include selecting a planar 6R parallel mechanism as the research object and exploring the selective degradation strategy of degrees of freedom based on motion/force transmission index. The remaining sections are organized as follows: In Sect. 2, we provide a brief description of the prototype under study and analyze its workspace. In Sect. 3, we establish the LTI of the mechanism and identify its good transmission workspace (GTW). In Sect. 4, we formulate the degree of freedom selective degradation strategy of the mechanism and the position accuracy and position repeatability of the mechanism before and after the selective degradation of redundant degrees of freedom is measured by experiments in Sect. 5. Finally, we conclude with our research findings.

2 Kinematics Analysis of Planar 6R Parallel Mechanism

2.1 Robot Prototype Introduction

Our team has developed a construction robot for handling building components and loading operations, as shown in Fig. 1(a). Since the cylinder pushes the corresponding joint to complete the rotational motion, the mechanism diagram shown in Fig. 1(b) can be equivalent to Fig. 1(c). This autonomous system comprises a planar 6R parallel mechanism as the primary functional component, a rotary shaft connected to the base, and an end wrist that can rotate around the x and y axes, respectively. In this paper, we focus our research on the planar 6R parallel mechanism of the construction robot.

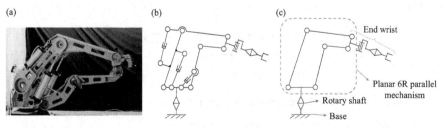

Fig. 1. (a) Robot prototype (b) Mechanism sketch (c) Equivalent mechanism structure sketch

2.2 Inverse Kinematics

Figure 2 illustrates the sketch of a planar 6R parallel mechanism. The active pair (represented by the red circle) is composed of joints A_1, B_1, and A_2, while the passive pair comprises joints B_2, C_1, and C_2. The moving platform of the mechanism is rod C_1C_2, with center point P (represented by the black circle) serving as its reference point. Rod A_1A_2 functions as the frame of the mechanism, while fixed reference coordinate system o-xy has its coordinate origin positioned at the center of A_1A_2. The dimensions of the rods are $A_1B_1 = A_2B_2 = r_1 = 1.2$ m, $C_1C_2 = 2r_3 = 0.3$ m, $B_1C_1 = B_2C_2 = r_2 = 1.2$ m, and $A_1A_2 = 2r_4 = 0.66$ m.

Suppose that the center of rod C_1C_2 is P, and its coordinates are denoted by $P = (x, y, \varphi)$. Based on the relationship of rod length, we can get

$$(x - r_3 \cos \varphi - r_1 \cos \theta_1 + r_4)^2 + (y - r_3 \sin \varphi - r_1 \sin \theta_1)^2 = r_2^2 \qquad (1)$$

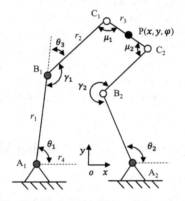

Fig. 2. Sketch of planar 6R parallel mechanism

Can be obtained from Eq. (1)

$$- 2r_1(y - r_3 \sin \varphi) \sin \theta_1 - 2r_1(x - r_3 \cos \varphi + r_4) \cos \theta_1$$
$$+ (x - r_3 \cos \varphi + r_4)^2 + (y - r_3 \sin \varphi)^2 + r_1^2 - r_2^2 = 0 \qquad (2)$$

Let

$$\begin{cases} A_1 = (x - r_3 \cos \varphi + r_4)^2 + (y - r_3 \sin \varphi)^2 + r_1^2 - r_2^2 \\ B_1 = -2r_1(x - r_3 \cos \varphi + r_4) \\ C_1 = -2r_1(y - r_3 \sin \varphi) \end{cases} \qquad (3)$$

Based on the double angle formula we can get

$$\begin{cases} \theta_1 = 2 \arctan \dfrac{-C_1 \pm \sqrt{C_1^2 + B_1^2 - A_1^2}}{A_1 - B_1} & A_1 \neq B_1 \\ \theta_1 = 2 \arctan \dfrac{-(A_1 + B_1)}{2C_1} & A_1 = B_1 \end{cases} \qquad (4)$$

Similarly, θ_2 can be get. Easily got by triangular relations

$$\theta_3 = \arctan \frac{y - r_3 \sin \varphi - r_1 \sin \theta_1}{x - r_3 \cos \varphi + r_4 - r_1 \cos \theta_1} \tag{5}$$

Similarly, γ_1, γ_1, μ_1, μ_1, can be obtained. From the preceding conclusions, it can be observed that the inverse kinematics of the parallel mechanism yields four solution sets. In subsequent calculations, we consider θ_1 as positive and θ_2 as negative.

2.3 Inverse Kinematics Workspace Analysis

Workspace analysis is a critical aspect of robot design, and the workspace is solved by the search method. To determine the workspace of the parallel mechanism, we initially establish a search range comprising all possible workspaces based on the mechanism's initial parameters. Next, each position point within this range undergoes a search process to determine whether it satisfies the inverse position discrimination condition of the parallel mechanism. If a position point satisfies this condition, it is identified as a workspace point. The primary variation range for the attitude angle of the end moving platform is $(-\pi, -\pi/2)$. As the attitude angle continuously varies within this range, the flexible workspace of the mechanism encompasses the motion range achievable by the reference point of the end moving platform at any attitude angle (Fig. 3).

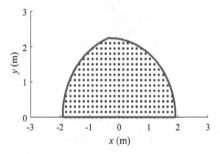

Fig. 3. Flexible workspaces of parallel mechanism

3 Motion/Force Transmission Performance Analysis

In this paper, the LTI proposed by Liu et al. [11] is used to measure the motion performance of the mechanism. The LTI can be analyzed from two perspectives: input and output, denoted as input transmission index (ITI) and output transmission index (OTI), respectively. The ITI is defined as

$$\lambda_i = \frac{\left| \$_{Ti} \circ \$_{Ii} \right|}{\left| \$_{Ti} \circ \$_{Ii} \right|_{\max}} \tag{6}$$

In the formula, $\$_{Ti}$ represents the unit transmission wrench screw (TWS) of the i-th limb, while $\$_{Ii}$ denotes the unit input twist screw (ITS) of the i-th limb.

The OTI is defined as

$$\eta_i = \frac{\left|\$_{Ti} \circ \$_{Oi}\right|}{\left|\$_{Ti} \circ \$_{Oi}\right|_{\max}} \tag{7}$$

In the formula, $\$_{Oi}$ represents the unit output twist screw (OTS) of the i-th limb.

The LTI of the mechanism is determined by taking the minimum value of the ITI and the OTI, which is defined as

$$\gamma = \min\{\lambda_i, \eta_i\} \tag{8}$$

3.1 Solving the TWS, ITS and OTS of Planar 6R Parallel Mechanism

For the <u>RRR</u> limb of 6R mechanism, its structure sketch is shown in Fig. 4.

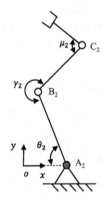

Fig. 4. <u>RRR</u> limb structure sketch

In the <u>RRR</u> limb, there are three twist screws, which are

$$\begin{cases} \$_1 = \left(0, 0, 1;\ \ 0, -r_4, 0\right) \\ \$_2 = \left(0, 0, 1;\ \ r_1 \sin\theta_2, -r_4 - r_1 \cos\theta_2, 0\right) \\ \$_3 = \left(0, 0, 1;\ \ r_1 \sin\theta_2 + r_2 \sin(\gamma_2 - \theta_2), r_2 \cos(\gamma_2 - \theta_2) - r_4 - r_1 \cos\theta_2, 0\right) \end{cases} \tag{9}$$

Their constraint screws are

$$\begin{cases} \$_1^r = \left(0, 0, 1; 0, 0, 0\right) \\ \$_2^r = \left(0, 0, 0; 1, 0, 0\right) \\ \$_3^r = \left(0, 0, 0; 0, 1, 0\right) \end{cases} \tag{10}$$

When the drive joint A_2 is locked. The $\$_{TA2}$ can be derived as

$$\$_{TA2} = (-\cos(\gamma_2 - \theta_2), \sin(\gamma_2 - \theta_2), 0; 0, 0, r_4\sin(\gamma_2 - \theta_2) + r_1\sin\gamma_2) \qquad (11)$$

Similarly, the TWS $\$_{TA1}$ and $\$_{TB1}$ corresponding to joints A_1 and B_1 in the limb RRR can be got.

For the planar 6R parallel mechanism, it is necessary to determine ITS and OTS. Since the three input joints of the parallel mechanism are single-degree-of-freedom motion pairs, the ITS are their respective corresponding twist screw. They are

$$\begin{cases} \$_{IA1} = \left(0, 0, 1; \quad 0, r_4, 0\right) \\ \$_{IB1} = \left(0, 0, 1; \quad r_1\sin\theta_1, r_4 - r_1\cos\theta_1, 0\right) \\ \$_{IA2} = \left(0, 0, 1; \quad 0, -r_4, 0\right) \end{cases} \qquad (12)$$

In a single-drive limb RRR, it is assumed that joints A_1 and B_1 are locked while only joint A_2 can be driven. We use the unit OTS $\$_{OA2}$ to represent the unit instantaneousmotion of the moving platform, we can get

$$\begin{cases} \$_{TA1} \circ \$_{OA2} = 0 \\ \$_{TB1} \circ \$_{OA2} = 0 \\ \$_i^r \circ \$_{OA2} = 0, (i = 1, 2, 3) \end{cases} \qquad (13)$$

Based on Eq. (10) and Eq. (13), we can get $\$_{OA2}$. Similarly, it can also be got that the OTS corresponding to joints A_1 and B_1 in the RRR limb are $\$_{OA1}$ and $\$_{OB1}$.

3.2 LTI and GTW of Planar 6R Parallel Mechanism

Based on (6)–(8), the LTI of the 6R mechanism can be obtained

$$\gamma = \min\{\lambda_i, \eta_i\} = \min\{\lambda_1, \lambda_2, \lambda_3, \eta_1, \eta_2, \eta_3\}$$

$$= \min\left\{|\sin\gamma_2|, \left|\frac{r_1\sin\gamma_1}{\sqrt{r_1^2 + r_2^2 - 2r_1r_2\cos\gamma_1}}\right|, |\sin\mu_2|\right\} \qquad (14)$$

The distribution of LTI in the flexible workspace is shown in Fig. 5(a). To ensure optimal overall performance of the mechanism, we define the area where LTI is greater than or equal to 0.7 as the GTW. It is recommended that the mechanism operates within this range. Figure 5(b) illustrates the distribution of GTW in the flexible workspace under a specific angle range, with the GTW area measuring 0.006.

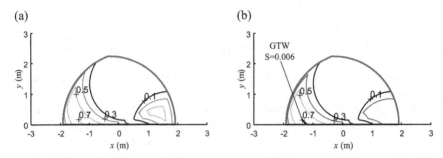

Fig. 5. (a) LTI distribution in flexible workspace (b) GTW distribution in flexible workspace

4 Selective Degradation of Degrees of Freedom

4.1 Degree of Freedom Selective Degradation Rule Research

Figure 6 shows the degree of freedom selective degradation of joints A_1, A_2, B_1, and B_2. The purple solid dots represent the rigid joints, while the connection part of the purple solid line represents the equivalent rigid part or equivalent moving platform of the new mechanism after rigidizing the corresponding joint. Meanwhile, the red solid dot serves as the driving joint of the mechanism. From 2.2, we can obtain the inverse kinematics of each joint after rigidization.

Figure 6(a) shows that after the joint A_1 is rigidized, the original mechanism becomes a planar 5R mechanism, the joints B_1 and A_2 are selected as the driving joints., the TWS corresponding to the joint B_1 in the limb $\underline{RR}$ is

$$\$_{TB1}=(\sin(\gamma_1 + \theta_1), - \cos(\gamma_1 + \theta_1), 0;\ 0, 0, r_4 \cos(\gamma_1 + \theta_1) + r_2 - r_1 \cos \gamma_1) \quad (15)$$

Similarly, the TWS $\$_{TA2}$ corresponding to the joint A_2 can be got.

Based on Eq. (8), we can calculate the LTI of the new mechanism after rigidizing joint A_1

$$LTI_{A1} = \min\{1, |\sin \gamma_2|, 1, |\sin \mu_2|\} \quad (16)$$

Similarly, the LTI_{A2}, LTI_{B1} and LTI_{B2} of the new mechanism formed after rigidizing joints A_2, B_1 and B_2 can be got. According to the optimal principle, the following selective degradation rules of redundant degrees of freedom are formulated

$$\begin{cases} \text{"Lock"}A_1: LTI_{A_1} \geq LTI_{A_1 B_1 A_2} \\ \text{"Lock"}A_2: LTI_{A_2} \geq LTI_{A_1 B_1 A_2} \\ \text{"Lock"}B_1: LTI_{B_1} \geq LTI_{A_1 B_1 A_2} \\ \text{"Lock"}B_2: LTI_{B_2} \geq LTI_{A_1 B_1 A_2} \end{cases} \quad (17)$$

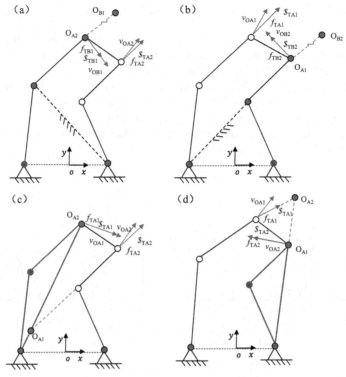

Fig. 6. Schematic diagram of mechanism performance analysis after selective degradation of redundant DOF: (a) Rigid joint A_1; (b) Rigid joint A_2; (c) Rigid joint B_1; (d) Rigid joint B_2

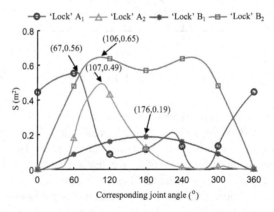

Fig. 7. Variation of workspace area with corresponding joint angle

4.2   Performance Analysis after Degree of Freedom Selective Degradation

After selectively degrading the mechanism's degree of freedom, the workspace of the reference point located at the end moving platform changes in a specific angle range correspondingly to the joint angle, as illustrated in Fig. 7.

As demonstrated in Fig. 7, the new mechanism's workspace is the most extensive when locking the four joints at the corresponding joint angles of 67°, 107°, 176°, 106°.

After implementing the degree of freedom degradation rule, the joint locks at the angle that corresponds to the maximum workspace. The distribution of the GTW of the new mechanism is presented in Fig. 8.

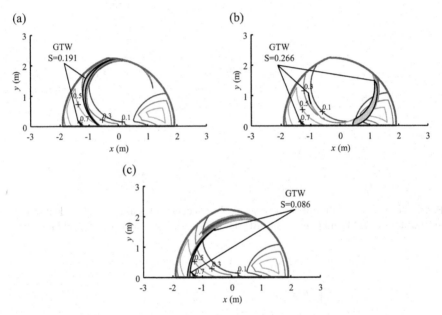

Fig. 8. GTW distribution after locking corresponding joints: (a) A_1; (b) A_2; (c) B_2

Compared to the mechanism driven by $A_1 B_2 A_2$ joints in Fig. 6, adopting the selective degradation rule of redundant degrees of freedom significantly increases the GTW in the flexible workspace under a specific rotation angle range. This suggests that the motion/force transmission performance of the mechanism can be fully improved through the selective degradation rule of redundant degrees of freedom. Through comparison, it can be seen that the mechanism adopts the selective degradation rule of redundant degrees of freedom for joints A_1, A_2 and B_2 respectively, the area of GTW is 0.185, 0.26 and 0.08 higher than that of $A_1 B_2 A_2$ joint drive, and the growth amplitude is 30.8, 43.3 and 13.3 times respectively.

5 Experiment

In order to detect the position accuracy and position repeatability of the parallel robot before and after the selective degradation of redundant degrees of freedom, three measurement points are selected in the flexible workspace of the robot, which are marked as $W_1 = (1203$ mm, 927 mm), $W_2 = (774$ mm, 1827 mm), $W_3 = (1455$ mm, 57 mm).

When the redundant degree of freedom selective degradation strategy is not adopted, the robot is controlled to execute W_1 point, W_2 point and W_3 point sequentially from W_1 point, and repeated 30 times. In the process of executing the pose point of the robot, the API-RADIAN laser tracker is used to measure and record the pose information of the robot end effector executing W_1, W_2 and W_3. The above steps are repeated when using the redundant degree of freedom selective degradation strategy. Figure 9 shows the detection scene photos of the W_2 point of the parallel robot measured and recorded by the laser tracker.

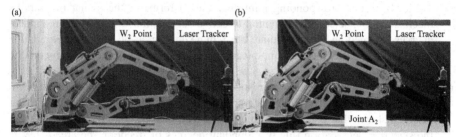

Fig. 9. Parallel robot execution accuracy test: (a) Before degradation (b) After degeneration of joint A2

The laser tracker is used to measure the same measurement point for many times, and the measured coordinate points can construct a circumscribed sphere that envelopes the three-dimensional coordinates of all measured points. The position accuracy of the robot refers to the distance between the command position point and the center of the circumscribed ball formed by the set of measured position points, and the radius of the constructed circumscribed ball is the position repeatability of the robot end effector. The position repeatability and position accuracy of the parallel robot before and after the selective degradation of redundant degrees of freedom are obtained (Table 1).

Table 1. The accuracy parameters of the parallel robot at each measurement point

point/mm	W_1	W_2	W_3
position repeatability before degradation/mm	0.049	0.043	0.051
position repeatability after degradation/mm	0.041	0.038	0.042
position accuracy before degradation/mm	0.520	0.514	0.577
position accuracy after degradation/mm	0.411	0.483	0.437

Taking the maximum value of position repeatability and position accuracy of each point, it can be seen that when the mechanism adopts the selective degradation of redundant degrees of freedom, the position repeatability and position accuracy of the mechanism are 0.042 and 0.483 respectively. Compared with the $A_1B_2A_2$ joint drive, the position repeatability and position accuracy of the mechanism are increased by 0.009 and 0.081 respectively, and the growth amplitudes are 18% and 14% respectively. The improvement effect is obvious.

6 Conclusion

This manuscript addresses the issue of optimizing the kinematic performance of parallel mechanisms. We conduct a thorough analysis of the kinematic performance exhibited by the planar 6R parallel mechanism, taking into account the selective degradation of redundant degrees of freedom. Our investigation yields the following conclusions.

(1) We analyze the corresponding joint degradation forms of the planar 6R parallel mechanism and select four potential selective degradation strategies for redundant degrees of freedom. We formulate the redundant degree of freedom degradation rules for the parallel mechanism, expanding the application range of the method to a certain extent.

(2) We compare and analyze the kinematic performance of the planar 6R parallel mechanism before and after selective degradation of redundant degrees of freedom. Our research shows that compared to the mechanism driven by $A_1B_2A_1$ joints, under the selective degradation rule of redundant degrees of freedom, the area GTW in the flexible workspace increases by 0.185, 0.26 and 0.08, respectively, with growth amplitudes of 30.8, 43.3 and 13.3 times, respectively. The improvement effect is significant.

(3) The position repeatability and position accuracy of planar 6R parallel mechanism before and after selective degradation of redundant degrees of freedom is studied experimentally. The experimental results show that when the parallel robot adopts the redundant degree of freedom selective degradation strategy, the position repeatability and position accuracy of the mechanism are increased by 0.009 and 0.081 respectively, and the growth amplitudes are 18% and 14% respectively. The improvement effect is obvious.

This paper proves that the redundant degree of freedom selective degradation strategy significantly improves the performance of the planar 6R parallel mechanism, providing a new approach to enhance the essential performance of the parallel mechanism.

References

1. Kardan, I., Akbarzadeh, A.: An improved hybrid method for forward kinematics analysis of parallel robots. Adv. Robot. **29**(6), 401–411 (2016)
2. Rahmani, A., Ghanbari, A.: Application of neural network training in forward kinematics simulation for a novel modular hybrid manipulator with experimental validation. Intel. Serv. Robot. **9**(1), 79–91 (2015). https://doi.org/10.1007/s11370-015-0188-8

3. Ren, H.H., Zhang, L.Z., Su, C.Z.: Design and research of a walking robot with two parallel mechanisms. Robotica **39**(9), 1634–1641 (2021)
4. Xie, F.G., Liu, X.J., Wang, J.S.: Conceptual design and optimization of a 3-dof parallel mechanism for a turbine blade grinding machine. Proc. Inst. Mech. Eng. C J. Mech. Eng. Sci. **230**(3), 406–413 (2016)
5. Wang, C., Fang, Y., Guo, S., et al.: Design and kinematic analysis of redundantly actuated parallel mechanisms for ankle rehabilitation. Robotica **33**(2), 366–384 (2014)
6. Wang, C., Fang, Y., Guo, S.: Multi-objective optimization of a parallel ankle rehabilitation robot using modified differential evolution algorithm. Chin. J. Mech. Eng. **28**(4), 702–715 (2015). https://doi.org/10.3901/CJME.2015.0416.062
7. Li, Y.M., Xu, Q.S.: Kinematic analysis of a 3-PRS parallel manipulator. Robot. Comput. Integrat. Manufac. **23**(4), 395–408 (2007)
8. Yang, H., Fang, H., Fang, Y., Li, X.: Dimensional synthesis of a novel 5-DOF reconfigurable hybrid perfusion manipulator for large-scale spherical honeycomb perfusion. Front. Mech. Eng. **16**(1), 46–60 (2021). https://doi.org/10.1007/s11465-020-0606-2
9. Chen, X.L., Sun, X.Y.: Dexterity analysis of a 4-UPS-RPS parallel mechanism. Int. J. Adv. Rob. Syst. **9**(4), 1–8 (2012)
10. Merlet, J.: Jacobian, manipulability, condition number and accuracy of parallel robots. J. Mech. Des. **128**(1), 199–206 (2006)
11. Wang, J.S., Wu, C., Liu, X.J.: Performance evaluation of parallel manipulators: motion/force transmissibility and its index. Mech. Mach. Theory **45**(10), 1462–1476 (2010)

Development and Analysis of a Wheel-Legged Mobile Robot for Ground and Rail Inspection

Shanwei Liu[1], Qiang Fu[2], Yisheng Guan[1(✉)], and Haifei Zhu[1]

[1] Biomimetic and Intelligent Robotics Lab (BIRL), School of Electromechanical Engineering, Guangdong University of Technology, Guangzhou 510006, China
ysguan@gdut.edu.cn
[2] School of Mechanical Engineering and Automation, Harbin Institute of Technology, Shenzhen 518055, China

Abstract. In order to combine the advantages of rail-type inspection robot and wheeled inspection robot, this paper proposes a modular wheel-legged robot (Mobot-H) for ground and rail inspection. The robot has the characteristics of high mobility, over-obstacle and multi-purpose. Firstly, The robot system is introduced. Mobot-H is composed of joint modules, wheel-footed modules, and body modules, which can be reconstructed into various configurations and has three different motion modes. Secondly, the over-obstacle motion of Mobot-H is introduced on the ground, and the limit and center of gravity of over-obstacle are deeply analyzed. The working principle of the robot is introduced on the rail, its motion characteristics are analyzed and its steering motion model is established. Finally, a series of prototype experiments and simulation experiments are designed.

Keywords: Mobile robot · Over-obstacle · Motion mode · Steering model

1 Introduction

Inspection robots can replace manual inspection and maintenance of equipment, reduce the labor intensity of workers, improve the efficiency, and has broad application prospects. According to the motion mode of the robot, the inspection robot can be divided into wheeled inspection robot, tracked inspection robot and rail-type inspection robot.

The tracked inspection robot is driven by the track and has a large contact surface. Yamauchi et al. proposed a track inspection robot [1], which can cross a variety of obstacles, adapt to sand and gravel roads. The robot carries

Supported by the Key Research and Development Program of Guangdong Province (Grant No. 2019B090915001).

© The Author(s), under exclusive license to Springer Nature Singapore Pte Ltd. 2023
H. Yang et al. (Eds.): ICIRA 2023, LNAI 14274, pp. 590–602, 2023.
https://doi.org/10.1007/978-981-99-6501-4_50

a pair of mechanical arms, which can be operated remotely in complex environments. Wang et al. proposed a tracked inspection robot. Each machine contains six tracks, which can be used for underground environmental monitoring in coal mines [2]. Baetz et al. proposed a tracked robot for automatic detection in the natural gas station environment, which can complete the thermal imaging detection of pipeline leakage and liquid leakage on the ground [3]. The above-mentioned robots have the disadvantages of slow moving speed, difficult steering, complex overall structure, large volume and weight, and are not suitable for aisles with narrow spaces.

The development of wheeled robot technology provides new ideas for the inspection. Wheeled mobile robots can carry relevant sensors to move on the ground to detect abnormal conditions in the environment. Based on the chassis of Clearpath Robotics Husky A200, the Hydro-Quebec Research Institute of Canada has designed a four-wheeled inspection robot. The camera and infrared camera on the robot are used to complete inspection tasks [4]. Xu et al. proposed a modular inspection robot, which consists of two driving wheels and two passive wheels [5]. Wang et al. proposed a floating mobile chassis of inspection robot, which was designed based on the Teoriya Resheniya Izobreatatelskikh Zadatch theory. The kinematic model and the over-obstacle analysis has been completed [6]. Leonidas et al. proposed a four-wheeled robot for detecting tunnel cracks, which carried ultrasonic sensors and cameras for cracks that appeared in the tunnel [7]. The wheeled mobile inspection robot has the advantages of fast moving speed, high inspection efficiency and flexible steering. Because it is susceptible to terrain and aisle space, the motion of the wheeled inspection robot is greatly limited.

In view of these situations, relevant research institutions have developed a rail-type inspection robot to replace the inspection robot that move on the ground. The rail-type inspection robot can carry various detection components, is not restricted by the unstructured environment, has a single driving route and is easy to control. Jiang et al. proposed a multi-functional rail-type inspection robot, which can walk on a special rail. The robot is characterized by stable mechanical performance, anti vibration and swing, and can be used for real-time monitoring of substations [8]. Bae et al. proposed a trajectory oriented mobile robot system with brushless DC (BLDC) motor as traction force. The camera can move up and down for monitoring [9]. A rail-type inspection robot is proposed, which can reduce the position error caused by turning [10]. Combined with the inspection requirements of coal mines, Zhang et al. designed a mine inspection robot system. With the connection of flexible transition mechanism, the robot can realize the transition from horizontal track to inclined track [11]. The rail-type inspection robot can be equipped with various detection equipment, and is not restricted by the unstructured environment. However, the moving route of the rail-type inspection robot is fixed, it needs to move along the pre-arranged rail, and the detection range is limited.

Therefore, the rail-type inspection robot and the wheeled inspection robot have their own advantages and disadvantages. It is of great significance to combine these two types of inspection robot and has a wide application prospect.

This paper develops a modular inspection robot (Mobot-H), which can move on the ground and rail. Firstly, the design and three different motion modes of Mobot-H is introduced. Then, the over-obstacle motion is deeply analyzed and the steering motion is introduced on the ground. The working principle of the robot is introduced, and the steering model is established to solve the speed distribution of the driving wheel on the rail. Finally, a series of prototype experiments and simulation experiments are designed.

2   Introduction of Robot System

The robot consists of four basic modules: T-joint module, I-joint module, body-module (B-module), and wheel-footed module (WF-module), as shown in Fig. 1.

2.1   Introduction of Basic Module

T-joint module provides a swinging motion, and the rotation axis is perpendicular to the center line of the module itself, and the rotation range are $-120°{\sim}120°$. I-joint module provides a rotary motion infinitely, and the rotation axis is collinear with the center line of the module itself. WF-module has two independently driving wheels, and the wheels can be swung symmetrically around the fixed support. The range of the swing are $0{\sim}110°$ [13]. It has three motors, one motor for swinging the wheels, the other two motors for driving the wheel rotation. B-module has four passive wheels that assist in over-obstacle and motion mode conversion, as shown in Fig. 1.

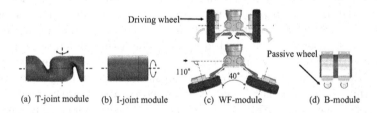

(a) T-joint module   (b) I-joint module   (c) WF-module   (d) B-module

Fig. 1. Four basic modules.

2.2   Control Architecture

The control architecture is hybrid, as shown in Fig. 2. For each joint module, the control system has three layers. A host PC is used as the top controller for task management, motion planning, and man-machine interface. The middle layer is the core of the control system, including the control unit of each module (the motion controller or driver of the joint module and the MCU of the WF-module). The bottom layer is the controlled unit, the servo motor of the modules [14].

Joint modules and WF-modules communicate with the top controller based on CAN-bus, which is used to control the joint rotation and the wheel swing.

The wheel rotation is controlled by the MCU, and the MCU communicates with the host PC through RS232. The depth camera Realsense D435i communicates with the host PC through USB3.0, so that the real-time inspection image can be displayed on the host PC.

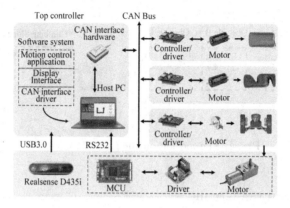

Fig. 2. The control architecture of Mobot-H.

2.3 Mechanical Configuration of Mobot-H

The design of Mobot-H is modular, so its configuration is flexible. It can be spliced into a variety of configurations from the four basic modules. Mobot-H in this paper has seven modules, includes two T-joint modules, two I-joint modules, one B-module, and two WF-modules.

Mobot-H has three different motion modes, which are the n-mode, I-mode, and U-mode. The n-mode and I-mode correspond to the ground-moving mode, and the U-mode corresponds to the rail-moving mode. Mobot-H can adjust the motion of each module to complete the motion mode conversion, over-obstacle motion and Steering motion and so on. Figure 3 is a model diagram of the three motion modes.

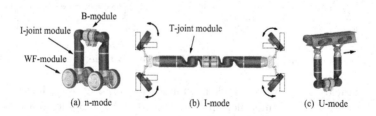

Fig. 3. Three motion modes of Mobot-H.

3   Inspection on the Ground and Rail

This section mainly introduces the motion characteristics of Mobot-H on the ground and rail, and analyzes its over-obstacle and the steering motion, as shown in Fig. 4.

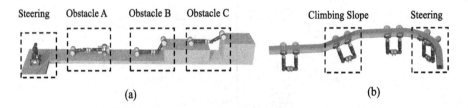

Fig. 4. The motion on the ground and rail.

3.1   Motion on the Ground

Steering on the Ground. Mobot-H can complete the steering motion by adjusting the angles of the two I-joint modules in the n-mode. When Mobot-H converts into the I-mode, it can turn in place and move laterally by adjusting the swinging angle of the driving wheels on WF-module. For more configuration information and characteristics of Mobot-H on the ground, please refer to [13].

Over-Obstacle Motion. As shown in Fig. 4(a), Mobot-H benefits from the configuration advantages, it can skilfully across the obstacle A, B, and C (Obstacle A is a unilateral convex, Obstacle B is a step, and Obstacle C is a gully).

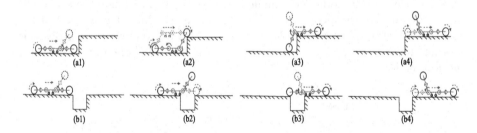

Fig. 5. The motion of the over-obstacle.

For obstacle A, the over-obstacle motion is shown in Fig. 4(a). The robot only needs to rotate a I-joint module, lifts one wheel of WF-module to a reasonable height, and the robot is driven by three driving wheels that touch the ground.

For obstacle B, the over-obstacle motion is shown in Fig. 5(a1~a4). The T-joint module is adjusted to lift the front WF-module to a reasonable height, and the robot is driven by the back WF-module until the front WF-module have a reliable contact with the surface of the step. By adjusting the two T-joint modules, B-module is at the same height as the step. The robot is then driven forward. The back WF-module is lifted after the upper surface of the step supports the passive wheels on the B-module. Finally, after the robot is driven by the front WF-module, the back WF-module is lowered. Therefore, Mobot-H goes up the step, the motion of down the step is similar.

For obstacle C, the over-obstacle motion is shown in Fig. 5(b1~b4). The over-obstacle motion also relies on the support of the passive wheels and T-joint modules to adjust the posture of Mobot-H, so as to cross the gully conveniently and reliably.

Over-Obstacle Analysis. For obstacle A, its over-obstacle ability is mainly limited by the lifting height of a driving wheel. For obstacle C, its over-obstacle ability depends on its arm length l_2. For obstacle B, the maximum height over which it crosses is limited by the process (a2) in Fig. 5. For the consideration of obstacle stability, the reliable over-obstacle condition of the process (a2) is that the tangent at the contact point between the front driving wheels and the step coincides with the upper surface of the step. As shown in Fig. 6(a), this posture is the limit posture for crossing steps, and the maximum height h can be expressed as:

$$\begin{cases} h = r_1 + h_1 + h_2 \\ h_1 = l_1 sin(\theta_{pitch}) \\ h_2 = l_2 cos[arcsin(\frac{r_1}{r})] - r \end{cases} \tag{1}$$

where r_1 is the radius of the joint module, r is the radius of the driving wheel, and θ_{pitch} is the pitch angle of B-module. l_1 is the length of the rod.

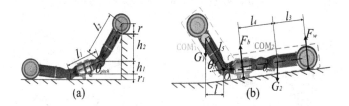

Fig. 6. Analysis of over-obstacle motion.

When Mobot-H relies on passive wheels to cross an obstacle, there is one WF-module that is suspended. The other WF-module is in contact with the ground and drives the robot forward, as shown in process (a1)(a3)(b1)(b3) in Fig. 5. In this case, the friction force of the driving wheel f may be insufficient because of the reduction of the supporting force on the driving wheel. Therefore, it is necessary to adjust the T-joint module angle θ_T to adjust the center of gravity of Mobot-H so as to ensure sufficient friction between the driving wheel and the ground.

As shown in Fig. 6(b), Mobot-H is divided into two parts, each of which is axisymmetric, so that its center of gravity is on its symmetric axis. The first part is the suspended end, including the suspended WF-module, one I-joint module and one T-joint module. The remaining modules are the second part. The center of gravity position of each part COM_1, COM_2 was measured by the suspension method. The force points of the four passive wheels are simplified to the midpoint. According to the stability criterion, the net force and moment acting on the robot must be zero. The relationship between the T-joint module angle θ_T and the friction force f at the wheel-ground contact can be expressed as follows:

$$\begin{cases} G_1 cos(\theta_{pitch}) + G_2 cos(\theta_{pitch}) = F_w + F_b \\ G_1 l + F_b \frac{l_1}{2} + F_w(l_3 + l_4 + \frac{l_1}{2}) = G_2 cos(\theta_{pitch})(l_4 + \frac{l_1}{2}) \\ l = l_5 sin(\theta_T - \theta_{pitch}) \\ f = \mu F_w \end{cases} \quad (2)$$

where G_1, G_2 is the gravity on the center of Mass. F_w is the supporting force of the ground to the driving wheel. F_b is the supporting force of the ground to passive wheels. μ is the friction coefficient between the driving wheel and the ground.

3.2   Motion on the Rail

The Principle of Motion on the Rail. As shown in Fig. 4(b), Mobot-H uses WF-modules to grasp the rail in the U-mode, so the robot is hung on the special rail and moves forward. As shown in Fig. 7, the designed rail has a trapezoidal cross-section. The WF-module can grasp on the rail, and the wheel surface can fit the web of the rail. In addition, the rim of the wheel just fits the flange of the rail, and the flange gives the WF-module a supporting force.

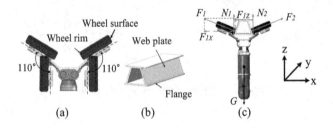

Fig. 7. The principle of motion on the rail and the designed rail.

Reliability Analysis on the Rail. It is very necessary for the robot to run safely and stably on the rail. Figure 7(c) shows the force analysis diagram of Mobot-H. The robot is subjected to three forces: its own gravity (G, the mass is 20.6kg), the force of the web on the wheel surface (F_1, F_2) and the support force of the flange on the wheel rim (N_1, N_2). The force on the left and right wheels is symmetrical, $F_1 \cos 20° = F_2 \cos 20°$, $N_1 = N_2$, so the force on the robot needs to meet:

$$F_1 \cos 70° + F_2 \cos 70° + N_1 + N_2 \geq G \qquad (3)$$

If the WF-module uses its maximum unfold-fold force to clamp the rail, the unfold-fold force is 350N [15], there is

$$350 \times 2 \times \cos 70° + 2N_1 \geq 20.6 \times 9.8 \qquad (4)$$

It can be seen that the above equation is completely satisfied.

Steering Analysis on the Rail. The steering function of Mobot-H can be realized through the differential speed of four driving wheels and the rotatable I-joint modules. Therefore, the relationship between the speed of the four driving wheels and the rail radius, the motion of I-joint modules and the robot body should be fully considered.

As shown in Fig. 8, the steering is divided into the following three stages: (1) The four driving wheels rotate at the same speed before entering the bend. Then the front WF-module enters the bend, the two driving wheels generate a speed difference. v_1, v_2 conforms to Eq. (5). The two driving wheels of the back WF-module rotate at the same angular speed, $v_4 = v_3 = v/\cos(\theta_{I_2})$. (2) Both WF-modules enter the bend, the four driving wheels generate a speed difference. v_1, v_2, v_3, v_4 conforms to Eq. (5). (3) The front WF-module out of the bend, the two driving wheels rotate at the same speed, $v_2 = v_2 = v/\cos(\theta_{I_2})$. The two driving wheels of the back WF-module still generate a speed difference. v_3, v_4 conforms to Eq. (5).

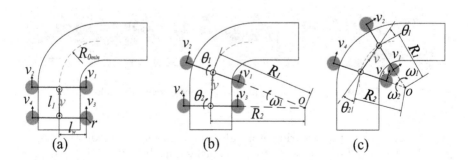

Fig. 8. Steering analysis of Mobot-H on the rail.

The speed v_i of driving wheels moving in the bend can be expressed as:

$$\begin{cases} \frac{R_1}{sin(\frac{\pi}{2}-\theta_2)} = \frac{R_2}{sin(\frac{\pi}{2}-\theta_1)} = \frac{l_1}{sin(\theta_1+\theta_2)} \\ \omega_j = \frac{v}{R_j cos(\theta_j)} \\ v_i = \omega_j(R_j + (-1)^i l_w) \end{cases} \tag{5}$$

where v_i is the wheel speed. w_j is the angular velocity of the I-joint module around the center O. R_j is the vertical distance from the axis of the I-joint module to the center O. θ_j is the rotation angle of the I-joint module. l_w is the length of the rod. When $j = 1$, $i \in (1,2)$, When $j = 2$, $i \in (3,4)$.

As shown in Fig. 8(c), during the steering process of Mobot-H, the two driving wheels in the inner circle of the rail may touch. According to the similar triangular nature, the minimum rail radius R_{0min} through which the robot can pass can be obtained as:

$$\frac{2r}{l_1} = \frac{R_{0min} - l_w}{R_{0min}} \tag{6}$$

Therefore, The minimum radius R_{0min} is calculated to be 368.16 mm.

4   Experiment

To verify the feasibility and mobility of Mobot-H, a series of experiments and simulations are conducted.

4.1   Over-Obstacle Experiment

As shown in Fig. 9, various obstacle environments are constructed to verify the feasibility of over-obstacle motion planning and the ability of over-obstacle. The length, width and height of obstacle A are $400 \times 320 \times 150$ mm. The length, width and height of obstacle B are $1800 \times 750 \times 350$ mm. The length and width of obstacle C are 400×750 mm, the height difference is 150 mm.

Fig. 9. The experimental environment of over-obstacle.

Figure 10 shows the experimental video screenshots of over-obstacle on the ground. MOBOT-H can cross the three obstacles quickly and reliably, which validates the over-obstacle motion in the third part. The experiments have verified to cross the unilateral convex, up and down steps and cross gullies.

4.2   Motion Mode Conversion

Mobot-H can switch three different motion modes during the inspection. Figure 11 shows the experiment of the mode conversion. Figure 11(1)~(3) shows the conversion from n-mode to I-mode. The process is accomplished by the coordinated motion of T-joint modules and the driving wheel. Figure 11(4)~(10) shows the conversion from I-mode to U-mode. Mobot-H first lifts one WF-module, then opens the wheels of the WF-module to grasp the rail, which serves as a support point for the robot. Finally, it lifts another WF-module to grasp the rail. The conversion from I mode to U mode has been done.

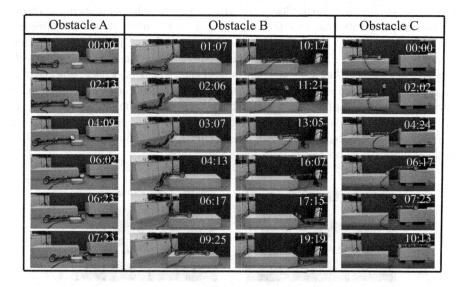

Fig. 10. The experimental video screenshot of over-obstacle.

Fig. 11. The experimental of motion mode conversion.

4.3   Simulation on Curved Rail

In order to verify the feasibility of Mobot-H moving on the rail and show the wheel differential speed phenomenon when it moves on the curved rail, several Adams simulation environments are designed to carry out the simulation experiments. The rail radius in Fig. 12(a) is set to 370 mm according to the minimum radius R_{0min} in Sect. 3. The rail radius in Fig. 12(b) is set to 1300 mm.

In the simulation environment, Mobot-H moves at a constant speed of 470 mm/s in the straight rail. The speed is reduced to 250 mm/s before entering the curved rail. Figure 13 shows the simulation results of Mobot-H under two curved rail respectively. Turn_370 and Turn_370_V are the simulation results of the rail radius of 370 mm, Turn_1300 and Turn_1300_V are the simulation results of the rail radius of 1300 mm. B_V is the speed of the robot body, that is, the speed of the B-module. Theta_I1 and Theta_I2 are the angles of the I-joint module motion respectively. LB_V, LF_V, RB_V and RF_V are the speed of the left back wheel, the left front wheel, the right back wheel, and the right front wheel respectively.

According to the experimental results, Mobot-H can move steadily on a curved rail with a radius of 370 mm. At the same time, the motion of the four driving wheels accords with the three stages analyzed in Sect. 3. By comparing the motion of Mobot-H in different radius curved rail, the motion of the robot body is more stable on the rail with a larger radius.

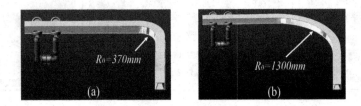

Fig. 12. Steering simulation experiment of Mobot-H.

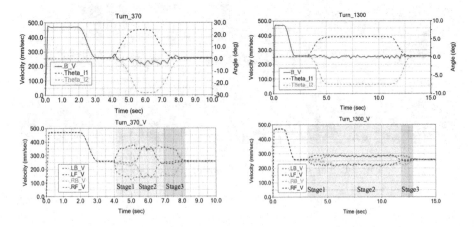

Fig. 13. Simulation results of Moobt-H steering.

5   Conclusions

This paper proposes a wheel-legged mobile robot that can be used for inspection on the ground and rail, and its prototype is manufactured. The motion characteristics of Mobot-H are introduced. The over-obstacle motion and steering motion are analyzed. Finally, the feasibility of the proposed over-obstacle method is verified and the process of the motion mode conversion is demonstrated on the prototype. The feasibility of the system moving on the rail was fully verified by setting up various simulation experiments. In the future, Fully combined with the principle of motion control, the robot can adjust joint modules motion adaptively on the rail and realize the adaptive steering control.

References

1. Yamauchi, B.M.: PackBot: a versatile platform for military robotics. In: Unmanned Ground Vehicle Technology VI, pp. 228–237 (2004)
2. Li, I.H., Wang, W.Y., Tseng, C.K.: A Kinect-sensor-based tracked robot for exploring and climbing stairs. Int. J. Adv. Rob. Syst. **11**(5), 80 (2014)
3. Baetz, W., Kroll, A., Bonow, G.: Mobile robots with active IR-optical sensing for remote gas detection and source localization. In: IEEE International Conference on Robotics and Automation, pp. 2773–2778 (2009)
4. Beaudry, J., Allan, J.F.: Electrical substation inspection and intervention robot, field experiments. In: IEEE International Conference on Applied Robotics for the Power Industry, pp. 1–2 (2014)
5. Xu, W., Yang, S., Mu, S.: Modularization design of inspection robot based on substation. In: IEEE Advanced Information Technology, Electronic and Automation Control Conference, pp. 2230–2233 (2018)
6. Wang, C., Wang, Z., Hu, H., Li, L.: Innovative design and kinematic characteristics analysis of floating mobile chassis of inspection robot. Mechines **11**(1) (2023)
7. Leonidas, E., Xu, Y.: The development of an automatic inspection system used for the maintenance of rail tunnels. In: IEEE International Conference on Automation and Computing, pp. 1–6 (2018)
8. Jiang, K., Sun, Z., Liu, Y., Sui, J., Fu, C., Li, Y.: Development and application of the rail-type inspection robot used in substation rooms. In: MATEC Web of Conferences, vol. 139, p. 00210 (2017)
9. Bae, J., Lee, D.H.: Position control of a rail guided mover using a low-cost BLDC motor. IEEE Trans. Ind. Appl. **54**(3), 2392–2399 (2018)
10. Ok, S., Bae, J., Lee, D.H.: Novel curving control scheme of rail-type monitoring robot system using two BLDC motors and IMU sensor. In: IEEE International Conference on Electrical Machines and Systems, pp. 515–519 (2021)
11. Zhang, X., Huo, X., Du, Y.: Robot control system for inspection of fully mechanized coal mining face. In: IEEE International Conference on Ubiquitous Robots, pp. 397–403 (2021)
12. Guan, Y., Zhu, H., Wu, W., Zhou, X., Jiang, L.: A modular biped wall-climbing robot with high mobility and manipulating function. IEEE/ASME Trans. Mechatron. **18**(6), 1787–1798 (2013)
13. Fu, Q., Guan, Y., Liu, S., Zhu, H.: A novel modular wheel-legged mobile robot with high mobility. In: IEEE International Conference on Robotics and Biomimetics, pp. 577–582 (2021)

14. Zhou, X., et al.: Bibot-u6: a novel 6-DoF biped active walking robot-modeling, planning and control. Int. J. Humanoid Robot. **11**(02) (2014)
15. Guan, Y., et al.: Climbot: a bio-inspired modular biped climbing robot-system development, climbing gaits, and experiments. J. Mech. Robot. **8**(02) (2016)

Author Index

© The Editor(s) (if applicable) and The Author(s), under exclusive license
to Springer Nature Singapore Pte Ltd. 2023
H. Yang et al. (Eds.): ICIRA 2023, LNAI 14274, pp. 603–605, 2023.
https://doi.org/10.1007/978-981-99-6501-4

Printed in the United States
by Baker & Taylor Publisher Services.

Printed in the United States
by Baker & Taylor Publisher Services